www.wadsworth.com

wadsworth.com is the World Wide Web site for Wadsworth Publishing Company and is your direct source to dozens of online resources.

At *wadsworth.com* you can find out about supplements, demonstration software, and student resources. You can also send e-mail to many of our authors and preview new publications and exciting new technologies.

wadsworth.com
Changing the way the world learns®

Twentieth-Century WORLD HISTORY

WILLIAM J. DUIKER

The Pennsylvania State University

WEST/WADSWORTH

I(T)P® An International Thomson Publishing Company

Belmont, CA • Albany, NY • Boston • Cincinnati • Detroit • Johannesburg • London • Madrid • Melbourne
Mexico City • New York • Pacific Grove, CA • Scottsdale, AZ • Singapore • Tokyo • Toronto

History Editor: *Clark Baxter*
Senior Development Editor: *Sharon Adams Poore*
Editorial Assistant: *Melissa Gleason*
Marketing Manager: *Jay Hu*
Print Buyer: *Barbara Britton*
Permissions Manager: *Robert Kauser*
Production: *Anne Draus, Scratchgravel Publishing Services*

Text and Cover Designer: *Diane Beasley*
Copy Editor: *Margaret C. Tropp*
Photo Researcher: *Sarah Evertson/Image Quest*
Compositor: *Scratchgravel Publishing Services*
Cover Image: *People's Republic of China calendar illustration, circa 1960. Artist unknown.*
Printer: *R.R. Donnelley & Sons, Crawfordsville*

Printed in the United States of America
    2   3   4   5   6   7   8   9   10

For more information, contact Wadsworth Publishing Company, 10 Davis Drive, Belmont, CA 94002,
or electronically at http://www.wadsworth.com

International Thomson Publishing Europe
Berkshire House
168-173 High Holborn
London WC1V 7AA, United Kingdom

Nelson ITP, Australia
102 Dodds Street
South Melbourne
Victoria 3205 Australia

Nelson Canada
1120 Birchmount Road
Scarborough, Ontario
Canada M1K 5G4

International Thomson Publishing Southern Africa
Building 18, Constantia Square
138 Sixteenth Road, P.O. Box 2459
Halfway House, 1685 South Africa

International Thomson Editores
Seneca 53
Colonia Polanco
11560 México D. F. México

International Thomson Publishing Asia
60 Albert Street
#15-01 Albert Complex
Singapore 189969

International Thomson Publishing Japan
Hirakawa-cho Kyowa Building, 3F
2-2-1 Hirakawa-cho, Chiyoda-ku
Tokyo 102 Japan

Library of Congress Cataloging-in-Publication Data

Duiker, William J.
    Twentieth-century world history / William J. Duiker
        p.   cm.
    Includes bibliographical references and index.
    ISBN 0-534-54873-3 (alk. paper)
    1. History, Modern—20th century.   I. Title.
D421.D86   1999
909.82—dc21   98-39244

*This book is printed on
acid-free recycled paper.*

To Kirsten and Zachary,
as you face the challenges of the next century

✦

Contents

Maps

Preface

The twentieth century has been an era of paradox. When it began, Western civilization was a region of squabbling states that bestrode the world like a colossus. As the century comes to an end, the West is prosperous and increasingly united, yet there are signs that—despite the recent financial crisis—global economic and political hegemony are beginning to shift to the East. The era of Western dominance is over. It has been an era marked by war and revolution but also by rapid industrial growth and widespread economic prosperity, a time of growing interdependence but also of burgeoning ethnic and national consciousness, a period that witnessed the rising power of science but also fervent religiosity and growing doubts about the impact of technology on the human experience.

Twentieth-Century World History attempts to chronicle the key events in our revolutionary century while seeking to throw light on some of the underlying issues that have shaped the times. Does the beginning of a new millennium mark the end of an extended period of Western dominance? If so, will recent decades of European and American superiority be followed by a "Pacific Century" with economic and political power shifting to the nations of eastern Asia? Will the end of the Cold War lead to what has been called a "new world order" marked by global cooperation, or are we on the verge of an unstable era of ethnic and national conflict? Why has a time of unparalleled prosperity and technological advancement been accompanied by deep pockets of poverty and widespread doubts about the role of government and the capabilities of human reason? Although this book does not promise final answers to such questions, it can provide a framework for analysis and a better understanding of some of the salient issues of our time.

A number of decisions must be made by any author sufficiently foolhardy to seek to encompass in a single volume the history of a turbulent century. First in importance is whether to present the topic as an integrated whole or with a focus on individual cultures and societies. The world that we live in today is in many respects an interdependent one in terms of economics as well as culture and communications, a reality that is often ex-

pressed by the familiar phrase "global village." At the same time, the process of globalization is by no means complete, as ethnic, religious, and regional differences continue to exist and to shape the course of our times. The tenacity of these differences is reflected not only in the rise of internecine conflicts in such divergent areas as Africa, South Asia, and Eastern Europe, but also in the emergence in recent years of such regional organizations as the Organization of African Unity, the Association for the Southeast Asian Nations, and the European Economic Community. Political leaders in various parts of the world speak routinely (if sometimes wistfully) of "Arab unity," the "African road to socialism," and the "Confucian path to economic development."

A second problem is a practical one. College students today are all too often not well informed about the distinctive character of civilizations such as China, India, and sub-Saharan Africa. Without sufficient exposure to the historical evolution of such societies, students will assume all too readily that the peoples in these countries have had historical experiences similar to their own and respond to various stimuli in a similar fashion to those living in Western Europe or the United States. If it is a mistake to ignore those forces that link us together, it is equally erroneous to underestimate those factors that continue to divide us and to differentiate us into a world of diverse peoples.

My response to this challenge has been to adopt an overall global approach to the history of the twentieth century, while at the same time attempting to do justice to the distinctive character and recent development of individual civilizations and regions in the world. The opening chapters focus on issues that have a global impact, such as the Industrial Revolution, the era of imperialism, and the two world wars. Later chapters center on individual regions of the world, although two separate chapters are devoted to the international implications of the Cold War and its aftermath. The book is divided into five parts. The first four parts are each followed by a short section labeled "Reflections," which attempts to link events together in a broad comparative and global framework. The final chapter examines some of the common problems of our time—including environmental pollution, the population explosion, and spiritual malaise—and takes a cautious look into the future to explore how such issues will evolve in the next century.

Another issue that requires attention is the balance of the treatment of Western civilization and its counterparts in Asia and Africa. The modern world is often viewed essentially as the history of Europe and the Western hemisphere, with other regions treated as appendages of the industrial countries. It is certainly true that much of this century has been dominated by events in Europe and North America, and in recognition of this fact, the opening chapters focus primarily on issues related to the rise of the West, including the Industrial Revolution and the age of imperialism. In recent decades, however, other parts of the world have assumed greater importance, thus restoring a global balance that had existed prior to the scientific and technological revolution that transformed the West in the eighteenth and nineteenth centuries. Later chapters examine this phenomenon, according to regions such as Africa, Asia, and Latin America the importance that they merit as the world prepares to enter a new millennium.

This book seeks balance in another area as well. Many textbooks tend to simplify the content of history courses by emphasizing an intellectual or political perspective or, most recently, a social perspective, often at the expense of providing sufficient details in a chronological framework. This approach is confusing to students whose high school social studies programs have often neglected a systematic study of world history. I have attempted to write a well-balanced work in which political, economic, social, and cultural history have been integrated into a chronologically ordered synthesis. A strong narrative, linking together key issues in a broad interpretative framework, is still the most effective way to present the story of the past to young minds.

To enliven the text, I have included a number of boxed essays that explore key issues within each chapter, citing important works in the field. Extensive maps and illustrations—each placed at the appropriate place in the chapter—serve to deepen the reader's understanding of the text. An annotated bibliography at the end of the book reviews the most recent literature on each period while referring also to some of the older, "classical" works in the field.

The following supplements are available for instructors' use:

- **Instructor's Manual and Test Bank**—prepared by Dmitry Shlapentokh, Indiana University, South Bend—includes chapter outlines, chapter summaries, identifications, true/false, multiple choice, and essay questions.
- **Computerized Test Bank**—available in Macintosh and Windows formats. Call-in testing is also available.
- **Four-color acetate package**—includes all the maps from the text along with a full-page commentary for each image, prepared by James Harrison, Siena College.
- Also, visit our **Web site** at www.thomson.com/Wadsworth.html.

I would like to express my appreciation to those reviewers who have read individual chapters and provided me with useful suggestions for improvement: Dmitry Shlapentokh, Indiana University, South Bend; John W. Cell, Duke University; Larry D. Wilcox, The University of Toledo; William J. Brazill, Wayne State University; Constance McGovern, Frostburg State University; and Alexander Rudhart, Villanova University. Jackson Spielvogel, who is co-author of our textbook, *World History* (now in its second edition), has been kind enough to permit me to use some of his sections in that book for the purposes of writing this one. Several of my other colleagues at Penn State—including Kumkum Chatterjee, On-cho Ng, and Arthur F. Goldschmidt—have provided me with invaluable assistance in understanding parts of the world that are beyond my own area of concentration. To Clark Baxter, whose unfailing good humor, patience, and sage advice has so often eased the trauma of textbook publishing, I offer my heartfelt thanks. I am also grateful to Sharon Adams Poore and Hal Humphrey of Wadsworth Publishing, and to Amy Guastello, for their assistance in bringing this project to fruition, and to Anne Draus of Scratchgravel Publishing for editorial advice. As always, Sarah Evertson has been helpful in obtaining illustrations for the book.

Finally, I am eternally grateful to my wife, Yvonne V. Duiker, Ph.D. Her research and her written contributions on art, architecture, literature, and music have added sparkle to this book. Her presence at my side has immeasurably added sparkle to my life.

William J. Duiker
The Pennsylvania State University

Twentieth-Century
WORLD HISTORY

PART

I

New World in the Making

The Rise of Industrial Society in the West

As the twentieth century began, the world appeared to be falling increasingly under the domination of Europe. During the previous century, much of the Asian and African continents had come under European colonial rule. Those areas that had so far escaped European conquest—notably China and Japan—remained under heavy European pressure. The world appeared to be entering a phase of Western global dominance.

The rise of Europe, and the Western world in general, to a position of global hegemony was a product, above all, of the Industrial Revolution. The rise of modern industry began in England in the eighteenth century and spread to the Continent a few decades later. By the beginning of the twentieth century, it had transformed the economic and social structure of Europe and led to a degree of economic and technological achievement that was unprecedented in the history of the world.

The Industrial Revolution in Great Britain

Why the Industrial Revolution broke out in Great Britain rather than in another part of the world has been a subject for debate among historians for many decades. A number of factors certainly contributed to the rapid transformation of eighteenth-century British society from a predominantly agricultural to an industrial and commercial economy. First, improvements in agriculture during the eighteenth century had led to a significant increase in food production. British agriculture could now feed more people at lower prices with less labor; even ordinary British families no longer had to use most of their income to buy food, giving them the potential to purchase manufactured goods. At the same time, a rapid growth of population in the second half of the eighteenth century provided a pool of surplus labor for the new factories of the emerging British industrial sector.

A second factor was the rapid increase in national wealth. Two centuries of expanding trade had provided Britain with a ready supply of capital for investment in the new industrial machines and the factories that were required to house them. In addition to profits from trade, Britain possessed an effective central bank and well-developed, flexible credit facilities. Many early factory owners were merchants and entrepreneurs who had profited from the eighteenth-century cottage industry. The country also possessed what might today be described as a "modernization elite"—individuals who were interested in making profits if the opportunity presented itself. In that objective they were generally supported by the government.

Third, Britain was richly supplied with important mineral resources, such as coal and iron ore, needed in the manufacturing process. Britain was also a small country, and the relatively short distances made transportation facilities readily accessible. In addition to nature's provision of abundant rivers, from the mid-seventeenth century onward, both private and public investment poured into the construction of new roads, bridges, and canals. By 1780, roads, rivers, and canals linked the major industrial centers of the north, the Midlands, London, and the Atlantic coast.

Finally, foreign markets gave British industrialists a ready outlet for their manufactured goods. British exports quadrupled between 1660 and 1760. In the course of its eighteenth-century wars and conquests (see Chapter 2), Great Britain had developed a vast colonial empire at the expense of its leading continental rivals, the Dutch Republic and France. Britain also possessed a well-developed merchant marine that was able to transport goods to any place in the world. A crucial factor in Britain's successful industrialization was the ability to produce cheaply those articles most in demand abroad. And the best markets abroad were not in Europe, where countries protected their own incipient industries, but in the Americas, Africa, and Asia, where people wanted sturdy, inexpensive clothes rather than costly, highly finished, luxury items. Britain's machine-produced textiles fulfilled that demand. Nor should we overlook the British domestic market. Britain had the highest standard of living in Europe and a rapidly growing population. It was the demand from both domestic and foreign markets and the inability of the old system to meet it that led entrepreneurs to seek and accept the new methods of manufacturing that a series of inventions provided. In so doing, these individuals produced the Industrial Revolution.

During the last decades of the century, technological innovations, including the flying shuttle, the spinning jenny, and the power loom, led to a significant increase in production (see box on p. 4). The cotton textile industry achieved even greater heights of productivity with the invention of the steam engine, which proved invaluable to Britain's Industrial Revolution. The steam engine was a tireless source of power and depended for fuel on a substance—namely, coal—that seemed then to be available in unlimited quantities. The success of the steam engine increased the demand for coal and led to an expansion in coal production. In turn, new processes using coal furthered the development of an iron industry, the production of machinery, and the invention of the railroad.

By the mid-nineteenth century, Great Britain had become the world's first and richest industrial nation. Britain was the "workshop, banker, and trader of the world." It produced half of the world's coal and manufactured goods; in 1850, its cotton industry alone was equal in size to the industries of all other European countries combined. No doubt, Britain's certainty about its mission in the world in the nineteenth century was grounded in its incredible material success story.

The Spread of Industrialization

Beginning first in Great Britain, industrialization spread to the continental countries of Europe and the United States at different times and speeds during the nineteenth century. First to be industrialized on the Continent were Belgium, France, and the German states and in North America, the new nation of the United States. Not until after 1850 did the Industrial Revolution spread to the rest of Europe and other parts of the world.

Industrialization on the Continent faced numerous hurdles, and as it proceeded in earnest after 1815, it did so along lines that were somewhat different from Britain's. Lack of technical knowledge was a first major obstacle to industrialization. But the continental countries possessed an advantage here; they could simply borrow British techniques and practices. By the 1840s, a new generation of skilled mechanics from Belgium and France was spreading their knowledge east and south. More important, however, continental countries, especially France and the German states, began to establish a wide range of technical schools to train engineers and mechanics.

That government played an important role in this regard brings us to a second difference between British and continental industrialization. Governments on much of the Continent were accustomed to playing a significant role in economic affairs. Furthering the development of industrialization was a logical extension of that attitude. Hence governments provided for the costs of technical education, awarded grants to inventors and foreign entrepreneurs, exempted foreign industrial equipment from import duties, and in some places even financed factories. Of equal if not greater importance in the long run, governments actively bore much of the cost of building roads and canals, deepening and widening river channels, and constructing railroads. By 1850, a network of iron rails had spread across Europe, although only Germany and Belgium had completed major parts of their systems by that time.

Like Belgium, France, and the German states, the United States experienced the first stages of an industrial revolution and the urbanization that accompanied it during the first half of the nineteenth century. In 1800, society in the United States was agrarian. The new nation had no cities over 100,000, and six out of every seven American workers were farmers. By 1860, however, the population had grown from 5 to 30 million people, larger than Great Britain, and nine American cities had populations over 100,000. Only 50 percent of American workers were farmers.

❧ Discipline in the New Factories ❧

The Industrial Revolution led to changes not only in the economic structure of Western society, but also in work habits. The most visible symbol of the Industrial Revolution was the factory, which became the chief means of organizing labor for the new machines. From its beginning, the factory system demanded a new type of discipline from its employees. Once factory owners purchased machinery, it had to be used as much as possible to enable them to profit from their investment. Workers were forced to work regular hours, often in shifts, to keep the machines producing at a steady pace for maximum output.

The new system thus represented a massive adjustment for the first generation of factory workers. In the cottage industry that had preceded it, workers spun thread and wove cloth in their own rhythm and time. Now factory workers were forced to adhere to a new and rigorous discipline geared to the requirements of their machines. Typical of the disciplinary regulations enforced in such factories were those that were established for a factory in Berlin, Germany, in the 1840s. Employees at the factory were required to report for work at 6 A.M. precisely. With short breaks for meals, they remained on the job until 7 in the evening.

Regulations for employees at the factory were strictly enforced. All conversation with fellow workers was prohibited, as was smoking or leaving the premises without permission before the end of the working day. Drunkenness, disobedience, dishonesty, or "repeated irregular arrival at work" were all grounds for immediate dismissal.

During the early stages of the Industrial Revolution, child labor was common, and working conditions for underage workers were often abysmal. According to a report commissioned in 1832 to inquire into the conditions for child factory workers in Great Britain, children as young as six years of age began work before dawn. Those who were drowsy or fell asleep were tapped on the head, doused with cold water, or even strapped to a chair or flogged with a stick. In one case, according to the report,

> provided a child should be drowsy, the overlooker walks round the room with a stick in his hand, and he touches that child on the shoulder, and says, "Come here." In a corner of the room there is an iron cistern; it is filled with water; he takes this boy, and takes him up by the legs, and dips him over head in the cistern, and sends him to work for the remainder of the day.

Sources: Sidney Pollard and Colin Holmes, eds., *Documents of European Economic History* (New York and London: St. Martin's Press, 1968); E. Royston Pike, ed., *Human Documents of the Industrial Revolution* (London: Unwin Hyman, 1966).

The initial application of machinery to production was accomplished—as it had been in continental Europe—by borrowing from Great Britain. Soon, however, Americans began to equal or surpass British technical inventions. The Harpers Ferry arsenal, for example, built muskets with interchangeable parts. Because all the individual parts of a musket were identical (for example, all triggers were the same), the final product could be put together quickly and easily; this innovation enabled Americans to avoid the more costly system in which skilled craftsmen fitted together individual parts made separately. The so-called American system reduced costs and revolutionized production by saving labor, an important consideration in a society that had few skilled artisans.

Unlike Britain, the United States was a large country. The lack of a good system of internal transportation seemed to limit American economic development by making the transport of goods prohibitively expensive. This difficulty was gradually remedied, however. Thousands of miles of roads and canals were built linking east and west. The steamboat facilitated transportation on the Great Lakes, Atlantic coastal waters, and rivers. Most important of all in the development of an American transportation system was the railroad. Beginning with 100 miles in 1830, by 1860 more than 27,000 miles of railroad track covered the United States. This transportation revolution turned the United States into a single massive market for the manufactured goods of the Northeast, the early center of American industrialization, and by 1860, the United States was well on its way to being an industrial nation.

The Second Industrial Revolution

During the fifty years before the outbreak of World War I in 1914, the Western world witnessed a dynamic age of material prosperity. With new industries, new sources of energy, and new goods, a second Industrial Revolution transformed the human environment and led people to believe that their material progress meant human progress. Scientific and technological achievements, many believed, would improve humanity's condition and solve all human problems. They led, in fact, in a quite different direction

New Products and New Patterns

The first major change in industrial development between 1870 and 1914 was the substitution of steel for iron. New methods for rolling and shaping steel made it useful in the construction of lighter, smaller, and faster machines and engines as well as for railways, shipbuilding, and armaments. In 1860, Great Britain, France, Germany, and Belgium produced 125,000 tons of steel; by 1913, the total was 32 million tons. By 1910, German steel production was double that of Great Britain, and both had been surpassed by the United States.

Electricity was a major new form of energy that proved to be of great value since it could be easily converted into other forms of energy, such as heat, light, and motion, and moved relatively effortlessly through space by means of transmitting wires. The first commercially practical generators of electrical current were not developed until the 1870s. By 1910, hydroelectric power stations and coal-fired steam-generating plants enabled entire districts to be tied into a single power distribution system that provided a common source of power for homes, shops, and industrial enterprises.

Electricity spawned a whole series of new products. The invention of the incandescent filament lamp by the American Thomas Edison and the Briton Joseph Swan opened homes and cities to illumination by electric lights. A revolution in communications ensued when Alexander Graham Bell invented the telephone in 1876 and Guglielmo Marconi sent the first radio waves across the Atlantic in 1901. Although most electricity was initially used for lighting, it was eventually put to use in transportation. By the 1880s, streetcars and subways had appeared in major European cities. Electricity also transformed the factory. Conveyor belts, cranes, machines, and machine tools could all be powered by electricity and located anywhere. Thanks to electricity, all countries could now enter the industrial age.

The development of the internal combustion engine had a similar effect. The processing of liquid fuels—namely, petroleum and its distilled derivatives—made possible the widespread use of the internal combustion engine as a source of power in transportation. An oil-fired engine was made in 1897, and by 1902, the

◆ **The Colossus of Paris.** When it was completed for the World's Fair in Paris in 1889, the Eiffel Tower became, at 1,056 feet, the tallest man-made monument in the world. The colossus, which seemed to be rising from the shadows of the city's feudal past like some new technological giant, symbolized the triumph of the Industrial Revolution and machine-age capitalism, proclaiming the dawn of a new era possessing endless possibilities and power. Constructed of wrought iron and comprising more than 2.5 million rivet holes, the structure was completed in two years and was paid for entirely by the builder himself, the engineer Gustave Eiffel. From the outset, the monument was wildly popular. Nearly 2 million people lined up at the fair to visit this gravity-defying marvel.

Hamburg-Amerika Line had switched from coal to oil on its new ocean liners. By the beginning of the twentieth century, some naval fleets had been converted to oil burners as well.

The internal combustion engine gave rise to the automobile and airplane. In 1900, world production stood at 9,000 cars; by 1906, Americans had overtaken the initial lead of the French. It was an American, Henry Ford, who revolutionized the car industry with the mass production of the Model T. By 1916, Ford's factories were producing 735,000 cars a year. In the meantime, air transportation had emerged with the Zeppelin airship in 1900. In 1903, at Kitty Hawk, North Carolina, the Wright brothers made the first flight in a fixed-wing plane powered by a gasoline engine. It took World War I, however, to stimulate the aircraft industry, and it was not until 1919 that the first regular passenger air service was established.

The growth of industrial production depended upon the development of markets for the sale of manufactured

✷ Map 1.1   The Industrial Regions of Europe by 1914

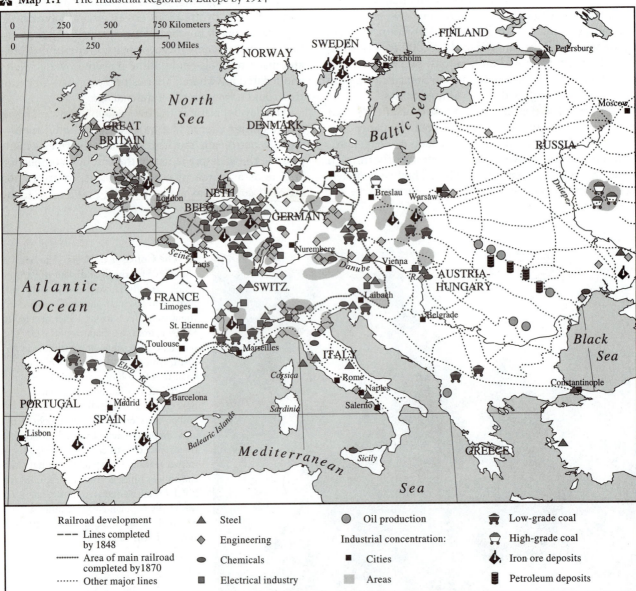

goods. After 1870, the best foreign markets were already heavily saturated, forcing Europeans to take a renewed look at their domestic markets. Between 1850 and 1900, real wages had increased in Britain by two-thirds and in Germany by one-third. A decline in the cost of food combined with lower prices for manufactured goods because of reduced transportation costs made it easier for Europeans to buy consumer products. In the cities, new methods for retail distribution—in particular, the department store—were used to expand sales of a whole new range of consumer goods made possible by the development of the steel and electrical industries. The desire to own sewing machines, clocks, bicycles, electric lights, and typewriters was rapidly generating a new consumer ethic that has been a crucial part of the modern economy.

Meanwhile, increased competition for foreign markets and the growing importance of domestic demand led to a reaction against the free trade that had characterized much of the European economy between 1820 and 1870. To many industrial and political leaders, protective tariffs guaranteed domestic markets for the products of their own industries. By the 1870s, Europeans were returning to the practice of tariff protection. At the same time, cartels were being formed to decrease competition internally. In a cartel, independent enterprises worked together to control prices and fix production quotas, thereby restraining the kind of competition that led to reduced prices. Cartels were especially strong in Germany, where banks moved to protect their investments by eliminating the "anarchy of competition." Founded in 1893, the Rhenish-Westphalian Coal Syndicate controlled 98 percent of Germany's coal production by 1904.

The formation of cartels was paralleled by a move toward ever-larger manufacturing plants, especially in the iron and steel, machinery, heavy electrical equipment, and chemical industries. This growth in the size of industrial plants led to pressure for greater efficiency in factory production at the same time that competition led to demands for greater economy. The result was a desire to streamline or rationalize production as much as possible. The development of precision tools enabled manufacturers to produce interchangeable parts, which in turn led to the creation of the assembly line for production. First used in the United States for small arms and clocks, the assembly line had moved to Europe by 1850. In the second half of the nineteenth century, it was primarily used in manufacturing nonmilitary goods, such as sewing machines, typewriters, bicycles, and finally the automobile.

The emergence of protective tariffs and cartels was clearly a response to the growth of the multinational industrial system. Economic competition intensified the political rivalries of the age. The growth of the national state, which had seemed in the mid-nineteenth century to be the answer to old problems, now seemed to be creating new ones.

Between 1870 and 1914, Germany replaced Great Britain as the industrial leader of Europe. Already in the 1890s, Germany's superiority was evident in new areas of manufacturing, such as organic chemicals and electrical equipment, and increasingly apparent in its ever-greater share of worldwide trade. But the struggle for economic (and political) supremacy between Great Britain and Germany should not cause us to overlook the other great polarization of the age. By 1900, Europe was divided into two economic zones. Great Britain, Belgium, France, the Netherlands, Germany, the western part of the Austro-Hungarian Empire, and northern Italy constituted an advanced industrialized core that had a high standard of living, decent systems of transportation, and relatively healthy and educated peoples. Another part of Europe, the backward and little industrialized area to the south and east, consisting of southern Italy, most of Austria-Hungary, Spain, Portugal, the Balkan kingdoms, and Russia, was still largely agricultural and relegated by industrial countries to the function of providing food and raw materials. The presence of Romanian oil, Greek olive oil, and Serbian pigs and prunes in Western Europe served as reminders of an economic division of Europe that continued well into the twentieth century.

Toward a World Economy

The economic developments of the late nineteenth century, combined with the transportation revolution that saw the growth of marine transport and railroads, fostered a true world economy. By 1900, Europeans were receiving beef and wool from Argentina and Australia, coffee from Brazil, nitrates from Chile, iron ore from Algeria, and sugar from Java. European capital was also invested abroad to develop railways, mines, electrical power plants, and banks. High rates of return, such as 11.3 percent on Latin American banking shares that were floated in London, provided plenty of incentive. Of course, foreign countries also provided markets for the surplus manufactured goods of Europe. With its capital, industries, and military might, Europe dominated the world economy by the beginning of the nineteenth century.

Trade among various regions of the world, of course, had taken place for centuries. As early as the first millennium C.E., China and the Roman Empire had traded with each other through intermediaries on both the maritime route across the Indian Ocean and over the famous Silk Road through the parched deserts of central Asia. Trade across the Eurasian supercontinent increased with the rise of the Arab Empire in the Middle East in the ninth century, and then reached a peak during the thirteenth and fourteenth centuries, when the Mongol Empire stretched from the shores of the Pacific to the steppes of Russia and the borders of eastern Europe. Trade routes also snaked across the Sahara Desert to central and western Africa and along the eastern coast from the Red Sea to the island of Madagascar.

Not until the beginning of the sixteenth century, however, was a truly global economy created—a product of the circumnavigation of the globe by the Portuguese adventurer Ferdinand Magellan and the voyages of exploration that followed. With the establishment of contacts between the Old World and the societies in the Western Hemisphere, trade now literally spanned the globe. New crops from the Americas, such as corn, potatoes, and manioc, entered the world market and changed eating habits and social patterns as far away as China. Tobacco from the New World and coffee and tea from the Orient became the new craze in affluent circles in Europe and the Middle East.

In the view of some contemporary historians, it was this process that enabled a resurgent Europe to launch the economic and technological revolution that led to the Industrial Revolution. According to the historian Immanuel Wallerstein, one of the leading proponents of this theory, the age of exploration led to the creation of a new "world system" characterized by the emergence of global trade networks dominated by the rising force of European capitalism. This commercial revolution, in fact, operated much to the advantage of the European countries. Profits from the spice trade with eastern Asia, along with gold and silver from the Americas, flowed into state treasuries and the pockets of private traders in London, Paris, and Amsterdam. The wealth and power of Europe increased rapidly during this period, thus laying the groundwork for the economic revolution of the nineteenth century.

The Structure of Mass Society

The new world created by the Industrial Revolution has led historians to speak of the emergence of a mass society by the end of the nineteenth century. A mass society meant new forms of expression for the lower classes as they benefited from the extension of voting rights, an improved standard of living, and compulsory elementary education. But it also brought problems. Urbanization led to overcrowding in the burgeoning cities and increasing public health problems. The development of expanded means of communication resulted in the emergence of new organizations that sought to manipulate and control the population for their own purposes. A mass press, for example, swayed popular opinion by flamboyant journalistic practices.

As the number and size of cities continued to mushroom, governments by the 1880s came to the conclusion—although reluctantly—that private enterprise could not solve the housing crisis. In 1890, a British Housing Act empowered local town councils to construct cheap housing for the working classes. London and Liverpool were the first communities to take advantage of their new powers. Similar activity had been set in motion in Germany by 1900. Everywhere, however, these lukewarm measures failed to do much to meet the real housing needs of the working classes. Nevertheless, by the start of World War I, the need for planning had been recognized, and after the war municipal governments moved into housing construction on a large scale. In housing, as in so many other areas of life in the late nineteenth and early twentieth centuries, the liberal principle that the government that governs least governs best (discussed later in this chapter) had simply proven untrue. More and more, governments were stepping into areas of activity that they would have never touched earlier.

The Social Structure of Mass Society

At the top of European society stood a wealthy elite, constituting but 5 percent of the population but controlling between 30 and 40 percent of its wealth. This nineteenth-century elite was an amalgamation of the traditional landed aristocracy that had dominated European society for centuries and the emerging upper middle class. In the course of the nineteenth century, aristocrats coalesced with the most successful industrialists, bankers, and merchants to form a new elite. The growth of big business had created this group of wealthy plutocrats while aristocrats, whose income from landed estates declined, invested in railway shares, public utilities, government bonds, and even businesses, sometimes on their own estates. Gradually, the greatest fortunes shifted into the hands of the upper middle class. In Great Britain, for example, landed aristocrats constituted 73 percent of the country's millionaires in mid-century while the commercial and financial magnates made up 14 percent. By the period 1900–1914, landowners had declined to 27 percent.

Increasingly, aristocrats and plutocrats fused as the members of the wealthy upper middle class purchased landed estates to join the aristocrats in the pleasures of country living while the aristocrats bought lavish town houses for part-time urban life. Common bonds were also created when the sons of wealthy middle-class families were admitted to the elite schools dominated by the children of the aristocracy. This educated elite, whether aristocratic or middle class in background, assumed leadership roles in government bureaucracies and military hierarchies. Marriage also served to unite the two groups. Daughters of tycoons gained titles while aristocratic heirs gained new sources of cash. Wealthy American heiresses were in special demand. When the American heiress Consuelo Vanderbilt married the duke of Marlborough, the new duchess brought £2 million (approximately $10 million) to her husband.

The middle classes consisted of a variety of groups. Below the upper middle class was a middle level that included such traditional groups as professionals in law, medicine, and the civil service as well as moderately well-to-do industrialists and merchants. The industrial expansion of the nineteenth century also added new groups to the middle middle class. These newcomers included business managers and new professionals, such as engineers, architects, accountants, and chemists, who formed professional associations as the symbols of their newfound importance. Beneath this solid and comfortable middle middle class was a lower middle class of small shopkeepers, traders, manufacturers, and prosperous peasants. Their chief preoccupation was the provision of goods and services for the classes above them.

Standing between the lower middle class and the lower classes were new groups of white-collar workers who were the product of the second Industrial Revolution. They were the traveling salesmen, bookkeepers, bank tellers, telephone operators, department store salespeople, and secretaries. Although largely propertyless and often paid little more than skilled laborers, these white-collar workers were often committed to middle-class ideals and optimistic about improving their status.

The moderately prosperous and successful middle classes shared a certain style of life, one whose values tended to dominate much of nineteenth-century society. The members of the middle class were especially active in preaching their worldview to their children and to the upper and lower classes of their society. This was es-

pecially evident in Victorian Britain, often considered a model of middle-class society. It was the European middle classes who accepted and promulgated the importance of progress and science. They believed in hard work, which they viewed as the primary human good, open to everyone and guaranteed to have positive results. They were also regular churchgoers who believed in the good conduct associated with traditional Christian morality.

The working classes of European society constituted almost 80 percent of the population. Many of them were landholding peasants, agricultural laborers, and sharecroppers, especially in eastern Europe. This was less true, however, in western and central Europe. About 10 percent of the British population worked in agriculture, while in Germany the figure was 25 percent.

There was no such thing as a homogeneous urban working class. The elite of the working class included, first of all, skilled artisans in such traditional handicraft trades as cabinetmaking, printing, and jewelry making. As the production of more items was mechanized in the course of the nineteenth century, these highly skilled workers found their economic security threatened. The second Industrial Revolution, however, also brought new entrants into the group of highly skilled workers, including machine-tool specialists, shipbuilders, and metalworkers. Many of the skilled workers attempted to pattern themselves after the middle class by seeking good housing and educating their children.

Semiskilled laborers, including such people as carpenters, bricklayers, and many factory workers, earned wages that were about two-thirds of those of highly skilled workers. At the bottom of the working-class hierarchy stood the largest group of workers, the unskilled laborers. They included day laborers, who worked irregularly for very low wages, and large numbers of domestic servants. One out of every seven employed persons in Great Britain in 1900 was a domestic servant. Most of them were women.

Urban workers did experience a real betterment in the material conditions of their lives after 1870. For one thing, urban improvements meant better living conditions. A rise in real wages, accompanied by a decline in many consumer costs, especially in the 1880s and 1890s, made it possible for workers to buy more than just food and housing. Workers' budgets now included money for more clothes and even leisure at the same time that strikes and labor agitation were winning ten-hour days and Saturday afternoons off. The combination of more income and more free time produced whole new patterns of mass leisure.

The "Woman Question": Female Experiences

One of the most important social consequences of the Industrial Revolution was the changing role of women. During much of the nineteenth century, many women adhered to the ideal of femininity popularized by writers and poets. Alfred Lord Tennyson's *The Princess* expressed it well:

> Man for the field and woman for the hearth:
> Man for the sword and for the needle she:
> Man with the head and woman with the heart:
> Man to command and woman to obey;
> All else confusion.

The reality was somewhat different. Under the impact of the second Industrial Revolution, which created a wide variety of service and white-collar jobs, women began to accept employment as clerks, typists, secretaries, and salesclerks. Compulsory education opened the door to new opportunities in the medical and teaching professions. In some countries in Western Europe, women's legal rights increased.

Still, most women remained confined to their traditional roles of homemaking and child rearing. The less fortunate were still compelled to undertake marginal work at home or as pieceworkers in sweatshops. By the end of the century, strikes and labor agitations led to the enactment of laws that ended child labor, reduced working hours to ten per day, and eliminated work on Saturday afternoons, which enabled working-class parents to devote more attention to their children (see box on p. 11).

Many of these improvements occurred as the result of the rise of Europe's first feminist movement. The movement had its origins in the social upheaval of the French Revolution, when some women advocated equality for women based on the doctrine of natural rights. In the 1830s, a number of women in the United States and Europe sought improvements for women by focusing on family and marriage law to strengthen the property rights of wives and enhance their ability to secure a divorce. Later in the century, attention shifted to the issue of equal political rights. Many feminists believed that the right to vote was the key to all other reforms to improve the position of women.

The British women's movement was the most vocal and active in Europe, but it was divided over tactics. Moderates believed that women must demonstrate that they would use political power responsibly if they wanted Parliament to grant them the right to vote. Another group, however, favored a more radical approach.

Emmeline Pankhurst (1858–1928) and her daughters, Christabel and Sylvia, in 1903 founded the Women's Social and Political Union, which enrolled mostly middle- and upper-class women. Pankhurst's organization realized the value of the media and used unusual publicity stunts to call attention to its demands. Derisively labeled suffragettes by male politicians, its members pelted government officials with eggs, chained themselves to lampposts, smashed the windows of department stores on fashionable shopping streets, burned railroad cars, and went on hunger strikes in jail.

Before World War I, demands for women's rights were being heard throughout Europe and the United States, although only in Norway and some American states did women actually receive the right to vote before 1914. It would take the dramatic upheaval of World War I before male-dominated governments capitulated on this basic issue.

Reaction and Revolution: The Decline of the Old Order

While the Industrial Revolution shook the economic and social foundations of European society, similar revolutionary developments were reshaping the political map of the continent. These developments were the product of a variety of factors, including not only the Industrial Revolution itself, but also the Renaissance, the Enlightenment, and the French Revolution at the end of the eighteenth century. The influence of these new forces resulted in a redefinition of political conditions in Europe. The conservative order—based on the principle of hereditary monarchy and the existence of great multinational states such as Austria-Hungary, Russia, and the Ottoman Empire—had emerged intact from the defeat of Napoleon Bonaparte at the Battle of Waterloo in 1815, but by mid-century it had come under attack along a wide front. Arraigned against the conservative forces were a set of new political ideas that began to come into their own in the first half of the nineteenth century and continue to affect the entire world today.

Liberalism and Nationalism

One of these new political ideas was liberalism. Liberalism owed much to the Enlightenment of the eighteenth century and the American and French Revolutions that erupted at the end of that century. In addition, liberalism became increasingly important as the Industrial Revolution progressed because the developing industrial

❧ Escaping the Doll's House ❧

The role of women in Europe during the early stages of the Industrial Revolution was filled with contradictions. During the nineteenth century, the traditional characterization of the sexes, based on gender-defined social roles, was virtually elevated to the status of universal male and female attributes, largely because of the impact of the Industrial Revolution on the family. As the chief family wage earners, men were expected to work outside the home, while women were assigned the responsibility of caring for home and family. The ideal, however, did not always match reality, for with the advent of the Industrial Revolution many women, especially those from the lower classes, were driven by the need for supplemental income to seek employment outside the home, often in the form of menial labor. Marriage, then, was widely viewed as the only honorable and available career during the nineteenth century. In fact, for many women it was a financial necessity, since the lack of meaningful work and the lower wages paid to women made it difficult for single women to earn a living.

Given the pervasiveness of such views, it is not surprising that many women accepted the traditional ideal and sought to make the best of it. In her book *Woman in Her Social and Domestic Character*, the American writer Elizabeth Poole Sanford counseled her contemporaries to accept their lot and play their role as effectively and as gracefully as possible. Domestic life, she noted, was the chief source of women's influence. A woman "may make a man's home delightful, and may thus increase his motives for virtuous exertion." In so doing, she would in turn "be esteemed and loved" and merit the deference which in the past would have been "conceded to her as a matter of course." Above all, women must ac-

cept their position of dependence. A woman, she noted, does what she can, but "she is conscious of inferiority, and therefore grateful for support. She knows that she is the weaker vessel, and that as such she should receive honor."

Such views were by no means universal. Although a majority of women probably accepted the nineteenth-century ideal of women as keepers of the household and nurturers of husband and children, a growing number spoke out for the rights of women. None was more famous than the fictional character Nora Helmer in Danish writer Henrik Ibsen's *A Doll's House*. In his play, published in 1879, Nora declared her independence from her husband's control and announced her intention to leave home to start her life anew. To her husband, Torvald, Nora's decision was monstrous. How, he declared in outrage, could she forsake her holiest duties to husband and children? "I have other duties just as sacred," she retorted—duties to herself. When Torvald declared that "before all else" she was a wife and mother, Nora retorted that above all she was a human being. "I can no longer content myself with what most people say, or with what is found in books. I must think over things for myself and get to understand them."

In rejecting traditional assumptions about female dependency, Henrik Ibsen's Nora reflected the dramatic changes that would eventually take place in the role of women in Western society.

Sources: Elizabeth Poole Sanford, *Woman in Her Social and Domestic Character* (Boston: Otis Boradors & Co., 1842); Henrik Ibsen, *Plays* (New York: Macmillan, 1927), p. 85.

---

middle class largely adopted the idea as its own. Opinions diverged among people classified as liberals, but all began with a common denominator, a conviction that people should be as free from restraint as possible. This belief is evident in both economic and political liberalism. Economic liberalism, also known as classical economics, was based on the tenet of laissez-faire—the belief that the state should not interrupt the free play of natural economic forces, especially supply and demand. Political liberalism was based on the concept of a constitutional monarchy or a constitutional state, with limits on the powers of government and a written charter to protect the basic civil rights of the people.

Nineteenth-century liberals, however, were not democrats in the modern sense. Although all people were entitled to equal civil rights, they should not have equal political rights. The right to vote and to hold office would be open only to men who met certain property qualifications. As a political philosophy, liberalism was tied to middle-class, and especially industrial middle-class, men who favored the extension of voting rights so that they could share power with the landowning classes.

They had little desire to let the lower classes share that power.

Nationalism was an even more powerful ideology for change in the nineteenth century. Nationalism arose out of an awareness of being part of a community that had common institutions, traditions, language, and customs. In some cases, that sense of identity was based on shared ethnic or linguistic characteristics. In others, it was a consequence of a common commitment to a religion or a culture. In any event, such a community came to be called a "nation," and the primary political loyalty of individuals would be to the nation rather than to a dynasty or a city-state or other political unit. Nationalism did not become a popular force for change until the French Revolution, and even then nationalism was not so much political as cultural, with its emphasis upon the uniqueness of a particular nationality. Cultural nationalism, however, evolved into political nationalism, the claim advocated that governments should coincide with nationalities. Thus, a divided people such as the Germans wanted national unity in a German nation-state with one central government. Subject peoples, such as the Hungarians, wanted national self-determination, or the right to establish their own autonomy rather than be subject to a German minority in a multinational empire.

Liberalism and nationalism began to exert a measurable impact on the European political scene in the 1830s, when a revolt led by progressive forces installed a constitutional monarchy in France, and nationalist uprisings took place in Belgium (which was then attached to the Dutch Republic), in Italy, and in Poland (then part of the Russian Empire). Only the Belgians were successful, as Russian forces crushed the Poles' attempt to liberate themselves from foreign domination, while Austrian troops intervened in Italy to uphold reactionary governments in a number of Italian states.

In the spring of 1848, a new series of uprisings against established authority broke out in several countries in central and western Europe. The most effective was in France, where an uprising centered in Paris overthrew the so-called bourgeois monarchy of King Louis Philippe and briefly brought to power a new republic composed of an alliance of workers, intellectuals, and progressive representatives of the urban middle class.

The Unification of Germany and Italy

Within a few months, however, it became clear that optimism about the imminence of a new order in Europe had not been justified. In France, the shaky alliance between workers and the urban bourgeoisie was ruptured when workers' groups and their representatives in the government began to demand extensive social reforms to provide guaranteed benefits to the poor. Moderates, frightened by rising political tensions in Paris, resisted such demands. Facing the specter of class war, the French nation drew back and welcomed the rise to power of Louis Napoleon, a nephew of the great Napoleon Bonaparte. Within three years, he declared himself Emperor Napoleon III. Elsewhere in Europe—in Germany, in the Hapsburg Empire, and in Italy—popular uprisings failed to unseat autocratic monarchs and destroy the existing political order.

But the rising force of nationalism was not to be quenched. Italy, long divided into separate kingdoms, was finally united in the early 1860s. Germany followed a few years later. Unfortunately, the rise of nation-states in central Europe did not herald the onset of greater stability within the continent. To the contrary, it inaugurated a period of heightened tensions, as an increasingly aggressive Germany now began to dominate the politics of Europe. In 1870, German Prime Minister Otto von Bismarck (1815–1898) provoked a war with France. After the latter's defeat, a new German Empire was declared in the Hall of Mirrors at the Palace of Versailles, just outside of Paris.

Many German liberals were delighted at the unification of their country after centuries of division. But they were soon to discover that the new German Empire would not usher in a new era of peace and freedom. Under Prussian leadership, the new state quickly proclaimed the superiority of authoritarian and militaristic values and abandoned the principles of liberalism and constitutional government.

Liberal principles made similarly little headway elsewhere in central and eastern Europe. After the transformation of the Hapsburg Empire into the dual monarchy of Austria-Hungary in 1867, the Austrian part received a constitution that theoretically recognized the equality of the nationalities and established a parliamentary system with the principle of ministerial responsibility. However, Emperor Francis Joseph (1848–1916) largely ignored ministerial responsibility by personally appointing and dismissing his ministers and ruling by decree when parliament was not in session.

The problem of reconciling the interests of the various nationalities remained a difficult one. The German minority that governed Austria felt increasingly threatened by the Czechs, Poles, and other Slavic groups within the empire. The granting of universal male suffrage in 1907 served only to exacerbate the problem when nationalities that had played no rote in the gov-

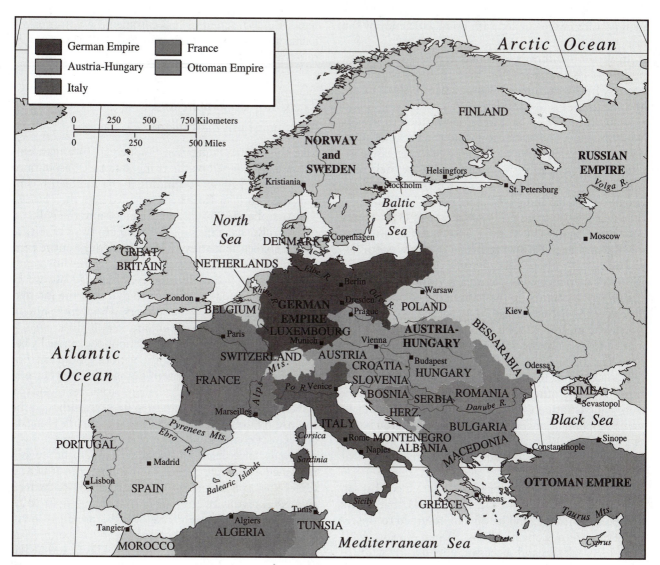

�֍ **Map 1.2** Europe in 1871

ernment now agitated in the parliament for autonomy. This led prime ministers after 1900 to ignore the parliament and rely increasingly on imperial emergency decrees to govern. On the eve of World War I, the Austro-Hungarian Empire was far from solving its minorities problem.

Roots of Revolution in Russia

Further to the east, in the vast Russian Empire, neither the Industrial Revolution nor the European Enlightenment had exerted much impact. At the beginning of the nineteenth century, Russia was overwhelmingly rural,

agricultural, and autocratic. The Russian tsar was still regarded as a divine-right monarch with unlimited power, although the physical extent of the empire made the claim impracticable. For centuries, Russian farmers had groaned under the yoke of an oppressive feudal system that tied the peasant to poverty conditions and the legal status of a serf under the authority of his manor lord. An enlightened tsar, Alexander II (r. 1855–1881), had emancipated the serfs in 1861, but under conditions that left most Russian peasants still poor and with little hope for social or economic betterment. In desperation, the *muzhik* (the Russian term for peasant) periodically lashed out at his oppressors in sporadic rebellions, but all such uprisings were quelled with brutal efficiency by the tsarist regime.

In Western Europe, as we have seen, it was the urban middle class that took the lead in the struggle for change. In Russia, the bourgeoisie was still small in size and lacking in self-confidence. A few, however, had traveled to the West and were determined to import Western values and institutions into the backward Russian environment. At mid-century, a few progressive intellectuals went out to the villages to arouse their rural brethren to the need for change. Known as narodniks (from the Russian term narod, for "people" or "nation"), they sought to energize the Russian peasant as a force for the transformation of Russian society. Although many saw the answer to Russian problems in the Western European model, others insisted on the uniqueness of the Russian experience and sought to bring about a revitalization of the country on the basis of the communal traditions of the native village.

For the most part, such efforts achieved little. The muzhik (Russian peasant) was resistant to change and suspicious of outsiders. In desperation, some radical intellectuals turned to terrorism in the hope that assassinations of public officials would spark tsarist repression, thus demonstrating the brutality of the system and galvanizing popular anger. Chief among such groups was the Narodnaya Volya ("the People's Will"), a terrorist organization that carried out the assassination of Tsar Alexander II in 1881.

The assassination of Alexander II convinced his son and successor, Alexander III (r. 1881–1894), that reform had been a mistake, and he quickly returned to the repressive measures of earlier tsars. When Alexander III died, his weak son and successor, Nicholas II (r. 1894–1917) began his rule armed with his father's conviction that the absolute power of the tsars should be preserved.

But it was too late, for conditions were changing. Although industrialization came late to Russia, it progressed rapidly after 1890, especially with the assistance of foreign investment capital. By 1900, Russia had become the fourth largest producer of steel behind the United States, Germany, and Great Britain. At the same time, Russia was turning out half of the world's production of oil. Conditions for the working class, however, were abysmal, and opposition to the tsarist regime from workers, peasants, and intellectuals finally exploded into revolt in 1905. Faced with an exhaustive war with Japan in Asia (see Chapter 3), Tsar Nicholas reluctantly granted civil liberties and agreed to create a Duma, or legislative assembly, elected directly by a broad franchise. But real constitutional monarchy proved short-lived. By 1907, the tsar had curtailed the power of the Duma and fell back on the army and the bureaucracy to rule Russia.

The Ottoman Empire and Nationalism in the Balkans

Like the Austro-Hungarian Empire, the Ottoman Empire was threatened by the rising nationalist aspirations of its subject peoples. Beginning in the fourteenth century, the Ottoman Turks had expanded from their base in the Anatolian peninsula and expanded into the Balkans, southern Russia, and along the northern coast of Africa. By the sixteenth century, they controlled the entire eastern half of the Mediterranean Sea. But by the nineteenth century, corruption and inefficiency had gradually weakened the once powerful empire so that only the interference of the great European powers, who were fearful of each other's designs on the empire, kept it alive.

But the emotional appeal of nationhood gradually began to make inroads among the various ethnic and linguistic groups in southeastern Europe. In the course of the nineteenth century, the Balkan provinces of the Ottoman Empire began to gain their freedom, although the intense rivalry in the region between Austria-Hungary and Russia complicated the process. Serbia had already received a large degree of autonomy in 1829, although it remained a province of the Ottoman Empire until 1878. Greece became an independent kingdom in 1830 after a successful revolt. By the Treaty of Adrianople in 1829, Russia received a protectorate over the principalities of Moldavia and Walachia, but was forced to give them up after the Crimean War. In 1861, Moldavia and Walachia were merged into the state of Romania. Not until Russia's defeat of the Ottoman Empire in 1878, however, was Romania recognized as completely independent, as was Serbia at the same time. Although freed from Turkish rule, Montenegro was placed under an Austrian protectorate, while Bulgaria achieved autonomous status under Russian protection. The other Balkan territories of Bosnia and Herzegovina were placed under Austrian protection; Austria could occupy but not annex them. Despite these gains, by the end of the nineteenth century, the force of Balkan nationalism was by no means stilled.

Meanwhile, other parts of the empire began to break away from central control. In Egypt, the ambitious governor Muhammed Ali declared the region's autonomy from Istanbul and initiated a series of reforms designed to promote economic growth and government efficiency. During the 1830s, he sought to improve agricultural production and reform the educational system, and he imported machinery and technicians from Europe to carry out the first industrial revolution on African soil. In the end, however, the effort failed, partly because Egypt's manufactures could not compete with those of Europe, and also because much of the profit from the export of cash crops went into the hands of conservative landlords.

Measures to promote industrialization elsewhere in the empire had even less success. By mid-century, a small industrial sector, built with equipment imported from Europe, took shape, and a modern system of transport and communications began to make its appearance. By the end of the century, however, the results were meager.

Liberalism Triumphant

In Western Europe and North America, liberal principles experienced a better fate. By 1871, Great Britain had a functioning two-party parliamentary system. For fifty years, the Liberals and Conservatives alternated in power at regular intervals, although they also shared some common features. Both were dominated by a ruling class comprised of a coalition of aristocratic landowners frequently involved in industrial and financial activities and upper-middle-class businessmen. And both competed with each other in supporting legislation that expanded the right to vote. Reform Acts in 1867 and 1884 greatly expanded the number of adult males who could vote, and by the end of World War I, all males over twenty-one and women over thirty could vote. In 1911, parliamentary legislation curtailed the power of the House of Lords and instituted the payment of salaries to members of the House of Commons, which further democratized that institution by at least opening the door to people other than the wealthy. By the beginning of World War I, political democracy had become well entrenched and was soon accompanied by social welfare measures for the working class.

The growth of trade unions, which began to advocate more radical change of the economic system, and the emergence in 1900 of the Labour party, which dedicated itself to workers' interests, put pressure on the Liberals. The Liberals, who held the government from 1906 to 1914, perceived that they would have to initiate a program of social welfare or lose the support of the workers. Therefore, they abandoned the classical principles of laissez-faire and voted for a series of social reforms. The

National Insurance Act of 1911 provided benefits for workers in case of sickness or unemployment, to be paid for by compulsory contributions from workers, employers, and the state. Additional legislation provided a small pension for those over seventy and compensation for those injured in accidents while at work. While the program benefits and tax increases were both modest, they were the first hesitant steps toward the future British welfare state.

A similar process was under way in France, where the overthrow of Napoleon III's Second Empire in 1870 led to the creation of a republican form of government. France failed, however, to develop a strong parliamentary system on the British two-party model because the existence of a dozen political parties forced the premier to depend upon a coalition of parties to stay in power. The Third Republic was notorious for its changes of government. Between 1875 and 1914, there were no fewer than fifty cabinet changes; during the same period, the British had eleven. Nevertheless, the government's moderation gradually encouraged more and more middle-class and peasant support, and by 1914, the Third Republic commanded the loyalty of most French people.

By 1870, Italy had emerged as a geographically united state with pretensions to great-power status. Its internal weaknesses, however, gave that claim a particularly hollow ring. Sectional differences—a poverty-stricken south and an industrializing north—weakened any sense of community. Chronic turmoil between labor and industry undermined the social fabric. The Italian government was unable to deal effectively with these problems because of the extensive corruption among government officials and the lack of stability created by ever-changing government coalitions. Abroad, Italy's pretensions to great-power status proved equally hollow when Italy became the first European power to lose a war to an African state, Ethiopia, a disgrace that later led to the costly (but successful) attempt to compensate by conquering Libya in 1911 and 1912.

The United States and Canada

Between 1860 and World War I, the United States made the shift from an agrarian to a mighty industrial nation. American heavy industry stood unchallenged in 1900. In that year, the Carnegie Steel Company alone produced more steel than Great Britain's entire steel industry. Industrialization also led to urbanization. While established cities, such as New York, Philadelphia, and Boston, grew even larger, other moderate-size cities, such as

Pittsburgh, grew by leaps and bounds because of industrialization. Whereas 20 percent of Americans lived in cities in 1860, more than 40 percent did in 1900.

By 1900, the United States had become the world's richest nation and greatest industrial power. Yet serious questions remained about the quality of American life. In 1890, the richest 9 percent of Americans owned an incredible 71 percent of all the wealth. Labor unrest over unsafe working conditions, strict work discipline, and periodic cycles of devastating unemployment led workers to organize. By the turn of the century, one national organization, the American Federation of Labor, emerged as labor's dominant voice. Its lack of real power, however, is reflected in its membership figures. In 1900, it constituted but 8.4 percent of the American industrial labor force. One part of the U.S. labor force remained almost entirely disenfranchised. Although the victory of the North in the Civil War led to the abolition of slavery, political, economic, and social opportunities for the country's African American population remained limited, and racist attitudes were widespread.

During the so-called Progressive Era after 1900, the reform of many features of American life became a primary issue. At the state level, reforming governors sought to achieve clean government by introducing elements of direct democracy, such as direct primaries for selecting nominees for public office. State governments also enacted economic and social legislation, including laws that governed hours, wages, and working conditions, especially for women and children. The realization that state laws were ineffective in dealing with nationwide problems, however, led to a progressive movement at the national level.

National progressivism was evident in the administrations of both Theodore Roosevelt and Woodrow Wilson. Under Roosevelt (1901–1909), a Meat Inspection Act and Pure Food and Drug Act provided for a limited degree of federal regulation of corrupt industrial practices. Roosevelt's expressed principle, "We draw the line against misconduct, not against wealth," guaranteed that public protection would have to be within limits tolerable to big corporations. Wilson (1913–1921) was responsible for the creation of a graduated federal income tax and a Federal Reserve System that permitted the federal government to have a role in important economic decisions formerly made by bankers. Like European states, the United States was moving slowly into policies that extended the functions of the state.

By the end of the nineteenth century, many Americans believed that the United States was ready to expand abroad. The Pacific islands were the scene of great-

power competition and witnessed the entry of the United States on the imperialist stage. The Samoan Islands became the first important American colony; the Hawaiian Islands were the next to fall. Soon after Americans had made Pearl Harbor into a naval station in 1887, American settlers gained control of the sugar industry on the islands. When Hawaiian natives tried to reassert their authority, the U.S. Marines were brought in to "protect" American lives. Hawaii was annexed by the United States in 1898 during the era of American nationalistic fervor generated by the Spanish-American War. The American defeat of Spain encouraged Americans to extend their empire by acquiring Puerto Rico, Guam, and the Philippine Islands. Although the Filipinos hoped for independence, the Americans refused to grant it. According to President William McKinley, the United States had a duty "to educate the Filipinos and uplift and Christianize them"—a remarkable statement in view of the fact that most of them had been Roman Catholics for centuries. It took three years and 60,000 troops to pacify the Philippines and establish American control. By the first decade of the twentieth century, American possessions in the Caribbean and Asia had made the United States another Western imperialist power.

Canada, too, faced problems of national unity between 1870 and 1914. At the beginning of 1870, the Dominion of Canada had only four provinces: Quebec, Ontario, Nova Scotia, and New Brunswick. With the addition of two more provinces in 1871—Manitoba and British Columbia—the Dominion of Canada now extended from the Atlantic Ocean to the Pacific. But real unity was difficult to achieve because of the distrust between the English-speaking and French-speaking peoples of Canada. Fortunately for Canada, Wilfred Lanier, who became the first French-Canadian prime minister in 1896, was able to reconcile Canada's two major groups and resolve the issue of separate schools for French-Canadians. Lanier's administration also witnessed increased industrialization and successfully encouraged immigrants from central and eastern Europe to help populate Canada's vast territories.

Change and Tradition in Latin America

Encouraged by liberal and nationalist ideas prevalent in Europe, the peoples of Latin American began to free themselves from colonial rule and established independent states in the first decades of the nineteenth century. As industrialization progressed in Europe and the United States, those countries experienced an ever-greater need for food and raw materials. Latin American nations provided these goods. Their increasing prosperity was based to a large extent on the export of one or two commodities from each region, such as wheat and beef from Argentina, coffee from Brazil, nitrates from Chile, coffee and bananas from Central America, and sugar and silver from Peru. Exports from Argentina doubled between 1873 and 1893; Mexican exports quadrupled between 1877 and 1900. These foodstuffs and raw materials were largely exchanged for finished goods—textiles, machines, and luxury products—from Europe and the United States. With economic growth came a boom in foreign investment. Between 1870 and 1913, British investments—mostly in railroads, mining, and public utilities—grew from £85 million to £757 million, which constituted two-thirds of all foreign investment in Latin America. As Latin Americans struggled to create more balanced economies after 1900, they concentrated on increasing industrialization, especially by building textile, food-processing, and construction-material factories.

Nevertheless, the growth of the Latin American economy came largely from the export of raw materials, and economic modernization in Latin America simply added to the growing dependency of Latin America on the capitalist nations of the West. Modernization was basically a surface feature of Latin American society, where past patterns still largely prevailed. Rural elites dominated their estates and their rural workers. Although slavery was abolished by 1888, former slaves and their descendants were still at the bottom of society. The Indians remained poverty-stricken, debt servitude was still a way of life, and Latin America remained economically dependent on foreigners. Despite its economic growth, Latin America was still an underdeveloped region of the world.

The prosperity that resulted from the development of an export economy had both social and political repercussions. One result socially was the modernization of the elites, who grew determined to pursue their vision of modern progress. Large landowners increasingly sought ways to rationalize their production methods in order to make greater profits. As a result, cattle ranchers in Argentina and coffee barons in Brazil became more aggressive entrepreneurs.

Another result of the new prosperity was the growth of a small but increasingly visible middle class—lawyers, merchants, shopkeepers, businessmen, schoolteachers, professors, bureaucrats, and military officers. Regardless of the country, they shared some common characteristics. They lived in the cities, sought education and de-

cent incomes, and increasingly saw the United States as the model to emulate, especially in regard to industrialization and education.

As Latin American export economies boomed, the working class expanded, which in turn led to the growth of labor unions, especially after 1914. Radical unions often advocated the use of the general strike as an instrument for change. By and large, however, the governing elites succeeded in stifling the political influence of the working class by restricting their right to vote. The need for industrial labor also led Latin American countries to encourage European immigrants. Between 1880 and 1914, 3 million Europeans, primarily Italians and Spaniards, settled in Argentina. More than 100,000 Europeans, mostly Italian, Portuguese, and Spanish, arrived in Brazil each year between 1891 and 1900.

As in Europe and the United States, industrialization led to urbanization, evident in both the emergence of new cities and the rapid growth of old ones. Buenos Aires (the "Paris" of South America) had 750,000 inhabitants by 1900 and 2 million by 1914—a fourth of Argentina's population. By that time, urban dwellers made up 53 percent of Argentina's population overall. Brazil and Chile also witnessed a dramatic increase in the number of urban dwellers.

Latin America also experienced a political transformation after 1870. Large landowners began to take a more direct interest in national politics, sometimes expressed by a direct involvement in governing. In Argentina and Chile, for example, landholding elites controlled the governments, and although they produced constitutions similar to those of the United States and Europe, they were careful to ensure their power by regulating voting rights.

In some countries, large landowners made use of dictators to maintain the interests of the ruling elite. Porfirio Díaz, who ruled Mexico from 1876 to 1910, established a conservative, centralized government with the support of the army, foreign capitalists, large landowners, and the Catholic Church, all of whom benefited from their alliance. But there were forces for change in Mexico that sought to precipitate a true social revolution.

The Rise of the Socialist Movement

One of the less desirable consequences of the Industrial Revolution was the yawning disparity in the distribution of wealth. If industrialization brought increasing affluence to an emerging middle class, to millions of others it brought grinding hardship in the form of low-paying jobs in mines or factories characterized by long working hours under squalid conditions. The underlying cause was clear: Under the circumstances prevailing in most industrializing societies in Europe, factory owners remained largely free to hire labor on their own terms based on market forces.

Beginning in the last decades of the eighteenth century, radical groups began to seek the means to rectify the problem. Some found the answer in intellectual schemes that envisaged a classless society based on the elimination of private property. Others prepared for an armed revolt to overthrow the ruling order and create a new society controlled by the working masses. Still others began to form trade unions to fight for improved working conditions and reasonable wages. Only one group sought to combine all of these factors into a comprehensive program to destroy the governing forces and create a new egalitarian society based on the concept of "scientific socialism." The founder of that movement was Karl Marx, a German Jew who had abandoned an academic career in philosophy to take up radical political activities in Paris.

Marxism made its first appearance on the eve of the revolutions of 1848 with the publication of a short treatise, *The Communist Manifesto*, written by Karl Marx (1818–1883) and his close collaborator, Friedrich Engels (1820–1895). In the *Manifesto*, the two authors predicted the outbreak of a massive uprising that would overthrow the existing ruling class and bring to power a new revolutionary regime based on their ideas (see box on p. 19).

When revolutions broke out all over Europe in that eventful year of 1848, Marx and Engels eagerly but mistakenly predicted that the uprisings would spread throughout Europe and lead to a new revolutionary regime led by workers, dispossessed bourgeoisie, and communists. What had gone wrong? In the aftermath of defeat, they realized that they had been unduly optimistic about the prospects for social revolution in mid-century Europe.

Sobered by reality, Marx now realized that his expectation that Europe was on the verge of social revolution was premature. The urban merchants and the peasants, he concluded, were too conservative to support the workers and would oppose revolution once their own immediate economic demands were satisfied. As for the worker movement itself, it was clearly still too weak to seize power and could not expect to achieve its own objectives until the workers had become politically more sophisticated and better organized. In effect, revolution would not take place in Western Europe until capitalism

had "ripened," leading to a concentration of capital in the hands of a wealthy minority and an "epidemic of overproduction" because of inadequate purchasing power by the impoverished lower classes. Then, a large and increasingly alienated proletariat could drive the capitalists from power and bring about a classless utopia.

For the remainder of his life, Marx acted out the logic of these conclusions. From his base in London, he undertook a massive study of the dynamics of the capitalist system, a project that resulted in the publication of the first volume of his most famous work, *Das Kapital* ("Capital"), in 1869. In the meantime, he attempted to prepare for the future revolution by organizing the scattered radical parties throughout Europe into a cohesive revolutionary movement that would be ready to arouse the workers to action when the opportunity came. That organization, called the International Workingmen's Association (usually known today as the First International), was founded in 1864 in London and included radical groups from Great Britain and Spain to imperial Russia.

Unity was short-lived. Although all members of the First International shared a common distaste for the capitalist system, some preferred to reform it from within (many of the labor groups from Great Britain), whereas others were convinced that only violent insurrection would suffice to destroy the existing ruling class (Karl Marx and the Anarchists around the Russian revolutionary Mikhail Bakunin). Even the radicals could not agree. Marx believed that revolution could not succeed without a core of committed communists to organize and lead the masses; Bakunin contended that the general insurrection should be a spontaneous uprising from below. Such differences over strategy were exacerbated by personality conflicts (Marx, in particular, could not tolerate an intellectual rival), and in 1871, the First International disintegrated.

While Marx was grappling with the problems of preparing for the coming revolution, capitalism in Europe was itself undergoing significant changes. The advanced capitalist states such as Great Britain, France, and the Low Countries (Belgium, Luxembourg, and the Netherlands) were gradually evolving into mature, politically stable societies in which Marx's dire predictions were not being borne out. His forecast of periodic economic crises was correct enough, but his warnings of concentration of capital and the impoverishment of labor were somewhat wide of the mark, as capitalist societies began to eliminate or at least reduce some of the more flagrant inequities apparent in the early stages of capitalist development. Antitrust laws limited the growth of powerful monopolies that would strangle competition; social leg-

❧ A Communist Manifesto ❦

"A spectre is haunting Europe—the spectre of Communism." *With these portentous words, penned in 1847, Karl Marx began his most famous work,* The Communist Manifesto. *With the assistance of his close collaborator, Friedrich Engels, Marx wrote the pamphlet at the request of a British labor union group seeking to publicize its activities among factory workers in London.*

In writing the pamphlet, Marx and Engels hoped to promote their own efforts not simply to improve working conditions in Great Britain, but also to arouse popular support for a vast revolution that would sweep away the capitalist system and create a new, classless society. In their view, the motive force in human history was class struggle. Marx believed that whoever owned the sources of economic wealth in a given society—whether that wealth consisted of factories, raw materials, domesticated animals, or land—controlled the state and defined the culture and beliefs of that society. When the tensions between the oppressors and the exploited masses in a given society had become too glaring, the existing ruling class would be overthrown and a new form of society would emerge into being. That new society, in turn, would be dominated by a new ruling class based on new economic relationships, leading to the growth of new tensions that would result in its own eventual destruction. Only when the oppression of one class by another came to an end in the final stage of communism would the cycle be broken and a utopian society take shape.

According to Marx and Engels, then, human society passes through several stages en route to its final resting place in the classless society of utopian communism. European society during the Middle Ages had given rise to the landholding feudal class, but feudalism was now giving way to capitalism under the Industrial Revolution, which led to the introduction of new technology and the rise of the bourgeoisie as the dominant class in society. Capitalism was itself essentially oppressive, however, because it was based on the ability of the ruling capitalist class to exploit the workers (known in Marxist parlance as the proletariat). According to Marx, the political system of emerging capitalism—which he called bourgeois democracy—was a tool of the capitalist class, for although it promised freedom and equality, it actually permitted a level of economic inequality and exploitation equal to, if different in form from, that which had existed under feudalism.

In *The Communist Manifesto,* Marx and Engels set out these ideas in simple terms accessible to understanding by unsophisticated readers. "The proletariat," it said, "will use its political supremacy to wrest, by degrees, all capital from the bourgeoisie, to centralize all instruments of production in the hands of the State, i.e., of the proletariat organized as the ruling class." Once that had been achieved, a program would be adopted to abolish private ownership of property and bring to an end the exploitation of man by man. Once that had been achieved, the State itself would begin to wither away. "In place of the old bourgeois society, with its classes and class antagonisms," it concluded, "we shall have an association, in which the free development of each is the condition of the free development of all."

Source: Karl Marx and Friedrich Engels, *The Communist Manifesto,* ed. A. J. P. Taylor (New York: Viking Penguin, 1967).

---

islation protected the right of workers to organize for collective bargaining and to provide for improved working conditions and health benefits. These reforms occurred because workers and their representatives had begun to use the democratic political process to their own advantage, organizing labor unions and political parties to improve working conditions and enhance the role of workers in the political system. Many of these political parties were led by Marxists, who were learning that in the absence of a social revolution to bring the masses to power, the capitalist democratic system could be reformed from within to improve the working and living conditions of their constituents. In 1889, after Marx's death, several such parties (often labeled social democratic parties) formed the Second International, dominated by reformist elements committed to achieving socialism within the bounds of the Western parliamentary system.

Why had Marx misread the path of capitalism in Western Europe? Perhaps his main mistake was in failing to see the self-corrective elements in the capitalist system that would rectify some of the more glaring abuses brought about by the Industrial Revolution. Marx predicted that the ruling capitalist class, motivated by blind greed, would rush headlong to its doom. He did not envisage the capacity of political leaders in capitalist countries to see the need for a more equitable sharing of the wealth and power created by the capitalist machine. Perhaps, too, Marx had misread the mind of his own sacred class, the proletariat. He did not see the degree to which workers would be satisfied with economic, social, and political reforms that would provide them with a share (albeit a small one) of the West's growing wealth and power. Nor did he realize the degree to which workers in most European countries would be attracted to the appeal of nationalism. Marx had viewed nation and culture as false idols diverting the interests of the oppressed from their true concern—the struggle against the ruling class. In his view, the proletariat would throw off its chains and unite in the sacred cause of "internationalist" world revolution. In reality, workers joined peasants and urban merchants in defending the cause of the nation against its foreign enemies. A generation later, French workers would die in the trenches defending France from workers across the German border.

A historian of the late nineteenth century might have been forgiven for predicting that Marxism, as a revolutionary ideology, was dead. In fact, however, the new century would see a rapid revival of the Marxist vision as one of the dominant political and ideological forces of the new era. While Western European states were evolving into mature capitalist societies, the evolving situation in Russia was creating conditions that, over time, would put Marxist parties in power in much of Eastern Europe. If Marx's radical vision seemed dead in Western Europe, in the East it was about to be reborn.

Toward the Modern Consciousness: Intellectual and Cultural Developments

Before 1914, most Westerners continued to believe in the values and ideals that had been generated by the impact of the scientific revolution and the Enlightenment. Reason, science, and progress were still important words in the European vocabulary. The ability of human beings to improve themselves and achieve a better society seemed to be well demonstrated by a rising standard of living, urban improvements, and mass education. Such products of modern technology as electric lights, phonographs, and automobiles reinforced the popular prestige of science and the belief in the ability of the human mind to understand the universe. Between 1870 and 1914, however, a dramatic transformation in the realm of ideas and culture challenged many of these assumptions. A new view of the physical universe, alternative views of human nature, and radically innovative forms of literary and artistic expression shattered old beliefs and opened the way to a modern consciousness. Although the real impact of many of these ideas was not felt until after World War I, they served to provoke a sense of confusion and anxiety before 1914 that would become even more pronounced after the war.

Developments in the Sciences: The Emergence of a New Physics

Science was one of the chief pillars underlying the optimistic and rationalistic view of the world that many Westerners shared in the nineteenth century. Supposedly based on hard facts and cold reason, science offered a certainty of belief in the orderliness of nature that was comforting to many people for whom traditional religious beliefs no longer had much meaning. Many optimistically believed that the application of already known scientific laws would give humanity a complete understanding of the physical world and an accurate picture of reality. The new physics dramatically altered that perspective.

Throughout much of the nineteenth century, Westerners adhered to the mechanical conception of the universe postulated by the classical physics of Isaac Newton. In this perspective, the universe was viewed as a giant machine in which time, space, and matter were objective realities that existed independently of those observing them. Matter was thought to be composed of indivisible and solid material bodies called atoms.

These views were first seriously questioned at the end of the nineteenth century. Some scientists had discovered that certain elements such as radium and polonium spontaneously gave off rays or radiation that apparently came from within the atom itself. Atoms were not simply hard, material bodies but small worlds containing such subatomic particles as electrons and protons that behaved in seemingly random and inexplicable fashion. Inquiry into the disintegrative process within atoms became a central theme of the new physics.

Building upon this work, in 1900, a Berlin physicist, Max Planck (1858–1947), rejected the belief that a heated body radiates energy in a steady stream but maintained instead that it did so discontinuously, in irregular packets of energy that he called "quanta." The quantum theory raised fundamental questions about the subatomic realm of the atom. By 1900, the old view of atoms as the basic building blocks of the material world was being seriously questioned, and the world of Newtonian physics was in trouble.

Albert Einstein (1879–1955), a German-born patent officer working in Switzerland, pushed these new theories of thermodynamics into new terrain. In 1905, Einstein published a paper, "The Electrodynamics of Moving Bodies," setting forth his special theory of relativity. According to relativity theory, space and time are not absolute but relative to the observer, and both are interwoven into what Einstein called a four-dimensional space-time continuum. Neither space nor time has an existence independent of human experience. As Einstein later explained to a journalist: "It was formerly believed that if all material things disappeared out of the universe, time and space would be left. According to the relativity theory, however, time and space disappear together with the things."[1] Moreover, matter and energy reflect the relativity of time and space. Einstein concluded that matter was nothing but another form of energy. His epochal formula $E = mc^2$—each particle of matter is equivalent to its mass times the square of the velocity of light—was the key theory explaining the vast energies contained within the atom. It led to the atomic age.

Sigmund Freud and the Emergence of Psychoanalysis

Although poets and mystics had revealed a world of unconscious and irrational behavior, many scientifically oriented intellectuals under the impact of Enlightenment thought continued to believe that human beings responded to conscious motives in a rational fashion. At the end of the nineteenth and beginning of the twentieth century, the Viennese doctor Sigmund Freud (1856–1939) put forth a series of theories that undermined optimism about the rational nature of the human mind. Freud's thought, like the new physics, added to the uncertainties of the age. His major ideas were published in 1900 in his *Interpretation of Dreams*, which laid the basic foundation for what came to be known as psychoanalysis.

According to Freud, human behavior is strongly determined by the unconscious—former experiences and inner drives of which people are largely oblivious. To explore the contents of the unconscious, Freud relied not only on hypnosis but also on dreams, which were dressed in an elaborate code that needed to be deciphered if the contents were to be properly understood.

Why do some experiences whose influence persists in controlling an individual's life remain unconscious? Ac-

◆ **The Scream.** Although the Norwegian artist Evard Munch probably never heard of Sigmund Freud, his painting *The Scream* (1893) graphically illustrates the Viennese psychotherapist's studies on human hysteria and neurosis. Fascinated by a withered Inca mummy shown at the Great Exposition in Paris in 1889, Munch was inspired in his painting to express the human condition, as though, in his words, "the colors were real blood." Although the primal scream portrayed in this canvas was produced at the end of the nineteenth century, it seems to be crying out in prophetic horror at the coming era's mass atrocities.

cording to Freud, repression is a process by which unsettling experiences are blotted from conscious awareness but still continue to influence behavior because they have become part of the unconscious. To explain how repression works, Freud elaborated an intricate theory of the inner life of human beings.

According to Freud, a human being's inner life is a battleground of three contending forces: the id, ego, and superego. The id is the center of unconscious drives and is ruled by what Freud termed the pleasure principle. As creatures of desire, human beings direct their energy toward pleasure and away from pain. The id contains all kinds of lustful drives and desires, crude appetites and impulses, loves and hates. The ego is the seat of reason and hence the coordinator of the inner life. It is governed by the reality principle. Although humans are dominated by the pleasure principle, a true pursuit of pleasure is not feasible. The reality principle means that people become willing to forgo or postpone pleasure so that they might live together in society; reality thwarts the unlimited pursuit of pleasure. The superego is the locus of conscience and represents the inhibitions and moral values that society in general and parents in particular impose upon people. The superego serves to force the ego to curb the unacceptable pressures of the id.

Thus, the conflict among id, ego, and superego dominates the human being's inner life. The ego and superego exert restraining influences on the unconscious id and repress, or keep out of consciousness, what they want to. Repression begins in childhood. Psychoanalysis is thus a dialogue between psychotherapist and patient in which the therapist probes deeply into memory in order to retrace the chain of repression all the way back to its childhood origins. By making the conscious mind aware of the unconscious and its repressed contents, the therapist enables the patient to resolve the psychic conflict.

Literature and the Arts: The Culture of Modernity

The revolution in physics and psychology was paralleled by a revolution in literature and the arts. Before 1914, writers and artists had begun to rebel against the traditional literary and artistic styles that had dominated European cultural life since the Renaissance. The changes that they produced have since been called modernism.

Throughout much of the late nineteenth century, literature was dominated by naturalism. Naturalists accepted the material world as real and believed that literature should be realistic. By addressing social problems, writers could contribute to an objective understanding of the world. Although naturalism was a continuation of realism, it lacked the underlying note of liberal optimism about people and society that had still been prevalent in the 1850s. The naturalists were pessimistic about Europe's future. They doubted the existence of free will and portrayed characters caught in the grip of forces beyond their control.

The novels of the French writer Émile Zola (1840–1902) provide a good example of naturalism. Against a backdrop of the urban slums and coalfields of northern France, Zola showed how alcoholism and different environments affected people's lives. The materialistic science of his age had an important influence on Zola. He had read Darwin's *Origin of Species* and had been impressed by its emphasis on the struggle for survival and the importance of environment and heredity. These themes are central to his *Rougon-Macquart*, a twenty-volume series of novels on the "natural and social history of a family." Zola maintained that the artist must analyze and dissect life as a biologist would a living organism. He said, "I have simply done on living bodies the work of analysis which surgeons perform on corpses."

At the turn of the century, a new group of writers, known as the symbolists, reacted against realism. Primarily interested in writing poetry, the symbolists believed that an objective knowledge of the world was impossible. The external world was not real but only a collection of symbols that reflected the true reality of the individual human mind. Art, they believed, should function for its own sake instead of serving, criticizing, or seeking to understand society. In the works of the symbolist poets W. B. Yeats and Rainer Maria Rilke, poetry ceased to be part of popular culture because only through a knowledge of the poet's personal language could one hope to understand what the poet was saying. Symbolism began in France, and its founder, Stéphane Mallarmé (1842–1898), attempted to summarize its poetic theory in one sentence: "It is not description which can unveil the efficacy and beauty of monuments, seas, or the human face in all their maturity and native state, but rather evocation, allusion, suggestion."

By the beginning of the twentieth century, the belief that the task of art was to represent "reality" had lost much of its meaning. By that time, the new psychology and the new physics had made it evident that many people were not sure what constituted reality anyway. Then, too, the growth of photography gave artists another reason to reject visual realism. First invented in the 1830s, photography became popular and widespread after George Eastman created the first Kodak camera for the mass market in 1888. What was the point of an artist's doing what the camera did better? Unlike the camera, which could only mirror reality, artists could create reality. As in literature, so also in modern art, individual consciousness became the source of meaning. Between the beginning of the new century and the outbreak of World War I in 1914, this search for individual expression produced a great variety of painting schools—including impressionism, expressionism, and cubism—that would have a significant impact on the world of art for decades to come (see box on p. 24).

Modernism in the arts also revolutionized architecture and architectural practices. A new principle known as functionalism motivated this revolution. Functionalism meant that buildings, like the products of machines, should be "functional" or useful, fulfilling the purpose for which they were constructed. Art and engineering were to be unified, and all unnecessary ornamentation was to be stripped away.

The United States was a leader in these pioneering architectural designs. Unprecedented urban growth and the absence of restrictive architectural traditions allowed for new building methods, especially in the relatively new city of Chicago. The Chicago school of the 1890s, led by Louis H. Sullivan (1856–1924), used reinforced concrete, steel frames, electric elevators, and sheet glass to build skyscrapers virtually free of external ornamentation. One of Sullivan's most successful pupils was Frank Lloyd Wright (1869–1959), who became known for innovative designs in domestic architecture. Wright's private houses, built chiefly for wealthy patrons, featured geometric structures with long lines, overhanging roofs, and severe planes of brick and stone. The interiors were open spaces and included cathedral ceilings and built-in furniture and lighting features. Wright pioneered the modern American house.

At the beginning of the twentieth century, developments in music paralleled those in painting. Expressionism in music was a Russian creation, the product of composer Igor Stravinsky (1882–1971) and the Ballet Russe, the dance company of Sergei Diaghilev (1872–1929). Together they revolutionized the world of music with Stravinsky's ballet *The Rite of Spring*. When it was performed in Paris in 1913, the savage and primitive sounds and beats of the music and dance caused a near riot from an audience outraged at its audacity.

Just as artists began to experiment with new revolutionary ways to represent reality in painting, so musicians searched for new revolutionary sounds. In 1907 the Austrian composer Arnold Schoenberg (1874–1991) rejected the traditional tonal system based on the harmonic triad that had dominated Western music since the Renaissance. In order to free the Western ear from traditional harmony and progression, Schoenberg substituted a radically new "atonal" system in which each piece established its own individual set of relationships and structure. In 1923, he devised his twelve-tone system in which he placed the twelve pitches of the chromatic scale found on the piano in a set sequence for a musical composition. The ordering of these twelve tones was to be repeated throughout the piece, for all instrumental parts, constituting its melody and harmony. The series of notes could be reversed, inverted, or transposed but otherwise not altered. Even today, such atonal music

♦ **Les Demoiselles d'Avignon.** In this 1907 painting, Pablo Picasso presents reality in geometric shapes and from several perspectives simultaneously. He uses the African mask, with its elongated shape, to accentuate the violence and impersonality of women—whores who stare dispassionately at us, waiting to be chosen, representing venereal disease and, for Picasso, the impending threat of impotence and castration.

sounds alien and incomprehensible to the uninitiated. Yet, Schoenberg, perhaps more than any other composer, influenced the development of twentieth-century music.

By the end of the nineteenth century, then, traditional forms of literary, artistic, and musical expression were in a state of rapid retreat. Freed from conventional tastes, and responding to the intellectual and social revolution that was getting under way throughout the Western world, painters, writers, composers, and architects launched a variety of radical new ideas that would revolutionize Western culture in coming decades.

Conclusion

During the course of the nineteenth century, Western society underwent a number of dramatic changes. Countries that in 1750 were still predominantly agricultural had by 1900 been transformed into essentially industrial and urban societies. The amount of material

❧ A Revolution in the Arts ❧

Since the Renaissance, artists had attempted to represent reality in painting through the optical illusion of a static three-dimensional perspective. By the late nineteenth century, however, artists began to respond to ongoing investigations into the nature of optics and human perception by experimenting with radical new techniques to represent the multiplicity of reality. They were fascinated with how the eye moves as its focuses on an object or a landscape. How, indeed, could this shifting and multidimensional perspective be captured on a flat piece of canvas? Their passionate search for a new way to represent reality defined new directions for art and literature in the entire twentieth century.

The first to embark on the challenge were the impressionists. Originating in France in the 1870s, they rejected indoor painting and preferred to go out to the countryside to paint nature directly. As Camille Pissarro (1830–1903), one of the movement's founders, expressed it: "Don't proceed according to rules and principles, but paint what you observe and feel. Paint generously and unhesitatingly, for it is best not to lose the first impression."

Although impressionism was ridiculed by the Parisian art establishment at its first exhibition in 1874, it has proven to be the most popular of all art movements in the twentieth century, and its paintings often command millions of dollars on the world market. Most influential of the impressionists was Claude Monet (1840–1926). Fascinated by the transaction between the eye and the mind when viewing a landscape, he painted several series of canvases on the same object—such as haystacks, the Rouen cathedral, and water lilies in the garden of his house on the Seine River—in the hope of breaking down the essential lines, planes, colors, and shadows of what the eye observed. He was especially fascinated with water and painted many pictures in an effort to capture the interplay of light, water, and reflection. The illusion of the water's movement and the luminosity of his landscapes figure as one of the wonders of painting.

In expressionism, the era witnessed another innovative approach to visual representation. Expressionists employed an exaggerated use of colors and distorted shapes in order to achieve emotional expression. This technique, called the "pathetic fallacy," enabled the artist to attribute human emotions to inanimate objects. Painters such as the Dutchman Vincent Van Gogh (1853–1890) and the Swede Edvard Munch (1863–1944) were not interested in capturing the optical play of light on a landscape, but in projecting their inner selves onto the hostile universe around them. Who cannot be affected by the intensity of Van Gogh's dazzling sunflowers, or by the ominous swirling stars above a church steeple in his *Starry Night* (1890)?

One of the most important artists obsessed with finding a new way to portray reality was the French painter Paul Cézanne (1839–1906). Scorning the photographic duplication of a landscape, he sought to isolate the pulsating structure beneath the surface. During the last years of his life, he produced several paintings of Mont Saint Victoire, located near Aix-en-Provence in the south of France. Although each canvas differed in perspective, composition, and color, they all reflect the same technique of reducing the landscape to virtual geometric slabs of color to represent the interconnection of trees, earth, tiled roofs, mountain, and sky. Although at the end of his life he confessed his failure to capture the "magnificent richness" of nature, more than any other artist of his time he influenced modern art, propelling it to seek new ways to express reality.

Following Cézanne was Pablo Picasso (1881–1973), one of the giants of twentieth-century painting. Settling in Paris in 1904, he and the French artist Georges Braque (1882–1963) collaborated in founding cubism, the first truly radical approach in representing visual reality since the Renaissance. To the cubist, any perception of an object was a composite of simultaneous and different perspectives. Their paintings accordingly sought to present a synthesized view of an object from all sides simultaneously. Even today, Picasso's *Les Demoiselles d'Avignon* (1907) is still disturbing, with its geometrical women staring out at the viewer with questioning yet indifferent stares. Picasso had intended the painting to call attention to the problem of venereal disease, as the five women represented prostitutes on display, waiting for the viewer-client to select one of them for his pleasure. To some critics, the women's threatening presence reflected Picasso's own fear of women and his underlying anxiety about impotence and castration. Others have pointed to the influence of African art, and in particular to the African mask, which cubists saw as a means of distorting reality and expressing the underlying role of violence in human existence.

Source: Robert Hughes, *The Shock of the New* (New York: Knopf, 1996).

goods available to consumers had increased manyfold, and machines were rapidly replacing labor-intensive methods of production and distribution. The social changes were equally striking. Human beings were becoming more mobile, and enjoyed more creature comforts, than at any time since the Roman Empire. A mass society, based on the principles of universal education, limited government, and an expanding franchise, was in the process of creation.

The Industrial Revolution had thus vastly expanded the horizons and the potential of the human race. It had also broken down many walls of aristocratic privilege and opened the door to a new era based on merit. Yet the costs had been high. The distribution of wealth was as unequal as ever, and working and living condi-tions for millions of Europeans had probably deterio-rated. The psychological impact of such rapid changes had also produced feelings of anger, frustration, and alienation on the part of many who lived through them. With the old certainties of religion and science now increasingly under challenge, many faced the future with doubt or foreboding.

Meanwhile, along the borders of Europe—in Russia, in the Balkans, and in the vast Ottoman Empire—the Industrial Revolution had not yet made an impact, or was just getting underway. Old autocracies found themselves under increasing pressure from ethnic minorities and other discontented subjects, but continued to resist pressure for reform. As the world prepared to enter a new century, the stage was set for dramatic change.

NOTES

1. Quoted in Arthur E. E. McKenzie, *The Major Achievements of Science* (New York, 1960), 1:310.

CHAPTER

2

The High Tide of Imperialism: Africa and Asia in an Era of Western Dominance

During the nineteenth and early twentieth centuries, Western colonialism spread throughout much of the non-Western world. Spurred by the demands of the Industrial Revolution, a few powerful Western states—notably Great Britain, France, Germany, Russia, and the United States—competed avari- *ciously for consumer markets and raw materials for their expanding economies. By the end of the nineteenth century, virtually all of the traditional societies in Asia and Africa were under direct or indirect colonial rule.*

The Myth of European Superiority

To many Western observers at the time, the ease of the European conquest provided a clear affirmation of the innate superiority of Western civilization to its counterparts in Asia and Africa. Historians in Europe and the United States began to view world history essentially as the story of the inexorable rise of the West from the glories of ancient Greece to the emergence of modern Europe after the Enlightenment and the Industrial Revolution. Under the circumstances, it was easy to conclude that the extension of Western influence to Africa and Asia, a process that began with the arrival of European fleets in the Indian Ocean in the early sixteenth century, was a reflection of Western cultural superiority and represented a necessary step in bringing civilization to the peoples of that area.

The truth, however, was quite different, for Western global hegemony was a relatively recent phenomenon. Prior to the age of Christopher Columbus, Europe was only an isolated appendage of a much larger world system of states stretching from the Atlantic to the Pacific oceans. The center of gravity in this trade network was not in Europe or even in the Mediterranean Sea, but much further to the east, in the Persian Gulf, and in Central Asia. The most sophisticated and technologically advanced region in the world was not Europe but China, whose proud history could be traced back several thousand years to the rise of the first Chinese state in the Yellow River Valley. As for the transcontinental trade network that linked the continent of Europe with the nations of the Middle East, South Asia, and the Pacific basin, it had not been created by Portuguese and Spanish navigators but had already developed under the Arab Empire of the Abbasids, with its capital in Baghdad. Later, the Mongols took control of the land trade routes during their conquest of much of the Eurasian continent in the thirteenth and fourteenth centuries. During the long centuries of Arabic and Mongolian hegemony, the caravan routes and sea lanes stretching across the Eurasian continent and the Indian Ocean between China, Africa, and Europe carried not only commercial goods, but also ideas and inventions such as the compass, printing, Arabic numerals, and gunpowder. It was inventions such as these, many of them originating in China or India, which would later play a major role in the emergence of Europe as a major player on the world's stage.

Commercial and cultural relations between Europe and the societies of Africa and Asia, of course, were not a new phenomenon and had indeed existed for centuries. The ancient Greeks had maintained trade relations with Egypt and the countries beyond the Red Sea. China and the Roman Empire had established at least indirect commercial relations with each other, and although those links were broken with the collapse of Rome and the rise of the Arab Empire, they resumed in the fifteenth and sixteenth centuries, when Portuguese fleets, led by the famous adventurer Vasco da Gama, sailed down the coast of Africa and into the Indian Ocean in search of the Spice Islands. For the next three centuries, the ships of several European nations crossed the seas in quest of the spices, silks, precious metals, and porcelains of the Orient.

In a few cases, Europeans engaged in military conquest as a means of seeking their objective. The islands of the Indonesian archipelago were gradually brought under Dutch colonial rule, while the British inexorably extended their political hegemony over the South Asian subcontinent. Spain, Portugal, and later other nations of Western Europe divided up the New World into separate colonial territories. For the most part, however, European nations were satisfied to trade with their Asian and African counterparts from coastal enclaves that they had established along the trade routes that threaded across the seas en route from the ports along the Atlantic and the Mediterranean Sea to their far-off destinations.

The Spread of Colonial Rule

In the nineteenth century, a new phase of Western expansion into Asia and Africa began. Whereas European aims in the East before 1800 could be summed up in Vasco da Gama's famous phrase "Christians and spices," in the early nineteenth century a new relationship took shape: European nations began to view Asian and African societies as a source of industrial raw materials and a market for Western manufactured goods. No longer were Western gold and silver exchanged for cloves, pepper, tea, silk, and porcelain. Now the prodigious output of European factories was sent to Africa and Asia in return for oil, tin, rubber, and the other resources needed to fuel the Western industrial machine.

The reason for this change, of course, was the Industrial Revolution. Now industrializing countries in the West needed vital raw materials that were not available at home as well as a reliable market for the goods produced in their factories. The latter factor became increasingly crucial as capitalist societies began to discover that their home markets could not always absorb domestic output. When consumer demand lagged, economic depression threatened.

As Western economic expansion into Asia and Africa gathered strength during the last quarter of the nineteenth century, it became fashionable to call the process imperialism. Although the term *imperialism* has many meanings, in this instance it referred to the efforts of capitalist states in the West to seize markets, cheap raw materials, and lucrative sources for the investment of capital in the countries beyond Western civilization. In this interpretation, the primary motives behind the Western expansion were economic. The best-known promoter of this view was the British political economist John A. Hobson, who published a major analysis, *Imperialism: A Study,* in 1902. In this influential book, Hobson maintained that modern imperialism was a direct consequence of the modern industrial economy.

As in the earlier phase of Western expansion, however, the issue was not simply an economic one. As Hobson himself conceded, economic concerns were inevitably tinged with political ones and with questions of national grandeur and moral purpose as well. In nineteenth-century Europe, economic wealth, national status, and political power went hand in hand with the possession of a colonial empire, at least in the minds of observers at the time. To nineteenth-century global strategists, colonies brought tangible benefits in the world of balance-of-power politics as well as economic profits, and many nations became involved in the pursuit of colonies as much to gain advantage over their rivals as to acquire territory for its own sake.

The relationship between colonialism and national survival was expressed directly in a speech by French politician Jules Ferry in 1885. A policy of "containment or abstinence," he warned, would set France on "the broad road to decadence" and initiate its decline into a "third- or fourth-rate power." British imperialists agreed. To Cecil Rhodes, the most famous empire builder of his day, the extraction of material wealth from the colonies was only a secondary matter. "My ruling purpose," he remarked, "is the extension of the British Empire."[1] That British Empire, on which (as the saying went) "the sun never set," was the envy of its rivals and was viewed as the primary source of British global dominance during the latter half of the nineteenth century.

With the change in European motives for colonization came a corresponding shift in tactics. Earlier, when their economic interests were more limited, European states had generally been satisfied to deal with existing independent states rather than attempt to establish direct control over vast territories. There had been exceptions where state power at the local level was on the point of collapse (as in India), where European economic interests were especially intense (as in Latin America and the East Indies), or where there was no centralized authority (as in North America and the Philippines). But for the most part, the Western presence in Asia and Africa had been limited to controlling the regional trade network and establishing a few footholds where the foreigners could carry on trade and missionary activity.

After 1800, the demands of industrialization in Europe created a new set of dynamics. Maintaining access to industrial raw materials, such as oil and rubber, and setting up reliable markets for European manufactured products required more extensive control over colonial territories. As competition for colonies increased, the colonial powers sought to solidify their hold over their territories to protect them from attack by their rivals. During the last two decades of the nineteenth century, the quest for colonies became a scramble, as all the major European states, now joined by the United States and Japan, engaged in a global land grab. In many cases, economic interests were secondary to security concerns or the requirements of national prestige. In Africa, for example, the British engaged in a struggle with their rivals to protect their interests in the Suez Canal and the Red Sea. In Southeast Asia, the United States seized the Philippines from Spain at least partly to keep them out of the hands of the Japanese, while the French took over Indochina for fear that it would otherwise be occupied by Germany, Japan, or the United States.

By 1900, virtually all the societies of Africa and Asia were either under full colonial rule or, as in the case of China and the Ottoman Empire, on the point of virtual collapse. Only a handful of states, such as Japan in East Asia, Thailand in Southeast Asia, Afghanistan and Iran in the Middle East, and mountainous Ethiopia in East Africa, managed to escape internal disintegration or political subjection to colonial rule. For the most part, the exceptions were the result of good fortune rather than design. Thailand escaped subjugation primarily because officials in London and Paris found it more convenient to transform the country into a buffer state than to fight over it. Ethiopia and Afghanistan survived because of their remote location and mountainous terrain. Only Ja-

pan managed to avoid the common fate through a concerted strategy of political and economic reform. As the new century began, European hegemony over the ancient civilizations of Asia and Africa seemed complete.

The British Conquest of India

The first of the major Asian civilizations to fall victim to European predatory activities was India. The first organized society (commonly known today as Harappan civilization) had emerged in the Indus River Valley in the fourth and third millennia B.C.E. After the influx of Aryan peoples across the Hindu Kush in the Indian subcontinent around 1500 B.C.E., a new civilization based on sedentary agriculture and a regional trade network gradually emerged with its central focus in the Ganges River basin, in north central India. The unity of the subcontinent was first established by the empire of the Mauryas in the third century B.C.E. Although the Mauryan state eventually collapsed, it had laid the foundation for the creation of a technologically advanced and prosperous civilization, and its concept of political unity was later reasserted by the Guptas, who ruled the region for nearly two hundred years until they too were overthrown in about 500 C.E. Under the Guptas, Hinduism, a religious faith brought to the subcontinent by the Aryan people, evolved into the dominant religion of the Indian people.

Beginning in the eleventh century, much of northern India fell under the rule of Turkic-speaking people who penetrated into the subcontinent from the northwest and introduced the people in the area to the Islamic religion and civilization. At the end of the fifteenth century, they were succeeded by the Mughals, a powerful new force from the mountains to the north. The Mughal rulers, although foreigners and Muslims like many of their immediate predecessors, nevertheless brought India to a level of political power and cultural achievement that inspired admiration and envy throughout the entire region.

The Mughal Empire reached the peak of its greatness under the famed Emperor Akbar (r. 1556–1605) and maintained its vitality under a series of strong rulers for another century. Then the dynasty began to weaken, as Hindu forces in southern India sought to challenge the authority of the Mughal court in Delhi. This process of fragmentation was probably hastened by the growing presence of European traders, who began to establish enclaves along the fringes of the subcontinent. Eventually the British and the French began to seize control of the regional trade routes and to meddle in the internal politics of the subcontinent. By the end of the eighteenth century, nothing remained of the empire but a shell. Into the vacuum left by its final decay stepped the British, who used a combination of firepower and guile to consolidate their power over the subcontinent.

The Colonial Takeover of Southeast Asia

Southeast Asia had been one of the first destinations for European adventurers en route to the East. Lured by the riches of the "Spice Islands" (located in the eastern islands of present-day Indonesia), European adventurers sailed to the area in the early sixteenth century in the hope of seizing control over the spice trade from Arab and Indian merchants. By the next century, the trade was fast becoming a monopoly of the Dutch, whose sturdy ships and ample supply of capital gave them a significant advantage over their rivals.

Well before the arrival of the first Europeans, however, Southeast Asia had been an active participant in the global trade network, purchasing textiles from India and luxury goods from China in return for spices, precious metals, and various tropical woods and herbs. Although no single empire had ever controlled the region in the manner of the Mauryas and the Mughals in India, several powerful states had emerged in the region since the early centuries of the first millennium C.E. Some, like Sailendra and Srivijaya in the Indonesian archipelago, were primarily trading states. Others, like Vietnam, Angkor (in present-day Cambodia), and the Burmese empire of Pagan on the subcontinent, were predominantly agricultural. Most had patterned their political systems and their religious beliefs after those of the Indian subcontinent. Vietnam alone was strongly influenced by China.

In 1800, only two societies in Southeast Asia were under effective colonial rule: the Spanish Philippines and the Dutch East Indies. The British had been driven out of the Spice Islands trade by the Dutch in the seventeenth century and possessed only a small enclave on the southern coast of the island of Sumatra in addition to territory on the Malay peninsula. The French had actively engaged in trade with states on the Asian mainland, but were eventually reduced to a small missionary effort run by the Society for Foreign Missions. The only legacy of Portuguese expansion in the region was their possession of half of the small island of Timor.

During the second half of the nineteenth century, however, European interest in Southeast Asia grew rapidly, and by 1900 virtually the entire area was under colonial rule. The process began after the end of the Napo-

leonic Wars, when the British, by agreement with the Dutch, abandoned their claims to territorial possessions in the East Indies in return for a free hand in the Malay peninsula. In 1819, the colonial administrator Sir Stamford Raffles founded a new British colony on a small island at the tip of the peninsula. Called Singapore (city of the lion), it had previously been used by Malay pirates to raid shipping passing through the Strait of Malacca. When the invention of steam power enabled merchant ships to save time and distance by passing through the strait rather than sailing with the westerlies across the southern Indian Ocean, Singapore became a major stopping point for traffic en route to and from China and other commercial centers in the region. Raffles showed an understandable paternal pride in "this my almost only child" and wrote to a friend in England that "here all is life and activity; and it would be difficult to name a place on the face of the globe with brighter prospects or more present satisfaction."[2]

During the next few decades, the pace of European penetration into Southeast Asia accelerated. At the beginning of the nineteenth century, the British had sought and received the right to trade with the kingdom of Burma. A few decades later, the British began to consolidate a more direct presence in the area to protect the eastern flank of their possessions in India and to explore the possibility of a land route into South China. The latter effort failed because of the tortuous terrain along the frontier between Burma and China and the inhospitable reception given to outsiders by hill peoples in the region (the members of the first British exploratory team, for example, were reportedly beheaded by natives). But British activities in the area did lead to the destruction of the Burmese monarchy and the establishment of British control over the entire country, which was eventually placed under the colonial administration in India.

The British advance into Burma was watched nervously in Paris, where French geopoliticians were ever anxious about British operations in Asia and Africa. The French still maintained a clandestine missionary organization in Vietnam despite harsh persecution by the local authorities, who viewed Christianity as a threat to Confucian doctrine. But Vietnamese efforts to prohibit Christian missionary activities were hindered by internal rivalries that had earlier divided the country into two separate and mutually hostile governments in the north and south.

French religious interests had intervened in the Vietnamese civil war in the late eighteenth century in the hope of regaining access to the country, but the Nguyen dynasty, which came to power with French assistance in

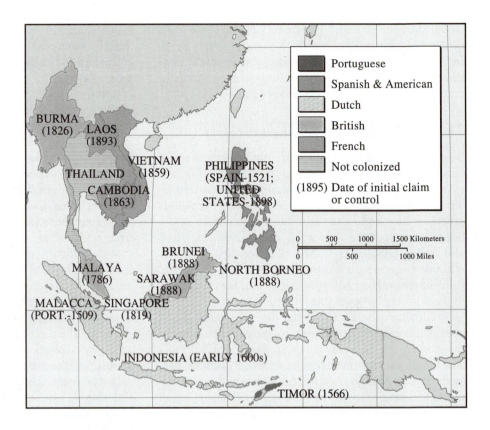

❋ **Map 2.1**   Colonial Southeast Asia

1802, continued to persecute French priests operating in Vietnam. In 1857, the French government decided to force the Vietnamese to accept French protection in order to prevent the British from obtaining a monopoly of trade in South China. A naval attack launched a year later was not a total success, but the French eventually forced the Vietnamese court to cede territories in the Mekong River delta. A generation later, French rule was extended over the remainder of the country. By the end of the century, French seizure of neighboring Cambodia and Laos had led to the creation of the French-ruled Indochinese Union.

With the French conquest of Indochina, Thailand was the only remaining independent state on the Southeast Asian mainland. During the last quarter of the century, British and French rivalry threatened to place the Thai, too, under colonial rule. But under the astute leadership of two remarkable rulers, King Mongkut (familiar to millions of theatergoers as the king in *The King and I*) and his son King Chulalongkorn, the Thai attempted to introduce Western learning and maintain relations with the major European powers without undermining internal stability or inviting an imperialist attack. In 1896,

the British and the French agreed to preserve Thailand as an independent buffer zone between their possessions in Southeast Asia.

The final piece of the colonial edifice in Southeast Asia was put in place in 1898, when U.S. naval forces under Commodore George Dewey defeated the Spanish fleet in Manila Bay. President William McKinley agonized over the fate of the Philippines, but ultimately decided that the moral thing to do was to turn the islands into an American colony to prevent them from falling into the hands of the Japanese. In fact, the Americans (like the Spanish before them) found the islands convenient as a jumping-off point for the China trade (see Chapter 3). This mixture of moral idealism and desire for profit was reflected in a speech given in the Senate in January 1900 by Senator Albert Beveridge of Indiana:

> Mr. President, the times call for candor. The Philippines are ours forever, "territory belonging to the United States," as the Constitution calls them. And just beyond the Philippines are China's illimitable markets. We will not retreat from either. We will not repudiate our duty in the archipelago. We will not abandon our opportunity in the Orient. We will not renounce our part in the mission of our

race, trustee, under God, of the civilization of the world. And we will move forward to our work, not howling out regrets like slaves whipped to their burdens, but with gratitude for a task worthy of our strength, and thanksgiving to Almighty God that He has marked us as His chosen people, henceforth to lead in the regeneration of the world.[3]

Not all Filipinos agreed with Senator Beveridge's portrayal of the situation. Under the leadership of Emilio Aguinaldo, guerrilla forces fought bitterly against U.S. troops to establish their independence from both Spain and the United States. But America's first war against guerrilla forces in Asia was a success, and the bulk of the resistance collapsed in 1901. President McKinley had his stepping-stone to the rich markets of China.

Empire Building in Africa

The last region in the equatorial regions of the world to be placed under European colonial rule was the continent of Africa. There is an apparent irony in that fact, since the area was the first to be encountered by the Europeans on their voyages to the East.

European navigators had first established contacts with African peoples below the Sahara Desert during the late fifteenth century, when Portuguese fleets sailed southward along the Atlantic coast en route to the Indian Ocean. During the next three centuries, European countries established port facilities along the coast of East and West Africa to facilitate their trade with areas farther to the east and to engage in limited commercial relations with African societies. Eventually, the slave trade took on predominant importance, and several million unfortunate Africans were eventually loaded onto European ships destined for the New World. For a variety of reasons, however, Europeans made little effort to penetrate the vast continent and were generally content to deal with African middlemen along the coast to maintain their trading relationship. Deeply ingrained in the Western psyche developed an image of "darkest Africa"—a continent without a history, its people living out their days bereft of any cultural contact with the outside world.

As with most generalizations, there was a glimmer of truth in the Western image of sub-Saharan Africa as a region outside the mainstream of civilization on the Eurasian land mass. Although Africa was the original seedbed of humankind and the site of much of its early evolutionary experience, the desiccation of the Sahara Desert during the fourth and third millennia B.C.E. had erected a major obstacle to communications between the peoples south of the desert and societies elsewhere in the world. The barrier was never total, however. From ancient times, caravans (known as the "fleets of the desert") crossed the Sahara from the Niger River basin to the shores of the Mediterranean carrying gold and other tropical products in exchange for salt, textile goods, and other manufactured articles from the north. By the seventh century C.E., several prosperous trading societies had begun to arise in the savanna belt in West Africa. Caravan routes crisscrossed the desert en route to and from the Mediterranean. In the baggage of merchants came not only commercial goods but also the religion and culture of Islam.

Farther to the east, the Sahara Desert posed no obstacle to communication beyond the seas. The long eastern coast of the African continent had played a role in the trade network of the Indian Ocean since the time of the pharaohs along the Nile. Ships from India, the Persian Gulf, and as far away as China made regular visits to the ports of Kilwa, Malindi, and Sofala, bringing textiles, metal goods, and luxury articles in return for gold, ivory, and various tropical products from Africa. With the settlement of traders from the Arabian Peninsula along the eastern coast, the entire region developed a new Swahili culture combining elements of Arabic culture with that of the Bantu-speaking indigenous peoples. Although the Portuguese briefly seized or destroyed most of the trading ports along the eastern coast, by the eighteenth century the Europeans had been driven out and local authority was restored.

THE GROWING EUROPEAN PRESENCE IN WEST AFRICA

Up to the beginning of the nineteenth century, the relatively limited nature of European economic interests in Africa had provided little temptation for the penetration of the interior or the political takeover of the coastal areas. The slave trade, the main source of European profit during the eighteenth century, could be carried on by using African rulers and merchants as intermediaries. Disease, political instability, lack of transportation, and the generally unhealthy climate (West Africa was known in the nineteenth century as the "White Man's Grave") all served as obstacles to European efforts to extort a profit from dealings in the area.

As the new century dawned, the slave trade itself was in a state of decline. One reason was the growing sense of outrage among humanitarians in several European

◆ **A Slave Raid on the Lualaba River.** By the mid-nineteenth century, most European nations had prohibited the trade in African slaves, but slavery continued in East Africa under the sponsorship of the sultan of Zanzibar. In this sketch, slave traders massacre Africans in an 1871 slave raid on the Lualaba River, just west of Lake Tanganyika. Wrote David Livingstone of the occasion, "It gave me the impression of being in Hell."

countries over the purchase, sale, and exploitation of human beings. Traffic in slaves by Dutch merchants effectively came to an end in 1795 and by Danes in 1803. A few years later, the slave trade was declared illegal in both Great Britain and the United States. The British began to apply pressure on other nations to follow suit, and most did so after the end of the Napoleonic Wars in 1815, leaving only Portugal and Spain as practitioners of the trade south of the equator. Meanwhile, the demand for slaves began to decline in the Western Hemisphere, and by the 1880s, slavery had been abolished in all major countries of the world.

Paradoxically, the decline of the slave trade in the Atlantic during the first half of the nineteenth century did not lead to an overall reduction in the European presence in West Africa. To the contrary, European interest in what was sometimes called "legitimate trade" in natural resources increased. Exports of peanuts, timber, hides, and palm oil increased substantially during the first decades of the century, while imports of textile goods and other manufactured products rose. The increasing pace of interregional commerce benefited rulers and merchants, of course, but in some cases also worked to the advantage of farmers and artisans who were fortunate enough to be involved in that trade.

Stimulated by growing commercial interests in the area, European governments began to push for a more permanent presence along the coast. During the first decades of the nineteenth century, the British established settlements along the Gold Coast (present-day Ghana) and in Sierra Leone, where they attempted to

set up agricultural plantations for freed slaves who had returned from the Western Hemisphere or had been liberated by British ships while en route to the Americas. A similar haven for ex-slaves was developed with the assistance of the United States in Liberia. The French occupied the area around the Senegal River near Cape Verde, where they attempted to develop peanut plantations.

The growing European presence in West Africa led to tensions with African governments in the area. British efforts to increase trade with Ashanti led to conflict in the 1820s, but British influence in the area intensified in later decades. Most African states, especially those with a fairly high degree of political integration, were able to maintain their independence from this creeping European encroachment, called "informal empire" by some historians, but the prospects for the future were ominous. When Afro-European groups attempted to organize to protect their own interests, the British stepped in and annexed the coastal states as the first British colony of Gold Coast in 1874. At about the same time, the British extended an informal protectorate over warring tribal groups in the Niger delta.

IMPERIALIST SHADOW OVER THE NILE

A similar process was under way in the Nile valley. Ever since the voyages of the Portuguese explorers at the close of the fifteenth century, European trade with the East had been carried on almost exclusively by the route around the Cape of Good Hope. But from the outset

there was some interest in shortening the route by digging a canal east of Cairo, where only a low, swampy isthmus separated the Mediterranean from the Red Sea. The Ottoman Turks, who controlled the area, had considered constructing a canal in the sixteenth century, but nothing was accomplished until 1854, when the French entrepreneur Ferdinand de Lesseps signed a contract to begin construction of the canal. The project, completed in 1869, brought little immediate benefit to Egypt, however. The costs of construction imposed a major debt on the Egyptian government and forced a growing level of dependence on foreign financial support. When an army revolt against growing foreign influence broke out in 1881, the British stepped in to protect their investment (they had bought Egypt's canal company shares in 1875) and set up an informal protectorate that would last until World War I.

The weakening of Turkish rule in the Nile valley had a parallel further to the west, where autonomous regions had begun to emerge under local viceroys in Tripoli, Tunis, and Algiers. In 1830, the French, on the pretext of reducing the threat of piracy to European shipping in the Mediterranean, seized the area surrounding Algiers and integrated it into the French Empire. By the mid-1850s, more than 150,000 Europeans had settled in the fertile region adjacent to the coast, while resistance from Berber elements continued unceasingly in the desert to the south. In 1881, the French imposed a protectorate on neighboring Tunisia. Only Tripoli and Cyrenaica (Ottoman provinces that comprise modern-day Libya) remained under Turkish rule until the Italians took them in 1911–1912.

BANTUS, BOERS, AND BRITISH IN SOUTH AFRICA

Nowhere in Africa did the European presence grow more rapidly than in the south. During the eighteenth century, European settlers expanded gradually and began to migrate eastward from the Cape Colony into territory inhabited by local Khoisan- and Bantu-speaking peoples entering the area from the north. Internecine warfare among the Bantus had largely depopulated the region, facilitating occupation of the land by the Boers, the Afrikaans-speaking farmers who were descended from the original Dutch settlers in the seventeenth century. But in the early nineteenth century, a local people called the Zulus, under a talented ruler named Shaka, counterattacked, setting off a series of wars between the Europeans and the Zulus. Eventually, Shaka was overthrown, and the Boers continued their advance northeastward during the so-called Great Trek of the mid-1830s. By 1865, the total European population of the area had risen to nearly 200,000 people.

The Boers' eastward migration was provoked in part by the British seizure of the Cape from the Dutch during the Napoleonic Wars. The British government was generally more sympathetic to the rights of the local African population than were the Afrikaners, many of whom saw white superiority as ordained by God and fled from British rule to control their own destiny. Eventually, the Boers formed their own independent republics, the Orange Free State and the South African Republic (usually known as Transvaal). Much of the African population in these areas was confined to reserves.

THE SCRAMBLE FOR AFRICA

At the beginning of the 1880s, most of Africa was still independent. European rule was still limited to the fringes of the continent, such as Algeria, the Gold Coast, and South Africa. Other areas, such as Egypt, lower Nigeria, Senegal, and Mozambique, were under various forms of loose protectorate. But the trends were ominous, as the pace of European penetration was accelerating, and the constraints that had limited European rapaciousness were fast disappearing.

The scramble began in the mid-1880s, when several European states, including Belgium, France, Germany, Great Britain, and Portugal, engaged in what today would be called a feeding frenzy to seize a piece of African territory before the carcass had been picked clean. By 1900, virtually all of the continent had been placed under one form or another of European rule. The British had consolidated their authority over the Nile valley and seized additional territories in East Africa. When the British received the German colony of Tanganyika as a trust territory after World War I, they had created an unbroken band from "Cape to Cairo" under the rule of the British crown. The French retaliated by advancing eastward from Senegal into the central Sahara, where they eventually came eyeball to eyeball with the British at Fashoda on the Nile. They also occupied the island of Madagascar and other coastal territories in West and Central Africa. In between, the Germans claimed the hinterland opposite Zanzibar, as well as coastal strips in West and Southwest Africa north of the Cape, while King Leopold II of Belgium claimed the Congo. Eventually, Italy entered the contest and seized modern-day Libya and some of the Somali coast.

What had happened to spark the sudden imperialist hysteria that brought an end to African independence? Clearly, economic interests in the narrow sense were not at stake as they had been in South and Southeast Asia. The level of trade between Europe and Africa was simply not sufficient to justify the risks and the expense of conquest.

There were, in fact, a number of other reasons. Clearly, one factor was the growing rivalry among imperialist powers for possessions in the non-Western world.

In some cases, European leaders might be provoked into an imperialist takeover not by strictly economic considerations, but by the fear that another state might do so, leaving them at a disadvantage.

Another consideration might be called the "missionary factor," as European missionary interests lobbied with their governments for a colonial takeover to facilitate their efforts to convert the African population to Christianity. In fact, considerable moral complacency was inherent in the process. The concept of social Darwinism and the "white man's burden" persuaded many that it was in the interests of the African people, as well as their conquerors, to be introduced more rapidly to the benefits of Western civilization. Even the highly respected Scottish missionary David Livingstone had become convinced that missionary work and economic development had to go hand in hand, pleading to his fellow Europeans to introduce the "three Cs" (Christianity, commerce, and civilization) to the continent. How much easier such a task would be if African peoples were under benevolent European rule!

There were more prosaic reasons as well. Advances in Western technology and European superiority in firearms made it easier than ever for a small European force to defeat superior numbers. Furthermore, life expectancy for Europeans living in Africa had improved. With the discovery that quinine (extracted from the bark of the cinchona tree) could provide partial immunity from the ravages of malaria, the mortality rate for Europeans living in Africa dropped dramatically in the 1840s. By the end of the century, European residents in tropical Africa faced only slightly higher risks of death by disease than individuals living in Europe.

As rivalry among competing powers heated up, a conference was convened at Berlin in 1884 to avert war and reduce tensions among European nations competing for the spoils of Africa. It proved reasonably successful at achieving the first objective but less so at the second. During the next few years, African territories were annexed without provoking a major confrontation between Western powers, but in the late 1890s, Britain and France reached the brink of conflict at Fashoda, a small town on the Nile River in the Sudan. The French had been advancing eastward across the Sahara with the transparent objective of controlling the regions around the upper Nile. In 1898, British and Egyptian troops seized the Sudan from successors of the Mahdi and then marched southward to head off the French. After a tense face-off between units of the two European countries at Fashoda, the French government backed down, and British authority over the area was secured. Except for

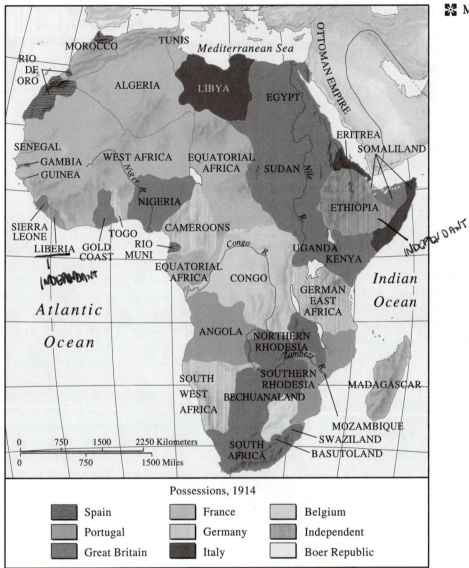

Map 2.2   Africa in 1914

Possessions, 1914

Spain	
Portugal	France
Great Britain	Germany
	Italy

Belgium	
Independent	
Boer Republic	

their small possessions of Djibouti and a portion of the Somali coast, the French were restricted to equatorial Africa.

Ironically, the only major clash between Europeans over Africa took place in South Africa, where competition among the powers was almost nonexistent. The discovery of gold and diamonds in the Boer republic of the Transvaal was the source of the problem. Clashes between the Afrikaner population and foreign (mainly British) miners and developers led to an attempt by Cecil Rhodes, prime minister of the Cape Colony and a prominent entrepreneur in the area, to subvert the Transvaal and bring it under British rule. In 1899, the so-called Boer War broke out between Britain and the Transvaal, which was backed by its fellow republic, the Orange Free State. Guerrilla resistance by the Boers was fierce, but the vastly superior forces of the British were able to prevail by 1902. To compensate the defeated Afrikaner population for the loss of independence, the British government agreed that only whites would vote in the now essentially self-governing colony. The Boers were placated, but the brutalities committed during the war (the British introduced an institution later to be known as the concentration camp) created bitterness on both sides that continued to fester through future decades.

The Colonial System

Now that they were in control of most of the world, what did the colonial powers do with it? As we have seen, their primary objective was to exploit the natural resources of the subject areas and to open up markets for manufactured goods and capital investment from the mother country. In some cases, that goal could be realized in cooperation with local political elites, whose loyalty could be earned (or purchased) by economic rewards or by confirming them in their positions of authority and status in a new colonial setting. Sometimes, however, this policy, known as "indirect rule," was not feasible because local leaders refused to cooperate with their colonial masters or even actively resisted the foreign conquest. In such cases, the local elites were removed from power and replaced with a new set of officials recruited from the mother country.

Several factors determined whether colonial rule would be direct or indirect. In general, active resistance to colonial conquest came primarily from societies with a long tradition of national cohesion and independence, such as China, Burma, and Vietnam in Asia and the African Muslim states in northern Nigeria and Morocco. In those areas, the colonial power was likely to dispense with local collaborators and govern directly. Indirect rule, on the other hand, was often applied in societies where the local authorities, for whatever reason, were willing to collaborate with the imperialist powers. Such was the case in parts of Africa and the Indian subcontinent and in the Malay peninsula.

The distinction between direct and indirect rule was not merely academic and often had fateful consequences for the peoples involved. Where colonial powers encountered resistance and were forced to overthrow local political elites, they often adopted policies designed to eradicate the source of resistance and destroy the traditional culture. Such policies often had quite corrosive effects on the indigenous societies and provoked resentment and resistance that not only marked the colonial relationship but even affected relations after the restoration of national independence. The bitter struggles after World War II in Algeria, the Dutch East Indies, and Vietnam can be ascribed in part to that phenomenon.

The Philosophy of Colonialism

To justify their conquests, the colonial powers appealed, in part, to the time-honored maxim of "might makes right." In a manner reminiscent of the Western attitude toward the oil reserves in the Persian Gulf today, the Eu-

ropean powers viewed industrial resources as vital to national survival and security and felt that no moral justification was needed for any action to protect access to them. By the end of the nineteenth century, that attitude received pseudoscientific validity from the concept of social Darwinism, which maintained that only societies that moved aggressively to adapt to changing circumstances would survive and prosper in a world governed by the Darwinist law of "survival of the fittest."

Some people, however, were uncomfortable with such a brutal view of the law of nature and sought a moral justification that appeared to benefit the victim. Here again, the concept of social Darwinism pointed the way. According to social Darwinists, human societies, like living organisms, must adapt to survive. Thus, the advanced nations of the West were obliged to assist the backward nations of Asia and Africa so that they, too, could adjust to the challenges of the modern world. Few expressed this view as graphically as the English poet Rudyard Kipling, who called on the Anglo-Saxon peoples (in particular, the United States) to take up the "white man's burden" in Asia (see box on p. 37).

Buttressed by such comforting theories, humane and sympathetic souls in Western countries could ignore the brutal aspects of the colonial process and persuade themselves that, in the long run, the results would be beneficial to both sides. Some, like their antecedents in the sixteenth and seventeenth centuries, saw the issue primarily in religious terms. During the nineteenth century, Christian missionaries by the thousands went to Asia and Africa to bring the Gospel to the "heathen masses." To others, the objective was the more secular one of bringing the benefits of Western democracy and capitalism to the feudalistic and tradition-ridden societies of the Orient. Either way, sensitive Western minds could console themselves with the belief that their governments were bringing civilization to the primitive peoples of the world. If commercial profit and national prestige happened to be by-products of that effort, so much the better.

Few were as good at expressing such a "civilizing mission" as the French administrator and twice governorgeneral of French Indochina, Albert Sarraut. Admitting that colonialism was originally an "act of force" undertaken for commercial profit, he declared that it resulted in a "work of human solidarity":

> More important than any other rights is the right of all human beings to live a better life on this planet through the more effective utilization of material goods and moral wealth susceptible to be distributed to all living persons. This process can only take place through the solid collabo-

White Man's Burden, Black Man's Sorrow

*O*ne of the justifications for European colonialism was the notion that the "more advanced" white peoples had the moral responsibility to raise allegedly primitive societies in Africa and Asia to a higher level of civilization. Few captured this notion better than the British poet Rudyard Kipling (1865–1936) in his famous poem "The White Man's Burden." His appeal, addressed primarily to the United States, became one of the most famous set of verses in the English-speaking world:

> Take up the White Man's burden—
> Send forth the best ye breed—
> Go bind your sons to exile
> To serve your captives' need;
> To wait in heavy harness,
> On fluttered folk and wild—
> Your new-caught sullen peoples,
> Half-devil and half-child.

Yet that sense of moral responsibility was often misplaced or, even worse, laced with hypocrisy. Not only was it virtually self-evident that the underlying motive for colonial conquest was the drive for national or personal wealth and power, but it was also clear that the consequences of imperial rule all too often were detrimental to those living under colonial authority. Nowhere was this harsh reality more clearly displayed than in the continent of Africa, which had already suffered for centuries from the European slave trade.

Few observers described the destructive effects of Western imperialism on native Africans as well as Edward Morel, a British journalist who spent time in the Belgian Congo. In his book *The Black Man's Burden*, Morel pointed out that the power of what he called "modern capitalistic exploitation, assisted by modern engines of destruction," might manage to accomplish what even the slave trade and imperial conquest had failed to do. Colonial rule, he charged,

> kills not the body merely, but the soul. It breaks the spirit. It attacks the African at every turn, from every point of vantage. It wrecks his polity, uproots him from his land, invades his family life, destroys his natural pursuits and occupations, claims his whole time, enslaves him in his own home.

The most harmful aspect of colonialism, in the author's view, was the pervasive and corrosive character of capitalist exploitation, which relentlessly undermined the foundations of traditional society and allowed no recourse for African workers against long hours of "monotonous, uninterrupted labour," often involving a lengthy separation from home, family, and community. Violent resistance, he lamented, provided no answer because of the "killing power of modern armament."

Morel's book, combined with other searing attacks on the system, such as British writer Joseph Conrad's famous novel, *Heart of Darkness*, represented a terrible indictment of the colonial system and the alleged benefits extolled by its defenders.

Sources: Rudyard Kipling, *Verse* (New York: Doubleday, 1920); Louis L. Snyder, ed., *The Imperialism Reader* (Princeton, NJ: Van Nostrand, 1962).

---

ration of all races, liberally exchanging their natural resources and the creative faculties of their own genius. Nature has divided these faculties and these resources unequally across the surface of the globe through the unequal influence of climate, of fertility and hereditary values. Its arbitrary devolution has localized, here and there, one from another, in the diversity, the dispersion and the contrast. Is it just, is it legitimate that such a state of things should be indefinitely prolonged? In the name of humanity, one can respond forcefully: No! A right which results in undermining the right of universal well-being is not a right. Humanity is universal throughout the globe. No race, no people has the right or the power to isolate itself egotistically from the movements and necessities of the universal life.[4]

Here, claimed Sarraut, was the "broad and generous idea" on which colonialism, "the agent of civilization," must be founded as it took charge of the wealth of the earth so that it could be distributed to the profit of all.

But what about the possibility that historically and culturally the societies of Asia and Africa were fundamentally different from those of the West and could not, or would not, be persuaded to transform themselves along Western lines? After all, even Kipling had remarked that "East is East and West is West, and ne'er the twain shall meet." Was the human condition universal, in which case the Asian and African peoples could be transformed, in the quaint American phrase for their subject Filipinos, into "little brown Americans"? Or were human beings so shaped by their history and geographic environment that their civilizations would inevitably remain distinctive from those of the West? In that case, a policy of cultural transformation could not be expected to succeed and could even lead to disaster.

In fact, colonial theory never decided this issue one way or the other. The French, who were most inclined to philosophize about the problem, adopted the terms *assimilation* (which implied an effort to transform colonial societies in the Western image) and *association* (collaborating with local elites while leaving local traditions alone) to describe the two alternatives and then proceeded to vacillate between one and the other. French policy in Indochina, for example, began as one of association, but switched to assimilation under pressure from liberal elements who felt that colonial powers owed a debt to their subject peoples. But assimilation (which in any case was never accepted as feasible or desirable by many colonial officials) aroused resentment among the local population, many of whom opposed the destruction of their native traditions. In the end, the French abandoned the attempt to justify their presence and fell back on a policy of ruling by force of arms.

Not all colonial powers were as inclined to debate the theory of colonialism as were the French. The British, whether out of a sense of pragmatism or of racial superiority, refused to entertain the possibility of assimilation and treated their subject peoples as culturally and racially distinctive. In formulating a colonial policy for the Philippines, the United States adopted a policy of assimilation in theory, but was not always so quick to put it into practice.

To many colonial peoples, such questions must have appeared academic; clearly, the primary objectives of all the colonial states were economic exploitation and the retention of power. Like the British soldier in Kipling's poem "On the Road to Mandalay," all too many Westerners living in the colonies believed that the Great Lord Buddha was nothing but a "bloomin' idol made of mud, what they call the great god Bud."

The Dilemmas of Colonial Responsibility

Whatever their ultimate intentions, most colonial governments sought to justify their presence by promising to introduce the blessings of advanced Western civilization. In the United States and Britain, the task was commonly known as the "white man's burden." In France and the Netherlands, it was called the "civilizing mission."

EXPORTING DEMOCRACY

The problem with such a lofty goal was that all too often it conflicted with practical considerations. That was certainly the case in the area of political reform. The civilizing mission postulated that the colonial powers would introduce representative institutions and educate the native peoples in the democratic process. In fact, however, colonial officials understandably feared that native elements with full powers of political representation (especially educated ones) would be only too likely to demand full participation in the government or even the restoration of national independence.

Faced with a contradiction between moral purpose and practical needs, colonial governments routinely opted for the latter. In directly ruled societies, power was placed entirely in the hands of high European officials appointed by the colonial government and assisted by an advisory council composed mainly of Europeans. In societies under indirect rule, the colonial power ruled through the native rulers, who retained at least a semblance of their formerly supreme authority. Key decisions, however, were usually made by the ruler's colonial advisers.

In time, pressure from educated elements within the indigenous population compelled colonial governments to introduce political reforms. In the early years of the twentieth century, legislative councils with limited representation for native elements were established in Egypt, India, the Dutch East Indies, French Indochina, and the Gold Coast. The powers of these fledgling parliamentary bodies were limited, however, and the franchise was restricted to a wealthy elite. As time passed, such advisory councils gradually evolved into full legislative assemblies. Native participation in the colonial bureaucracies also tended to increase, although senior positions were usually held by Europeans and salaries for native officials were lower than for their European counterparts.

A key aspect of the colonial enterprise, of course, was education, and all colonial governments set up a new school system to introduce the subject peoples to the rudiments of Western culture and institutions. In general, only native elites attended such schools, where the primary goal was to train native officials for the colonial bureaucracy. Some went abroad to receive higher education at Oxford, Cambridge, the Sorbonne, or similar institutions in Belgium, the Netherlands, or the United States. A few were sent by their governments, but more commonly they went at their families' expense.

Educational opportunities for the common people were harder to come by. In French-controlled Vietnam, for example, as of 1917, only 3,000 out of a total of

23,000 villages in the country had a public school. The French had opened a university in Hanoi, but it was immediately closed as a result of student demonstrations. In some cases, missionary schools filled the gap, providing sound instruction at the elementary and secondary level for the fortunate few in many colonial societies.

By the second quarter of the twentieth century, then, a framework of representative government had been put into place in most if not all the colonial territories, and a native elite trained in the democratic process was beginning to play a role in decision making. Yet most decisions continued to be reached by and for the interests of the colonial power. In that sense, colonial rule had not essentially transformed the traditional political culture. It was still fundamentally paternalistic and elitist. The main difference now was that the new ruling class was not only foreign but also lacked the mystique and semidivine quality that had been a characteristic of traditional leadership. Where authority in traditional societies in Asia and Africa had been legitimized by religion or hallowed tradition, authority in colonial societies was based on military force alone.

BETWEEN OLD AND NEW:
COLONIAL ECONOMIC POLICY

In the field of economics, the objective of the civilizing mission was to integrate native societies into the global economic market. Those believing in Adam Smith's philosophy of laissez-faire economics maintained that the division of labor on the basis of free trade principles would eventually redound to the benefit of all. "Open new channels," advised one British writer in the 1830s, "for the most productive employment of English capital. Let the English buy bread from every people that has bread to sell cheap. Make England, for all that is produced by steam, the workshop of the world. If, after this, there be capital and people to spare, . . . find room for both by means of colonization."[5] In this view, the increasing wealth accumulated in colonial territories would nurture a native middle class, which in turn would spur the growth and maturation of democratic institutions. Many Western observers believed that a strong middle class was a prerequisite for the emergence of liberal democracy.

It was therefore in the interests of the general good that the economic relationship between the mother country and the colonial society should be governed by the laws of the marketplace. In practice, these laws generally decreed that manufactured goods from the former would be exchanged for raw materials exported by the latter. The problem with this relationship was that because of high labor costs, prices of manufactured goods were much higher than of the raw materials exported from the colonies, and it was obviously in the interest of the colonial government to keep them that way. Simply put, the system exploited the colonial peoples.

To native producers, the obvious answer was to develop their own technology for refining raw materials and producing their own manufactured goods, which could then be exported on a competitive basis to other countries. But such a policy would threaten the economic interests of the colonial power, which benefited from keeping the price of raw materials low and maintaining a lucrative colonial market for the manufactures of the home country. Not surprisingly, in this clash of economic interests, those of the colonial power triumphed. Colonial governments generally located refining facilities in the home country and discouraged the development of a native manufacturing sector.

This is not to say that no economic changes took place in the colonies. To facilitate the production and flow of goods, colonial governments built railroads and highways, telegraph lines, radio transmitters, modern power plants, and airports. Although these facilities were designed primarily for the benefit of European interests, they did provide an economic infrastructure that future independent governments would inherit and could use for the benefit of the native peoples.

Moreover, in major urban conglomerations from Dakar to Batavia, Saigon to Bombay, and Calcutta to Cairo, a lively commercial and manufacturing sector began to develop almost despite the restrictive efforts of the colonial bureaucracy. Some of the wealth resulting from increased economic activity enriched an affluent and well-educated middle class. All too often, however, the most enterprising and successful entrepreneurs were not members of the majority population. In some cases, they were Europeans. In others, they were Indians in East Africa and Burma; Persian Parsis in Bombay; Jews, Syrians, Armenians, Greeks, and Italians in Egypt; and Chinese in Kuala Lumpur, Batavia, and Saigon. In most colonial cities, foreign interests controlled banking, major manufacturing activities, and the import-export trade. The natives were more apt to work in a family business, at handicrafts, in factory or assembly plants, or as peddlers, day laborers, or rickshaw drivers—that is, at less profitable and less capital-intensive businesses. Many of them lived in dismal conditions in urban slums or in squatter settlements along the edge of the cities.

Despite the growth of an urban economy, the vast majority of colonial peoples continued to farm the land.

Many continued to live by subsistence agriculture, growing dry crops or wet rice as they had for centuries. But the colonial era brought changes here as well. In some areas, the livelihood of the rural population was affected by the colonial power's interest in producing cash crops for the export market. Peasants in the Dutch East Indies, for example, were forced to devote some of their ricelands to growing sugarcane in order to pay their taxes. Other areas previously occupied by private farms were turned into plantations for growing cotton, rubber, palm oil, tropical fruits, or spices. In some cases, farmers benefited from the new situation. But others, who had previously possessed tenure rights to their land, risked eviction by landlords who turned the land to commercial use.

The situation was made even more difficult by the steady growth of the population. Peasants in Asia and Africa had always had large families, on the assumption that a high proportion of their children would die in infancy. Large families, and especially sons, provided labor for the present and security for old age. But improved sanitation and medical treatment resulted in lower rates of infant mortality and a staggering increase in population. The population of the island of Java, for example, increased from about 1 million in the precolonial era to about 40 million at the end of the nineteenth century.

Under these conditions, the rural areas could no longer support the growing population, and many young people fled to the cities to seek jobs in factories or shops. This migratory pattern gave rise to the squatter settlements in the suburbs of the major cities. A similar process had occurred in Europe during the early stages of the Industrial Revolution, when changes in agricultural practices forced many peasants off the land. At first, the transition had been painful, but eventually it led to more efficient farming and an available labor force for the growing industrial base.

The problem in colonial societies was that there was no such light at the end of the tunnel. Because colonial policies limited the growth of the domestic industrial economy, no jobs were available for the migrants to the cities. At the same time, the lack of capital and a local manufacturing base meant that few farmers could afford to mechanize. The end result was that the colonial peoples, unlike their Western counterparts, suffered for nothing. As the sociologist Clifford Geertz has said, the colonial peoples were caught between the old and new. The old system was collapsing, but a new system did not emerge to take its place.

SOCIAL AND CULTURAL CHANGES

The Western presence also had an impact on the social mores and religious beliefs of the colonial peoples. It was difficult for many Westerners who visited or lived in Asia or Africa to avoid an attitude of condescension toward the customs and institutions of non-Western societies. Even well-meaning European or American observers viewed strange customs as the remnants of a primitive or feudal legacy destined to be wiped out by the inexorable march of modern civilization. In some cases, the results were beneficial, as in the efforts to end child marriage and *sati* (widow burning) in India and the practice of cannibalism among upland peoples on the island of Sumatra. All too often, however, the Western attitude was expressed in blatant cultural arrogance personified by the colonial habit of addressing natives by their first names or calling an adult male "boy."

Nowhere were such attitudes more pronounced than in South Africa, where a sense of racial superiority among Afrikaners was deeply rooted, and virtually the entire black population in the Cape Colony was maintained in conditions of slavery. After the British government abolished slavery throughout the empire in 1838, many black Africans sought employment in cities and towns, but racial prejudice and lack of job skills condemned them to menial jobs and ghetto conditions.

Although such attitudes were often bitterly resented, at the same time many Asian and African elites found European civilization irresistible and began to hold their own traditional cultures in contempt. In the colonial cities, many native elites aped the behavior and dress of their rulers, speaking European languages, drinking European wines, and dancing to Western tunes in modern nightclubs built for the pleasure of the affluent. Outside the urban areas, though, traditional mores continued to survive.

How is one to evaluate the colonial experience? Defenders of colonialism point to the undeniable technological benefits that it brought to many a preindustrial society. They note that, however painful, the experience represented the first stage in the nation-building process. Critics deny that colonialism was the handmaiden of modernization and argue that in many ways it actively delayed the process of change. No final answer to this controversy is likely to appear because, unlike a scientific experiment, history can never be reproduced. What can be said is that because economic self-interest usually had more power than high moral purpose, the colonial experience for most of the peoples of Asia and Africa was unnecessarily painful and protracted. It is a keen historical irony that most of the major colonial powers were practicing democracies. But their constituencies were in London and Paris, Birmingham and Brussels, Amsterdam, Pittsburgh, and Dubuque—not in Jakarta, Dakar, Cairo, or Manila.

Colonialism in Action

In practice, colonialism in India, Southeast Asia, and Africa exhibited many similarities but also some differences. Some of these variations can be traced to political or social differences among the colonial powers. The French, for example, often tried to impose a centralized administrative system on their colonies that mirrored the system in use in France, while the British sometimes attempted to transform local aristocrats into the equivalent of the landed gentry at home in Britain. Other differences stemmed from conditions in the colonies and the colonizers' aspirations for them. For instance, the Western powers believed that their economic interests were far more limited in Africa than elsewhere and therefore treated their African colonies somewhat differently than those in India or Southeast Asia. The result was to introduce a degree of variation within the general pattern of colonialism that we have described.

INDIA UNDER THE BRITISH RAJ

At the beginning of the nineteenth century, Indian society was at one of the lowest points in its historical development. The once glorious empire of the Mughals had been debased and humiliated and was now reduced by British military power to a shadow of its former greatness. During the next few decades, the British sought to consolidate their control over the subcontinent, expanding from their base areas along the coast into the interior. Some territories were taken over directly, first by the East India Company and later by the British crown, while others were ruled indirectly through their local maharajas and rajas. In the 1820s, the British began to move into lower Burma in an attempt to find a land route to China, and twenty years later British troops fought in Afghanistan to solidify India's northwestern frontier against Russian penetration.

Not all of the effects of British rule were bad. British governance over the subcontinent brought order and stability to a society that had been rent by civil war even before the effects of Western intrusion had been strongly felt. By the early nineteenth century, British control had been consolidated and led to a relatively honest and efficient government that in many respects operated to the benefit of the average Indian. One of the benefits of the period was the heightened attention given to education. Through the efforts of the British administrator and historian Lord Macaulay, a new school system was established to train the children of Indian elites, and the British civil service examination was introduced. Macaulay's attitude was unashamedly Anglocentric. Although admitting the value of Indian philosophy, he argued that "all the historical information which has been

◆ **Gateway to India?** Built by the British to commemorate the visit to India of King George V and Queen Mary in 1911, the Gateway of India was erected at the water's edge in the harbor of Bombay, India's greatest port city. For thousands of British citizens arriving in India, the Gateway of India was the first view of their new home and a symbol of the power and majesty of the British raj.

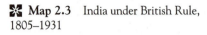 **Map 2.3** India under British Rule, 1805–1931

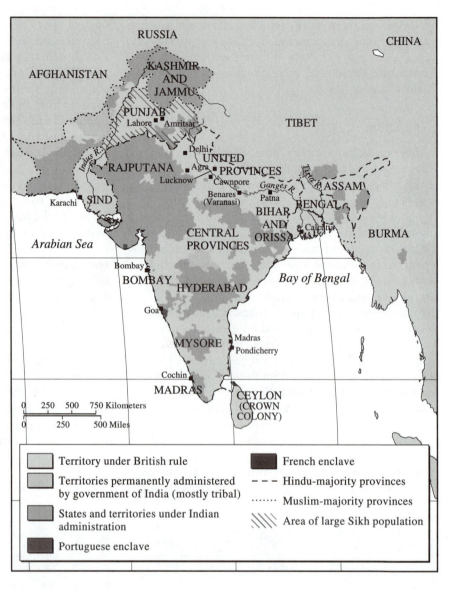

Territory under British rule		French enclave	
Territories permanently administered by government of India (mostly tribal)		– – – Hindu-majority provinces	
States and territories under Indian administration		⋯⋯ Muslim-majority provinces	
Portuguese enclave		⫽⫽⫽ Area of large Sikh population	

collected from all the books written in the Sanskrit language is less valuable than what may be found in the most paltry abridgements used at preparatory schools in England." Better, then, to teach Indian elites about Western civilization "to form a class who may be interpreters between us and the millions whom we govern; a class of persons, Indian in blood and color, but English in taste, in opinions, in morals, and in intellect."[6] (See box on p. 43.)

British rule also brought an end to some of the more inhumane aspects of Indian tradition. The practice of *sati* was outlawed, and widows were legally permitted to

remarry. The British also attempted to put an end to the endemic brigandage (known as *thuggee*, which gave rise to the English word "thug") that had plagued travelers in India since time immemorial. Railroads, the telegraph, and the postal service were introduced to India shortly after they appeared in Great Britain itself. Work began on the main highway from Calcutta to Delhi in 1839, and the first rail network was opened in 1853. A new penal code based on the British model was adopted, and health and sanitation conditions were improved.

But the Indian people paid a high price for the peace and stability brought by the British raj (from the Indian

Indian in Blood, English in Taste and Intellect

One of the most difficult dilemmas faced by administrators serving in the colonial societies of Asia and Africa was whether to introduce Western institutions and values to the native population, or to permit them to retain their own local traditions and customs. The first approach conformed better with the ideal of the civilizing mission, but it was more costly and sometime provoked resentment or even violent resistance. Nowhere was this dilemma more acute than in the sphere of education, which served as the primary vehicle for introducing young Asians and Africans to the responsibilities of adulthood.

One British administrator who deliberated on this issue in public was the colonial official Thomas Babington Macaulay (1800–1859), later to become one of Britain's foremost historians. Appointed a member of the Supreme Council of India in the early 1830s, he became responsible for drawing up a new educational policy for the area. One of the questions before the Council was whether English or one of the various local languages was to become the vehicle for educational training in the Indian school system.

In his *Minute on Education*, Macaulay presented his own views on the issue to members of the Council. Dismissing the local dialects spoken in various parts of the subcontinent as lacking in literary value or scientific terminology, he noted that the only serious candidates to serve as the chief language of instruction were English, Arabic (widely spoken throughout the Middle East and parts of the subcontinent), and Sanskrit (the classical language from which most modern Indian tongues derived).

In making a selection, Macaulay argued, the standard for choice should be which language was "the best worth knowing." Using that standard, he unhesitatingly settled on English. "I have read translations," he said,

of the most celebrated Arabic and Sanskrit works. I have conversed both here and at home with men distinguished by their proficiency in the Eastern tongues. I am quite ready to take the Oriental learning at the valuation of the Orientalists [European scholars of Asian civilizations] themselves. I have never found one among them who could deny that a single shelf of a good European library was worth the whole native literature of India and Arabia.

Macaulay concluded that English was more worth knowing than either Sanskrit or Arabic, and that many Indians had reached the same conclusion. Declaring that it was possible "to make natives of this country thoroughly good English scholars," he declared that it was to that end that the Council's efforts should be directed.

In his cavalier dismissal of the value of Arabic or Sanskrit literature, both of which are now acknowledged to be rich in tradition and subtle in their power of expression, Macaulay reflected the racial and cultural arrogance that characterized the attitudes of colonial administrators throughout the world. In any event, English gradually became the common language of communication for educated Indians throughout the colonial era.

The decision was momentous, and still has an impact on the subcontinent well over a century later. The use of the English language enabled colonial authorities to set up the Indian Civil Service on the British model, thus providing a future independent India with a powerful tool for creating a stable government based on an efficient and honest bureaucracy. On the other hand, by rejecting Sanskrit, the British lost an opportunity to provide the Indian people with a language based on the local heritage that could serve as a common tongue throughout the entire subcontinent. As we shall see, the lack of a common language continues to bedevil the Indian people even today.

Source: Michael Edwards, *A History of India: From the Earliest Times to the Present Day* (London: Thames and Hudson, 1961), pp. 261–265.

raja, or prince). Perhaps the most flagrant cost was economic. While British entrepreneurs and a small percentage of the Indian population attached to the imperial system reaped financial benefits from British rule, it brought hardship to millions of others in both the cities and the rural areas. The introduction of British textiles put thousands of Bengali women out of work and severely damaged the local textile industry.

In rural areas, the British introduced the *zamindar* system, according to which local landlords were authorized to collect taxes from peasants and turn the taxes over to the government, in the misguided expectation that it would not only facilitate the collection of agricultural taxes but would also create a new landed gentry that could, as in Britain itself, become the conservative foundation of imperial rule. But the local gentry took advantage of their new authority to increase taxes and force the less fortunate peasants to become tenants or lose their land entirely. When rural unrest threatened, the government passed legislation protecting farmers against eviction and unreasonable rent increases, but this measure had little effect outside the southern provinces, where it had originally been enacted.

British colonialism was also remiss in bringing the benefits of modern science and technology to India. Some limited forms of industrialization took place, notably in the manufacturing of textiles and jute (used in making rope). The first textile mill opened in 1856; seventy years later, there were eighty mills in the city of Bombay alone. Nevertheless, the lack of local capital and the advantages given to British imports prevented the emergence of other vital new commercial and manufacturing operations.

Foreign rule also had a psychological effect on the psyche of the Indian people. While many British colonial officials sincerely tried to improve the lot of the people under their charge, British arrogance and contempt for native tradition cut deeply into the pride of many Indians, especially those of high caste who were accustomed to a position of superior status in India. Educated Indians trained in the Anglo-Indian school system for a career in the civil service, as well as Eurasians born to mixed marriages, rightfully wondered where their true cultural loyalties lay. This cultural collision is poignantly described in the novel *A Passage to India* by the British writer E. M. Forster.

COLONIAL REGIMES IN SOUTHEAST ASIA

In Southeast Asia, economic profit was the immediate and primary aim of colonial enterprise. For that purpose, colonial powers tried wherever possible to work with local elites to facilitate the exploitation of natural resources. Indirect rule reduced the cost of training European administrators and had a less corrosive impact on the local culture. In the Dutch East Indies, for example, officials of the Dutch East India Company (VOC) entrusted local administration to the indigenous landed aristocracy, known as the *priyayi*. The *priyayi* maintained law and order and collected taxes in return for a payment from the VOC. The British followed a similar practice in Malaya. While establishing direct rule over areas of crucial importance, such as the

commercial centers of Singapore and Malacca and the island of Penang, the British signed agreements with local Muslim rulers to maintain princely power in the interior of the peninsula.

Indirect rule, however convenient and inexpensive, was not always feasible. In some instances, local resistance to the colonial conquest made such a policy impossible. In Burma, faced with staunch opposition from the monarchy and other traditionalist forces, the British abolished the monarchy and administered the country directly through their colonial government in India. In Indochina, the French used both direct and indirect means. They imposed direct rule on the southern provinces in the Mekong delta, which had been ceded to France as a colony after the first war in 1858–1860. The northern parts of the country, seized in the 1880s, were governed as a protectorate, with the emperor retaining titular authority from his palace in Hue. The French adopted a similar policy in Cambodia and Laos, where local rulers were left in charge with French advisers to counsel them. Even the Dutch were eventually forced into a more direct approach. When the development of plantation agriculture and the extraction of oil in Sumatra made effective exploitation of local resources more complicated, they dispensed with indirect rule and tightened their administrative control over the archipelago.

Whatever method was used, colonial regimes in Southeast Asia, as elsewhere, were slow to create democratic institutions. The first legislative councils and assemblies were composed almost exclusively of European residents in the colonies. The first representatives from the indigenous population were wealthy and conservative in their political views. When Southeast Asians began to complain, colonial officials gradually and reluctantly began to broaden the franchise, but even such liberal thinkers as Albert Sarraut advised patience in awaiting the full benefits of colonial policy. "I will treat you like my younger brothers," he promised, "but do not forget that I am the older brother. I will slowly give you the dignity of humanity."[7]

There was some logic to the view that education in democratic institutions must precede the granting of greater political rights. But here, too, concerns that more knowledge of Western freedoms might spark greater resistance to foreign rule led colonial officials to adopt a cautious attitude toward educational reform. While the introduction of Western educational systems was one of the dominant themes of the concept of civilizing missions, colonial officials soon discovered that educating native elites could backfire. Often there were few jobs for highly trained lawyers, engineers, and architects in colonial societies, leading to the threat of an indigestible mass of unemployed intellectuals who would take out their frustrations on the colonial regime. By the mid-1920s, many colonial governments in Southeast Asia began to limit education to a small and, they hoped, docile elite. As one French official noted in voicing his opposition to increasing the number of schools in Vietnam, educating the natives did not mean "one coolie less, but one rebel more."

Colonial powers were equally reluctant to take up the "white man's burden" in the area of economic development. As we have seen, their primary goals were to secure a source of cheap raw materials and to maintain markets for manufactured goods. Such objectives would be undermined by the emergence of advanced industrial economies. So colonial policy concentrated on the export of raw materials—teakwood from Burma; rubber and tin from Malaya; spices, tea, coffee, and palm oil from the East Indies; and sugar and copra from the Philippines. In many instances, this policy led to a form of plantation agriculture in which peasants were recruited to work as wage laborers on rubber and tea plantations owned by foreign interests.

In some Southeast Asian colonial societies, a measure of industrial development did take place to meet the needs of the European population and local elites. Major manufacturing cities, including Rangoon in lower Burma, Batavia on the island of Java, and Saigon in French Indochina, grew rapidly. Such forms of light industry as textile-processing plants, cement and brick works, and factories for bicycle and auto assembly were established, and some were run by local entrepreneurs. New lands were opened for cultivation in the Mekong and Irrawaddy deltas, and modern banking and transportation networks began to appear.

Despite such fragile signs of economic development, in practice colonial policy tended to lock the local population into a status of permanent economic inferiority relative to their colonial masters. To slake their desire for profits and maintain a competitive edge, plantation owners kept their workers' wages at poverty levels. Many plantation workers were "shanghaied" (the English term originated from the practice of recruiting laborers, often from the docks and streets of Shanghai, by unscrupulous means, such as the use of force, alcohol, or drugs) to work on plantations where conditions were often so inhumane that thousands died. High taxes, enacted by colonial governments to pay for administrative costs or improvements in the local infrastructure, were a heavy burden for poor peasants.

✦ **A Rubber Tree.** Natural rubber was one of the most important cash crops in European colonies in Asia. Rubber trees, native to the Amazon River basin in Brazil, had been transplanted to Southeast Asia, where they became a major source of profit. Workers on the plantations received few benefits, however, for once the sap of the tree (known as latex and shown here) was extracted, the bulk of the refining process took place in Europe.

Colonial policy was often equally harmful in urban areas. There was usually a local middle class that benefited in various ways from the Western presence, but most industrial and commercial establishments were owned and managed by Europeans or, in some cases, by Indian or Chinese merchants. In Saigon, for example, even the manufacture of *nuoc mam*, the traditional Vietnamese fish sauce, was under Chinese ownership. Most urban residents were coolies (the term itself, used contemptuously by Westerners, means "bitter labor" in Chinese), factory workers, or rickshaw drivers or eked out a living in family shops as they had during the traditional era.

As in India, colonial rule did bring some benefits to Southeast Asia. It led to the beginnings of a modern economic infrastructure and what is sometimes called a "modernizing elite" dedicated to the creation of an advanced industrialized society. The development of an export market helped to create an entrepreneurial class in rural areas. On the outer islands of the Dutch East Indies (such as Borneo and Sumatra), for example, small growers of rubber, palm oil, coffee, tea, and spices began to share in the profits of the colonial enterprise. A Dutch sociologist, reporting on conditions in western Sumatra in the 1920s, noted that the development of small coffee plantations in the area had brought considerable benefits to local planters. Children and even teachers stayed away from school, he remarked, because "they see that a coffee farmer earns more than a miserable petty official, who is, moreover, obliged to work away from his native village."[8] Local residents who had previously migrated to Malaya to find employment were now returning to work in their native villages.

A balanced assessment of the colonial legacy in Southeast Asia must take into account that the early stages of industrialization are difficult in any society. Even in Western Europe, industrialization led to the creation of an impoverished and powerless proletariat, urban slums, and displaced peasants driven from the land. In much of Europe and Japan, however, the bulk of the population eventually enjoyed better material conditions as the profits from manufacturing and plantation agriculture were reinvested in the national economy and gave rise to increased consumer demand. In contrast, in Southeast Asia, most of the profits were repatriated to the colonial mother country, while displaced peasants fleeing to cities such as Rangoon, Batavia, and Saigon found little opportunity for employment. Many were left with seasonal employment, with one foot on the farm and one in the factory. The old world was being destroyed, while the new had yet to be born.

COLONIALISM IN AFRICA

Colonialism had similar consequences in Africa, although with some changes in emphasis. As we have seen, European economic interests were more limited in Africa than elsewhere. Having seized the continent in what could almost be described as a fit of hysteria, the European powers had to decide what to do with it. With economic concerns relatively limited except for isolated areas, such as gold mines in the Transvaal and copper deposits in the Belgian Congo, interest in Africa declined, and most European governments settled down to govern their new territories with the least effort and expense possible. In many cases, this meant a form of indirect rule reminiscent of the British approach to the princely states in the Indian peninsula. The British, with their tradition of decentralized government at home, were especially prone to adopt this approach.

In the minds of British administrators, the stated goal of indirect rule was to preserve African political traditions. The desire to limit cost and inconvenience was one reason for this approach, but it may also have been based on the conviction that Africans were inherently inferior to the white race and thus incapable of adopting European customs and institutions. In any event, indirect rule entailed relying to the greatest extent possible on existing political elites and institutions. Initially, in some areas, the British simply asked a local ruler to formally accept British authority and to fly the Union Jack over official buildings. Sometimes it was the Africans who did the asking, as in the case of the African leaders in the Cameroon who wrote to Queen Victoria:

> We *wish* to have your laws in our towns. We want to have every *fashion* altered, also we will do according to your Consul's *word*. Plenty wars here in our country. Plenty murder and plenty idol worshippers. Perhaps these *lines* of our writing will *look* to you as an *idle* tale.
>
> We have *spoken* to the English consul plenty times about having an English *government* here. We never have answer from you, so we wish to write you *ourselves*.
>
> We are, etc.
> King Acqua
> Prince Dido Acqua
> Prince Blakc
> Prince Go Garner
> etc.[9]

The concept of indirect rule was introduced in the Islamic state of Sokoto in northern Nigeria in 1900. British administration under European officials operated at the central level, but local authority was assigned to native chiefs, with British district officers serving as intermediaries with the central administration. Where a local aristocracy did not exist, the British assigned administrative responsibility to clan heads from communities in the vicinity. The local authorities were expected to maintain law and order and to collect taxes from the native population. As a general rule, indigenous customs were left undisturbed; a dual legal system was instituted that applied African laws to Africans and European laws to foreigners.

One advantage of such an administrative system was that it did not severely disrupt local customs and institutions. In fact, however, it had several undesirable consequences. In the first place, it was essentially a fraud, because all major decisions were made by the British administrators while the native authorities served primarily as the means of enforcing decisions. Moreover, indirect rule served to perpetuate the autocratic system that often existed prior to colonial takeover. It was official policy to inculcate respect for authority in areas under British rule, and there was a natural tendency to view the local aristocracy as the African equivalent of the traditional British ruling class. Such a policy provided few opportunities for ambitious and talented young Africans from outside the traditional elite and thus sowed the seeds for class tensions after the restoration of independence in the twentieth century.

The situation was somewhat different in East Africa, especially in Kenya, which had a relatively large European population attracted by the temperate climate in the central highlands. The local government had encouraged Europeans to migrate to the area as a means of promoting economic development and encouraging financial self-sufficiency. To attract them, fertile farmlands in the central highlands were reserved for European settlement while, as in South Africa, specified reserve lands were set aside for Africans. The presence of a substantial European minority (although, in fact, they represented only about 1 percent of the entire population) had an impact on Kenya's political development. The European settlers actively sought self-government and dominion status similar to that granted to such former British possessions as Canada and Australia. The British government, however, was not willing to run the risk of provoking racial tensions with the African majority and agreed only to establish separate government organs for the European and African populations.

The situation in South Africa, of course, was unique, not only because of the high percentage of European settlers but also because of the division between English-speaking and Afrikaner elements within the European population. In 1910, the British agreed to the creation of an independent Union of South Africa that combined the old Cape Colony and Natal with the Boer republics. The new union adopted a representative government, but only for the European population, while the African reserves of Basutoland (now Lesotho), Bechuanaland (now Botswana), and Swaziland were subordinated directly to the crown. The union was now free to manage its own domestic affairs and possessed considerable autonomy in foreign relations. Remaining areas south of the Zambezi River, eventually divided into the territories of Northern and Southern Rhodesia, were also placed under British rule. British immigration into Southern Rhodesia was extensive, and in 1922, after a popular referendum, it became a crown colony.

Most other European nations governed their African possessions through a form of direct rule. The prototype was the French system, which reflected the centralized administrative system introduced in France by Napo-

leon. As in the British colonies, at the top of the pyramid was a French official, usually known as a governor-general, who was appointed from Paris and governed with the aid of a bureaucracy in the capital city. At the provincial level, French commissioners were assigned to deal with local administrators, but the latter were required to be conversant in French and could be transferred to a new position at the needs of the central government.

The French ideal was to assimilate their African subjects into French culture rather than preserving their native traditions. Africans were eligible to run for office and to serve in the French National Assembly, and a few were appointed to high positions in the colonial administration. Such policies reflected the relative absence of racist attitudes in French society, as well as the French conviction of the superiority of Gallic culture and their revolutionary belief in the universality of human nature.

After World War I, European colonial policy in Africa entered a new and more formal phase. The colonial administrative network extended into outlying areas, where it was represented by a district official and defended by a small native army under European command. Colonial governments paid more attention to improving social services, including education, medicine, sanitation, and communications. The colonial system was now viewed more formally as a moral and social responsibility, a "sacred trust" to be maintained by the civilized countries until the Africans became capable of self-government. Governments placed more emphasis on economic development and the exploitation of natural resources to provide the colonies with the means of achieving self-sufficiency. More Africans were now serving in colonial administrations, though relatively few in positions of responsibility. At the same time, race consciousness probably increased during this period. Segregated clubs, schools, and churches were established as more European officials brought their wives and began to raise families in the colonies.

Conclusion

By the first quarter of the twentieth century, virtually all of Africa and a good part of South and Southeast Asia were under some form of colonial rule. With the advent of the age of imperialism, a global economy was finally established, and the domination of Western civilization over those of Africa and Asia appeared to be complete.

Defenders of colonialism argue that the system was a necessary if sometimes painful stage in the evolution of human societies. Although its immediate consequences were admittedly sometimes unfortunate, Western imperialism was ultimately beneficial to colonial powers and subjects alike, because it created the conditions for global economic development and the universal application of democratic institutions. Critics, however, charge that the Western colonial powers were driven by an insatiable lust for profits. They dismiss the Western civilizing mission as a fig leaf to cover naked greed and reject the notion that imperialism played a salutary role in hastening the adjustment of traditional societies to the demands of industrial civilization. In the blunt words of two recent Western critics of imperialism: "Why is Africa (or for that matter Latin America and much of Asia) so poor? ... The answer is very brief: we have made it poor."[10]

Between these two irreconcilable views, where does the truth lie? This chapter has suggested that neither extreme position is justified. The sources of imperialism lie not simply in the demands of industrial capitalism, but also in the search for security, national greatness, and even such psychological factors as the spirit of discovery and the drive to excel. Whereas some regard the concept of the "white man's burden" as a hypocritical gesture to moral sensitivities, others see it as a meaningful reality justifying a lifelong commitment to the colonialist enterprise. Although the "civilizing urge" of missionaries and officials may have been tinged with self-interest, it was nevertheless often sincerely motivated.

Similarly, the consequences of colonialism have been more complex than either its defenders or its critics would have us believe. Although the colonial peoples received little immediate benefit from the imposition of foreign rule, overall the imperialist era brought about a vast expansion of the international trade network and created at least the potential for societies throughout Africa and Asia to play an active and rewarding role in the new global economic arena. If, as world historian William McNeill believes, the introduction of new technology through cross-cultural encounters is the driving force of change in world history, then Western imperialism, whatever its faults, served a useful purpose in open-ing the door to such change, much as the rise of the Arab Empire and the Mongol invasions hastened the process of global economic development in an earlier time.

Still, the critics have a point. Although colonialism did introduce the peoples of Asia and Africa to new technology and the expanding economic marketplace, it was unnecessarily brutal in its application and all too often failed to realize the exalted claims and objectives of its promoters. Existing economic networks—often potentially valuable as a foundation for later economic development—were ruthlessly swept aside in the interests of providing markets for Western manufactured goods. Potential sources of native industrialization were nipped in the bud to avoid competition for factories in Amsterdam, London, Pittsburgh, or Manchester. Training in Western democratic ideals and practices was ignored out of fear that the recipients might use them as weapons against the ruling authorities.

The fundamental weakness of colonialism, then, was that it was ultimately based on the self-interests of the citizens of the colonial powers. Where those interests collided with the needs of the colonial peoples, those of the former always triumphed. Much the same might be said about earlier periods in history, when Assyrians, Arabs, Mongols, and Chinese turned their conquests to their own profit. Where modern imperialism differed was in its tendency to cloak naked self-interest in the cloak of moral obligation. However sincerely the David Livingstones, Albert Sarrauts, and William McKinleys of the world were convinced of the rightness of their civilizing mission, the ultimate result was to deprive the colonial peoples of the right to make their own choices about their own destiny.

In one area of Asia, the spreading tide of imperialism did not result in the establishment of formal Western colonial control. In East Asia, the traditional societies of China and Japan were buffeted by the winds of Western expansionism during the nineteenth century but successfully resisted foreign conquest. In the next chapter, we will see how they managed this and how they fared in their encounter with the West.

NOTES

1. Quoted in Henry Braunschwig, *French Colonialism, 1871–1914* (London, 1961), p. 80.

2. From C. M. Turnbull, *A History of Singapore, 1819–1975* (Kuala Lumpur, 1977), p. 19.

3. Quoted in Ruhl Bartlett, ed., *The Record of American Diplomacy: Documents and Readings in the History of American Foreign Relations* (New York, 1952), p. 385.

4. From Georges Garros, *Forgeries Humaines* (Paris, 1926).

5. Quoted in Winfred Baumgart, *Imperialism: The Idea and Reality of British and French Colonial Expansion, 1880–1914* (Oxford, 1982), p. 137.

6. Quoted in Stanley Wolpert, *A New History of India* (New York, 1977), p. 215.

7. Sarraut's comment is from Louis Roubaud, *Vietnam: La Tragédie Indochinoise* (Paris, 1926), p. 80.

8. Quoted in Clifford Geertz, *Agricultural Involution: The Process of Ecological Change in Indonesia* (Berkeley, 1963), p. 119.

9. Quoted in Thomas Pakenham, *The Scramble for Africa, 1876–1912* (New York, 1991), p. 13.

10. Quoted in Tony Smith, *The Pattern of Imperialism: The United States, Great Britain, and the Late-Industrial World since 1815* (Cambridge, 1981), p. 81.

CHAPTER
3

Shadows over the Pacific: East Asia under Challenge

In August 1793, a British ambassadorial mission led by Lord Macartney arrived at the North Chinese port of Taku and embarked on the road to Beijing. His caravan, which included 600 cases bearing presents for the emperor, bore flags and banners provided by the Chinese which proclaimed in Chinese characters "Ambassador bearing tribute from the country of England." Macartney chose to ignore the slight, but on arrival in the capital he refused his hosts' demand that he perform the kowtow, a traditional symbol of submission to the emperor. Eventually a compromise was reached, according to which he agreed to bend on one knee, a courtesy that he displayed to his own sovereign, and the dispute over protocol was resolved.

In other respects, however, the mission was a failure. Macartney carried a British request for an increase in trade between the two countries, but the appeal was flatly rejected, and he left Beijing in October with nothing to show for his efforts. It would not be until half a century later that the Qing dynasty—at the point of a gun—agreed to the British demand for an expansion of commercial ties.

The failure of the Macartney mission has often been interpreted by historians as a reflection of the disdain of Chinese rulers toward their counterparts in other countries and their serene confidence in the superiority of Chinese civilization in a world inhabited by barbarians, and of course it was. But, in retrospect, it is clear that the imperial concern over the aggressive behavior of the European barbarians was justified, for in the decades immediately following the abortive Macartney mission to Beijing, China was faced with a growing challenge from the escalating power and ambitions of the West. Backed by European guns, European merchants and missionaries pressed insistently for the right to carry out their activities in China and the neighboring islands of Japan. Despite their initial reluctance, the Chinese and Japanese governments were eventually forced to open their doors to the foreigners, whose presence and threat to the local way of life escalated rapidly during the final years of the century.

. . . .

China at Its Apex

In 1800, the Qing or Manchu dynasty (1644–1911) appeared to be at the height of its power. China had experienced a long period of peace and prosperity under the rule of two great emperors, Kangxi (1661–1722) and Qianlong (1736–1795). Its borders were secure, and its

culture and intellectual achievements were the envy of the world. Its rulers, hidden behind the walls of the Forbidden City in Beijing, had every reason to describe their patrimony as the Central Kingdom, China's historical name for itself. But a little over a century later, humiliated and harassed by the black ships and big guns of the Western powers, the Qing dynasty, the last in a series that had endured for more than two thousand years, collapsed in the dust.

Historians once assumed that the primary reason for the rapid decline and fall of the Manchu dynasty was the intense pressure applied to a proud but somewhat complacent traditional society by the modern West. There is indeed some truth in that allegation. On the surface, China had long appeared to be an unchanging society patterned after the Confucian vision of a Golden Age in the remote past. This, in fact, was the image presented by China's rulers, who referred constantly to tradition as a model for imperial institutions and cultural values. That tradition was based firmly on a set of principles that were identified with the ancient philosopher Confucius (551–479 B.C.E.) and emphasized such qualities as obedience, hard work, rule by merit, and the subordination of the individual to the interests of the community. Such principles, which had emerged out of the conditions of a continental society based on agriculture as the primary source of national wealth, had formed the basis for Chinese political and social institutions and values since the early years of the great Han dynasty in the second century B.C.E.

When European ships first began to arrive off the coast of China in the sixteenth and seventeenth centuries, they brought with them revolutionary new ideas and values that were strikingly at variance with those of imperial China. China's rulers soon came to recognize the nature of the threat represented by European missionaries and merchants and attempted to expel the former while restricting the latter to a limited presence in the southern coastal city of Canton. For the next two centuries, China was, at least in intent, an essentially closed society.

It was the hope of influential figures at the imperial court in Beijing that by expelling the barbarians, they could protect the purity of Chinese civilization from the virus of foreign ideas. Their effort to freeze time was fruitless, however, for in reality Chinese society was already beginning to change under their feet—and changing rather rapidly. Although few observers may have been aware of it at the time, by the beginning of the Manchu era in the seventeenth century, Confucian precepts were becoming increasingly irrelevant in a society that was becoming ever more complex.

Nowhere was change more evident than in the economic sector. During the early modern period, China was a predominantly agricultural society, as it had been throughout recorded history. Nearly 85 percent of the population were farmers. In the south, the main crop was rice; in the north, it was wheat or dry crops. As always, most Chinese were small farmers, although a few large landowners hired out their land to tenants. But although China was still a country of villages with a few scattered urban centers, the economy was changing and was by no means the same as it had been under previous glorious dynasties, such as the Tang, the Song, or the Ming.

In the first place, the population was beginning to increase rapidly. A long era of peace and stability, the introduction of new crops from the Americas, and the cultivation of new, fast-ripening strains of rice enabled the Chinese population to double between the time of the early Qing and the end of the eighteenth century. The population continued to grow during the nineteenth century, reaching the unprecedented level of 400 million by 1900.

Of course, this population increase meant much greater population pressure on the land, smaller farms, and a razor-thin margin of safety in case of climatic disaster. The imperial court had attempted to deal with the problem by a variety of means—most notably by preventing the concentration of land in the hands of wealthy landowners—but by the end of the eighteenth century, almost all the land that could be irrigated was already under cultivation, and the problems of rural hunger and landlessness became increasingly serious. Not surprisingly, economic hardship was quickly translated into rural unrest.

Another change that took place during the early modern period in China was the steady growth of manufacturing and commerce. Trade and manufacturing had existed in China since early times, of course, but they had been limited by a number of factors, including social prejudice, official restrictions, and state monopolies on mining and on the production of such commodities as alcohol and salt. Now, taking advantage of the long era of peace and prosperity, merchants and manufacturers began to expand their operations beyond their immediate provinces. Trade in silk, metal and wood products, porcelain, cotton goods, and cash crops such as cotton and tobacco developed rapidly, and commercial networks began to operate on a regional and sometimes even a national basis. A Portuguese visitor in the sixteenth century viewed the process from the environs of Canton:

> This country of China is great, and its commerce is between certain provinces of it and others. Cantao [Canton] has iron, which there is not in the whole of the rest of the country of China, according to what I am informed. From here it goes inland to the other side of the mountain range;

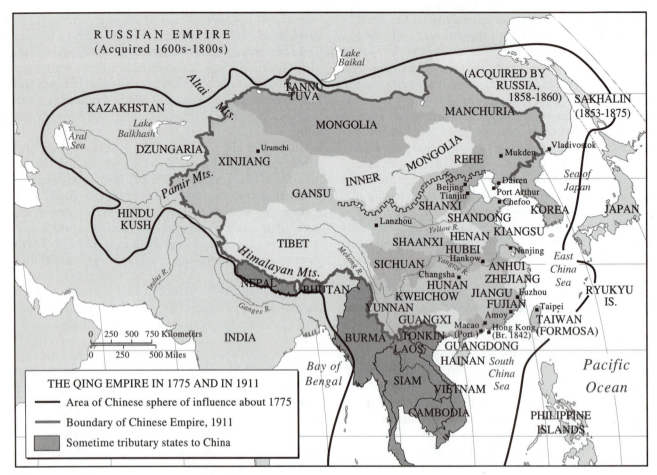

Map 3.1 The Qing Empire in the Early Twentieth Century

and the rest lies in the vicinity of this city of Cantao. From this they manufacture pots, nails, Chinese trade of goods from the provinces to Cantao and from Cantao arms and everything else of iron. They have also cordage, thread and silk, and cotton cloths. By reason of trade all goods come here, because this is the port whither foreigners come for this trade of goods from the provinces to Cantao and from Cantao to the interior, and the people are more numerous than in the other provinces.[1]

With the expansion of trade came an extension of commercial contacts and guild organizations on a nationwide basis. Merchants began establishing guilds in cities and market towns throughout the country to provide legal protection, an opportunity to do business, and food and lodging for merchants from particular provinces. Foreign trade also expanded, with Chinese merchants, mainly from the coastal provinces of the south, setting up extensive contacts with countries in Southeast Asia. In many instances, the contacts in Southeast

Asia were themselves Chinese who had settled in the area during the seventeenth and eighteenth centuries.

Some historians have interpreted this rise in industrial and commercial activity as a process that would have led under other circumstances to an indigenous industrial revolution and the emergence of a capitalist society such as that already taking shape in Europe. By this reasoning, the arrival of Western imperialism in the nineteenth century not only failed to hasten economic change, but may actually have hindered it.

But the significance of these changes should not be exaggerated. In fact, there were some key differences between China and Western Europe that would have hindered the emergence of capitalism in China. In the first place, the bourgeoisie in China were not as independent as their European counterparts. Free cities, such as had long existed in the West, had not emerged in China, and trade and manufacturing remained under the firm control of the state. In addition, political and social prejudices against commercial activity remained strong at court and in society at large. Reflecting an ancient preference for agriculture over manufacturing and trade, the state levied heavy taxes on manufacturing and commerce while attempting to keep agricultural taxes low. Such attitudes were still shared by key groups in the population. Although much money could be made in commerce, most gentry resisted the temptation, and many merchants who accumulated wealth used it to buy their way into the ranks of the gentry. The most that can really be said, then, is that during the late Ming and Qing dynasties, China was beginning to undergo major economic and social changes that might have led, in due time, to the emergence of an industrialized society.

Traditional China in Decline

When Western pressure on the Manchu empire began to increase during the early nineteenth century, it served to exacerbate the existing strains in Chinese society. By 1800, the trade relationship that restricted Western merchants to a small commercial outlet at Canton was no longer acceptable to the British, who chafed at the growing trade imbalance resulting from a growing appetite for Chinese tea. Their solution was opium. A product more addictive than tea, opium was grown under company sponsorship in northeastern India and then shipped directly to the Chinese market. Soon demand for the product in South China became insatiable, despite an official prohibition on its use. Bullion now flowed out of the Chinese imperial treasury into the pockets of British merchants and officials.

Opium and Rebellion

When the Chinese attempted to prohibit the opium trade, the British declared war (see box on p. 54). The Opium War (1839–1842) lasted three years and graphically demonstrated the superiority of British firepower and military tactics to those of the Chinese. China sued for peace, and in the Treaty of Nanjing agreed to open five coastal ports to British trade, limit tariffs on imported British goods, grant extraterritorial rights to British citizens in China, and pay a substantial indemnity to cover the British costs of the war. Beijing also agreed to cede the island of Hong Kong (dismissed by a senior British official as a "barren rock") to Great Britain. Nothing was said in the treaty about the opium trade.

The Opium War has traditionally been considered the beginning of modern Chinese history. This view

seems plausible because the war marked the first major stage in the Western penetration of China, a process that eventually led to the virtual collapse of the Qing dynasty at the hands of foreign imperialists in the early twentieth century. At the time, however, it is unlikely that many Chinese would have seen it that way. This was not the first time that a ruling dynasty had been forced to make concessions to foreigners, and the opening of five coastal ports to the British hardly constituted a serious threat to the security of the empire. Although a few concerned Chinese argued that the court should learn more about European civilization to find the secret of British success, others contended that China had nothing to learn from the barbarians and that borrowing foreign ways would undercut the purity of Confucian civilization.

For the time being, the Manchus attempted to deal with the problem in the traditional way of playing the foreigners off against each other. Concessions granted to the British were offered to other Western nations, including the United States, and soon thriving foreign concession areas were operating in treaty ports along the southern Chinese coast from Canton in the south to Shanghai, a bustling new port on a tributary of the Yangtze, in the center.

In the meantime, the Qing court's failure to deal with pressing internal economic problems led to a major peasant revolt that shook the foundations of the empire. On the surface, the so-called Taiping (T'ai p'ing) Rebellion owed something to the Western incursion; the leader of the uprising, Hong Xiuquan (Hung Hsiu-ch'uan), a failed examination candidate, was a Christian convert who viewed himself as a younger brother of Jesus Christ and hoped to establish what he referred to as a "Heavenly Kingdom of Supreme Peace" in China. Its ranks swelled by impoverished peasants and other discontented elements throughout the southern provinces, the Taiping Rebellion swept northward while Hong Xiuquan proclaimed his intention of destroying the corrupt Qing and founding a new dynasty. The rebels seized the old Ming capital of Nanjing in March 1853. The revolt continued for ten more years, but the seizure of the central Yangtze valley was its high-water mark. Plagued by factionalism that led to an internal civil war and the death of thousands, the rebellion gradually lost momentum, and in 1864 the Qing, although weakened, retook Nanjing and destroyed the remnants of the rebel force.

One reason for the dynasty's failure to deal effectively with internal unrest was its continuing difficulties with the Western imperialists. In 1856, the British and the

⋟ *The Tribute System in Action* ⋞

During the imperial era, China's view of the outside world was essentially hierarchical. China was assumed to be the Central Kingdom, and rulers of all friendly societies were expected to place themselves in a tributary relationship with the "son of Heaven" in Beijing. In return, such countries were granted commercial privileges in China and their monarchs received the blessing of the Chinese emperor as the legitimate sovereigns over their subjects.

During the nineteenth century, the tribute system came under severe challenge. First to question the practice had been the British, whose emissary, Lord Macartney, refused to perform the traditional kowtow during his visit to Beijing in 1793. Macartney's action, however, had little effect. When, four decades later, the imperial commissioner Lin Zexu wrote to Queen Victoria to protest against British efforts to market opium in China, his letter reflected the familiar tone of condescension that Chinese officials customarily used in their dealings with other governments. Noting that "the kings of your honorable country" had always been noted for their "politeness and submissiveness," he warned that the sale of opium in China must come to an end, on the pain of losing the "Celestial grace." Commissioner Lin's threat of retaliation had a distinctly modern ring. Your country, he declared, depends for its prosperity on trade relations with China. As for us, however, "articles coming from the outside to China can only be used as toys. We can take them or get along without them. Since they are not needed by China, what difficulty would there be if we closed the frontier and stopped the trade?"

China's defeat in the ensuing conflict with Great Britain forced the Qing court to deal with the European powers as equals, but the tribute system continued to serve as a guideline for relations with neighboring states in Asia. By the end of the century, however, even the latter were sometimes emboldened to challenge the system. When China and Japan clashed over interests in the Korean peninsula, the Qing attempted to intimidate its new rival by insisting on its tributary relationship with Korea and referring to Japan by the contemptuous Chinese term *wojen* ("dwarf people"). But it was too late. Japanese leaders, now convinced by Western actions that a colonial empire was the key to national greatness, were no longer willing to accept the grandiose pretensions of their larger neighbor. In his declaration of war against China in 1894, the Japanese emperor declared that although it was China's habit "to designate Korea as her dependency," the latter was in fact "an independent state" that "had been first introduced into the family of nations by the advice and guidance of Japan."

The Koreans would later have cause to question the benevolence of their new protector. A few years after Japan's victory over China, Korea was assimilated into the Japanese Empire.

Sources: Ssu-yu Teng and John K. Fairbank, *China's Response to the West: A Documentary Survey, 1839–1923* (New York: Atheneum, 1970), p. 19; Franz Schurmann and Orville Schell, eds., *The China Reader: Imperial China* (New York: Vintage, 1967), pp. 251–259.

French, still smarting from trade restrictions and limitations on their missionary activities, launched a new series of attacks against China and seized the capital of Beijing in 1860. As punishment, British troops destroyed the imperial summer palace just outside the city. In the ensuing Treaty of Tianjin (Tientsin), the Qing agreed to humiliating new concessions: legalization of the opium trade, the opening of additional ports to foreign trade, and cession of the peninsula of Kowloon (opposite the island of Hong Kong) to the British. Additional territories in the north were ceded to Russia.

The Climax of Imperialism in China

The continuing failure of traditional methods to deal with the Western threat gradually persuaded some thoughtful officials and intellectuals that China must learn from the West in order to survive. At first that point of view had little impact at court, where the initial reaction to the occupation of the capital was to seek a return to Confucian purity. But Confucian precepts by themselves were of little use against European guns, and the glories of the past could not be conjured

⯈ An Appeal for Change in China ⯇

After the humiliating defeat at the hands of the British in the Opium War, a few Chinese intellectuals began to argue that China must change its ways in order to survive. Among such reformist thinkers was the journalist and author Wang Tao (1828–1897). After a trip to Europe in the late 1860s, Wang returned to China convinced of the technological superiority of the West and the need for his country to adopt reforms to enable it to compete effectively in a changing world. During the remainder of his life devoted to journalism and publishing, he actively promoted his reformist views.

By the mid-1870s, the Qing court had already recognized the need to match Western technological achievements, a decision that resulted in the "self-strengthening" movement. But conservative officials at court remained convinced of the innate superiority of Chinese political and social institutions and were reluctant to tamper with any aspect of the Chinese "essence" inherited from the past. Wang Tao vigorously disagreed. The techniques and skills of the Westerners, he argued, "develop without bound. . . . The foreign nations come from afar with their superior techniques, contemptuous of us in our deficiencies." Yet arrogant Chinese officials, he lamented, regard these achievements as unworthy and refuse to pay attention, arguing that "we should use our own laws to govern the empire, for that is the Way of the sages." But the Way of the sages, Wang retorted, is valued only because it can make proper accommodations according to the times. "If Confucius lived

today," he declared, "we may be certain that he would not cling to antiquity and oppose making changes."

For Wang Tao, then, reform went beyond such practical innovations as railroads, steamships, and modern weapons. It also involved the development of a modern industrial and commercial sector, abolition of the civil service examination and the adoption of a modern system of education, and above all, a new relationship between the government and the people. "The real strength of England," he pointed out, "lies in the fact that there is a sympathetic understanding between the governing and the governed, a close relationship between the ruler and the people."

Wang Tao had only limited success in persuading his contemporaries of the need for dramatic change. Undoubtedly many Chinese were reluctant to believe his claim that China was not the Middle Kingdom and "all under Heaven," but only one nation among many in a rapidly changing world. Just before his death, Wang met the man whose ideas would eventually bring the old system to its knees. His name was Sun Yat-sen.

Sources: William Theodore De Bary, ed., *Sources of Chinese Tradition* (New York: Columbia University Press, 1958); Paul A. Cohen, *Between Tradition and Modernity: Wang T'ao and Reform in Late Ch'ing China* (Cambridge: Harvard University Press, 1974), p. 225; and Wang Ke-wen, ed., *Modern China: An Encyclopedia of History, Culture, and Nationalism* (New York: Garland Publishers, 1998).

---

up at will to restore China to the Golden Age of ancient days.

In its weakened state, the court finally began to listen to the appeals of reform-minded officials, who called for a new policy of "self-strengthening," in which Western technology would be adopted while Confucian principles and institutions were maintained intact. This policy, popularly known by its slogan "East for essence, West for practical use," remained the guiding standard for Chinese foreign and domestic policy for nearly a quarter of a century. Some even called for reforms in education and in China's hallowed political institutions, but such radical proposals were rejected.

During the last quarter of the century, the Manchus attempted to modernize their military establishment and build up an industrial base without touching the essential elements of traditional Chinese civilization. Railroads, weapons arsenals, and shipyards were built, but the value system remained essentially unchanged (see box above).

In the end, the results spoke for themselves. During the last two decades of the nineteenth century, the European penetration of China, both political and military, intensified. At the outer edges of the Qing Empire, rapacious imperialists began to bite off territory. The Gobi Desert north of the Great Wall, Chinese Central

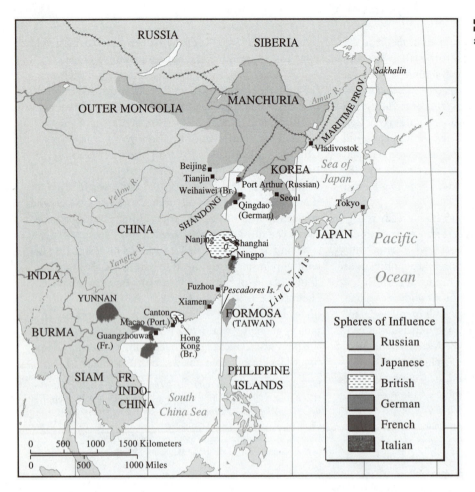

Map 3.2 Foreign Possessions and Spheres of Influence about 1900

Asia, and Tibet, all inhabited by non-Chinese peoples and never fully assimilated into the Chinese Empire, were now gradually removed totally from Beijing's control. In the north and northwest, the main beneficiary was Russia, which took advantage of the dynasty's weakness to force the cession of territories north of the Amur River in Siberia. In Tibet, competition between Russia and Great Britain prevented either power from seizing the territory outright, but at the same time enabled Tibetan authorities to revive local autonomy never recognized by the Chinese. On the southern borders of the empire, British and French advances in mainland Southeast Asia removed Burma and Vietnam from their traditional vassal relationship to the Manchu court.

Even more ominous developments were taking place in the Chinese heartland, where European economic penetration led to the creation of so-called spheres of influence dominated by diverse foreign powers. These spheres, normally composed of one or more Chinese administrative provinces, had originated with the rise of autonomous regional forces after the Taiping Rebellion. Local commanders began to negotiate directly with foreign political and economic interests, providing them with exclusive commercial, railroad-building, or mining privileges in return for financial compensation. Although the imperial court retained theoretical sovereignty throughout the country, in practice its political, economic, and administrative influence beyond the region of the capital was increasingly circumscribed.

The breakup of the Manchu dynasty accelerated during the last five years of the nineteenth century. In 1894, the Qing went to war with Japan over Japanese incursions into the Korean peninsula, which threatened China's long-held suzerainty over the area. To the surprise of many observers, the Chinese were roundly defeated, confirming to some critics the devastating failure of the policy of self-strengthening by halfway measures. As a reward, Japan demanded and received the island of Taiwan (known to Europeans at the time as Formosa) and the Liaodong (Liaotung) peninsula, strategically located at the entrance to the Gulf of Bohai in southern Manchuria. The emergence of Japan as an imperialist power aroused concern in European capitals, and a consortium composed of Germany, France, and Russia forced the Japanese to renounce their seizure of the Liaodong peninsula. But European statesmen were not concerned with preventing the collapse of the Chinese Empire. Before the end of the century, the peninsula once again fell under foreign control.

The process began in 1897, when Germany, a new entry in the race for spoils in East Asia, used the pretext of the murder of two German missionaries by Chinese rioters to demand the cession of territories in the Shandong (Shantung) peninsula. The imperial court's approval of this demand set off a scramble for territory by other interested powers. Russia now demanded the Liaodong peninsula with its ice-free port at Port Arthur, and Great Britain weighed in with a request for a coaling station in North China at Weihaiwei, near the eastern tip of the Shandong peninsula.

The latest scramble for territory had taken place at a time of internal crisis in China. In the spring of 1898, an outspoken advocate of reform, the progressive Confucian scholar Kang Youwei (K'ang Yu-wei), won the support of the young Emperor Guangxu (Kuang Hsu) for a comprehensive reform program patterned after recent changes initiated in Japan. During the next several weeks, the emperor issued edicts calling for major

♦ **The Empress Dowager's Navy.** Historians have often interpreted the stone pavilion shown here as a symbol of the Qing dynasty's inability to comprehend the nature of the threat to its survival. Funds meant to strengthen the Chinese navy against imperious Westerns were used instead to construct this stone pleasure boat on the shore of a lake at the Summer Palace west of Beijing. Today, the lake is a popular place for Chinese tourists.

political, administrative, and educational reforms. Kang's appeal to the emperor was simple and direct:

> A survey of all states in the world will show that those states which undertook reforms became strong while those states which clung to the past perished. The consequences of clinging to the past and the effects of opening up new ways are thus obvious. If Your Majesty, with your discerning brilliance, observes the trends in other countries, you will see that if we can change, we can preserve ourselves. But if we cannot change, we shall perish. Indeed, if we can make a complete change, we shall become strong, but if we only make limited changes, we shall still perish. If Your Majesty and his ministers investigate the source of the disease, you will know that this is the right prescription.[2]

Not surprisingly, Kang's ideas for reform were opposed by many conservatives, who saw little advantage to copying the West. "An examination of the causes of success and failure in government," said one, "reveals that in general the upholding of Confucianism leads to good government while the adoption of foreignism leads to disorder."[3] What was necessary, he concluded, was to reform existing ways (to follow the "Kingly Way") rather than abandoning the tried-and-true rules of the past.

Most important, the new program was opposed by the emperor's aunt, the Empress Dowager Cixi (Tz'u Hsi), the real source of power at court. Cixi had begun her political career as a concubine to an earlier emperor. After his death, she became a dominant force at court and in 1878 placed her infant nephew Guangxu on the throne. For two decades, she ruled in his name as regent. Cixi interpreted Guangxu's action as a British-supported effort to reduce her influence at court. With the aid of conservatives in the army, she arrested and executed several of the reformers and had the emperor incarcerated in the palace. Kang Youwei succeeded in fleeing abroad. With Cixi's palace coup, the so-called One Hundred Days of reform came to an end.

The Open Door

During the next two years, foreign pressure on the dynasty intensified. With encouragement from the British, who hoped to avert a total collapse of the Manchu Empire, U.S. Secretary of State John Hay presented the other imperialist powers with a proposal to ensure equal economic access to the China market for all nations. Hay also suggested that all powers join together to guarantee the territorial and administrative integrity of the Chinese Empire. He requested that each power, within its own sphere of influence:

1. Will in no way interfere with any treaty port or any vested interest within any so-called sphere of interest or leased territory it may have in China.
2. That only the Chinese government should collect duty and according to the Chinese treaty tariff.
3. That no preferential harbour dues or railway charges should benefit its own subjects.[4]

When none of the other governments flatly opposed the idea, Hay issued a second note declaring that all major nations with economic interests in China had agreed to an "Open Door" policy in China.

In later years, the Open Door policy would be praised in American history books as an indication of U.S. benevolence and support for the survival of China. While many Americans did sympathize with China's struggle against rapacious colonial powers, it is undeniable that the United States was also motivated by self-interest. Trading interests in the United States preferred to operate in open markets and disliked the existing division of China into separate spheres of influence dominated by individual powers. The Open Door policy did not formally end the system of spheres of influence, but it did reduce the number of tariffs or quotas on foreign imports imposed by the dominating power within each sphere.

Whatever its underlying motivation, the Open Door policy did have the practical effect of reducing the imperialist hysteria over access to the China market. That hysteria—a product of decades of mythologizing among Western commercial interests about the "400 million" Chinese customers—had accelerated at the end of the century, as fear over China's imminent collapse increased. The "gentlemen's agreement" about the Open Door (it was not a treaty, but merely a pious and nonbinding expression of intent) served to deflate fears in Britain, France, Germany, and Russia that other powers would take advantage of China's weakness to dominate the China market for themselves.

In the long run, then, the Open Door was a positive step that brought a measure of sanity to imperialist behavior in East Asia. Unfortunately, it came too late to stop the domestic explosion known as the Boxer Rebellion. The Boxers, so called because of the physical exercises they performed, were members of a secret society operating primarily in rural areas in North China. Provoked by a damaging drought and high levels of unemployment, caused in part by foreign economic activity (the introduction of railroads and steamships, for example, undercut the livelihood of boatworkers who traditionally carried merchandise on the rivers and canals), the Boxers attacked foreign residents and besieged the

◆ **Justice or Mercy: Uncle Sam Decides.** In the summer of 1900, Chinese rebels called Boxers besieged Western embassies in the imperial capital of Beijing. Western nations, including the United States, dispatched troops to North China to rescue their compatriots. In the cartoon, which appeared in a contemporary American newsmagazine, China figuratively seeks pardon from a stern Uncle Sam.

foreign legation quarter in Beijing until the foreigners were rescued by an international expeditionary force in the late summer of 1900. As punishment, the foreign troops destroyed a number of temples in the capital suburbs, and the Chinese government was compelled to pay a heavy indemnity to the foreign governments involved in suppressing the uprising.

The Collapse of the Old Order

During the next few years, the old dynasty tried desperately to reform itself. The empress dowager, who had long resisted change, now embraced a number of reforms in education, administration, and the legal system. The venerable civil service examination system was replaced by a new educational system based on the Western

model. In 1905, a commission was formed to study constitutional changes, and over the next few years, legislative assemblies were established at the provincial level. Elections for a national assembly were held in 1910.

These moves won at least temporary support for the dynasty among progressive elements in the country. But history shows that the most dangerous period for an authoritarian system is when it begins to reform itself, because change breeds instability and performance rarely matches rising expectations. Such was the case in China. The emerging new provincial elite, composed of merchants, professionals, and reform-minded gentry, soon became impatient with the slow pace of political change. They were disillusioned to find that the new assemblies, severely limited in their franchise in any case, were intended to be primarily advisory rather than legislative. The government also alienated influential elements by financing railway development projects through lucrative contracts to foreign firms rather than by turning to local investors.

These reforms also had little meaning for peasants, artisans, miners, and transportation workers, whose living conditions were being eroded by rising taxes and official venality. Rising rural unrest, as yet poorly organized and often centered on secret societies such as the Boxers, was an ominous sign of deep-seated resentment to which the dynasty would not, or could not, respond.

To China's reformist elite, such signs of social unrest were a threat to be avoided; to its tiny revolutionary movement, they were a harbinger of promise. The first physical manifestations of future revolution appeared during the last decade of the nineteenth century with the formation of the Revive China Society by the young radical Sun Yat-sen (1866–1925). Born to a peasant family in a village south of Canton, Sun was educated in Hawaii and returned to China to practice medicine. Soon he turned his full attention to the ills of Chinese society.

Sun Yat-sen disagreed with Kang Youwei's plan to use the young Manchu emperor as the engine of change. When you decide to build a railroad, he pointed out, you should find the most modern locomotive. He was convinced that the Qing dynasty was in a state of irreparable decay, incapable of becoming the vehicle for an effective program of national revival. The Chinese people, he lamented, are like "a sheet of loose sand."[5] Until they were united under a strong government, they would be at the mercy of other countries. Accordingly, Sun believed that China should follow the pattern of the Western democracies.

Gathering support from radical students, merchants, and secret society members in South China—as well as

Chinese living in Europe, the United States, and elsewhere in Asia—Sun launched a series of local insurrections to topple the Qing and establish a republic on the Western model. Acknowledging Kang's point that the Chinese people were not yet sophisticated enough to put Western democracy into practice, he called for a three-stage process beginning with a military takeover and ending with a constitutional democracy. Thus, he would replace the monarchy with his own revolutionary party as the vehicle for change during a transitional stage that he labeled the period of political tutelage. During that stage, the revolutionary party would try to repair the defects in Chinese society and prepare the people for the next stage of constitutionalism.

At first, Sun's efforts yielded few positive results other than creating a symbol of resistance and a pantheon of revolutionary martyrs. But at a convention in Tokyo in 1905, Sun managed to unite radical groups from across China in a Revolutionary Alliance (Tongmenghui, or T'ung Meng Hui). The new organization's program was based on Sun's Three People's Principles: nationalism (meaning primarily the destruction of Manchu rule over China), democracy, and "people's livelihood" (an ambiguous term referring to a program to improve social and economic conditions). Although the new organization was small and relatively inexperienced, it benefited from rising popular discontent with the failure of Manchu reforms to improve conditions in China.

The dynasty, in fact, was about to commit suicide. In 1908, the dowager empress died. Mysteriously, her nephew Guangxu, imprisoned in the imperial palace since the failure of the One Hundred Days of reform, had died the day before. The throne was now occupied by China's "last emperor," the infant Henry Puyi (P'u Yi).

In October 1911, followers of Sun Yat-sen launched yet another uprising, in the industrial center of Wuhan, on the Yangtze River in central China. With Sun traveling in the United States, the insurrection lacked leadership, but the decrepit government's inability to react quickly encouraged political forces at the provincial level to take measures into their own hands. The dynasty was now in a state of virtual collapse, opening the way for new political forces to fill the vacuum. Sun's party, however, had neither the military strength nor the political base necessary to seize the initiative and was forced to turn to a representative of the old order, General Yuan Shikai (Yuan Shih-k'ai). A prominent figure in military circles since the beginning of the century, Yuan had been placed in charge of the imperial forces sent to suppress the rebellion, but now he abandoned the Manchus and acted on his own behalf. In negotiations with representatives of Sun Yat-sen's party (Sun himself had arrived in China in January 1912), he agreed to serve as president of a new Chinese republic. The old dynasty and the age-old system it had attempted to preserve were no more.

Propagandists for Sun Yat-sen's party have often portrayed the events of 1911 as a glorious revolution that brought two thousand years of imperial tradition to an end, and indeed they did finish off the old dynastic system. But a true revolution does not just destroy an old order; it also brings new political and social forces into power and creates new institutions and values that provide a new framework for a changing society. If these are the criteria of revolution, then the 1911 revolution did not live up to its name. Sun Yat-sen and his followers were unable to consolidate their gains. The Revolutionary Alliance found the bulk of its support in an emerging urban middle class and set forth a program based generally on Western liberal democratic principles. That class and that program had provided the foundation for the capitalist democratic revolutions in Western Europe and North America in the late eighteenth and nineteenth centuries, but the bourgeois class was still too small in China to form the basis for a new, post-Confucian political order. The vast majority of the Chinese people still lived on the land. Although Sun Yat-sen had hoped to win their support with a land reform program that relied on fiscal incentives to persuade landlords to sell excess lands to their tenants, few had participated in the 1911 revolution, although rural unrest was on the rise. In effect, then, the events of 1911 were less a revolution than a collapse of the old order. Undermined by imperialism and its own internal weaknesses, the old dynasty had come to an abrupt end before new political and social forces were ready to fill the vacuum.

What China had experienced was part of a historical process that was bringing down traditional empires across the globe, both in those regions threatened by Western imperialism and in Europe itself, where tsarist Russia, the Austro-Hungarian Empire, and the Ottoman Empire all came to an end within a few years of the collapse of the Qing. The circumstances of their demise were not all the same. The Austro-Hungarian Empire, for example, was dismembered by the victorious allies after World War I, while the fate of tsarist Russia was directly linked to that conflict. Still, all four regimes shared the responsibility for their common fate because they had failed to meet the challenges posed by the times. All had responded to the forces of industrialization and popular participation in the political process with hesitation and reluctance, and their attempts at reform were too little and too late. All paid the supreme price for their folly.

Chinese Society in Transition

The growing Western presence in China during the late nineteenth and early twentieth centuries obviously had a major impact on Chinese society; hence many historians have asserted that the arrival of the Europeans shook China out of centuries of slumber and launched it on the road to revolutionary change. In fact, when the European economic penetration into China began to accelerate in the mid-nineteenth century, Chinese society was already in a state of transition. The growth of industry and trade was particularly noticeable in the cities, where a national market for such commodities as oil, copper, salt, tea, and porcelain had developed. The foundation of an infrastructure more conducive to the rise of a money economy appeared to be in place. In the countryside, new crops introduced from abroad significantly increased food production and aided population growth. The Chinese economy had never been more productive or complex.

Whether these changes by themselves would eventually have led to an industrial revolution and the rise of a capitalist society on the Western model in the absence of Western intervention is a question that historians cannot answer with assurance. Certainly, a number of obstacles would have made it difficult for China to embark on the Western path if it had wished to do so.

Although industrial production was on the rise, it was still based almost entirely on traditional methods of production. China had no uniform system of weights and measures, and the banking system was still primitive by European standards. The use of paper money, invented by the Chinese centuries earlier, had essentially been abandoned. The transportation system, which had been neglected since the end of the Yuan dynasty, was increasingly chaotic. There were few paved roads, and the Grand Canal, long the most efficient means of carrying goods from north to south, was silting up. As a result, merchants had to rely more and more on the coastal route, where they faced increasing competition from foreign shipping.

Although foreign concession areas in the coastal cities provided a conduit for the importation of Western technology and modern manufacturing methods, the Chinese borrowed less than they might have. Foreign manufacturing enterprises could not legally operate in China until the last decade of the nineteenth century, and their methods had little influence beyond the con-

cession areas. Chinese efforts to imitate Western methods, notably in shipbuilding and weapons manufacture, were dominated by the government and often suffered from mismanagement.

Equally serious problems persisted in the countryside. The rapid increase in population had led to smaller plots and growing numbers of tenant farmers. Whether per capita consumption of food was on the decline is not clear from the available evidence, but apparently rice as a staple of the diet was increasingly being replaced by less nutritious foods. Some farmers benefited from switching to commercial agriculture to supply the markets of the growing coastal cities. The shift entailed a sizable investment, however, and many farmers went so deeply into debt that they eventually lost their land. At the same time, the traditional patron-client relationship was frayed, as landlords moved to the cities to take advantage of the glittering urban lifestyle.

Most important, perhaps, the Qing dynasty was still locked into a traditional mindset that discouraged commercial activities and prized the time-honored virtues of preindustrial agrarian society. China also lacked the European tradition of a vigorous and self-confident merchant class based in cities that were autonomous or even independent of the feudal political leadership of the surrounding areas.

In any event, the advent of the imperialist era in the second half of the nineteenth century made such questions academic; imperialism created serious distortions in the local economy that resulted in massive changes in Chinese society during the twentieth century. Whether the Western intrusion was beneficial or harmful is debated to this day. The Western presence undoubtedly accelerated the development of the Chinese economy in some ways: the introduction of modern means of production, transport, and communications; the appearance of an export market; and the steady integration of the Chinese market into the nineteenth-century global economy. To many Westerners at the time, it was self-evident that such changes would ultimately benefit the Chinese people. Western civilization represented the most advanced stage of human development. By supplying (in the catch phrase of the day) "oil for the lamps of China," it was providing a backward society with an opportunity to move up a notch or two on the ladder of human evolution.

Not everyone agreed. The Marxist Vladimir Lenin contended that Western imperialism actually hindered the process of structural change in preindustrial societies because it thwarted the rise of a local industrial and commercial sector in order to maintain colonies and semicolonies as a market for Western manufactured goods and a source of cheap labor and materials. Fellow Marxists in China, such as Mao Zedong, later took up Lenin's charge and asserted that if the West had not intervened, China would have found its own road to capitalism and thence to socialism and communism.

Many historians today would say that the answer was a little of both. By shaking China out of its traditional mindset, imperialism accelerated the process of change that had begun in the late Ming and early Qing periods and forced the Chinese to adopt new ways of thinking and acting. At the same time, China paid a heavy price in the destruction of its local industry, while many of the profits flowed abroad. Although industrial revolution is a painful process whenever and wherever it occurs, the Chinese found the experience doubly painful because it was foisted on China from the outside.

*T*raditional Japan and the End of Isolation

While Chinese rulers were coping with the dual problems of external threat and internal instability, similar developments were taking place in Japan. An agricultural society like its powerful neighbor, Japan had borrowed extensively from Chinese civilization for more than a millennium; its political institutions, religious beliefs, and cultural achievements all bore the clear imprint of the Chinese model. Nevertheless, throughout the centuries, the Japanese were able to retain not only their political independence but also their cultural uniqueness, and had created a civilization quite distinct from those elsewhere in the region.

One reason for the historical differences between China and Japan is that China is a large continental country and Japan a small island nation. Proud of their own considerable cultural achievements and their dominant position throughout the region, the Chinese have traditionally been reluctant to dilute the purity of their culture with foreign innovations. Often subject to invasion by nomadic peoples from the north, for the Chinese, culture rather than race became a symbol of their sense of identity. By contrast, the island character of Japan probably had the effect of strengthening the Japanese sense of ethnic and cultural distinctiveness. Although the Japanese self-image of ethnic homogeneity may not be entirely justified, it enabled them to import ideas from abroad without the risk of destroying the uniqueness of their own culture.

In any event, although the Japanese borrowed liberally from China over the centuries, Japanese civilization retained its distinctive character. In contrast to China, where a centralized and authoritarian political system was viewed as crucial to protect the vast country from foreign conquest or internal fractionalization, a decentralized political system reminiscent of the feudal system in medieval Europe held sway in Japan under the hegemony of a powerful military leader, or shogun (translated by one prominent Western historian into "English" as "generalissimo"), who ruled with varying degrees of effectiveness in the name of the hereditary emperor. This system lasted until the early seventeenth century, when a strong shogunate called the Tokugawa rose to power after a protracted civil war. The Tokugawa shogunate managed to revitalize the traditional system in a somewhat more centralized form that enabled it to survive for another 250 years.

One of the many factors involved in the rise of the Tokugawa was the impending collapse of the old system. Another was contact with the West, which had begun with the arrival of Portuguese ships in Japanese ports in the middle of the sixteenth century. Japan initially opened its doors eagerly to European trade and missionary activity, but later Japanese elites became concerned at the corrosive effects of Western ideas and practices and attempted to evict the foreigners. For the next two centuries, the Tokugawa adopted a policy of "closed country" (to use the contemporary Japanese phrase) to keep out foreign ideas and protect native values and institutions. In spite of such efforts, however, Japanese society was changing from within, and by the early nineteenth century was quite different from what it had been two centuries earlier. Traditional institutions and the feudal aristocratic system were under increasing strain, not only from the emergence of a new merchant class, but also from the centralizing tendencies of the powerful shogunate.

Some historians have seen strong parallels between Tokugawa Japan and early modern Europe, which gave birth to centralized empires and a strong merchant class during the same period. Certainly there were signs that the shogunate system was becoming less effective. Factionalism and corruption plagued the central bureaucracy. Feudal lords in the countryside (known as *daimyo*, or "great names") reacted to increasing economic pressures by intensifying their exactions from the peasants who farmed their manor holdings and by engaging in manufacturing and commercial pursuits, such as the sale of textiles, forestry products, and *sake* (Japanese rice wine). As peasants were whipsawed by rising manorial exactions and a series of poor harvests caused by bad weather, rural unrest swept the countryside.

Japan, then, was ripe for change. Some historians maintain that the country was poised to experience an industrial revolution under the stimulus of internal conditions. As in China, the resumption of contacts with the West in the middle of the nineteenth century rendered the question somewhat academic. To the Western powers, the continued isolation of Japanese society was an affront and a challenge. Driven by growing rivalry among themselves and convinced by their own propaganda and the ideology of world capitalism that the expansion of trade on a global basis would benefit all na-

tions, Western nations began to approach Japan in the hope of opening up the hermit kingdom to foreign economic interests.

The first to succeed was the United States. American whalers and clipper ships following the northern route across the Pacific needed a fueling station before completing their long journey to China and other ports in the area. The first efforts to pry the Japanese out of their cloistered existence in the 1830s and 1840s failed, but the Americans persisted. In the summer of 1853, an American fleet of four warships under Commodore Matthew C. Perry arrived in Edo Bay (now Tokyo Bay) with a letter from President Millard Fillmore addressed to the shogun. The letter requested better treatment for sailors

◆ **Commodore Perry Arrives in Japan.** In July 1853, U. S. Commodore Matthew Perry arrived in Tokyo Bay in command of a fleet of black ships. His goal was to open Japan to Western trade. In this painting by a Japanese artist, Perry is greeted by his Japanese host, both in full regalia. The U.S. fleet sits at anchor in the background.

shipwrecked on the Japanese islands and the opening of foreign relations between the two countries.

A few months later, Perry returned with an even larger fleet for an answer. In his absence, shogunate officials had discussed the issue, but without reaching a decision. Now the big black guns of Commodore Perry's ships proved decisive, and Japan agreed to the Treaty of Kanagawa, providing for the return of American sailors, the opening of two ports, and the establishment of a U.S. consulate on Japanese soil. In 1858, U.S. Consul Townsend Harris signed a more elaborate commercial treaty calling for the opening of several ports to U.S. trade and residence, an exchange of ministers, and extraterritorial privileges for U.S. residents in Japan. The Japanese soon signed similar treaties with several European nations.

The decision to open relations with the Western barbarians was highly unpopular in some quarters, particularly in regions distant from the shogunate headquarters in Edo. Resistance was especially strong in two of the key outside daimyo territories in the south: Satsuma and Choshu. Both had strong military traditions—Satsuma, on Kyushu, was a center of pirate activity; Choshu dominated the strategically located Strait of Shimonoseki, leading into the Sea of Japan—and neither was at first exposed to heavy Western military pressure. In 1863, the "Sat-Cho" alliance forced the hapless shogun to promise to bring relations with the West to an end. The shogun eventually reneged on the agreement, but the rebellious groups soon disclosed their own weakness. When Choshu troops fired on Western ships in the Strait of Shimonoseki, the Westerners fired back and destroyed the Choshu fortifications. The incident convinced the rebellious samurai ("retainers," the traditional warrior class) of the need to strengthen their own military and intensified their unwillingness to give in to the West. Accordingly, Sat-Cho elements continued to harass the shogunate to take a stronger line with the foreigners. Having strengthened their influence at the imperial court in Kyoto, they demanded the resignation of the shogunate and the restoration of the power of the emperor. The reigning shogun agreed to resign in favor of a council of daimyo that would function under the chairmanship of the emperor, with the shogun serving as prime minister. But this arrangement was unsatisfactory to leading members of the Sat-Cho faction, and in January 1868, rebel armies attacked the shogunate's palace in Kyoto and proclaimed the restored authority of the emperor. After a few weeks, resistance collapsed, and the venerable shogunate system was brought to an end.

Rich Country and Strong State

Although the victory of the Sat-Cho faction over the shogunate appeared on the surface to be a struggle between advocates of tradition and proponents of conciliation toward the West, in fact the new leadership soon embarked on a policy of comprehensive reform that would lay the foundations of a modern industrial nation within a generation. Although the Sat-Cho leaders genuinely mistrusted the West, they soon realized that Japan must change to survive.

The symbol of the new era was the young emperor himself, who had taken the reign name Meiji ("enlightened rule") on ascending the throne after the death of his father in 1867. Although the post-Tokugawa period was termed a "restoration," the Meiji ruler, who shared the modernist outlook of the Sat-Cho group, was controlled by the new leadership just as the shogunate had controlled his predecessors. In tacit recognition of the real source of political power, the new capital was located at Edo (now renamed Tokyo, or "Eastern Capital"), and the imperial court was moved to the shogun's palace in the center of the city.

The Transformation of Japanese Politics

Once in power, the new leaders launched a comprehensive reform of Japanese political, social, economic, and cultural institutions and values. They moved first to abolish the remnants of the old order and strengthen executive power in their hands. To undercut the power of the daimyo, hereditary privileges were abolished in 1871, and the great lords lost title to their lands. Noble titles were retained, but the *eta* (the traditional slave class) were granted legal equality. The samurai received a lump-sum payment to replace their traditional stipends but were forbidden to wear the sword, the symbol of their hereditary status.

The abolition of the legal underpinnings of the Tokugawa system permitted the Meiji modernizers to embark on the creation of a modern political system based on the Western model. In 1868, the new leaders enacted a Charter Oath, in which they promised to create a new deliberative assembly within the framework of continued imperial rule. An advisory council of state was established the same year. Although senior positions in the new government were given to the daimyo, the key posts were dominated by modernizing samurai from the Sat-Cho clique. The leading faction in the new, highly centralized government was known as the *genro*, or elder statesmen. The country was divided into seventy-five prefectures (the number was reduced to forty-five in 1889 and remains at that number today).

During the next two decades, the Meiji government undertook a systematic study of Western political systems. A constitutional commission under Prince Ito Hirobumi traveled to several Western countries to study their political systems and expressed particular interest in those of Great Britain, Germany, Russia, and the United States. As the process evolved, a number of factions appeared, each representing different political ideas within the ruling clique. The most prominent were the Liberals, who favored political reform on the Western liberal democratic model, with supreme authority vested in a parliament as the representative of the people, and the Progressives, who called for a distribution of power between the legislative and executive branches, with a slight nod to the latter. There was also an imperial party that advocated the retention of supreme authority exclusively in the hands of the emperor.

During the 1870s and 1880s, these factions competed for preeminence. In the end, the Progressives emerged victorious. The Meiji constitution, adopted in 1890, was based on the Bismarckian model, with authority vested in the executive branch, although the imperialist faction was pacified by the statement that the constitution was the gift of the emperor. Members of the cabinet were to be handpicked by the Meiji oligarchs. The upper house of parliament was to be appointed and have equal legislative powers with the lower house, called the Diet, whose members would be elected. An interesting feature of the new constitution was that the Diet had the power to appropriate funds, but if no agreement was reached, the budget would remain the same as in the previous year, thus permitting the executive branch to continue in operation. The core ideology of the state was called the *kokutai* (national polity), which embodied (although in very imprecise form) the concept of the uniqueness of the Japanese system based on the supreme authority of the emperor.

The result was a system that was democratic in form but despotic in practice, modern in external appearance but still recognizably traditional in that power remained in the hands of a ruling oligarchy. The system permitted the traditional ruling class to retain its influence and economic power while acquiescing in the emergence of a new set of institutions and values. In fact, some historians have contended that the Meiji ruling clique deliberately exaggerated the hierarchical character of Japanese society during the Tokugawa era in order to further its goal of strengthening the state and increasing its wealth and power.

Meiji Economics

With the end of the daimyo domains, the government needed to establish a new system of land ownership that would transform the mass of the rural population from indentured serfs into citizens. To do so, it enacted a land reform program that redefined the domain lands as the private property of the tillers, while compensating the previous owner with government bonds. One reason for the new policy was that the government needed operating revenues. At the time, public funds came mainly from customs duties, which were limited by agreement with the foreign powers to 5 percent of the value of the product. To remedy the problem, the Meiji leaders added a new agriculture tax, which was set at an annual rate of 3 percent of the estimated value of the land. The new tax proved to be a lucrative and dependable source of income for the government, but it was quite onerous for the farmers, who previously had paid a fixed percentage of their harvest to the landowner. As a result, in bad years, many taxpaying peasants were unable to pay their taxes and were forced to sell their lands to wealthy neighbors. Eventually, the government reduced the tax to 2.5 percent of the land value. Still, by the end of the century, about 40 percent of all farmers were tenants.

With its budget needs secured, the government turned to the promotion of industry. The basic objective of the Meiji reformers was to create a "rich country and strong state" (*fukoku kyohei*) in order to guarantee Japan's survival against the challenge of Western imperialism. In a broad sense, they very single-mindedly copied the process of development followed by the nations of Western Europe.

An advantage, of course, was that a small but growing industrial economy already existed under the Tokugawa. In its early stages, manufacturing in Japan had been the exclusive responsibility of an artisan caste, who often worked for the local daimyo. Eventually, these artisans began to expand their activities, hiring workers and borrowing capital from merchants. By the end of the seventeenth century, substantial manufacturing centers had developed in Japan's growing cities, such as Edo, Kyoto, and Osaka. According to one historian, by 1700, Japan had four cities with a population over 100,000 and was one of the most urbanized societies in the world.

Japan's industrial revolution received a massive stimulus from the Meiji Restoration. The government provided financial subsidies to needy industries, training, foreign advisers, improved transport and communications, and a universal system of education emphasizing applied science. In contrast to China, Japan was able to achieve results with minimum reliance on foreign capital. Although the first railroad—built in 1872—was financed by a loan from Great Britain, future projects were all financed by local funds. The foreign currency holdings came largely from tea and silk, which were exported in significant quantities during the latter half of the nineteenth century.

During the late Meiji era, Japan's industrial sector began to grow. Besides tea and silk, other key industries were weaponry, shipbuilding, and *sake*. From the start, the distinctive feature of the Meiji model was the intimate relationship that existed between government and private business in terms of operations and regulations. Once an individual enterprise or industry was on its feet (or, sometimes, when it had ceased to make a profit), it was turned over entirely to private ownership, although the government often continued to play some role even after its direct involvement in management was terminated.

Also noteworthy is the effect that the Meiji reforms had on rural areas. As we have seen, the new land tax provided the government with funds to subsidize the industrial sector, but it imposed severe hardship on the rural population, many of whom abandoned their farms and fled to the cities in search of jobs. This influx of people, in turn, benefited Japanese industry, because it provided an abundant source of cheap labor. As in early modern Europe, the industrial revolution was built on the strong backs of the long-suffering peasantry.

Building a Modern Social Structure

The Meiji reformers also transformed several other feudal institutions. A key focus of their attention was the army. The Sat-Cho reformers had been struck by the weakness of the Japanese armed forces in clashes with the Western powers and embarked on a major program to create a modern military force that could compete in a Darwinist world governed by survival of the fittest. The old feudal army based on the traditional warrior class was abolished, and an imperial army based on universal conscription was formed in 1871. The army also played an important role in Japanese society, becoming a route of upward mobility for many rural males.

Education also underwent major changes. The Meiji leaders recognized the need for universal education including instruction in modern technology. After a few years of experiment, they adopted the American model of a three-tiered system culminating in a series of universities and specialized institutes. In the meantime, they sent bright students to study abroad and brought foreign specialists to Japan to teach in their new schools. Much of the content of the new system was Western in inspiration. Yet, in a Japanese equivalent to the Chinese "essence versus practical use" concept, its ethical foundations had a distinctly Confucian orientation, emphasizing such values as filial piety and loyalty to the emperor (see box on p. 67).

Joining the Imperialist Club

Japan's rapid advance was an impressive achievement and was viewed with proprietary pride and admiration by sympathetic observers in the United States. Unfortunately, the Japanese did not just imitate the domestic policies of their Western mentors; they also emulated the latter's aggressive approach to foreign affairs. That they adapted this course is perhaps not surprising. In their own minds, the Japanese were particularly vulnerable in the world economic arena. Their territory was small, lacking in resources, and densely populated, and they had no natural outlet for expansion. To observant Japanese, the lessons of history were clear. Western nations had amassed wealth and power not only because of their democratic systems and high level of education, but also because of their colonies, which provided them with sources of raw materials, cheap labor, and markets for their manufactured products.

Traditionally, Japan had not been an expansionist country. The Japanese had generally been satisfied to remain on their home islands and had even deliberately isolated themselves from their neighbors during the Tokugawa era. Perhaps the most notable exception was a short-lived attempt at the end of the sixteenth century to extend Japanese control over the Korean peninsula.

The Japanese began their program of territorial expansion close to home. In 1874, they claimed compensation from China for fifty-four sailors from the Ryukyu Islands who had been killed by aborigines on the island of Taiwan and sent a Japanese fleet to Taiwan to punish the perpetrators. When the Qing dynasty evaded responsibility for the incident while agreeing to pay an indemnity to Japan to cover the cost of the expedition, it weakened its claim to ownership of the island of Taiwan. Japan was then able to claim suzerainty over the Ryukyu Islands, long tributary to the Chinese Empire. Two years later, Japanese naval pressure forced the opening of Korean ports to Japanese commerce.

During the 1880s, Sino-Japanese rivalry over Korea intensified. In 1894, China and Japan intervened on opposite sides of an internal rebellion in Korea. When hostilities broke out between the two powers, Japanese ships

The Rules of Good Citizenship in Meiji Japan

After seizing power from the Tokugawa shogunate in 1868, the Meiji reformers turned their attention to the creation of a new political system that would bring their country into the modern world. After exploring various systems currently in use in the West, a constitutional commission decided to adopt the system used in imperial Germany because of its paternalistic character. To promote civic virtue and obedience among the citizenry, the government drafted an imperial rescript that was to be taught to every schoolchild in the country. The rescript instructed all children to obey their sovereign and place the interests of the community and the state above their own personal desires.

Significantly, the text contained a strong Confucian flavor, signaling that the reformist leadership was determined to build a new nation on solid traditional foundations. The "glory of the fundamental character of Our Empire," Emperor Meiji declared, lay in the loyalty and filial piety of the people. Japanese citizens were thus instructed to be filial to their parents and benevolent to all, to pursue learning and cultivate the arts, to advance the public good and promote common interests, and to respect the Constitution and obey the laws. In so doing, they would "not only be Our good and faithful subjects, but render illustrious the best traditions of Your forefathers."

Source: Ryusaku Tsunoda et al., eds., *Sources of Japanese Tradition* (New York: Columbia University Press, 1958), vol. 2, p. 139.

---

destroyed the Chinese fleet and seized the Manchurian city of Port Arthur. In the Treaty of Shimonoseki, the Manchus were forced to recognize the independence of Korea and to cede Taiwan and the Liaodong peninsula, with its strategic naval base at Port Arthur, to Japan.

Shortly thereafter, under pressure from the European powers, the Japanese returned the Liaodong peninsula to China, but in the early twentieth century they returned to the offensive. Rivalry with Russia over influence in Korea led to increasingly strained relations between the two countries. In 1904, Japan launched a surprise attack on the Russian naval base at Port Arthur, which Russia had taken from China in 1898. The Japanese armed forces were weaker, but Russia faced difficult logistical problems along its new Trans-Siberian Railway and severe political instability at home. In 1905, after Japanese warships sank almost the entire Russian fleet off the coast of Korea, the Russians agreed to a humiliating peace, ceding the strategically located Liaodong peninsula back to Japan, along with southern Sakhalin and the Kurile Islands. Russia also agreed to abandon its political and economic influence in Korea and southern Manchuria, which now came increasingly under Japanese control. The Japanese victory stunned the world, including the colonial peoples of Southeast Asia, who now began to realize that Europeans were not necessarily invincible.

During the next few years, the Japanese consolidated their position in northeastern Asia, annexing Korea in 1908 as an integral part of Japan. When the Koreans protested the seizure, Japanese reprisals resulted in thousands of deaths. The United States was the first nation to recognize the annexation in return for Tokyo's declaration of respect for U.S. authority in the Philippines. In 1908, the two countries reached an agreement in which

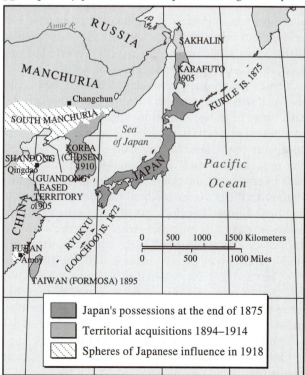

Map 3.3 Japanese Overseas Expansion during the Meiji Era

the United States recognized Japanese interests in the region in return for Japanese acceptance of the principles of the Open Door. But mutual suspicion between the two countries was growing, sparked in part by U.S. efforts to restrict immigration from all Asian countries. President Theodore Roosevelt, who mediated the Russo-Japanese War, had aroused the anger of many Japanese by turning down a Japanese demand for reparations from Russia. In turn, some Americans began to fear the rise of a "yellow peril" manifested by Japanese expansion in East Asia.

The Meiji Restoration:
A Revolution from Above

Japan's transformation from a feudal, agrarian society to an industrializing, technologically advanced society in little more than half a century has frequently been described by outside observers (if not by the Japanese themselves) in almost miraculous terms. Some historians have questioned this characterization, pointing out that the achievements of the Meiji leaders were spotty. In his book, *Japan's Emergence as a Modern State*, the Canadian historian E. H. Norman laments that the Meiji Restoration was an "incomplete revolution" because it did not end the economic and social inequities of feudal society or enable the common people to participate fully in the governing process. Although the *genro* were enlightened in many respects, they were also despotic and elitist, and the distribution of wealth remained as unequal as it had been under the old system.[6]

These criticisms are persuasive, although they could also be applied to most other societies going through the early stage of industrialization. In any event, from an economic perspective, the Meiji Restoration was certainly one of the great success stories of modern times. Not only did the Meiji leaders put Japan firmly on the path to economic and political development, they also managed to remove the unequal treaty provisions that had been imposed at mid-century. Japanese achievements are especially impressive when compared with the difficulties experienced by China, which was not only unable to effect significant changes in its traditional society, but had not even reached a consensus on the need for doing so. Japan's achievements more closely resemble those of Europe, but whereas the West needed a century and a half to achieve a significant level of industrial development, the Japanese achieved it in forty years.

One of the distinctive features of Japan's transition from a traditional to a modern society during the Meiji era was that it took place for the most part without violence or the kind of major social or political revolution that occurred in so many other countries. The Meiji Restoration, which began the process, has been called a "revolution from above"—a comprehensive restructuring of Japanese society by its own ruling group.

Technically, of course, the Meiji Restoration was not a revolution, since it was not violent and did not result in the displacement of one ruling class by another. The existing elites undertook to carry out a series of major reforms that transformed society but left their own power intact. In that respect, the Meiji Restoration resembles the American Revolution more than the French Revolution; it was a "conservative revolution" that resulted in gradual change rather than rapid and violent upheaval.

The differences between the Japanese response to the West and that of China and many other nations in the region have sparked considerable debate among students of comparative history. Some have argued that Japan's success was partly due to good fortune; lacking abundant natural resources, it was exposed to less pressure from the West than many of its neighbors. That argument is problematical, however, and would probably not have been accepted by Japanese observers at the time. Nor does it explain why nations under considerably less pressure, such as Laos and Nepal, did not advance even more quickly. All in all, the "good luck" hypothesis is not very persuasive.

One possible explanation has already been suggested: Japan's unique geographical position in Asia. China, a continental nation with a heterogeneous ethnic composition, was distinguished from its neighbors by its Confucian culture. By contrast, Japan was an island nation, ethnically and linguistically homogeneous, which had never been conquered. Unlike the Chinese or many other peoples in the region, the Japanese had little to fear from cultural change in terms of its effect on their national identity. If Confucian culture, with all its accoutrements, was what defined the Chinese gentleman, his Japanese counterpart, in the familiar image, could discard his sword and kimono and don a modern military uniform or a Western business suit and still feel comfortable in both worlds.

Whatever the case, as the historian W. G. Beasley has noted, the Meiji Restoration was possible because aristocratic and capitalist elements managed to work together in a common effort to achieve national wealth and power. The nature of the Japanese value system, with its emphasis on practicality and military achievement, may also have contributed. Finally, the Meiji benefited from the fact that the pace of urbanization and commercial

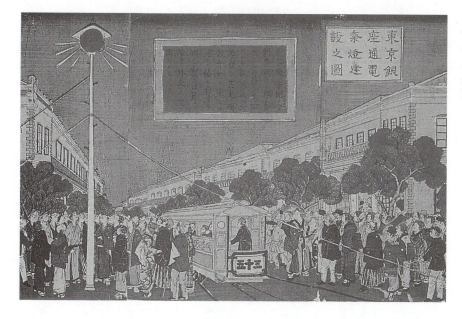

♦ **The Ginza in Downtown Tokyo.**
This 1877 woodblock print shows the Ginza area—the bustling shopping district in downtown Tokyo—with modern brick buildings, rickshaws, and a horse-drawn streetcar.

and industrial development had already begun to quicken under the Tokugawa. Japan, it has been said, was ripe for change, and nothing could have been more suitable as an antidote for the collapsing old system than the Western emphasis on wealth and power. It was a classic example of challenge and response.

The final product was an amalgam of old and new, native and foreign, forming a new civilization that was still uniquely Japanese. It did have some undesirable consequences, however. Because Meiji politics were essentially despotic, Japanese leaders were able to fuse key traditional elements such as the warrior ethic and the concept of feudal loyalty with the dynamics of modern industrial capitalism to create a state totally dedicated to

the possession of material wealth and national power. This combination of *kokutai* and capitalism, which one scholar has described as a form of "Asian fascism," was highly effective, but explosive in its international manifestation. Like modern Germany, which also entered the industrial age directly from feudalism, Japan eventually engaged in a policy of repression at home and expansion abroad in order to achieve its national objectives. In Japan, as in Germany, it took defeat in war to disconnect the drive for national development from the feudal ethic and bring about the transformation to a pluralistic society dedicated to living in peace and cooperation with its neighbors. Whether that transformation has been completed in Japan only the future will tell.

NOTES

1. Quoted in J. H. Parry, ed., *The European Reconnaissance: Selected Documents* (New York, 1968), pp. 135–136.
2. Quoted in William Theodore de Bary et al., eds., *Sources of Chinese Tradition* (New York, 1963), p. 733.
3. Ibid., p. 472.
4. From Hosea Ballou Morse, *The International Relations of the Chinese Empire* (Shanghai and London, 1910–1918), vol. 3, p. 126.
5. Quoted in Ssu-yu Teng and John K. Fairbank, eds., *China's Response to the West, 1839–1923* (New York, 1970), p. 263.
6. John Dower, *The Origins of the Modern Japanese State: Selected Writings of E. H. Norman* (New York, 1975), p. 13.

PART I

Reflections

The late nineteenth century witnessed two major developments: the Industrial Revolution and European domination of the world. Of these two factors, the first was clearly the more important, for it created the conditions for the latter. It was, of course, the major industrial powers—Great Britain, France, and later Germany, Japan, and the United States—that took the lead in building large colonial empires. Those European nations that did not achieve a high level of industrial advancement, such as Spain and Portugal, clearly declined in importance as colonial powers.

Why some societies were able to master the challenge of industrialization and others were not has been a matter of considerable scholarly debate. Some observers have found the answer in the cultural characteristics of individual societies, such as the Protestant work ethic in parts of Europe or the tradition of social discipline and class hierarchy in Japan. Others have placed more emphasis on practical considerations, such as the lack of an urban market for agricultural goods in China (which reduced the landowners' incentives to introduce mechanized farming) or the absence of a foreign threat in Japan (which provided increased opportunities for local investment). In the view of some theorists of the "world systems" school, it was in fact as a result of the successes achieved during the early stages of European expansion during the sixteenth and seventeenth centuries that major European powers amassed the capital, developed the experience, and built the trade networks that would later fuel the Industrial Revolution. In that interpretation, the latter event is less important as the driving force of the modern age than the period that immediately preceded it.

The advent of the industrial age had a number of lasting consequences for the world at large. On the one hand, the material wealth of those nations that successfully passed through the process increased significantly. In many cases, the creation of advanced industrial societies strengthened democratic institutions and led to a higher standard of living for the majority of the population. The spread of technology and trade outside of Europe created the basis for a new international economic order based on the global exchange of goods.

On the other hand, as we have seen, not all the consequences of the Industrial Revolution were beneficial. In the industrializing societies themselves, rapid economic change often led to resentment over the vast disparities in the distribution of wealth and a sense of rootlessness and alienation among much of the population. While some societies were able to manage these problems with some degree of success, others experienced a breakdown of social values and the rise of widespread political instability. Industrialization also had destabilizing consequences on the global scene. Rising economic competition among the industrial powers was a major contributor to heightened international competition on the world scene.

Elsewhere in Europe, old empires found it increasingly difficult to respond to new problems. The Ottoman Empire appeared increasingly helpless to curb unrest in the Balkans. In imperial Russia, internal tensions became too much for the traditional landholding elites to handle, leading to significant political and social unrest in the first decade of the twentieth century. In Austria-Hungary, deep-seated ethnic and class antagonisms remained under the surface, but clearly had reached a point where they might eventually threaten the survival of that multinational state.

In the meantime, the Industrial Revolution was creating the technological means by which the Western world would achieve domination of much of the rest of the world by the end of the nineteenth century. Europeans had begun to explore the world in the fifteenth century, but even as late as 1870, they had not yet completely penetrated North America, South America, and Australia. In Asia and Africa, with a few notable exceptions, the Western presence was limited to trading posts. Between 1870 and 1914, Western civilization expanded into the rest of the Americas and Australia, while most of Africa and Asia was divided into European colonies or spheres of influence. Two major factors explain this remarkable expansion: the migration of many Europeans to other parts of the world as a result of population growth and the revival of imperialism made possible by the West's technological advances.

The European population increased dramatically between 1850 and 1910, rising from 270 million to 460 million by 1910. Although growing agricultural and industrial prosperity supported an increase in the European population, it could not do so indefinitely, especially in areas that had little industry and a severe problem of rural overpopulation. Some of the excess labor from underdeveloped areas migrated to the industrial regions of Europe. By 1913, for example, more than 400,00 Poles were working in the heavily industrialized Ruhr region of western Germany. But the industrialized regions of Europe could not absorb the entire surplus population of the agricultural regions. A booming American economy after 1898 and cheap shipping fares after 1900 led to mass emigration from southern and eastern Europe to North America at the beginning of the twentieth century. In 1880, on average, around 500,000 people departed annually from Europe, but between 1906 and 1910, their numbers increased to 1,300,000, many of them from southern and eastern Europe. Altogether, between 1846 and 1932, probably 60 million Europeans left Europe, half of them bound for the United States and most of the rest for Canada or Latin America.

Beginning in the 1880s, European states began an intense scramble for overseas territory. This revival of imperialism—the "new imperialism," as some have called it—led Europeans to carve up Asia and Africa. Imperialism was not a new phenomenon. Since the crusades of the Middle Ages and the overseas expansion of the sixteenth and seventeenth centuries, when Europeans established colonies in North and South America and trading posts around Africa and the Indian Ocean, Europeans had shown a marked proclivity for the domination of less technologically oriented, non-European peoples. Nevertheless, the imperialism of the late nineteenth century was different from that of earlier periods. First, it occurred after a period in which Europeans had reacted against imperial expansion. Between 1775 and 1875, European states actually lost more colonial territory than they acquired, as many Europeans had actually come to regard colonies as expensive and useless. Second, the new imperialism was more rapid and resulted in greater and deeper penetrations into non-European societies. Finally, most of the new imperialism was directed toward Africa and Asia, two regions that had been largely ignored until then.

The new imperialism had a dramatic effect on Africa and Asia as European powers competed for control of these two continents. In contrast, Latin America was able to achieve political independence from its colonial rulers in the course of the nineteenth century and embark upon the process of building new nations. Like the Ottoman Empire, however, Latin America remained subject to commercial penetration by Western merchants.

Another part of the world that escaped total domination by the West was East Asia, where China and Japan were able to maintain at least the substance of national independence during the height of the Western onslaught at the end of the nineteenth century. For China, once the most advanced country in the world, survival was very much in doubt for many decades as the waves of Western political, military, and economic influence lapped at the edges of the Chinese Empire and appeared on the verge of dividing up the Chinese heartland into separate spheres of influence. Only Japan responded with vigor and effectiveness, launching a comprehensive reform program that by the end of the century had transformed the island nation into an emerging member of the imperialist club.

PART

II

Cultures in Collision

War and Revolution: World War I and Its Aftermath

$\mathcal{A}$ccording to the First Futurist Manifesto:

> We intend to sing the love of danger, the habit of energy and fearlessness. Courage, audacity and revolt will be essential ingredients of our poetry. We affirm that the world's magnificence has been enriched by a new beauty; the beauty of speed. A racing car whose hood is adorned by great pipes, like serpents of explosive breath—a roaring car that seems to run on shrapnel—is more beautiful than the Victory of Samothrace. We will glorify war—the world's only hygiene.[1]

From the tone of this manifesto, with its emphasis on speed, violence, and revolt, the contemporary reader might assume that it had been composed in the 1990s—the product of a generation raised on MTV that craves excitement and danger as a diversion from the humdrum reality of a boring existence. In fact, it was published in 1909 by a group of European writers, artists, and intellectuals, thrilled by the potential power and force represented by the advent of the industrial age, who looked forward to a future cut off completely from the past, in which modern technology would create a new type of human being. Their reference to the glory of war was eerily prophetic. Several leading members of the movement would soon lose their lives in the Great War, which erupted only five years later.

International Rivalry and the Coming of War

Between 1871 and 1914, Europeans experienced a long period of peace. There were wars (including wars of conquest in the non-Western world), but none involved the great powers. There were, however, a series of crises that might easily have led to general war. Until 1890, Bismarck, the chancellor of Germany, exercised a restraining influence on Europeans. He realized that the emergence in 1871 of a unified Germany as the most powerful state on the Continent had upset the balance of power established at Vienna in 1815. Bismarck knew that Germany's success frightened Europeans. Fearful of a possible anti-German alliance between France and Russia and possibly even Austria, Bismarck made a defensive alliance with Austria in 1879. Both powers agreed to support each other in the event of an attack by Russia. In 1882, this German-Austrian alliance was enlarged with the entrance of Italy, angry with the French over conflicting colonial ambitions in North Africa. The Triple Alliance of 1882 committed the three powers to support the existing political and social order while providing a defensive alliance against France. At the same time, Bismarck maintained a separate treaty with Russia and tried to remain on good terms with Great Britain.

When Emperor William II cashiered Bismarck in 1890, he embarked upon an activist foreign policy dedicated to enhancing German power by finding, as he put it, Germany's rightful "place in the sun." One of his changes in Bismarck's foreign policy was to drop the treaty with Russia, which he viewed as being at odds with Germany's alliance with Austria. The ending of the alliance achieved what Bismarck had feared: it brought France and Russia together. Republican France leapt at the chance to draw closer to tsarist Russia, and in 1894 the two powers concluded a military alliance. During the next ten years, German policies abroad caused the British to draw closer to France. By 1907, a loose confederation of Great Britain, France, and Russia—known as the Triple Entente—stood opposed to the Triple Alliance of Germany, Austria-Hungary, and Italy. Europe became divided into two opposing camps that became more and more inflexible and unwilling to compromise. When the members of the two alliances became involved in a new series of crises between 1908 and 1913 over the remnants of the Ottoman Empire in the Balkans, the stage was set for World War I.

Crises in the Balkans, 1908–1913

The Bosnian crisis of 1908–1909 began a chain of events that eventually spun out of control. Since 1878, Bosnia and Herzegovina had been under the protection of Austria, but in 1908 Austria took the drastic step of annexing these two Slavic-speaking territories. Serbia was outraged at this action because it dashed the Serbs' hopes of creating a large Serbian kingdom that would include most of the south Slavs. But this possibility was precisely why the Austrians had annexed Bosnia and Herzegovina. The creation of a large Serbia would be a threat to the unity of their empire with its large Slavic population. The Russians, as protectors of their fellow Slavs and also desiring to increase their own authority in the Balkans, supported the Serbs and opposed the Austrian action. Backed by the Russians, the Serbs prepared for war against Austria. At this point, William II intervened and demanded that the Russians accept Austria's annexation of Bosnia and Herzegovina or face war with Germany. Weakened from their defeat in the Russo-Japanese War in 1904–1905, the Russians were afraid to risk war and backed down. Humiliated, the Russians vowed revenge.

European attention returned to the Balkans in 1912 when Serbia, Bulgaria, Montenegro, and Greece organized a Balkan League and defeated the Turks in the First Balkan War. When the victorious allies were unable to agree on how to divide the conquered Turkish provinces of Macedonia and Albania, a second Balkan War erupted in 1913. Greece, Serbia, Romania, and the Ottoman Empire attacked and defeated Bulgaria. As a result, Bulgaria obtained only a small part of Macedonia, and most of the rest was divided between Serbia and Greece. Yet Serbia's aspirations remained unfulfilled. The two Balkan wars left the inhabitants embittered and created more tensions among the great powers.

By now, Austria-Hungary was convinced that Serbia was a mortal threat to its empire and must at some point be crushed. Meanwhile, the French and Russian governments renewed their alliance and promised each other that they would not back down at the next crisis. Britain drew closer to France. By the beginning of 1914, two armed camps viewed each other with suspicion. The European "age of progress" was about to come to an inglorious and bloody end.

The Road to World War I

On June 28, 1914, the heir to the Austrian throne, the Archduke Francis Ferdinand, and his wife, Sophia, were assassinated in the Bosnian city of Sarajevo. The assassination was carried out by a Bosnian activist who worked for the Black Hand, a Serbian terrorist organization dedicated to the creation of a pan-Slavic kingdom. Although the Austrian government did not know whether the Serbian government had been directly involved in the archduke's assassination, it saw an opportunity to "render Serbia innocuous once and for all by a display of force," as the Austrian foreign minister put it. Fearful of Russian intervention on Serbia's behalf, Austrian leaders sought the backing of their German allies. Emperor William II and his chancellor gave their assurance that Austria-Hungary could rely on Germany's "full support," even if "matters went to the length of a war between Austria-Hungary and Russia."

Bolstered by German support, Austrian leaders issued an ultimatum to Serbia on July 23 in which they made such extreme demands that Serbia felt it had little choice but to reject some of them in order to preserve its sovereignty. Austria then declared war on Serbia on July 28. Still smarting from its humiliation in the Bosnian crisis of 1908, Russia was determined to support Serbia's cause. On July 28, Tsar Nicholas II ordered partial mobilization of the Russian army against Austria. At this point, the rigidity of the military war plans played havoc with diplomatic and political decisions. The Russian general staff informed the tsar that their mobilization plans were based on a war against both Germany and Austria simultaneously. They could not execute partial mobilization without creating chaos

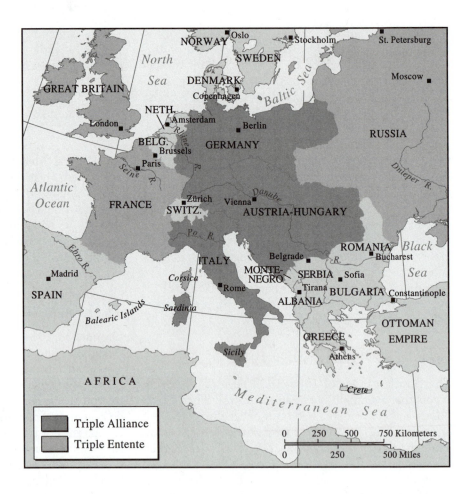

Map 4.1 Europe in 1914

in the army. Consequently, the Russian government ordered full mobilization of the Russian army on July 29, knowing that the Germans would consider this an act of war against them. Germany responded to Russian mobilization with its own ultimatum that the Russians must halt their mobilization within twelve hours. When the Russians ignored it, Germany declared war on Russia on August 1.

At this stage of the conflict, German war plans determined whether or not France would become involved in the war. Under the guidance of General Alfred von Schlieffen, chief of staff from 1891 to 1905, the German general staff had devised a military plan based on the assumption of a two-front war with France and Russia, which had formed a military alliance in 1894. The Schlieffen Plan called for only a minimal troop deployment against Russia. Most of the German army would execute a rapid invasion of France before Russia could become effective in the east or the British could cross

the English Channel to help France. To achieve this rapid invasion, the Germans would advance through neutral Belgium, with its level coastal plain, where the army could move faster than on the rougher terrain to the southeast. After the planned quick defeat of the French, the German army would then redeploy to the east against Russia. Under the Schlieffen Plan, Germany could not mobilize its troops solely against Russia; therefore, on August 2, Germany issued an ultimatum to Belgium demanding the right of German troops to pass through Belgian territory and, on August 3, declared war on France. On August 4, Great Britain declared war on Germany, officially in response to this violation of Belgian neutrality, but in fact because of Britain's desire to maintain its world power. As one British diplomat argued, if Germany and Austria were to win the war, "What would be the position of a friendless England?" Thus, by August 4, all the great powers of Europe were at war.

The War

Before 1914, many political leaders had become convinced that war involved so many political and economic risks that it was not worth fighting. Others believed that "rational" diplomats could control any situation and prevent the outbreak of war. At the beginning of August 1914, both of these prewar illusions were shattered, but the new illusions that replaced them soon proved to be equally foolish.

1914–1915: Illusions and Stalemate

Europeans went to war in 1914 with remarkable enthusiasm. Government propaganda had been successful in stirring up national antagonisms before the war. Now, in August of 1914, the urgent pleas of governments for defense against aggressors fell on receptive ears in every belligerent nation. Most people seemed genuinely convinced that their nation's cause was just. A new set of illusions also fed the enthusiasm for war. In August 1914, almost everyone believed that the war would be over in a few weeks. People were reminded that all European wars since 1815 had, in fact, ended in a matter of weeks, conveniently overlooking the American Civil War (1861–1865), which was the real prototype for World War I. Both the soldiers who exuberantly boarded the trains for the war front in August 1914 and the jubilant citizens who bombarded them with flowers as they departed believed that the warriors would be home by Christmas.

German hopes for a quick end to the war rested upon a military gamble. The Schlieffen Plan had called for the German army to make a vast encircling movement through Belgium into northern France that would sweep around Paris and encircle most of the French army. But the German advance was halted only 20 miles from Paris at the First Battle of the Marne (September 6–10). The war quickly turned into a stalemate as neither the Germans nor the French could dislodge the other from the trenches they had begun to dig for shelter. Two lines of trenches soon extended from the English Channel to the frontiers of Switzerland. The Western Front had become bogged down in a trench warfare that kept both sides immobilized in virtually the same positions for four years.

In contrast to the west, the war in the east was marked by much more mobility, although the cost in lives was equally enormous. At the beginning of the war, the Russian army moved into eastern Germany but was

◆ **The Excitement of War.** World War I was greeted with incredible enthusiasm. Each of the major belligerents was convinced of the rightness of its cause. Everywhere in Europe, jubilant civilians sent their troops off to war with joyous fervor. Their belief that the soldiers would be home by Christmas proved to be a pathetic illusion.

decisively defeated at the battles of Tannenberg on August 30 and the Masurian Lakes on September 15. The Russians were no longer a threat to German territory.

The Austrians, Germany's allies, fared less well initially. After they were defeated by the Russians in Galicia and thrown out of Serbia as well, the Germans came to their aid. A German-Austrian army defeated and routed the Russian army in Galicia and pushed the Russians back 300 miles into their own territory. Russian casualties stood at 2.5 million killed, captured, or wounded; the Russians had almost been knocked out of the war. Buoyed by their success, the Germans and Austrians, joined by the Bulgarians in September 1915, attacked and eliminated Serbia from the war.

1916–1917: The Great Slaughter

The successes in the east enabled the Germans to move back to the offensive in the west. The early trenches dug in 1914 had by now become elaborate systems of defense.

Both lines of trenches were protected by barbed-wire entanglements 3 to 5 feet high and 30 yards wide, concrete machine-gun nests, and mortar batteries, supported further back by heavy artillery. Troops lived in

The Excitement and the Reality of War

The incredible outpouring of patriotic enthusiasm that greeted the declaration of war at the beginning of August 1914 in many European countries demonstrated the power that nationalistic feeling had attained at the beginning of the twentieth century. Many Europeans seemingly believed that the war had given them a higher purpose, a renewed dedication to the greatness of their nation. As the Austrian writer Stefan Zweig put it at the time:

> To be truthful, I must acknowledge that there was a majestic, rapturous, and even seductive something in this first outbreak of the people from which one could escape only with difficulty. And in spite of all my hatred and aversion for war, I should not like to have missed the memory of those days. As never before, thousands and hundreds of thousands felt what they should have felt in peace time, that they belonged together.

Statesmen, of course, were quick to use this situation to their advantage. Some probably opted for war in 1914 because they believed that "prosecuting an active foreign policy," as one Austrian leader expressed it, would smother "internal troubles" such as labor strife and ethnic divisions. In St. Petersburg, as we shall see later in this chapter, Tsar Nicholas happily sent Russian troops off to war against Germany in sublime ignorance of the fact that before the conflict had ended, he would no longer have a throne to sit upon.

The reality of war, however, was quite different. World War I was the first conflict that combined modern weaponry with the concept of the conscripted army to create a vast war machine that would bring death and destruction to millions, civilian as well as military. Nowhere was the reality of war more dreadful than in the trenches. Soldiers who had left for the front in August 1914 in the belief that they would be home by Christmas found themselves shivering and dying in the vast networks along the battlefront. Few expressed the horror of trench warfare as well as the German writer Erich Maria Remarque in his famous novel *All Quiet on the Western Front*, written in 1929:

> We wake up in the middle of the night. The earth booms. Heavy fire is falling on us. We crouch into corners. . . . Every man is aware of the heavy shells tearing down the parapet, rooting up the embankment and demolishing the upper layers of concrete. . . . Already by morning a few of the recruits are green and vomiting. . . .
>
> No one would believe that in this howling waste there could still be men, but steel helmets now appear on all sides out of the trench, and fifty yards from us a machine-gun is already in position and barking.

Finally the attack begins.

> The wire-entanglements are torn to pieces. Yet they offer some obstacle. We see the storm-troops coming. . . . We recognize the distorted faces, the smooth helmets: they are French. They have already suffered heavily when they reach the remnants of the barbed wire entanglements.
>
> I see one of them, his face upturned, fall into a wire cradle. His body collapses, his hands remain suspended as thought he were praying. Then his body drops clear away and only his hands with the stumps of his arms, shot off, now hang in the wire.

It seems incredible that only two decades later, Europe would once again embark on total war. Yet the relative ease by which nations continued to enter into conflict throughout the century, and the patriotic frenzy that had accompanied so many declarations of war, suggests that each generation can only understand the true horror of war through its own experience.

Sources: Stefan Zweig, *The World of Yesterday*, trans. Helmut Ripperger (New York: Viking Penguin Books, 1943); Erich Maria Remarque, *All Quiet on the Western Front* (Boston: Little, Brown and Co., 1957, 1958).

holes in the ground, separated from each other by a "no-man's-land."

The unexpected development of trench warfare baffled military leaders who had been trained to fight wars of movement and maneuver. The only plan generals could devise was to attempt a breakthrough by throwing masses of men against enemy lines that had first been battered by artillery barrages. Once the decisive breakthrough had been achieved, they thought, they could then return to the war of movement that they knew best. Periodically, the high command on either side would order an offensive that would begin with an artillery barrage to flatten the enemy's barbed wire and leave the enemy in a state of shock. After "softening up" the enemy in this fashion, a mass of soldiers would climb out of their trenches with fixed

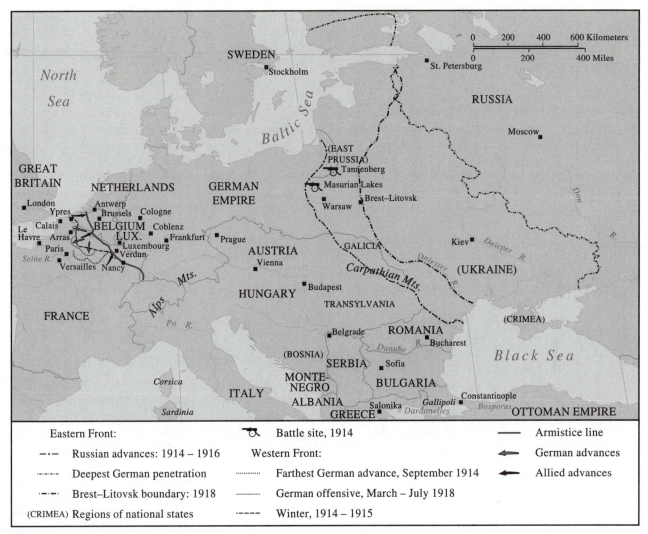

Map 4.2 World War I, 1914–1918

Eastern Front:
- – · – Russian advances: 1914 – 1916
- – · · · – Deepest German penetration
- – · – Brest–Litovsk boundary: 1918
- (CRIMEA) Regions of national states

Battle site, 1914

Western Front:
- ············· Farthest German advance, September 1914
- ———— German offensive, March – July 1918
- – – – – Winter, 1914 – 1915

——— Armistice line
⟵ German advances
⟵ Allied advances

bayonets and hope to work their way toward the opposing trenches. The attacks rarely worked, as the machine gun put hordes of men advancing unprotected across open fields at a severe disadvantage. In 1916 and 1917, millions of young men were sacrificed in the search for the elusive breakthrough. In ten months at Verdun, 700,000 men lost their lives over a few miles of terrain.

Warfare in the trenches of the Western Front produced unimaginable horrors (see box on p. 78). Battlefields were hellish landscapes of barbed wire, shell holes, mud, and injured and dying men. The introduction of poison gas in 1915 produced new forms of injuries, as described by one British writer:

I wish those people who write so glibly about this being a holy war could see a case of mustard gas . . . could see the poor things burnt and blistered all over with great mustard-coloured suppurating blisters with blind eyes all sticky . . . and stuck together, and always fighting for breath, with voices a mere whisper, saying that their throats are closing and they know they will choke.[2]

Soldiers in the trenches also lived with the persistent presence of death. Since combat went on for months, soldiers had to carry on in the midst of countless bodies of dead men or the remains of men dismembered by artillery barrages. Many soldiers remembered the stench of decomposing bodies and the swarms of rats that grew fat in the trenches.

The Yanks Are Comin'

As another response to the stalemate on the Western Front, both sides looked for new allies who might provide a winning advantage. The Ottoman Empire had already come into the war on Germany's side in August 1914. Russia, Great Britain, and France declared war on the Ottoman Empire in November. Although the Allies attempted to open a Balkan front by landing forces at Gallipoli, southwest of Constantinople, in April 1915, the entry of Bulgaria into the war on the side of the Central Powers (as Germany, Austria-Hungary, and the Ottoman Empire were called) and a disastrous campaign at Gallipoli caused them to withdraw. The Italians also entered the war on the Allied side after France and Britain promised to further their acquisition of Austrian territory. In the long run, however, Italian military incompetence forced the Allies to come to the assistance of Italy.

By 1917, the war that had originated in Europe had truly become a world conflict. In the Middle East, a British officer who came to be known as Lawrence of Arabia (1888–1935) incited Arab princes to revolt against their Ottoman overlords in 1917. In 1918, British forces from Egypt destroyed the rest of the Ottoman Empire in the Middle East. For their Middle East campaigns, the British mobilized forces from India, Australia, and New Zealand. The Allies also took advantage of Germany's preoccupations in Europe and lack of naval strength to seize German colonies in the rest of the world. Japan seized a number of German-held islands in the Pacific while Australia took over German New Guinea (see Chapter 5).

Most important to the Allied cause was the entry of the United States into the war. At first, the United States tried to remain neutral, but that became more difficult as the war dragged on. The immediate cause of U.S. involvement grew out of the naval conflict between Germany and Great Britain. Britain used its superior naval power to maximum effect by imposing a naval blockade on Germany. Germany retaliated with a counterblockade enforced by the use of unrestricted submarine warfare. Strong U.S. protests over the German sinking of passenger liners—especially the British ship *Lusitania* on May 7, 1915, in which more than 100 Americans lost their lives—forced the German government to suspend unrestricted submarine warfare in September 1915 to avoid further antagonizing the Americans.

In January 1917, however, eager to break the deadlock in the war, the Germans decided on another military gamble. German naval officers convinced Emperor William II that the renewed use of unrestricted submarine warfare could starve the British into submission within five months, certainly before the Americans could act. The return to unrestricted submarine warfare brought the United States into the war on April 6, 1917. Although American troops did not arrive in Europe in large numbers until 1918, U.S. entry into the war gave the Allied powers a badly needed psychological boost. The year 1917 was not a good year for them. Allied offensives on the Western Front were disastrously defeated. The Italian armies were smashed in October, and in November 1917 the Bolshevik Revolution in Russia (discussed later in this chapter) led to Russia's withdrawal from the war, leaving Germany free to concentrate entirely on the Western Front. The cause of the Central Powers looked favorable, although war weariness in the Ottoman Empire, Bulgaria, Austria-Hungary, and Germany was beginning to take its toll. The home front was rapidly becoming a cause for as much concern as the war front.

The Home Front: The Impact of Total War

The prolongation of World War I transformed it into a total conflict that affected the lives of all citizens, however remote they might be from the battlefields. The need to organize masses of men and matériel for years of combat (Germany alone had 5.5 million men in active units in 1916) led to increased centralization of government powers, economic regimentation, and manipulation of public opinion to keep the war effort going.

Because the war was expected to be short, little thought had been given to economic problems and long-term wartime needs. Governments had to respond quickly, however, when the war machines failed to achieve their knockout blows and made ever-greater demands for men and matériel. The extension of government power was a logical outgrowth of these needs. Most European countries had already devised some system of mass conscription or military draft. It was now carried to unprecedented heights as countries mobilized tens of millions of young men for that elusive breakthrough to victory. Even countries that continued to rely on volunteers (Great Britain had the largest volunteer army in modern history—1 million men—in 1914 and 1915) were forced to resort to conscription, especially to ensure that skilled laborers did not enlist but remained in factories that were important to the production of munitions. In 1916, despite widespread resistance to this extension of government power, compulsory military service was introduced in Great Britain.

Throughout Europe, wartime governments expanded their powers over their economies. Free-market capitalistic systems were temporarily shelved as governments experimented with price, wage, and rent controls, the rationing of food supplies and materials, the regulation of imports and exports, and the nationalization of transportation systems and industries. Some governments even moved toward compulsory labor employment. In effect, in order to mobilize the entire resources of the nation for the war effort, European countries had moved toward planned economies directed by government agencies. Under total war mobilization, the distinction between soldiers at war and civilians at home was narrowed. In the view of political leaders, all citizens constituted a national army dedicated to victory. As the American president Woodrow Wilson expressed it, the men and women "who remain to till the soil and man the factories are no less a part of the army than the men beneath the battle flags."

As the Great War dragged on and both casualties and privations worsened, internal dissatisfaction replaced the patriotic enthusiasm that had marked the early stages of the conflict. By 1916, there were numerous signs that civilian morale was beginning to crack under the pressure of total war. War governments, however, fought back against the growing opposition to the war. Authoritarian regimes, such as those of Germany, Russia, and Austria-Hungary, had always relied on force to subdue their populations. Under the pressures of the war, however, even parliamentary regimes resorted to an expansion of police powers to stifle internal dissent. The British Parliament passed a Defence of the Realm Act (DORA) at the very beginning of the war that allowed the public authorities to arrest dissenters as traitors. The act was later extended to authorize public officials to censor newspapers by deleting objectionable material and even to suspend newspaper publication. In France, government authorities had initially been lenient about public opposition to the war, but by 1917 they began to fear that open opposition to the war might weaken the French will to fight. When Georges Clemenceau (1841–1929) became premier near the end of 1917, the lenient French policies came to an end, and basic civil liberties were suppressed for the duration of the war. When a former premier publicly advocated a negotiated peace, Clemenceau's government had him sentenced to prison for two years for treason.

Wartime governments made active use of propaganda to arouse enthusiasm for the war. At the beginning, the task was easy. The British and French, for example, exaggerated German atrocities in Belgium and found that their citizens were only too willing to believe these accounts. But as the war dragged on and morale sagged, governments were forced to devise new techniques for stimulating declining enthusiasm. In one British recruiting poster, for example, a small daughter asked her father, "Daddy, what did YOU do in the Great War?" while her younger brother played with toy soldiers and cannon.

Total war made a significant impact on European society, most visibly by bringing an end to unemployment. The withdrawal of millions of men from the labor market to fight, combined with the heightened demand for wartime products, led to jobs for everyone able to work.

World War I also created new roles for women. Because so many men went off to fight at the front, women were called upon to take over jobs and responsibilities that had not been available to them before. Overall, the number of women employed in Britain who held new jobs or replaced men rose by 1,345,000. Women were also now employed in jobs that had been considered beyond the "capacity of women." These included such occupations as chimney sweeps, truck drivers, farm laborers, and, above all, factory workers in heavy industry. By 1918, 38 percent of the workers in the Krupp armaments works in Germany were women.

While male workers expressed concern that the employment of females at lower wages would depress their own wages, women began to demand equal pay legislation. A law passed by the French government in July 1915 established a minimum wage for women homeworkers in textiles, an industry that had grown dramatically thanks to the demand for military uniforms. Later in 1917, the government decreed that men and women should receive equal rates for piecework. Despite the noticeable increase in women's wages that resulted from government regulations, women's industrial wages still were not equal to men's wages by the end of the war.

Even worse, women's place in the workforce was far from secure. Both men and women seemed to assume that many of the new jobs for women were only temporary, an expectation quite evident in the British poem "War Girls," written in 1916:

There's the girl who clips your ticket for the train,
And the girl who speeds the lift from floor to floor,
There's the girl who does a milk-round in the rain,
And the girl who calls for orders at your door.
Strong, sensible, and fit,
They're out to show their grit,
And tackle jobs with energy and knack.
No longer caged and penned up,

They're going to keep their end up
Till the khaki soldier boys come marching back.[3]

At the end of the war, governments moved quickly to remove women from the jobs they had encouraged them to take earlier. By 1919, there were 650,000 unemployed women in Britain, and wages for women who were still employed were lowered. The work benefits for women from World War I seemed to be short-lived as demobilized men returned to the job market.

Nevertheless, in some countries, the role played by women in the wartime economy did have a positive impact on the women's movement for social and political emancipation. The most obvious gain was the right to vote, granted to women in Britain in January 1918 and in Germany and Austria immediately after the war. Contemporary media, however, tended to focus on the more noticeable, yet in some ways more superficial, social emancipation of upper- and middle-class women. In ever-larger numbers, these young women took jobs, had their own apartments, and showed their new independence by smoking in public and wearing shorter dresses, cosmetics, and new hairstyles.

The Last Year of the War

For Germany, the withdrawal of the Russians from the war in March 1918 offered renewed hope for a favorable end to the war. The victory over Russia persuaded Erich von Ludendorff (1865–1937), who guided German military operations, and most German leaders to make one final military gamble—a grand offensive in the west to break the military stalemate. The German attack was launched in March and lasted into July, but an Allied counterattack, supported by the arrival of 140,000 fresh American troops, defeated the Germans at the Second Battle of the Marne on July 18. Ludendorff's gamble had failed. With the arrival of 2 million more American troops on the Continent, Allied forces began to advance steadily toward Germany.

On September 29, 1918, General Ludendorff informed German leaders that the war was lost and demanded that the government sue for peace at once. When German officials discovered that the Allies were unwilling to make peace with the autocratic imperial government, reforms were instituted to create a liberal government. But these constitutional reforms came too late for the exhausted and angry German people. On November 3, naval units in Kiel mutinied, and within days councils of workers and soldiers were forming throughout northern Germany and taking over civilian

and military administrations. William II, capitulating to public pressure, abdicated on November 9, and the Socialists under Friedrich Ebert (1871–1925) announced the establishment of a republic. Two days later, on November 11, 1918, the new German government agreed to an armistice. The war was over.

The Peace Settlement

In January 1919, the delegations of twenty-seven victorious Allied nations gathered in Paris to conclude a final settlement of the Great War. Some delegates believed that this conference would avoid the mistakes made at Vienna in 1815 by aristocrats who rearranged the map of Europe to meet the selfish desires of the great powers. Harold Nicolson, one of the British delegates, expressed what he believed this conference would achieve instead: "We were journeying to Paris not merely to liquidate the war, but to found a New Order in Europe. We were preparing not Peace only, but Eternal Peace. There was about us the halo of some divine mission. . . . For we were bent on doing great, permanent and noble things."[4]

National expectations, however, made Nicolson's quest for "eternal peace" a difficult one. Over the years, the reasons for fighting World War I had been transformed from selfish national interests to idealistic principles. No one expressed the latter better than Woodrow Wilson. The American president outlined to the U.S. Congress "Fourteen Points" that he believed justified the enormous military struggle then being waged. Later, Wilson spelled out additional steps for a truly just and lasting peace. Wilson's proposals included "open covenants of peace, openly arrived at" instead of secret diplomacy; the reduction of national armaments to a "point consistent with domestic safety"; and the self-determination of people so that "all well-defined national aspirations shall be accorded the utmost satisfaction." Wilson characterized World War I as a people's war waged against "absolutism and militarism," two scourges of liberty that could only be eliminated by creating democratic governments and a "general association of nations" that would guarantee "political independence and territorial integrity to great and small states alike." As the spokesman for a new world order based on democracy and international cooperation, Wilson was enthusiastically cheered by many Europeans when he arrived in Europe for the peace conference.

Wilson soon found, however, that other states at the Paris Peace Conference were guided by considerably more pragmatic motives. The secret treaties and agreements that had been made before and during the war could not be totally ignored, even if they did conflict with the principle of self-determination enunciated by Wilson (see Chapter 5). National interests also complicated the deliberations of the Paris Peace Conference. David Lloyd George (1863–1945), prime minister of Great Britain, had won a decisive electoral victory in December of 1918 on a platform of making the Germans pay for this dreadful war.

France's approach to peace was primarily determined by considerations of national security. To Georges Clemenceau, the feisty French premier who had led his country to victory, the French people had borne the brunt of German aggression. They deserved revenge and security against future German aggression. Clemenceau wanted a demilitarized Germany, vast German reparations to pay for the costs of the war, and a separate Rhineland as a buffer state between France and Germany—demands that Wilson viewed as vindictive and contrary to the principle of national self-determination.

Although twenty-seven nations were represented at the Paris Peace Conference, the most important decisions were made by Wilson, Clemenceau, and Lloyd George. Italy was considered one of the so-called Big Four powers, but played a much less important role than the other three countries. Germany, of course, was not invited to attend, and Russia could not because of its civil war.

In view of the many conflicting demands at Versailles, it was inevitable that the Big Three would quarrel. Wilson was determined to create a League of Nations to prevent future wars. Clemenceau and Lloyd George were equally determined to punish Germany. In the end, only compromise made it possible to achieve a peace settlement. Wilson's wish that the creation of an international peacekeeping organization be the first order of business was granted, and on January 25, 1919, the conference adopted the principle of a League of Nations; the details of its structure were left for later sessions; Wilson willingly agreed to make compromises on territorial arrangements to guarantee the establishment of the League, believing that a functioning League could later rectify bad arrangements. Clemenceau also compromised to obtain some guarantees for French security. He renounced France's desire for a separate Rhineland and instead accepted a defensive alliance with Great Britain and the United States, both of which pledged to help France if it were attacked by Germany.

The final peace settlement of Paris consisted of five separate treaties with the defeated nations—Germany, Austria, Hungary, Bulgaria, and Turkey. The Treaty of Versailles with Germany, signed on June 28, 1919, was by far the most important one. The Germans considered it a harsh peace and were particularly unhappy with Article 231, the so-called war guilt clause, which declared Germany (and Austria) responsible for starting the war and ordered Germany to pay reparations for all the damage to which the Allied governments and their people had been subjected as a result of the war "imposed upon them by the aggression of Germany and her allies."

The military and territorial provisions of the treaty also rankled the Germans, although they were by no means as harsh as the Germans claimed. Germany had to lower its army to 100,000 men, reduce its navy, and eliminate its air force. German territorial losses included the return of Alsace and Lorraine to France and sections of Prussia to the new Polish state. German land west and as far as 30 miles east of the Rhine was established as a demilitarized zone and stripped of all armaments or fortifications, to serve as a barrier to any future German military moves westward against France. Outraged by the "dictated peace," the new German government complained but accepted the treaty.

The separate peace treaties made with the other Central Powers (Austria, Hungary, Bulgaria, and Turkey) extensively redrew the map of eastern Europe. Many of these changes merely ratified what the war had already accomplished. Both the German and Russian Empires lost considerable territory in eastern Europe; the Austro-Hungarian Empire disappeared altogether. New nation-states emerged from the lands of these three empires: Finland, Latvia, Estonia, Lithuania, Poland, Czechoslovakia, Austria, and Hungary. Territorial rearrangements were also made in the Balkans. Romania acquired additional lands from Russia, Hungary, and Bulgaria. Serbia formed the nucleus of a new South Slav state, called Yugoslavia, which combined Serbs, Croats, and Slovenes. Although the Paris Peace Conference was supposedly guided by the principle of self-determination, the mixtures of peoples in eastern Europe made it impossible to draw boundaries along neat ethnic lines. Compromises had to be made, sometimes to satisfy the national interest of the victors. France, for example, had lost Russia as its major ally on Germany's eastern border and wanted to strengthen and expand Poland, Czechoslovakia, Yugoslavia, and Romania as much as possible so that those states could serve as barriers against Germany and Communist Russia. As a result of compromises, virtually every eastern Europe state was left with a minorities problem that could lead to future conflicts. Germans in Poland; Hungarians, Poles, and Germans in Czechoslovakia; and the combination of Serbs, Croats, Slovenes, Macedonians, and Albanians in Yugoslavia all became

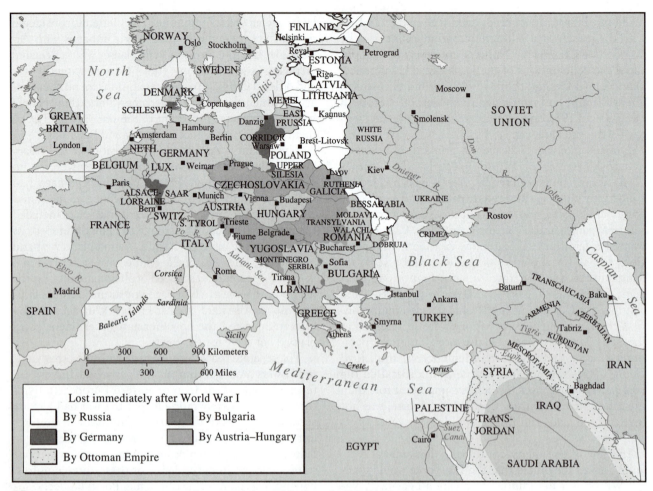

Map 4.3 Territorial Changes in Europe and the Middle East after World War I

sources of later conflict. Moreover, the new map of eastern Europe was based upon the temporary collapse of power in both Germany and Russia. As neither country accepted the new eastern frontiers, it seemed only a matter of time before a resurgent Germany or Russia would make changes.

Yet another centuries-old empire—the Ottoman Empire—was dismembered by the peace settlement after the war. To gain Arab support against the Turks during the war, the Western allies had promised to recognize the independence of Arab states in the Middle Eastern lands of the Ottoman Empire. But the imperialist habits of Western nations died hard. After the war, France took control of Lebanon and Syria while Britain received Iraq and Palestine. Officially, both acquisitions were called mandates. Because Woodrow Wilson had opposed the outright annexation of colonial territories by the Allies,

the peace settlement had created a system of mandates whereby a nation officially administered a territory on behalf of the League of Nations. The system of mandates could not hide the fact that the principle of national self-determination at the Paris Peace Conference was largely for Europeans.

The peace settlement negotiated at Paris soon came under attack, not only by the defeated Central Powers, but by others who felt that the peacemakers had been shortsighted. The famous British economist John Maynard Keynes, for example, condemned the preoccupation with frontiers at the expense of economic issues that left Europe "inefficient, unemployed, disorganized." Despite the criticisms, the peace settlement may have been the best that could be achieved under the circumstances. Self-determination had served reasonably well as a central organizing principle, and the establishment of the League of Nations gave some hope that future conflicts could be resolved peacefully. And yet, within twenty years after the signing of the peace treaties, Europe was again engaged in deadly conflict. As some historians have suggested, perhaps the cause of the failure of the peace of 1919 was less in its structure than in its lack of enforcement.

Successful enforcement of the peace necessitated the active involvement of its principal architects, especially in assisting the new German state in developing a peaceful and democratic republic. The failure of the U.S. Senate to ratify the Treaty of Versailles, however, meant that the United States never joined the League of Nations. In addition, the U.S. Senate also rejected Wilson's defensive alliance with Great Britain and France. By the end of 1919, the United States was already retreating into isolationism.

This retreat had dire consequences. American withdrawal from the defensive alliance with Britain and France led Britain to withdraw as well. By removing itself from European affairs, the United States forced France to face its old enemy alone, leading the embittered nation to take strong actions against Germany that only intensified German resentment. By the end of 1919, it appeared that the peace of 1919 was already beginning to unravel.

The Russian Revolution

One area of Europe where a durable peace appeared unlikely was in Russia.

During the early years of the twentieth century, Russia entered the Industrial Revolution. As elsewhere, it was a wrenching experience, marked by rapid social change and political unrest. Demonstrations during the Russo-Japanese War of 1904–1905 forced the tsar to agree to political reforms (including the creation of Russia's first legislative assembly, called the Duma) that for the first time limited his supreme authority. For a brief time, radicals harbored hopes that revolution was imminent, but the monarchy survived, though shaken, and the nation entered a brief period of relative stability.

Marxism made its first appearance in the Russian environment in the 1880s. Early Marxists were aware of the primitive conditions in their country and asked Karl Marx himself for advice. The Russian proletariat was oppressed—indeed brutalized—but small in numbers and unsophisticated. Could agrarian Russia make the transition to socialism without an intervening stage of capitalism? Marx, who always showed more flexibility than the

rigid determinism of his system suggested, replied that it was possible that Russia could avoid the capitalist stage by building on the communal traditions of the Russian village, known as the *mir*.

As the Russian Marxist organization grew, however, its ideas turned more toward Marxist orthodoxy. Founder and leader George Plekhanov saw signs in the early stages of the Industrial Revolution that Russia would follow the classic pattern. He predicted, however, that the weak Russian bourgeoisie would be unable to consolidate its power, thus opening the door for a rapid advance from the capitalist to the socialist stage of the revolution. In 1898, Plekhanov's Russian Social Democratic Labor Party (RSDLP) held its first congress.

During the last decade of the nineteenth century, a new force entered the Russian Marxist movement in the figure of Vladimir Ulyanov, later to be known as Lenin. Initially radicalized by the execution of his older brother for terrorism in 1886, he became a revolutionary and a member of Plekhanov's RSDLP. Like Plekhanov, Lenin believed in the revolution but unlike him, he was a man in a hurry. Whereas Plekhanov wanted to prepare patiently for revolution by education and mass work, Lenin wanted to build up the party rapidly as a vanguard instrument to galvanize the masses and spur the workers to revolt. In his pamphlet "What Is to Be Done?" he proposed the transformation of the RSDLP into a compact and highly disciplined group of professional revolutionaries that would unleash the storm clouds of revolt and not merely ride the crest of the revolutionary wave.

At the Second National Congress of the RSDLP, held in 1903 in Brussels and London, Lenin's ideas were supported by a majority of the delegates (thus the historical term Bolsheviks, or "majorityites," for his followers). His victory was short-lived, however, and for the next decade Lenin, living in exile, was a brooding figure on the fringe of the Russian revolutionary movement, which was now dominated by the Mensheviks ("minorityites"), who opposed Lenin's single-minded pursuit of violent revolution.

It was World War I that broke the trajectory of Russian economic growth and laid the foundation for the collapse of the old order. There is a supreme irony in this fact, for Tsar Nicholas II almost appeared to welcome war with Germany as a means of uniting the people behind their sovereign. In fact, war often erodes the underpinnings of a declining political system and hastens its demise. This was certainly the case with Russia.

After stirring victories in the early stages of the war, news from the battlefield turned increasingly grim, as poorly armed and poorly led Russian soldiers were slaughtered by the modern armies of the kaiser. The conscription of peasants from the countryside caused food prices to rise and led, by late 1916, to periodic bread shortages in the major cities. Workers grew increasingly restive at the wartime schedule of long hours with low pay and joined army deserters in angry marches through the capital of St. Petersburg (now renamed Petrograd). It was a classic scenario for revolution—discontent in the big cities fueled by mutinous troops streaming home from the battlefield, and a rising level of lawlessness in rural areas as angry peasants seized land and burned the manor houses of the wealthy. Even the urban middle class, always a bellwether on the political scene, grew impatient with the economic crisis and the bad news from the front and began to question the competence of the tsar and his advisers. In late February 1917, government troops fired at demonstrators in the streets of the capital and killed several. An angry mob marched to the Duma, where restive delegates demanded the resignation of the tsar's cabinet. Nicholas II, lacking in self-confidence at the best of times, continued to refuse to share the supreme power he had inherited with the throne. After a brief period of hesitation, he abdicated, leaving a vacuum that was quickly seized by leading elements in the Duma, who formed a provisional government to steer Russia through the crisis. On the left, reformist and radical political parties—including the Social Revolutionaries (the legal successors of the outlawed terrorist organization Narodnaya Volya) and the two wings of the RSDLP, the Mensheviks and the Bolsheviks—cooperated in creating a shadow government, called the St. Petersburg Soviet. This shadow government supported the provisional government in pursuing the war but attempted to compel it to grant economic and social reforms that would benefit the masses.

The so-called February Revolution of 1917 had forced the collapse of the monarchy, but it showed little promise of solving the deeper problems that had led Russia to the brink of civil war. Finally convinced that a real social revolution was at hand, Lenin returned from exile in Switzerland in April and, on his arrival in Petrograd, laid out a program for his followers: all power to the Soviets, an end to the war, and the distribution of land to poor peasants. But Lenin's April Theses were too radical even for his fellow Bolsheviks, and his demands were ignored by other Soviet leaders, who continued to cooperate with the provisional government while attempting to push it to the left.

The Bolshevik Revolution

During the summer, the crisis worsened, and in July, riots by workers and soldiers in the capital led the provisional government to outlaw the Bolsheviks and call for Lenin's arrest. The "July Days," raising the threat of disorder and class war, aroused the fears of conservatives and split the fragile political consensus within the provisional government. In September, General Lavr Kornilov, commander in chief of Russian imperial forces, launched a coup d'etat to seize power from Alexander Kerensky, now the dominant figure in the provisional government. The revolt was put down with the help of so-called Red Guard units, formed by the Bolsheviks within army regiments in the capital area (these troops would later be viewed as the first units of the Red Army), but Lenin now sensed the weakness of the provisional government and persuaded his colleagues to prepare for revolt. On the night of the 25th of October (according to the old-style Gregorian calendar), forces under the command of Lenin's lieutenant, Leon Trotsky, seized key installations in the capital area. Alexander Kerensky fled from Russia in disguise. The following morning, at a national congress of delegates from Soviet organizations throughout the country, the Bolsheviks declared the opening of a new socialist order. Moderate elements from the Menshevik faction and the Social Revolutionary Party protested the illegality of the Bolshevik action and left the conference hall in anger. They were derided by Trotsky, who proclaimed that they were relegated "to the dustbin of history."

With the Bolshevik Revolution of October 1917, Lenin was now in command. His power was tenuous and extended only from the capital to a few of the larger cities, such as Moscow and Kiev, that had waged their own insurrections. There were, in fact, few Bolsheviks in rural areas, where most peasants supported the moderate leftist Social Revolutionaries. On the fringes of the Russian Empire, restive minorities prepared to take advantage of the anarchy to seize their own independence, while "White Russian" supporters of the monarchy began raising armies to destroy the "Red menace" in St. Petersburg. Lenin was in power, but for how long?

The Russian Revolution of 1917 has been the subject of vigorous debate by scholars and students of world affairs. Could it have been avoided if the provisional government had provided more effective leadership, or was it inevitable? Did Lenin stifle Russia's halting progress toward a Western-style capitalist democracy, or was the Bolshevik victory preordained by the autocratic condi-

⇒ The State and Revolution ⇐

According to Karl Marx, the state (the government) had throughout history served as the instrument of the ruling class. As such it was an oppressive institution and should eventually "wither away" as world society reached the stage of utopian communism, when centralized authority would no longer by required because the oppression of one class over another had been finally eliminated. But Marx also recognized that the mere overthrow of capitalism could not lead immediately to the "withering away" of the state, because surviving elements of the ruling order must be destroyed. In the meantime, the Communists (the leaders of the masses in the world revolution) would indoctrinate the people in the principles of communism, based on the slogan "From each according to his ability, to each according to his need."

For that reason, Marx and his collaborator, Friedrich Engels, predicted that between the capitalist and communist stages of human society there would appear "a political transition period in which the state can be nothing but the revolutionary dictatorship of the proletariat." That proletarian dictatorship would consist of representatives of the working masses wielding power in their name. During this period, which Marx labeled "raw communism," surviving class enemies would be eliminated and the groundwork for the new communist man would be laid.

Karl Marx did not survive to see the creation of the first state organized on Marxist principles, but his disciple Lenin did. In his pamphlet "State and Revolution" (1916), Lenin sought to interpret Marx's words and give them practical reality. He noted that because of the complexity of the postrevolutionary situation, the "withering away" predicted by his mentor would be "a lengthy process." The instrument that would carry out the dictatorship of the proletariat would be his own Bolshevik organization—later to be called the Communist Party of the Soviet Union, or CPSU. It would be the duty of the Communists to suppress counterrevolutionary elements (in Leninist parlance, "who defeats whom"). Suppression was justified in this case, he asserted, because it was now "the suppression of the exploiting minority by the exploited majority." Because the state would not have majority support, this "special machine" of suppression, as he called it, would gradually begin to disappear. Communism, he concluded, would make the state completely unnecessary, for then "there is nobody to suppress" in the form of an oppressing class.

On coming to power in the fall of 1917, the Bolsheviks immediately established the proletarian dictatorship and began to eliminate the class enemy. But they would eventually decide that striking workers and poor peasants, too, sometimes had to be suppressed if they protested against conditions in Soviet society. And they would eventually discover that the Communist Party could itself become corrupted by power and take on the characteristics of the ruling classes of the past. In the end, under Communist rule, the state did not wither away at all, but continued in existence as the result of a continuing need to suppress its enemies within Soviet society.

Sources: Karl Marx, *Critique of the Gotha Programme*, in Marx-Engels, *Selected Works* (Moscow: Foreign Languages Press, 1950), vol. 2, p. 30; Lenin, "State and Revolution," in *Works*, vol. 25 (Moscow, 1950).

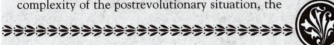

tions and lack of democratic traditions in imperial Russia? Such questions have no simple answers, but some hypotheses are possible. The weakness of the moderate government created by the February Revolution was probably predictable, given the political inexperience of the urban middle class and the deep divisions within the ruling coalition over issues of peace and war. On the other hand, it seems highly unlikely that the Bolsheviks would have possessed the self-confidence to act without the presence of their leader, Vladimir Lenin, who employed his strength of will to urge his colleagues almost single-handedly to make their bid for power. Without Lenin, then, there would have been no political force with the sense of purpose to fill the vacuum in Petrograd. In that case, as in so many cases elsewhere during the turbulent twentieth century, it would probably have been left to the army to intervene in an effort to maintain law and order.

In any event, the October Revolution was a momentous development, not only for Russia, but for the entire world. Not only did it present Western capitalist societies with a brazen new challenge to their global supremacy, it also demonstrated that Lenin's concept of revolution, carried through at the will of a determined minority of revolutionary activists "in the interests of the masses," could succeed in a society going through the difficult early stages of the Industrial Revolution. It was a repudiation of orthodox "late Marxism" and a return to Marx's pre-1848 vision of a multiclass revolt leading rapidly from a capitalist to a proletarian takeover (see Chapter 1). It was, in short, a lesson that would not be ignored by radical intellectuals throughout the world.

The Civil War

The Bolshevik seizure of power in Petrograd (soon to be renamed Leningrad after Lenin's death in 1924) was only the first, and not necessarily the most difficult, stage in the Russian Revolution. Although the Bolshevik slogan of "peace, land, and bread" had earned considerable appeal among workers, petty merchants, and soldiers in the vicinity of the capital and other major cities, the party—only 50,000 strong in October—had little representation in the rural areas, where the moderate leftist Social Revolutionary Party received majority support from the peasants. On the fringes of the Russian Empire, ethnic minority groups took advantage of the confusion in Petrograd to launch movements to restore their own independence or achieve a position of autonomy within the Russian state. In the meantime, supporters of the deposed Romanov dynasty and other political opponents of the Bolsheviks attempted to mobilize support to drive the Bolsheviks out of the capital and reverse the verdict of Red October. And, beyond all that, the war with Germany continued.

Lenin was aware of these problems and hoped that a wave of socialist revolutions in the economically advanced countries of central and western Europe would bring the world war to an end and usher in a new age of peace, socialism, and growing economic prosperity. In the meantime, his first priority was to consolidate the rule of the working class and its party vanguard (now to be renamed the Communist Party) in Russia. The first step was to set up a new order in Petrograd to replace the provisional government that itself had been created after the February Revolution. For lack of a better alternative, outlying areas were simply informed of the change in government—a "revolution by telegraph," as Leon Trotsky termed it. Then Lenin moved to create new organs of proletarian power, setting up a Council of People's Commissars to serve as a provisional government. Lenin was unwilling to share power with moderate leftists who had resisted the Bolshevik coup in October, and he created security forces (popularly called the Cheka or "extraordinary commission"), which imprisoned and sometimes executed opponents of the new regime. In January 1918, the Constituent Assembly,

which had been elected on the basis of plans established by the previous government, convened in Petrograd. Composed primarily of delegates from the Social Revolutionary Party and other parties opposed to the Bolsheviks, it showed itself critical of the new regime and was immediately abolished.

In foreign affairs, Lenin's first major decision was to seek peace with Germany in order to permit the new Soviet government to focus its efforts on the growing threat posed by White Russian forces within the country. In March 1918, a peace settlement with Germany was reached at Brest-Litovsk, although at enormous cost. Soviet Russia lost nearly one-fourth of the territory and one-third the population of the prewar Russian Empire. In retrospect, however, Lenin's controversial decision to accept a punitive peace may have been a stroke of genius, for it gained time for the regime to build up its internal strength and defeat its many adversaries in the Russian Civil War (1918–1920). The White Russian forces were larger than those of the Red Army; they were supported by armed contingents sent by Great Britain, France, and the United States to assist in the extinction of the "Red menace"; but they were also rent by factionalism and hindered by the tendency of White Russian leaders to return conquered land to the original landowners, thus driving many peasants to support the Soviet regime. By 1920, the civil war was over, and Soviet power was secure.

The Search for Stability in Europe

Only twenty years after the Treaty of Versailles, the world was again at war. Yet, in the 1920s, many people continued to assume that Europe and the world were about to enter a new era of international peace, economic growth, and political democracy. In all of these areas, the optimistic hopes of the 1920s failed to be realized.

An Uncertain Peace: The Search for Security

The peace settlement at the end of World War I had tried to fulfill the nineteenth-century dream of nationalism by creating new boundaries and new states. From its inception, however, this peace settlement had left nations unhappy. Conflicts over disputed border regions between Germany and Poland, Poland and Lithuania, Poland and Czechoslovakia, Austria and Hungary, and Italy and Yugoslavia poisoned mutual relations in eastern Europe for years. Many Germans viewed the Peace of Versailles as a dictated peace and vowed to seek its revision.

The American president Woodrow Wilson had recognized that the peace treaties contained unwise provisions that could serve as new causes for conflicts and had placed many of his hopes for the future in the League of Nations. The League, however, was not particularly effective in maintaining the peace. The failure of the United States to join the League and the subsequent American retreat into isolationism undermined the effectiveness of the League from its beginning. Moreover, the League could use only economic sanctions to halt aggression. The French attempt to strengthen the League's effectiveness as an instrument of collective security by creating some kind of international army was rejected by nations that feared giving up any of their sovereignty to a larger international body.

The weakness of the League of Nations and the failure of both the United States and Great Britain to honor their defensive military alliances with France left France embittered and alone. France's search for security between 1919 and 1924 was founded primarily upon a strict enforcement of the Treaty of Versailles. This tough policy toward Germany began with the issue of reparations—the payments that the Germans were supposed to make to compensate for the "damage done to the civilian population of the Allied and Associated Powers and to their property," as the treaty asserted. In April 1921, the Allied Reparations Commission settled on a sum of 132 billion marks ($33 billion) for German reparations, payable in annual installments of 2.5 billion (gold) marks. Allied threats to occupy the Ruhr valley, Germany's chief industrial and mining center, induced the new German republic to accept the reparations settlement and to make its first payment in 1921. By the following year, however, faced with rising inflation, domestic turmoil, and lack of revenues because of low tax rates, the German government announced that it was unable to pay more. Outraged by what they considered to be Germany's violation of one aspect of the peace settlement, the French government sent troops to occupy the Ruhr valley. If the Germans would not pay reparations, the French would collect reparations in kind by operating and using the Ruhr mines and factories.

French occupation of the Ruhr seriously undermined the fragile German economy. The German government adopted a policy of passive resistance to French occupation that was largely financed by printing more paper money, thus intensifying the inflationary pressures that had already begun in Germany by the end of the war.

The German mark became worthless. Economic disaster fueled political upheavals as Communists staged uprisings in October and Adolf Hitler's band of Nazis attempted to seize power in Munich in 1923. All the nations, including France, were happy to cooperate with the American suggestion for a new conference of experts to reassess the reparations problem. By the time the conference did its work in 1924, both France and Germany were opting to pursue a more conciliatory approach toward each other.

The formation of liberal-socialist governments in both Great Britain and France opened the door to conciliatory approaches to Germany and the reparations problem. At the same time, a new German government led by Gustav Stresemann (1878–1929) ended the policy of passive resistance and committed Germany to carry out the provisions of the Versailles Treaty while seeking a new settlement of the reparations question.

In August 1924, an international commission produced a new plan for reparations. Named the Dawes Plan after the American banker who chaired the commission, it reduced reparations and stabilized Germany's payments on the basis of its ability to pay. The Dawes Plan also granted an initial $200 million loan for German recovery, which opened the door to heavy American investments in Europe that helped create a new era of European prosperity between 1924 and 1929.

A new age of European diplomacy accompanied the new economic stability. A spirit of international cooperation was fostered by the foreign ministers of Germany and France, Gustav Stresemann and Aristide Briand (1862–1932), who concluded the Treaty of Locarno in 1925. This treaty guaranteed Germany's new western borders with France and Belgium. Although Germany's new eastern borders with Poland were conspicuously absent from the agreement, the Locarno pact was viewed by many as the beginning of a new era of European peace. On the day after the pact was concluded, the headline in the *New York Times* read "France and Germany Ban War Forever," and the London *Times* declared "Peace at Last."[5]

Germany's entry into the League of Nations in March 1926 soon reinforced the new spirit of conciliation engendered at Locarno. Two years later, similar optimistic attitudes prevailed in the Kellogg-Briand Pact, drafted by the American secretary of state Frank B. Kellogg and the French foreign minister Aristide Briand. Sixty-three nations signed this accord, in which they pledged "to renounce war as an instrument of national policy." Nothing was said, however, about what would be done if anyone violated the treaty.

The spirit of Locarno was based on little real substance. Germany lacked the military power to alter its western borders even if it wanted to. Pious promises to renounce war without mechanisms to enforce them were virtually worthless. And the issue of disarmament soon proved that even the spirit of Locarno could not bring nations to cut back on their weapons. The League of Nations Covenant had suggested the "reduction of national armaments to the lowest point consistent with national safety." Germany, of course, had been disarmed with the expectation that other states would do likewise. Numerous disarmament conferences, however, failed to achieve anything substantial as states proved unwilling to trust their security to anyone but their own military forces. When a World Disarmament Conference finally met in Geneva in 1932, the issue was already dead.

The Great Depression

After World War I, most European states hoped to return to the liberal ideal of a private-enterprise, market economy largely free of state intervention. But the war had vastly strengthened business cartels and labor unions, making some government regulation of these powerful organizations necessary. At the same time, reparations and war debts had severely damaged the postwar international economy, making the prosperity that did occur between 1924 and 1929 at best a fragile one and the dream of returning to the liberal ideal of a self-regulating market economy merely an illusion. What destroyed the concept altogether was the Great Depression.

Two factors played a major role in the coming of the Great Depression: a downturn in domestic economies and an international financial crisis created by the collapse of the American stock market in 1929. Already in the mid-1920s, prices for agricultural goods were beginning to decline rapidly as a result of the overproduction of basic commodities, such as wheat. In 1925, states in central and eastern Europe began to impose tariffs to close their markets to other countries' goods. An increase in the use of oil and hydroelectricity led to a slump in the coal industry even before 1929.

Meanwhile, much of the European prosperity between 1924 and 1929 was built upon American bank loans to Germany. Twenty-three billion marks had been invested in German municipal bonds and German industries since 1924. In 1928 and 1929, American investors began to pull money out of Germany in order to invest in the booming New York stock market. With the crash of the American stock market in October 1929,

panicky American investors withdrew even more of their funds from Germany and other European markets. The withdrawal of funds seriously weakened the banks of Germany and other central European states. The Credit-Anstalt, Vienna's most prestigious bank, collapsed on May 31, 1931. By that time, trade was slowing down, industrialists were cutting back production, and unemployment was increasing as the ripple effects of international bank failures had a devastating impact on domestic economies.

Economic depression was by no means a new phenomenon in European history. But the depth of the economic downturn after 1929 fully justifies the label Great Depression. During 1932, the worst year of the depression, one British worker in four was unemployed, while 6 million Germans or 40 percent of the labor force, were out of work. Between 1929 and 1932, industrial production plummeted almost 50 percent in the United States and more than 40 percent in Germany. The unemployed and homeless filled the streets of cities throughout the advanced industrial countries.

Governments seemed powerless to deal with the crisis. The classical liberal remedy for depression—a deflationary policy of balanced budgets, which involved cutting costs by lowering wages and raising tariffs to exclude other countries' goods from home markets—only served to worsen the economic crisis and create even greater mass discontent. This failure in turn, led to serious political repercussions. Increased government activity in the economy was one reaction, even in countries such as the United States that had a strong laissez-faire tradition. Another effect was a renewed interest in Marxist doctrines because Marx had predicted that capitalism would destroy itself through overproduction. Communism took on new popularity, especially with workers and intellectuals. Finally, the Great Depression increased the attractiveness of simplistic dictatorial solutions, especially from a new movement known as fascism. Everywhere, democracy seemed on the defensive in the 1930s.

The Democratic States

According to Woodrow Wilson, World War I had been fought to make the world safe for democracy. In 1919, there seemed to be some justification for his claim. Four major European states and a host of minor ones had functioning political democracies. In a number of states, universal male suffrage had even been replaced by universal suffrage as male politicians rewarded women for their contributions to World War I by granting them the right to vote (except in Italy, Switzerland, France, and Spain, where women had to wait until the end of World War II). In the 1920s, Europe seemed to be returning to the political trends of the prewar era—the broadening of parliamentary regimes and the fostering of individual liberties. But it was not an easy process; four years of total war and four years of postwar turmoil made the desire for a "return to normalcy" a difficult and troublesome affair.

After World War I, Great Britain went through a period of painful readjustment and serious economic difficulties. During the war, Britain had lost many of the markets for its industrial products, especially to the United States and Japan. The postwar decline of such staple industries as coal, steel, and textiles led to a rise in unemployment, which reached the 2 million mark in 1921. Britain soon rebounded, experiencing an era of renewed prosperity between 1925 and 1929, but this prosperity was relatively superficial. British exports in the 1920s never compensated for the overseas investments lost during the war, and even in these so-called prosperous years, unemployment remained at a startling 10 percent. Coal miners were especially affected by the decline of the antiquated and inefficient British coal mines, which also suffered from a world glut of coal.

By 1929, Britain was faced with the growing effects of the Great Depression. The Labour Party, which had now become the largest party in Britain, failed to solve the nation's economic problems and fell from power in 1931. A national government, dominated by the Conservatives, claimed credit for bringing Britain out of the worst stages of the depression, primarily by using the traditional policies of balanced budgets and protective tariffs. British politicians largely ignored the new ideas of a Cambridge economist, John Maynard Keynes (1883–1946). In 1936, Keynes published his *General Theory of Employment, Interest, and Money*. Contrary to the traditional view that depressions should be left to work themselves out through the self-regulatory mechanisms of a free economy, Keynes argued that unemployment stemmed not from overproduction but from a decline in demand, and that demand could be increased by public works, financed, if necessary, through deficit spending to stimulate production. These policies, however, could only be accomplished by government intervention in the economy, and Britain's political leaders were unwilling to go that far in the 1930s.

After the defeat of Germany and the demobilization of the German army, France became the strongest power on the European continent. Its biggest problem involved the reconstruction of the devastated areas of northern and eastern France. But neither the conservative National Bloc government nor a government coalition of leftist parties (the Cartel of the Left) seemed capable of solving France's financial problems between 1921 and 1926. The failure of the Cartel of the Left led to the return of the conservative Raymond Poincaré (1860–1934), whose government from 1926 to 1929 stabilized the French economy by means of a substantial increase in taxes during a period of relative prosperity.

France did not feel the effects of the depression as soon as other countries because of its more balanced economy. The French population was almost evenly divided between urban and agricultural pursuits, and a slight majority of French industrial plants were small enterprises. Consequently, France did not begin to feel the full effects of the Great Depression until 1932, but then economic instability soon had political repercussions. During a nineteen-month period in 1932 and 1933, six different cabinets were formed as France faced political chaos.

When the imperial Germany of William II came to an end with Germany's defeat in World War I, a German democratic state known as the Weimar Republic was established. From its beginnings, the Weimar Republic was plagued by a series of problems. The republic had no truly outstanding political leaders, and those who were relatively able—including Friedrich Ebert, who served as president, and Gustav Stresemann, the foreign minister and chancellor—died in the 1920s. When Ebert died in 1925, Paul von Hindenburg (1847–1934), the World War I military hero, was elected president. Hindenburg was a traditional military man, monarchist in sentiment, who at heart was not in favor of the republic. The young republic also suffered politically from attempted uprisings and attacks from both the left and right.

The Weimar Republic also faced serious economic difficulties. Germany experienced runaway inflation in 1922 and 1923, with grave social effects. Widows, orphans, the retired elderly, army officers, teachers, civil servants, and others who lived on fixed incomes all watched their monthly stipends become worthless or their lifetime savings disappear. Their economic losses increasingly pushed the middle class to the rightist parties that were hostile to the republic. To make matters worse, after a period of prosperity from 1924 to 1929, Germany faced the Great Depression. Unemployment increased to 3 million in March 1930 and 4.38 million by December of the same year. The depression paved the way for social discontent, fear, and extremist parties. The political, economic, and social problems of the Weimar Republic help us to understand the environment in which Adolf Hitler and the Nazis were able to rise to power.

After Germany, no Western nation was more affected by the Great Depression than the United States. The full force of the depression had struck the United States by 1932. In that year, industrial production fell to 50 percent of what it had been in 1929. By 1933, there were 15 million unemployed. Under these circumstances, the Democrat Franklin Delano Roosevelt (1882–1945) was able to win a landslide electoral victory in 1932. Following the example of the American experience during World War I, he and his advisors pursued a policy of active government intervention in the economy that came to be known as the New Deal.

Initially, the New Deal attempted to restore prosperity by creating the National Recovery Administration (NRA), which required government, labor, and industrial leaders to work out regulations for each industry. Declared unconstitutional by the Supreme Court in 1935, the NRA was soon superseded by other efforts collectively known as the Second New Deal. Its programs included the Works Progress Administration (WPA), established in 1935, which employed between 2 and 3 million people building bridges, roads, post offices, airports, and other public works. The Roosevelt administration was also responsible for new social legislation that launched the American welfare state. In 1935, the Social Security Act created a system of old-age pensions and unemployment insurance. At the same time, the National Labor Relations Act of 1935 encouraged the rapid growth of labor unions.

The New Deal undoubtedly provided some social reform measures and may even have averted social revolution in the United States; it did not, however, solve the unemployment problems of the Great Depression. In May 1937, during what was considered a period of full recovery, American unemployment still stood at 7 million; a recession the following year increased that number to 11 million. Only World War II and the subsequent growth of armaments industries brought American workers back to full employment.

Socialism in One Country

With their victory over the White Russians in 1920, Soviet leaders now could turn for the first time to the challenging task of building the first socialist society in a world dominated by their capitalist enemies. In his writings, Karl Marx had said little about the nature of the final communist utopia or how to get there. He had spoken briefly of a transitional phase, variously known as "raw communism" or "socialism," that would precede the final stage of communism. During this phase, the Communist Party would establish a "dictatorship of the proletariat" to rid society of the capitalist oppressors, set up the institutions of the new order, and indoctrinate the population in the communist ethic. In recognition of the fact that traces of "bourgeois thinking" would remain among the population, profit incentives would be used to encourage productivity (in the slogan of Marxism, payment would be on the basis of "work" rather than solely on "need"), but major industries would be nationalized and private landholdings eliminated. Lenin had briefly sketched out his own ideas on the subject in a pamphlet, "State and Revolution," written just before the Bolshevik Revolution. After seizing power, however, the Bolsheviks were too preoccupied with survival to give much attention to the future nature of Soviet society. "War communism"—involving the government seizure of major industries, utilities, and sources of raw materials, and the requisition of grain from private farmers—was, by Lenin's own admission, just a makeshift policy to permit the regime to mobilize resources for the civil war.

In 1920, it was time to adopt a more coherent approach. The realities were sobering. Soviet Russia was not an advanced capitalist society in the Marxist image, blessed with modern technology and an educated and politically aware population imbued with the desire to advance to socialism. It was poor and primarily agrarian, and its small but growing industrial sector had been ravaged by years of war. Under the circumstances, Lenin called for caution. He won his party's approval of a moderate program of social and economic development known as the New Economic Policy, or NEP. The program was based on a combination of capitalist and socialist techniques designed to increase production through the use of incentives while at the same time promoting the concept of socialist ownership and maintaining firm party control over the political system and the overall direction of the economy. The "commanding heights" of the Soviet economy (heavy industry, banking, utilities, and foreign trade) remained in the hands of the state, while private industry and commerce were allowed to operate at the lower levels. The forced requisition of grain, which had caused serious unrest among the peasantry, was replaced by a tax, and land remained firmly in private hands. The theoretical justification for the program was that Soviet Russia now needed to go through its own "capitalist stage" (albeit under the control of the party) before beginning the difficult transition to socialism.

✦ *Lenin at the Tribune.* In the Soviet Union, as in all Marxist-Leninist states, artists were required to glorify the socialist system and its leaders, a style that was known as socialist realism. In this fine example by the Soviet painter Alexander Gerasimov, the Bolshevik leader Vladimir Lenin appears in a heroic mold.

As an economic strategy, the NEP succeeded brilliantly. During the early and mid-1920s, the Soviet economy recovered rapidly from the doldrums of war and civil war. A more lax hand over the affairs of state allowed a modest degree of free expression of opinion within the ranks of the party, and in Soviet society at large. Under the surface, however, trouble loomed. Lenin had been increasingly disabled by a bullet lodged in his neck from an attempted assassination, and he began to lose his grip over a fractious party. Even before his death in 1924, potential successors had begun to scuffle for precedence in the struggle to assume his position as party leader, the most influential position in the state. The main candidates were Leon Trotsky and a rising young figure from the state of Georgia, Joseph Djugashvili, better known by his revolutionary name of Stalin. Lenin

had misgivings about candidates to succeed him and suggested that a collective leadership best represented the interests of the party and the revolution. After his death in 1924, factional struggle among the leading figures in the party intensified. Although in some respects it was a pure power struggle, it did have policy ramifications, as party factions debated about the NEP and its impact on the future of the Russian Revolution.

At first, the various factions were relatively evenly balanced, but Stalin proved adept at using his position as general secretary of the party to outmaneuver his rivals. By portraying himself as a centrist opposed to the extreme positions of his "leftist" (too radical in pursuit of revolutionary goals) or "rightist" (too prone to adopt moderate positions contrary to Marxist principles) rivals, he gradually concentrated power in his own hands.

In the meantime, the relatively moderate policies of the NEP continued in operation, as the party and the state vocally encouraged the Soviet people, in a very un-Marxist manner, to enrich themselves. Capital investment and technological assistance from Western capitalist countries were actively welcomed. An observer at the time might reasonably have concluded that the Marxist vision of a world characterized by class struggle had become a dead letter.

$\mathcal{T}$he Search for a New Reality in the Arts

The mass destruction brought on by World War I precipitated a general disillusionment with Western civilization on the part of artists and writers throughout Europe. Avant-garde art, which had sought to discover alternative techniques to portray reality, now gained broader acceptance, as Europeans began to abandon classical traditions in an attempt to come to grips with the anxieties of the new age.

Although there were many different schools of artistic expression during the postwar era, a common denominator for all modernist art was its unrelenting crusade for absolute freedom of expression. Some artists opted for open revolt against the past, whereas others wished to liberate the darker impulses of the spirit from rational constraints in order to reveal the whole individual underneath. Others still, renouncing the apparent chaos of Western civilization, sought refuge in a new world of abstract painting. Some abandoned painting and sculpture altogether, preferring to focus on ameliorating social conditions through utopian architecture and interior designs for everyday living.

A number of the artistic styles that gained popularity during the 1920s originated during the war in neutral Switzerland, where alienated intellectuals congregated at cafés to decry the insanity of the age and to exchange ideas on how to create a new and better world. One such group was the Dadaists, who sought to destroy the past with a vengeance, proclaiming their right to complete freedom of expression in art. As one put it, "repelled by the slaughterhouses of the world war, . . . we searched for an elementary art that would, we thought, save mankind from the furious madness of these times."[6] A flagrant example of Dada's innovative approach was the decision by the French artist Marcel Duchamp (1887–1968) to enter a urinal in an art exhibit held in 1917 in New York City. By signing it and giving it a title, Duchamp proclaimed that he had transformed the urinal into a work of art. Duchamp's "ready-mades" (as such art would henceforth be labeled) declared that whatever the artist proclaimed to be art, was art.

While Dadaism flourished in Germany during the Weimar era, a school of surrealism was established in Paris to liberate the total human experience from the restraints of the rational world. By using the subconscious, surrealists hoped to resurrect the whole personality and reveal a submerged and illusive reality. Normally unrelated objects and people were placed in juxtaposition in dreamlike and frequently violent paintings that were intended to shock the viewer into approaching reality from a totally fresh perspective. Most famous of the surrealists was the Spaniard Salvadore Dali (1904–1989), who subverted the sense of reality in his painting by using near photographic detail in presenting a fantastic and irrational world.

Yet another modernist movement born on the eve of World War I was abstract painting. As one of its founders, the Swiss artist Paul Klee (1879–1940) observed, "the more fearful this world becomes, . . . the more art becomes abstract."[7] Two of the movement's principal founders, Wassily Kandinsky (1866–1944) and Piet Mondrian (1872–1944), were followers of Theosophy, a religion that promised the triumph of the spirit in a new millennium. Since they viewed matter as an obstacle to salvation, the art of the new age would totally abandon all reference to the material world. Only abstraction, in the form of colorful forms and geometric shapes floating in space, could express the bliss and spiritual beauty of this terrestrial paradise.

Other fields of artistic creativity, including sculpture, ballet, and architecture, reflected these new directions. In Germany, a group of imaginative architects called the Bauhaus school created what is widely known as the in-

◆ *Black Lines No. 189,* Wassily Kandinsky, 1913. Abstract painting was a renunciation of the material world and a glorification of the spiritual realm. Deeming it no longer necessary to represent objects and people, artists chose to express emotions solely through color and abstract form. In this painting by Kandinsky, we rejoice in the springlike swirling splashes of color of the artist's abstract world.

ternational school, which soon became the dominant school of modern architecture. Led by the famous German architect Ludwig Mies van der Rohe (1881–1969), the internationalists promoted a new functional and unadorned style (van der Rohe was widely known for his pithy remark, "Less is more") characterized by high-rise towers of steel and glass that have been reproduced endlessly throughout the second half of the century all around the world.

For many postwar architects, the past was the enemy of the future. In 1925, the famous French architect Le Corbusier (1877–1965) advocated razing much of the old city of Paris, to be replaced by modern towers of glass. In his plan, which called for neat apartment complexes separated by immaculate areas of grass, there was no room for people, pets, or nature. Fortunately, it was rejected by municipal authorities.

During the postwar era, writers followed artists and architects in rejecting traditional forms in order to explore the subconscious. In his novel *Ulysses,* published in 1922, the Irish author James Joyce (1882–1941) invented the "stream of consciousness" technique to por-

♦ **Chrysler Building, New York, 1929.** America's greatest expression of modernist art was the city of New York itself, with its vertiginous vertical forest of shiny steel and glass skyscrapers. Most exuberant was William van Alen's Chrysler Building, a monument to American ingenuity, industry, and power. Here, the ornamentation suggests the Chrysler's hubcaps in the seven-tiered fringe, with radiator caps as gargoyles; the elegance and power of the building itself reflect the owner's luxurious car and impressive fortune.

tray the lives of ordinary people through the use of inner monologue. Joyce's technique exerted a powerful influence on literature for the remainder of the century. Other writers, such as Ernest Hemingway (1899–1961), Theodore Dreiser (1871–1945), and Sinclair Lewis (1885–1951), reflected the rising influence of mass journalism in a new style designed to "tell it like it is." Such writers sought to report the "whole truth" in an effort to reproduce the authenticity of modern photography.

For much of the Western world, however, the best way to find (or escape) reality was in the field of mass entertainment. The 1930s represented the heyday of the Hollywood studio system, which in the single year of 1937 turned out nearly 600 feature films. Supplementing the movies were cheap paperbacks and radio, which brought sports, soap operas, and popular music to the mass of the population. The radio was a great social leveler, speaking to all classes with the same voice. Such new technological wonders offered diversion even to the poor, while helping to define the twentieth century as the era of the common people.

Conclusion

World War I shattered the liberal, rational society of late nineteenth- and early twentieth-century Europe. The incredible destruction and the death of almost 10 million people undermined the whole idea of progress. New propaganda techniques had manipulated entire populations into sustaining their involvement in a meaningless slaughter.

World War I was a total war, involving an unprecedented mobilization of resources and populations and increased government centralization of power over the lives of its citizens. Civil liberties, such as freedom of the press, speech, assembly, and movement, were circumscribed in the name of national security. World War I made the practice of strong central authority a way of life.

What had happened to tarnish the bright dreams aroused by the Enlightenment and the technological revolution? In the first half of the nineteenth century, liberals had maintained that the organization of European states along national lines would lead to a peaceful Europe based on a sense of international fraternity. They had been very wrong. The system of nation-states that emerged in Europe in the second half of the nineteenth century led not to cooperation but to competition. Rivalries over colonial and commercial interests intensified during an era of frenzied imperialist expansion; the division of Europe's great powers into two loose alliances (Germany, Austria, and Italy versus France, Great Britain, and Russia) only added to the tensions. The series of crises that tested these alliances left European states with a dangerous lesson. Those governments that exercised restraint in order to avoid war wound up being publicly humiliated; those that went to the brink of war to maintain their national interests were often praised for having preserved national honor. In either case, by 1914, the major European states had come to believe that their allies were important and that their security depended on supporting those allies, even when they took foolish risks.

Diplomacy based on brinkmanship was especially frightening in view of the nature of the European state system. Each nation-state regarded itself as sovereign, subject to no higher interest or authority. Each was motivated by its own self-interest and success. Such attitudes made war an ever-present possibility, particularly since most statesmen at the time considered war an acceptable way to preserve national wealth and power.

The growth of nationalism in the nineteenth century had yet another serious consequence. Not all ethnic groups had achieved the goal of nationhood. Slavic minorities in the Balkans and the polyglot Austro-Hungarian Empire, for example, still dreamed of creating their own national states. So did the Irish in the British Empire and the Poles in the Russian Empire, not to speak of the subject peoples living in colonial areas elsewhere around the globe. To a close observer of the global scene, the future must have looked ominous.

A mounting sense of insecurity led to increased military expenditures. The growth of large mass armies after 1900 not only heightened the existing tensions in Europe, but made it inevitable that if war did come it would be highly destructive. Conscription had been established as a regular practice in most Western countries before 1914 (the United States and Britain were major exceptions). European military machines had doubled in size between 1890 and 1914. With its 1.3 million men, the Russian army had grown to be the largest, but the French and Germans were not far behind with 900,000 each. The British, Italian, and Austrian armies numbered between 250,000 and 500,000 soldiers.

Militarism, however, involved more than just large armies. As armies grew, so too did the influence of military leaders, who drew up vast and complex plans for quickly mobilizing millions of men and enormous quantities of supplies in the event of war. Fearful that changing these plans would cause chaos in the armed forces,

military leaders insisted that the plans could not be altered. In the crises during the summer of 1914, the generals' lack of flexibility forced European political leaders to make decisions for military rather than political reasons.

To make matters worse, the very industrial and technological innovations that brought the prospect of increased material prosperity for millions also led to the manufacture of new weapons of mass destruction that would make war a more terrible prospect for those involved, whether military or civilian. It was World War I that introduced long-range artillery, the tank, poison gas, and the airplane.

Victorious world leaders gathering at Versailles hoped to forge a peace settlement that would say good-bye to all that. But, as it turned out, the turmoil wrought by World War I seemed to open the door to even greater insecurity. Revolutions in Russia and the Middle East dismembered old empires and created new states that gave rise to unexpected problems. Expectations that Europe and the world would return to normalcy were soon dashed by the failure to achieve a lasting peace, economic collapse, and the rise of authoritarian governments that not only restricted individual freedoms, but sought even greater control over the lives of their subjects in order to manipulate and guide them to achieve the goals of their totalitarian regimes.

Finally, World War I brought an end to the age of European hegemony over world affairs. By virtually demolishing their own civilization on the battlegrounds of Europe in World War I, Europeans inadvertently encouraged the subject peoples of their vast colonial empires to initiate movements for national independence. In the next chapter, we examine some of those movements.

NOTES

1. Robert Hughes, *The Shock of the New* (New York, 1996), p. 43.
2. Quoted in J. M. Winter, *The Experience of World War I* (New York, 1989), p. 142.
3. From Catherine W. Reilly, ed., *Scars upon My Heart: Women's Poetry and Verse of the First World War* (London, 1981), p. 90.
4. Harold Nicolson, *Peacemaking, 1919* (Boston and New York, 1933), pp. 31–32.
5. Quoted in Robert Paxton, *Europe in the Twentieth Century*, 2d ed. (San Diego, 1985), p. 237.
6. Hughes, *Shock of the New*, p. 61.
7. Nikos Stangos, *Concepts of Modern Art: From Fauvism to Postmodernism*, 3d ed. (London, 1994), p. 44.

Nationalism, Revolution, and Dictatorship: Africa, Asia, and Latin America from 1919 to 1939

In the spring of 1913, the Bolshevik leader Vladimir Lenin wrote an article in the party newspaper Pravda *on the awakening of Asia. "Was it so long ago," he asked his readers, "that China was considered typical of the lands that had been standing still for centuries? Today China is a land of seething political activity, the scene of a virile social movement and of a democratic upsurge." Similar conditions, he added, were spreading the democratic revolution to other parts of Asia—to Turkey, Persia, and China. Ferment was even on the rise in British India.[1]*

A year later, the Great War erupted and Lenin, like millions of others, turned his eyes to events in Europe. In February 1917, riots in the streets of Petrograd (the old St. Petersburg) marked the onset of the Russian Revolution. By the end of the year, the Bolsheviks were in power in Moscow. For the next few years, Lenin and his colleagues were preoccupied with consolidating their control over the vast territories of the old tsarist Russian Empire. But he had not forgotten his earlier prediction that the colonial world was on the verge of revolt. Now, with the infant Soviet state virtually surrounded by its capitalist enemies, Lenin argued that the oppressed masses of Asia and Africa were potential allies in the bitter struggle against the brutal yoke of world imperialism. For the next two decades, the leaders in Moscow periodically turned their eyes to China and other parts of Asia in an effort to ride what they hoped would be a mounting wave of revolt against foreign domination.

. . . .

The Rise of Nationalism

Although the West had emerged from its recent bloodletting relatively intact, its political and social foundations and its self-confidence had been severely undermined by the experience. Within Europe, doubts about the future viability of Western civilization were widespread, especially among the intellectual elite. These doubts were quick to reach the attention of perceptive observers in Asia and Africa, and contributed to a rising tide of unrest against Western political domination throughout the colonial and semicolonial world. That unrest took a variety of forms, but was most notably displayed in increasing worker activism, rural protest, and a rising sense of national fervor among anticolonialist intellectuals. In those areas of Asia, Africa, and Latin America where independent states had successfully resisted the Western onslaught, the discontent fostered by the war and later by the Great Depression led to a loss of confidence in democratic institutions and the rise of political dictatorships.

Nationalism, of course, is not a uniquely twentieth-century phenomenon, nor is it the exclusive preserve of the non-Western world. Some historians believe that the concept of nationalism first emerged with the rise of linguistic and ethnic consciousness in eighteenth-century Europe. It eventually resulted in the breakup of the multiracial empires of the Ottomans and Austria-Hungary and the creation of such modern "nations" as Italy, Germany, Hungary, and Poland. Others see the origins of nationalism in the decline of religious belief and the need for a new sense of community to replace the concept of heavenly salvation.

As we have seen, nationalism refers to a state of mind rising out of an awareness of being part of a community that possesses common institutions, traditions, language, and customs. Unfortunately, few nations in the world today meet such criteria. Most modern states contain a variety of ethnic, religious, and linguistic communities, each with its own sense of cultural and national identity. How does nationalism differ from tribal, religious, linguistic, or other forms of affiliation? Should every group that resists assimilation into a larger cultural unity be called nationalist?

Such questions complicate the study of nationalism even in Europe and North America and make agreement on a definition elusive. They create even greater dilemmas in discussing Asia and Africa, where most societies are deeply divided by ethnic, linguistic, and religious differences and the very term *nationalism* is a foreign phenomenon imported from the West. Prior to the colonial era, most traditional societies in Africa and Asia were formed on the basis of religious beliefs, tribal loyalties, or devotion to hereditary monarchies. Whereas individuals in some countries may have identified themselves as members of a particular national group, others viewed themselves as subjects of a king, members of a tribe, or adherents of a particular religion.

The advent of European colonialism brought the consciousness of modern nationhood to many of the societies of Asia and Africa. The creation of European colonies with defined borders and a powerful central government led to the weakening of tribal and village ties and a significant reorientation in the individual's sense of political identity. The introduction of Western ideas of citizenship and representative government produced a new sense of participation in the affairs of government. At the same time, the appearance of a new elite class based not on hereditary privilege or religious sanction but on alleged racial or cultural superiority aroused a shared sense of resentment among the subject peoples who felt a common commitment to the creation of an independent society. By the first quarter of the twentieth century, political movements dedicated to the

overthrow of colonial rule had arisen throughout much of the non-Western world.

Modern nationalism, then, was a product of colonialism and, in a sense, a reaction to it. But a sense of nationhood does not emerge full-blown in a given society. The rise of modern nationalism is a process that begins among a few members of the educated elite (most commonly among articulate professionals such as lawyers, teachers, journalists, and doctors) and then spreads only gradually to the mass of the population. Even after national independence has been realized, as we shall see, it is often questionable whether a mature sense of nationhood has been created.

Traditional Resistance: A Precursor to Nationalism

If we view the concept of nationalism as a process by which people in a given society gradually become aware of themselves as members of a particular nation with its own culture and aspirations, then it is reasonable to seek the beginnings of modern nationalism in the initial resistance by the indigenous peoples to the colonial conquest itself. Strictly speaking, such resistance cannot be described as "nationalist," because it was essentially motivated by the desire to defend traditional institutions. Still, at a minimum, it reflected a primitive concept of nationhood in that it aimed at protecting the homeland from the invader; later spokespersons for patriotic groups have often hailed such resistance movements as the precursors of more modern nationalist movements that have arisen in the twentieth century. Thus, traditional resistance to colonial conquest may logically be viewed as the first stage in the development of modern nationalism.

Such resistance took various forms. For the most part, it was led by the existing ruling class. In the Ashanti kingdom in West Africa and in Burma and Vietnam in Southeast Asia, the resistance to Western domination was initially directed by the imperial courts themselves. In some cases, however, traditionalist elements continued to oppose foreign conquest even after resistance had collapsed at the center. In Japan, conservative elements led by nobles under Saigo Takamori opposed the decision of the Tokugawa shogunate in Tokyo to accommodate the Western presence and launched an abortive movement to defeat the foreigners and restore Japan to its previous policy of isolation (see Chapter 3). In India, Tipu Sultan resisted the British in the Deccan after the collapse of the Mughal dynasty. Similarly, after the decrepit monarchy in Vietnam had bowed to French pressure and agreed to the concession of territory in the south and the establishment of a protectorate over the remainder of the country, a number of civilian and military officials set up an organization called Can Vuong (literally, "Save the King") and continued their resistance without imperial sanctions.

Sometimes traditional resistance went beyond elite circles. Most commonly, it appeared in the form of peasant revolts. Rural rebellions were not uncommon in traditional Asian societies as a means of expressing peasant discontent with high taxes, official corruption, rising rural debt, and famine in the countryside. Under colonialism, rural conditions often deteriorated, as land hunger increased and peasants were driven off the land to make way for plantation agriculture. Angry peasants then vented their frustration at the foreign invaders. For example, in Burma, the Buddhist monk Saya San led a peasant uprising against the British many years after they had completed their takeover. Similar forms of unrest occurred in various parts of India, where *zamindars* and rural villagers alike resisted government attempts to increase tax revenues. Yet another peasant uprising took place in Algeria in 1840 under the leadership of Abdel Qadir.

Sometimes the resentment had a religious basis, as in the Sudan where a revolt against the growing British presence had strong Islamic overtones, although it was initially provoked by Turkish misrule in Egypt. More significant than Roy's Brahmo Samaj in its impact on British policy was the famous Sepoy Mutiny of 1857 in India. The sepoys (derived from *sipahi*, a Turkish word meaning horseman or soldier) were native troops hired by the East India Company to protect British interests in the region. Unrest within Indian units of the colonial army had been common since early in the century, when it had been sparked by economic issues, religious sensitivities, or nascent anticolonial sentiment. Such attitudes intensified in the mid-1850s when the British instituted a new policy of shipping Indian troops abroad—a practice that exposed Hindus to pollution by foreigners. In 1857, tension erupted when the British adopted the new Enfield rifle for use by sepoy infantrymen. The new weapon was a muzzle-loader that used paper cartridges covered with animal fat and lard; because the cartridge had to be bitten off, it broke strictures against high-caste Hindus' eating animal products and Muslim prohibitions against eating pork. Protests among sepoy units in northern India turned into a full-scale mutiny, supported by risings in rural districts in various parts of the country. But the revolt lacked clear goals, while rivalries between Hindus and Muslims and discord

among leaders within each community prevented coordination of operations. Although Indian troops often fought bravely and outnumbered the British by 240,000 to 40,000, they were poorly organized, and the British forces (supplemented in many cases by sepoy troops) suppressed the rebellion.

Still, the revolt frightened the British and led to a number of major reforms. The proportion of native troops relative to those from Great Britain was reduced, and precedence was given to ethnic groups likely to be loyal to the British, such as the Sikhs of Punjab and the Gurkhas, an upland people from Nepal in the Himalaya Mountains. To avoid religious conflicts, ethnic groups were spread throughout the service rather than assigned to special units. The British also decided to suppress the final remnants of the hapless Mughal dynasty, which had supported the mutiny.

As we have noted, such forms of resistance cannot properly be called nationalist because they were essentially attempts to protect or restore traditional society and its institutions and were not motivated by the desire to create a "nation" in the modern sense of the word. In any event, such movements rarely met with success. Peasants armed with pikes and spears were no match for Western armies possessing the most terrifying weapons then known to human society. In a few cases, as with the Muslim revolt in the Sudan, the natives were able to defeat the invaders temporarily. But such successes were rare, and the late nineteenth century witnessed the seemingly inexorable march of the Western powers, armed with the Gatling gun (the first rapid-fire weapon and the precursor of the modern machine gun), to mastery of the globe.

Modern Nationalism

The first stage of resistance to the West in Asia and Africa had met with humiliation and failure and must have confirmed many Westerners' conviction that colonial peoples lacked both the strength and the know-how to create modern states and govern their own destinies. In fact, the process was just beginning. The next phase, which can be described as the rise of modern nationalism, began to take shape at the beginning of the twentieth century and was the product of the convergence of several factors. The primary sources of anticolonialist sentiment were found in a new class of Westernized intellectuals in the urban centers created by colonial rule. In many cases, this new urban middle class, composed of merchants, petty functionaries, clerks, students, and professionals, had been educated in Western-style schools.

A few had spent time in the West. In either case, they were the first generation of Asians and Africans to possess more than a rudimentary understanding of the institutions and values of the modern West. Many spoke Western languages, wore Western clothes, and worked in occupations connected with the colonial regime. Some, like Mahatma Gandhi in India, José Rizal in the Philippines, and Kwame Nkrumah in the Gold Coast, even wrote in the languages of their colonial masters.

The results were paradoxical. On the one hand, this "new class" admired Western culture and sometimes harbored a deep sense of contempt for traditional ways. On the other hand, many strongly resented the foreigners and their arrogant contempt for colonial peoples. While eager to introduce Western ideas and institutions into their own society, these intellectuals often resented the gap between ideal and reality, theory and practice, in colonial policy. Although Western political thought exalted democracy, equality, and individual freedom, these values were generally not applied in the colonies. Democratic institutions were primitive or nonexistent, and colonial subjects usually had access to only the most menial positions in the colonial bureaucracy. Equally important, the economic prosperity of the West was only imperfectly reflected in the colonies. To many Asians and Africans, colonialism meant the loss of their farmlands or demeaning and brutal employment on plantations or in sweatshops and factories run by foreigners.

Normally, middle-class Asians did not suffer in the same manner as impoverished peasants or menial workers on sugar or rubber plantations, but they, too, had complaints. They usually qualified only for menial jobs in the government or business. Even when employed, their salaries were normally lower than those of Europeans in similar occupations. The superiority of the Europeans over the natives was expressed in a variety of ways, including "whites only" clubs and the forms of language used to address colonial subjects. For example, Europeans would characteristically use the familiar form (normally used by adults to children) when talking to members of the local population.

Under these conditions, many of the new urban educated class were very ambivalent toward their colonial masters and the civilization that they represented. While willing to concede the superiority of many aspects of Western culture, these new intellectuals fiercely resented colonial rule and were determined to assert their own nationality and cultural destiny. Out of this mixture of hopes and resentments emerged the first stirrings of modern nationalism in Asia and Africa. During the first quarter of the century, in colonial and semicolonial societies across the entire arc of Asia from the Suez Canal to the shores of the Pacific Ocean, educated native peoples began to organize political parties and movements seeking reforms or the end of foreign rule and the restoration of independence.

RELIGION AND NATIONALISM

At first, many of the leaders of these movements did not focus clearly on the idea of nationhood, but tried to defend the economic interests or religious beliefs of the native population. In Burma, for example, the first expression of modern nationalism came from students at the University of Rangoon, who formed an organization to protest against official persecution of the Buddhist religion and British lack of respect for local religious traditions. Calling themselves Thakin (a polite term in the Burmese language meaning "lord" or "master," thus emphasizing their demand for the right to rule themselves), they protested against British arrogance and failure to observe local customs in Buddhist temples (visitors are expected to remove their footwear in a temple, a custom that was widely ignored by Europeans in colonial Burma). Only in the 1930s did they begin to focus specifically on the issue of national independence.

A similar example occurred in the Dutch East Indies, where the first quasi-political organization dedicated to the creation of a modern Indonesia, the Sarekat Islam (Islamic Association), began as a self-help society among Muslim merchants to fight against domination of the local economy by Chinese interests. Eventually, activist elements began to realize that the source of the problem was not the Chinese merchants but the colonial presence, and in the 1920s, Sarekat Islam was transformed into a new organization—the Nationalist Party of Indonesia (PNI)—that focused on the issue of national independence. Like the Thakins in Burma, this party would eventually lead the country to independence after World War II.

INDEPENDENCE OR MODERNIZATION? THE NATIONALIST QUANDARY

Building a new nation, however, requires more than a shared sense of grievances against the foreign invader. By what means was independence to be achieved? Was independence or modernization the more important objective? What kind of political and economic system should be adopted once colonial rule had been overthrown? What national or cultural concept should be adopted as the symbol of the new nation, and which institutions and values should be preserved from the past?

Questions such as these created lively and sometimes acrimonious debate among patriotic elements throughout the colonial world. If national independence was the desired end, how could it be achieved? Could the Westerners be persuaded to leave by nonviolent measures, or would force be required? If the Western presence could be beneficial in terms of introducing much-needed reforms in traditional societies, then a gradualist approach made sense. On the other hand, if the colonial regime was primarily an impediment to social and political change, then the first priority was to bring it to an end.

Another problem was how to adopt modern Western ideas and institutions while at the same time preserving the essential values that defined the indigenous culture. The vast majority of patriotic intellectuals were convinced that to survive, their societies must move with the times and adopt much of the Western way of life. The programs adopted by most nationalist parties displayed a devotion to such Western concepts as political democracy, economic industrialization, and national unity. Yet many were equally determined that the local culture could not, and should not, simply become a carbon copy of the West. What was the national identity, after all, if it did not incorporate some elements inherited from the traditional way of life?

One of the reasons for using traditional values was to provide ideological symbols that the common people could understand. If the desired end was national independence, then, almost by definition, the new political parties needed to enlist the mass of the population in the common struggle. But how could ignorant peasants, plantation workers, fishermen, and sheepherders be made to understand complicated and unfamiliar concepts like democracy, industrialization, and nationhood? The problem was often one of communication, for most urban intellectuals had little in common with the teeming population in the countryside. As the Indonesian intellectual Sutan Sjahrir lamented, many Westernized intellectuals had more in common with their colonial rulers than with the native population in the rural villages (see box on p. 102). As one French colonial official remarked in some surprise to a Vietnamese reformist, "Why, Monsieur, you are more French than I am!"

GANDHI AND THE INDIAN NATIONAL CONGRESS

Nowhere in the colonial world were these issues debated more vigorously than in India. Before the Sepoy Mutiny, Indian consciousness had focused primarily on the question of religious identity. But in the latter half of the nineteenth century, a stronger sense of national consciousness began to arise, provoked by the conservative policies and racial arrogance of the British colonial authorities.

The first Indian nationalists were almost invariably upper class and educated. Many of them were from urban areas such as Bombay, Madras, and Calcutta. Some were trained in law and were members of the civil service. At first, many tended to prefer reform to revolution and accepted the idea that India needed modernization before it could handle the problems of independence. Otherwise, it would slip back into traditionalism. An exponent of this view was Gopal Gokhale (1866–1915), a moderate nationalist who hoped that he could convince the British to bring about needed reforms in Indian society. Gokhale and other like-minded reformists did have some effect. In the 1880s, the government launched a series of reforms introducing a measure of self-government for the first time. All too often, however, such efforts were sabotaged by local British officials.

The slow pace of reform convinced many Indian nationalists that relying on British benevolence was futile. In 1885, a small group of Indians, with some British participation, met in Bombay to form the Indian National Congress (INC). They hoped to speak for all India, but most were high-caste English-trained Hindus. Like their reformist predecessors, members of the INC did not demand immediate independence and accepted the need for reforms to end traditional abuses like child marriage and *sati*. At the same time, they called for an Indian share in the governing process and more spending on economic development and less on military campaigns along the frontier.

The British responded with a few concessions, such as accepting the principle of elective Indian participation on government councils, but in general change was glacially slow. As impatient members of the INC became disillusioned, radical leaders such as Balwantrao Tilak (1856–1920) openly criticized the British while defending traditional customs like child marriage to solicit support from conservative elements within the local population. Tilak's activities split the INC between moderates and radicals, and he and his followers formed the New Party, which called for the use of terrorism and violence to achieve national independence. Tilak was eventually convicted of sedition.

The INC also had difficulty reconciling religious differences within its ranks. The stated goal of the INC was to seek self-determination for all Indians regardless of class or religious affiliation, but many of its leaders were

⟫ The Meeting of East and West ⟪

One of the most painful dilemmas for many thoughtful nationalist leaders in Asia during the colonial era was whether to import Western ways or seek to preserve traditional institutions and customs. Although the famous British poet Rudyard Kipling had remarked that "East is East and West is West, and ne'er the twain shall meet," in fact the situation was by no means so clear-cut. Many intellectuals were genuinely attracted to some of the more appealing elements of Western culture and felt that they should be adopted for use in their own countries. Others were offended by the crass materialist worldview that characterized much of Western culture and sought to preserve the superior qualities of their own civilization. Some, while arguing that some degree of Westernization was needed, recognized the emotional appeal of traditional culture and its symbolic importance in appealing for support from the mass of the population.

In virtually every colonial society in Asia, nationalist leaders were divided on how to resolve the dilemma. Some called for wholehearted Westernization, taking the view that the traditional heritage would be an impediment to creating a modern and independent society. Others sought their own unique "national" road to development, arguing that the inherent "spirituality" of Asian culture was superior to the alleged "materialism" of the West.

Few articulated the dilemma as poignantly as Sutan Sjahrir (1909–1966), an Indonesian nationalist leader who served briefly as prime minister of the Republic of Indonesia in the 1950s. Like many Western-educated Asian intellectuals, he was tortured by the realization that by education and outlook he was closer to his colonial masters than to his own people. "Am I perhaps estranged from my people?" he lamented in a letter to his wife in 1935. "Why am I vexed by the things that fill their lives, and to which they are so attached? Why are the things that contain beauty for them and aroused their gentler emotions only senseless and displeasing for me?"

The problem, as Sjahrir perceptively noted, was that citizens of Western countries saw the concept of modernity as arising naturally from within their own national cultures. In Holland, he pointed out, "They build—both consciously and unconsciously—on what is already there." Even those who oppose their own past and tradition "do so as a method of application or as a starting point." Western-educated Asians, he lamented, did not have that option, because most of them believed that their own "feudal" cultures could not possibly provide a realistic starting point for building a modern society.

In the end, he concluded, many Asian intellectuals like himself wanted to have it both ways—both Western science and Eastern philosophy. Unfortunately, as Sjahrir and other Asian intellectuals of his generation would discover after the restoration of national independence following World War II, materialism and spirituality are difficult to synthesize. Once set in motion, the powerful force of materialism inevitably clashes with the traditional spiritual outlook.

Source: Sutan Sjahrir, *Out of Exile*, quoted in *The World of Southeast Asia: Selected Historical Readings*, Harry J. Benda and John A. Larkin, eds. (New York: Harper & Row, 1967).

Hindu and inevitably reflected Hindu concerns. By the first decade of the twentieth century, Muslims began to call for the creation of a separate Muslim League to represent the interests of the millions of Muslims in Indian society.

In 1913, the return of a young Hindu lawyer from South Africa to become active in the INC transformed the movement and galvanized India's struggle for independence and identity. Mohandas Gandhi was born in 1869 in Gujarat, in western India, the son of a government minister. In the late nineteenth century, he studied in London and became a lawyer. In 1893, he went to South Africa to work in a law firm serving Indian emigrés working as laborers there. He soon became aware of the racial prejudice and exploitation experienced by Indians living in the territory and tried to organize them to protect their living conditions.

On his return to India, Gandhi immediately became active in the independence movement. Using his experience in South Africa, he set up a movement based on nonviolent resistance (the Indian term was *satyagraha*, "hold fast to the truth") to try to force the British to improve the lot of the poor and grant independence to India. His goal was twofold: to convert the British to his views while simultaneously strengthening the unity and sense of self-respect of his compatriots. Gandhi was particularly concerned about the plight of the millions of untouchables, whom he called *harijans*, or "children of God." When the British attempted to suppress dissent, he called on his followers to refuse to obey British regulations. He began to manufacture his own clothes (Gandhi now dressed in a simple *dhoti* made of coarse homespun cotton) and adopted the spinning wheel as a symbol of Indian resistance to imports of British textiles.

Gandhi, now increasingly known as India's "Great Soul" (*Mahatma*), organized mass protests to achieve his aims, but in 1919 they got out of hand and led to violence and British reprisals. British troops killed hundreds of unarmed protesters in the enclosed square in the city of Amritsar in northwestern India. When the protests spread, Gandhi was horrified at the violence and briefly retreated from active politics. Nevertheless, he was arrested for his role in the protests and spent several years in prison.

Gandhi combined his anticolonial activities with an appeal to the spiritual instincts of all Indians. Though born and raised a Hindu, he possessed a universalist approach to the idea of God that transcended individual religion, although it was shaped by the historical themes of Hindu religious belief. At a speech given in London in September 1931, he expressed his view of the nature of God as "an indefinable mysterious power that pervades everything . . ., an unseen power which makes itself felt and yet defies all proof."[2]

While Gandhi was in prison, the political situation continued to evolve. In 1921, the British passed the Government of India Act to expand the role of Indians in the governing process and transform the heretofore advisory Legislative Council into a bicameral parliament, two-thirds of whose members would be elected. Similar bodies were created at the provincial level. In a stroke, 5 million Indians were enfranchised. But such reforms were no longer enough for many members of the INC, which under its new leader, Motilal Nehru, wanted to push aggressively for full independence. The British exacerbated the situation by increasing the salt tax and prohibiting the Indian people from manufacturing or harvesting their own salt. Gandhi, now released from prison, returned to his earlier policy of civil disobedience by openly joining several dozen supporters in a 200-mile walk to the sea, where he picked up a lump of salt and urged Indians to ignore the law. Gandhi and many other members of the INC were arrested (see box on p. 104).

In the 1930s, a new figure entered the movement in the person of Jawaharlal Nehru, son of the INC leader Motilal Nehru. Educated in the law in Great Britain and

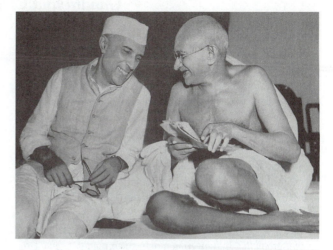

◆ **Gandhi and Nehru.** Mahatma Gandhi (on the right), India's "Great Soul," became the emotional leader of India's struggle for independence from British colonial rule. Unlike many other nationalist leaders, Gandhi rejected the materialistic culture of the West and urged his followers to return to the native traditions of the Indian village. To illustrate his point, Gandhi dressed in the simple Indian *dhoti* rather than in the Western fashion favored by many of his colleagues. Along with Gandhi, Jawaharlal Nehru was a leading figure in the Indian struggle for independence. Unlike Gandhi, however, his goal was to transform India into a modern industrial society. After independence, he became the nation's prime minister until his death in 1964.

a brahmin by birth, Nehru personified the new Anglo-Indian politician: secular, rational, upper class, and intellectual. In fact, he appeared to be everything that Gandhi was not. With his emergence, the independence movement embarked on two paths, religious and secular, native and Western, traditional and modern. The dual character of the INC leadership may well have strengthened the movement by bringing together the two primary impulses behind the desire for independence: elite nationalism and the primal force of Indian traditionalism. But it portended trouble for the nation's new leadership in defining India's future path in the contemporary world. In the meantime, Muslim discontent with Hindu dominance over the INC was increasing. In 1930, the Muslim League called for the creation of a separate Muslim state of Pakistan (meaning "the land of the pure") in the northwest. As communal strife between Hindus and Muslims increased, many Indians came to realize with sorrow (and some British colonialists with satisfaction) that British rule was all that stood between peace and civil war.

❧ Gandhi and Civil Disobedience ❧

In 1930, Mohandas Gandhi, the sixty-one-year-old leader of the movement for Indian independence from British rule, began a march to the sea with seventy-eight followers. Their destination was Dandi, a little coastal town more than 200 miles away. The group covered about 12 miles a day. As they went, Gandhi preached his doctrine of nonviolent resistance to British rule in every village he passed through: "Civil disobedience is the inherent right of a citizen. He dare not give it up without ceasing to be a man." By the time he reached Dandi, twenty-four days later, his small group had become a nonviolent army of thousands. On the beach, Gandhi picked up a pinch of salt from the sand. All along the coast, thousands did likewise, openly breaking British laws that prohibited Indians from making their own salt. The British government had long profited from its monopoly on the making and sale of salt, an item much in demand in a tropical country. By their simple act of disobedience, Gandhi and his followers had taken yet another step on their long march to independence,

After his return to India in 1913, Gandhi had gradually became convinced that only a policy of civil disobedience could effectively bring an end to British rule in the subcontinent. In a letter to Lord Irwin, the viceroy of India, he sought to persuade the British to adopt the necessary measures to avoid future conflict. If the curse of British rule were not brought to an end, he warned, the "party of violence" would soon have the upper hand. While conceding that its objectives were the same as his, Gandhi declared his conviction that violence could not bring the desired relief to "the dumb millions."

Gandhi admitted that many of his colleagues dismissed his program of nonviolence as inadequate, but he argued that, properly led, it could become an intensely active force. It was his purpose to set that force in motion, both against the organized violence of British rule and the disorganized force of the growing Indian party of violence.

Gandhi's policy of nonviolence won respect throughout the world, and India eventually achieved its independence without the bitter conflicts that marked the transition in many other parts of Asia. But, as the "great soul" undoubtedly feared, violence remained just beneath the surface in colonial Indian society and, as we shall see, broke out in an orgy of fratricidal bloodletting at the virtual moment of the restoration of independence.

Source: Martin Green, ed., *Gandhi in India: In His Own Words* (Hanover, NH: University Press of New England, 1987), pp. 113–118.

The Nationalist Revolt in the Middle East

In the Middle East, as in Europe, World War I hastened the collapse of old empires. The Ottoman Empire, which had dominated the eastern Mediterranean since the seizure of Constantinople in 1453, had been growing steadily weaker since the end of the eighteenth century, troubled by rising governmental corruption, a decline in the effectiveness of the sultans, and the loss of considerable territory in the Balkans and southwestern Russia. In North Africa, Ottoman authority, tenuous at best, had disintegrated in the nineteenth century, enabling the French to seize Algeria and Tunisia and the British to establish a protectorate over the Nile River valley.

MUSTAPHA KEMAL AND THE MODERNIZATION OF TURKEY

Reformist elements in Istanbul, to be sure, had tried to resist the trend. The first phase had taken place in the eighteenth century, when Westernizing forces, concerned at the shrinkage of the empire, had tried to modernize the army. But, as other traditional forces would later discover, a modern army cannot compensate for decrepit political and social institutions. One energetic sultan, Selim III (r. 1789–1807), tried to establish a "new order" that would streamline both the civilian and military bureaucracies, but janissary forces (the emperor's private guard recruited from among Christian subjects in the Balkans), alarmed at the potential loss of their power, revolted and brought the experiment to an end. Further efforts during the first half of the nineteenth century were somewhat more successful and resulted in the removal of the janissaries from power and the institution of a series of bureaucratic, military, and educational reforms. New roads were built, the power of local landlords was reduced, and an Imperial Rescript issued in 1856 granted equal rights to all subjects of the empire, whatever their religious preference.

But military defeats continued: Greece declared its independence, and Ottoman power declined steadily in the Middle East. A rising sense of nationality among

Serbs, Armenians, and other minority peoples threatened the internal stability and cohesion of the empire. In the 1870s, a new generation of Ottoman reformers seized power in Istanbul and pushed through a constitution aimed at forming a legislative assembly that would represent all the peoples in the state. But the sultan they placed on the throne, Abdulhamid (r. 1876–1909), suspended the new charter and attempted to rule by traditional authoritarian means.

By the end of the nineteenth century, the defunct 1876 constitution had become a symbol of change for reformist elements, now grouped together under the common name Young Turks (undoubtedly borrowed from the Young Italy nationalist movement earlier in the century). Leading members of the group established a Committee of Union and Progress (CUP), which found support within the Ottoman army and administration and among Turks living in exile. In 1908, Young Turk elements forced the sultan to restore the constitution, and he was removed from power the following year.

But the Young Turks had appeared at a moment of extreme fragility for the empire. Internal rebellions, combined with Austrian annexations of Ottoman territories in the Balkans, undermined support for the new government and provoked the army to step in. With most minorities from the old empire now removed from Istanbul's authority, many ethnic Turks began to embrace a new concept of a Turkish state based on all those of Turkish nationality.

The final blow to the old empire came in World War I, when the Ottoman government decided to ally with Germany in the hope of driving the British from Egypt and restoring Ottoman rule over the Nile valley. The new sultan called for a holy war by Muslim subjects in Russia and in British- and French-ruled territories in the Middle East. In response, the British declared an official protectorate over Egypt and, aided by the efforts of the dashing if eccentric British adventurer T. E. Lawrence (popularly known as Lawrence of Arabia), sought to undermine Ottoman rule in the Arabian peninsula by encouraging Arab nationalist activities there. In 1916, the local governor of Mecca, encouraged by the British, declared Arabia independent from Ottoman rule, while British troops, advancing from Egypt, seized Palestine. In October 1918, having suffered more than 300,000 casualties during the war, the Ottoman Empire negotiated an armistice with the Allied powers.

During the next few years, the tottering empire began to fall apart, as the British and the French made plans to divide up Ottoman territories in the Middle East and the Greeks won Allied approval to seize the western parts of the Anatolian peninsula for their dream of recreating the substance of the old Byzantine Empire. The impending collapse energized key elements in Turkey under the leadership of war hero Colonel Mustapha Kemal (1881–1938), who had commanded Turkish forces in their heroic defense of the Dardanelles against a British invasion during World War I. Now he resigned from the army and convoked a national congress that called for the creation of an elected government and the preservation of the remaining territories of the old empire in a new Republic of Turkey. Establishing his new capital at Ankara, Kemal's forces drove the Greeks from the Anatolian peninsula and persuaded the British to agree to a new treaty. In 1923, the last of the Ottoman sultans fled the country, which was now declared a Turkish republic. The Ottoman Empire had finally come to an end.

During the next few years, President Mustapha Kemal (now popularly known as Ataturk, or "father Turk") attempted to transform Turkey into a modern secular republic. The trappings of a democratic system were put in place, centered on an elected Grand National Assembly, but the president was relatively intolerant of opposition and harshly suppressed critics of his rule. Turkish nationalism was emphasized, and the Turkish language, now written in the Roman alphabet, was shorn of many of its Arabic elements. Popular education was emphasized, old aristocratic titles like pasha and bey were abolished, and all Turkish citizens were given family names in the European style.

Ataturk also took steps to modernize the economy, overseeing the establishment of a light industrial sector producing textiles, glass, paper, and cement and instituting a five-year plan on the Soviet model to provide for state direction over the economy. Ataturk was no admirer of Soviet communism, however, and the Turkish economy can be better described as a form of state capitalism. He also encouraged the modernization of the agricultural sector through the establishment of training institutions and model farms, but such reforms had relatively little effect on the nation's predominantly conservative peasantry.

Perhaps the most significant aspect of Ataturk's reform program was his attempt to break the power of the Islamic religion and transform Turkey into a secular state. The caliphate was formally abolished in 1924, and the Shari'ya (Islamic law) was replaced by a revised version of the Swiss law code. The fez (the brimless cap worn by Turkish Muslims) was abolished as a form of headdress, and women were forbidden to wear the veil in the traditional Islamic custom. Women received the

♦ **Mustapha Kemal Ataturk.** The war hero Mustapha Kemal took the initiative in creating a new Republic of Turkey. As president of the new republic, Ataturk (or "father Turk," as he came to be called) worked hard to transform Turkey into a modern secular state by modernizing the economy, adopting Western styles of dress and breaking the powerful hold of Islamic traditions.

cepted in practice, especially by devout Muslims, the bulk of the changes that he introduced were retained after his death in 1938. In virtually every respect, the Turkish republic was the product of his determined efforts to create a modern Turkish nation.

MODERNIZATION IN IRAN

In the meantime, a similar process was under way in Persia. Under the Qajar dynasty (1794–1925), the country had not been very successful in resisting Russian advances in the Caucasus or resolving its domestic problems. To secure themselves from foreign influence, the shahs moved the capital from Tabriz to Tehran, in a mountainous area just south of the Caspian Sea. During the mid-nineteenth century, one modernizing shah attempted to introduce political and economic reforms, but was impeded by resistance from tribal and religious—predominantly Shi'ite—forces. To buttress its rule, the dynasty turned increasingly to Russia and Great Britain to protect itself from its own people.

Eventually, the growing foreign presence led to the rise of a native Persian nationalist movement. Its efforts were largely directed against Russian advances in the northwest and the growing European influence within the small modern industrial sector, the profits from which left the country or disappeared into the hands of the dynasty's ruling elite. Supported actively by Shi'ite religious leaders, opposition to the regime rose steadily among both peasants and merchants in the cities, and in 1906 popular pressures forced the reigning shah to grant a constitution on the Western model. It was an eerie foretaste of the revolution of 1979.

As in the Ottoman Empire and Manchu China, however, the modernizers had moved too soon, before their power base was secure. With the support of the Russians and the British, the shah was able to retain control, while the two foreign powers began to divide the country into separate spheres of influence. One reason for the growing foreign presence in Persia was the discovery of oil reserves in the southern part of the country in 1908. Within a few years, oil exports increased rapidly, with the bulk of the profits going into the pockets of British investors.

In 1921, an officer in the Persian army by the name of Reza Khan (1878–1944) led a mutiny that seized power in Tehran. The new ruler's original intention had been to establish a republic, but resistance from traditional forces impeded his efforts, and in 1925 a new Pahlavi dynasty, with Reza Khan as shah, replaced the now defunct Qajar dynasty. During the next few years, Reza

right to vote in 1934 and were legally guaranteed equal rights with men in all aspects of marriage and inheritance. Education and the professions were now open to citizens of both sexes, and some women even began to take part in politics. All citizens were given the right to convert to another religion at will.

Finally, Ataturk attempted to break the waning power of the various religious orders of Islam, abolishing all monasteries and brotherhoods and declaring,

> The straightest, truest way is the way of civilization. To be a man, it is enough to do as civilization requires. The heads of the brotherhoods will understand this truth I have uttered in all its clarity, and will of their own accord at once close their convents, and accept the fact that their disciples have at last come of age.[3]

The legacy of Mustapha Kemal Ataturk was enormous. Although not all of his reforms were widely ac-

Khan attempted to follow the example of Mustapha Kemal Ataturk in Turkey, introducing a number of reforms to strengthen the central government, modernize the civilian and military bureaucracy, and establish a modern economic infrastructure.

Unlike Mustapha Kemal Ataturk, Reza Khan did not attempt to destroy the power of Islamic beliefs, but he did encourage the establishment of a Western-style educational system and forbade women to wear the veil in public. To strengthen the sense of Persian nationalism and reduce the power of Islam, he attempted to popularize the symbols and beliefs of pre-Islamic times. Like his Qajar predecessors, however, Reza Khan was hindered by strong foreign influence. When the Soviet Union and Great Britain decided to send troops into the country during World War II, he resigned in protest and died three years later.

THE RISE OF ARAB NATIONALISM AND THE PROBLEM OF PALESTINE

As we have seen, the Arab uprising during World War I helped bring about the demise of the Ottoman Empire. Actually, unrest against Ottoman rule had existed in the Arabian peninsula since the eighteenth century, when the Wahhabi revolt attempted to drive out the outside influences and cleanse Islam of corrupt practices that had developed in past centuries. The revolt was eventually suppressed, but the influence of the Wahhabi movement persisted, revitalized in part by resistance to the centralizing and modernizing efforts of reformist elements in the nineteenth century.

World War I offered an opportunity for the Arabs to throw off the shackles of Ottoman rule—but what would replace them? The Arabs were not a nation, but an idea, a loose collection of peoples who often do not see eye to eye on what constitutes their common sense of community. Disagreement over what constitutes an Arab has plagued generations of political leaders who have sought unsuccessfully to knit together the disparate peoples of the region into a single Arab nation.

When the Arab leaders in Mecca declared their independence from Ottoman rule in 1916, they had hoped for British support, but they were to be sorely disappointed. At the close of the war, the British and French agreed to create a number of mandates in the area to be placed under the general supervision of the League of Nations. Iraq and Jordan were assigned to the British; Syria and Lebanon (the two areas were separated so that Christian peoples in Lebanon could be placed under Christian administration) were given to the French.

The land of Palestine—once the home of the Jews but now inhabited primarily by Muslim Palestinians—became a separate mandate. According to the Balfour Declaration, issued by the British foreign secretary Lord Balfour in November 1917, Palestine was to be a national home for the Jews. The declaration was ambiguous on the legal status of the territory and promised that the decision would not undermine the rights of the non-Jewish peoples currently living in the area. But Arab nationalists were incensed. How could a national home for the Jewish people be established in a territory where 90 percent of the population was Muslim?

In the early 1920s, a leader of the Wahhabi movement, Ibn Saud (1880–1953), united Arab tribes in the northern part of the Arabian peninsula and drove out the remnants of Ottoman rule. Ibn Saud was a descendant of the family that had led the Wahhabi revolt in the eighteenth century. Devout and gifted, he won broad support among Arab tribal peoples and established the kingdom of Saudi Arabia throughout much of the peninsula in 1932.

At first his new kingdom, consisting essentially of the vast wastes of central Arabia, was desperately poor. Its financial resources were limited to the income from Muslim pilgrims visiting the holy sites in Mecca and Medina. But during the 1930s, American companies began to explore for oil, and in 1938, Standard Oil made a successful strike at Dahran, on the Persian Gulf. Soon an Arabian-American oil conglomerate, popularly called Aramco, was established, and the isolated kingdom was suddenly inundated by Western oilmen and untold wealth.

In the meantime, Jewish settlers began to arrive in Palestine in response to the promises made in the Balfour Declaration. As tensions between the new arrivals and existing Muslim residents began to escalate during the 1930s, the British tried to restrict Jewish immigration into the territory and rejected the concept of a separate state. The stage was set for the conflicts that would take place in the region after World War II.

Nationalism and Revolution in Asia and Africa

Before the Russian Revolution, to most intellectuals in Asia and Africa, Westernization meant the capitalist democratic civilization of Western Europe and the United States, not the doctrine of social revolution developed by Karl Marx. Until 1917, Marxism was regarded as a utopian idea rather than a concrete system of government. Moreover, to many intellectuals, Marxism appeared to have little relevance to conditions in Asia and Africa. Marxist doctrine, after all, declared that a communist society would arise only from the ashes of an advanced capitalism that had already passed through the stage of industrial revolution. From the perspective of Marxist historical analysis, most societies in Asia and Africa were still at the feudal stage of development; they lacked the economic conditions and political awareness to achieve a socialist revolution that would bring the working class to power. Finally, the Marxist view of nationalism and religion had little appeal to many patriotic intellectuals in the non-Western world. Marx believed that nationhood and religion were essentially false ideas that diverted the attention of the oppressed masses from the critical issues of class struggle and, in his phrase, the exploitation of one person by another. Instead, Marx stressed the importance of an "internationalist" outlook based on class consciousness and the eventual creation of a classless society with no artificial divisions based on culture, nation, or religion.

For these reasons, many patriotic non-Western intellectuals initially found Marxism to be both irrelevant and unappealing. That situation began to change after the Russian Revolution in 1917. The rise to power of Lenin's Bolsheviks demonstrated that a revolutionary party espousing Marxist principles could overturn a corrupt, outdated system and launch a new experiment dedicated to ending human inequality and achieving a paradise on earth. In 1920, Lenin proposed a new revolutionary strategy designed to relate Marxist doctrine and practice to non-Western societies. His reasons were not entirely altruistic. Soviet Russia, surrounded by capitalist powers, desperately needed allies in its struggle to survive in a hostile world. To Lenin, the anticolonial movements emerging in North Africa, Asia, and the Middle East after World War I were natural allies of the beleaguered new regime in Moscow. Lenin was convinced that only the ability of the imperialist powers to find markets, raw materials, and sources of capital investment in the non-Western world kept capitalism alive. If the tentacles of capitalist influence in Asia and Africa could be severed, then imperialism itself would ultimately weaken and collapse.

Establishing such an alliance was not easy, however. Most nationalist leaders in colonial countries belonged to the urban middle class, and many abhorred the idea of a comprehensive revolution to create a totally egalitarian society. In addition, many still adhered to traditional religious beliefs and were opposed to the atheistic principles of classical Marxism.

Since it was unrealistic to expect bourgeois nationalist support for social revolution, Lenin sought a compromise by which Communist parties could be organized among the working classes in the preindustrial societies of Asia and Africa. These parties would then forge informal alliances with existing middle-class parties to struggle against the common enemies of feudal reaction (the remnants of the traditional ruling class) and Western imperialism. Such an alliance, of course, could not be permanent because many bourgeois nationalists in Asia and Africa would reject an egalitarian, classless society. Once the imperialists had been overthrown, therefore, the Communist parties would turn against their erstwhile nationalist partners to seize power on their own and carry out the socialist revolution. Lenin thus proposed a two-stage revolution: an initial "national democratic" stage followed by a "proletarian socialist" stage.

Lenin's strategy became a major element in Soviet foreign policy in the 1920s. Soviet agents fanned out across the world to carry Marxism beyond the boundaries of industrial Europe. The primary instrument of this effort was the Communist International, or Comintern for short. Formed in 1919 at Lenin's prodding, the Comintern was a worldwide organization of Communist parties dedicated to the advancement of world revolution. At its headquarters in Moscow, agents from around the world were trained in the precepts of world communism and then sent back to their own countries to form Marxist parties and promote the cause of social revolution. By the end of the 1920s, almost every colonial or semicolonial society in Asia had a party based on Marxist principles. The Soviets had less success in the Middle East, where Marxist ideology appealed mainly to minorities such as Jews and Armenians in the cities, or in black Africa, where Soviet strategists in any case did not feel conditions were sufficiently advanced for the creation of Communist organizations. Later on, they had some success in the labor unions of countries such as Sudan and the Ivory Coast.

According to Marxist doctrine, the rank and file of Communist parties should be urban factory workers alienated from capitalist society by inhuman working conditions. In practice, many of the leading elements even in European Communist parties tended to be urban intellectuals or members of the lower middle class (in Marxist parlance, the "petty bourgeoisie"). That phenomenon was even more true in the non-Western world, where most early Marxists were rootless intellectuals. Some were probably drawn into the movement for patriotic reasons and saw Marxist doctrine as a new, more effective means of modernizing their societies and removing the power of exploitative colonialism (see box on p. 109). Others were attracted by the basic message of

The Path to Liberation

In 1919, the Vietnamese patriot Ho Chi Minh was living in exile in France, where he sought to find the means to liberate his country from French colonial rule. In the summer of 1920, he read a French translation of Vladimir Lenin's report, "Theses on the National and Colonial Questions," which had just been presented at a meeting of Communist parties from various countries held in Moscow. The effect on the young Ho Chi Minh was electric. Although sitting alone in his small flat in Paris, he shouted aloud as if addressing large crowds: "Dear martyrs, compatriots! This is what we need, this is the path of our liberation!"

As he pointed out in an article many years later, Ho Chi Minh was less interested in the utopian aspects of Marxist doctrine than in the strategy that Marx's disciple Lenin had outlined for promoting revolution in the colonial societies in Asia and Africa. In his "Theses," Lenin had proposed a strategy calling for future Communist parties in colonial areas to ally with middle-class nationalist elements in a common struggle against the ruling colonial regimes. Lenin's goal was to link the class struggle in Western industrialized societies with the anticolonial struggle in preindustrial colonial and semicolonial areas in Asia and North Africa. In classical Marxism, such economically backward societies would not be ripe for a socialist revolution until they had passed through the stage of capitalism, but Lenin realized that rising anticolonial sentiment among Asian peoples could make them a worthy ally against global imperialism. In Lenin's view, without access to the markets and resources of their colonies, which guaranteed profits to the industrialists, the capitalist regimes of Europe were bound to collapse.

Lenin thus proposed that Communist parties based on the small local working class and led by radical intellectuals be established in colonial territories. Although such parties would lack the experience and mass base sufficient to triumph on their own over the entrenched power of colonial regimes, with the support of angry peasants and nationalist elements within the middle class, they might hope to overthrow colonial governments and restore true national independence. Once that "first stage" of the revolution had been carried through, local Communist parties could then mobilize progressive forces within the alliance to isolate their erstwhile middle-class allies and seize power on their own.

To Ho Chi Minh, Lenin's strategy was tailor-made to assist colonial peoples like those in Southeast Asia in liberating themselves from foreign domination. Returning to Asia in the mid-1920s, he founded a Vietnamese Communist party and began to seek support from nationalist forces and the oppressed peasantry to lead the peoples of Indochina in a struggle against French colonial rule. As we shall see, Ho applied Lenin's strategy with considerable effectiveness against the French, and later against the United States, and it became a model for liberation struggles throughout the Third World.

Source: Ho Chi Minh, "The Path Which Led Me to Leninism," in *Vietnam: History, Documents, and Opinions on a Major World Crisis*, ed. Marvin Gettelman (New York: Fawcett Publications, 1965), pp. 30–32.

egalitarian communism and the utopian dream of a classless society. All who joined found it a stirring message of release from oppression and a practical strategy for the liberation of their society from colonial rule. For those who had lost their faith in traditional religion, it often served as a new secular ideology, dealing not with the hereafter but with the here and now or, indeed, with a remote future when the state would wither away and the "classless society" would replace the lost truth of traditional faiths.

Of course, the new doctrine's appeal was not the same in all non-Western societies. In Confucian societies such as China and Vietnam, where traditional belief systems had been badly discredited by their failure to counter the Western challenge, communism had an immediate impact and rapidly became a major factor in the anticolonial movement. In Buddhist and Muslim societies, where traditional religion remained strong and actually became a cohesive factor within the resistance movement, communism had less success and was forced to adapt to local conditions in order to survive.

Sometimes, as in Malaya (where the sense of nationhood was weak) or Thailand (which, alone in Southeast Asia, had not fallen under colonial rule), support for the local Communist party came from minority groups such as the overseas Chinese community in the cities. In Egypt and Syria, the Marxists often found adherents among the sons of wealthy merchants and landowners. To maximize their appeal and minimize potential conflict with traditional ideas, Communist parties frequently attempted to adjust Marxist doctrine to indigenous values and institutions. In the Middle East, for example, the Ba'ath party in Syria adopted a hybrid socialism combining Marxism with Arab nationalism. In Africa, radical intellectuals talked vaguely of a uniquely "African road to socialism."

The degree to which these parties were successful in establishing alliances with existing nationalist parties and building a solid base of support among the mass of the population also varied from place to place. In some instances, the local Communists were briefly able to establish a cooperative relationship with bourgeois parties in the struggle against Western imperialism. The most famous example was the alliance between the Chinese Communist party (CCP) and Sun Yat-sen's Nationalist Party (discussed in the next section).

In the Dutch East Indies, the Indonesian Communist Party (known as the PKI) allied with the middle-class nationalist group Sarekat Islam, but later broke loose in an effort to organize its own mass movement among the poor peasants. Similar problems were encountered in French Indochina, where Vietnamese Communists organized by the Moscow-trained revolutionary Ho Chi Minh sought to cooperate with bourgeois nationalist parties against the colonial regime. In 1928, these efforts were abandoned when the Comintern, reacting to Chiang Kai-shek's betrayal of the alliance with the Chinese Communist Party, declared that Communist parties should restrict their recruiting efforts to the most revolutionary elements in society—notably, the urban intellectuals and the working class. Harassed by colonial authorities and saddled with strategic directions from Moscow that often had little relevance to local conditions, Communist parties in most colonial societies had little success in the 1930s and failed to build a secure base of support among the mass of the population.

Revolution in China

Overall, revolutionary Marxism had its greatest impact in China, where a group of young radicals, including several faculty and staff members from prestigious Peking University, founded the Chinese Communist Party (CCP) in 1921. The rise of the CCP was a consequence of the failed revolution of 1911. When political forces are too weak or divided to consolidate their power during a period of instability, the military usually steps in to fill the vacuum. In China, Sun Yat-sen and his colleagues had accepted General Yuan Shikai as president of the new Chinese republic in 1911 because they lacked the military force to compete with his control over the army. Moreover, many feared, perhaps rightly, that if the revolt lapsed into chaos, the Western powers would intervene and the last shreds of Chinese sovereignty would be lost. But some had misgivings about Yuan's intentions. As one remarked in a letter to a friend, "We don't know whether he will be a George Washington or a Napoleon."

As it turned out, he was neither. Understanding little of the new ideas sweeping into China from the West, Yuan ruled in a traditional manner, reviving Confucian rituals and institutions and eventually trying to found a new imperial dynasty. Yuan's dictatorial inclinations rapidly led to clashes with Sun's party, now renamed the *Guomindang (Kuomintang)* or Nationalist Party. When Yuan dissolved the new parliament, the Nationalists launched a rebellion. When it failed, Sun Yat-sen fled to Japan.

Yuan was strong enough to brush off the challenge from the revolutionary forces, but not to turn back the clock of history. He died in 1916 (apparently of natural causes, although legend holds that his heart was broken by growing popular resistance to his imperial pretensions) and was succeeded by one of his military subordinates. For the next several years, China slipped into semi-anarchy, as the power of the central government disintegrated and military warlords seized power in the provinces.

Mr. Science and Mr. Democracy: The New Culture Movement

Although the failure of the 1911 revolution was a clear sign that China was not yet ready for radical change, discontent with existing conditions continued to rise in various sectors of Chinese society. The most vocal protests came from radical intellectuals who opposed Yuan Shikai's conservative rule but were now convinced that political change could not take place until the Chinese people were more familiar with trends in the outside world. Braving the displeasure of Yuan Shikai and his successors, progressive intellectuals at Peking University launched the New Culture Movement, aimed at abolishing the remnants of the old system and introducing Western values and institutions into China. Using the classrooms of China's most prestigious university as well as the pages of newly established progressive magazines and newspapers, Chinese intellectuals presented the Chinese people with a bewildering mix of new ideas, from the philosophy of Friedrich Nietszche and Bertrand

Russell to the educational views of the American John Dewey and the feminist plays of Henrik Ibsen. As such ideas flooded into China, they stirred up a new generation of educated Chinese youth, who chanted "Down with Confucius and sons" and talked of a new era dominated by "Mr. Sai" (Mr. Science) and "Mr. De" (Mr. Democracy). No one was a greater defender of free thought and speech than the chancellor of Peking University, Cai Yuanpei (Ts'ai Yuan-p'ei):

> So far as theoretical ideas are concerned, I follow the principles of "freedom of thought" and an attitude of broad tolerance in accordance with the practice of universities the world over. . . . Regardless of what school of thought a person may adhere to, so long as that person's ideas are justified and conform to reason and have not been passed by through the process of natural selection, although there may be controversy, such ideas have a right to be presented.[4]

The problem was that appeals for American-style democracy and women's liberation had little relevance to Chinese peasants, most of whom were still illiterate and concerned above all with survival. Consequently, the New Culture Movement did not win widespread support outside the urban areas. It certainly earned the distrust of conservative military officers, one of whom threatened to lob artillery shells into Peking University to destroy the poisonous new ideas and their advocates.

Discontent among intellectuals, however, was soon joined by the rising chorus of public protest against Japan's efforts to expand its influence on the mainland. During the first decade of the twentieth century, Japan had taken advantage of the Qing's decline to extend its domination over Manchuria and Korea (see Chapter 3). In 1915, the Japanese government insisted that Yuan Shikai accept a series of "twenty-one demands" that would have given Japan a virtual protectorate over the Chinese government and economy. Yuan was able to fend off the most far-reaching Japanese demands by arousing popular outrage in China, but at the Paris Peace Conference four years later, Japan received Germany's sphere of influence in Shandong Province as a reward for its support of the Allied cause in World War I. On hearing the news that the Chinese government had accepted the decision, on May 4, 1919, patriotic students, supported by other sectors of the urban population, demonstrated in Beijing and other major cities of the country. Although this May Fourth Movement did not result in a reversal of the decision to award Shandong to Japan, it did alert a substantial part of the politically literate population to the threat to national survival and the incompetence of the warlord government.

By 1920, central authority had almost ceased to exist in China. Two political forces now began to emerge as competitors for the right to bring order to the chaos of the early republican era. One was Sun Yat-sen's Nationalist Party. Driven from the political arena seven years earlier by Yuan Shikai, the party now reestablished itself on the mainland by making an alliance with the warlord ruler of Guangdong (Kwangtung) Province in South China. From Canton, Sun sought international assistance to carry out his national revolution. The other was the Chinese Communist Party (CCP). Following Lenin's strategy, Comintern agents soon advised the new party to link up with the more experienced Nationalists. Sun Yat-sen needed the expertise and the diplomatic support that the Soviet Union could provide, because his anti-imperialist rhetoric had alienated many Western powers; one English-language newspaper in the international concession in Shanghai remarked, "All his life, all his influence, are devoted to ideas which keep China in turmoil, and it is utterly undesirable that he should be allowed to prosecute those aims here."[5] In 1923, the two parties formed an alliance to oppose the warlords and drive the imperialist powers out of China.

For three years, with the assistance of a Comintern mission in Canton, the two parties submerged their mutual suspicions and mobilized and trained a revolutionary army to march north and seize control over China. The so-called Northern Expedition began in the summer of 1926. By the following spring, revolutionary forces were in control of all Chinese territory south of the Yangtze River, including the major river ports of Wuhan and Shanghai. But tensions between the two parties now surfaced. Sun Yat-sen had died of cancer in 1925 and was succeeded as head of the Nationalist Party by his military subordinate, Chiang Kai-shek. Chiang feigned support for the alliance with the Communists but actually planned to destroy them. In April 1927, he struck against the Communists and their supporters in Shanghai, killing thousands. The CCP responded by encouraging revolts in central China and Canton, but the uprisings were defeated and their leaders were killed or forced into hiding.

The Nanjing Republic

In 1928, Chiang Kai-shek founded a new Chinese republic at Nanjing, and over the next three years, he managed to reunify China by a combination of military operations and inducements (known as "silver bullets") to various northern warlords to join his movement. One of his key targets was the warlord Zhang Zuolin (Chang

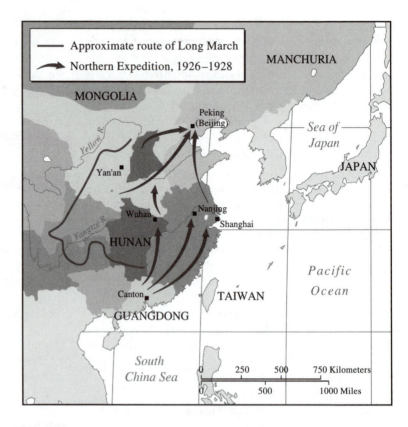

✖ Map 5.1 The Northern Expedition

Legend:
— Approximate route of Long March
→ Northern Expedition, 1926–1928

MANCHURIA

MONGOLIA

Yellow R.

Peking (Beijing)

Yan'an

Sea of Japan

JAPAN

Wuhan

Yangtze R.

Nanjing

Shanghai

HUNAN

Canton

TAIWAN

Pacific Ocean

GUANGDONG

South China Sea

0   250   500   750 Kilometers

0   500   1000 Miles

Tso-lin), who controlled Manchuria under the tutelage of Japan. When Zhang allegedly agreed to throw in his lot with the Nationalists, the Japanese had him assassinated by placing a bomb under his train as he was returning to Manchuria. The Japanese hoped that Zhang Zuolin's son and successor, Zhang Xueliang (Chang Hsueh-liang), would be more cooperative, but they had miscalculated. Promised a major role in Chiang Kai-shek's government, Zhang began instead to integrate Manchuria politically and economically into the Nanjing Republic.

Chiang Kai-shek saw the Japanese as a serious threat to Chinese national aspirations, but considered them less dangerous than the Communists. (He once remarked to an American reporter that "the Japanese are a disease of the skin, but the Communists are a disease of the heart.") After the Shanghai massacre of April 1927, most of the Communist leaders went into hiding in the city, where they attempted to revive the movement in its traditional base among the urban working class. Shanghai was a rich recruiting ground for the party. A city of millionaires, paupers, prostitutes, gamblers, and adventurers, it had led one pious Christian missionary to

comment, "If God lets Shanghai endure, He owes an apology to Sodom and Gomorrah."[6] Some party members, however, led by the young Communist organizer Mao Zedong (Mao Tse-Tung), fled to the hilly areas south of the Yangtze River.

Unlike most other CCP leaders, Mao was convinced that the Chinese revolution must be based on the impoverished peasants in the countryside. The son of a prosperous peasant, Mao had helped to organize a peasant movement in South China during the early 1920s, and then served as an agitator in rural villages in his native province of Hunan during the Northern Expedition in the fall of 1926. At that time, he wrote a famous report to the party leadership suggesting that the CCP support peasant demands for a land revolution. But his superiors refused, fearing that adopting excessively radical policies would destroy the alliance with the Nationalists.

After the spring of 1927, the CCP-Nationalist alliance ceased to exist. Chiang Kai-shek attempted to root the Communists out of their urban base in Shanghai and their rural redoubt in the rugged hills of Jiangxi (Kiangsi) Province. He succeeded in the first task in 1931, when most party leaders were forced to flee

Shanghai for Mao's base in South China. Three years later, using their superior military strength, Chiang's troops surrounded the Communist base in Jiangxi, inducing Mao's young People's Liberation Army (PLA) to abandon its guerrilla lair and embark on the famous Long March, an arduous journey of thousands of miles on foot through mountains, marshes, and deserts to the small provincial town of Yan'an (Yenan) 200 miles north of the modern-day city of Xian in the dusty hills of North China. Of the 90,000 who embarked on the journey in October 1934, only 10,000 arrived in Yan'an a year later. Contemporary observers must have thought that the Communist threat to the Nanjing regime had been averted forever.

Meanwhile, Chiang Kai-shek was trying to build a new nation. When the Nanjing republic was established in 1928, Chiang publicly declared his commitment to Sun Yat-sen's Three People's Principles. In a program announced in 1918, Sun had written about the all-important second stage of "political tutelage":

> China . . . needs a republic government just as a boy needs school. As a schoolboy must have good teachers and helpful friends, so the Chinese people, being for the first time under republican rule, must have a farsighted revolutionary government for their training. This calls for the period of political tutelage, which is a necessary transitional stage from monarchy to republicanism. Without this, disorder will be unavoidable.[7]

In keeping with Sun's program, Chiang announced a period of political indoctrination to prepare the Chinese people for a final stage of constitutional government. In the meantime, the Nationalists would use their dictatorial power to carry out a land reform program and modernize the urban industrial sector.

But it would take more than paper plans to create a new China. Years of neglect and civil war had severely frayed the political, economic, and social fabric of the nation. There were faint signs of an impending industrial revolution in the major urban centers, but most of the people in the countryside, drained by warlord exactions and civil strife, were still grindingly poor and overwhelmingly illiterate. A Westernized middle class had begun to emerge in the cities and formed much of the natural constituency of the Nanjing government. But this new Westernized elite, preoccupied with bourgeois values of individual advancement and material accumulation, had few links with the peasants in the countryside or the rickshaw drivers "running in this world of suffering," in the poignant words of a Chinese poet. In an expressive phrase, some critics dismissed Chiang Kai-

◆ **Mao Zedong at Yan'an.** In 1934, Mao Zedong led his bedraggled forces on a famous "Long March" from South China to a new location at Yan'an, in the hills just south of the Gobi Desert. Here Chairman Mao, next to one of his generals, poses for a photograph at his new headquarters. Note the thick padded jackets to keep out the cold.

shek and his chief followers as "banana Chinese"—yellow on the outside, white on the inside.

Chiang Kai-shek was aware of the difficulty of introducing exotic foreign ideas into a society still culturally conservative. While building a modern industrial sector, he attempted to synthesize modern Western ideas with traditional Confucian values of hard work, obedience, and moral integrity. In the officially promoted New Life Movement, sponsored by his Wellesley-educated wife, Mei-ling Soong, Chiang sought to propagate traditional Confucian social ethics such as integrity, propriety, and righteousness, while rejecting what he considered the excessive individualism and material greed of Western capitalism.

Unfortunately for Chiang Kai-shek, Confucian ideas—at least in their institutional form—had been widely discredited by the failure of the traditional system to solve China's growing problems. With only a tenuous hold over the Chinese provinces (the Nanjing government had total control over only a handful of provinces in the Yangtze valley), a growing Japanese threat in the north, and a world suffering from the Great Depression, Chiang made little progress with his program. Lacking the political sensitivity of Sun Yat-sen and fearing Communist influence, Chiang repressed all opposition and censored free expression, thereby alienating many intellectuals and political moderates. Since the urban middle class and landed gentry were his natural political constituency, he shunned programs that would lead to a redistribution of wealth. A land reform program was enacted in 1930 but had little effect.

Chiang Kai-shek's government had little more success in promoting industrial development. During the decade of precarious peace following the Northern Expedition, industrial growth averaged only about 1 percent annually. Much of the national wealth was in the hands of the so-called four families, composed of senior officials and close subordinates of the ruling elite. Military expenses consumed half the budget, and distressingly little was devoted to social and economic development.

The new government, then, had little success in dealing with the deep-seated economic and social problems that affected China during the interwar years. The deadly combination of internal disintegration and foreign pressure now began to coincide with the virtual collapse of the global economic order during the Great Depression and the rise of militant political forces in Japan determined to extend Japanese influence and power in an unstable Asia. These forces and the turmoil they unleashed will be examined in the next chapter.

Down with Confucius and Sons: Economic and Social Change in Republican China

The transformation of the old order that had commenced at the end of the Qing era continued into the period of the early Chinese republic. The industrial sector, sparked in part by the decline in European investment during World War I, continued to grow, albeit slowly. Although many Chinese firms faced severe competition from Western rivals, they enjoyed some advantages in terms of experience and local connections and in general were able to hold their own. Still, about 75 percent of all industrial production was still craft-produced in the early 1930s.

Mechanization, however, was gradually beginning to replace manual labor in a number of traditional industries, notably in the manufacture of textile goods. Sometimes, technological advances undoubtedly led to a loss of jobs, but as in many other industrializing societies, the overall impact was probably beneficial in terms of cheaper products and increased output. Traditional Chinese exports, such as silk and tea, were hard-hit by the Great Depression, and manufacturing suffered a decline during the 1930s.

It is difficult to gauge conditions in the countryside during the early republican era. Scholars disagree over whether overall per capita consumption declined during this period, and if so, what the primary causes were. Whatever the statistical evidence regarding agricultural production, there is no doubt that farmers were often victimized by high taxes imposed by local warlords and the endemic political and social conflict that marked the period.

Social changes followed shifts in the economy and the political culture. By 1915, the assault on the old system and values by educated youth was intense. The main focus of the attack was the Confucian concept of the family—in particular, filial piety and the subordination of women. Young people demanded the right to choose their own mates and their own careers. Women demanded rights and opportunities equal to those enjoyed by men.

More broadly, progressives called for an end to the concept of duty to the community and praised the Western individualist ethos. The prime spokesman for such views was the popular writer Lu Xun (Lu Hsun), whose short stories criticized the Confucian concept of family as a "man-eating" system that degraded humanity. In a famous short story entitled "Diary of a Madman," the protagonist remarks:

> I remember when I was four or five years old, sitting in the cool of the hall, my brother told me that if a man's parents were ill, he should cut off a piece of his flesh and boil it for them if he wanted to be considered a good son. I have only just realized that I have been living all these years in a place where for four thousand years they have been eating human flesh.[8]

Such criticisms did have some beneficial results. During the early republic, the tyranny of the old family system began to decline, at least in urban areas, under the impact of economic changes and the urgings of the New Culture intellectuals. Women, long consigned to an inferior place in the Confucian world order, began to escape their cloistered existence and seek education and

An Arranged Marriage

One of the key elements in the reformist program of the New Culture movement in early republican China was the concept of freeing children from the domination of their parents, as called for by the concept of filial piety in Confucian ethics. According to traditional practice, for example, parents were expected to select marriage partners for their children as a means of enhancing the economic or social status of the family. Professional matchmakers were employed to negotiate the arrangement with the prospective in-laws.

During the early republican era, many young Chinese rejected the idea of an arranged marriage and set out to find a love match on their own initiative. But the power of traditional ways remained strong, especially in the countryside, and many young Chinese returned from schooling in the modern cities to find that their parents had already made arrangements for them to marry the son or daughter of a family in their native village.

One of the most poignant treatments of this issue is the novel *Family,* written by the respected Chinese novelist Ba Jin. In the novel, the young Chueh-hsin has fallen in love with a young female classmate while studying in middle school in the provincial capital. But on his return home after graduation, his dreams are cruelly shattered when his father announces:

Now that you've graduated, I want to arrange your marriage. . . . You're old enough to be married; I won't feel easy until I fulfill my obligation to find you a wife. Although I didn't accumulate much money in my years away from home as an official, still I've put by enough for us to get along on. My health isn't what it used to be; I'm thinking of spending my time at home and having you help me run the household affairs. All the more reason you'll be needing a wife. I've already arranged a match with the Li family. . . . You can be married within the year.

The announcement is a terrible shock to Chueh-hsin, but he does not protest, nor does it ever occur to him to do so. Such was the power of traditional family ethics, even in the heady days of the early republic when many young Chinese were boldly urging reforms to bring their country into the modern world. But the bitterness aroused by such conditions created severe tensions between the older and younger generations in China, and undoubtedly contributed to the powerful desire for revolutionary change that would later bring the Communist Party to power after World War II.

Source : Ba Jin, *Family* (Peking: Foreign Languages Press, 1964), pp. 28–29.

---

employment alongside their male contemporaries. Free choice in marriage and a more relaxed attitude toward sex became commonplace among affluent families in the cities, where the teenage children of Westernized elites aped the clothing, social habits, and even the musical tastes of their contemporaries in Europe and the United States.

But as a rule, the new consciousness of individualism and women's rights that marked the early republican era in the major cities did not penetrate to the villages. Here traditional attitudes and customs held sway. Arranged marriages continued to be the rule rather than the exception, and concubinage remained common. According to a survey taken in the 1930s, well over two-thirds of the marriages even among urban couples had been arranged by their parents (see box above), while in one rural area, only 3 out of 170 villagers interviewed had even heard of the idea of "modern marriage." Even

the tradition of binding the feet of female children continued despite efforts by the Nationalist government to eradicate the practice.

China's Changing Culture

Nowhere was the struggle between traditional and modern more visible than in the field of culture. Beginning with the New Culture era during the early years of the first Chinese republic, radical reformists criticized traditional culture as the symbol and instrument of feudal oppression that must be entirely eradicated in order to create a new China that could stand on its feet with dignity in the modern world.

The first cracks in the edifice of traditional culture had actually come in the late nineteenth century, when progressive elements began to introduce Western books, paintings, music, and ideas into China. By the first quarter of the new century, the trickle became a flood, as progressive intellectuals called for a new culture based on that of the modern West. During the 1920s and 1930s, Western literature and art became highly popular in China, especially among the urban middle class. Traditional culture continued to prevail among more conservative elements of the population, while some intellectuals argued for the creation of a new art that would synthesize the best of Chinese and foreign culture. But the most creative artists were interested in imitating foreign trends, while traditionalists were more concerned with preservation.

Literature in particular was influenced by foreign ideas, as Western genres like the novel and the short story attracted a growing audience. Although most Chinese novels written after World War I dealt with Chinese subjects, they reflected the Western tendency toward social realism and often dealt with the new Westernized middle class (Mao Dun's *Midnight,* for example, describes the changing mores of Shanghai's urban elites) or the disintegration of the traditional Confucian family (Ba Jin's famous novel *Family* is an example). Most of China's modern authors displayed a clear contempt for the past.

Japan between the Wars

During the first two decades of the twentieth century, Japan made remarkable progress toward the creation of an advanced society on the Western model. The political system based on the Meiji Constitution of 1890 began to evolve along Western pluralistic lines, and a multiparty system took shape, while the economic and social reforms launched during the Meiji era led to increasing prosperity and the development of a modern industrial and commercial sector. Optimists had reason to hope that Japan was on the road to becoming a full-fledged democracy.

Experiment in Democracy

During the first quarter of the twentieth century, the Japanese political system appeared to evolve significantly toward the Western democratic model. Political parties expanded their popular following and became increasingly competitive, and universal male suffrage was instituted in the 1920s. Individual pressure groups began to appear in Japanese society, along with an independent press and a bill of rights. The influence of the old ruling oligarchy, the *genro,* had not yet been significantly challenged, however, nor had that of its ideological foundation, the *kokutai.*

The fragile flower of democratic institutions was able to survive throughout the 1920s (often called the era of Taisho democracy from the reign title of the ruling emperor). During that period, the military budget was reduced, and a suffrage bill enacted in 1925 continued the process of democratization that had begun earlier in the century.

But the era was also marked by growing social turmoil, and two opposing forces within the system were gearing up to challenge the prevailing wisdom. On the left, a Marxist labor movement, which reflected the tensions within the working class and the increasing radicalism among the rural poor, began to take shape in the early 1920s in response to growing economic difficulties. Attempts to suppress labor disturbances led to further radicalization. On the right, ultranationalist groups called for a rejection of Western models of development and a more militant approach to realizing national objectives. In 1919, the radical nationalist Kita Ikki called for a military takeover and the establishment of a new system bearing strong resemblance to what would later be called National Socialism in Germany.

This cultural conflict between old and new, native and foreign, was reflected in the world of literature. Japanese self-confidence had been somewhat restored after their victories over China and Russia, and this resurgence sparked a great age of creativity in the early twentieth century. Now more adept at handling European literary forms, Japanese writers blended Western psychology with Japanese sensibility in exquisite novels reeking with nostalgia for the old Japan. A well-known example is Junichiro Tanizaki's *Some Prefer Nettles,* published in 1928, which delicately juxtaposes the positive aspects of both traditional and modern Japan. By the 1930s, however, military censorship increasingly inhibited free literary expression. Many authors continued to write privately, producing works that reflected the gloom of the era. This attitude is perhaps best exemplified by Shiga Naoya's *A Dark Night's Journey,* written during the early 1930s and capturing a sense of the approaching global catastrophe. It is regarded as the masterpiece of modern Japanese literature.

A Zaibatsu Economy

Japan also continued to make impressive progress in economic development. Spurred by rising domestic demand as well as a continued high rate of government investment in the economy, the production of raw materials tripled between 1900 and 1930, while industrial production increased more than twelvefold. Much of the increase went into the export market, and Western manufacturers began to complain about the rising competition for markets from the Japanese.

As often happens, rapid industrialization was accompanied by some hardship and rising social tensions. A characteristic of the Meiji model was the concentration of various manufacturing processes within a single enterprise, the so-called *zaibatsu*, or financial clique. Some of these firms were existing merchant companies, such as Mitsui and Sumitomo, that had the capital and the foresight to move into new areas of opportunity. Others were formed by enterprising samurai, who used their status and experience in management to good account in a new environment. Whatever their origins, these firms gradually developed, often with official encouragement, into large conglomerates that controlled a major segment of the Japanese industrial sector. According to one source, by 1937 the four largest *zaibatsu* (Mitsui, Mitsubishi, Sumitomo, and Yasuda) controlled 21 percent of the banking industry, 26 percent of mining, 35 percent of shipbuilding, 38 percent of commercial shipping, and more than 60 percent of paper manufacturing and insurance.

This concentration of power and wealth in the hands of a few major industrial combines created problems in Japanese society. In the first place, it resulted in the emergence of a form of dual economy: on the one hand, a modern industry characterized by up-to-date methods and massive government subsidies and on the other, a traditional manufacturing sector characterized by conservative methods and small-scale production techniques.

Concentration of wealth also led to growing economic inequalities. As we have seen, economic growth had been achieved at the expense of the peasants, many of whom fled to the cities to escape rural poverty. That labor surplus benefited the industrial sector, but the urban proletariat was still poorly paid and ill-housed. Rampant inflation in the price of rice led to food riots shortly after World War I. A rapid increase in population (the total population of the Japanese islands increased from an estimated 43 million in 1900 to 73 million in 1940) led to food shortages and the threat of rising unemployment. Intense competition and the global recession in the early 1920s led to an increased concentration of industry and a perceptible rise in urban radicalism, marked by the appearance of a Marxist labor movement. In the meantime, those left on the farm continued to suffer. As late as the beginning of World War II, an estimated one-half of all Japanese farmers were tenants.

Shidehara Diplomacy

A final problem for Japanese leaders in the post-Meiji era was the familiar colonial dilemma of finding sources of raw materials and foreign markets for the nation's manufactured goods. Until World War I, Japan had dealt with the problem by seizing territories such as Formosa, Korea, and southern Manchuria and transforming them into colonies or protectorates of the growing Japanese Empire. That policy had succeeded brilliantly, but it had also begun to arouse the concern and in some cases the hostility of the Western nations. China was also becoming apprehensive; as we have seen, Japanese demands for Shandong Province at the Paris Peace Conference in 1919 aroused massive protests in major Chinese cities.

The United States was especially concerned about Japanese aggressiveness. Although the United States had been less active than some European states in pursuing colonies in the Pacific, it had a strong interest in keeping the area open for U.S. commercial activities. American anxiety about Tokyo's "twenty-one demands" on China in 1915 led to a new agreement in 1917, which essentially repeated the compromise provisions of the agreement reached nine years earlier.

In 1922, in Washington, D.C., the United States convened a major conference of nations with interests in the Pacific to discuss problems of regional security. The Washington Conference led to agreements on several issues, but the major accomplishment was the conclusion of a nine-power treaty recognizing the territorial integrity of China and the Open Door. The other participants induced Japan to accept these provisions by accepting its special position in Manchuria.

During the remainder of the 1920s, Japanese governments attempted to play by the rules laid down at the Washington Conference. Known as Shidehara diplomacy, after the foreign minister (and later prime minister) who attempted to carry it out, this policy sought to use diplomatic and economic means to realize Japanese interests in Asia. But this approach came under severe pressure as Japanese industrialists began to move into new areas of opportunity, such as heavy industry, chemicals, mining, and the manufacturing of appliances and automobiles. Because such industries desperately needed resources not found in abundance locally, the Japanese government came under increasing pressure to find new sources abroad.

The fragile flower of democratic institutions was able to survive growing social turmoil throughout the 1920s, while Japan sought to operate within a cooperative framework with other nations. In the early 1930s, however, with the onset of the Great Depression and growing tensions in the international arena, nationalist forces rose to dominance in the government. As one historian has recently noted, the changes taking place in the 1930s were not in the constitution or the institutional structure, which remained essentially intact, but in the composition and attitudes of the ruling group. Party leaders during the 1920s had attempted to realize Japanese aspirations within the existing global political and economic framework. The dominant elements in the government in the 1930s, a mixture of military officers and ultranationalist politicians, were convinced that the diplomacy of the 1920s had failed and advocated a more aggressive approach to protecting national interests in a brutal and competitive world.

Historians argue over whether Taisho democracy was merely a fragile period of comparative liberalization within a framework dominated by the Meiji vision of empire and *kokutai* or whether the militant nationalism of the 1930s was an aberration brought on by the depression, which caused the emerging Japanese democracy to wilt. Perhaps both contentions contain a little truth. A process of democratization was taking place in Japan during the first decades of the twentieth century, but without shaking the essential core of the Meiji concept of the state. When the "liberal" approach of the 1920s failed to solve the problems of the day, the shift toward a more aggressive approach was inevitable.

Nationalism and Dictatorship in Latin America

Although the nations of Latin America played little role in World War I, that conflict nevertheless exerted an impact on the region, and especially on its economy. By the end of the following decade, the region was also strongly influenced by another event of global proportions—the Great Depression.

The Economy and the United States

At the beginning of the twentieth century, the economy of Latin America was based largely on the export of foodstuffs and raw materials. Some countries were compelled to rely on the export earnings of only one or two products. Argentina, for example, relied on the sale of beef and wheat; Chile exported nitrates and copper; Brazil and the Caribbean nations sold sugar; and the Central American states relied on the export of bananas.

Such exports brought large profits to a few, but for the majority of the population, the returns were meager.

During World War I, the export of some products, such as Chilean nitrates (used to produce explosives), increased dramatically. In general, however, the war led to a decline in European investment in Latin America and a rise in the U.S. role in the local economies. By the late 1920s, the United States had replaced Great Britain as the foremost source of investment in Latin America. Unlike the British, however, U.S. investors placed funds directly into production enterprises, causing large segments of the area's export industry to fall into American hands. A number of Central American states, for example, were popularly labeled "banana republics" because of the power and influence of the U.S.–owned United Fruit Company. American firms also dominated the copper mining industry in Chile and Peru, as well as the oil industry in Mexico, Peru, and Bolivia.

Increasing economic power served to reinforce the traditionally high level of U.S. political influence in Latin America. This influence was especially evident in Central America and the Caribbean, regions that many Americans considered their backyard and thus vital to U.S. national security. The growing U.S. presence in the region provoked hostility among Latin Americans and a growing national consciousness that viewed the United States as an aggressive imperialist power. Some charged that Washington used its influence to keep ruthless dictators, such as Juan Vicente Gómez of Venezuela and Fulgencio Batista of Cuba, in power in order to preserve U.S. economic influence, sometimes through U.S. military intervention. In a bid to improve relations with Latin American countries, in 1935, President Franklin D. Roosevelt promulgated the Good Neighbor policy, which rejected the use of U.S. military force in the region. To underscore his sincerity, Roosevelt ordered the withdrawal of U.S. marines from the island nation of Haiti in 1936. For the first time in thirty years, there were no U.S. occupation troops in Latin America.

Because so many Latin American nations depended for their livelihood on the export of raw materials and food products, the Great Depression of the 1930s was a disaster for the region. The total value of Latin American exports in 1930 was almost 50 percent below the figure for the previous five years. Spurred by the decline in foreign revenues, Latin American governments began to encourage the development of new industries to reduce dependency on imports. In some cases—the steel industry in Chile and Brazil, the oil industry in Argentina and Mexico—government investment made up for the absence of local sources of capital.

Map 5.2 Latin America in the First Half of the Twentieth Century

The Move to Authoritarianism

During the late nineteenth century, most governments in Latin America had been increasingly dominated by landed or military elites, who controlled the mass of the population—mostly impoverished peasants—by the blatant use of military force. This trend toward authoritarianism increased during the 1930s, as domestic instability caused by the effects of the Great Depression led to the creation of military dictatorships throughout the region. This trend was especially evident in Argentina, Brazil, and Mexico—three countries that together possessed more than half of the land and wealth of Latin America.

The political domination of the country by an elite minority often had disastrous effects. The government of Argentina, controlled by landowners who had benefited from the export of beef and wheat, was slow to recognize the growing importance of establishing a local industrial base. In 1916, Hipólito Irigoyen (1852–1933), head of the Radical Party, was elected president on a program to improve conditions for the middle and lower classes. Little was achieved, however, as the party became increasingly corrupt and drew closer to the large landowners. In 1930, the army overthrew Irigoyen's government and reestablished the power of the landed class. But their effort to return to the previous export economy and suppress the growing influence of labor unions failed, and in 1946 General Juan Perón—claiming the support of the *descamisados* ("shirtless ones")—seized sole power (see Chapter 10).

Brazil followed a similar path. In 1889, the army overthrew the Brazilian monarchy, installed by Portugal years before, and established a republic. But it was dominated by landed elites, many of whom had grown wealthy through their ownership of coffee plantations. By 1900, three-quarters of the world's coffee was grown in Brazil. As in Argentina, the ruling oligarchy ignored the importance of establishing an urban industrial base. When the Great Depression ravaged profits from coffee exports, a wealthy rancher, Getúlio Vargas (1883–1954), seized power and ruled the country as president from 1930 to 1945. At first, Vargas sought to appease workers by declaring an eight-hour day and a minimum wage but, influenced by the apparent success of Fascist regimes in Europe, he ruled by increasingly autocratic means and relied on a police force that used torture to silence his opponents. His industrial policy was relatively enlightened, however, and by the end of World War II, Brazil had become Latin America's major industrial power. In 1945, the army, fearing that Vargas might prolong his power illegally after calling for new elections, forced him to resign.

Mexico, in the years after World War I, was not an authoritarian state, but neither was it democratic. Under the rule of the dictator Porfirio Díaz (wee Chapter 1), the real wages of the working class had declined. Moreover, 95 percent of the rural population owned no land while about 1,000 families ruled almost all of Mexico. When a liberal landowner, Francisco Madero, forced Diaz from power in 1910, he opened the door to a wider revolution. Madero's ineffectiveness triggered a demand for agrarian reform led by Emiliano Zapata, who aroused the masses of landless peasants and began to seize the haciendas of wealthy landholders. Between 1910 and 1920, the revolution caused untold destruction to the Mexican economy. Finally, a new constitution in 1917 established a strong presidency, initiated land reform policies, established limits on foreign investors, and set

◆ **Emiliano Zapata.** The inability of Francisco Madero to carry out far-reaching reforms led to a more radical upheaval in the Mexican countryside. Emiliano Zapata led a band of Indians in a revolt against the large landowners of southern Mexico and issued his own demands for land reform.

an agenda for social welfare workers. The revolution, however, was democratic in form only, as the official political party, known as the Institutional Revolutionary Party (PRI), controlled the levers of power throughout society. Every six years, PRI bosses chose the party's presidential candidate, who was then dutifully elected by the people.

The situation began to change with the election of Lázaro Cárdenas (1895–1970) as president in 1934. Cárdenas won wide popularity with the peasants by ordering the redistribution of 44 million acres of land controlled by landed elites. He also won popular support by adopting a stronger stand against the United States, seizing control over the oil industry, which had hitherto been dominated by major U.S. oil companies. Alluding to the Good Neighbor policy, President Roosevelt refused to intervene, and eventually Mexico agreed to compensate U.S. oil companies for their lost property. It then set up PEMEX, a state-run organization, to run the oil industry.

Latin American Culture

During the early twentieth century, the influence of modern European artistic and literary movements began to penetrate Latin America. Symbolism and surrealism were especially important in setting new directions in both painting and literature. In major cities, such as Buenos Aires and São Paulo, wealthy elites supported avant-garde trends, but other artists returned from abroad to adapt modern techniques to their native roots.

For many artists and writers, their creative work provided a means of promoting the emergence of a new national essence. Such was the case, for example, in Mexico, where the government provided financial support for the painting of murals on public buildings, including schools and government offices. Especially prominent in the development of Mexico's mural art was the painter Diego Rivera (1886–1957). Rivera had studied in Europe, where he was influenced by fresco painting in Italy. After his return to Mexico, he began to produce a monumental style of mural art that served two purposes: to illustrate the national past by portraying Aztec legends as well as Mexican festivals and folk customs, but also to promote a political message in favor of realizing the social goals of the Mexican Revolution. Rivera's murals can be found in such diverse locations as the Ministry of Education and the Social Security Hospital in Mexico City and the chapel of the Agricultural School at Chapingo.

Conclusion

The turmoil brought about by World War I not only resulted in the destruction of several of the major Western empires and a redrawing of the map of Europe, it also opened the door to political and social upheavals elsewhere in the world. In the Middle East, the decline and fall of the Ottoman Empire led, first of all, to the creation of a new secular Republic of Turkey. A new state of Saudi Arabia emerged in the Arabian peninsula, while Palestine became a source of tension between newly ar-

rived Jewish settlers and longtime Muslim Palestinians. Yet it was clear that the grip of European colonialism had been weakened, but not destroyed. Although a number of new states were created in the region between the Mediterranean Sea and the Persian Gulf, they were given only mandates status under the tutelage of the British and the French.

Other parts of Asia and Africa also witnessed the rise of movements for national independence. In Africa, these movements were led by native leaders educated in Europe or the United States. In India, Gandhi and his campaign of civil disobedience played a crucial role in his country's bid to be free of British rule. Communist movements also began to emerge in Asian societies, as radical elements sought new methods of bringing about the overthrow of Western imperialism. Japan continued to follow its own path to modernization which, although successful from an economic point of view, took a menacing turn during the 1930s, when Japanese leaders adopted an authoritarian political system and began to brandish military force to achieve their objectives abroad.

Between 1919 and 1939, China experienced a dramatic struggle to establish a modern nation. In the ashes of the disintegrating empire of the Qing, two dynamic political organizations—the Nationalists and the Communists—competed for legitimacy as the rightful heirs of the old order. At first, they were able to form an alliance in an effort to defeat their common adversaries, but cooperation turned to conflict during the Northern Expedition in the late 1920s. The Nationalists under Chiang Kai-shek emerged supreme, but Chiang found it difficult to control the remnants of the warlord regime in China, while the Great Depression undermined his efforts to build an industrial nation. During the 1930s, Japanese interference in Chinese affairs added a new complexity to the situation.

During the interwar years, the nations of Latin America faced severe economic problems because of their dependence on the export of foodstuffs and raw materials. Increasing U.S. investments in Latin America contributed to growing hostility against the powerful neighbor to the north. The Great Depression forced the region to begin developing new industries, but it also led to the rise of authoritarian governments, some of them modeled after the Fascist regimes of Italy and Germany.

By demolishing the remnants of their old civilization on the battlefields of Europe in World War I, Europeans had inadvertently encouraged the subject peoples of their vast colonial empires to begin their own movements for national independence. The process was by no means completed in the two decades following the Treaty of Versailles, but the bonds of imperial rule had been severely strained, and once Europeans began to weaken themselves in the even more destructive conflict of World War II, the hopes of African and Asian peoples for national independence and freedom could at last be realized. It is to that devastating world conflict that we must now turn.

NOTES

1. Vladimir I. Lenin, "The Awakening of Asia," in *The Awakening of Asia: Selected Essays* (New York, 1963–1968), p. 22.
2. Speech by Mahatma Gandhi, delivered in London in September 1931 during his visit for the first Roundtable Conference.
3. Quoted in Bernard Lewis, *The Emergence of Modern Turkey,* 2d ed. (London, 1968), pp. 410–411.
4. Ts'ai Yuan-p'ei, "Ta Lin Ch'in-nan Han," in *Ts'ai Yuan-p'ei Hsien-sheng Ch'uan-chi* [Collected Works of Mr. Ts'ai Yuan-p'ei] (Taipei, 1968), pp. 1057–1058.
5. Quoted in Nicholas Rowland Clifford, *Spoilt Children of Empire: Westerners in Shanghai and the Chinese Revolution of the 1920s* (Hanover, 1991), p. 93.
6. Ibid., p. 16.
7. Quoted in William Theodore de Bary et al., eds., *Sources of Chinese Tradition* (New York, 1963), p. 783.
8. Lu Xun, "Diary of a Madman," in *Selected Works of Lu Hsun* (Peking, 1957), 1:20.

CHAPTER

6

The Crisis Deepens: The Coming of World War II

In September 1931, acting on the pretext that Chinese troops had attacked a Japanese railway near the northern Chinese city of Mukden, Japanese military units stationed in the area seized control throughout Manchuria. Although Japanese military authorities in Manchuria announced that China had provoked the action, the "Mukden incident," as it was called, had actually been carried out by Japanese saboteurs. Eventually, worldwide protests against the Japanese action led the League of Nations to send an investigative commission to Manchuria. When the commission issued a report condemning the seizure, Japan withdrew from the League. Over the next several years, the Japanese consolidated their hold on Manchuria, renaming it Manchukuo and placing it under the titular authority of the former Chinese emperor and now Japanese puppet, Henry Pu Yi.

Although no one knew it at the time, the Manchurian incident would later be singled out by some observers as the opening shot of World War II. The failure of the League of Nations to take decisive action sent a strong signal to Japan and other potentially aggressive states that they might seek their objectives without the risk of united opposition by the major world powers. Despite its agonizing efforts to build a system of peace and stability that would prevent future wars, the League had failed dismally, and the world was once again about to slide inexorably into a new global conflict.

The problem had first begun to appear in the late 1920s, when the military forces of Chiang Kai-shek crossed the Yangtze and began to march north in the hope of unifying all of China under his Nanjing republic. When the Manchurian warlord Zhang Zuolin allegedly agreed to abandon his prior ties with Japan and integrate Manchuria into Chiang's government, elements in the Japanese army, fearing a loss of influence on the mainland, had him assassinated. But, as we saw in Chapter 5, Zhang Zuolin's son and successor, Zhang Xueliang, continued to integrate Manchuria into the Nanjing republic. Appeals from Tokyo to Washington for a U.S. effort to restrain Chiang Kai-shek were rebuffed.

Already suffering from the decline of its business interests on the mainland, after 1929 Japan began to feel the impact of the Great Depression, when the United States and major European nations raised their tariff rates against Japanese imports in a desperate effort to protect local businesses and jobs. Militant elements in Tokyo began to argue that what Japan could not obtain by peaceful means it must secure by violent action. It was undoubtedly that vision that had motivated the decisions reached about Mukden in the early fall of 1931.

The Retreat from Democracy: The Rise of Dictatorial Regimes

On February 3, 1933, only four days after he had been appointed chancellor of Germany, Adolf Hitler met secretly with Germany's leading generals. He revealed to them his desire to remove the "cancer of democracy," create a new authoritarian leadership, and forge a new domestic unity. All Germans would need to realize that "only a struggle can save us and that everything else must be subordinated to this idea." Youth especially must be trained and their wills strengthened "to fight with all means." Since Germany's living space was too small for its people, Hitler said, above all Germany must rearm and prepare for "the conquest of new living space in the east and its ruthless Germanization." Even before he had consolidated his power, Adolf Hitler had a clear vision of his goals, and their implementation meant another war.

There was thus a close relationship between the rise of dictatorial regimes in the 1930s and the coming of World War II. The apparent triumph of liberal democracy in 1919 proved extremely short-lived. By 1939, only two major states in Europe, France and Great Britain, and a host of minor ones remained democratic. Italy and Germany had succumbed to the political movement called fascism, while Soviet Russia under Joseph Stalin moved toward a repressive totalitarian state. A host of other European states and Latin American countries as well adopted authoritarian structures of various kinds, while a militarist regime in Japan moved that country down the path of war.

The dictatorial regimes between the wars assumed both old and new forms. Dictatorship was by no means a new phenomenon, but the modern totalitarian state was. The totalitarian regimes, whose best examples can be found in Stalinist Russia and Nazi Germany, extended the functions and power of the central state far beyond what they had been in the past. The immediate origins of totalitarianism can be found in the total warfare of World War I, when governments exercised controls over economic, political, and personal freedom in order to achieve victory.

The modern totalitarian state soon moved beyond the ideal of passive obedience expected in a traditional dictatorship or authoritarian monarchy. The new "total states" expected the active loyalty and commitment of their citizens to the regime's goals. They used modern mass propaganda techniques and high-speed communications to conquer the minds and hearts of their subjects. The total state aimed to control not only the eco-nomic, political, and social aspects of life, but the intellectual and cultural aspects as well. But that control also had a purpose: the active involvement of the masses in the achievement of the regime's goals, whether they be war, a classless utopia, or a thousand-year Reich.

The modern totalitarian state was to be led by a single leader and single party. It ruthlessly rejected the liberal ideal of limited government power and constitutional guarantees of individual freedoms. Indeed, individual freedom was to be subordinated to the collective will of the masses, organized and determined for them by a leader or leaders. Modern technology also gave total states the ability to use unprecedented police powers to impose their wishes on their subjects.

Totalitarianism is an abstract term, and no state followed all its theoretical implications. The Fascist states—Italy and Nazi Germany—as well as the Soviet Union of Joseph Stalin have all been labeled totalitarian, although their regimes exhibited significant differences and met with varying degrees of success. Totalitarianism transcended traditional political labels. Fascism in Italy and Nazism in Germany grew out of extreme rightist preoccupations with nationalism and, in the case of Germany, racism. Communism in the Soviet Union emerged out of Marxism and the concept of the dictatorship of the proletariat. Thus, totalitarianism could and did exist in what were perceived as extreme right-wing and extreme left-wing regimes. This fact helped bring about a new concept of the political spectrum in which the extremes were no longer seen as opposites on a linear scale, but came to be viewed as being similar to each other in at least some respects.

The Birth of Fascism

In the early 1920s, in the wake of economic turmoil, political disorder, and the general insecurity and fear stemming from World War I, Benito Mussolini burst upon the Italian scene with the first Fascist movement in Europe. Mussolini (1883–1945) began his political career as a socialist, but was expelled from the Socialist Party after supporting Italy's entry into World War I, a position contrary to the socialist principle of ardent neutrality in imperialist wars. In 1919, Mussolini established a new political group, the *Fascio di Combattimento,* or League of Combat. It received little attention in the elections of 1919, but political stalemate within Italy's parliamentary system and strong nationalist sentiment saved Mussolini and the Fascists.

The new parliament elected in November 1919 quickly proved to be incapable of governing Italy, as the three major parties were unable to form an effective governmental coalition. When socialists began to speak of the need for revolution, provoking worker strikes and a general climate of class violence, alarmed conservatives turned to the Fascists, who formed armed squads to attack socialist offices and newspapers. By 1922, Mussolini's nationalist rhetoric and ability to play to middle-class fears of socialism, Communist revolution, and disorder were attracting ever more adherents. On October 29, 1922, after Mussolini and the Fascists threatened to march on Rome if they were not given power, King Victor Emmanuel III (1900–1946) capitulated and made Mussolini prime minister of Italy.

By 1926, Mussolini had established the institutional framework for his Fascist dictatorship. Press laws gave the government the right to suspend any publication that fostered disrespect for the Catholic Church, the monarchy, or the state. The prime minister was made "head of government" with the power to legislate by decree. A police law empowered the police to arrest and confine anybody for both nonpolitical and political crimes without due process of law. The government was given the power to dissolve political and cultural associations. In 1926, all anti-Fascist parties were outlawed. A secret police, known as the OVRA, was also established. By the end of 1926, Mussolini ruled Italy as *Il Duce*, the leader.

Mussolini left no doubt of his intentions. Fascism, he said, "is totalitarian, and the Fascist State, the synthesis and unity of all values, interprets, develops and gives strength to the whole life of the people."[1]

Mussolini and the Fascists attempted to mold Italians into a single-minded community by developing Fascist organizations. Because the secondary schools maintained considerable freedom from Fascist control, the regime relied more and more on the activities of youth organizations known as the Young Fascists to indoctrinate the young people of the nation in Fascist ideals. By 1939, about 6,800,000 children, teenagers, and young adults of both sexes, or 66 percent of the population between eight and eighteen, were enrolled in some kind of Fascist youth group. Activities for these groups included Saturday afternoon marching drills and calisthenics, seaside and mountain summer camps, and youth contests. An underlying motif for all of these activities was the Fascist insistence on militarization. Beginning in the 1930s, all male groups were given some kind of premilitary exercises to develop discipline and provide training for war. Results were mixed. Many Italian teenagers, who liked neither military training nor routine discipline of any kind, simply refused to attend Fascist youth group meetings on a regular basis.

The Fascist organizations hoped to create a new Italian, who would be hardworking, physically fit, disciplined, intellectually sharp, and martially inclined. In practice, the Fascists largely reinforced traditional social attitudes in Italy, as is evident in their policies toward women. The Fascists portrayed the family as the pillar of the state and women as the foundation of the family. "Woman into the home" became the Fascist slogan. Women were to be homemakers and baby producers, "their natural and fundamental mission in life," according to Mussolini, who viewed population growth as an indicator of national strength. Employment outside the home was an impediment, distracting from conception. "It forms an independence and consequent physical and moral habits contrary to child bearing."[2] A practical consideration also underlay the Fascist attitude toward women: Working women would compete with males for jobs in the depression economy of the 1930s. Eliminating women from the market reduced male unemployment.

In all areas of Italian life under Mussolini and the Fascists, there was a noticeable dichotomy between Fascist ideals and practice. The Italian Fascists promised much but actually delivered considerably less, and they were soon overshadowed by a much more powerful Fascist movement to the north. Adolf Hitler was a great admirer of Benito Mussolini, but the German pupil soon proved to be far more adept in the use of power than his Italian teacher.

Hitler and Nazi Germany

In 1923, a small south German rightist party, led by an obscure Austrian rabble-rouser named Adolf Hitler, created a stir when it tried to seize power in southern Germany in conscious imitation of Mussolini's march on Rome in 1922. Although the attempt failed, Adolf Hitler and his followers, known as the National Socialists, achieved sudden national prominence.

Born on April 20, 1889, Adolf Hitler was the son of an Austrian customs official. He had done poorly in secondary school and eventually made his way to Vienna to become an artist. While there, Hitler established the basic ideas of an ideology from which he never deviated for the rest of his life. At the core of Hitler's belief system was a passionate commitment to the German "race" and a fervent hatred of Jews. While in Vienna, Hitler became an extreme German nationalist who learned from his experience in mass politics there how political parties could use propaganda and terror effectively. He also developed a strong belief in the importance of struggle, which he saw as the "granite foundation of the world."

Anti-Semitism, of course, was not new to European civilization. Since the Middle Ages, Jews had been portrayed as the murderers of Christ and were often subjected to mob violence and official persecution. Their rights were restricted, and they were physically separated from Christians in residential quarters known as ghettos. By the nineteenth century, as a result of the ideals of the Enlightenment and the French Revolution, Jews were increasingly granted legal equality in many European countries. Nevertheless, Jews were not completely accepted, and this ambivalence was apparent throughout Europe.

Nowhere in Europe was suspicion of Jews more prevalent than in Germany and in German-speaking areas of Austria-Hungary. During the nineteenth century, many Jews in both countries had left the ghetto and become assimilated into the surrounding Christian population. Some entered what had previously been the closed world of politics and the professions. Many Jews became eminently successful as bankers, lawyers, scientists, scholars, journalists, and stage performers. In 1880, for example, Jews made up 10 percent of the population of Vienna, but accounted for 39 percent of its medical students and 23 percent of its law students.

Envy now blended with distrust. During the last two decades of the century, conservatives in Germany and Austria founded right-wing anti-Semitic parties that used dislike of Jews to win the votes of traditional lower-middle-class groups who felt threatened by changing times. Such parties also played on the rising sentiment of racism in German society. Spurred by Social Darwinist ideas that nations, like human species, were engaged in a brutal struggle for survival, rabid German nationalists promoted the concept of the Volk (nation, people, or race) as an underlying idea in Germany history since the medieval era. Portraying the German people as the successors of the pure Aryan race, the true and original creators of Western culture, such groups called for Germany to take the lead in a desperate struggle to fight for European civilization and save it from the destructive assaults of such lower races as Jews, Negroes, and Orientals.

HITLER'S RISE TO POWER, 1919–1933

At the end of World War I, after four years of military service on the Western front, Hitler went to Munich and decided to enter politics. He joined the obscure German Workers' Party, one of a number of right-wing nationalist parties in Munich. By the summer of 1921,

he had assumed total control over the party, which he renamed the National Socialist German Workers' Party (NSDAP), or Nazi for short. His idea was that the party's name would distinguish the Nazis from the socialist parties while gaining support from both working-class and nationalist circles. Hitler worked assiduously to develop the party into a mass political movement with flags, party badges, uniforms, its own newspaper, and its own police force or party militia known as the SA—the *Sturmabteilung*, or Storm Troops. The SA was used to defend the party in meeting halls and break up the meetings of other parties. It added an element of force and terror to the growing Nazi movement. Hitler's own oratorical skills were largely responsible for attracting an increasing number of followers. By 1923, the party had grown from its early hundreds into a membership of 55,000, with 15,000 SA members.

In a burst of overconfidence, Hitler staged an armed uprising against the government in Munich in November 1923. The Beer Hall Putsch was quickly crushed, and Hitler was sentenced to prison. During his brief stay in jail, he wrote *Mein Kampf*, an autobiographical account of his movement and its underlying ideology. Virulent German nationalism, anti-Semitism, and anti-communism were linked together by a Social Darwinian theory of struggle that stressed the right of superior nations to *Lebensraum* ("living space") through expansion and the right of superior individuals to secure authoritarian leadership over the masses. What is perhaps most remarkable about *Mein Kampf* is its elaboration of a series of ideas that directed Hitler's actions once he took power. That opponents refused to take Hitler and his ideas seriously was one of his greatest advantages.

During his imprisonment, Hitler also came to the realization that the Nazis would have to come to power by constitutional means, not by overthrowing the Weimar Republic. This strategy implied the formation of a mass political party that would actively compete for votes with the other political parties. After his release from prison, Hitler worked assiduously to build such a party. He reorganized the Nazi Party on a regional basis and expanded it to all parts of Germany, growing in size from 27,000 members in 1925 to 178,000 by the end of 1929. Especially noticeable was the youthfulness of the regional, district, and branch leaders of the Nazi organization. Many were between the ages of twenty-five and thirty and were fiercely committed to Hitler because he gave them the kind of active politics they sought. As one recruit remarked,

For me this was the start of a completely new life. There was only one thing in the world for me and that was service in the movement. All my thoughts were centered on the movement. I could talk only politics.[3]

By 1932, the Nazi Party had 800,000 members and had become the largest party in the Reichstag. No doubt, Germany's economic difficulties were a crucial factor in the Nazi rise to power. Unemployment rose dramatically, from 4.35 million in 1931 to 6 million by the winter of 1932. The economic and psychological impact of the Great Depression made extremist parties more attractive. The Nazis were especially effective in developing modern electioneering techniques. In their election campaigns, party members pitched their themes to the needs and fears of different social groups. In working-class districts, for example, the Nazis attacked international high finance, while in middle-class neighborhoods, they exploited fears of a Communist revolution and its threat to private property. At the same time that the Nazis made blatant appeals to class interests, they were denouncing conflicts of interest and maintaining that they stood above classes and parties. Hitler, in particular, claimed to stand above all differences and promised to create a new Germany free of class differences and party infighting. His appeal to national pride, national honor, and traditional militarism struck chords of emotion in his listeners.

Increasingly, the right-wing elites of Germany—the industrial magnates, landed aristocrats, military establishment, and higher bureaucrats—came to see Hitler as the man who had the mass support to establish a right-wing, authoritarian regime that would save Germany and their privileged positions from a Communist takeover. Under pressure, since the Nazi Party had the largest share of seats in the Reichstag, President Paul von Hindenburg agreed to allow Hitler to become chancellor on January 30, 1933 and form a new government.

Within two months, Hitler had laid the foundations for the Nazis' complete control over Germany. On the day after a fire broke out in the Reichstag building (February 27), supposedly caused by the Communists, Hitler convinced President Hindenburg to issue a decree giving the government emergency powers. The decree suspended all basic rights for the full duration of the emergency, thus enabling the Nazis to arrest and imprison anyone without redress. The crowning step in Hitler's "legal" seizure of power came on March 23, when the Reichstag passed the Enabling Act by a two-thirds vote. This legislation, which empowered the government to dispense with constitutional forms for four years while it

issued laws that dealt with the country's problems, provided the legal basis for Hitler's subsequent acts. He no longer needed either the Reichstag or President Hindenburg. In effect, Hitler became a dictator appointed by the parliamentary body itself.

With their new source of power, the Nazis acted quickly to enforce *Gleichschaltung*, the coordination of all institutions under Nazi control. The civil service was purged of Jews and democratic elements, concentration camps were established for opponents of the new regime, the autonomy of the federal states was eliminated, trade unions were dissolved, and all political parties except the Nazis were abolished. By the end of the summer of 1933, within seven months of being appointed chancellor, Hitler and the Nazis had established the foundations for a totalitarian state. When Hindenburg died on August 2, 1934, the office of Reich president was abolished, and Hitler became sole ruler of Germany. Public officials and soldiers were all required to take a personal oath of loyalty to Hitler as the "Führer of the German Reich and people."

THE NAZI STATE, 1933–1939

Having smashed the parliamentary state, Hitler now felt the real task was at hand: to develop the "total state." Hitler's aim had not been simply power for power's sake or a tyranny based on personal power. He had larger ideological goals. The development of an Aryan racial state that would dominate Europe and possibly the world for generations to come required a movement in which the German people would be actively involved, not passively cowed by force. "There are no longer any free realms in which the individual belongs to himself," Hitler stated. "The time of personal happiness is over."[4]

The Nazis pursued the creation of this totalitarian state in a variety of ways. Most dramatic were the mass demonstrations and spectacles employed to integrate the German nation into a collective fellowship and to mobilize it as an instrument for Hitler's policies. These mass demonstrations, especially the Nuremberg party rallies that were held every September, combined the symbolism of a religious service with the merriment of a popular amusement. They had great appeal and usually evoked mass enthusiasm and excitement.

In the economic sphere, Hitler and the Nazis also established control. Although the regime pursued the use of public works projects and "pump-priming" grants to private construction firms to foster employment and end the depression, there is little doubt that rearmament contributed far more to solving the unemployment problem. Unemployment, which had stood at 6 million in 1932, dropped to 2.6 million in 1934 and less than 500,000 in 1937. The regime claimed full credit for solving Germany's economic woes, and this was undoubtedly an important factor in convincing many Germans to accept the new regime, despite its excesses.

For its enemies, the Nazi total state had its instruments of terror and repression. Especially important was the SS (*Schutzstaffel,* or "protection echelon"). Originally created as Hitler's personal bodyguard, the SS, under the direction of Heinrich Himmler (1900–1945), came to control all of the regular and secret police forces. Himmler and the SS functioned on the basis of two principles: ideology and terror. Terror included the instruments of repression and murder: the secret police, criminal police, concentration camps, and later the execution squads and death camps for the extermination of the Jews.

Other institutions, including the Catholic and Protestant churches, primary and secondary schools, and universities, were also brought under the control of the state. Nazi professional organizations and leagues were formed for civil servants, teachers, women, farmers, doctors, and lawyers. Because the early indoctrination of youth would create the foundation for a strong totalitarian state in the future, youth organizations—the *Hitler Jugend* (Hitler Youth) and its female counterpart, the *Bund Deutscher Mädel* (League of German Maidens)— were given special attention. The oath required of Hitler Youth members demonstrates the degree of dedication expected of youth in the Nazi state: "In the presence of this blood banner, which represents our Führer, I swear

to devote all my energies and my strength to the savior of our country, Adolf Hitler. I am willing and ready to give up my life for him, so help me God."

The creation of the new system also had an impact on women. The Nazi attitude toward women was largely determined by ideological considerations. Women played a crucial role in the Aryan racial state as bearers of the children who would ensure the triumph of the Aryan race. To the Nazis, the differences between men and women were quite natural. Men were warriors and political leaders, while women were destined to be wives and mothers. By maintaining this clear distinction, each could best serve to "maintain the whole community."

Nazi ideas determined employment opportunities for women. The Nazis hoped to drive women out of certain areas of the labor market, including heavy industry or other jobs that might hinder women from bearing healthy children. Certain professions, including university teaching, medicine, and law, were also considered inappropriate for women, especially married women. Instead, the Nazis encouraged women to pursue professional occupations that had direct practical application, such as social work and nursing. In addition to restrictive legislation against females, the Nazi regime pushed its campaign against working women with such poster slogans as "Get ahold of pots and pans and broom and you'll sooner find a groom!"

The Nazi total state was intended to be an Aryan racial state. From its beginning, the Nazi Party reflected the strong anti-Semitic beliefs of Adolf Hitler. Once in power, the Nazis translated anti-Semitic ideas into anti-Semitic policies. In September 1935, the Nazis announced new racial laws at the annual party rally in

◆ **The Nazi Mass Spectacle.** Hitler and the Nazis made clever use of mass spectacles to rally the German people behind the Nazi regime. These mass demonstrations evoked intense enthusiasm, as is evident in this photograph of Hitler arriving at the Bückeberg near Hamelin for the Harvest Festival in 1937. Almost 1 million people were present for the celebration.

Nuremberg. These Nuremberg laws excluded German Jews from German citizenship and forbade marriages and extramarital relations between Jews and German citizens. The Nuremberg laws essentially separated Jews from the Germans politically, socially, and legally and were the natural extension of Hitler's stress upon the creation of a pure Aryan race.

Another, considerably more violent phase of anti-Jewish activity took place in 1938 and 1939. It was initiated on November 9–10, 1938, the infamous *Kristallnacht*, or night of shattered glass. The assassination of a third secretary in the German embassy in Paris became the occasion for a Nazi-led destructive rampage against the Jews, in which synagogues were burned, 7,000 Jewish businesses were destroyed, and at least 100 Jews were killed. Moreover, 20,000 Jewish males were rounded up and sent to concentration camps. *Kristallnacht* also led to further drastic steps. Jews were barred from all public buildings and prohibited from owning, managing, or working in any retail store. Finally, under the direction of the SS, Jews were encouraged to "emigrate from Germany." After the outbreak of World War II, the policy of emigration was replaced by a more gruesome one.

Authoritarian States in Europe

A number of other European states were not totalitarian but did possess conservative authoritarian governments. These states adopted some of the trappings of totalitarian states, especially their wide police powers. However, their greatest concern was not the creation of a mass movement aimed at the establishment of a new kind of society, but rather the defense of the existing social order. Consequently, the authoritarian states tended to limit the participation of the masses and were content with passive obedience rather than demanding active involvement in the goals of the regime.

Nowhere had the map of Europe been more drastically altered by World War I than in eastern Europe. The new states of Austria, Poland, Czechoslovakia, and Yugoslavia (known until 1929 as the kingdom of the Serbs, Croats, and Slovenes) adopted parliamentary systems, and the preexisting kingdoms of Romania and Bulgaria gained new parliamentary constitutions in 1920. Greece became a republic in 1924. Hungary's government was parliamentary in form, but controlled by its landed aristocrats. Thus, at the beginning of the 1920s, political democracy seemed well established. Yet almost everywhere in eastern Europe, parliamentary governments soon gave way to authoritarian regimes.

Several problems helped to create this situation. Eastern European states had little tradition of liberalism or parliamentary politics and no substantial middle class to support them. Then, too, these states were largely rural and agrarian in character. While many of the peasants were largely illiterate, much of the land was still dominated by large landowners who feared the growth of agrarian peasant parties with their schemes for land redistribution. Ethnic conflicts also threatened to tear these countries apart. Fearful of land reform, communist agrarian upheaval, and ethnic conflict, powerful landowners, the churches, and even some members of the small middle class looked to authoritarian governments to maintain the old system. Only Czechoslovakia, with its substantial middle class, liberal tradition, and strong industrial base, maintained its political democracy.

In Spain, political democracy also failed to survive. Fearful of the rising influence of left-wing elements in the government, Spanish military forces led by General Francisco Franco (1892–1995) launched a brutal and bloody civil war that lasted three years. Foreign intervention complicated the Spanish Civil War. Franco's forces were aided by arms, money, and men from the fascist regimes of Italy and Germany, while the government was assisted by 40,000 foreign volunteers and trucks, planes, tanks, and military advisers from the Soviet Union. After Franco's forces captured Madrid on March 28, 1939, the Spanish Civil War finally came to an end. General Franco soon established a dictatorship that favored large landowners, businessmen, and the Catholic clergy.

The Soviet Union

During the mid-1920s, Soviet society gradually recovered from the enormous damage caused by the Great War. As he consolidated his power at the expense of rivals within the party, Joseph Stalin followed a centrist policy that avoided confrontation with his capitalist enemies abroad while encouraging capitalist forces at home under the careful guidance of the state. But Stalin—fearful that the rising influence of the small Russian bourgeoisie could undermine the foundations of party rule—had no intention of permitting the NEP to continue indefinitely. In the late 1920s, he used the issue to bring the power struggle to a head.

Stalin had previously joined with the moderate Bukharin and other members of the party to defend the NEP against Leon Trotsky, whose "left opposition" wanted a more rapid advance toward socialism. Then, in

◆ **Picasso's *Guernica* (1937).** In 1937, Picasso painted *Guernica*, his diatribe against the violence of war, inspired by the bombing of a Basque town during the Spanish Civil War. It screams with pain and suffering and stands as one of the most expressive paintings in Western art. *Guernica* was to be the last great painting portraying the horrors of war, soon to be followed by war photography. How could painting compete any longer with those black and white frozen images of Auschwitz, with the quiet mountains of discarded eyeglasses, false teeth, and shoes?

1928, Stalin reversed course: he now claimed that the NEP had achieved its purpose and called for a rapid advance to socialist forms of ownership. Beginning in 1929, a series of new programs changed the face of Soviet society. Private capitalism in manufacturing and trade was virtually abolished, and party and state control over the economy was extended. The first of several Five-Year Plans was launched to promote rapid "socialist industrialization" and, in a massive effort to strengthen the state's hold over the agricultural economy, all private farmers were herded into collective farms (see box on p. 131).

The bitter campaign to collectivize the countryside aroused the antagonism of many peasants and led to a decline in food production and, in some areas, to mass starvation. It also further divided the Communist Party, and led to a massive purge of party members at all levels who opposed Stalin's effort to achieve rapid economic growth and the socialization of Russian society. A series of brutal purge trials eliminated thousands of "Old Bolsheviks" (people who had joined the party before the 1917 Revolution) and resulted in the conviction and death of many of Stalin's chief rivals. Trotsky, driven into exile, was dispatched by Stalin's assassin in 1940. Of the delegates who had attended the National Congress of the CPSU (Communist Party of the Soviet Union) in 1934, 70 percent had been executed by the time of the National Congress in 1939.

By the late 1930s, as the last of the great purge trials came to an end, the Russian Revolution had been in existence for more than two decades. It had achieved some successes. Stalin's policy of forced industrialization had led to rapid growth in the industrial sector, surpassing in many respects what had been achieved in the capitalist years prior to World War I. Between 1918 and 1937, steel production increased from 4 to 18 million tons per year, while hard coal output went from 36 to 128 million tons. New industrial cities sprang up overnight in the Urals and Siberia. The Russian people in general were probably better clothed, better fed, and better educated than they had ever been before. The cost had been enormous, however. Millions had died by bullet or by starvation. Thousands, perhaps millions, more languished in Stalin's concentration camps. The remainder of the population lived in a society now officially described as socialist, under the watchful eye of a man who had risen almost to the rank of a deity, the great leader of the Soviet Union, Joseph Stalin.

❧ Life on the Kolkhoz ❧

One of the key elements in the Bolshevik program to build a socialist society in Soviet Russia was the collective farm (known in Russian as the kolkhoz, or collective economy). Private farmlands throughout the country were to be gathered into larger agricultural units in which the land and livestock were owned by the collective, rather than by the individual farm family.

The process began in 1928, when Joseph Stalin launched the first Soviet Five-Year Plan to build the foundations of an advanced industrial economy. Representatives of the Communist Party arrived in individual villages and announced the new policy. Those who resisted were frequently sent off to concentration camps or even shot. One of Stalin's primary motives in launching the program was to destroy the power of prosperous private farmers (traditionally known in Russian as *kulaks*, or "fists," for their grasping ways) in the countryside. Rural officials were therefore ordered to "liquidate the kulaks as a class."

Lenin had declared that the program should not be undertaken until sufficient agricultural machinery had been provided from Soviet factories (a program known by the slogan "Mechanization before collectivization"), so that peasants could be persuaded that their income would be increased by transferring their land to collective ownership. In fact, the amount of mechanized equipment available—to be sold through government-run Machine Tractor Stations—was vastly inadequate to serve the need. During the early 1930s, almost 90 percent of all collective farms had no tractors of their own. Tractor maintenance was poor, and one foreign observer noted that Soviet-produced machinery had "a very short life."

At first, progress was rapid, but resistance was mounting. Many farmers, ordered to turn over their cattle to the collective, killed them instead and used the meat to feed their families. Horses were simply released by their owners to roam the countryside. Those that remained under collective ownership were usually ill-cared-for. During the early 1930s, the number of cattle in the Soviet Union decreased from over 70 million to under 40 million, while the supply of horses available dropped from 30 million to 15 million.

Agricultural output dropped precipitously, due partly to the lack of draft animals or farm machinery and also to the resistance of peasants who saw no reason to work hard on collective land. During the early 1930s, an estimated 10 million people died of hunger. One Soviet activist who visited a collective village in the Ukraine reported that only eight men were preparing the harvest, while the remainder did nothing. When he pointed out that the grain would be destroyed, they agreed with him. "I cannot believe that the loss of bread grains was of no consequence to the peasants. Their feelings must have been terribly strong for them to go to the extreme of leaving the grain in the fields."

In the end, Stalin had his way, and by the mid-1930s, virtually all of the 26 million farm families in the Soviet Union had been herded into 250,000 collective farms. As a concession to the peasants, each farmworker was allowed to have a tiny, privately owned garden plot. But the damage was done. Long after the end of World War II, farm output had still not recovered to pre–World War I levels, and the agricultural sector remained the Achilles' heel of the Soviet economy.

Sources: Robert Conquest, *The Harvest of Sorrow: Soviet Collectivization and the Terror-Famine* (New York: Oxford University Press, 1986), pp. 179–182; Max Belov, "The History of a Collective Farm," excerpted in *Readings in Russian History*, ed. Sidney Harcave (New York: Thomas Crowell and Co., 1962), pp. 208–210.

The impact of Joseph Stalin on Soviet society in one decade had been enormous. If Lenin had brought the party to power and nursed it through the difficult years of the Civil War, it was Stalin, above all, who had mapped out the path to economic modernization and socialist transformation. To many foreign critics of the regime, the Stalinist terror and autocracy were an inevitable consequence of the concept of the vanguard party and the centralized state built by Lenin. Others traced Stalinism back to Marx and Engels. It was they, after all, who had formulated the idea of the dictatorship of the proletariat, which now provided ideological justification for the Stalinist autocracy. Still others found the ultimate cause in the Russian political culture, which had been characterized by political autocracy since the emergence of Russian society from Mongol control in the fifteenth century.

Was Stalinism an inevitable outcome of Marxist-Leninist doctrine and practice? Or, as Mikhail Gorbachev has claimed, were Stalin's crimes "alien to the nature of socialism" and a departure from the course charted by V. I. Lenin before his death? Certainly Lenin had not envisaged a party dominated by a figure who became even larger than the organization itself and who, in the 1930s, almost destroyed the party. On the other hand, recent evidence shows that Lenin was capable of the brutal suppression of perceived enemies of the revolution in a way that is reminiscent in manner, if not in scope, of that of his successor, Stalin.

It is clear from the decade of the 1920s that there were other models for development in Soviet society than that adopted by Stalin; the NEP program, so ardently supported by Bukharin, is testimony to that fact. But it is also true that the state created by Lenin provided the conditions for a single-minded leader like Stalin to rise to absolute power. The great danger that neither Marx nor Lenin had foreseen had come to pass: the party itself, the vanguard organization leading the way into the utopian future, had become corrupted.

The Rise of Militarism in Japan

The rise of militant forces in Japan resulted not from a seizure of power by a new political party, but from the growing influence of such elements at the top of the political hierarchy. During the 1920s, a multiparty system based on democratic practices appeared to be emerging. Two relatively moderate political parties, the Minseito and the Seiyukai, dominated the Diet and took turns providing executive leadership in the cabinet. In 1925, universal male suffrage was declared. Radical elements existed at each end of the political spectrum, but neither militant nationalists nor violent revolutionaries appeared to present a threat to the stability of the system.

In fact, the political system was probably weaker than it seemed at the time. Both of the major parties were deeply dependent upon campaign contributions from powerful corporations (the *zaibatsu*), and conservative forces connected to the military or the old landed aristocracy were still highly influential behind the scenes. As in the Weimar Republic in Germany during the same period, the actual power base of moderate political forces was weak, and politicians unwittingly undermined the fragility of the system by engaging in bitter attacks on each other.

The growing confrontation with China in Manchuria, combined with the onset of the Great Depression, brought an end to the fragile stability of the immediate postwar years. The depression, which had started in the West, had a disastrous effect on Japan during the early 1930s. The value of Japanese exports dropped by 50 per-

cent from 1929 to 1931, while wages dropped nearly as much. Hardest hit were the farmers, as the price of rice and other staple food crops plummeted. At the same time, militant nationalists, outraged at Japan's loss of influence in Manchuria, began to argue that the Shidehara policy of peaceful cooperation with other nations in maintaining the existing international economic order (see Chapter 5) had been a failure.

During the early 1930s, civilian cabinets managed to cope with the economic challenges presented by the Great Depression. By abandoning the gold standard, Prime Minister Inukai Tsuyoshi was able to lower the price of Japanese goods on the world market, and exports climbed back to earlier levels. But the political parties were no longer able to stem the growing influence of militant nationalist elements. Despite its doubts about the wisdom of the Mukden incident, the cabinet was too divided to disavow it, and military officers in Manchuria increasingly acted on their own initiative.

In May 1932, Inukai Tsuyoshi was assassinated by right-wing extremists. He was succeeded by a moderate, Admiral Saito Makoto, but extremist patriotic societies composed of ultranationalists began to terrorize opponents, assassinating businessmen and public figures identified with the Shidehara policy of conciliation toward the outside world. Some, like the publicist Kita Ikki, were convinced that the parliamentary system had been corrupted by materialism and Western values and should be replaced by a system that would return to traditional Japanese values and imperial authority. His message, "Asia for the Asians," had not won widespread support during the relatively prosperous 1920s, but increased in popularity after the Great Depression, which convinced many Japanese that capitalism was unsuitable for Japan.

During the mid-1930s, the influence of the military and extreme nationalists over the government steadily increased. Minorities and left-wing elements were persecuted, and moderates were intimidated into silence. Terrorists tried for their part in assassination attempts portrayed themselves as selfless patriots and received light sentences. Japan continued to hold national elections, and moderate candidates continued to receive substantial popular support, but the cabinets were dominated by the military or advocates of Japanese expansionism. In February 1936, junior officers in the army led a coup in the capital city of Tokyo, briefly occupying the Diet building and other key government installations and assassinating several members of the cabinet. The ringleaders were quickly tried and convicted of treason, but under conditions that strengthened even further the influence of the military halls of power.

The Path to War

Only twenty years after the war to end war, the world plunged back into a new era of heightened international tension. The efforts at collective security in the 1920s—the League of Nations, the attempts at disarmament, the pacts and treaties—all proved meaningless in view of the growth of Nazi Germany and the rise of Japan.

The Path to War in Europe

World War II in Europe had its beginnings in the ideas of Adolf Hitler, who believed that only the Aryans were capable of building a great civilization. But Hitler was only expressing the frustrations of many Germans, who resented the punitive peace of Versailles and feared that their country was being threatened from all sides—from the west in the vengeful policies of the French, and from the east by a large mass of inferior peoples, the Slavs, who had learned to use German weapons and technology. Germany needed more land to support a larger population and be a great power. In the 1920s, in the second volume of *Mein Kampf*, Hitler had indicated where a National Socialist regime would find this land:

> And so we National Socialists . . . take up where we broke off six hundred years ago. We stop the endless German movement to the south and west, and turn our gaze toward the land in the east. . . . If we speak of soil in Europe today, we can primarily have in mind only Russia and her vassal border states.[5]

Once Russia had been conquered, its land could be resettled by German peasants while the Slavic population could be used as slave labor to build the Aryan racial state that would dominate Europe for a thousand years.

When Hitler became chancellor on January 30, 1933, Germany's situation in Europe seemed weak. The Versailles treaty had created a demilitarized zone on Germany's western border that would allow the French to move into the heavily industrialized parts of Germany in the event of war. To Germany's east, the smaller states, such as Poland and Czechoslovakia, had defensive treaties with France. The Versailles treaty had also limited Germany's army to 100,000 troops with no air force and only a small navy.

Posing as a man of peace in his public speeches, Hitler emphasized that Germany wished only to revise the unfair provisions of Versailles by peaceful means and occupy Germany's rightful place among the European states. On March 9, 1935, he announced the creation of a new air force and, one week later, the introduction of a military draft that would expand Germany's army from 100,000 to 550,000 troops. Hitler's unilateral repudiation of the Versailles treaty brought a swift reaction as France, Great Britain, and Italy condemned Germany's action and warned against future aggressive steps. But nothing concrete was done.

On March 7, 1936, buoyed by his conviction that the Western democracies had no intention of using force to maintain the Treaty of Versailles, Hitler sent German troops into the demilitarized Rhineland. According to the Versailles treaty, the French had the right to use force against any violation of the demilitarized Rhineland. But France would not act without British support, and the British viewed the occupation of German territory by German troops as reasonable action by a dissatisfied power. The London *Times* noted that the Germans were only "going into their own back garden."

Meanwhile, Hitler gained new allies. In October 1935, Benito Mussolini committed Fascist Italy to imperial expansion by invading Ethiopia. Angered by French and British opposition to his invasion, Mussolini welcomed Hitler's support and began to draw closer to the German dictator he had once called a buffoon. The joint intervention of Germany and Italy on behalf of General Francisco Franco in the Spanish Civil War in 1936 also drew the two nations closer together. In October 1936, Mussolini and Hitler concluded an agreement that recognized their common political and economic interests, and one month later, Mussolini referred publicly to the new Rome-Berlin Axis. Also in November, Germany and Japan (the rising military power in the Far East) concluded the Anti-Comintern Pact and agreed to maintain a common front against communism.

STALIN SEEKS A UNITED FRONT

From behind the walls of the Kremlin in Moscow, Joseph Stalin undoubtedly observed the effects of the Great Depression in the capitalist states with a measure of satisfaction. During the early 1920s, once it became clear that the capitalist states in Europe, although badly shaken by the war, had managed to survive without socialist revolutions, Stalin decided to improve relations with the outside world as a means of obtaining capital and technological assistance in promoting economic growth in the Soviet Union. But Lenin had predicted that after a brief period of stability in Europe, a new crisis brought on by overproduction and intense competition was likely to occur in the capitalist world. That, he added, would mark the beginning of the next wave of revolution. In the meantime, he declared: "We will give the capitalists the shovels with which to bury themselves."

To Stalin, the onset of the Great Depression was a signal that the next era of turbulence in the capitalist world was at hand, and during the early 1930s, Soviet foreign policy returned to the themes of class struggle and social revolution. When the influence of the Nazi Party reached significant proportions in the early 1930s, Stalin viewed it as a pathological form of capitalism and ordered the Communist Party in Germany not to support the fragile Weimar Republic. Hitler would quickly fall, he reasoned, leading to a Communist takeover.

By 1935, Stalin became uneasily aware that Hitler was not only securely in power in Berlin, but also represented a serious threat to the Soviet Union. That summer, at a major meeting of the Communist International held in Moscow, Soviet officials announced a shift in policy. The Soviet Union would now seek to form a united front with capitalist democratic nations throughout the world against the common danger of Naziism and fascism. Communist parties in capitalist countries, and in colonial areas, were instructed to cooperate with "peace-loving democratic forces" in forming coalition governments called Popular Fronts.

In most capitalist countries, Stalin's move was greeted with suspicion, but in France, a coalition of leftist parties—Communists, Socialists, and Radicals—fearful that rightists intended to seize power, formed a Popular Front government in June 1936. The Popular Front government succeeded in launching a program for workers that some called the French New Deal. It included the right of collective bargaining, a forty-hour workweek, two-week paid vacations, and minimum wages. But the Popular Front's policies failed to solve the problems of the depression, and although it survived until 1938, the Front was for all intents and purposes dead before then. Moscow signed a defensive treaty with France and reached an agreement with three noncommunist states in Eastern Europe (Czechoslovakia, Romania, and Yugoslavia), but talks with Great Britain achieved little result. The Soviet Union, rebuffed by London and disappointed by Paris, feared that it might be forced to face the might of Hitler's *Wehrmacht* alone.

DECISION AT MUNICH

By the end of 1936, Hitler and Nazi Germany had achieved a "diplomatic revolution" in Europe. The Treaty of Versailles had been virtually scrapped, and Germany was once more a "world power," as Hitler proclaimed. Hitler was convinced that neither the French nor the British would provide much opposition to his plans and decided in 1938 to move on Austria. By threat-

ening Austria with invasion, Hitler coerced the Austrian chancellor into putting Austrian Nazis in charge of the government. The new government promptly invited German troops to enter Austria and assist in maintaining law and order. One day later, on March 13, 1938, after his triumphal return to his native land, Hitler formally annexed Austria to Germany. Great Britain's ready acknowledgment of Hitler's action only increased the German dictator's contempt for Western weakness.

The annexation of Austria improved Germany's strategic position in central Europe and put Germany in position for Hitler's next objective—the destruction of Czechoslovakia. This goal might have seemed unrealistic because democratic Czechoslovakia was quite prepared to defend itself and was well supported by pacts with France and the Soviet Union. Hitler believed, however, that France and Britain would not use force to defend Czechoslovakia.

He was right again. On September 15, 1938, Hitler demanded the cession to Germany of the Sudetenland (an area in northwestern Czechoslovakia that was inhabited largely by ethnic Germans) and expressed his willingness to risk "world war" to achieve his objective. Instead of objecting, the British, French, Germans, and Italians—at a hastily arranged conference at Munich—reached an agreement that essentially met all of Hitler's demands. German troops were allowed to occupy the Sudetenland as the Czechs, abandoned by their Western allies, stood by helplessly. The Munich Conference was the high point of Western appeasement of Hitler. When Neville Chamberlain, the British prime minister, returned to England from Munich, he boasted that the Munich agreement meant "peace in our times." Hitler had promised Chamberlain that he had made his last demand. Like scores of German politicians before him, Chamberlain believed Hitler's promises (see box on p. 135).

In fact, Munich confirmed Hitler's perception that the Western democracies were weak and would not fight. Increasingly, Hitler was convinced of his own infallibility, and he had by no means been satisfied at Munich. In March 1939, Hitler occupied the Czech lands (Bohemia and Moravia) while the Slovaks, with his encouragement, declared their independence of the Czechs and created the German puppet state of Slovakia. On the evening of March 15, 1939, Hitler triumphantly declared in Prague that he would be known as the greatest German of them all.

At last, the Western states reacted vigorously to the Nazi threat. Hitler's naked aggression had made it clear that his promises were utterly worthless. When he began

⇒ *The Perils of Appeasement* ⇐

In the fall of 1938, the prime ministers of Great Britain and France traveled to Munich, a city in southern Germany, where they consulted with Adolf Hitler over the latter's demand for the return of the Sudetenland to the Third Reich. The Sudetenland was a hilly region inhabited by ethnic Germans that had been turned over by the victorious powers to the new state of Czechoslovakia after World War I in the belief that by controlling that strategic region, Czechoslovakia would be able to defend itself against a possible future German invasion.

To Hitler, the loss of the Sudetenland was an insult to all Germans, and in his talks with British Prime Minister Neville Chamberlain and French Premier Edouard Daladier, he bluntly demanded its return to German control. Although France was linked to Czechoslovakia by a treaty of mutual defense, Chamberlain and Daladier capitulated to Hitler's demand in a desperate effort to avert a general war. On his return to London, Chamberlain defended his action in the House of Commons. "When we were convinced, as we became convinced, that nothing any longer would keep the Sudetenland within the Czechoslovakian State, we urged the Czech Government as strongly as we could to agree to the cession of territory, and to agree promptly." It was a difficult decision, Chamberlain conceded, but it was the only way to save Czechoslovakia from annihilation and so save all of Europe "from Armageddon."

Chamberlain expressed the hope that he had returned from Munich with the promise of "peace in our times." But to rival Conservative Party politician Winston Churchill, the Munich Conference was "a disaster of the first magnitude." In his own speech in Parliament, Churchill warned:

> And do not suppose that this is the end. This is only the beginning of the reckoning. This is only the first sip, the first foretaste of a bitter cup which will be proferred to us year by year unless by a supreme recovery of moral health and martial vigor, we arise again and take our stand for freedom as in the olden time.

History has recorded that Churchill was correct. The last-minute attempt to appease Hitler was a failure, as the German attack on Poland the following year amply demonstrated. For those generations of Americans and Europeans who lived through World War II, Munich became a symbol of the futility of appeasing an aggressor to avoid a confrontation. After the end of the war, the lesson of Munich began to be applied to the Cold War between the capitalist nations and the communist bloc led by the Soviet Union. Political leaders in the United States frequently invoked the "Munich syndrome" to argue against the loss of territory anywhere in the world to the forces of international communism.

But could the lessons from Europe be applied elsewhere in the world, under different conditions? For many, the answer to that question lay in Vietnam.

Sources: Neville Chamberlain, *In Search of Peace* (New York: Putnam, 1939), pp. 215, 217; *Parliamentary Debates, House of Commons* (London: His Majesty's Stationery Office, 1938), vol. 339, pp. 361–369.

to demand the return to Germany of Danzig (which had been made a free city by the Treaty of Versailles to serve as a seaport for Poland), Britain recognized the danger and offered to protect Poland in the event of war. At the same time, both France and Britain realized that only the Soviet Union was powerful enough to help contain Nazi aggression and began political and military negotiations with Joseph Stalin and the Soviets. Their distrust of Soviet communism, however, made an alliance unlikely.

Meanwhile, Hitler pressed on in the belief that Britain and France would not really fight over Poland. To preclude an alliance between the western European states and the Soviet Union, which would create the danger of a two-front war, Hitler, ever the opportunist, approached Stalin, who had given up hope of any alliance with Britain and France. The announcement on August 23, 1939, of the Nazi-Soviet Nonaggression Pact shocked the world. The treaty with the Soviet Union gave Hitler the freedom he sought and on September 1, German forces invaded Poland. Two days later, Britain and France declared war on Germany. Europe was again at war.

The Path to War in Asia

In the years immediately following the Japanese seizure of Manchuria in the fall of 1931, Japanese military forces began to expand gradually into North China. Using the tactics of military intimidation and diplomatic bullying rather than all-out attack, Japanese military authorities began to carve out a new "sphere of influence" south of the Great Wall.

Not all politicians in Tokyo agreed with this aggressive policy, but right-wing terrorists assassinated some of the key critics and intimidated others into silence. By the mid-1930s, militants connected with the government and the armed forces were effectively in control of Japanese politics. The United States refused to recognize the Japanese takeover of Manchuria, which Secretary of State Henry L. Stimson declared an act of "international outlawry," but was unwilling to threaten the use of force. Instead, the Americans attempted to appease Japan in the hope of encouraging moderate forces in Japanese society. As one senior U.S. diplomat with long experience in Asia warned in a memorandum to the president:

> Utter defeat of Japan would be no blessing to the Far East or to the world. It would merely create a new set of stresses, and substitute for Japan the USSR—as the successor to Imperial Russia—as a contestant (and at least an equally unscrupulous and dangerous one) for the mastery of the East. Nobody except perhaps Russia would gain from our victory in such a war.[6]

For the moment, the prime victim of Japanese aggression was China. Chiang Kai-shek attempted to avoid a confrontation with Japan so that he could deal with what he considered the greater threat from the Communists. When clashes between Chinese and Japanese troops broke out, he sought to appease the Japanese by granting them the authority to administer areas in North China. But as Japan moved steadily southward, popular protests in Chinese cities against Japanese aggression intensified. In December 1936, Chiang was briefly kidnapped by military forces commanded by General Zhang Xueliang, who compelled him to end his military efforts against the Communists in Yan'an and form a new united front against the Japanese. After Chinese and Japanese forces clashed at Marco Polo Bridge, south of Beijing, in July 1937, China refused to apologize, and hostilities spread.

Japan had not planned to declare war on China, but neither side would compromise, and the 1937 incident eventually turned into a major conflict. The Japanese advanced up the Yangtze valley and seized the Chinese capital of Nanjing, raping and killing thousands of innocent civilians in the process. But Chiang Kai-shek refused to capitulate and moved his government upriver to Hankou. When the Japanese seized that city, he moved on to Chongqing, in remote Sichuan Province. Japanese

strategists had hoped to force Chiang to join a Japanese-dominated New Order in East Asia, comprising Japan, Manchuria, and China. This aim was part of a larger plan to seize Soviet Siberia with its rich resources and create a new "Monroe Doctrine for Asia," in which Japan would guide its Asian neighbors on the path to development and prosperity (see box p. 137). After all, who better to instruct Asian societies on modernization than the one Asian country that had already achieved it?

During the late 1930s, Japan began to cooperate with Nazi Germany on the assumption that the two countries would ultimately launch a joint attack on the Soviet Union and divide up its resources between them. But when Germany surprised the world by signing a nonaggression pact with the Soviets in August 1939, Japanese strategists were compelled to reevaluate their long-term objectives. Japan was not strong enough to defeat the Soviet Union alone, as a small but bitter border war along the Siberian frontier near Manchukuo had amply demonstrated. So the Japanese began to shift their gaze southward to the vast resources of Southeast Asia—the oil of the Dutch East Indies, the rubber and tin of Malaya, and the rice of Burma and Indochina.

A move southward, of course, would risk war with the European colonial powers and the United States. Japan's attack on China in the summer of 1937 had already aroused strong criticism abroad, particularly from the United States, where President Franklin D. Roosevelt threatened to "quarantine" the aggressors after Japanese military units bombed an American naval ship operating in China. Public fear of involvement forced the president to draw back, but when Japan suddenly demanded the right to occupy airfields and exploit economic resources in French Indochina in the summer of 1940, the United States warned the Japanese that it would impose economic sanctions unless Japan withdrew from the area and returned to its borders of 1931.

The Japanese viewed the American threat of retaliation as an obstacle to their long-term objectives. Japan badly needed liquid fuel and scrap iron from the United States. Should they be cut off, Japan would have to find them elsewhere. The Japanese were thus caught in a vise. To obtain guaranteed access to the natural resources that were necessary to fuel the Japanese military machine, Japan must risk being cut off from its current source of the raw materials that would be needed in case of a conflict. After much debate, the Japanese decided to launch a surprise attack on U.S. and European colonies in Southeast Asia in the hope of a quick victory that would evict the United States from the region.

☙ Manchuria and the Third Door ☙

Advocates of Japanese expansion in the 1920s and 1930s justified their proposals by citing a combination of practical and moralistic motives. One good example was a publication titled "The Need for Emigration and Expansion," written by nationalist figure Hashimoto Kingoro in the late 1930s.

One reason for expansion, the author declared, was the need to find an outlet for an expanding population, then a source of considerable worry among Japanese leaders. "We are like a great crowd of people packed into a small and narrow room," Kingoro noted, "and there are only three doors through which we might escape, namely, emigration, advance into world markets, and expansion of territory." Since emigration had been limited by anti-Japanese immigration policies in other countries, and the second door had been shut by high tariff barriers, it was "quite natural that Japan should rush upon the last remaining door."

Conceding that territorial expansion might appear risky, Kingoro countered that Japan did not seek to annex foreign territories, but simply to find locations abroad where "Japanese capital, Japanese skills and Japanese labor can have free play, free from the oppression of the white race." What right, he complained, did foreigners have to close off two of the country's op-tions and then criticize Japan's attempt to use the third and last door?

Kingoro sought to counter foreign criticisms of the Japanese occupation of Manchuria. That action, he claimed, "was not in the least a selfish one," because the result was "the establishment of the splendid new nation of Manchuria." Whether or not other countries granted recognition to Manchukuo [as it was formally known], it had already been established with the aid of its friend and supporter, Japan. As for the charge that Japanese actions in Manchuria were excessively violent, the author asked pointedly, "just which country it was that sent warships and troops to India, South Africa, and Australia and slaughtered innocent natives, bound their hands and feet with iron chains, lashed their backs with iron whips, proclaimed these territories as their own, and still continues to hold them to this very day."

Hashimoto Kingoro's arguments were written in the 1930s, but they continue to reflect the views of many Japanese today, who charge that Japanese actions were judged by a different standard than were those of the European colonial nations and the United States.

Source: William Theodore de Bary, *Sources of Japanese Tradition* (New York: Columbia University Press, 1958).

The Course of World War II

Using *Blitzkrieg*, or "lightning war," Hitler stunned Europe with the speed and efficiency of the German attack. Armored columns, or panzer divisions (a panzer division was a strike force of about 300 tanks and accompanying forces and supplies), supported by airplanes broke quickly through Polish lines and encircled the bewildered Polish troops. Conventional infantry units then moved in to hold the newly conquered territory. Within four weeks, Poland had surrendered. On September 28, 1939, Germany and the Soviet Union officially divided Poland between diem.

Europe at War

Although Hitler's hopes to avoid a war with the western European states were dashed when France and Britain declared war on September 3, he was confident that he could control the situation. After a winter of waiting (called the "phony war"), Hitler resumed the war on April 9, 1940, with another *Blitzkrieg* against Denmark and Norway. One month later, on May 10, the Germans launched their attack on the Netherlands, Belgium, and France. The main assault through Luxembourg and the Ardennes forest was completely unexpected by the French and British forces. German panzer divisions broke through the weak French defensive positions there and raced across northern France, splitting the Allied armies and trapping French troops and the entire British army on the beaches of Dunkirk. Only by heroic efforts did the British succeed in a gigantic evacuation of 330,000 Allied (mostly British) troops. The French capitulated on June 22. German armies occupied about three-fifths of France while the French hero of World War I, Marshal Henri Pétain (1856–1951), established an authoritarian regime (known as Vichy France) over the remainder. Germany was now

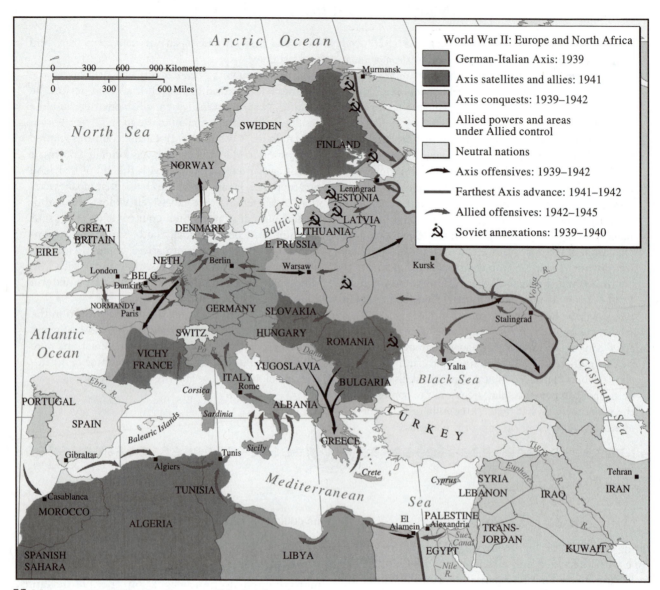

Map 6.1 World War II in Europe and North Africa

in control of western and central Europe, but Britain had still not been defeated.

As Hitler realized, an amphibious invasion of Britain would only be possible if Germany gained control of the air. At the beginning of August 1940, the *Luftwaffe* (the German air force) launched a major offensive against British air and naval bases, harbors, communication centers, and war industries. The British fought back doggedly, supported by an effective radar system that gave them early warning of German attacks. Nevertheless, the British air force suffered critical losses by the end of

August and was probably saved by Hitler's change in strategy. In September, in retaliation for a British attack on Berlin, Hitler ordered a shift from military targets to massive bombing of British cities to break British morale. The British rebuilt their air strength quickly and were soon inflicting major losses on *Luftwaffe* bombers. By the end of September, Germany had lost the Battle of Britain, and the invasion of the British Isles had to be postponed.

At this point, Hitler pursued the possibility of a Mediterranean strategy, which would involve capturing

Egypt and the Suez Canal and closing the Mediterranean to British ships, thereby shutting off Britain's supply of oil. Hitler's commitment to the Mediterranean was never wholehearted, however. His initial plan was to let the Italians defeat the British in North Africa, but this strategy failed when the British routed the Italian army. Although Hitler then sent German troops to the North African theater of war, his primary concern lay elsewhere; he had already reached the decision to fulfill his lifetime obsession with the acquisition of territory in the east.

Although he had no desire for a two-front war, Hitler became convinced that Britain was remaining in the war only because it expected Soviet support. If the Soviet Union were smashed, Britain's last hope would be eliminated. Moreover, Hitler had convinced himself that the Soviet Union, with what he regarded as its Jewish-Bolshevik leadership and a pitiful army, could be defeated quickly and decisively. Although the invasion of the Soviet Union was scheduled for spring 1941, the attack was delayed because of problems in the Balkans. Hitler had already obtained the political cooperation of Hungary, Bulgaria, and Romania, but Mussolini's disastrous invasion of Greece in October 1940 exposed Hitler's southern flank to British air bases in Greece. To secure his Balkan flank, German troops seized both Yugoslavia and Greece in April 1941. Now reassured, Hitler turned to the east and invaded the Soviet Union on June 22, 1941, in the belief that the Soviets could still be decisively defeated before winter set in.

The massive attack stretched out along an 1,800-mile front. German troops advanced rapidly, capturing 2 million Russian soldiers. By November, one German army group had swept through Ukraine, while a second was besieging Leningrad; a third approached within 25 miles of Moscow, the Russian capital. An early winter and unexpected Soviet resistance, however, brought a halt to the German advance. For the first time in the war, German armies had been stopped. A Soviet counterattack in December 1941 by a Soviet army supposedly exhausted by Nazi victories came as an ominous ending to the year for the Germans. By that time, another of Hitler's decisions—the declaration of war on the United States—had turned another European conflict into a global war.

Asia at War

On December 7, 1941, Japanese carrier-based aircraft attacked the U.S. naval base at Pearl Harbor in the Hawaiian Islands. The same day, other units launched assaults on the Philippines and began advancing toward the British colony of Malaya. Shortly thereafter, Japanese forces invaded the Dutch East Indies and occupied a number of islands in the Pacific Ocean. In some cases, as on the Bataan peninsula and the island of Corregidor in the Philippines, resistance was fierce, but by the spring of 1942, almost all of Southeast Asia and much of the western Pacific had fallen into Japanese hands. Japan declared the creation of a Great East Asia Co-prosperity Sphere out of the entire region under Japanese tutelage and announced its intention to liberate the colonies of Southeast Asia from Western rule. For the moment, however, Japan needed the resources of the region for its war machine and placed its conquests under its rule on a wartime basis.

Japanese leaders had hoped that their lightning strike at American bases would destroy the U.S. Pacific Fleet and persuade the Roosevelt administration to accept Japanese domination of the Pacific. The American people, in the eyes of Japanese leaders, had been made soft by material indulgence. But the Japanese had miscalculated. The attack on Pearl Harbor galvanized American opinion and won broad support for Roosevelt's war policy. The United States now joined with European nations and Nationalist China in a combined effort to defeat Japan and bring an end to its hegemony in the Pacific. Believing the American involvement in the Pacific would render the United States ineffective in the European theater of war, Hitler declared war on the United States four days after Pearl Harbor.

The Turning Point of the War, 1942–1943

The entry of the United States into the war created a coalition (the Grand Alliance) that ultimately defeated the Axis powers (Germany, Italy, and Japan). Nevertheless, the three major Allies—Britain, the United States, and the Soviet Union—had to overcome mutual suspicions before they could operate as an effective alliance. Two factors aided that process. First, Hitler's declaration of war on the United States made it easier for the Americans to accept the British and Russian contention that the defeat of Germany should be the first priority of the United States. For that reason, the United States, under its Lend-Lease program, sent large amounts of military aid, including $50 billion worth of trucks, planes, and other arms, to the British and Soviets. Also important to the alliance was the tacit agreement of the three chief Allies to stress military operations while ignoring political differences and larger strategic issues concerning any postwar settlement. At the beginning of

1943, the Allies agreed to fight until the Axis powers surrendered unconditionally. Although this principle of unconditional surrender prevented a repeat of the mistake of World War I, which was ended in 1918 with an armistice rather than a total victory, it likely discouraged dissident Germans and Japanese from overthrowing their governments in order to arrange a negotiated peace. At the same time, it did have the effect of cementing the Grand Alliance by making it nearly impossible for Hitler to divide his foes.

Defeat, however, was far from Hitler's mind at the beginning of 1942. As Japanese forces advanced into Southeast Asia and the Pacific after crippling the American naval fleet at Pearl Harbor, Hitler and his European allies continued the war in Europe against Britain and the Soviet Union. Until the fall of 1942, it appeared that the Germans might still prevail on the battlefield. Reinforcements in North Africa enabled the Afrika Korps under General Erwin Rommel to break through the British defenses in Egypt and advance toward Alexandria. In the spring of 1942, a renewed German offensive in the Soviet Union led to the capture of the entire Crimea, causing Hitler to boast in August 1942:

> As the next step, we are going to advance south of the Caucasus and then help the rebels in Iran and Iraq against the English. Another thrust will be directed along the Caspian Sea toward Afghanistan and India. Then the English will run out of oil. In two years we'll be on the borders of India. Twenty to thirty elite German divisions will do. Then the British Empire will collapse.[7]

But this would be Hitler's last optimistic outburst. By the fall of 1942, the war had turned against the Germans.

In North Africa, British forces stopped Rommel's troops at El Alamein in the summer of 1942 and then forced them back across the desert. In November 1942, British and American forces invaded French North Africa and forced the German and Italian troops to surrender in May 1943. On the Eastern Front, the turning point of the war occurred at Stalingrad. After capturing the Crimea, Hitler's generals wanted him to concentrate on the Caucasus and its oil fields, but Hitler decided that Stalingrad, a major industrial center on the Volga, should be taken first. Between November 1942 and February 1943, German troops were stopped, then encircled, and finally forced to surrender on February 2, 1943. The entire German Sixth Army of 300,000 men was lost. By February 1943, German forces in Russia were back to their positions of June 1942. By the spring of 1943, long before Allied troops returned to the European continent, even Hitler knew that the Germans would not defeat the Soviet Union.

The tide of battle in the Far East also turned dramatically in 1942. In the Battle of the Coral Sea on May 7–8, 1942, American naval forces stopped the Japanese advance and temporarily relieved Australia of the threat of invasion. On June 4, at the Battle of Midway Island, American carrier planes destroyed all four of the attacking Japanese aircraft carriers and established American naval superiority in the Pacific. The victory was especially remarkable in that almost all the American planes were shot down in the encounter. By the fall of 1942, Allied forces were beginning to gather for offensive operations into South China from Burma, through the Indonesian islands by a process of "island hopping" by troops commanded by the American general Douglas MacArthur, and across the Pacific with a combination of U.S. Army, Marine, and Navy attacks on Japanese-held islands. After a series of bitter engagements in the waters off the Solomon Islands from August to November 1942, Japanese fortunes began to fade.

The Last Years of the War

By the beginning of 1943, the tide of battle had turned against Germany, Italy, and Japan. After the Axis forces had surrendered in Tunisia on May 13, 1943, the Allies crossed the Mediterranean and carried the war to Italy. After taking Sicily, Allied troops began the invasion of mainland Italy in September. In the meantime, following the ouster and arrest of Benito Mussolini, a new Italian government offered to surrender to Allied forces. But the Germans, in a daring raid, liberated Mussolini and set him up as the head of a puppet German state in northern Italy, while German troops moved in and occupied much of Italy. The new defensive lines established by the Germans in the hills south of Rome were so effective that the Allied advance up the Italian peninsula was a painstaking affair accompanied by heavy casualties. Rome did not fall to the Allies until June 4, 1944. By that time, the Italian war had assumed a secondary role anyway, as the Allies opened their long-awaited "second front" in western Europe.

Since the autumn of 1943, the Allies had been planning a cross-channel invasion of France from Britain. Under the direction of the American general Dwight D. Eisenhower (1890–1969), the Allies landed five assault divisions on the Normandy beaches on June 6, 1944, in history's greatest naval invasion. An initially indecisive German response enabled the Allied forces to establish a

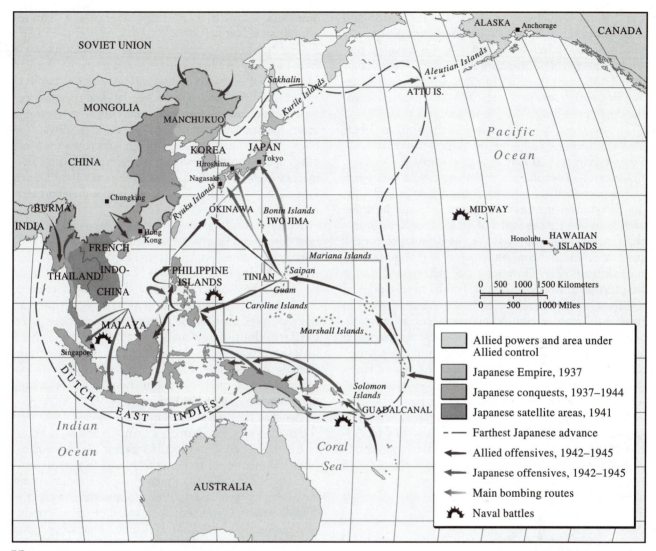

Map 6.2 World War II in Asia and the Pacific

beachhead. Within three months, they had landed 2 million men and a half-million vehicles that pushed inland and broke through German defensive lines.

After the breakout, Allied troops moved south and east, liberating Paris by the end of August. By March 1945, they had crossed the Rhine River and advanced further into Germany. At the end of April 1945, Allied armies in northern Germany moved toward the Elbe River, where they finally linked up with the Soviets. The Soviets had come a long way since the Battle of Stalingrad in 1943. In the summer of 1943, Hitler gambled on taking the offensive by making use of newly developed heavy tanks. At the Battle of Kursk (July 5–12), the greatest tank battle of World War II, the Soviets soundly defeated the German forces. Soviet forces now began a relentless advance westward. The Soviets reoccupied Ukraine by the end of 1943, lifted the siege of Leningrad, and moved into the Baltic states by the beginning of 1944. Advancing along a northern front, Soviet troops occupied Warsaw in January 1945 and entered Berlin in April. Meanwhile, Soviet troops along a southern front swept through Hungary, Romania, and Bulgaria.

In January 1945, Adolf Hitler moved into a bunker 55 feet under Berlin to direct the final stages of the war. In his final political testament, Hitler, consistent to the end in his rabid anti-Semitism, blamed the Jews for the war: "Above all I charge the leaders of the nation and those under them to scrupulous observance of the laws of race and to merciless opposition to the universal poisoner of all peoples, international Jewry."[8] Hitler committed suicide on April 30, two days after Mussolini was shot by partisan Italian forces. On May 7, German commanders surrendered. The war in Europe was over.

The war in Asia continued. Beginning in 1943, American forces had gone on the offensive and advanced their way, slowly at times, across the Pacific. American forces took an increasing toll of enemy resources, especially at sea and in the air. As Allied military power drew inexorably closer to the main Japanese islands in the first months of 1945, President Harry Truman, who had succeeded to the presidency on the death of Franklin Roosevelt in April, had an excruciatingly difficult decision to make. Should he use atomic weapons (at the time, only two bombs were available, and their effectiveness had not been demonstrated) to bring the war to an end without the necessity of an Allied invasion of the Japanese homeland? As the world knows, Truman answered that question in the affirmative. The first bomb was dropped on the city of Hiroshima on August 6. Truman then called on Japan to surrender or expect a "rain of ruin from the air." When the Japanese did not respond, a second bomb was dropped on Nagasaki. Japan surrendered unconditionally on August 14. World War II, in which 17 million combatants died in battle and perhaps 18 million civilians perished as well (some estimate total losses at 50 million), was finally over.

The New Order

The initial victories of the Germans and Japanese gave them the opportunity to create new orders in Europe and Asia. Although both countries presented positive images of these new orders for publicity purposes, in practice both followed policies of ruthless domination of their subject peoples.

The New Order in Europe

After the German victories in Europe, Nazi propagandists created glowing images of a new European order based on "equal chances" for all nations and an integrated economic community. Hitler's conception of a European New Order was rather different. He saw the Europe he had conquered simply as subject to German

domination. Only the Germans, he once said, "can really organize Europe."

The Nazi empire stretched across continental Europe from the English Channel in the west to the outskirts of Moscow in the east. In no way was this empire organized systematically or governed efficiently. Nazi-occupied Europe was generally organized in one of two ways. Some areas, such as western Poland, were directly annexed by Nazi Germany and made into German provinces. Most of occupied Europe, however, was administered by German military or civilian officials in combination with varying degrees of indirect control from collaborationist regimes.

Racial considerations played an important role in how conquered peoples were treated. German civil administrations were established in Norway, Denmark, and the Netherlands because the Nazis considered their peoples to be Aryan, or racially akin to the Germans, and hence worthy of more lenient treatment. "Inferior" Latin peoples, such as the occupied French, were given military administrations. By 1943, however, as Nazi losses continued to multiply, all the occupied territories of northern and western Europe were ruthlessly exploited for material goods and manpower for Germany's labor needs.

Because the conquered lands in the east contained the living space for German expansion and were populated in Nazi eyes by racially inferior Slavic peoples, Nazi administration there was considerably more ruthless. Hitler's racial ideology and his plans for an Aryan racial empire were so important to him that he and the Nazis began to implement their racial program soon after the conquest of Poland. Heinrich Himmler, a strong believer in Nazi racial ideology and the leader of the SS, was put in charge of German resettlement plans in the east. Himmler's task was to evacuate the inferior Slavic peoples and replace them with Germans, a policy first applied to the new German provinces created from the lands of western Poland. One million Poles were uprooted and dumped in southern Poland. Hundreds of thousands of ethnic Germans (descendants of Germans who had migrated years ago from Germany to different parts of southern and eastern Europe) were encouraged to colonize designated areas in Poland. By 1942, 2 million ethnic Germans had been settled in Poland.

The invasion of the Soviet Union inflated Nazi visions of German colonization in the east. Hitler spoke to his intimate circle of a colossal project of social engineering after the war, in which Poles, Ukrainians, and Russians would become slave labor while German peasants settled on the abandoned lands and Germanized them. Nazis involved in this kind of planning were well aware of the human costs. Himmler, unconcerned, told a gathering of SS officers that the destruction of 30 million Slavs was a prerequisite for German plans in the east. "Whether nations live in prosperity or starve to death interests me only insofar as we need them as slaves for our culture. Otherwise it is of no interest."[9]

Labor shortages in Germany led to a policy of ruthless mobilization of foreign labor. After the invasion of the Soviet Union, the 4 million Russian prisoners of war captured by the Germans, along with more than 2 million workers conscripted in France, became a major source of heavy labor—much of it wasted by allowing more than 3 million of them to die from neglect. In 1942, a special office was created to recruit labor for German farms and industries. By the summer of 1944, 7 million foreign workers were laboring in Germany, constituting 20 percent of Germany's labor force. At the same time, another 7 million workers were supplying forced labor in their own countries on farms, in industries, and even in military camps. Forced labor, however, often proved counterproductive because it created economic chaos in occupied countries and disrupted industrial production that could have helped Germany. The brutal character of Germany's recruitment policies often led more and more people to resist the Nazi occupation forces.

The Holocaust

No aspect of the Nazi New Order was more terrifying than the deliberate attempt to exterminate the Jewish people of Europe. Racial struggle was a key element in Hitler's ideology and meant to him a clearly defined conflict of opposites: the Aryans, creators of human cultural development, against the Jews, parasites who were trying to destroy the Aryans. By the beginning of 1939, Nazi policy focused on promoting the "emigration" of German Jews from Germany. Once the war began in September 1939, the so-called Jewish problem took on new dimensions. For a while there was discussion of the Madagascar Plan—a mass shipment of Jews to the African island of Madagascar. When war contingencies made this plan impractical, an even more drastic policy was conceived.

Heinrich Himmler and the SS organization closely shared Hitler's racial ideology. The SS was given responsibility for what the Nazis called their Final Solution to the Jewish problem—that is, the annihilation of the

Jewish people. Reinhard Heydrich (1904–1942), head of the SS's Security Service, was given administrative responsibility for the Final Solution. After the defeat of Poland, Heydrich ordered the special strike forces (Einsatzgruppen) that he had created to round up all Polish Jews and concentrate them in ghettos established in a number of Polish cities.

In June 1941, the Einsatzgruppen were given new responsibilities as mobile killing units. These SS death squads followed the regular army's advance into the Soviet Union. Their job was to round up Jews in the villages and execute and bury them in mass graves, often giant pits dug by the victims themselves before they were shot. Such constant killing produced morale problems among the SS executioners. During a visit to Minsk in the Soviet Union, Himmler tried to build morale by pointing out that

> he would not like it if Germans did such a thing gladly. But their conscience was in no way impaired, for they were soldiers who had to carry out every order unconditionally. He alone had responsibility before God and Hitler for everything that was happening, . . . and he was acting from a deep understanding of the necessity for this operation.[10]

Although it has been estimated that as many as 1 million Jews were killed by the Einsatzgruppen, this approach to solving the Jewish problem was soon perceived as inadequate. Instead, the Nazis opted for the systematic annihilation of the European Jewish population in specially built death camps. The plan was basically simple. Jews from countries occupied by Germany (or sympathetic to Germany) would be rounded up, packed like cattle into freight trains, and shipped to Poland, where six extermination centers were built for this purpose. The largest and most famous was Auschwitz-Birkenau. Medical technicians chose Zyklon B (the commercial name for hydrogen cyanide) as the most effective gas for quickly killing large numbers of people in gas chambers designed to took like "shower rooms" to facilitate the cooperation of the victims. After gassing, the corpses would be burned in specially built crematoria.

By the spring of 1942, the death camps were in operation. Although initial priority was given to the elimination of the ghettos in Poland, by the summer of 1942, Jews were also being shipped from France, Belgium, and Holland. Even as the Allies were making significant advances in 1944, Jews were being shipped from Greece and Hungary. These shipments depended on the cooperation of Germany's Transport Ministry, but despite desperate military needs, the Final Solution had priority in using railroad cars to transport Jews to death camps.

A harrowing experience awaited the Jews when they arrived at one of the six death camps. Rudolf Höss, commandant at Auschwitz-Birkenau, described it:

> We had two SS doctors on duty at Auschwitz to examine the incoming transports of prisoners. The prisoners would be marched by one of the doctors who would make spot decisions as they walked by. Those who were fit for work were sent into the camp. Others were sent immediately to the extermination plants. Children of tender years were invariably exterminated since by reason of their youth they were unable to work. . . . at Auschwitz we endeavored to fool the victims into thinking that they were to go through a delousing process. Of course, frequently they realized our true intentions and we sometimes had riots and difficulties due to that fact.[11]

About 30 percent of the arrivals at Auschwitz were sent to a labor camp, while the remainder went to the gas chambers. After they had been gassed, the bodies were burned in the crematoria. The victims' goods and even their bodies were used for economic gain. Women's hair was cut off, collected, and turned into mattresses or cloth. Some inmates were also subjected to cruel and painful "medical" experiments. The Germans killed between 5 and 6 million Jews, more than 3 million of them in the death camps. Virtually 90 percent of the Jewish populations of Poland, the Baltic countries, and Germany were exterminated. Overall, the Holocaust was responsible for the death of nearly two out of every three European Jews.

The Nazis were also responsible for another Holocaust—the death by shooting, starvation, or overwork of at least another 9 to 10 million people. Because the Nazis considered the Gypsies of Europe (like the Jews) an alien race, they were systematically rounded up for extermination. About 40 percent of Europe's 1 million Gypsies were killed in the death camps. The leading elements of the "subhuman" Slavic peoples—the clergy, intelligentsia, civil leaders, judges, and lawyers—were arrested and deliberately killed. Probably an additional 4 million Poles, Ukrainians, and Belorussians lost their lives as slave laborers for Nazi Germany, and at least 3 to 4 million Soviet prisoners of war were killed in captivity. The Nazis also singled out homosexuals for persecution, and thousands lost their lives in concentration camps.

The New Order in Asia

Once the Japanese takeover was completed, Japanese policy in the occupied areas of Asia became essentially defensive, as Japan hoped to use its new possessions to meet its burgeoning needs for raw materials, such as tin, oil, and rubber, as well as an outlet for Japanese manufactured goods. To provide an organizational structure for the arrangement, Japanese leaders set up the Great East Asia Co-prosperity Sphere, a self-sufficient economic community designed to provide mutual benefits to the occupied areas and the home country. A Ministry for Great East Asia, staffed by civilians, was established in Tokyo in October 1942 to handle relations between Japan and the conquered territories.

The Japanese conquest of Southeast Asia had been accomplished under the slogan "Asia for the Asiatics," and many Japanese probably sincerely believed that their government was bringing about the liberation of the Southeast Asian peoples from European colonial rule. Japanese officials in the occupied territories quickly made contact with anticolonialist elements and promised that independent governments would be established under Japanese tutelage. Such governments were eventually established in Burma, the Dutch East Indies, Vietnam, and the Philippines.

In fact, however, real power rested with the Japanese military authorities in each territory, and the local Japanese military command was directly subordinated to the Army General Staff in Tokyo. The economic resources of the colonies were exploited for the benefit of the Japanese war machine, while natives were recruited to serve in local military units or conscripted to work on public works projects. In some cases, the people living in the occupied areas were subjected to severe hardships. In Indochina, for example, forced requisitions of rice by the local Japanese authorities for shipment abroad created a food shortage that caused the starvation of more than a million Vietnamese in 1944 and 1945.

The Japanese planned to implant a new moral and social order as well as a new political and economic order in the occupied areas. Occupation policy stressed traditional values such as obedience, community spirit, filial piety, and discipline that reflected the prevailing political and cultural bias in Japan, while supposedly Western values such as materialism, liberalism, and individualism were strongly discouraged. In order to promote the creation of this New Order, as it was called, occupation authorities gave particular support to local religious organizations, but discouraged the formation of formal political parties.

At first, many Southeast Asian nationalists took Japanese promises at face value and agreed to cooperate with their new masters. In Burma, an independent government was established in 1943 and subsequently declared war on the Allies. But as the exploitative nature of Japanese occupation policies became increasingly clear, sentiment turned against the New Order. Japanese officials sometimes unwittingly provoked resentment by their arrogance and contempt for local customs. In the Dutch East Indies, for example, Indonesians were required to bow in the direction of Tokyo and recognize the divinity of the Japanese emperor, practices that were repugnant to Muslims. In Burma, Buddhist pagodas were sometimes used as military latrines.

Such Japanese behavior created a dilemma for many nationalists, who had no desire to see the return of the colonial powers. Some turned against the Japanese, while others lapsed into inactivity. Indonesian patriots tried to have it both ways, feigning support for Japan while attempting to sabotage the Japanese administration. In French Indochina, Ho Chi Minh's Indochinese Communist Party established contacts with American military units in South China and agreed to provide information on Japanese troop movements and rescue downed American fliers in the area. In Malaya, where Japanese treatment of ethnic Chinese residents was especially harsh, many joined a guerrilla movement against the occupying forces. By the end of the war, little support remained in the region for the erstwhile "liberators."

The Home Front: Two Examples

World War II was even more of a total war than World War I. Fighting was much more widespread and covered most of the world. Economic mobilization was more extensive; so too was the mobilization of women. The number of civilians killed was far higher; almost 20 million were killed from bombing raids, mass extermination policies, and attacks by invading armies.

The home fronts of the major belligerents varied considerably, based on local circumstances. World War II had an enormous impact on the Soviet Union. Two out of every five persons killed in World War II were Soviet citizens. Leningrad experienced 900 days of siege, during which its inhabitants became so desperate for food that they ate dogs, cats, and mice. As the German army made its rapid advance into Soviet territory, the factories in the western part of the Soviet Union were dismantled and shipped to the interior—to the Urals, western Siberia, and the Volga region.

Soviet women played a major role in the war effort. Women and girls worked in industries, mines, and rail-

roads. Overall, the number of women working in industry increased almost 60 percent. Soviet women were also expected to dig antitank ditches and work as air-raid wardens. Finally, the Soviet Union was the only country to use women as combatants in World War II. Soviet women functioned as snipers and also as aircrews in bomber squadrons. The female pilots who helped to defeat the Germans at Stalingrad were known as the "Night Witches."

The home front in the United States was quite different from those of its chief wartime allies, largely because the United States faced no threat of war on its own territory. Although the economy and labor force were slow to mobilize, eventually the United States became the arsenal of the Allied powers, producing the military equipment they needed. At the height of war production in 1943, the nation was constructing six ships a day and $6 billion worth of war-related goods a month.

The mobilization of the U.S. economy produced social problems. The construction of new factories created boomtowns where thousands came to work but then faced shortages of housing, health facilities, and schools. More than 1 million African Americans migrated from the rural South to the industrial cities of the North and West, looking for jobs in industry. The presence of African Americans in areas where they had not been present before led to racial tensions and sometimes even race riots.

Japanese Americans were treated shabbily. On the West Coast, 110,000 Japanese Americans, 65 percent of them born in the United States, were removed to camps encircled by barbed wire and made to take loyalty oaths. Although public officials claimed this policy was necessary for security reasons, no similar treatment of German Americans or Italian Americans ever took place.

In Japan, society was placed on a wartime footing even before the attack on Pearl Harbor. A conscription law was passed in 1938, and economic resources were placed under strict government control. Two years later, all political parties were merged into an Imperial Rule Assistance Association. Labor unions were dissolved, and education and culture were purged of all "corrupt" Western ideas in favor of traditional values emphasizing the divinity of the emperor and the higher spirituality of Japanese civilization. During the war, individual rights were severely curtailed, as the entire population was harnessed to the needs of the war effort. Thousands of women—many from among the Korean residents of Japan and the Korean peninsula, or from occupied areas in

Southeast Asia and China—were conscripted to serve as "comfort women" for brothels set up for the use of the Japanese troops.

The Aftermath of the War

The total victory of the Allies in World War II was not followed by a real peace, but by the beginnings of a new conflict, known as the Cold War, that dominated world politics until the end of the 1980s. The Cold War stemmed from the military, political, and ideological differences, especially between the Soviet Union and the United States, that became apparent at the Allied war conferences held in the last years of the war. Although Allied leaders were mostly preoccupied with how to end the war, they were also strongly motivated by differing, and often conflicting, visions of the postwar world.

Stalin, Roosevelt, and Churchill, the leaders of the Big Three of the Grand Alliance, met at Tehran (the capital of Iran) in November 1943 to decide the future course of the war. Their major strategic decision concerned the final assault on Germany. Stalin and Roosevelt argued successfully for an American-British invasion of the Continent through France, which they scheduled for the spring of 1944. The acceptance of this plan had important consequences. It meant that Soviet and British-American forces would meet in defeated Germany along a north-south dividing line and that, most likely, Eastern Europe would be liberated by Soviet forces. The Allies also agreed to a partition of postwar Germany until denazification could take place. Roosevelt privately assured Stalin that Soviet borders in Europe would be moved westward to compensate for the loss of territories belonging to the old Russian Empire after World War I. Poland would receive lands in eastern Germany to make up for territory lost in the east to the Soviet Union.

By the time of the conference at Yalta in southern Russia in February 1945, the defeat of Germany was a foregone conclusion. The Western powers, who had earlier believed that the Soviets were in a weak position, were now faced with the reality of 11 million Red Army soldiers taking possession of eastern and much of central Europe. Stalin was still operating under the notion of spheres of influence. He was deeply suspicious of the Western powers and desired a buffer to protect the Soviet Union from possible future Western aggression. At the same time, Stalin was eager to obtain economically important resources and strategic military positions. Roosevelt by this time was moving away from the no-

tion of spheres of influence to the more Wilsonian ideal of self-determination. He called for "the end of the system of unilateral action, exclusive alliances, and spheres of influence." The Grand Alliance approved a "Declaration on Liberated Europe," pledging to assist liberated Europe in the creation of "democratic institutions of their own choice." Liberated countries were to hold free elections to determine their political systems.

At Yalta, Roosevelt sought Soviet military help against Japan. The atomic bomb was not yet assured, and American military planners feared the possible loss of as many as 1 million men in amphibious assaults on the Japanese home islands. Roosevelt therefore agreed to Stalin's price for military assistance against Japan: possession of Sakhalin and the Kurile Islands, as well as two warm-water ports and railroad rights in Manchuria.

The creation of the United Nations was a major American concern at Yalta. Roosevelt hoped to ensure the participation of the Big Three powers in a postwar international organization before difficult issues divided them into hostile camps. After a number of compromises, both Churchill and Stalin accepted Roosevelt's plans for a United Nations organization and set the first meeting for San Francisco in April of 1945.

The issues of Germany and eastern Europe were treated less decisively. The Big Three reaffirmed that Germany must surrender unconditionally and created four occupation zones. German reparations were set at $20 billion. A compromise was also worked out in regard to Poland. Stalin agreed to free elections in the future to determine a new government. But the issue of free elections in eastern Europe caused a serious rift between the Soviets and the Americans. The principle was that eastern European governments would be freely elected, but they were also supposed to be pro-Soviet. As Churchill expressed it: "The Poles will have their future in their own hands, with the single limitation that they must honestly follow in harmony with their allies, a policy friendly to Russia."[12] This attempt to reconcile the irreconcilable was doomed to failure. Even before the conference at Potsdam took place in July 1945, Western relations with the Soviets had begun to deteriorate rapidly. The Grand Alliance had been one of necessity, in which ideological incompatibility had been subordinated to the pragmatic concerns of the war. The Allied powers' only common aim was the defeat of Nazism. Once this aim had been all but accomplished, the many differences that antagonized East-West relations came to the surface.

The Potsdam conference of July 1945, the last Allied conference of World War II, consequently began under a

◆ **The Victorious Allied Leaders at Yalta.** Even before World War II ended, the leaders of the Big Three of the Grand Alliance—Churchill, Roosevelt, and Stalin (shown seated from left to right)—met in wartime conferences to plan the final assault on Germany and negotiate the outlines of the postwar settlement. At the Yalta meeting (February 5–11, 1945), the three leaders concentrated on postwar issues. The American president, who died two months later, was already a worn-out man at Yalta.

cloud of mistrust. Roosevelt had died on April 12 and had been succeeded as president by Harry Truman. During the conference, Truman received word that the atomic bomb had been successfully tested. Some historians have argued that this knowledge stiffened Truman's resolve against the Soviets. Whatever the reasons, there was a new coldness in the relations between the Soviets and Americans. At Potsdam, Truman demanded free elections throughout eastern Europe. Stalin responded: "A freely elected government in any of these East European countries would be anti-Soviet, and that we cannot allow."[13] After a bitterly fought and devastating war, Stalin sought absolute military security, which in his view could only be ensured by the presence of communist states in eastern Europe. Free elections might result in governments hostile to the Soviet Union. By the middle of 1945, only an invasion by Western forces could undo developments in eastern Europe and, in the immediate aftermath of the world's most destructive conflict, few people favored such a policy. But the stage was set for a new confrontation, this time between the two major victors of World War II.

Conclusion

World War II was the most devastating total war in human history. Germany, Italy, and Japan had been utterly defeated. Perhaps as many as 40 million people—both soldiers and civilians—had been killed in only six years. In Asia and Europe, cities had been reduced to rubble, and millions of people faced starvation as once fertile lands stood neglected or wasted. Untold millions of people had become refugees.

What were the underlying causes of the war? Certainly one direct cause of the conflict was the effort by two rising capitalist powers, Germany and Japan, to make up for their relatively late arrival on the scene to carve out their own global empires. Key elements in both countries had resented the agreements reached after the end of World War I that divided the world in a manner favorable to their rivals, and hoped to overturn them at the earliest opportunity. Neither Germany nor Japan possessed a strong tradition of political pluralism; to the contrary, in both countries the legacy of a feudal past marked by a strong military tradition still wielded strong influence over the political system and the mindset of the entire population. It is no surprise that under the impact the Great Depression, the effects of which were severe in both countries, fragile democratic institutions were soon overwhelmed by militant forces determined to enhance national wealth and power.

Given this perspective, there has long been a broad consensus within the victorious nations that—unlike the case of World War I, where responsibility for causing the war has often been placed on the entire system, rather than solely on the leaders of the Central Powers—responsibility for World War II falls squarely on the shoulders of leaders in Berlin and Tokyo who were willfully determined to reverse the verdict of Versailles and divide the world between them. But the argument has occasionally been made that World War II, like its predecessor, was a product of the intense rivalries among the imperialist powers, and that Germany and Japan (and Italy as well) were only among the more active players in this great game. That view is especially prevalent in postwar Japan, where conservative elements argue that Japan was only attempting to realize the same imperialist ambitions as its rivals in the West and, because it was an Asian country itself, with more justification.

There is some plausibility to the argument that World War II was a product of imperialist rivalries in the same way that its predecessor was a consequence of balance-of-power tensions in Europe. But the blatant attempt by Hitler's Germany to dominate all of Europe was clearly a step beyond the ambitions of the great powers before World War I, while Hitler's program of Aryanization was unique in its ferocity. Although Japan was not guilty of carrying out a program of systematic ethnic cleansing, its treatment of subject populations in occupied areas was frequently brutal and earned the lasting enmity of many of the people in neighboring regions of Asia.

Whatever the causes of World War II, the consequences were soon to be evident. European hegemony over the world was at an end, and two new superpowers had emerged on the fringes of Western civilization to take its place. Even before the last battles had been fought, the United States and the Soviet Union had arrived at different visions of the postwar world. No sooner had the war ended than their differences created a new and potentially even more devastating Cold War. Though Europeans seemed merely pawns in the struggle between the two superpowers, they managed to stage a remarkable recovery of their own civilization. In Asia, defeated Japan made a miraculous economic recovery, while an era of European domination finally came to an end.

NOTES

1. Benito Mussolini, "The Doctrine of Fascism," in *Italian Fascisms from Pareto to Gentile,* ed. Adrian Lyttleton, (London, 1973), p. 42.
2. Quoted in Alexander De Grand, "Women under Italian Fascism," *Historical Journal* 19 (1976): 958–59.
3. Quoted in Jeremy Noakes and Geoffrey Pridham, eds., *Nazism, 1919–1945* (Exeter, 1983), 1:50–51.
4. Quoted in Joachim Fest, *Hitler,* trans. Richard and Clara Winston (New York, 1974), p. 418.
5. Adolf Hitler, *Mein Kampf,* trans. Ralph Manheim (Boston, 1971), p. 654.
6. Memorandum by John Van Antwerp MacMurray, quoted in Arthur Waldron, *How the Peace Was Lost: The 1935 Memorandum* (Stanford, CA, 1992), p. 5.
7. Quoted in Albert Speer, *Spandau,* trans. Richard and Clara Winston (New York, 1976), p. 50.
8. *Nazi Conspiracy and Aggression* (Washington, 1946), 6:262.
9. International Military Tribunal, *Trial of the Major War Criminals* (Nuremberg, 1947–1949), 22:480.
10. Quoted in Raul Hilberg, *The Destruction of the European Jews,* rev. ed. (New York, 1985), 1:332–33.
11. *Nazi Conspiracy and Aggression,* 6:789.
12. Quoted in Norman Graebner, *Cold War Diplomacy, 1945–1960* (Princeton, 1962), p. 117.
13. Ibid.

PART II

Reflections

*B*y 1945, the era of European hegemony over world affairs was severely shaken. As World War I was followed by revolutions, the Great Depression, the mass murder machines of totalitarian regimes, and the destructiveness of World War II, it appeared to many that European civilization had become a nightmare. Europeans, accustomed to dominating the world at the beginning of the twentieth century, now watched helplessly at mid-century as the two new superpowers—the United States and the Soviet Union—created by their two world wars took control of their destinies. Moreover, the power of the European states had been destroyed by the exhaustive struggles of World War II, and the colonial powers no longer had the energy or wealth to maintain their colonial empires after the war. With the decline of Western power, a new era of global relationships was about to begin.

What were the underlying causes of the astounding spectacle of self-destruction that engaged the European powers in two bloody internecine conflicts that broke out within a period of less than a quarter of a century? One factor was the rise of the spirit of nationalism. Modern nationalism, of course, had developed first in Europe during the French Revolution, and it proved to be an especially powerful force. But its political orientation varied according to time and place. In the first half of the nineteenth century, nationalism in Europe was closely identified with liberals, who pursued both individual rights and national unification and independence. Liberal nationalists maintained that unified, independent nation-states could best preserve individual rights.

After the unification of Italy and Germany in 1871, however, nationalism entered a new stage of development. The new nationalism of the late nineteenth century, tied to conservatism, was loud and chauvinistic. As one exponent expressed it, "a true nationalist places his country above everything"; he believes in the "exclusive pursuit of national policies" and "the steady increase in national power—for a nation declines when it loses military might." It was sentiments such as these that resulted in bitter disputes and civil strife in a number of

countries and contributed to the competition among nations that eventually erupted into world war.

Another factor that contributed to the violent character of the early twentieth century was the Industrial Revolution, with its accompanying technological improvements. Technology transformed the nature of war itself. New weapons of mass destruction created the potential for a new kind of warfare that reached beyond the battlefield into the very heartland of the enemy's territory, while the concept of nationalism transformed war from the sport of kings to a matter of national honor and commitment. Since the French Revolution, when the revolutionary government in Paris had mobilized the entire country by a levy-in-mass (mass conscription) to fight against the forces that opposed the revolution, governments had relied on mass conscription to defend the national cause while their engines of destruction reached far into enemy territory to destroy the industrial base and undermine the will to fight. This trend was amply demonstrated in the two world wars of the twentieth century. Each was a product of antagonisms that had been unleashed by economic competition and growing national consciousness. Each resulted in a level of destruction that severely damaged the material foundations and eroded the popular spirit of the participants, the victors as well as the vanquished.

In the end, then, industrial power and the driving force of nationalism, the very factors that had created the conditions for European global dominance, contained the seeds for the decline of that dominance. These seeds germinated during the 1930s, when the Great Depression sharpened international competition and mutual antagonisms, and then sprouted in the ensuing conflict, which for the first time embraced the entire globe. By the time World War II came to an end, the once-powerful countries of Europe were exhausted, leaving the door ajar for the emergence of two new global superpowers, the United States and the Soviet Union, who dominated the postwar political scene. Although the new superpowers were both products of modern European civilization, they were physically and politically separate from it, and their intense competition, which marked the postwar period, threatened to transform the old map of Europe into a battleground for a new and even more destructive ideological conflict.

If in Europe the dominant fact of the era was the Industrial Revolution, in the rest of the world it was undoubtedly the sheer fact of Western imperialism. Between the end of the Napoleonic wars and the end of the nineteenth century, European powers, or their rivals in Japan and the United States, achieved political mastery over virtually the entire remainder of the world.

What was the overall effect of imperialism on the subject peoples? It seems clear from this narrative that for most of the population in colonial areas, Western domination was rarely beneficial and was often destructive. Although a limited number of merchants, large landowners, and traditional hereditary elites undoubtedly prospered under the umbrella of the expanding imperialist economic order, the majority of people, urban and rural alike, probably suffered considerable hardship as a result of the policies adopted by their foreign rulers. The effects of the Industrial Revolution on the poor had been felt in Europe, too, but there the pain was eased somewhat by the fact that the industrial era had laid the foundations for future technological advances and material abundance. In the colonial territories, the importation of modern technology was limited, while most of the profits from manufacturing and commerce fled abroad. For too many, the "white man's burden" was shifted to the shoulders of the colonial peoples.

Some historians point out, however, that for all the inequities of the colonial system, the colonial experience had another side as well. It provided some economic benefits such as expanded markets and the beginnings of a modern transportation and communications network. The Western intruders also introduced a number of new ideas to the peoples of Asia and Africa and provided new ways of looking at human society and its relationship to the individual.

Perhaps the most influential concept introduced from the West was nationalism. The concept of nationalism served a useful role in many countries in Asia and Africa, where it provided colonial peoples with a sense of common purpose that later proved vital in knitting together diverse elements in their societies to oppose colonial regimes and create the conditions for future independent states. At first, such movements achieved relatively little success, but they began to gather momentum in the second quarter of the twentieth century, when full-fledged nationalist movements began to appear throughout the colonial world to lead their people in the struggle for independence.

Another idea that gained currency in colonial areas was that of democracy. As a rule, colonial regimes did not make a serious attempt to introduce democratic institutions to their subject populations; understandably, they feared that such institutions would inevitably undermine colonial authority. Nevertheless, Western notions of representative government and individual freedom had their advocates in India, Vietnam, China, and Japan well before the end of the nineteenth century. Later, countless Asians and Africans were exposed to such ideas in schools set up by the colonial regime or in the course of travel to Europe or the United States. Most of the nationalist parties founded in colonial territories espoused democratic principles and attempted to apply them when they took power after the restoration of independence.

As we shall see later, in most instances such programs were premature. For the most part, the experiment with democracy in postwar African and Asian societies was a brief one. But the popularity of democratic ideals among educated elites in colonial societies was a clear indication of democracy's universal appeal and a sign that it would become a meaningful part of the political culture after the dismantling of the colonial regimes. The idea of the nation, composed of free, educated, and politically active citizens, was now widely accepted throughout much of the non-Western world.

In an earlier chapter, we attempted to draw up a final balance sheet on the era of Western imperialism. To its defenders, it was a necessary stage in the evolution of the human race, a flawed but essentially humanitarian effort to provide the backward peoples of Africa and Asia with a boost up the ladder of social evolution. To its critics, it was a tragedy of major proportions. The insatiable drive of the advanced economic powers for access to raw materials and markets resulted in the widespread destruction of traditional cultures and created an exploitative environment that transformed the vast majority of colonial peoples into a permanent underclass while restricting the benefits of modern technology to a privileged few. Sophisticated, age-old societies that should have been left to respond to the technological revolution in their own way were subjected to foreign rule and squeezed dry of precious national resources under the guise of the "civilizing mission."

In this debate, the critics surely have the best of the argument. Although the ruling colonial powers did make a halfhearted gesture toward introducing the technology and ideas that had accompanied the rise of modern Europe, all in all, the colonial experience was a brutal one whose benefits accrued almost entirely to citizens of the ruling power. The argument that the Western societies had a "white man's burden" to civilize the world was all too often a hypocritical gesture to salve the guilty feelings of those who recognized imperialism for what it was—a savage act of rape.

The final judgment on the age of European dominance, then, must be a mixed one. It was a time of unfulfilled expectations, of altruism and greed, of bright promise and tragic failure. The fact is, human beings had learned how to master some of the forces of nature before they had learned how to order relations among themselves or temper their own natures for the common good. The consequences were painful, for European and non-European peoples alike.

Did the system serve the interests of the colonial powers? On the face of it, the answer seems obvious, since it provided cheap raw materials and markets for Western manufactured goods, both essential to the effective operation of the capitalist system. But some recent observers of the phenomenon have concluded that the possession of colonies was not always beneficial to those who possessed them. According to the French economic historian Jacques Marseille, for example, the cost of maintaining the French colonial empire, on balance, exceeded the economic benefits it provided, especially since the maintenance of a protected market in the colonies hindered the French effort to create an industrial sector capable of competing in the global marketplace. Such costs did not become fully apparent until after World War II, however, as we shall see in subsequent chapters.

Across the Ideological Divide

CHAPTER
7

In the Grip of the Cold War:
The Breakdown of the Yalta System

Our meeting here in the Crimea has reaffirmed our common determination to maintain and strengthen in the peace to come that unity of purpose and of action which has made victory possible and certain for the United Nations in this war. We believe that this is a sacred obligation which our Governments owe to our peoples and to all the peoples of the world.[1]

With these ringing words, drafted at the Yalta Conference in February 1945, President Franklin D. Roosevelt, Generalissimo Joseph Stalin, and Prime Minister Winston Churchill affirmed their common hope that the Grand Alliance which had brought their countries to victory in World War II could be sustained into the postwar era. Only through the continuing and growing cooperation and understanding among the three victorious allies, the statement asserted, could a secure and lasting peace be realized which, in the words of the Atlantic Charter, would "afford assurance that all the men in all the lands may live out their lives in freedom from fear and want."

President Franklin D. Roosevelt hoped that the decisions reached at Yalta would provide the basis for a stable peace in the postwar era. Allied occupation forces—American, British, and French in the West and Soviet in the East—were to bring about the end of Axis administration and the holding of free elections to create democratic governments throughout Europe. To foster an attitude of mutual trust and an end to the suspicions that had marked relations between the capitalist world and the USSR prior to World War II, Roosevelt tried to reassure Generalissimo Stalin that Moscow's legitimate territorial aspirations and genuine security needs would be adequately met in a durable peace settlement.

It was not to be. Within months after the German surrender, the attitude of mutual trust among the victorious allies—if it had ever existed—rapidly disintegrated, and the dream of a stable peace was replaced by the specter of a nuclear holocaust. As the Cold War conflict between Moscow and Washington intensified, Europe was divided into two armed camps, while the two superpowers, glaring at each other across a deep ideological divide, held the survival of the entire world in their hands.

The Collapse of the Grand Alliance

The problem started in Europe. At the end of the war, Soviet military forces occupied all of Eastern Europe and the Balkans (except for Greece, Albania, and Yugoslavia), while U.S. and other allied forces completed their occupation of the western part of the continent. Roosevelt had assumed that free elections administered by "democratic and peace-loving forces" would bring about the creation of democratic governments responsive to the aspirations of the local population. But it soon be-

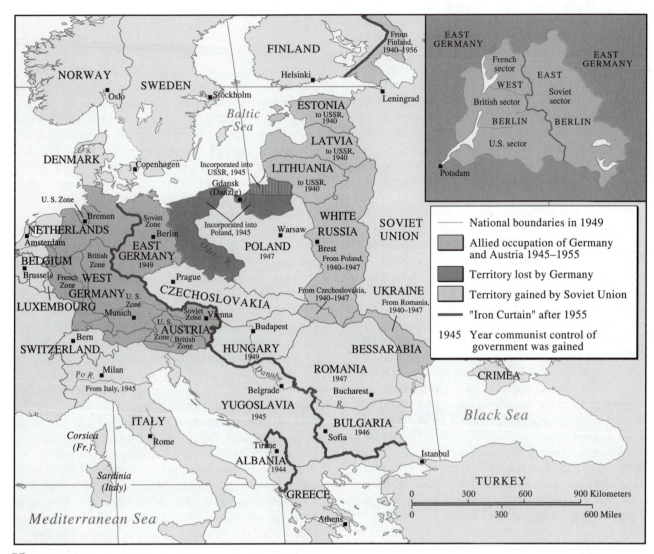

Map legend:

National boundaries in 1949

Allied occupation of Germany and Austria 1945–1955

Territory lost by Germany

Territory gained by Soviet Union

"Iron Curtain" after 1955

1945 Year communist control of government was gained

❊ Map 7.1   Territorial Changes in Europe after World War II

came clear that Moscow and Washington disagreed in their interpretation of the Yalta agreement. When Soviet occupation authorities turned their attention to forming a new Polish government in Warsaw, Stalin refused to accept the legitimacy of the Polish government-in-exile—headquartered in London during the war, it was composed primarily of representatives of the landed aristocracy who harbored a deep distrust of the USSR—and instead created a government composed of Communists who had spent the war in Moscow. Roosevelt complained to Stalin, but FDR was preoccupied with other problems and eventually he agreed to a compromise solution whereby two members of the exile government in London were included in a new regime dominated by

the Communists. A week later, Roosevelt was dead of a cerebral hemorrhage.

Similar developments took place elsewhere in Eastern Europe, as all of the states occupied by Soviet troops became part of Moscow's sphere of influence. Coalitions of all political parties (except fascist or right-wing parties) were formed to run the government, but within a year or two, the Communist parties in these coalitions had assumed the lion's share of power. The next step was the creation of one-party Communist governments. The timetables for these takeovers varied from country to country, but between 1945 and 1947, Communist governments became firmly entrenched in East Germany, Bulgaria, Romania, Poland, and

Hungary. In Czechoslovakia, with its strong tradition of democratic institutions, the Communists did not achieve their goals until 1948. In the elections of 1946, the Communist Party of Czechoslovakia became the largest party. But it was not all-powerful and shared control of the government with the non-Communist parties. When it appeared that the latter might win new elections early in 1948, the Communists seized control of the government on February 25. All other parties were dissolved, and the Communist leader Klement Gottwald became the new president of Czechoslovakia.

Albania and Yugoslavia were notable exceptions to the pattern of growing Soviet dominance in Eastern Europe. The Communist Party had led resistance to the Nazis in both countries during the war, and both parties easily took over power when the war ended. In Albania, local Communists established a rigidly Stalinist regime, but one that grew increasingly independent of the Soviet Union.

In Yugoslavia, Josip Broz, known as Tito (1892–1980), the leader of the Communist resistance movement, appeared to be a loyal Stalinist. After the war, however, he moved toward the establishment of an independent Communist state in Yugoslavia. Stalin hoped to take control of Yugoslavia, just as he had done in other Eastern European countries. But Tito refused to capitulate to Stalin's demands and gained the support of the people (and some sympathy in the West) by portraying the struggle as one of Yugoslav national freedom. In 1958, the Yugoslav party congress asserted that Yugoslav Communists did not see themselves as deviating from communism, only from Stalinism. They considered their way closer to the Marxist-Leninist ideal, including a more decentralized economic and political system in which workers could manage themselves and local communes could exercise some political power.

To Joseph Stalin (who had once boasted "I will shake my little finger, and there will be no more Tito"), the creation of pliant pro-Soviet regimes throughout Eastern Europe may simply have represented his interpretation of the Yalta peace agreement and a reward for sacrifices suffered during the war, while satisfying Moscow's aspirations for a buffer zone against the capitalist West. If the Soviet leader had any intention of promoting future Communist revolutions in Western Europe—and there is some indication that he did—such developments would have to await the appearance of a new capitalist crisis a decade or more into the future. As Stalin undoubtedly recalled, Lenin had always maintained that revolutions come in waves.

The Truman Doctrine and the Beginnings of Containment

In the United States, however, the Soviet takeover of Eastern Europe represented an ominous development that threatened Roosevelt's vision of a durable peace. Public suspicion of Soviet intentions grew rapidly, especially among the millions of Americans who still had relatives living in Eastern Europe. Winston Churchill was quick to put such fears into words. In a highly publicized speech given to an American audience at Fulton College in Fulton, Missouri, in March 1946, the former British prime minister declared that an "Iron Curtain" had "descended across the continent," dividing Germany and Europe itself into two hostile camps. Stalin responded by branding Churchill's speech a "call to war with the Soviet Union." But he need not have worried. Although public opinion in the United States placed increasing pressure on Truman to devise an effective strategy to counter Soviet advances abroad, the American people were in no mood for another war.

A civil war in Greece created another potential arena for confrontation between the superpowers and an opportunity for the Truman administration to take a stand. Communist guerrilla forces supported by Tito's Yugoslavia had taken up arms against the pro-Western government in Athens. Great Britain had initially assumed primary responsibility for promoting postwar reconstruction in the eastern Mediterranean, but in 1947 continued postwar economic problems caused the British to withdraw from the active role they had been playing in both Greece and Turkey. President Harry S Truman (1884-1972) of the United States, alarmed by British weakness and the possibility of Soviet expansion into the eastern Mediterranean, responded with the Truman Doctrine (see box on p. 158).

According to President Truman, "It must be the policy of the United States to support free peoples who are resisting attempted subjugation by armed minorities or by outside pressures." The president made this statement to the Congress in March 1947 in connection with a request for $400 million in economic and military aid for Greece and Turkey. The Truman Doctrine said in essence that the United States would provide money to countries that claimed they were threatened by communist expansion. If the Soviets were not stopped in Greece, the Truman argument ran, then the United States would have to face the spread of communism throughout the free world. As Dean Acheson, the American secretary of state, explained, "Like apples in a barrel infected by disease, the corruption of Greece would infect Iran and all the East . . . likewise Africa . . . Italy . . . France. . . . Not since Rome and Carthage has there been such a polarization of power on this earth."[2]

The proclamation of the Truman Doctrine was soon followed in June 1947 by the European Recovery Program, better known as the Marshall Plan. Intended to rebuild prosperity and stability, this program included $13 billion for the economic recovery of war-torn Europe. Underlying the program was the belief that communist aggression fed off economic turmoil. General George C. Marshall noted in his commencement speech at Harvard, "Our policy is not directed against any country or doctrine but against hunger, poverty, desperation and chaos."[3]

From the Soviet perspective, the Marshall Plan was nothing less than capitalist imperialism, a thinly veiled attempt to buy the support of the smaller European countries, which in return would be expected to submit to economic exploitation by the United States. A Soviet spokesman described the United States as the "main force in the imperialist camp," whose ultimate goal was "the strengthening of imperialism, preparation for a new imperialist war, a struggle against socialism and democracy, and the support of reactionary and antidemocratic, pro-fascist regimes and movements." The White House indicated that the Marshall Plan was open to the Soviet Union and its Eastern European satellite states, but they refused to participate. According to the Soviet view, the Marshall Plan aimed at "the construction of a bloc of states bound by obligations to the USA" and guaranteed "the American loans in return for the relinquishing by the European states of their economic and later also their political independence."[4] The Soviets, however, were in no position to compete financially with the United States and could do little to counter the Marshall Plan.

Europe Divided

By 1947, the split in Europe between East and West had become a fact of life. At the end of World War II, the United States had favored a quick end to its commitments in Europe. But American fears of Soviet aims caused the United States to play an increasingly important role in European affairs. In an important article in *Foreign Affairs* in July 1947, George Kennan, a well-known U.S. diplomat with much knowledge of Soviet affairs, advocated a policy of containment against further aggressive Soviet moves. Kennan favored the "adroit and vigilant application of counter-force at a series of constantly shifting geographical and political points, corresponding to the shifts and maneuvers of Soviet policy." After the Soviet blockade of Berlin in 1948, containment of the Soviet Union became formal U.S. policy.

The fate of Germany had become a source of heated contention between East and West. Besides denazification and the partitioning of Germany (and Berlin) into four occupied zones, the Allied powers had agreed on

✦ **A Call to Arms.** In March 1946, former British Prime Minister Winston Churchill gave a speech before a college audience in Fulton, Missouri, that electrified the world. Soviet occupation of the countries of Eastern Europe, he declared, had divided the continent into two conflicting halves, separated by an "Iron Curtain." Churchill's speech has often been described as the opening salvo in the Cold War. In the photo at the left, Churchill, with President Harry S Truman behind him, prepares to give his address.

❧ The Truman Doctrine ❧

By 1947, the battlelines had been clearly drawn in the Cold War. In Western capitals, the establishment of Communist governments throughout Eastern Europe had aroused doubts about Stalin's future intentions. To Stalin, whose own distrust of leaders of the capitalist world was a core element in his worldview, Churchill's famous "Iron Curtain" speech in March 1946 confirmed his own fears of an attempted capitalist encirclement of the Soviet Union. As Stalin's colleague Andrei Zhdanov remarked in a speech given at Wiliza Gora in Poland in September 1947, two camps had emerged in the postwar era—the capitalist and the socialist. To counter the danger, Zhdanov declared, Communist parties throughout the world "must rally their ranks and unite their efforts on the basis of a common anti-imperialist and democratic platform, and gather around them all the democratic and patriotic forces of the people."

In Washington, the Truman administration took its own steps to rally support from allies and contain the further spread of communism in the postwar world. Containment, however, would be costly, since it would require an increased level of military expenditure at a time when the American people hoped to return to peacetime pursuits. How could the White House persuade the public to rearm against a new aggressor potentially as dangerous as those that had just been vanquished in the Second World War?

The answer was the Truman Doctrine, enunciated in a speech given before both houses of Congress in March 1947. At that time, one of the areas most vulnerable to Communist penetration was the eastern Mediterranean, where Soviet pressure on Turkey and a Communist-led guerrilla war against the pro-Western government in Greece raised the specter of Soviet domination of the entire region. Recognizing that the American people, and their representatives in Congress, would be reluctant to provide military and economic assistance to the two countries, Truman decided to couch his appeal in broad terms to demonstrate the importance of containing the Soviet threat throughout the world. "The peoples of a number of countries of the world," he declared, "have recently had totalitarian regimes forced upon them against their will." It must be the policy of the United States, he declared, "to support free peoples who are resisting attempted subjugation by armed minorities or by outside pressures. I believe that we must assist free people to work out their own destinies in their own way."

Thus President Truman enunciated the fundamental principle of containment of Communism that would serve to define U.S. foreign policy for the next four decades. Truman and his advisers were well aware that in couching the issue in such broad terms they were somewhat overstating the problem, but they believed that only when Congress and the American people recognized that they were about to embark upon a sacred mission of saving the free world would they be willing to assume the burden.

That assumption was correct. Congress agreed to provide assistance to Greece and Turkey, and the Truman Doctrine, as it would become known, would now serve to define the fundamental security interests of the United States for a generation.

Sources: Charles B. McLane, *Soviet Strategies in Southeast Asia* (Princeton, NJ: Princeton University Press, 1966); U.S. Congress, *Congressional Record*, 80th Congress, first session (Washington, DC: U.S. Government Printing Office, 1947), 93:1981.

---

little with regard to the conquered nation. Even denazification proceeded differently in the various zones of occupation. The Americans and British proceeded methodically—the British had tried 2 million cases by 1948—while the Soviets (and French) went after major criminals and allowed lesser officials to go free. The USSR, hardest hit by the war, took reparations from Germany in the form of booty. The technology-starved Soviets dismantled and removed to Russia 380 factories from the western zones of Berlin before transferring their control to the Western powers. By the summer of 1946, 200 chemical, paper, and textile factories in the East German zone had likewise been shipped to the Soviet Union. At the same time, the German Communist Party was reestablished under the control of Walter Ulbricht (1893–1973) and was soon in charge of the political reconstruction of the Soviet zone in eastern Germany.

Although the foreign ministers of the four occupying powers (the United States, the Soviet Union, Great Britain, and France) kept meeting in an attempt to arrive at a final peace treaty with Germany, they moved further and further apart. At the same time, the British, French, and Americans gradually began to merge their zones economically and, by February 1948, were making plans for the unification of these three western sections of Germany and the formal creation of a West German federal government. The Soviet Union responded with a blockade of West Berlin that allowed neither trucks nor trains to enter the city's three western zones through Soviet-controlled territory in East Germany. The Soviets hoped to secure economic control of all Berlin and force the Western powers to stop the creation of a separate West German state.

The Western powers were faced with a dilemma. Direct military confrontation seemed dangerous, and no one wished to risk World War III. Therefore, an attempt to break through the blockade with tanks and trucks was ruled out. The solution was the Berlin Airlift, as supplies for the city's inhabitants were brought in by plane. At its peak, the airlift flew 13,000 tons of supplies daily into Berlin. The Soviets, also not wanting war, did not interfere and finally lifted the blockade in May 1949. The blockade of Berlin had severely increased tensions between the United States and the Soviet Union and brought the separation of Germany into two states. The German Federal Republic (FRG) was formally created from the three Western zones in September 1949, and a month later, a separate German Democratic Republic (GDR) was established in East Germany. Berlin remained a divided city and the source of much contention between East and West.

The search for security in the new world of the Cold War also led to the formation of military alliances. The North Atlantic Treaty Organization (NATO) was formed in April 1949 when Belgium, Luxembourg, the Netherlands, France, Britain, Italy, Denmark, Norway, Portugal, and Iceland signed a treaty with the United States and Canada. All the powers agreed to provide mutual assistance if any one of them was attacked. A few years later, West Germany and Turkey joined NATO.

The Eastern European states soon followed suit. In 1949, they formed the Council for Mutual Economic Assistance (COMECON) for economic cooperation. Then, in 1955, Albania, Bulgaria, Czechoslovakia, East Germany, Hungary, Poland, Romania, and the Soviet Union organized a formal military alliance, the Warsaw Pact. Once again, Europe was tragically divided into hostile alliance systems.

By the end of the decade, then, the dream of a stable peace in Europe had been obliterated. There has been considerable historical debate over who bears the most responsibility for starting what would henceforth be called the Cold War. In the 1950s, most scholars in the West assumed that the bulk of the blame must fall on the shoulders of Joseph Stalin, whose determination to impose Soviet rule on the countries of Eastern Europe snuffed out hopes for freedom and self-determination there and aroused justifiable fears of Communist expansion in the Western democracies. During the next decade, however, a new school of revisionist historians—influenced in part by aggressive U.S. policies to prevent a Communist victory in Southeast Asia—began to argue that the fault lay primarily in Washington, where President Truman and his anti-Communist advisers abandoned the precepts of Yalta and sought to encircle the USSR with a tier of pliant U.S. client states.

No doubt, both the United States and the Soviet Union took steps at the end of World War II that were unwise or might have been avoided. Both nations, however, were working within a framework conditioned by the past. Ultimately, the rivalry between the two superpowers stemmed from their different historical perspectives and their irreconcilable political ambitions. Intense competition for political and military supremacy had long been a regular feature of Western civilization. The United States and the Soviet Union were the heirs of that European tradition of power politics, and it should not surprise us that two such different systems would seek to extend their way of life to the rest of the world. Because of its need to feel secure on its western border, the Soviet Union was not prepared to give up the advantages it had gained in Eastern Europe from Germany's defeat. But neither were Western leaders prepared to accept without protest the establishment of a system of Soviet satellites that not only threatened the security of Western Europe but also deeply offended Western sensibilities because of its blatant disregard of the Western concept of human rights.

This does not necessarily mean that neither side bears primary responsibility for starting the Cold War: Some revisionist historians have claimed that the U.S. doctrine of containment was a provocative action that aroused Stalin's suspicions and drove Moscow into a position of hostility to the West. This charge lacks credibility. As information from the Soviet archives and other sources has become available, it is increasingly clear that Stalin's suspicions of the West were rooted in his Marxist-Leninist worldview and long predated Washington's enunciation of the doctrine of containment. As his foreign minister Vyacheslav Molotov once remarked, Soviet policy was inherently aggressive in nature, and would be triggered whenever the opportunity offered. While Stalin apparently had no master plan to advance Soviet power into Western Europe, he was probably prepared to make every effort to do so once the next

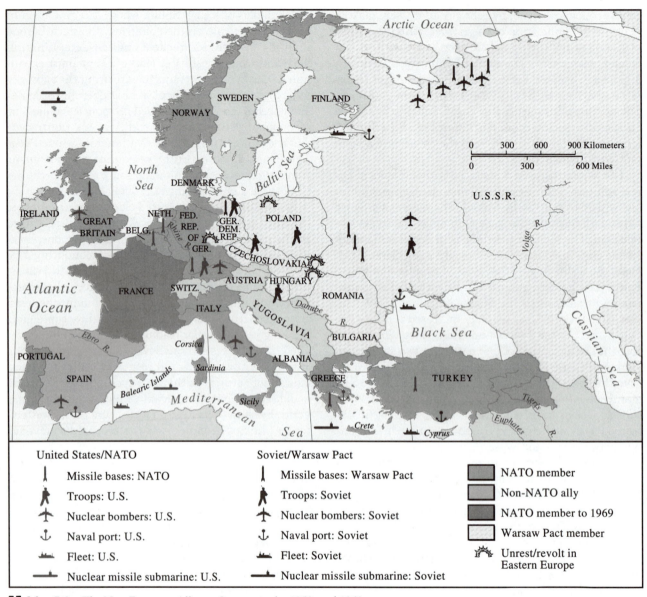

⁜ Map 7.2   The New European Alliance Systems in the 1950s and 1960s

revolutionary wave appeared on the horizon. Western leaders were fully justified in reacting to this possibility by strengthening their own lines of defense.

On the other hand, a case can be made that in deciding to respond to the Soviet challenge in a primarily military manner, Western leaders overreacted to the situation and virtually guaranteed that the Cold War would be transformed into an arms race that could quite conceivably result in a new and uniquely destructive war.

Cold War in Asia

The Cold War was somewhat slower to make its appearance in Asia. At Yalta, Stalin formally agreed to enter the Pacific War against Japan three months after the close of the conflict with Germany. As a reward for Soviet participation in the struggle against Japan, Roosevelt promised that Moscow would be granted "preeminent interests" in Manchuria (interests reminiscent of those possessed by imperial Russia prior to its defeat at the hands of Japan in 1904–1905) and the establishment of a Soviet naval base at Port Arthur. In return, Stalin promised to sign a treaty of alliance with the Republic of China, thus implicitly committing the USSR not to provide the Chinese Communists with support in a possible future civil war.

Although many observers would later question Stalin's sincerity in making such a commitment to the vocally anti-Communist Chiang Kai-shek, in Moscow the decision probably had a logic of its own. The Soviet Union had provided diplomatic support and military assistance to Nanjing during the 1930s, when Stalin viewed Chiang as a potentially useful bulwark against Japanese expansion in East Asia. Although that policy was abandoned in 1941, when the USSR signed a treaty of nonaggression with Tokyo to protect its eastern flank, Stalin had good reason to seek to resurrect that relationship after the close of the Pacific conflict. He had no particular liking for the independent-minded Mao Zedong, and indeed did not anticipate a Communist victory in the eventuality of a civil war in China. Only an agreement with Chiang Kai-shek could provide the Soviet Union with a strategically vital economic and political presence in North China.

Despite these commitments, Allied agreements on creating a stable peace in East Asia soon broke down, and the region was sucked into the vortex of the Cold War by the end of the decade. The root of the problem lay in the underlying weakness of the Chiang Kai-shek regime, which threatened to create a political vacuum in East Asia that both Moscow and Washington would be tempted to fill.

The Chinese Civil War

As World War II came to an end in the Pacific, the government of Chiang Kai-shek in China had a powerful ally. During the two years after the Japanese attack on Pearl Harbor, the United States had attempted to strengthen Chiang to provide a base in southern and central China from which to attack Japan. President Franklin D. Roosevelt also hoped that republican China would be the keystone of his plan for peace and stability in Asia after the war. Eventually, however, U.S. officials became disillusioned with the corruption of Chiang's government and his unwillingness to risk his forces against the Japanese (he hoped to save them for use against the Communists after the war in the Pacific ended), and China became a backwater as the war came to a close. Nevertheless, U.S. military and economic aid to China had been substantial, and at war's end the new

Truman administration still hoped that it could rely on Chiang to support U.S. postwar goals in the region.

While Chiang Kai-shek wrestled with Japanese aggression and problems of national development, the Communists were building up their liberated base in North China. An alliance with Chiang in December 1936 had relieved them from the threat of immediate attack from the south, although Chiang was chronically suspicious of the Communists and stationed troops near Xi'an to prevent them from infiltrating into areas under his control.

He had good reason to fear for the future. During the war, the Communists patiently penetrated Japanese lines and built up their strength in North China. To enlarge their political base, they carried out a "mass line" policy (from the masses, to the masses), reducing land rents and confiscating the lands of wealthy landlords. By the end of World War II, according to Communist estimates, 20 to 30 million Chinese were living under their administration, and their People's Liberation Army (PLA) included nearly 1 million troops.

As the war came to an end, world attention began to focus on the prospects for renewed civil strife in China. Members of a U.S. liaison team stationed in Yan'an during the last months of the war were impressed by the performance of the Communists, and some recommended that the United States should support them or at least remain neutral in a possible conflict between Communists and Nationalists for control of China. The Truman administration, though skeptical of Chiang's ability to forge a strong and prosperous country, was increasingly concerned over the spread of communism in Europe and tried to find a peaceful solution through the formation of a coalition government of all parties in China.

The effort failed. By 1946, full-scale war between the Nationalist government, now reinstalled in Nanjing, and the Communists resumed. The Communists, having taken advantage of the Soviet occupation of Manchuria in the last days of the war, occupied rural areas in the region and laid siege to Nationalist garrisons hastily established there. Now Chiang Kai-shek's errors came home to roost. In the countryside, millions of peasants, attracted to the Communists by promises of land and social justice, flocked to serve in Mao Zedong's People's Liberation Army. In the cities, middle-class Chinese, who were normally hostile to communism, were alienated by Chiang's brutal suppression of all dissent and his government's inability to slow the ruinous rate of inflation or solve the economic problems it caused. With morale dropping in the cities, Chiang's troops began to

◆ **Chiang Kai-shek and Mao Zedong Exchange a Toast.** After World War II, the United States sent General George C. Marshall to China in an effort to prevent civil war between Chiang Kai-shek's government and the Communists. Marshall's initial success was symbolized by this toast between Chiang and Mao. But suspicion ran too deep, and soon conflict ensued, leading to a Communist victory in 1949. Chiang Kai-shek's government retreated to the island of Taiwan.

defect to the Communists. Sometimes whole divisions, officers as well as ordinary soldiers, changed sides. By 1948, the People's Liberation Army was advancing south out of Manchuria and had encircled Beijing. Communist troops took the old imperial capital, crossed the Yangtze the following spring, and occupied the commercial hub of Shanghai. During the next few months, Chiang's government and 2 million of his followers fled to Taiwan, which the Japanese had returned to Chinese control after World War II.

The Truman administration reacted to the spread of Communist power in China with acute discomfort. Washington had no desire to see a Communist government on the mainland, but it had little confidence in Chiang Kai-shek's ability to realize Roosevelt's dream of a strong, united, and prosperous China. In December 1945, President Truman sent General George C. Marshall to China in a last-ditch effort to avoid civil war and bring about a peaceful settlement. But anti-Communist elements within the Republic of China resisted U.S. ef-

forts to create a coalition government with the Chinese Communist Party (CCP), and the following December Marshall sought and received permission from the White House to abandon his mission, arguing that neither side was cooperating in the effort. During the next two years, the United States gave limited military support to the Chiang Kai-shek regime, but refused to commit U.S. power to guarantee its survival. The administration's hands-off policy deeply angered many in Congress, who charged that the White House was "soft on communism" and declared further that Roosevelt had betrayed Chiang Kai-shek at Yalta by granting privileges in Manchuria to the USSR. In their view, Soviet troops had hindered the dispatch of Chiang's forces to the area and provided the PLA with weapons to use against their rivals.

In later years, sources in both Moscow and Beijing suggested that the Soviet Union gave little assistance to the CCP in its struggle against the Nanjing regime. In fact, Stalin periodically advised Mao against undertaking the effort. Although Communist forces undoubtedly

Who Lost China?

In 1949, with China about to fall under the control of the Communists, assigning responsibility for "the loss of China" became a major issue in U.S. national politics. Critics of the Democratic administration of President Harry S Truman, including many leaders of the Republican Party in Congress, charged that, by failing to provide adequate assistance to the Nationalist government of Chiang Kai-shek, the Truman administration was to blame. Some went even further and claimed that treasonous elements within the U.S. government had deliberately betrayed Chiang's government in order to bring about a Communist victory.

Seeking to deflect such criticism, U.S. Secretary of State Dean Acheson instructed the State Department to prepare a White Paper that would explain why the U.S. policy of seeking to avoid a Communist victory in China had failed. The authors' conclusion was that responsibility lay at the feet of Chinese leader Chiang Kai-shek and that there was nothing the United States could have reasonably done to alter the result. After the close of the war, it stated, the Nationalists were "weakened, demoralized, and unpopular. . . . Because of the ineffectiveness of the Nationalist forces which was later to be tragically demonstrated, the Communists probably could have been dislodged only by American arms."

It was obvious, the authors continued, that the American people "would not have sanctioned such a colossal commitment of our armies" so soon after the end of World War II. The only reasonable alternative was to seek to bring an end to the civil war by reducing the distrust between the Nationalists and their Communist rivals and creating a coalition government composed of all political forces in China. That, however, proved impossible. Not only was the mutual suspicion between the two parties too deep-seated to bring about a final agreement, but the Nationalists embarked on "an overly ambitious military campaign" in the face of U.S. warnings that it would plunge the country into economic chaos and "eventually destroy the Nationalist government." That warning was eventually confirmed.

"The unfortunate but inescapable fact," the White Paper concluded,

> is that the ominous result of the civil war in China was beyond the control of the government of the United States. Nothing that this country did or could have done within the reasonable limits of its capabilities could have changed that result; nothing that was left undone by this country has contributed to it. It was the product of internal Chinese forces, forces which this country tried to influence but could not. A decision was arrived at within China, if only a decision by default.

Most historians of China today would accept that assessment, but it had little effect at the time in deflecting criticism of the Truman administration for "selling out" the interests of its ally in China. The debate about China policy became a major feature of U.S. politics for the next decade.

Source: *United States Relations with China* (Washington, DC: Department of State, 1949), pp. iii–xvii.

---

received some assistance from Soviet occupation troops in Manchuria, the underlying causes of their victory stemmed from conditions inside China, not from the intervention of outside powers. So indeed argued the Truman administration, when in 1949 it issued a White Paper that placed most of the blame for the debacle at the foot of the Chiang Kai-shek regime. There was essentially nothing that the United States could have done, it claimed, that would have reversed the verdict (see box above).

Many Americans, however, did not agree. The Communist victory on the mainland of China injected Asia directly into American politics as an integral element of the Cold War. During the spring of 1950, under pressure from Congress and public opinion to define U.S. interests in Asia, the Truman administration adopted a new national security policy which implied that the United States would take whatever steps were necessary to stem the further expansion of communism in the region.

The Korean War

Communist leaders in China, from their new capital of Beijing, hoped that their accession to power in 1949 would bring about an era of peace in the region and permit their new government to concentrate on domestic goals. But the desire for peace was tempered by their determination to erase a century of humiliation at the hands of imperialist powers and to restore the traditional outer frontiers of the empire. In addition to recovering territories that had been part of the Manchu Empire, such as Manchuria, Taiwan, and Tibet, the Chinese leaders also hoped to restore Chinese influence in former tributary areas such as Korea and Vietnam.

It soon became clear that these two goals were not always compatible. Negotiations with the Soviet Union led to Soviet recognition of Chinese sovereignty over Manchuria and Xinjiang (the desolate lands north of Tibet that were known as Chinese Turkestan because many of the peoples in the area were of Turkish origin), although the Soviets retained a measure of economic influence in both areas. Chinese troops occupied Tibet in 1950 and brought it under Chinese administration for the first time in more than a century. But in Korea and Taiwan, China's efforts to recreate the imperial buffer zone provoked new conflicts with foreign powers.

The problem of Taiwan was a consequence of the Cold War. As the civil war in China came to an end, the Truman administration appeared determined to avoid entanglement in China's internal affairs and indicated that it would not prevent a Communist takeover of the island, now occupied by Chiang Kai-shek's Republic of China. But as tensions between the United States and the new Chinese government escalated during the winter of 1949–1950, influential figures in the United States began to argue that Taiwan was crucial to U.S. defense strategy in the Pacific.

The outbreak of war in Korea also helped bring the Cold War to East Asia. After the Sino-Japanese War in 1894–1895, Korea, long a Chinese tributary, had fallen increasingly under the rival influences of Japan and Russia. After the Japanese defeated the Russians in 1905, Korea became an integral part of the Japanese Empire and remained so until 1945. The removal of Korea from Japanese control had been one of the stated objectives of the Allies in World War II, and on the eve of Japanese surrender in August 1945, the Soviet Union and the United States agreed to divide the country into two separate occupation zones at the 38th parallel. They originally planned to hold national elections after the restoration of peace to reunify Korea under an independent government. But as U.S.–Soviet relations deteriorated, two separate governments emerged in Korea, a Communist one in the north and an anti-Communist one in the south.

Tensions between the two governments ran high along the dividing line, and on June 25, 1950, with the apparent approval of Joseph Stalin, North Korean troops invaded the south. The Truman administration immediately ordered U.S. naval and air forces to support South Korea, and the United Nations Security Council passed a resolution calling on member nations to jointly resist the invasion. By September, United Nations (UN) forces under the command of U.S. General Douglas MacArthur marched northward across the 38th parallel with the aim of unifying Korea under a single, non-Communist government.

President Harry Truman worried that by approaching the Chinese border at the Yalu River, the UN troops could trigger Chinese intervention, but was assured by MacArthur that China would not respond. In November, however, Chinese "volunteer" forces intervened in force on the side of North Korea and drove the UN troops southward in disarray. A static defense line was eventually established near the original dividing line at the 38th parallel, although the war continued.

To many Americans, the Chinese intervention in Korea was clear evidence that China intended to promote communism throughout Asia, and recent evidence suggests that Mao Zedong was convinced that a revolutionary wave was on the rise in Asia. In fact, however, China's decision to enter the war was probably motivated in large part by the fear that hostile U.S. forces might be stationed on the Chinese frontier and perhaps even launch an attack across the border. MacArthur intensified such fears by calling publicly for air attacks on Manchurian cities in preparation for an attack on Communist China. In any case, the outbreak of the Korean War was particularly unfortunate for China. Immediately after the invasion, President Truman dispatched the U.S. Seventh Fleet to the Taiwan Strait to prevent a possible Chinese invasion of Taiwan. Even more unfortunate, the invasion hardened Western attitudes against the new Chinese government and led to China's isolation from the major capitalist powers for two decades. As a result, China was cut off from all forms of economic and technological assistance and was forced to rely almost entirely on the Soviet Union, with which it had signed a pact of friendship and cooperation in early 1950.

Conflict in Indochina

During the mid-1950s, China sought to build contacts with the nonsocialist world. A cease-fire agreement brought the Korean War to an end in July 1953, and China signaled its desire to live in peaceful coexistence with other independent countries in the region. But a relatively minor conflict now began to intensify on Beijing's southern flank, in French Indochina. The struggle had begun after World War II, when Ho Chi Minh's Indochinese Communist Party, at the head of a multiparty nationalist alliance called the Vietminh

Front, seized power in northern and central Vietnam after the surrender of imperial Japan. After abortive negotiations between Ho's government and the returning French, war broke out in December 1946. French forces occupied the cities and the densely populated lowlands, while the Vietminh took refuge in the mountains.

For three years, the Vietminh gradually increased in size and effectiveness. What had begun as an anticolonial struggle by Ho Chi Minh's Vietminh Front against the French after World War II became entangled in the Cold War in the early 1950s when both the United States and the new Communist government in China began to intervene in the conflict to promote their own national security objectives. China began to provide military assistance to the Vietminh to protect its own borders from hostile forces. The Americans supported the French, but pressured the French government to prepare for an eventual transition to non-Communist governments in Vietnam, Laos, and Cambodia.

At the Geneva Conference in 1954, with the French public tired of fighting the "dirty war" in Indochina, the French agreed to a peace settlement with Ho Chi Minh's Vietminh. Vietnam was temporarily divided into a northern Communist half (known as the Democratic Republic of Vietnam, or DRV) and a non-Communist southern half based in Saigon (eventually to be known as the Republic of Vietnam, or RVN). Elections were to be held in two years to create a unified government. Cambodia and Laos were both declared independent under neutral governments.

China had played an active role in bringing about the settlement, and clearly hoped that a settlement would lead to a reduction of tensions in the area, but subsequent efforts to bring about improved relations between China and the United States foundered on the issue of Taiwan. In the fall of 1954, the United States signed a mutual security treaty with the Republic of China guaranteeing U.S. military support in case of an invasion of Taiwan. When Beijing demanded U.S. withdrawal from Taiwan as the price for improved relations, diplomatic talks between the two countries collapsed.

From Confrontation to Coexistence

The decade of the 1950s opened with the world teetering on the edge of a nuclear holocaust. The Soviet Union had detonated its first nuclear device in 1949, and the two blocs—capitalist and socialist—viewed each other across an ideological divide that grew increasingly bitter with each passing year. Yet as the decade drew to a close,

a measure of sanity crept into the Cold War, and the leaders of the major world powers began to seek ways to coexist in a peaceful and stable world.

Khrushchev and the Era of Peaceful Coexistence

The first clear sign occurred after Stalin's death in early 1953. His successor, Georgy Malenkov, openly hoped to improve relations with the Western powers in order to reduce defense expenditures and shift government spending to growing consumer needs. During his campaign to replace Malenkov two years later, Nikita Khrushchev appealed to powerful pressure groups in the party Politburo (the governing body of the CPSU) by calling for higher defense expenditures, but once in power, he resumed his predecessor's efforts to reduce tensions with the West and improve the living standards of the Soviet people.

In an adroit public relations touch, Khrushchev publicized Moscow's appeal for a new policy of "peaceful coexistence" with the West. In 1955, he surprisingly agreed to negotiate an end to the postwar occupation of Austria by the victorious allies and allow the creation of a neutral country with strong cultural and economic ties with the West. He also called for a reduction in defense expenditures and reduced the size of the Soviet armed forces.

At first, Washington was suspicious of Khrushchev's motives, especially after the Soviet crackdown in Hungary in the fall of 1956 (see Chapter 8). A new crisis over Berlin added to the tension. The USSR had launched its first intercontinental ballistic missile (ICBM) in August 1957, arousing U.S. fears—fueled by a partisan political debate—of a missile gap between the United States and the Soviet Union. Khrushchev attempted to take advantage of the U.S. frenzy over missiles to solve the problem of West Berlin, which had remained a "Western island" of prosperity inside the relatively poverty-stricken state of East Germany. Many East Germans sought to escape to West Germany by fleeing through West Berlin, a serious blot on the credibility of the GDR and a potential source of instability in East-West relations. In November 1958, Khrushchev announced that unless the West removed its forces from West Berlin within six months, he would turn over control of the access routes to the East Germans. Unwilling to accept an ultimatum that would have abandoned West Berlin to the Communists, President Eisenhower and the West stood firm, and Khrushchev eventually backed down.

Despite such periodic crises in East-West relations, there were tantalizing signs that an era of true peaceful coexistence between the two power blocs could be achieved. In the late 1950s, the United States and the Soviet Union initiated a cultural exchange program, thus helping to acquaint the peoples of one bloc with the nature of life in the other. While the Leningrad Ballet appeared at theaters in the United States, Benny Goodman and the film of Leonard Bernstein's *West Side Story* played in Moscow. In 1958, Nikita Khrushchev visited the United States and had a brief but friendly encounter with President Eisenhower at his presidential retreat in northern Maryland. Predictions of improved future relations led reporters to laud "the spirit of Camp David."

Yet Khrushchev could rarely avoid the temptation to gain an advantage over the United States in the competition for influence throughout the world, and this resulted in an unstable relationship that prevented a lasting accommodation between the two superpowers. West Berlin was an area of persistent tension (a boil on the foot of the United States, Khrushchev derisively termed it), and in January 1961, just as the newly elected president John F. Kennedy came into office, Moscow threatened once again to turn over responsibility for access to the East German government.

Moscow also took every opportunity to promote its interests in the Third World, as the countries of Asia, Africa, and Latin America were now popularly called. Unlike Stalin, Khrushchev viewed the dismantling of colonial regimes in the area as a potential advantage for the Soviet Union, and sought especially to exploit the deep suspicions of the United States in Latin America. To improve Soviet influence in such areas, Khrushchev established alliances with key Third World leaders such as Sukarno in Indonesia, Gamel Abdul Nasser in Egypt, Jawaharlal Nehru in India, and Fidel Castro in Cuba. In January 1961, just as John F. Kennedy assumed the presidency, Khrushchev unnerved the new president at an informal summit meeting in Vienna by declaring that the Soviet Union would provide active support to national liberation movements throughout the world. There were rising fears in Washington of Soviet meddling in such sensitive trouble spots as Southeast Asia, Central Africa, and the Caribbean.

The Cuban Missile Crisis and the Move toward Détente

The Cold War confrontation between the United States and the Soviet Union reached frightening levels during the Cuban Missile Crisis. In 1959, a left-wing revolutionary named Fidel Castro (b. 1927) overthrew the Cuban dictator Fulgencio Batista and established a Soviet-supported totalitarian regime. After the utter failure of a U.S.–supported attempt (the "Bay of Pigs" incident) to overthrow Castro's regime in 1961, the Soviet Union decided to place nuclear missiles in Cuba in 1962. The United States was not prepared to allow nuclear weapons within such close striking distance of the American mainland, despite the fact that it had placed nuclear weapons in Turkey within easy range of the Soviet Union. Khrushchev was quick to point out that "your rockets are in Turkey. You are worried by Cuba . . . because it is 90 miles from the American coast. But Turkey is next to us."[5] When U.S. intelligence discovered that a Soviet fleet carrying missiles was heading to Cuba, President Kennedy decided to blockade Cuba and prevent the fleet from reaching its destination. This approach to the problem had the benefit of delaying confrontation and giving the two sides time to find a peaceful solution. Khrushchev agreed to turn back the fleet if Kennedy pledged not to invade Cuba. In a conciliatory letter to Kennedy, Khrushchev wrote:

> We and you ought not to pull on the ends of the rope in which you have tied the knot of war, because the more the two of us pull, the tighter that knot will be tied. And a moment may come when that knot will be tied too tight that even he who tied it will not have the strength to untie it. . . . Let us not only relax the forces pulling on the ends of the rope, let us take measures to untie that knot. We are ready for this.[6]

The intense feeling that the world might have been annihilated in a few days had a profound influence on both sides. A hotline communications system between Moscow and Washington was installed in 1963 to expedite rapid communications between the two superpowers in time of crisis. In the same year, the two powers agreed to ban nuclear tests in the atmosphere, a step that at least served to lessen the tensions between the two nations.

The Sino-Soviet Dispute

Nikita Khrushchev had launched his slogan of peaceful coexistence as a means of improving relations with the capitalist powers; ironically, one result of the campaign was to undermine Moscow's ties with its close ally China. During the lifetime of Joseph Stalin, Beijing had accepted the USSR as the acknowledged leader of the socialist camp. After Stalin's death, however, relations began to deteriorate. Part of the reason may have been Mao Zedong's contention that he, as the most experi-

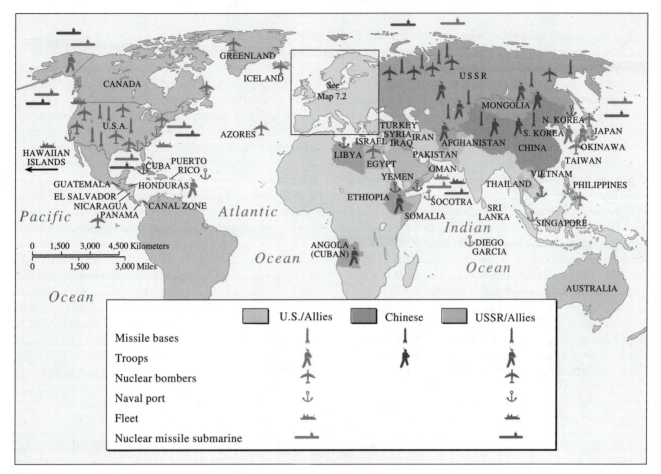

Map 7.3 The Global Cold War in the 1950s and 1960s

enced Marxist leader, should now be acknowledged as the most authoritative voice within the socialist community. But another determining factor was that just as Soviet policies were moving toward moderation, China's were becoming more radical.

Several other issues were involved, including territorial disputes and China's unhappiness with limited Soviet economic assistance. But the key sources of disagreement involved ideology and the Cold War. Chinese leaders were convinced that the successes of the Soviet space program confirmed that the socialists were now technologically superior to the capitalists (the East wind, trumpeted the Chinese official press, had now triumphed over the West wind), and they urged Soviet leader Nikita Khrushchev to go on the offensive to promote world revolution. Specifically, China wanted Soviet assistance in retaking Taiwan from Chiang Kai-shek. But Khrushchev was trying to improve relations

with the West and rejected Chinese demands for support against Taiwan (see box on p. 168).

By the end of the 1950s, the Soviet Union had begun to remove its advisers from China, and in 1961 the dispute broke into the open. Increasingly isolated, China voiced its hostility to what Mao described as the "urban industrialized countries" (which included the Soviet Union) and portrayed itself as the leader of the "rural underdeveloped countries" of Asia, Africa, and Latin America in a global struggle against imperialist oppression. In effect, China had applied Mao Zedong's famous concept of people's war in an international framework.

The Second Indochina War

China's radicalism was intensified in the early 1960s by the outbreak of renewed war in Indochina. The Eisenhower administration had opposed the peace settlement

A Plea for Peaceful Coexistence

Soviet leader Vladimir Lenin had asserted that war between the socialist and imperialist camps was inevitable because the imperialists would never give up without a fight. That assumption probably guided the thoughts of Joseph Stalin, who told colleagues shortly after World War II that a new imperialist war would break out in fifteen to twenty years. But Stalin's successor Nikita Khrushchev feared that a new world conflict could result in a nuclear holocaust and contended that the two sides must learn to coexist, although peaceful competition would continue.

In a speech in Beijing in 1959, Khrushchev attempted to persuade Chinese leaders to accept his views. "Comrades!" he declared. "Socialism brings to the people peace—that greatest blessing. The greater the strength of the camp of socialism grows, the greater will be its possibilities for successfully defending the cause of peace on this earth. The forces of socialism are already so great that real possibilities are being created for excluding war as a means of solving international disputes."

Khrushchev recognized that his Chinese listeners, whose armies had just fought against Americans in the Korean peninsula, were skeptical of his proposal. Pointing out that the leaders of the capitalist countries were now uneasily aware of the power and influence of the socialist camp, he argued that "cold warriors" who

pushed the world toward a new world war would only be moving toward their own destruction. As for those—like the Chinese—who might argue that the "East wind" should now take the offensive against the "West wind" to test the strength of the capitalist nations by force of arms, Khrushchev countered that "the peoples would not understand and would never support those who would think of acting in this way." Marxists, he said, recognize only "just wars," not "wars of conquest." "Even such a noble and progressive system as socialism," he said, "cannot be imposed by force of arms." The socialist countries must therefore concentrate on a policy of peace abroad and building socialism at home.

Chinese leaders, including Mao Zedong, were not persuaded. The "imperialist nature" of the United States would never change, they said, and they would never accept any peace agreement in which they had no part. China was undoubtedly angered that the United States continued to station military forces on Taiwan, which Beijing considered part of its own sacred territory. Khrushchev's words thus fell on deaf ears, and two years later the Sino-Soviet conflict burst into the open upon an astonished world.

Source: G. F. Hudson et al., eds., *The Sino-Soviet Dispute* (New York, 1961), pp. 61–63, citing *Peking Review*, no. 40, 1959.

---

at Geneva in 1954, which divided Vietnam temporarily into two separate regroupment zones, specifically because the provision for future national elections opened up the possibility of placing the entire country under Communist rule. But President Eisenhower had been unwilling to introduce U.S. military forces to continue the conflict without the full support of the British and the French, who preferred to seek a negotiated settlement. In the end, Washington promised not to break the provisions of the agreement but refused to commit itself to the results.

During the next several months, the United States began to provide aid to a new government in South Vietnam. Under the leadership of the anticommunist politician Ngo Dinh Diem, the South Vietnamese government began to root out dissidents. With the tacit approval of the United States, Diem refused to hold the national elections called for by the Geneva Accords. It was widely anticipated, even in Washington, that the Communists would win such elections. In 1959, Ho Chi Minh, despairing of the peaceful unification of the

country under Communist rule, returned to a policy of revolutionary war in the south.

By 1963, South Vietnam was on the verge of collapse. Diem's autocratic methods and inattention to severe economic inequality had alienated much of the population, and revolutionary forces, popularly known as the Viet Cong (Vietnamese Communists), expanded their influence throughout much of the country. In the fall of 1963, with the approval of the Kennedy administration, senior military officers overthrew the Diem regime. But factionalism kept the new military leadership from reinvigorating the struggle against the insurgent forces, and the situation in South Vietnam grew worse. By early 1965, the Viet Cong, whose ranks were now swelled by military units infiltrating from North Vietnam, were on the verge of seizing control of the entire country. In March, President Lyndon Johnson decided to send U.S. combat troops to South Vietnam to prevent a total defeat for the anticommunist government in Saigon.

Chinese leaders observed the gradual escalation of the conflict in South Vietnam with mixed feelings.

They were undoubtedly pleased to have a firm Communist ally—and indeed one that had in so many ways followed the path of Mao Zedong—just beyond their southern frontier. Yet they could not relish the possibility that renewed bloodshed in South Vietnam might enmesh China in a new conflict with the United States. Nor could they have welcomed the specter of a powerful and ambitious united Vietnam that might wish to extend its influence throughout mainland Southeast Asia, an area that Beijing considered as its own backyard.

Chinese leaders therefore tiptoed delicately through the minefield of the Indochina conflict, seeking to maintain good relations with their ally in Hanoi while avoiding a confrontation with the United States. As the war escalated in 1964 and 1965, Beijing publicly announced that the Chinese people would give their full support to their fraternal comrades seeking national liberation in South Vietnam, but privately assured Washington that China would not directly enter the conflict unless U.S. forces threatened its southern border. Beijing also refused to cooperate fully with Moscow in shipping Soviet goods to North Vietnam through Chinese territory.

Despite its dismay at the lack of full support from China, the Communist government in North Vietnam responded to U.S. escalation by infiltrating more of its own regular force troops into the south, and by 1968 the war had reached a stalemate. The Communists were not strong enough to overthrow the government in Saigon, but President Lyndon Johnson was reluctant to engage in all-out war on North Vietnam for fear of provoking a global nuclear conflict. In the fall, after the Communist-led Tet offensive aroused heightened antiwar protests in the United States, peace negotiations began in Paris.

Richard Nixon came into the White House in 1969 on a pledge to bring an honorable end to the Vietnam War. With U.S. public opinion sharply divided on the issue, he began to withdraw U.S. troops while continuing to hold peace talks in Paris. But the centerpiece of his strategy was to improve relations with China, and thus undercut Chinese support for the North Vietnamese war effort. During the 1960s, relations between Moscow and Beijing had reached a point of extreme tension, and thousands of troops were stationed on both sides of their long common frontier. To intimidate their Communist rivals, Soviet sources dropped the hint that they might decide to launch a preemptive strike to destroy Chinese nuclear facilities in Xinjiang. Sensing an opportunity to split the two onetime allies, Nixon sent his emissary Henry Kissinger on a secret trip to China. Responding to assurances from Washington that the United States was determined to withdraw from Indochina and hoped to improve relations with the mainland regime, Chinese leaders invited President Nixon to visit China in early 1972.

◆ **A Bridge across the Cold War Divide.** In January 1972, U.S. President Richard Nixon startled the world by visiting mainland China and beginning the long process of restoring normal relations between the two countries. Despite Nixon's reputation as a devout anti-Communist, the visit was a success, as the two sides agreed to put aside their most bitter differences in an effort to reduce tensions in Asia. Here, Nixon and Chinese leader Mao Zedong exchange a historic handshake in Beijing.

Incensed at the apparent betrayal by their close allies, North Vietnamese leaders decided to seek a peaceful settlement of the war in the south. In January 1973, a peace treaty was signed in Paris calling for the removal of all U.S. forces from South Vietnam. In return, the Communists agreed to seek a political settlement of their differences with the Saigon regime. But negotiations between north and south over the political settlement soon broke down, and in early 1975, the Communists resumed the offensive. At the end of April, under a massive assault by North Vietnamese military forces, the South Vietnamese government surrendered. A year later, the country was unified under Communist rule.

The Communist victory in Vietnam was a severe humiliation for the United States, but its strategic impact was limited because of the new relationship with China. During the next decade, Sino-American relations continued to improve. In 1979, diplomatic ties were established between the two countries under an arrangement whereby the United States renounced its mutual security treaty with the Republic of China in return for a pledge from China to seek reunification with Taiwan by peaceful means. By the end of the 1970s, China and the United States had forged a "strategic relationship" in which each would cooperate with the other against the common threat of Soviet "hegemonism" (as China described Soviet policy) in Asia.

An Era of Equivalence

The Johnson administration sent U.S. combat troops to South Vietnam in 1965 in an effort to prevent the expansion of communism in Southeast Asia. Washington's concern, however, was directed not at Moscow, but at Beijing. By the mid-1960s, U.S. officials viewed the Soviet Union as an essentially conservative power, more concerned with protecting its vast empire than with expanding its borders. In fact, U.S. policymakers periodically sought Soviet assistance in helping to bring about a peaceful settlement of the Vietnam War. So long as Khrushchev was in power, they found a receptive ear in Moscow. Khrushchev was firmly dedicated to promoting the cause of peaceful coexistence (at least on his terms) and sternly advised the North Vietnamese against a resumption of revolutionary war in South Vietnam.

After October 1964, when Khrushchev was replaced by a new leadership headed by party chief Leonid Brezhnev and Prime Minister Alexei Kosygin, Soviet attitudes about Vietnam became more ambivalent. On the one hand, the new Soviet leadership had no desire to see the Vietnam conflict poison relations between the great powers. On the other hand, Moscow was anxious to demonstrate its support for the North Vietnamese and their struggle for reunification with the south in order to deflect Chinese charges that the USSR had betrayed the interests of the oppressed peoples of the world. As a result, Soviet officials publicly voiced sympathy for the U.S. predicament in Vietnam, but put no pressure on their allies to bring an end to the war. Indeed, the USSR became Hanoi's main supplier of advanced military equipment in the final years of the war.

Still, under Brezhnev and Kosygin, the Soviet Union continued to pursue the Khrushchev line of peaceful coexistence with the West and adopted a generally cautious posture in foreign affairs. By the early 1970s, a new age in Soviet-American relations had emerged, often referred to by the French term *détente*, meaning reduction of tensions between the USSR and the United States. One appropriate symbol of the new relationship was the Antiballistic Missile (ABM) Treaty, often called SALT I (for Strategic Arms Limitation Talks), signed in 1972. Despite some lessening of tensions after the Cuban missile crisis, both superpowers had continued to expand their nuclear arsenals, while seeking to enhance the destructive power of their missiles by arming them with multiple warheads. By 1970, the United States had developed the capacity to arm its intercontinental ballistic missiles (ICBMs) with "multiple independently targeted reentry vehicles" (MIRVs) that enabled one missile to hit ten different targets. The Soviet Union soon followed suit. Between 1968 and 1972, both sides had also developed antiballistic missiles whose purpose was to hit and destroy incoming missiles. In the 1972 SALT I treaty, the two nations agreed to limit their antiballistic missile systems.

Washington's objective in pursuing such a treaty was to make it unprofitable for either superpower to believe that it could win a nuclear exchange by launching a preemptive strike against the other. U.S. officials believed that a policy of "equivalence," according to which there was a roughly equal power balance on each side of the Cold War, was the best way to avoid a nuclear confrontation. Détente was pursued in other ways as well. When President Nixon took office in 1969, he sought to increase trade and cultural contacts with the Soviet Union. His purpose was to set up a series of "linkages" in U.S.–Soviet relations that would persuade Moscow of the economic and social benefits of maintaining good relations with the West.

A symbol of that new relationship was the Helsinki Agreement, signed in 1975. Signed by the United States,

Canada, and all European nations on both sides of the Iron Curtain, these accords recognized all borders in central and eastern Europe that had been established since the end of World War II, thereby formally acknowledging for the first time the Soviet sphere of influence in Eastern Europe. The Helsinki Agreement also committed the signatory powers to recognize and protect the human rights of their citizens, a clear effort by the Western states to improve the performance of the Soviet Union and its allies in that arena.

An End to Détente?

Protection of human rights became one of the major foreign policy goals of the next U.S. president, Jimmy Carter (b. 1924). Ironically, just at the point when U.S. involvement in Vietnam came to an end and relations with China began to improve, the mood in U.S.–Soviet relations began to sour. During the 1976 presidential campaign, the Republican nominee, Gerald Ford, who had replaced Richard Nixon after the latter's resignation under pressure in August 1974, refused to categorize the relationship with the USSR under the label of détente.

A variety of factors were involved. On the one hand, some Americans had become increasingly concerned about aggressive new tendencies in Soviet foreign policy. The first indication came in Africa. Soviet influence was on the rise in Somalia, across the Red Sea in South Yemen, and later in Ethiopia. Soviet involvement was also on the increase in southern Africa, where an insurgent movement supported by Cuban troops came to power in Angola, once a colony of Portugal. Then, in 1979, Soviet troops were sent to neighboring Afghanistan to protect a newly installed Marxist regime faced with rising internal resistance from fundamentalist Muslims provoked by the Marxist government's effort to abolish traditional Islamic customs.

Some observers suspected that the Soviet advance into hitherto neutral Afghanistan was timed to take advantage of the revolution led by traditionalist Muslim forces loyal to the Ayatollah Khomeini in Iran (see Chapter 14) and that its ultimate objective was to extend Soviet power into the oil fields of the Persian Gulf. To deter such a possibility, the White House promulgated the Carter Doctrine, which stated that the United States would use its military power, if necessary, to safeguard Western access to the oil reserves in the Middle East. In fact, sources in Moscow later disclosed that the Soviet advance into Afghanistan had little to do with a strategic drive toward the Persian Gulf, but represented an effort to take advantage of the recent disarray in U.S.

foreign policy in the aftermath of defeat in Vietnam to increase Soviet influence in a sensitive region increasingly beset with Islamic fervor. Soviet officials feared that the wave of Islamic activism could spread to the Muslim populations in the Soviet republics in Central Asia and were confident that the United States was too distracted by the "Vietnam syndrome" (the public fear of U.S. involvement in another Vietnam-type conflict) to respond.

Other factors contributed to the growing suspicion of the USSR in the United States. During the era of détente, Washington officials had assumed that Moscow accepted the U.S. doctrine of equivalence—the idea that both sides possessed sufficient strength to destroy the other in the event of a surprise attack. By the end of the decade, however, some U.S. defense analysts began to charge that the USSR was seeking strategic superiority in nuclear weapons and argued for a substantial increase in U.S. defense spending. Such charges, combined with evidence of Soviet efforts in Africa and the Middle East and reports of the persecution of Jews and dissidents in the Soviet Union, helped to undermine public support for détente in the United States. These changing attitudes were reflected in the failure of the Carter administration to obtain congressional approval of a new arms limitation agreement (SALT II), signed with the USSR in 1979.

Countering the Evil Empire

The early years of the administration of President Ronald Reagan (b. 1911) witnessed a return to the harsh rhetoric, if not all of the harsh practices, of the Cold War. President Reagan's anti-Communist credentials were well known. In a speech given shortly after his election in 1980, he referred to the Soviet Union as an "evil empire" and frequently voiced his suspicion of its motives in foreign affairs. In an effort to eliminate perceived Soviet advantages in strategic weaponry, the White House began a military buildup that stimulated a renewed arms race. In 1982, the Reagan administration introduced the nuclear-tipped cruise missile, whose ability to fly at low altitudes made it difficult to detect by enemy radar. Reagan also became an ardent exponent of the Strategic Defense Initiative (SDI), nicknamed "Star Wars." Its purposes were to create a space shield that could destroy incoming missiles and to force Moscow into an arms race that it could not hope to win.

The Reagan administration also adopted a more activist, if not confrontational, stance in the Third World. The fruit of that attitude was most directly demonstrated in Central America, where the consolidation of power in Nicaragua by the revolutionary Sandinista regime (the Sandinistas had come to power with the overthrow of the Somoza dictatorship in 1979) aroused concern in the White House about the further spread of international communism in the Western Hemisphere. Charging that the Sandinista regime was supporting a guerrilla insurgency movement in nearby El Salvador, the Reagan administration began to provide material aid to the government in El Salvador, while simultaneously applying pressure on the Sandinistas by giving support to an anticommunist guerrilla movement (called the Contras) in Nicaragua. The administration's Central American policy caused considerable controversy in Congress, as some charged that growing U.S. involvement there could lead to a repeat of the nation's bitter experience in Vietnam.

The Reagan administration also took the offensive in other areas. By providing military support to the anti-Soviet insurgents in Afghanistan, the White House helped to maintain a Vietnam-like war in Afghanistan that would embed the Soviet Union in its own quagmire. Like the Vietnam War, the conflict in Afghanistan resulted in heavy casualties and demonstrated that the influence of a superpower was limited in the face of strong nationalist, guerrilla-type opposition.

Conclusion

At the end of World War II, a new conflict appeared in Europe, as the new superpowers, the United States and the Soviet Union, began to compete for political domination. This ideological division soon spread to the rest of the world, as the United States fought in Korea and Vietnam to prevent the spread of communism, promoted by the new Maoist government in China, while the Soviet Union used its influence to prop up pro-Soviet regimes in Asia, Africa, and Latin America.

What had begun, then, as a confrontation across the great divide of the Iron Curtain in Europe eventually took on global significance, much as the major European powers had jostled for position and advantage in African and eastern Asia prior to World War I. The result was that both Moscow and Washington became entangled in areas that, in themselves, had little importance in terms of real national security interests. To make matters worse, U.S. policymakers all too often applied the lessons of World War II (the so-called "Munich syndrome," according to which efforts to appease an aggressor only encourage his appetite for conquest) to crisis points in the Third World, where in reality conditions were not remotely comparable.

By the 1980s, however, there were tantalizing signs of a thaw in the Cold War. China and the United States, each hoping to gain leverage with Moscow, had agreed to establish diplomatic relations. Freed from its own concerns over Beijing's open support of revolutions in the Third World, the United States decided to withdraw from South Vietnam, and the war there came to an end without involving the great powers in a dangerous confrontation. While Washington and Moscow continued to compete for advantage all over the world, both sides gradually came to realize that the struggle for domination could best be carried out in the political and economic arena rather than on the battlefield.

NOTES

1. *Department of State Bulletin* 12 (February 11, 1945): pp. 213–216.
2. Quoted in Joseph M. Jones, *The Fifteen Weeks (February 21–June 5, 1947)*, 2d ed. (New York, 1964), pp. 140–141.
3. Quoted in Walter Laqueur, *Europe in Our Time* (New York, 1992), p. 111.
4. Quoted in Wilfried Loth, *The Division of the World, 1941–1955* (New York, 1988), pp. 160–161.
5. Quoted in Peter Lane, *Europe since 1945: An Introduction* (Totowa, NJ, 1985), p. 248.
6. Quoted in Robert F. Kennedy, *Thirteen Days: A Memoir of the Cuban Missile Crisis* (New York, 1969), pp. 89–90.

CHAPTER
8

Brave New World: Communism in the Soviet Union and Eastern Europe

According to Karl Marx, capitalism is a system that involves the exploitation of man by man; under socialism, it is the other way around. That wry joke, an ironic twist on the familiar Marxist remark a century previously, was typical of popular humor in post–World War II Moscow, where the dreams of a future communist utopia had faded in the grim reality of life in the Soviet Union.

Grim though life in the Soviet Union might be, the Communist monopoly on power seemed secure, as did Moscow's hold over its client states in Eastern

Europe. In fact, for three decades after the end of World War II, the Soviet Empire appeared to be a permanent feature of the international landscape. But by the early 1980s, it became clear that there were cracks in the facade of the Kremlin wall. The Soviet economy was stagnant, the minority nationalities were restive, and Eastern European leaders were increasingly emboldened to test the waters of the global capitalist marketplace. In the United States, newly elected president Ronald Reagan boldly predicted the imminent collapse of the "evil empire."

The Postwar Soviet Union

World War II had left the Soviet Union as one of the world's two superpowers and its leader, Joseph Stalin, at the height of his power. As a result of the war, Stalin and his Soviet colleagues were now in control of a vast empire that included Eastern Europe, much of the Balkans, and new territory gained from Japan in East Asia.

From Stalin to Khrushchev

World War II devastated the Soviet Union. Twenty million citizens lost their lives, and cities such as Kiev, Kharkov, and Leningrad suffered enormous physical destruction. As the lands that had been occupied by the German forces were liberated, the Soviet government turned its attention to restoring their economic structures. Nevertheless, in 1945, agricultural production was only 60 percent and steel output only 50 percent of prewar levels. The Soviet people faced incredibly difficult

conditions: they worked longer hours; they ate less; they were ill-housed and poorly clothed.

In the immediate postwar years, the Soviet Union removed goods and materials from occupied Germany and extorted valuable raw materials from its satellite states in Eastern Europe. More important, however, to create a new industrial base, Stalin returned to the method he had used in the 1930s—the extraction of development capital from Soviet labor. Working hard for little pay and for precious few consumer goods, Soviet laborers were expected to produce goods for export with little in return for themselves. The incoming capital from abroad could then be used to purchase machinery and Western technology. The loss of millions of men in the war meant that much of this tremendous workload fell upon Soviet women, who performed almost 40 percent of the heavy manual labor.

Economic recovery in the Soviet Union was nothing less than spectacular. By 1947, Russian industrial production had attained 1939 levels; three years later, it had surpassed those levels by 40 percent. New power plants, canals, and giant factories were built, while new industrial enterprises and oil fields were established in Siberia and Soviet Central Asia. Stalin's new five-year plan, announced in 1946, reached its goals in less than five years.

Although Stalin's economic recovery policy was successful in promoting growth in heavy industry, primarily for the benefit of the military, consumer goods remained scarce. While the development of thermonuclear weapons, MIG fighters, and the first space satellite (*Sputnik*) in the 1950s elevated the Soviet state's reputation as a world power abroad, domestically the Soviet people were shortchanged. Heavy industry grew at a rate three times that of personal consumption. Moreover, the housing shortage was acute. A British military attaché in Moscow reported that "all houses, practically without exception, show lights from every window after dark. This seems to indicate that every room is both a living room by day and a bedroom by night. There is no place in overcrowded Moscow for the luxury of eating and sleeping in separate rooms."[1]

When World War II ended in 1945, Stalin had been in power for more than fifteen years. During that time, he had removed all opposition to his rule and remained the undisputed master of the Soviet Union. Other lead-

ing members of the Communist Party were completely obedient to his will. Increasingly distrustful of competitors, Stalin exercised sole authority and pitted his subordinates against one another. One of these subordinates, Lavrenti Beria, head of the secret police, controlled a force of several hundred thousand agents.

Stalin's morbid suspicions added to the constantly increasing repression of the regime. In 1946, government decrees subordinated all forms of literary and scientific expression to the political needs of the state. Along with the anti-intellectual campaign came political terror. By the late 1940s, there were an estimated 9 million people in Siberian concentration camps. Distrust of potential threats to his power even spread to some of his closest colleagues. In 1948, Andrei Zhdanov, his presumed successor and head of the Leningrad party organization, died under mysterious circumstances, but presumably at Stalin's order. Within weeks, the Leningrad party organization was purged of several top leaders, many of whom were charged with traitorous connections with Western intelligence agencies. In succeeding years, Stalin directed his suspicion at other members of the inner circle, including Foreign Minister Vyacheslav Molotov. Known as "old stone butt" in the West for his stubborn defense of Soviet security interests, Molotov had been Stalin's loyal lieutenant since the early years of Stalin's rise to power.

◆ **The Portals of Doom.** Perhaps the most feared location in the Soviet Union was Lyubyanka Prison, an ornate prerevolutionary building in the heart of Moscow. Taken over by the Bolsheviks after the 1917 Revolution, it became the headquar-

ters of the Soviet secret police, the Cheka, later to be known as the KGB. It was here that many Soviet citizens accused of "counterrevolutionary acts" were imprisoned and executed.

Now Stalin distrusted Molotov and had his Jewish wife placed in a Siberian concentration camp.

Stalin died in 1953 and, after some bitter infighting within the party leadership, was succeeded by Georgy Malenkov, a veteran administrator and ambitious member of the Politburo. Malenkov came to power with a clear agenda. In foreign affairs, he hoped to promote an easing of Cold War tensions and improve relations with the Western powers. For Moscow's Eastern European allies, he advocated a "new course" in their mutual relations and a decline in Stalinist methods of rule. Inside the Soviet Union, he hoped to reduce defense expenditures and assign a higher priority to improving the standard of living. Such goals were laudable, and probably had the support of the majority of the Russian people, but they were not necessarily appealing to key pressure groups within the USSR—the army, the party, the managerial elite, and the security services (known as the Committee on Government Security, or KGB). In 1953, he was removed from his position as prime minister, and power shifted to his rival, the new party general secretary, Nikita Khrushchev

During his struggle for power with Malenkov, Khrushchev had outmaneuvered him by calling for heightened defense expenditures and a continuing emphasis on heavy industry. Once in power, however, Khrushchev showed the political dexterity displayed by many an American politician and reversed his priorities. He now resumed the efforts of his predecessor to reduce tensions with the West and improve the standard of living of the Russian people. He moved vigorously to improve the performance of the Soviet economy and revitalize Soviet society. By nature, Khrushchev was a man of enormous energy as well as an innovator. In an attempt to release the stranglehold of the central bureaucracy over the national economy, he abolished dozens of government ministries and split up the party and government apparatus. Khrushchev also attempted to rejuvenate the stagnant agricultural sector, long the Achilles' heel of the Soviet economy. He attempted to spur production by increasing profit incentives and opened "virgin lands" in Soviet Kazakhstan to bring thousands of acres of new land under cultivation.

Like any innovator, Khrushchev had to overcome the inherently conservative instincts of the Soviet bureaucracy, as well as of the mass of the Soviet population. His plan to remove the "dead hand" of the state, however laudable in intent, alienated much of the Soviet official class, while his effort to split the party angered those who saw it as the central force in the Soviet system.

Khrushchev's agricultural schemes inspired similar opposition. Although the Kazakhstan wheat lands would eventually demonstrate their importance in the overall agricultural picture, progress was slow, while his effort to persuade the Russian people to eat more corn (an idea he had apparently picked up during a visit to the United States) led to the mocking nickname of "Cornman." Disappointment in agricultural production, combined with high military spending, hurt the Soviet economy. The industrial growth rate, which had soared in the early 1950s, now declined dramatically, from 13 percent in 1953 to 7.5 percent in 1964.

Khrushchev was probably best known for his policy of de-Stalinization. Khrushchev had risen in the party hierarchy as a Stalin protégé but he had been deeply disturbed by his mentor's excesses and, once in a position of authority, moved to excise the Stalinist legacy from Soviet society. The kickoff of the campaign took place at the Twentieth National Congress of the Communist Party in February 1956, when Khrushchev gave a long secret speech criticizing some of Stalin's major shortcomings. The speech had apparently not been intended for public distribution, but it was quickly leaked to the Western press and created a sensation throughout the world (see box on p. 176). During the next few years, Khrushchev encouraged more freedom of expression for writers, artists, and composers, arguing that "readers should be given the chance to make their own judgments" regarding the acceptability of controversial literature and that "police measures shouldn't be used."[2] Under Khrushchev's instructions, thousands of prisoners were released from concentration camps, and in 1962, he allowed the publication of Alexander Solzhenitsyn's *One Day in the Life of Ivan Denisovich*, a grim portrayal of the horrors of Russia's forced-labor camps.

Khrushchev's personality, however, did not endear him to higher Soviet officials, who frowned at his tendency to crack jokes and play the clown. Nor were the higher members of the party bureaucracy pleased when Khrushchev tried to curb their privileges. Foreign policy failures further damaged Khrushchev's reputation among his colleagues. His plan to place missiles in Cuba was the final straw (see Chapter 7). While he was away on vacation in 1964, a special meeting of the Soviet Politburo voted him out of office (because of "deteriorating health") and forced him into retirement. Although a group of leaders succeeded him, real power came into the hands of Leonid Brezhnev (1906–1982), the "trusted" supporter of Khrushchev who had engineered his downfall.

⋟ Stalin the Terrible ⋞

Three years after Joseph Stalin's death in 1953, the new Soviet premier, Nikita Khrushchev, addressed the Twentieth Congress of the Communist Party of the Soviet Union and denounced the former Soviet dictator for his crimes. It had not been an easy decision. Many of Khrushchev's colleagues had served with Stalin for decades and continued to revere his memory. Others were aware of Stalin's brutality toward the Soviet people and the many shortcomings in his leadership, but feared that an exposé of the nature of his leadership would undermine the prestige of the Communist Party and the concept of the dictatorship of the proletariat. In the end, party leaders approved the speech, but ordered that it be presented in the middle of the night and not be disclosed to the Soviet people.

In his address, Khrushchev did not mince words. Stalin had ignored the Leninist concept of party collegiality and encouraged a "cult of personality." He "abandoned the method of ideological struggle for that of administrative violence, mass repressions and terror." He repressed his enemies with brutality, not only against actual enemies, but even against many individuals "who had not committed any crimes against the party and the Soviet government." During the 1930s, many "honest Communists" were unfairly charged with treason and exposed to torture and execution. In sum, the one-time Soviet leader was a "very distrustful man, sickly suspicious . . . , who saw enemies and spies everywhere."

Khrushchev's address, later to be known as the "de-Stalinization speech," was leaked to the press, and its contents soon became known to an astonished world. Many observers in the West (and undoubtedly in the Soviet Union as well) were delighted that Stalin's crimes against humanity had finally been publicly revealed, but some party cadres in the USSR and other socialist countries wept at learning the truth about their beloved leader. Khrushchev followed up his speech by seeking to rid the Soviet Union of Stalin's legacy. Writers and artists were encouraged to express their own views about life in Soviet society. Among those who took advantage of the new freedom was Alexander Solzhenitsyn, whose short novel One Day in the Life of Ivan Denisovich described the life of its chief character in a concentration camp in Siberia. Many Soviet citizens identified with Ivan as a symbol of the suffering that they themselves had endured under their "Great Leader" Stalin.

Sources: *Congressional Record*, 84th Congress, 2d session, Vol. 102, Part 7, pp. 9389–9402 (June 4, 1956); Alexander Solzhenitsyn, *One Day in the Life of Ivan Denisovich*, trans. Ralph Parker (New York: E. P. Dutton and Victor Gollancz, 1963).

The Brezhnev Years (1964–1982)

The overthrow of Nikita Khrushchev in October 1964 vividly demonstrated the challenges that would be encountered by any Soviet leader sufficiently bold to reform the Soviet system. In democratic countries, pressure on the executive and legislative branches comes from various sources within society at large—from the business community and labor unions, from innumerable pressure groups created to represent the particular needs of interest groups in society, and of course from the general public. In the Soviet Union, pressure on government and party leaders originated from sources essentially operating inside the system—from the government bureaucracy, the party apparatus, the KGB, and the armed forces.

Leonid Brezhnev, the new party chief, was undoubtedly aware of these realities of Soviet politics, and his long tenure in power was marked, above all, by the desire to avoid changes that might provoke instability, either at home or abroad. Brezhnev was himself a product of the Soviet system. He had entered the ranks of the party leadership under Joseph Stalin, and although he was not a particularly avid believer in party ideology—indeed, his years in power gave rise to innumerable stories about his addiction to "bourgeois pleasures," including expensive country houses in the elite Moscow suburb of Zhukovka and fast cars (many of them gifts from foreign leaders)—he was no partisan of reform.

Still, Brezhnev sought stability in the domestic arena. He and his prime minister, Alexei Kosygin, undertook what might be described as a program of "de-Khrushchevization," returning the responsibility for long-term planning to the central ministries and reuniting the Communist Party apparatus. Moscow did make some cautious attempts to stimulate the stagnant farm sector, increasing capital investment in agriculture and raising food prices to increase rural income and provide additional incentives to collective farmers, but there was no effort to revise the basic structure of the collective system. In the industrial sector, the regime launched a series of reforms designed to give factory managers (themselves employees of the state) more responsibility for setting prices, wages, and production quotas. These "Kosygin reforms" had little effect, however, because they were stubbornly resisted by the bureaucracy and were eventually adopted by relatively few enterprises within the vast state-owned industrial sector.

A CONTROLLED SOCIETY

Brezhnev also initiated a significant retreat from the policy of de-Stalinization adopted by Nikita Khrushchev. Criticism of the memory and record of the country's "Great Leader" had angered conservatives both within the party hierarchy and among the public at large, many of whom still revered Stalin as a hero of the Soviet system and a defender of the Russian people against Nazi Germany. Many influential figures in the Kremlin feared that de-Stalinization could lead to internal instability and a decline in public trust in the legitimacy of party leadership—the hallowed "dictatorship of the proletariat." Early in Brezhnev's reign, Stalin's reputation began to revive. Although his alleged "shortcomings" were not totally ignored, he was now described in the official press as "an outstanding party leader" who had been primarily responsible for the successes achieved by the Soviet Union.

The regime also adopted a more restrictive policy toward free expression and dissidence in Soviet society. Critics of the Soviet system, such as the physicist Andrei Sakharov, were harassed and arrested or, like the famous writer Alexander Solzhenitsyn, forced to leave the USSR. There was also a qualified return to the anti-Semitic policies and attitudes that had marked the Stalin era. Such indications of renewed repression aroused concern in the West, and were instrumental in the inclusion of a statement on human rights (the so-called "basket three") in the 1975 Helsinki Agreement, which guaranteed the sanctity of international frontiers throughout the continent of Europe (see Chapter 7). Performance in the area of human rights continued to be spotty, however, and the repressive character of Soviet society was not significantly alleviated.

The political stamp of the Brezhnev era was formally enshrined in a new state constitution, promulgated in 1977. Although the preamble declared that the Soviet Union was no longer a proletarian dictatorship, but a "state of all the people," comprising workers, farmers, and "socialist intellectuals," it confirmed the leading role of the party as "the predominant force" in Soviet society. Article 49 stated that "persecution for criticism shall be prohibited," but Article 39 qualified the rights of the individual by declaring that "the exercise by citizens of their rights and freedoms *should not harm the interests of society and the state* or the rights of other citizens [italics added]." Article 62 was even more explicit about the priority of national interests over those of the individual: "The citizens of the USSR shall be obligated to safeguard the interests of the Soviet state and to contribute to the strength of its might and prestige."

There were, of course, no interest groups to compete with the party and the government in defining national interests. The media were controlled by the state and presented only what the state wanted people to hear. The two major newspapers, *Pravda* (Truth) and *Izvestiya* (News), were the agents of the party and the government, respectively. Cynics joked that there was no news in *Pravda*, and no truth in *Izvestiya*. According to Western journalists, reports of airplane accidents in the USSR were rarely publicized, on the grounds that it would raise questions about the quality of the Soviet airline industry. The government made strenuous efforts to prevent the Soviet people from exposure to harmful foreign ideas, especially modern art, literature, and contemporary Western rock music. When the Summer Olympic Games were held in Moscow in 1980, Soviet newspapers advised citizens to keep their children indoors to keep them from being polluted with "bourgeois" ideas passed on by foreign visitors.

For citizens of Western democracies, such a political atmosphere would seem highly oppressive, but for the Russian people, an emphasis on law and order was an accepted aspect of everyday life inherited from the tsarist period. Conformism was the rule in virtually every corner of Soviet society, from the educational system (characterized at all levels by rote memorization and political indoctrination), to child rearing (it was forbidden, for example, to be left-handed), and even to yearly vacations (most workers took their vacations at resorts run by their employer, where the daily schedule of activities was highly regimented). Young Americans studying in the USSR reported that their Soviet friends were often shocked to hear U.S. citizens criticizing their own president, and to learn that they did not routinely carry identity cards. Clearly, the American "frontier spirit" did not exist in the Soviet Union.

A STAGNANT ECONOMY

Soviet leaders also failed to achieve their objective of revitalizing the national economy. Whereas growth rates during the early Khrushchev era had been impressive (prompting Khrushchev during one visit to the United States in the late 1950s to chortle "We will bury you"), during the Brezhnev years industrial growth declined to an annual rate of less than 4 percent in the early 1970s, and less than 3 percent in the period 1975–1980. Successes in the agricultural sector were equally meager. Grain production rose from less than 90 million tons in the early 1950s to nearly 200 million tons in the 1970s, but then stagnated at that level.

What were the major causes of the overall slowdown in the Soviet economy? One of the primary problems was certainly the absence of incentives. Under the Soviet system, people lacked the motivation to produce and to create, activities that Karl Marx had described as the most fundamental aspirations of human nature. Salary structures offered little reward in most sectors of the Soviet economy for hard labor and extraordinary achievement. Pay differentials in the USSR operated within a much narrower range than in most Western societies, and there was little danger of being dismissed. According to the Soviet Constitution, every Soviet citizen was guaranteed an opportunity to work.

There were, of course, some exceptions to this general rule. In a society such as the Soviet Union, where athletic achievement was highly prized, a gymnast of Olympic stature would receive great rewards in the form of prestige and lifestyle. Senior officials did not receive high salaries, but were provided with countless "perquisites," such as access to foreign goods, official automobiles with a chauffeur, and entry into prestigious institutions of higher learning for their children. For the elite, it was *blat* (influence) that most often differentiated them from the rest of the population. For the average citizen, however, whether clerk, factory laborer, collective farmer, or waitress, there was little material incentive to produce beyond the minimum acceptable level of effort. It is hardly surprising that overall per capita productivity was only about half that realized in most capitalist countries. At the same time, the rudeness of clerks and waiters toward their customers in Soviet society became legendary.

The problem of incentives existed at the managerial level as well, where the practice of centralized planning discouraged initiative and innovation. Factory managers, for example, were assigned monthly and annual quotas by the Gosplan (the "state plan," drawn up by the central planning commission). Because state-owned factories were not subjected to the level of competition characteristic of a free-market system, it was of relatively little concern to factory managers whether their products were competitive in terms of price and quality, so long as the quota was attained. One of the key complaints of Soviet citizens was the low quality of most locally made consumer goods. Knowledgeable consumers quickly discovered that products manufactured at the end of the month were often of lower quality (because factory workers had to rush to meet their quotas at the end of their production cycle) and attempted to avoid purchasing them.

Often, consumer goods were simply unavailable. Soviet citizens automatically got in line when they saw a queue forming in front of a store, because they never knew when something might be available again. When they reached the head of the line, most would purchase several of the same item in order to swap with their friends and neighbors. A popular joke at the time was that a Soviet inventor had managed to produce an airplane that was cheap enough to be purchased by every citizen. Everyone was delighted because now when they heard that there was a sale of a particular item anywhere in the country, they would be able to fly to the proper location to buy it. This "queue psychology," of course, was a time-consuming process and inevitably served to reduce the per capita rate of productivity.

Soviet citizens often tried to overcome the shortcomings of the system by operating "on the left" (the black market). Private economic activities, of course, were illegal in the socialized Soviet system, but many workers took to "moonlighting" to augment their meager salaries. An employee in a state-run appliance store, for example, would promise to repair a customer's television set on his own time in return for a payment "under the table." Otherwise, servicing of the set might require several weeks. Knowledgeable observers estimated that as much as one-third of the entire Soviet economy operated outside the legal system.

Another major obstacle to economic growth was inadequate technology. Except in the area of national defense, the overall level of Soviet technology was not comparable to that of the West or the advanced industrial societies of East Asia. Part of the problem, of course, stemmed from the issues already described. With no competition, factory managers had little incentive to improve the quality of their products. But another reason was the high priority assigned to defense. The military sector of the economy regularly received the most resources from the government and attracted the cream of the country's scientific talent.

♦ How to Shop in Moscow. Because of the policy of state control over the Soviet economy, the availability of goods was a consequence not of market factors but of decisions made by government bureaucrats. As a result, needed goods were often in short supply. When Soviet citizens heard that a shipment of a particular product had arrived at a state store, they queued up to buy it. Here, shoppers line up in front of a store selling dinnerware in Moscow.

There were still other reasons for the gradual slowdown in the Soviet economy. Coal mining was highly inefficient, and it was estimated that only one-third of the coal extracted actually reached its final destination. Although the USSR was estimated to possess the greatest liquid energy reserves of any country in the world, for the most part they were located in inaccessible areas of Siberia where extraction facilities and transportation were inadequate. U.S. intelligence reports estimated that a leveling off of oil and gas production could cause a severe problem for the future growth of the Soviet economy. Government planners hoped that nuclear energy could eventually take up the slack, but the highly publicized meltdown of a nuclear reactor at Chernobyl in 1986 vividly demonstrated that Soviet technology was encountering difficulties there as well. Finally, there were the serious underlying structural problems in agriculture.

Climatic difficulties (frequent flooding, drought, and a short growing season) and a lack of fertile soil (except in the renowned "black earth" regions of the Ukraine) combined with a chronic shortage of mechanized farm equipment and a lack of incentives to prevent the growth of an advanced agricultural economy.

PROBLEMS OF GERONTOCRACY

Such problems would be intimidating for any government; they were particularly so for the elderly generation of party leaders surrounding Leonid Brezhnev, many of whom were cautious to a fault. While some undoubtedly recognized the need for reform and innovation, they were paralyzed by the fear of instability and change. The problem worsened during the late 1970s, when Brezhnev's health began to deteriorate. According to one authoritative source in Moscow, during the last several years of his life, he was mentally as well as physically incapacitated, as the use of sedatives gradually destroyed his grip on reality. Brezhnev's mental and physical ailments inspired a new round of popular humor, but for the average citizen, conditions in Soviet society were no laughing matter.

Brezhnev died in November 1982 and was succeeded by Yuri Andropov (1914–1984), a party veteran and head of the Soviet secret services. During his brief tenure as party chief, Andropov was a vocal advocate of reform, but most of his initiatives were limited to the familiar nostrums of punishment for wrongdoers and moral exhortations to Soviet citizens to work harder. At the same time, material incentives were still officially discouraged and generally ineffective. Andropov had been ailing when he was selected to succeed Brezhnev as party chief, and when he died after only a few months in office, little had been done to change the system. He was succeeded, in turn, by a mediocre party stalwart, the elderly Konstantin Chernenko (1911–1985). With the Soviet system in crisis, Moscow seemed stuck in a time warp. As one concerned observer told an American journalist: "I had a sense of foreboding, like before a storm. That there was something brewing in people and there would be a time when they would say, 'That's it. We can't go on living like this. We can't. We need to redo everything.' "[3]

Ferment in Eastern Europe

The key to Moscow's security along the western frontier of the Soviet Union was the string of satellite states that had been created in Eastern Europe in the aftermath of World War II. Once Communist power had been assured in Warsaw, Prague, Sofia, Budapest, Bucharest, and East Berlin, a series of "little Stalins" put into power by Moscow instituted Soviet-type five-year plans that placed primary emphasis on heavy industry rather than consumer goods, on the collectivization of agriculture, and on the nationalization of industry. They also appropriated the political tactics that Stalin had perfected in the Soviet Union, eliminating all non-Communist parties and establishing the classical institutions of repression—the secret police and military forces. Dissidents were tracked down and thrown into prison, while "national Communists" who resisted total subservience to the USSR were charged with treason in mass show trials and executed.

Despite such repressive efforts, however, Soviet-style policies aroused growing discontent in several Eastern European societies. Countries such as Hungary, Poland, and Romania harbored bitter memories of past Russian domination and suspected that Stalin, under the guise of proletarian internationalism, was seeking to revive the empire of the Romanovs. For the vast majority of peoples in Eastern Europe, the imposition of the so-called "people's democracies" (a term invented by Moscow to define a society in the early stage of socialist transition) resulted in economic hardship and severe threats to the most basic political liberties.

The first indications of unrest appeared in 1953, when popular riots broke out against Communist rule in East Berlin. Georgy Malenkov, who had seized power in Moscow after Stalin's death in March, sought to deflect the discontent by announcing a "new course" in Soviet ties with its Eastern European allies. Malenkov's objective was to bring about political and economic reforms in the region before full-scale rebellion broke out.

The riots in East Berlin eventually subsided, but the virus had begun to spread to neighboring countries. Several of the "little Stalins" had ignored the ominous warnings of public discontent, and in 1956 popular dissatisfaction erupted in Poland and Hungary. In Poland, public demonstrations against an increase in food prices escalated into widespread protests against the regime's economic policies, restrictions on the freedom of Catholics to practice their religion, and the continued presence of Soviet troops (as called for by the Warsaw Pact) on Polish soil.

In a desperate effort to defuse the unrest, in October the first secretary of the Polish Workers' Party (the official name of the ruling party in Poland) stepped down and was replaced by Wladyslaw Gomulka (1905–1982), a popular figure who had previously been demoted for his "nationalist" tendencies. When Gomulka took steps to ease the crisis, the new Soviet party chief Nikita Khrushchev flew to Warsaw to warn his Polish colleague against adopting policies that could undermine the dictatorship of the proletariat (a classic Marxist phrase to express the political dominance of the party) and even weaken security links with the Soviet Union. After a brief confrontation, during which both sides threatened to use military force to punctuate their demands, Gomulka and Khrushchev reached a compromise according to which Poland would adopt a policy labeled "internal reform, external loyalty." Poland agreed to remain in the Warsaw Pact and to maintain the sanctity of party rule. In return, Warsaw was authorized to adopt

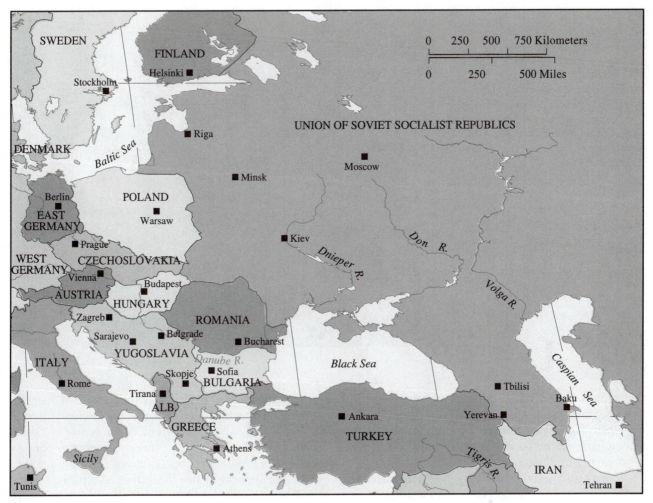

Map 8.1 The States of Eastern Europe and the Soviet Union

domestic reforms, such as easing restrictions on religious practice and ending the policy of forced collectivization in rural areas.

The developments in Poland sent shock waves throughout the region. The impact was the strongest in neighboring Hungary, where the methods of the local "little Stalin," Matyas Rakosi, were so brutal that he had been summoned to Moscow for a lecture. In late October, student-led popular riots broke out in the capital of Budapest and soon spread to other towns and villages throughout the country. Rakosi was forced to resign and was replaced by Imre Nagy (1896–1958), a "national Communist" who attempted to satisfy popular demands without arousing the anger of Moscow. Unlike Gomulka, however, Nagy was unable to contain the zeal of leading members of the protest movement, who sought major po-

litical reforms and the withdrawal of Hungary from the Warsaw Pact. On November 1, Nagy promised free elections which, given the mood of the country, would probably have brought an end to Communist rule. After a brief moment of uncertainty, Moscow decided on firm action. Soviet troops, recently withdrawn at Nagy's request, returned to Budapest and installed a new government under the more pliant party leader Janos Kadar (1912–1989). While Kadar rescinded many of Nagy's measures, Nagy sought refuge in the Yugoslav Embassy. A few weeks later, he left the embassy under the promise of safety, but was quickly arrested, convicted of treason, and executed.

The dramatic events in Poland and Hungary graphically demonstrated the vulnerability of the Soviet satellite system in Eastern Europe, and many observers

◆ **How the Mighty Have Fallen.**
In the fall of 1956, Hungarian freedom fighters rose up against Communist domination of their country in the short-lived Hungarian revolution. Their actions threatened Soviet hegemony in Eastern Europe, however, and in late October, Soviet leader Nikita Khrushchev dispatched troops to quell the uprising. In the meantime, the Hungarian people had voiced their discontent by toppling a gigantic statue of Joseph Stalin in the capital of Budapest.

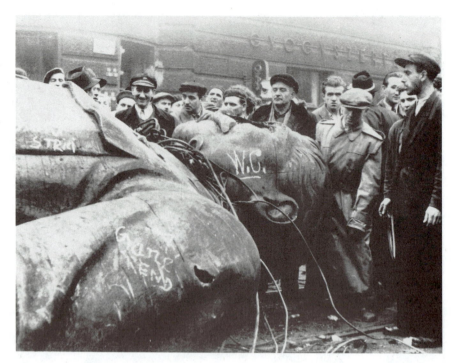

throughout the world anticipated an attempt by the United States to intervene on behalf of the freedom fighters in Hungary. After all, the Eisenhower administration had promised that it would "roll back" Communism, and radio broadcasts by the U.S.–sponsored Radio Liberty and Radio Free Europe had encouraged the peoples of Eastern Europe to rise up against Soviet domination. In reality, Washington was well aware that U.S. intervention could lead to nuclear war, and limited itself to protests against Soviet brutality in crushing the uprising.

The year of discontent was not without its consequences, however. Soviet leaders now recognized that Moscow could only maintain control over its satellites in Eastern Europe by granting them the leeway to adopt domestic policies appropriate to local conditions. Krushchev had already embarked on this path when, during a visit to Belgrade in 1955, he assured Josip Tito that there were "different roads to socialism." That compromise was confirmed to Gomulka in Warsaw the following year. Eastern European Communist leaders now took Khrushchev at his word and adopted reform programs to make socialism more palatable to their subject populations. Even Janos Kadar, derisively labeled the "butcher of Budapest," managed to preserve many of Imre Nagy's reforms to allow a measure of capitalist incentive and freedom of expression in Hungary.

Czechoslovakia did not share in the thaw of the mid-1950s and remained under the rule of Antonin Novotny (1904–1975), who had been placed in power by Stalin himself. By the late 1960s, however, Novotny's policies had led to widespread popular alienation, and in 1968, with the support of intellectuals and reformist party members, Alexander Dubcek was elected first secretary of the Communist Party. He immediately attempted to create what was popularly called "socialism with a human face," relaxing restrictions on freedom of speech and the press and the right to travel abroad. Reforms were announced in the economic sector, and party control over all aspects of society was reduced. A period of euphoria erupted that came to be known as the "Prague Spring."

It proved to be short-lived. Encouraged by Dubcek's actions, some called for more far-reaching reforms, including neutrality and withdrawal from the Soviet bloc. To forestall the spread of this "spring fever," the Soviet Red Army, supported by troops from other Warsaw Pact states, invaded Czechoslovakia in August of 1968 and crushed the reform movement. Gustav Husak (b. 1913), a committed Stalinist, replaced Dubcek and restored the old order (see box on p. 183).

Elsewhere in Eastern Europe, Stalinist policies continued to hold sway. In Romania, a Communist-dominated People's Democratic Front assumed complete

≽ *The Brezhnev Doctrine* ≼

*I*n the summer of 1968, when a new Communist Party leadership in Czechoslovakia was giving serious consideration to proposals for reforming the Stalinist system there, the Warsaw Pact nations met at the request of Soviet party chief Leonid Brezhnev to assess the threat to the socialist camp. Shortly after, military forces of several Soviet bloc nations entered Czechoslovakia and imposed a new government subservient to Moscow. The move was justified by the spirit of "proletarian internationalism" and was widely viewed as a warning to China and other socialist states not to stray too far from Marxist-Leninist orthodoxy, as interpreted by the USSR.

As Soviet and other Warsaw Pact forces prepared to enter the territory of Czechoslovakia to enforce Soviet will on the new leadership in the country, the Soviet Union published a letter which it had sent to the Czech party leaders in Prague. The letter invoked what would become known as the Brezhnev Doctrine. "The development of events in your country," it said, "evokes in us deep anxiety." Reactionary forces, it claimed,

backed by U.S. imperialism, were threatening the foundations of socialism in Czechoslovakia and jeopardizing the interests of the entire socialist camp.

Insisting that the Warsaw Pact signatories had no intention of interfering in the internal affairs of any member nation, the letter stated that "hostile forces" could not be allowed to "push your country from the road of socialism and create a threat of severing Czechoslovakia from the socialist community." That is why, it concluded, "a decisive rebuff to the anti-Communist forces, and decisive efforts for the preservation of the socialist system in Czechoslovakia" are "not only your task but ours as well."

The message—that the Soviet Union was prepared to use military force to protect its security interests, even against the will of a fraternal government, was undoubtedly not lost on Beijing.

Source: *Moscow News*, supplement to No. 30 (917), 1968, pp. 3–6.

---

power in 1948. In 1965, leadership passed into the hands of Nicolae Ceausescu (1918–1989), who with his wife Elena established a rigid and dictatorial regime. Ceausescu ruled Romania with an iron grip, using the secret police—the Securitate—as his personal weapon against any dissent.

The ruling Communist government in East Germany, led by Walter Ulbricht, consolidated its position in the early 1950s and became a faithful Soviet satellite. Industry was nationalized and agriculture collectivized. After the 1953 workers' revolt was crushed by Soviet tanks, a steady flight of East Germans to West Germany ensued, primarily through the city of Berlin. This exodus of mostly skilled laborers created economic problems and, in 1961, led the East German government to build the infamous Berlin Wall separating West from East Berlin, as well as equally fearsome barriers along the entire border with West Germany.

After building the Wall, East Germany succeeded in developing the strongest economy among the Soviet Union's Eastern European satellites. In 1971, Walter Ulbricht was succeeded by Erich Honecker (b. 1912), a party hard-liner who was deeply committed to the ideological battle against détente. Propaganda increased, and

the use of the Stasi, the secret police, became a hallmark of Honecker's virtual dictatorship. Honecker ruled unchallenged for the next eighteen years.

Culture and Society in the Soviet Bloc

In his occasional musings about the future communist utopia, Karl Marx had predicted the emergence of a new, classless society to replace the exploitative and hierarchical systems of feudalism and capitalism. Workers would take part in productive activities, but would share equally in the fruits of their labor. In their free time, they would help to produce a new, advanced culture, proletarian in character and egalitarian in content.

Cultural Expression

The reality in the post–World War II Soviet Union and in Eastern Europe was somewhat different. Under Stalin, the Soviet cultural scene was a wasteland. Beginning in 1946, a series of government decrees made all forms of literary and scientific expression dependent on the state. All Soviet culture was expected to follow the party line.

Historians, philosophers, and social scientists all grew accustomed to quoting Marx, Lenin, and, above all, Stalin as their chief authorities. Novels and plays, too, were supposed to portray Communist heroes and their efforts to create a better society. No criticism of existing social conditions was permitted. Even distinguished composers such as Dmitry Shostakovich were compelled to heed Stalin's criticisms, including his view that contemporary Western music was nothing but a "mishmash." Some areas of intellectual activity were virtually abolished; the science of genetics disappeared, and few movies were made during Stalin's final years.

Stalin's death brought a modest respite from cultural repression. Writers and artists banned during Stalin's years were again allowed to publish. Still, Soviet authorities, including Khrushchev, were reluctant to allow cultural freedom to move far beyond official Soviet ideology.

These restrictions, however, did not prevent the emergence of some significant Soviet literature, although authors paid a heavy price if they alienated the Soviet authorities. The writer Ilya Ehrenburg set the tone with his novel, significantly titled *The Thaw*. Boris Pasternak (1890–1960), who began his literary career as a poet, won the Nobel Prize in 1958 for his celebrated novel *Doctor Zhivago*, written between 1945 and 1956 and published in Italy in 1957. But the Soviet government condemned Pasternak's anti-Soviet tendencies, banned the novel from the USSR, and would not allow him to accept the prize. The author had alienated the authorities by describing a society scarred by the excesses of Bolshevik revolutionary zeal.

Alexander Solzhenitsyn (b. 1918) created an even greater furor than Pasternak. Solzhenitsyn had spent eight years in forced-labor camps for criticizing Stalin, and his *One Day in the Life of Ivan Denisovich*, which won him the Nobel Prize in 1970, was an account of life in those camps. Khrushchev allowed the book's publication as part of his de-Stalinization campaign. Later, Solzhenitsyn wrote *The Gulag Archipelago*, a detailed indictment of the whole system of Soviet oppression. Soviet authorities denounced Solzhenitsyn's efforts to inform the world of Soviet crimes against humanity and arrested and expelled him from the Soviet Union after he published *The Gulag Archipelago* abroad in 1973.

Exile abroad rather than imprisonment in forced-labor camps was perhaps a sign of modest progress. But even the limited freedom that had arisen during the Khrushchev years was rejected after his fall from power. Cultural controls were reimposed, de-Stalinization was halted, and authors were again sent to labor camps for expressing outlawed ideas. These restrictive policies continued until the late 1980s, when Gorbachev's policy of *glasnost* (see Chapter 16) opened the doors to a new cultural freedom and new opportunities for expression.

In the Eastern European satellites, cultural freedom varied considerably from country to country. In Poland, intellectuals had access to Western publications as well as greater freedom to travel to the West. Hungarian and Yugoslav Communists, too, tolerated a certain level of intellectual activity that was not liked, but at least not prohibited. Elsewhere, intellectuals were forced to conform to the regime's demands. After the Soviet invasion of Czechoslovakia in 1968, Czech Communists pursued a policy of strict cultural control. This control did not stop a number of intellectuals from opposing the regime, however. Dissident writers and professionals, including the dramatist Václav Havel, later to be elected president of the Czech Republic, formed Charter 77 in January 1977 to protest human rights violations by the Communist regime. Although the regime struck back by prohibiting them from working in their professions, members of Charter 77 persisted and eventually founded Civic Forum, the political organization that guided the ouster of the Communist regime in the revolution of 1989.

The socialist camp also experienced the many facets of modern popular culture. By the early 1970s, there were 28 million television sets in the Soviet Union, although state authorities controlled the content of the programs that the Soviet people watched. Modern tourism, too, made inroads into the Communist world, as state-run industries provided vacation time and governments facilitated the establishment of resorts for workers on the Black Sea and Adriatic coasts. In Poland, the number of vacationers who used holiday retreats increased from 700,000 in 1960 to 2.8 million in 1972.

Spectator sports became a large industry and were also highly politicized as the result of Cold War divisions. In 1948, the Soviet Communist Party called upon the nation "to spread physical culture and sport to every corner of the land, and to raise the level of skill, so that Soviet sportsmen might win world supremacy in the major sports in the immediate future." "Each new victory," one party leader stated, "is a victory for the Soviet form of society and the socialist sport system; it provides irrefutable proof of the superiority of socialist culture over the decaying culture of the capitalist states."[4] Accordingly, the state provided money for the construction of gymnasiums and training camps and portrayed athletes as superheroes.

Social Changes in the USSR and Eastern Europe

The imposition of Marxist systems in Eastern Europe had far-reaching social consequences. Most Eastern European countries made the change from peasant societies to modern, industrialized economies. In Bulgaria, for example, 80 percent of the labor force was in agriculture in 1950, but only 20 percent was still there in 1980. Although the Soviet Union and its Eastern European satellites never achieved the high standards of living of the West, they did experience some improvement. In 1960, the average real income of Polish peasants was four times higher than before World War II. Consumer goods also became more widespread. In East Germany, only 17 percent of families had television sets in 1960, but 75 percent had acquired them by 1972.

According to communist ideology, government control of industry and the elimination of private property were supposed to lead to a classless society. Although the classless society was never achieved, that ideal did have important social consequences in the Soviet Union and Eastern Europe. For one thing, traditional ruling classes in the Soviet Union and Eastern European countries were stripped of their special status after 1945. The Potocki family in Poland, for example, which had owned 9 million acres of land before the war, lost all of its possessions, and family members were reduced to the ranks of common laborers.

The desire to create a classless society led to noticeable changes in education. In some countries, the desire to provide equal educational opportunities led to laws that mandated quota systems based on class. In East Germany, for example, 50 percent of the students in secondary schools had to be children of workers and peasants. The sons of manual workers constituted 53 percent of university students in Yugoslavia in 1964 and 40 percent in East Germany, compared to only 15 percent in Italy and 5.3 percent in West Germany. Social mobility also increased. In Poland, in 1961, 50 percent of white-collar workers came from blue-collar families. A significant number of judges, professors, and industrial managers stemmed from working-class backgrounds.

Education became crucial in preparing for new jobs in the communist system and led to higher enrollments in both secondary schools and universities. In Czechoslovakia, for example, the number of students in secondary schools tripled between 1945 and 1970, while the number of university students quadrupled between the 1930s and the 1960s. The type of education that students received also changed. In Hungary before World War II, 40 percent of students studied law, 9 percent engineering and technology, and 5 percent agriculture. In 1970, the figures were 35 percent in engineering and technology, 9 percent in agriculture, and only 4 percent in law.

By the 1970s, the new managers of society, regardless of class background, realized the importance of higher education and used their power to gain special privileges for their children. By 1971, 60 percent of the children of white-collar workers attended university, and even though blue-collar families constituted 60 percent of the population, only 36 percent of their children attended institutions of higher learning. Even East Germany dropped its requirement that 50 percent of secondary students had to be the offspring of workers and peasants.

This shift in educational preferences demonstrates yet another aspect of the social structure in the communist world: the emergence of a new privileged class. This new ruling class comprised members of the Communist Party, state officials, high-ranking officers in the military and secret police, and a few special professional groups. The new elite not only possessed political power but also received special privileges, including the right to purchase high-quality goods in special stores (in Czechoslovakia, the elite could obtain organically grown produce not available to anyone else), paid vacations at special resorts, access to good housing and superior medical services, and advantages in education and jobs for their children. In 1980, in one province of the Soviet Union, 70 percent of Communist Party members came from the families of managers, technicians, and government and party bureaucrats.

Ideals of equality did not include women. Men dominated the leadership positions of the Communist parties in the Soviet Union and Eastern Europe. Women did have greater opportunities in the workforce and even in the professions, however. In the Soviet Union, women comprised 51 percent of the labor force in 1980; by the mid-1980s, they constituted 50 percent of the engineers, 80 percent of the doctors, and 75 percent of the teachers and teachers' aides. But many of these were low-paying jobs; most female doctors, for example, worked in primary care and were paid less than skilled machinists. The chief administrators in hospitals and schools were still men.

Moreover, although women were part of the workforce, they were never freed of their traditional roles in the home. Most women confronted what came to be known as the "double shift." After working eight hours in their jobs, they came home to face the housework and care of the children. They might spend two hours a day in long lines at a number of stores waiting to buy food and clothes. Because of the housing situation, they were forced to use kitchens that were shared by a number of families.

Nearly three-quarters of a century after the Bolshevik Revolution, then, the Marxist dream of an advanced, egalitarian society was as far away as ever. Although in some respects conditions in the socialist camp were a distinct improvement over those before World War II, many problems and inequities were as intransigent as ever.

Conclusion

The Soviet Union had emerged from World War II as one of the world's two superpowers. Its armies had played an instrumental role in the final defeat of the powerful German war machine and had installed pliant Communist regimes throughout Eastern Europe. No force of comparable strength had occupied the plains of western Russia since the Mongols in the thirteenth and fourteenth centuries.

During the next four decades, the Soviet Union appeared to be secure in its power. Its military and eco-

nomic performance during the first postwar decade was sufficiently impressive to produce an atmosphere of incipient panic in Washington. By the mid-1980s, however, fears that the Soviet Union would surpass the United States as an economic power had long since dissipated, and the Soviet system appeared to be mired in a state of near paralysis. Economic growth had slowed to a snail's pace, corruption had reached epidemic levels, and leadership had passed to a generation of elderly party apparatchiks who appeared incapable of addressing the burgeoning problems that affected Soviet society.

What had happened to tarnish the dream that had inspired Lenin and his fellow Bolsheviks to believe they could create a Marxist paradise? This chapter has hinted at a number of factors that contributed to the increasingly dysfunctional performance of the Soviet system. What seems clear is that the Soviet command economy proved better at launching the first stages of the Industrial Revolution than at moving to the next stage of an advanced technological society, and that the Leninist concept of democratic centralism failed to provide the quality of leadership and political courage needed to cope with the challenges of nation building. By the 1980s, behind the powerful shield of the Red Army, the system had become an empty shell.

NOTES

1. R. Hilton, *Military Attaché in Moscow* (London, 1949), p. 41.
2. Nikita Khrushchev, *Khrushchev Remembers*, trans. Strobe Talbott (Boston, 1970), p. 77.
3. Quoted in Hedrick Smith, *The New Russians* (New York, 1990), p. 30.
4. Quoted in Frank B. Tipton and Robert Aldrich, *An Economic and Social History of Europe from 1939 to the Present* (Baltimore, 1987), p. 193.

The East Is Red:
China under Communism

"A revolution is not a dinner party, or writing an essay, or painting a picture, or doing embroidery; it cannot be so refined, so leisurely and gentle, so temperate and kind, courteous, restrained, and magnanimous. A revolution is an insurrection, an act of violence by which one class overthrows another."[1] With these words—written in 1926, at a time when the Communists, in cooperation with Chiang Kai-shek's Nationalist Party, were embarked on their Northern Expedition to defeat the warlords and reunify China—the young revolutionary Mao Zedong warned his colleagues that the road to victory in the struggle to build a Communist society would be arduous and would inevitably involve acts of violence against the class enemy.

During the next twenty years, the mettle of the Communist Party was severely tested. It was harassed to near extinction by the Nationalist government, and then attacked by the armed forces of impe-

rial Japan. In the summer of 1949, it finally triumphed over Chiang Kai-shek in a bruising civil war that led to the latter's abandonment of the mainland and his final retreat to the island of Taiwan. By then, Mao Zedong had become the most powerful man in China, and people began to speculate about his future intentions. Did Mao's words two decades previously portend a new reign of terror that would—not for the first time—drown the Chinese Revolution in a sea of blood? Or were Mao and his colleagues—as some American observers had speculated in Mao's wartime capital of Yan'an—really "agrarian reformers," more patriots than revolutionaries, who would bind the wounds of war and initiate a period of peace and prosperity? As Mao and his colleagues mounted the rostrum of Beijing's Gate of Heavenly Peace in early October 1949 to declare their intentions, the fate of a nation lay in the balance.

. . . .

China under Mao Zedong

The first signs were reassuring. In the fall of 1949, China was at peace for the first time in twelve years. The newly victorious Communist Party, under the leadership of its chairman Mao Zedong, turned its attention to consolidating its power base and healing the wounds of war. Its long-term goal was to construct a socialist society, but its

leaders realized that popular support for the revolution was based on the party's platform of honest government, land reform, social justice, and peace rather than on the utopian goal of a classless society. Accordingly, the new regime followed Soviet precedent in adopting a moderate program of political and economic recovery known as New Democracy.

◆ **The Gate of Heavenly Peace.** Located at the southern entrance to the imperial city in Beijing, the Gate of Heavenly Peace was the portal through which the Chinese emperor passed on his way out of the imperial palace. It was from this gate that Mao Zedong announced the founding of the new People's Republic of China on October 1, 1949.

New Democracy

Under New Democracy—patterned after Lenin's New Economic Policy in Soviet Russia in the 1920s (see Chapter 4)—the capitalist system of ownership was retained in the industrial and commercial sectors. A program of land redistribution to the poor was adopted, but the collectivization of agriculture was postponed. Only after the party had consolidated its rule and brought a reasonable degree of prosperity to the national economy would the difficult transformation to a socialist society begin.

In following Soviet precedent, the new Chinese leadership tacitly recognized that time and extensive indoctrination would be needed to convince the Chinese people of the superiority of socialism. In the meantime, the party would rely on capitalist profit incentives to spur productivity. Manufacturing and commercial firms were permitted to remain under private ownership, although they were placed under stringent government regulations, and some were encouraged to form "joint enterprises" with the government. To win the support of the poorer peasants, who made up the majority of the population, the land reform program that had long been in operation in "liberated areas" was now expanded throughout the country. This strategy was designed not only to win the gratitude of the rural masses, but also to undermine the political and economic influence of counterrevolutionary elements still loyal to Chiang Kai-shek.

In a number of key respects, New Democracy was a success. About two-thirds of the peasant households in the country received land under the land reform program and thus had reason to be grateful to the new regime. Spurred by the benign official tolerance for capitalist activities and the end of internal conflict, the national economy began to rebound, although agricultural production still lagged behind both official targets and the growing population, which was increasing at an annual rate of more than 2 percent. But there was a darker side to the picture. In the course of carrying out land redistribution, thousands if not millions of landlords and rich farmers lost their lands, their personal property, their freedom, and sometimes their lives. Many of those who died were tried and convicted of "crimes against the people" in people's tribunals set up under official sponsorship in towns and villages around the country. As Mao himself later conceded, many were innocent of any crime, but in the eyes of the party, their deaths were necessary to destroy the power of the landed gentry in the countryside (see box on p. 189).

⇒ Land Reform in Action ⇐

The land reform program was the centerpiece of Mao Zedong's strategy of New Democracy. Through that program, the party hoped to achieve several things: to win the support of the peasants, who comprised more than 80 percent of China's population; to destroy the economic and political influence of the conservative landlord class at the village level; and to increase agricultural production in the countryside in preparation for a future advance to collective ownership of the land.

The land reform program became one of the great achievements of the new regime and resulted in the distribution of farmland to almost two-thirds of the rural population. It consequently won the gratitude of millions of Chinese peasants, and laid the groundwork for the collectivization effort that was launched in 1955. But it also had a dark side, as local land reform tribunals, composed of revolutionary elements in each village, routinely convicted "wicked landlords" of crimes against the people and then put them to death.

One of the best descriptions of the program is by William Hinton, author of the book *Fan Shen*, who observed the process at work in a village in Shanxi Province in 1948, just before the end of the civil war. His description shows how hard it was for poor peasants to muster the courage to criticize the landlords, who had long dominated their village. In one account, T'ien-ming, a party cadre, called a meeting of village residents to bring to trial Kuo Te-yu, the puppet village chief

T'ien-ming opened the tribunal by recounting the painful lives led by the villagers during the period of Japanese occupation and how, after the harvest, the puppet officials had seized the grain and turned it over to the Japanese authorities. He then turned to the crowd and asked who wished to give evidence against Kuo Te-yu. But the peasants gave no sign how they felt. Finally, one member of the new village leadership jumped up and struck Kuo on the jaw with the back of his hand. "The blow jarred the ragged crowd," Hinton wrote. "It was as if an electric spark had tensed every muscle. Not in living memory had any peasant ever struck an official."

From that point on, the trial moved forward rapidly, as "activists" singled out by local party leaders took the lead in speaking out against Kuo Te-yu's crimes. Other villagers soon followed, and as accusation followed accusation, some surged forward to beat him. Kuo was viewed only as a tool of the reactionary elements in the village, so his life was spared. But several landlords were subsequently placed on trial and summarily executed.

Such trials were carefully orchestrated by the party to mobilize the poor peasants to "speak their bitterness," to destroy the landlord class at the local level, and to forge a "blood tie" with the new revolutionary leadership. How many died in the course of carrying out the program is unknown, but they undoubtedly numbered in the millions. Chairman Mao later conceded that some innocent people had suffered along with the guilty, but justified it on the grounds that "you can't make an omelet without breaking eggs."

Sources: William Hinton, *Fan Shen: A Documentary of Revolution in a Chinese Village* (Berkeley: University of California Press, 1966), pp. 112–116.

The Transition to Socialism

Originally, party leaders intended to follow the Leninist formula of delaying the building of a fully socialist society until China had a sufficient industrial base to permit the mechanization of agriculture. In 1953, they launched the nation's first five-year plan (patterned after similar Soviet plans), which called for substantial increases in industrial output. Lenin had believed that the lure of mechanization would provide Russian peasants with an incentive to join collective farms, which, because of their greater size and efficiency, could better afford to purchase expensive farm machinery. But the enormity of the challenge of providing tractors and reapers for millions of rural villages eventually convinced Mao Zedong and some of his colleagues that it would take years, if not decades, for China's infant industrial base to meet the burgeoning needs of a modernizing agricultural sector. He therefore decided to change the equation and urged that collectivization be undertaken immediately, in the hope that collective farms would increase food production and release land, labor, and capital for the industrial sector.

Accordingly, in 1955, when it felt secure from foreign threats, the Chinese government launched a new program to build a socialist society. Beginning in that year, virtually all private farmland was collectivized, although

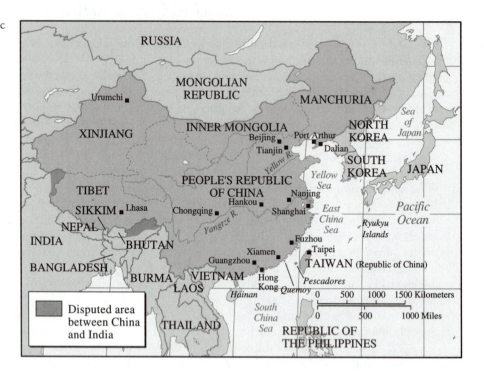

Map 9.1 The People's Republic of China

peasant families were allowed to retain small plots for their private use (a Chinese version of the private plots adopted in the Soviet Union). In addition, most industry and commerce were nationalized.

Collectivization was achieved without provoking the massive peasant unrest that had taken place in the Soviet Union during the 1930s, perhaps because the Chinese government followed a policy of persuasion rather than compulsion (Mao Zedong remarked that Stalin had "drained the pond to catch the fish") and because the Communist land redistribution program had already earned the support of millions of rural Chinese. But the hoped-for production increases did not materialize, and in 1958, at Mao's insistent urging, party leaders approved a more radical program known as the Great Leap Forward. Existing rural collectives, normally the size of a traditional village, were combined into vast "people's communes," each containing more than 30,000 people. These communes were to be responsible for all administrative and economic tasks at the local level. The party's official slogan promised "Hard work for a few years, happiness for a thousand."[2]

Mao Zedong hoped this program would mobilize the population for a massive effort to accelerate economic growth and ascend to the final stage of communism before the end of the twentieth century. It is better, he said, to "strike while the iron is hot" and advance the revolution without interruption. Some party members were concerned that this ambitious program would threaten the government's rural base of support, but Mao argued that Chinese peasants were naturally revolutionary in spirit. The Chinese rural masses, he said, are

first of all, poor, and secondly, blank. That may seem like a bad thing, but it is really a good thing. Poor people want change, want to do things, want revolution. A clean sheet of paper has no blotches, and so the newest and most beautiful words can be written on it, the newest and most beautiful pictures can be painted on it.[3]

Those words, of course, were *socialism* and *communism*.

The Great Leap Forward was a disaster. Administrative bottlenecks, bad weather, and peasant resistance to the new system (which, among other things, attempted to eliminate work incentives and destroy the traditional family as the basic unit of Chinese society) combined to drive food production downward, and over the next few years, as many as 15 million people may have died of starvation. Many peasants were reportedly reduced to eating the bark off trees and in some cases allowing infants to starve. In 1960, the commune experiment was essentially abandoned. Although the commune structure was retained, ownership and management were returned to the collective level. Mao Zedong was severely criticized by some of his more pragmatic colleagues (one remarked bitingly that "one cannot reach Heaven in a single step"), provoking him to complain that he had been relegated to the sidelines "like a Buddha on a shelf."

The Great Proletarian Cultural Revolution

But Mao was not yet ready to abandon either his power or his dream of a totally egalitarian society. In 1966, he returned to the attack, mobilizing discontented youth and disgruntled party members into revolutionary units known as Red Guards who were urged to take to the streets to cleanse Chinese society—from local schools and factories to government ministries in Beijing—of impure elements who (in Mao's mind, at least) were guilty of "taking the capitalist road." Supported by his wife Jiang Qing and other radical party figures, Mao launched China on a new forced march toward communism.

The so-called Great Proletarian Cultural Revolution (literally, great revolution to create a proletarian culture)

lasted for ten years, from 1966 to 1976. Some Western observers interpreted it as a simple power struggle between Mao Zedong and some of his key rivals such as Liu Shaoqi (Liu Shao-ch'i), Mao's designated successor, and Deng Xiaoping (Teng Hsiao-p'ing), the party's general secretary. Both were removed from their positions, and Liu later died, allegedly of torture, in a Chinese prison. But real policy disagreements were involved. One reason Mao Zedong had advocated the Great Leap Forward was to bypass the party and government bureaucracy, which, in his view, had lost their revolutionary zeal and were primarily concerned with protecting their power. Now he and his supporters feared that capitalist values and the remnants of "feudalist" Confucian ideas and practices would undermine ideological fervor and betray the revolutionary cause. Mao himself was convinced that only an atmosphere of constant revolutionary fervor (what he termed "uninterrupted revolution") could enable the Chinese to overcome the lethargy of the past and achieve the final stage of utopian communism. "I care

◆ **Punishing Chinese Enemies during the Cultural Revolution.** The Cultural Revolution, which began in 1966, was a massive effort by Mao Zedong and his radical supporters to eliminate rival elements within the Chinese Communist Party and the government. Accused of being "capitalist roaders," such individuals were subjected to public criticism and removed from their positions. Some were imprisoned or executed. Here, Red Guards parade a victim wearing a dunce cap through the streets of Beijing.

not," he once wrote, "that the winds blow and the waves beat. It is better than standing idly in a courtyard."

His opponents, on the other hand, worried that Mao's "heaven-storming" approach could delay economic growth and antagonize the people. They argued for a more pragmatic strategy that gave priority to nation building over the ultimate communist goal of spiritual transformation. But with Mao's supporters now in power, the party carried out vast economic and educational reforms that virtually eliminated any remaining profit incentives, established a new school system that emphasized "Maozedong Thought," and stressed practical education at the elementary level at the expense of specialized training in science and the humanities in the universities. School learning was discouraged as a legacy of capitalism, and Mao's famous *Little Red Book* (a slim volume of Maoist aphorisms to encourage good behavior and revolutionary zeal) was hailed as the most important source of knowledge in all areas.

The radicals' efforts to destroy all vestiges of traditional society were reminiscent of the Reign of Terror in revolutionary France, when the Jacobins sought to destroy organized religion and even reorganized the traditional Christian chronological system into a new revolutionary calendar. Red Guards rampaged through the country attempting to eradicate the "four olds" (old thought, old culture, old customs, and old habits). They destroyed temples and religious sculptures; they tore down street signs and replaced them with new ones carrying revolutionary names. At one point, the city of Shanghai even ordered that the significance of colors in stoplights be changed, so that red (the revolutionary color) would indicate that traffic could move.

But a mood of revolutionary ferment and enthusiasm is difficult to sustain. Key groups, including party bureaucrats, urban professionals, and many military officers, did not share Mao's belief in the benefits of "uninterrupted revolution" and constant turmoil. Many were alienated by the arbitrary actions of the Red Guards, who indiscriminately accused and brutalized their victims in a society where legal safeguards had almost entirely vanished (see box on p. 193). Whether the Cultural Revolution led to declining productivity is a matter of debate. Inevitably, however, the sense of anarchy and uncertainty caused popular support for the movement to erode, and when the end came with Mao's death in 1976, the vast majority of the population may well have welcomed its demise.

Personal accounts by young Chinese who took part in the Cultural Revolution clearly show that their initial enthusiasm often turned to disillusionment. According to Liang Heng, author of a book titled *Son of the Revolution*, at first he helped friends organize Red Guard groups:

> I thought it was a great idea. We would be following Chairman Mao just like the grownups, and Father would be proud of me. I suppose I too resented the teachers who had controlled and criticized me for so long, and I looked forward to a little revenge.[4]

Later, he had reason to repent. His sister ran off to join the local Red Guard group. Prior to her departure, she denounced her mother and the rest of her family as "rightists" and enemies of the revolution. Their home was regularly raided by Red Guards, and their father was severely beaten and tortured for having three neckties and "Western shirts." Books, paintings, and writings were piled in the center of the floor and burned before his eyes. On leaving, a few of the Red Guards helped themselves to his monthly salary and his transistor radio.

From Mao to Deng

In September 1976, Mao Zedong died at the age of eighty-three. After a short but bitter succession struggle, the pragmatists led by Deng Xiaoping seized power from the radicals and formally brought the Cultural Revolution to an end. Mao's widow, Jiang Qing, and three other radicals (derisively called the "gang of four" by their opponents) were placed on trial and sentenced to death or to long terms in prison. The egalitarian policies of the previous decade were reversed, and a new program emphasizing economic modernization was introduced.

Under the leadership of Deng Xiaoping, who placed his supporters in key positions throughout the party and the government, attention focused on what were called the "four modernizations": industry, agriculture, technology, and national defense. Deng Xiaoping had been a leader of the faction that opposed Mao's program of rapid socialist transformation, and during the Cultural Revolution he had been forced to perform menial labor to "sincerely correct his errors." But Deng continued to espouse the pragmatic approach and reportedly once remarked, "Black cat, white cat, what does it matter so long as it catches the mice?" Under the program of four modernizations, many of the restrictions against private activities and profit incentives were eliminated, and people were encouraged to work hard to benefit themselves and Chinese society. The familiar slogan "Serve the people" was replaced by a new one repugnant to the tenets of Maozedong Thought: "Create wealth for the people."

❧ Make Revolution! ❧

In 1966, Mao Zedong unleashed the power of revolution on China. Rebellious youth organized as Red Guards rampaged through all levels of society, exposing anti-Maoist elements, suspected "capitalist roaders," and those identified with the previous ruling class. Mao's purpose was to prevent the decline of revolutionary fervor in China by mobilizing activist elements in an "uninterrupted revolution" directed at building a fully communist society, and also to destroy those elements in China—from the rural areas up to and including Mao's rivals in the party leadership—who placed the demands of economic development at a higher level than revolutionary purity.

Initially, Mao won considerable support for his campaign from around the country. Millions of Chinese were disappointed at the failure of their living standards to improve after the civil war and found it easy to believe their "Great Leader" when he blamed "capitalist roaders" for opposing his policies. Especially vulnerable to his appeal were young people, millions of whom had been sent "to the village" to work on collective farms or on rural construction projects after leaving school. The program had been necessitated by the lack of job opportunities in urban areas, but many young Chinese resented it and felt that their talents were not being used effectively. One inside account of the movement was provided by the young Red Guard Liang Heng, who later described his experience in *Son of the Revolution*. His description of the ecstasy that he felt on first seeing Mao Zedong at the Gate of Heavenly Peace in Beijing shows the hysterical quality of the reverence shown to the Great Leader. "I was bawling like a baby, crying out incoherently again and again, 'You are our

hearts' reddest sun!' My tears blocked my vision, but I could do nothing to control myself ."

It was these young people, formed into Red Guard units throughout the country, who became the shock troops of the Cultural Revolution. In Mao's eyes, these revolutionary youths would cleanse China of its impurities and place it back on the road to a utopian society. But for the victims, it was a painful and sometimes a tragic experience. Few accounts of the Cultural Revolution are more poignant than that of Nien Cheng, the widow of an official of Chiang Kai-shek's regime. During the height of the campaign, Red Guards entered her home, systematically ransacked the house, and destroyed its contents, including valuable heirlooms from the imperial period. When she complained, one of the Red Guards retorted, "You shut up! These things belong to the old culture. They are the useless toys of the feudal emperors and the modern capitalist class and have no significance to us, the proletarian class." The old culture must be destroyed, he declared, "to make way for the new socialist culture."

In the end, the Cultural Revolution alienated the vast majority of the Chinese people by its violence and its arbitrary brutality. Many Red Guards used the campaign to enrich themselves or to settle old scores. Like so many previous revolutions, its radicalism exhausted the patience of many of its previous supporters, who now turned with relief to the pragmatic policies of Mao's eventual successor, Deng Xiaoping.

Sources: Liang Heng, with Judith Shapiro, *Son of the Revolution* (New York: Alfred A. Knopf, 1983); Nien Cheng, *Life and Death in Shanghai* (New York: Penguin, 1986).

Crucial to the program's success was the government's ability to attract foreign technology and capital. For more than two decades, China had been isolated from technological advances taking place elsewhere in the world. Although China's leaders understandably prided themselves on their nation's capacity for "self-reliance," their isolationist policy had been exceedingly costly for the national economy. China's post-Mao leaders blamed the country's backwardness on the "ten lost years" of the Cultural Revolution, but the "lost years," at least in technological terms, extended back to 1949 and in some respects even before. Now, to make up for lost time, the government encouraged foreign investment and sent

thousands of students and specialists abroad to study capitalist techniques.

By adopting this pragmatic approach in the years after 1976, China made great strides in ending its chronic problems of poverty and underdevelopment. Per capita income roughly doubled during the 1980s; housing, education, and sanitation improved; and both agricultural and industrial output skyrocketed. Clearly, China had begun to enter the industrial age.

But critics, both Chinese and foreign, complained that Deng Xiaoping's program had failed to achieve a "fifth modernization": that of democracy. Official sources denied such charges and spoke proudly of restoring "socialist legality" by doing away with the arbitrary punishments applied during the Great Proletarian Cultural Revolution. Deng Xiaoping himself encouraged the Chinese people to speak out against earlier excesses, particularly in the late 1970s when ordinary citizens pasted "big character posters" criticizing the abuses of the past on the so-called Democracy Wall near Tiananmen Square in downtown Beijing.

Yet it soon became clear that the new leaders would not tolerate any direct criticism of the Communist Party or of Marxist-Leninist ideology. Dissidents, such as the electrician Wei Jingsheng, were suppressed, and some were sentenced to long prison terms. Among them was the well-known astrophysicist Fang Lizhi (Fang Li-chih), a longtime critic of Stalinism and Maoist "left-ism." Fang spoke out publicly against official corruption and the continuing influence of Marxist-Leninist concepts in post-Mao China, telling an audience in Hong Kong that "China will not be able to modernize, if it does not break the shackles of Maoist and Stalinist-style socialism." Fang immediately felt the weight of official displeasure. He was refused permission to travel abroad, and articles that he submitted to official periodicals were rejected. Deng Xiaoping himself reportedly remarked, "We will not suppress people who hold differing political views from our own. But as for Fang Lizhi, he has been indulging in mudslinging and spreading slander without any basis, and we should take legal action against him." Replied Fang, "I have never criticized any Chinese leader by name, nor accused any of them of illegal acts or immoral activities. But some perhaps feel guilty. If the cap fits, wear it."[5]

The problem began to intensify in the late 1980s, as more Chinese began to study abroad and more information about Western society reached educated individuals inside the country. Rising expectations aroused by the economic improvements of the early 1980s led to increasing pressure from students and other urban residents for better living conditions, relaxed restrictions on study abroad, and increased freedom to select employment after graduation.

Serve the People: Chinese Society under Communism

Enormous changes took place in Chinese society after the Communist rise to power in 1949. Under the Nanjing regime, Sun Yat-sen's ideology of the Three People's Principles had replaced the Confucian values that had endured since the ancient Zhou dynasty. When that failed, China turned to the ideology of Marxism-Leninism, patterned after the socialist experiment in the Soviet Union. Under the urging of Mao Zedong, China launched its own version of the Industrial Revolution, with all of the political, social, and cultural implications that process entails.

Yet beneath the surface of rapid change were tantalizing hints of the survival of elements of the old China. Despite all the efforts of Mao Zedong and his colleagues, the ideas of Confucius and Sons had still not been irrevocably discarded. China under communism remained a society that in many respects was in thrall to its past.

The Politics of the Mass Line

Nowhere was this uneasy balance between the old and the new more clearly demonstrated than in politics and government.

The Chinese Communist Party (CCP) came to power in 1949 dedicated to eradicating what it described as the remnants of the feudalistic Confucian system and to building a set of political institutions based on Marxist principles. As Mao Zedong declared in a speech to the CCP Central Committee in March:

> The Chinese revolution is great, but the road after the revolution will be longer, the work greater and more arduous. This must be made clear now in the Party. The comrades must be helped to remain modest, prudent, and free from arrogance and rashness in their style of work. The comrades must be helped to preserve the style of plain living and hard struggle.[6]

In calling on Communist cadres to practice modesty, hard work, and plain living, Mao was pointedly making a distinction between the work style of the new revolutionary regime and that of the imperial governments of the past, whose Confucian officials had too often feathered their own nests and ignored the needs of the people under their charge.

In its broad outlines, the new political system followed the Soviet pattern. Yet from the start, the Communist leaders made it clear that the Chinese model would differ from the Soviet in important respects. Whereas the Bolsheviks had severely distrusted nonrevolutionary elements in Russia and established a minority government based on the radical left, Mao Zedong and his colleagues were more confident that they possessed the basic support of the majority of the Chinese people. Under New Democracy, the party attempted to reach out to all progressive classes in the population to maintain the alliance that had brought it to power in the first place.

As a symbolic confirmation of this broad-based policy, the CCP permitted minor political parties (the Democratic Party, the Socialist Party, and the so-called Revolutionary Branch of the Guomindang under Sun Yat-sen's widow, Soong Qingling) to represent the interests of progressive intellectuals and the bourgeoisie. But the primary link between the regime and the population was the system of "mass organizations," representing peasants, workers, women, religious groups, writers, and artists. The party had established these associations during the 1920s to mobilize support for the revolution. Now they served as a conduit between party and people, enabling the leaders to assess the attitude of the masses while at the same time seeking their support for the party's programs. Behind this facade of representative institutions stood the awesome power of the CCP.

Initially, this "mass line" system worked fairly well. True, opposition to the regime was ruthlessly suppressed, but on the positive side, China finally had a government that appeared to be for the people. Although there was no pretense at Western-style democracy, and official corruption and bureaucratic mismanagement and arrogance had by no means been entirely eliminated, the new ruling class came preponderantly from workers and peasants and, at least by comparison with its predecessors, was willing to listen to the complaints and aspirations of its constituents.

A good example of the party's "mass line" policy was the land reform program, which redistributed farmland to the poor. The program was carried out at the village level by land reform cadres who urged local farmers to establish tribunals to confiscate the lands of the landlord class and assign them to poor or landless peasants, thus giving the impression that the policy was locally inspired rather than imposed, Soviet-style, from the top down.

But the failure of the Great Leap Forward betrayed a fundamental weakness in the policy of the mass line. While party leaders declared their willingness to listen to the concerns of the population, they were also determined to build a utopian society based on Marxist-Leninist principles. Popular acceptance of nationalization and collectivization during the mid-1950s indicates that the Chinese people were not entirely hostile to socialism, but when those programs were carried to an extreme during the Great Leap Forward, many, even within the party, resisted and forced the government to abandon the program.

The failure of the Great Leap Forward split the CCP and led to the revolutionary disturbances of the following decade. The Cultural Revolution, which Mao launched in 1966, can be seen above all as his attempt to cleanse the system of its impurities and put Chinese society back on the straight road to egalitarian communism. Many of his compatriots evidently shared his beliefs. Young people in particular, alienated by the lack of job opportunities, flocked to his cause and served with enthusiasm in the Red Guard organizations that became the shock troops of the revolution. As we have seen, the enthusiasms aroused by the Cultural Revolution did not last. As in the French Revolution, the efforts to achieve revolutionary purity eventually alienated all except the most radical elements in the country, and a period of reaction inevitably set in. In China, revolutionary fervor gave way to a new era in which belief in socialist ideals was replaced by a more practical desire for material benefits.

After Mao's death, the new Chinese leadership under Deng Xiaoping recognized the need to restore a sense of "socialist legality" and credibility to a system that was on the verge of breakdown. Deng's encouragement of the Democracy Wall in 1979 was an attempt to rebuild the links between the party and the masses. But like other Communist leaders, Deng soon discovered that once the people have been encouraged to criticize current conditions, it is difficult to prevent them from focusing on the linchpin of the entire Marxist-Leninist system: the dictatorship of the proletariat and the party's domination of power.

The regime attempted to suppress the criticism by closing down the Democracy Wall and providing new guidelines—called the "Four Cardinal Principles"—that prohibited criticism of the socialist system, the dictatorship of the proletariat, Marxist-Leninist-Maoist thought, and the final goal of communism. But the credibility of Marxist thought, and of the CCP itself, had been severely shaken by recent events, and by the late 1980s, party leaders had good reason to fear that the vaunted mass line was a thing of the past.

Economics in Command

After their rise to power in 1949, Communist leaders quickly determined that for the time being, economic considerations would be foremost in their set of priorities for continuing the Chinese Revolution. The move was motivated by at least two considerations: to jump-start the economy into the first stage of the Industrial Revolution and to earn the support of the millions of uncommitted Chinese for whom the Communists and their ideology remained a mystery. To highlight their new policy, they declared that in making their selections of revolutionary cadres, "expertise" (technical competence) would take precedence over "redness" (ideological commitment).

That policy began to change in the late 1950s, when Mao Zedong decided that political considerations were more important than economic ones in building a socialist society. This attitude, symbolized by the well-known catch phrase "politics in command," was a major factor in the abandonment of the mass line policy in the late 1950s. During the Cultural Revolution, the policy of "red" over "expert" reached its logical extreme, as anyone possessing professional skills was suspected of harboring counterrevolutionary tendencies.

After 1976, Deng Xiaoping and other party leaders were obviously hoping that rapid economic growth would satisfy the Chinese people and prevent them from demanding political reforms. The post-Mao leadership demonstrated clear willingness to place economic performance over ideological purity. Deng Xiaoping and his colleagues rapidly dismantled many of the official restrictions on private economic activities that had hindered productivity since the mid-1950s. To stimulate the stagnant industrial sector, which had been under state control since the end of the era of New Democracy, they reduced bureaucratic controls over state industries and allowed local managers to have more say over prices, salaries, and quality control. Productivity was encouraged by permitting bonuses to be paid for extra effort, a policy that had been discouraged during the Cultural Revolution. State firms were no longer guaranteed access to precious resources and were told to compete with each other for public favor and even to export goods on their own initiative.

The regime also tolerated the emergence of a small private sector. Unemployed youth were encouraged to set up restaurants, bicycle or radio repair shops, and handicraft shops on their own initiative. At first, the government insisted that all participants should be considered joint owners, making the ventures a form of collective, but eventually the new businesses were permitted to hire workers. Attempts to restrict the number of salaried workers were generally ignored.

Finally, the regime opened up the country to foreign investment and technology. The Maoist policy of self-reliance was abandoned, and China openly sought the advice of foreign experts and the money of foreign capitalists. Special economic zones were established in urban centers near the coast (ironically, many were located in the old nineteenth-century treaty ports), where lucra-

tive concessions were offered to encourage foreign firms to build factories. The tourist industry was encouraged, and students were sent abroad to study.

The new leaders especially stressed educational reform. The system adopted during the Cultural Revolution, emphasizing practical education and ideology at the expense of higher education and modern science, was rapidly abandoned (the *Little Red Book* itself was withdrawn from circulation and could no longer be found on bookshelves), and a new system based generally on the Western model was instituted. Admission to higher education was based on success in merit examinations, and courses on science and mathematics received high priority.

No economic reform program could succeed unless it included the countryside. Three decades of socialism had done little to increase food production or to lay the basis for a modern agricultural sector. The initial effort to follow the Leninist-Stalinist model had been abandoned, and the Maoist attempt to utilize the labor power of the rural masses had fared no better. China, with a population now numbering 1 billion, could still barely feed itself. Peasants had little incentive to work and few opportunities to increase production through mechanization, the use of fertilizer, or better irrigation.

Under Deng Xiaoping, agricultural policy made a rapid about-face. Under the new "rural responsibility system," adopted shortly after Deng Xiaoping had consolidated his authority, collectives leased land on contract to peasant families, who paid a quota in the form of rent to the collective. Anything produced on the land above that payment could be sold on the private market or consumed. To soak up excess labor in the villages, the government encouraged the formation of so-called sideline industries, a modern equivalent of the traditional cottage industries in premodern China. Peasants raised fish or shrimp, made consumer goods, and even assembled living room furniture and appliances for sale to their newly affluent compatriots.

The reform program had a striking effect on rural production. Grain production increased rapidly, and farm income doubled during the 1980s. Yet it also created problems. In the first place, income at the village level became more unequal as some enterprising farmers (known locally as "ten thousand dollar" households) earned profits several times those realized by their less fortunate or industrious neighbors. When some farmers discovered they could earn more by growing cash crops or other specialized commodities, they devoted less land to rice and other grain crops, thus

◆ **Street Merchants.** In 1978, Deng Xiaoping began to introduce reforms aimed at stimulating economic production in China. One such reform was to permit the Chinese people, for the first time in over two decades, to engage in capitalist activities. In this photograph, a street-seller hawks a fast-food lunch to passers-by in a Chinese city.

threatening to reduce the supply of China's most crucial staple. Finally, the agricultural policy threatened to undermine the government's population control program, which party leaders viewed as crucial to the success of the four modernizations.

Since a misguided period in the mid-1950s when Mao Zedong had argued that more labor would result in higher productivity, China had been attempting to limit its population growth. By 1970, the government had launched a stringent family planning program—including education, incentives, and penalties for noncompliance—to persuade the Chinese people to limit themselves to one child per family. The program did have some success, and population growth was reduced drastically in the early 1980s. The rural responsibility system, however, undermined the program, because it encouraged farm families to pay the penalties for having additional children in the belief that their labor would increase family income and provide the parents with a form of social security for their old age.

Still, the overall effects of the modernization program were impressive. The standard of living improved for the majority of the population. Whereas a decade earlier the average Chinese had struggled to earn enough to buy a bicycle, radio, watch, or washing machine, by the late 1980s many were beginning to purchase videocassette

recorders, refrigerators, and color television sets. The government popularized the idea that all Chinese would prosper, although not necessarily at the same speed. Earlier slogans such as "Serve the people" and "Uphold the banner of Marxist-Leninist-Maoist thought" were replaced by others that announced that "Time is money" and instructed citizens to "Create wealth for the people." The party announced that China was still at the "primary stage of socialism" and might not reach the state of utopian communism for generations.

Yet the rapid growth of the economy created its own problems: inflationary pressures, greed, envy, increased corruption, and—most dangerous of all for the regime—rising expectations. Young people in particular resented restrictions on employment (most young people in China are still required to accept the jobs that are offered to them by the government or school officials) and opportunities to study abroad. Disillusionment ran high, especially in the cities, where high living by officials and rising prices for goods aroused widespread alienation and cynicism. Such attitudes undoubtedly contributed to the anger and frustration that burst out during the spring of 1989, when many workers, peasants, and functionaries joined the demonstrations against official corruption and one-party rule in Tiananmen Square (see Chapter 16).

The Legacy of the Past: Continuity and Change in Modern China

These events highlighted a serious dilemma facing China's aging leaders: how could they introduce Western technology and work habits without at the same time infecting the Chinese people with the virus of bourgeois individualism and the desire for personal profit and advancement? When the program of modernization was first launched in the late 1970s, conservative party officials warned that when the windows were opened, dust, flies, and all sorts of bad things would come in. Deng Xiaoping attempted to reassure them. In that case, he said, we will simply use our flyswatters. But would the flyswatters be enough? Or would the regime's effort to introduce Western technology while preserving the essence of Chinese socialism go the way of the nineteenth-century slogan of "East for essence, West for practical use" (see Chapter 3)?

From the start, the Chinese Communist Party intended to bring an end to the Confucian legacy in modern China. At the root of Marxist-Leninist ideology is the idea of building a new citizen free from the prejudices, ignorance, and superstition of the "feudal" era and the capitalist desire for self-gratification. This new citizen would be characterized not only by a sense of racial and sexual equality, but also by the selfless desire to contribute his or her utmost for the good of all. In the words of Mao Zedong's famous work "The Foolish Old Man Who Removed the Mountains," the people should "be resolute, fear no sacrifice, and surmount every difficulty to win victory."[7]

The new government wasted no time in keeping its promise. During the early 1950s, it took a number of steps to bring a definitive end to the old system in China. Women were permitted to vote and encouraged to become active in the political process. At the local level, an increasing number of women became active in the CCP and in collective organizations. In 1950, a new Marriage Law guaranteed women equal rights with men. Most important, perhaps, it permitted women for the first time to initiate divorce proceedings against their husbands. Within a year, nearly 1 million divorces had been granted.

The regime also undertook to destroy the influence of the traditional family system. To the Communists, loyalty to the family, a crucial element in the Confucian social order, undercut loyalty to the state and to the dictatorship of the proletariat. Such concerns had been raised by reform-minded Chinese long before the Communists' rise to power. At the beginning of the century, Sun Yat-sen had complained that China's family-oriented society lacked a concept of statehood, noting that the Chinese people were like "a sheet of loose sand." He believed loyalty to family undermined loyalty to the nation. Mao Zedong agreed. For Communist leaders, family loyalty contradicted the basic principle of Marxism—dedication to society at large.

At first, the new government moved carefully to avoid alienating its supporters in the countryside unnecessarily. When collective farms were established in the mid-1950s, each member of a collective accumulated "work points" based on the number of hours worked during a specified time period. Payment for work points was made not to the individual, but to the family head. The payments, usually in the form of ration coupons, could then be spent at the collective community store. Because the payments went to the head of the family, the traditionally dominant position of the patriarch was maintained. When people's communes were established in the late 1950s, payments went to the individual.

During the growing internal struggle and political radicalism of the Great Leap Forward, children were encouraged to report to the authorities any comments by their parents that criticized the system. Such practices continued during the Cultural Revolution, when young Red Guards were directed to root out all forms of reactionary thought from any source. Children were expected to report on their parents, students on their teachers, and employees on their superiors. Some have suggested that Mao deliberately encouraged such practices to bring an end to the traditional "politics of dependency." According to this theory, historically the famous "five relationships" forced individuals to swallow their anger and frustration and accept the hierarchical norms established by Confucian ethics (known in Chinese as "eat bitterness"). By encouraging the oppressed elements in society—the young, the female, and the poor—to voice their bitterness, Mao was helping to break the tradition of dependency. Such denunciations had been issued against landlords and other "local tyrants" in the land reform tribunals of the late 1940s and early 1950s. Later, during the Cultural Revolution, they were applied to other authority figures in Chinese society.

At the time, many outside observers feared that the Cultural Revolution would transform the Chinese people into a race of automatons mindlessly spouting the slogans and the class hatred fed to them by their leaders. After the decline of the movement in the early 1970s, it became clear that such fears were exaggerated. In the end, the chaotic character of the Cultural Revolution doomed it to failure. Mao's gamble that the Chinese

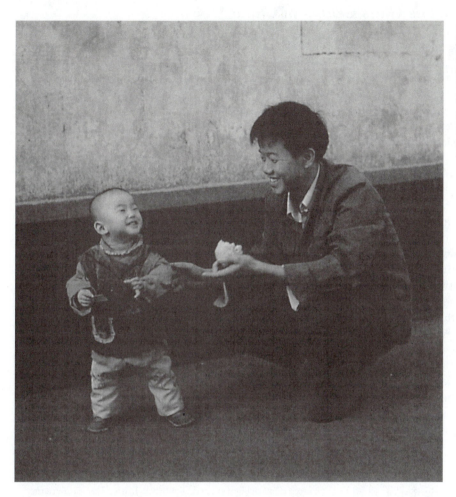

◆ **China's "Little Emperors."** Under Deng Xiaoping, Chinese leaders have launched a massive family planning program to curtail population growth. Urban families are restricted to a single child. In conformity with tradition, sons are especially prized, and some Chinese complain that many parents overindulge their children, turning them into spoiled "little emperors."

people would respond to his call for uninterrupted revolution did not take into account their craving for order and their ultimately practical approach to the problems of human existence. After a decade of fear, turmoil, growing economic hardship, and arbitrary arrests, most Chinese probably greeted the end of the era with a great sense of exhaustion and relief.

The post-Mao era brought a decisive shift away from revolutionary utopianism and a return to the pragmatic approach to nation building. For most people, it meant improved living conditions and a qualified return to family traditions. Spurred by Deng Xiaoping's slogan "Create wealth for the people," for the first time in more than a decade, enterprising Chinese began to concentrate on improving their standard of living. For the first time, millions of Chinese saw the prospect of a house or an urban flat with a washing machine, television set, and indoor plumbing. Young people whose parents had given patriotic names such as Build the Country, Protect Mao Zedong, Assist Korea began to choose more elegant

and cosmopolitan names for their own children. Some names, such as Surplus Grain or Bring a Younger Brother, expressed hope for the future. One Western observer reported that he had encountered a young Chinese named Dian Shi, or Color Television. When asked for an explanation, the father replied that if he had not had to pay a fine for having an extra child, he would have bought a color television set with the money.

The new attitudes were also reflected in physical appearance. For a generation after the civil war, clothing had been restricted to the traditional baggy "Mao suit" in olive drab or dark blue, but by the 1980s young people craved such fashionable Western items as designer jeans, trendy sneakers, and sweat suits (or reasonable facsimiles). Cosmetic surgery to create a more buxom figure or a more Western facial look became increasingly common among affluent young women in the cities. Many had the epicanthic fold over their eyelids removed or even added to their noses—a curious decision in view of the tradition of referring derogatorily to foreigners as "big noses."

The Glass Ceiling in China

"What men can do, women can do also." So said Chairman Mao Zedong as he sought to remove the age-old attitudes of male domination in Chinese society and provide women in the new China with opportunities equal to those of men. Such views were incorporated in a new Marriage Law passed in 1950 that attempted to remove some of the legal and social disabilities that women had often suffered during the imperial era.

An article in the magazine *China Youth Daily* in 1960 tried to describe the country's policy toward women and how it differed from past practices. For one thing, it said, China's basic premise is that "happiness should be shared by all. We advocate equal rights for man and woman, equal rights for husband and wife." Marriage, it continued, should be based on mutual consent, and on the foundation of mutual love between the partners. Such values differed from those of feudal China, where women belonged to men, and of the capitalist world, where love was "nothing but a merchandise; women trade their flesh for men's money."

In reality, sexual equality had not yet been realized in China, as the author of the article conceded. Some young Chinese, it lamented, in their thinking about marriage, were "still under the influence of the exploiting class." Such people "cannot do away with the thinking that man is superior to woman." They "love the new ones and forsake the old," pursuing extramarital relationships or seeking a divorce. Despite their new legal rights, women still suffered from discrimination in the workplace and, significantly, even in the upper ranks of the Communist Party, where few women occupied positions of authority.

Since the death of Mao Zedong, women have made steady progress in realizing some of the rights granted on paper during the earlier period. More women are found in professional positions, as well as in the ranks of the government and the Communist Party. But success has had a price. An oral history published in China highlighted the problems in many contemporary marriages, where the success of the wife in her chosen vocation has surpassed that of her spouse, creating difficult problems in the relationship and often leading to divorce. Spousal abuse, according to press estimates, is increasingly common. At the same time, in ironic contrast to the 1960 article, many marriages today—especially in rural areas—are once again arranged by the parents for the purposes of social or financial gain. As in the traditional era, weddings are often costly. As two young Americans who wrote an account of their experience teaching in China commented,

> the older generations have reasserted their control over marriage . . . , finding the return to older social conventions very reassuring. . . . So, the generation which benefited most from marriage reform is, according to their children, now making it difficult for love to survive, by insisting on elaborate weddings and many times selecting spouses for their children.

Clearly, forty years of revolution have not entirely erased some of the oldest traditions in Chinese society.

Sources: Franz Schurmann and Orville Schell, eds., *The China Reader*, Vol. 3 (New York: Vintage, 1967); Tani Barlow and Donald M. Lowe, *Teaching China's Lost Generation* (San Francisco: China Books and Periodicals, 1987), Zhang Xinxin and Sang Ye, *Chinese Lives: An Oral History of Contemporary China* (New York: Pantheon, 1987).

Religious practices and beliefs also changed. As the government became more tolerant, some Chinese began returning to the traditional Buddhist faith, and Buddhist and Taoist temples were once again crowded with worshipers. Christianity became increasingly popular; like the "rice Christians" (persons who supposedly converted for economic reasons) of the past, many viewed it as a symbol of success and cosmopolitanism.

Such changes have been much more prevalent among urban dwellers and China's still small middle class than among rural folk, who make up more than half the population. While prosperity has come to some parts of the countryside—notably in areas located near the major metropolitan centers—the vast majority of peasants have been only superficially affected by the events since Mao's death. In that sense, the yawning gap that has always separated town and country in China still remains. Because of the growing problem of youthful unemployment, for example, young people in rural areas have been told that if they were born and raised on a farm, they are likely to remain there for the rest of their lives.

As with all social changes, China's reintegration into the outside world has had a price (see box above). Arranged marriages, nepotism, and mistreatment of females (for example, many parents in rural areas reportedly have killed female infants in the hope of having a son) have come back, although such behavior likely had survived under the cloak of revolutionary purity for a generation. Materialistic attitudes are highly prevalent among young people, along with a corresponding cynicism about politics and the CCP. Expensive weddings are now increasingly common, and bribery and favoritism are all too frequent. Crime of all types, including an apparently growing incidence of prostitution and sex crimes against women, appears to be on the rise. To discourage sexual abuse, the government now seeks to provide free legal services for women living in rural areas.

China's Changing Culture

Like their contemporaries all over Asia, Chinese artists were strongly influenced by the revolutionary changes that were taking place in the art world of the West in the early twentieth century. The challenge proved to be enormous, for modern Western art differed from its Chinese counterpart not only in subject matter but in technique, and even in the materials used to produce a painting or sculpture. In the decades following the 1911 revolution, Chinese creative artists began to experiment with Western styles and with the new conviction that the purpose of art was to reveal reality, however unpleasant, rather than to encourage a certain state of mind or to entertain. For many, the challenge was too alien to be appreciated. Although some Chinese artists imitated Western styles, the more extreme schools such as surrealism and abstract painting had little impact.

The rise to power of the Chinese Communist Party in 1949 added a new dimension to the ongoing debate over the future of culture in China. Spurred by comments made by Mao Zedong at a cultural forum in Yan'an in 1942, leaders rejected the Western slogan of "Art for art's sake" and, like their Soviet counterparts, viewed culture as an important instrument of indoctrination. The standard would no longer be aesthetic quality or the personal preference of the artist, but "Art for life's safe," whereby culture would serve the interests of socialism. Through socialist realism, a concept borrowed from the Soviet Union, literature, art, and music would introduce the Chinese people to the superior virtues of socialist society.

At first, the new emphasis on socialist realism, which shared the Confucian conviction that culture must cultivate the mind, did not entirely extinguish the influence of traditional culture. Mao and his colleagues saw the importance of traditional values and culture in building a strong new China and tolerated—and in some cases even encouraged—efforts by artists to syn-

thesize traditional ideas with socialist concepts and Western techniques. Chinese painting and classical music in the 1950s, for example, were highly syncretic. Under the surface, however, the debate over the role of tradition continued. During the 1960s, the issue became entwined in the political struggle between radicals and moderates over the future course of the Chinese Revolution. The radicals around Mao Zedong who seized power during the Cultural Revolution viewed all forms of traditional culture as reactionary and wanted to create a new proletarian culture that would lead society toward communism. Socialist realism became the only standard of acceptability in literature, art, and music. All forms of traditional expression were forbidden.

Nowhere were the dilemmas of the new order more challenging than in literature. In the heady afterglow of the Communist victory in the civil war, many progressive writers supported the new regime and enthusiastically embraced Mao's exhortation to create a new Chinese literature for the edification of the masses. But in the harsher climate of the late 1950s and 1960s, many writers were criticized by the party for their excessive individualism and admiration for Western culture. Such writers either toed the new line and suppressed their doubts or were jailed and silenced.

Characteristic of the changing cultural climate in China was the experience of author Ding Ling. Born in 1904 and educated in a school for women set up by leftist intellectuals during the hectic years after the May Fourth Movement, she began writing in her early twenties. At first she was strongly influenced by prevailing Western styles, but after her husband, a struggling young poet and a member of the CCP, was executed by Chiang Kai-shek's government in 1931, she became active in party activities and sublimated her talent to the revolutionary cause.

In the late 1930s, Ding Ling settled in Yan'an, where she became a leader in the party's women's and literary associations. She remained dedicated to revolution, but years of service to the party had not stifled her individuality, and in 1942 she wrote critically of the incompetence, arrogance, and hypocrisy of many party officials, as well as the treatment of women in areas under Communist authority. Such conduct raised eyebrows, but she was able to survive criticism and in 1948 wrote her most famous novel, *The Sun Shines over the Sangan River*, which described the CCP's land reform program in favorable terms. It was awarded the Stalin Prize three years later.

During the early 1950s, Ding Ling was one of the most prominent literary lights of the new China, but in the more ideological climate at the end of the decade, she was attacked for her individualism and her previous criticism of the party. Although temporarily rehabilitated, during the Cultural Revolution she was sentenced to hard labor on a commune in the far north and was only released in the late 1970s after the death of Mao Zedong. Although crippled and in poor health, she began writing a biography of her mother that examined the role of women in twentieth-century China. She died in 1981.

Ding Ling's story is not unique and mirrors the fate of thousands of progressive Chinese intellectuals who, despite their efforts, were not able to satisfy the constantly changing demands of a repressive regime. Lionized during the conciliatory period of the early 1950s and encouraged to criticize society's shortcomings during a brief period of political relaxation called the One Hundred Flowers Movement in 1956, their voices were silenced during the Cultural Revolution, when only hymns of praise for revolutionary China and its "Great Helmsman" Mao Zedong were permitted.

After Mao's death, Chinese culture was once again released from the shackles of socialist realism. In painting, the new policies led to a revival of interest in both traditional and Western forms. The revival of traditional art was in part a matter of practicality, as talented young Chinese were trained to produce traditional paintings for export to earn precious foreign currency for the state. But the regime also showed a new tolerance for the imitation of Western styles as a necessary by-product of development, thus unleashing an impressive outpouring of artistic creativity later dubbed the "Beijing Spring." A new generation of Chinese painters began to emerge in the 1980s. Although some continued the attempt to blend Eastern and Western styles, others imitated trends from abroad, experimenting with a wide range of previously prohibited art styles including cubism and abstract expressionism.

An excellent illustration of Chinese artists' tireless battle for creative freedom is the painting My Dream (1988) by Xu Mangyao. On the canvas, an artist, having freed his hands from manacles, seeks to escape from the confinement of a red brick wall. The painting represents the worldwide struggle by all those twentieth-century artists who have been silenced by totalitarian regimes in the USSR, Latin America, and Africa.

In the late 1980s, two avant-garde art exhibits shocked the Chinese public and provoked the wrath of the party. An exhibition of nude paintings, the first ever held in China, attracted many viewers, but reportedly offended many Chinese for reasons of modesty. The second was an exhibit presenting the works of various schools of modern and postmodern art. The event resulted in considerable commentary, and some expressions of public hostility. After a Communist critic lambasted the works displayed as promiscuous and ideologically reactionary, the government declared that henceforth it would regulate all art exhibits.

In music, too, the post-Mao era brought significant changes. Music academies closed during the Cultural Revolution for sowing the seeds of the bourgeois mentality were reopened. Students were permitted to study both Chinese and Western styles, but the vast majority selected the latter. To provide examples, leading musicians and composers, such as violinist Isaac Stern, were invited to China to lecture and perform before eager Chinese students. Western visitors could not but be aware of the trend, as Chinese orchestras greeted foreign tourist groups with earnest renditions of such old favorites as the "Red River Valley" and "Auld Lang Syne."

The limits of freedom of expression were most apparent in literature. During the early 1980s, party leaders encouraged Chinese writers to express their views on the mistakes of the past, and a new "literature of the wounded" began to describe the brutal and arbitrary character of the Cultural Revolution. One of the most prominent writers was Bai Hua, whose script for the film Bitter Love described the life of a young Chinese painter who joined the revolutionary movement during the 1940s but was destroyed during the Cultural Revolution when his work was condemned as counterrevolutionary. The film depicts the condemnation through a view of a street in Beijing "full of people waving the Quotations of Chairman Mao, all those devout and artless faces fired by a feverish fanaticism." Driven from his home for posting a portrait of a third-century B.C.E. defender of human freedom on a Beijing wall, the artist flees the city. At the end of the film, he dies in a snowy field, where his corpse and a semicircle made by his footprints form a giant question mark.

In criticizing the excesses of the Cultural Revolution, Bai Hua was only responding to Deng Xiaoping's appeal for intellectuals to speak out, but like his counterparts during the Hundred Flowers era, he was soon criticized for failing to point out the essentially beneficial role of the CCP in recent Chinese history, and his film was withdrawn from circulation in 1981. Bai Hua was compelled to recant his errors and to state that the great ideas of Mao Zedong on art and literature were "still of universal guiding significance today."[8]

As the attack on Bai Hua illustrates, many party leaders remained suspicious of the impact that "decadent" bourgeois culture could have on the socialist foundations of Chinese society, and the official press periodically warned that China should adopt only the "positive" aspects of Western culture (notably, its technology and its work ethic) and not the "negative" elements such as drug use, pornography, and hedonism. Conservatives were especially incensed by the tendency of many writers to dwell on the shortcomings of the socialist system and to come uncomfortably close to direct criticism of the role of the CCP.

One author whose writings fell under the harsh glare of official disapproval is Zhang Xinxin (b. 1953). Her controversial novellas and short stories, which explored Chinese women's alienation and spiritual malaise, were viewed by many as a negative portrayal of contemporary society, provoking the government in 1984 to prohibit her from publishing for a year. Determined and resourceful, Zhang turned to reportage. With a colleague, she interviewed 100 "ordinary" people to record their views on all aspects of everyday life. (Some of their findings are included in the box on p. 200).

Conclusion

To the outside observer, since the Communist takeover of power on the mainland, China has projected an image of almost constant turmoil and rapid change. That portrayal is not an inaccurate one, for Chinese society has undergone a number of major transformations since the establishment of the People's Republic of China in the early fall of 1949. Even in the relatively stable 1980s, many a prudent China watcher undoubtedly wondered whether the prosperous and tolerant conditions of the era of Deng Xiaoping would long endure.

An extended period of political instability and domestic violence is hardly unusual in the years following a major revolutionary upsurge. Similar conditions existed in late eighteenth-century France after the revolt that overthrew the ancient régime, and in Russia after the Bolshevik seizure of power in 1917. In both cases, pragmatists in the pursuit of national wealth and power clashed with radicals who were determined to create a utopian society. In the end, the former were victorious, in a process sometimes known as the "routinization of the revolution." "The revolution," it has been astutely observed, "eats its own."

A similar course of events has been taking place in China since the Communist ascent to power. Radical elements grew restive at what they perceived as a relapse back into feudal habits by "capitalist roaders" within the party and launched the Great Proletarian Cultural Revolution. What was distinctive about the Chinese case was that the movement was led by Mao Zedong himself, who risked the destruction of the very organization that had brought him to power in the first place—the Communist Party. Clearly, much about the Chinese Revolution cannot be explained without an understanding of the complex personality of its great leader.

With the death of Mao Zedong in 1976, the virulent phase of the revolution appeared to be at an end, and a more stable era of economic development was launched by Mao's longtime colleague Deng Xiaoping. But under the surface, it eventually became clear, the forces of class struggle and cultural conflict that had marked the earlier period had not yet been blunted. Rapid economic and social development, party leaders were about to discover, exacted a price of its own. A century of revolution in China was not yet at an end.

NOTES

1. "Report on an Investigation of the Peasant Movement in Hunan (March 1927)," in Mao Tse-tung, *Selected Works*, Vol. I, p. 28, quoted in *Quotations from Chairman Mao Tse-tung* (Peking, 1976), p. 12.

2. Quoted in Stanley Karnow, *Mao and China: Inside China's Cultural Revolution* (New York, 1972), p. 95.

3. Quoted from an article by Mao Zedong in the June 1, 1958, issue of the journal *Red Flag*. See Stuart R. Schram, *The Political Thought of Mao Tse-tung* (New York, 1963), p. 253. The quotation "strike while the iron is hot" is from Karnow, *Mao and China*, p. 93.

4. Liang Heng with Judith Shapiro, *Son of the Revolution* (New York, 1983).

5. Quoted in *Time*, March 13, 1989, pp. 10–11.

6. *Quotations from Chairman Mao Tse-tung* (Peking, 1976), p. 195, quoting Mao's report to the CCP Central Committee, March 5, 1949.

7. "The Foolish Old Man Who Removed the Mountains," ibid., p. 182.

8. Quoted in Jonathan Spence, *Chinese Roundabout: Essays in History and Culture* (New York, 1992), p. 285.

CHAPTER

10

Europe and the Western Hemisphere

*B*etween 1945 and 1970, Europe not only recovered from the devastating effects of World War II, but experienced an economic resurgence that to many people seemed nothing less than miraculous. Economic growth and virtually full employment continued so long that the first postwar recession in 1973 came as a shock to Western Europe. Although economic growth resumed, Europeans faced a growing number of economic, social, and political problems in the 1980s and 1990s.

The most significant factor in the history of the Western world after 1945 was the emergence of the United States as the world's richest and most powerful nation. American prosperity reached new proportions in the two decades after World War II, but a series of economic and social problems—including racial division and staggering budget deficits—in the

1970s and 1980s left the nation with an imposing array of difficulties that weakened its ability to function as the world's only superpower.

To the south of the United States lay the vast world of Latin America with its own unique heritage. Although some Latin Americans in the nineteenth century had looked to the United States as a model for their own development, in the twentieth century, many attacked the United States for its military and economic domination of Central and South America. Some states, such as Cuba, even adopted a Marxist path to building a new society and broke completely with the United States. At the same time, many Latin American countries struggled with economic and political instability and all too often succumbed to military regimes.

. . . .

*W*estern Europe: Recovery and Renewal

In the summer of 1945, the nations of western and central Europe lay exhausted after five years of war. Their cities were in ruins, their economies were a shambles, their political institutions had been widely discredited, and the spirits of their people were heavily burdened by recent memories of the most destructive war in human history. In the immediate postwar era, the challenge to the region was clear, and intimidating. The peoples of Europe needed to rebuild their national economies and

reestablish and strengthen their democratic institutions. They needed to find the means to cooperate in the face of a potential new threat from the east in the form of the Soviet Union. Above all, they needed to restore their confidence in the continuing vitality and future promise of European civilization—a civilization whose image had been badly tarnished by two bitter internal conflicts in the space of a quarter century.

In confronting the challenge, the Europeans possessed one significant trump card—the support and assistance of the United States. The United States had entered World War II as a major industrial power, but its global influence had been limited by the effects of the Great Depression and a self-imposed policy of isolation which had removed it from active involvement in world affairs. Only the drift to war in the late 1930s had finally provoked President Franklin D. Roosevelt into action. As the conflict came to a close, the United States bestrode the world like a colossus. Its military power was enormous, its political influence was unparalleled, and its economic potential, fueled by the demands of building a war machine to defeat the Axis, seemed unlimited. When on June 5, 1947, Secretary of State George C. Marshall told the graduating class at Harvard University that the United States was prepared to assist the nations of Europe in the task of recovery from "hunger, poverty, desperation, and chaos," he offered a beacon of hope to a region badly in need of reasons for optimism.

The Triumph of Democracy in Postwar Europe

With the economic aid of the Marshall Plan, the countries of Western Europe recovered relatively rapidly from the devastation of World War II. Between 1947 and 1950, European countries received $9.4 billion to be used for new equipment and raw materials. Between the early 1950s and late 1970s, industrial production surpassed all previous records, and Western Europe experienced virtually full employment. Social welfare programs included affordable health care; housing; family allowances to provide a minimum level of material care for children; increases in sickness, accident, unemployment, and old-age benefits; and educational opportunities. Despite economic recessions in the mid-1970s and early 1980s, caused in part by a dramatic increase in the price of oil in 1973, the economies of Western Europe had never been so prosperous, leading some observers to label the period a "golden age" of political and economic achievement. Western Europeans were full participants in the technological advances of the age and seemed quite capable of standing up to competition from the other global economic powerhouses, Japan and the United States.

At the end of World War II, confidence in the ability of democratic institutions to meet the challenge of the industrial era was at an ebb. The Western democracies had been unable to confront the threat of Fascism until the armies of the Wehrmacht began their march across Europe at the end of the 1930s, and most succumbed rapidly to the Nazi juggernaut. As the war finally came to a close, many Europeans, their confidence shaken by bleak prospects for the future, turned their eyes to the Soviet model. In France and Italy, local Communist parties received wide support in national elections, raising fears that they might eventually be voted into power in Paris and Rome.

By the late 1940s, the Communist specter in Western Europe had subsided as economic conditions began to improve, and eventually the nations in the region became accustomed to democracy. Even Spain and Portugal, which retained their prewar dictatorial regimes until the mid-1970s, established democratic systems in the late 1970s. Moderate political parties, especially the Christian Democrats in Italy and Germany, played a particularly important role in achieving Europe's economic restoration. Overall, the influence of socialist parties declined, though reformist mass parties only slightly left of center, such as the Labour Party in Britain and the Social Democrats in West Germany, continued to share power. Western European Communist parties declined drastically. During the mid-1970s, a new variety of communism, called Eurocommunism, emerged briefly when Communist parties tried to work within the democratic system as mass movements committed to better government. But by the 1980s, internal political developments in Western Europe and events within the Communist world had combined to undermine the Eurocommunist experiment.

FRANCE: EXPECTATIONS OF GRANDEUR

The history of France for nearly a quarter century after the war was dominated by one man, Charles de Gaulle (1890–1970), who possessed an unshakable faith in his own historic mission to reestablish the greatness of the French nation. During the war, de Gaulle had assumed leadership of resistance groups known as the "Free French," and he played an important role in ensuring the establishment of a French provisional government after the war. But the creation immediately following the war of the Fourth Republic, with a return to a multiparty parliamentary system that de Gaulle considered inefficient, led him to withdraw from politics. Eventually, he formed the French Popular Movement, a political organization based on conservative principles, which blamed the party system for France's political mess and called for an even stronger presidency, a goal that de Gaulle finally achieved in 1958.

The fragile political stability of the Fourth Republic was badly shaken by a crisis in Algeria. The French army, having suffered a humiliating defeat in Indochina in 1954, was determined to resist Algerian demands for

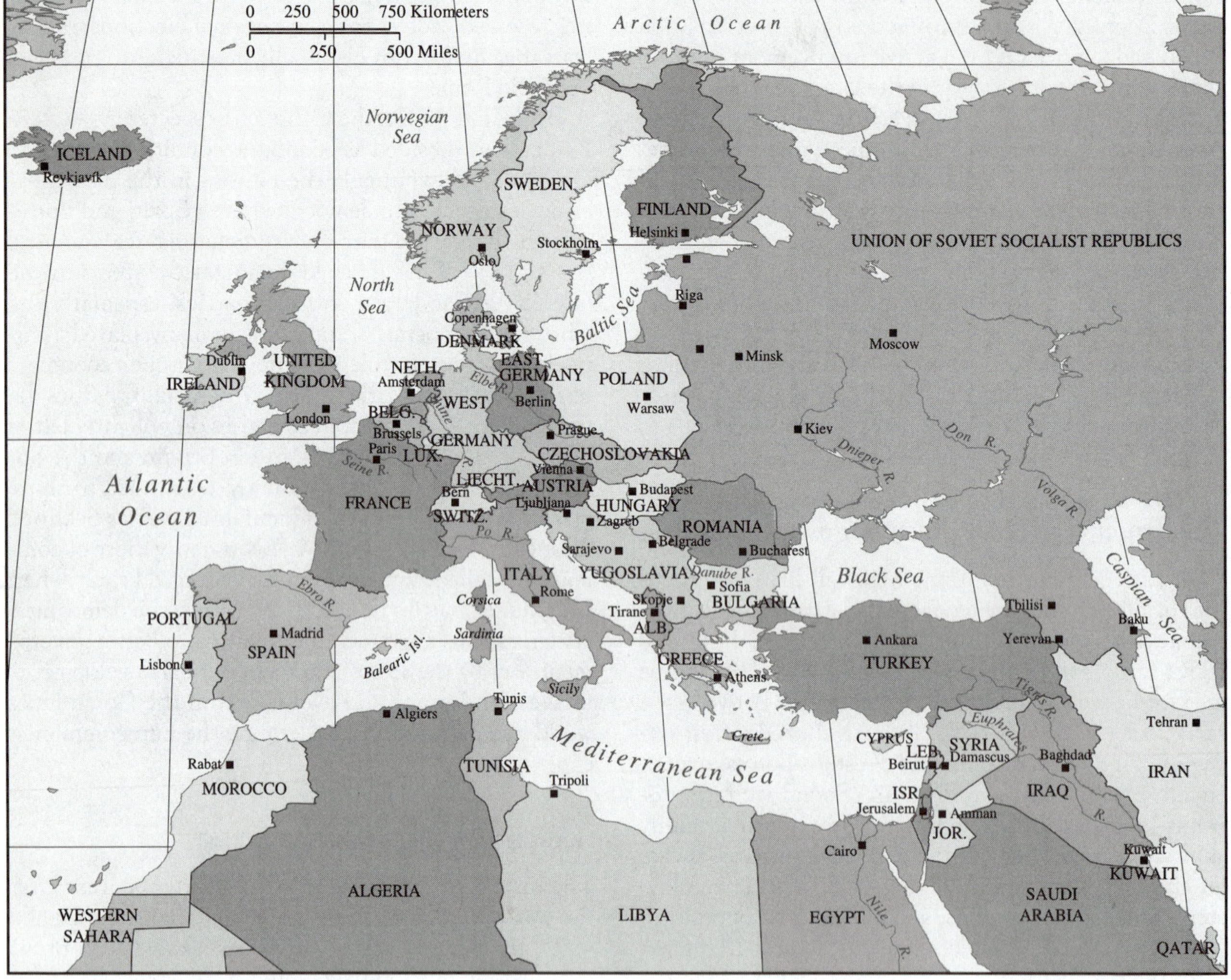

Map 10.1 Europe after World War II

independence. But a strong antiwar movement among French intellectuals and church leaders led to bitter divisions within France that opened the door to the possibility of civil war. The panic-stricken leaders of the Fourth Republic offered to let de Gaulle take over the government and revise the constitution.

In 1958, de Gaulle drafted a new constitution for a Fifth Republic that greatly enhanced the power of the French president, who now had the right to choose the prime minister, dissolve parliament, and supervise both defense and foreign policy. De Gaulle had always believed in strong leadership, and the new Fifth Republic was by no means a democratic system. As the new president, de Gaulle sought to return France to a position of great power. Believing that playing a pivotal role in the Cold War might enhance France's stature, he pulled France out of the NATO high command. He increased French prestige among the less-developed countries by consenting to Algerian independence despite strenuous opposition from the army. With an eye toward achieving the status of a world power, de Gaulle invested heavily in the nuclear arms race, and France exploded its first nuclear bomb in 1960. Despite his successes, however, de Gaulle did not really achieve his ambitious goals of world power. Although his successors maintained that France was the "third nuclear power" after the United States and the Soviet Union, in truth France was too small for such global ambitions.

◆ **Student Revolt in Paris, 1968.** The discontent of university students exploded in the late 1960s in a series of student revolts. Perhaps best known was the movement in Paris in 1968.

This photograph shows the barricades erected on a Parisian street on the morning of May 11 at the height of the revolt.

Although the cost of the nuclear program increased the defense budget, de Gaulle did not neglect the French economy. Economic decision making was centralized, a reflection of the overall centralization undertaken by the Gaullist government. Between 1958 and 1968, the French gross national product experienced an annual increase of 5.5 percent, faster than that of the United States. By the end of the Gaullist era, France was a major industrial producer and exporter, particularly in such areas as automobiles and armaments. Nevertheless, problems remained. The expansion of traditional industries, such as coal, steel, and railroads, which had all been nationalized, led to large government deficits. The cost of living increased faster than in the rest of Europe.

Growing dissatisfaction with the inability of de Gaulle's government to deal with these problems soon led to more violent action. In May 1968, a series of student protests, followed by a general strike by the labor unions, shook de Gaulle's government. Although he managed to restore order, the events of May 1968 seriously undermined the French people's respect for their aloof and imperious president. Tired and discouraged, de Gaulle resigned from office in April 1969 and died within a year.

During the 1970s, the French economic situation worsened, bringing about a political shift to the left. By 1981, the Socialists had become the dominant party in the National Assembly, and the veteran Socialist leader, François Mitterrand (1916–1996), was elected president. His first concern was to resolve France's economic difficulties. In 1982, Mitterrand froze prices and wages in the hope of reducing the huge budget deficit and high inflation. Mitterrand also passed a number of liberal measures to aid workers: an increased minimum wage, expanded social benefits, a mandatory fifth week of paid vacation for salaried workers, a thirty-nine-hour work-week, and higher taxes for the rich. Mitterrand's administrative reforms included both centralization (nationalization of banks and industry) and decentralization (granting local governments greater powers). Their victory also convinced the Socialists that they could enact some of their more radical reforms. Consequently, the government nationalized the steel industry, major banks, the space and electronics industries, and important insurance firms.

WEST GERMANY: THE ECONOMIC MIRACLE

As a result of the pressures of the Cold War, the unification of the three Western zones into the West German Federal Republic became a reality in 1949. Konrad Adenauer (1876–1967), the leader of the Christian Democratic Union (CDU), served as chancellor from 1949 to 1963 and became the "founding hero" of the Federal Republic. Adenauer, who had opposed Hitler and his tyrannical regime, sought respect for Germany by cooperating with the United States and the other Western European nations. He was especially desirous of reconciliation with France—Germany's longtime rival. The beginning of the Korean War in June 1950 had unexpected repercussions for West Germany. The fear that South Korea might fall to the Communists led many in the West to worry about the security of West Germany and inspired calls for German rearmament. Although some people, concerned about a revival of German militarism, condemned this proposal, Cold War tensions were decisive. West Germany rearmed in 1955 and became a member of NATO.

Adenauer's chancellorship was closely associated with the resurrection of the West German economy, often referred to as the "economic miracle." It was largely guided by the minister of finance, Ludwig Erhard. Although West Germany had only 75 percent of the population and 52 percent of the territory of prewar Germany, by 1955 the West German gross national product exceeded that of prewar Germany. Real wages doubled between 1950 and 1965, even though work hours were cut by 20 percent. Unemployment fell from 8 percent in 1950 to 0.4 percent in 1965. In order to maintain its economic expansion, West Germany imported hundreds of thousands of "guest" workers, primarily from Italy, Spain, Greece, Turkey, and Yugoslavia.

The capital of the Federal Republic had been placed at Bonn, a sleepy market town on the Rhine River, to erase memories of the Nazi era, when the capital was at Berlin. Still, the country was troubled by its past. The surviving major Nazi leaders had been tried and condemned as war criminals at the Nuremberg war crimes trials in 1945 and 1946. As part of the denazification of Germany, the victorious Allies continued to try lesser officials for war crimes, but these trials diminished in number as the Cold War produced a shift in attitudes. By 1950, German courts had begun to take over the war crimes trials, and the German legal machine persisted in prosecuting cases. Beginning in 1953, the West German government also began to make payments to Israel and to Holocaust survivors and their relatives in order to make some restitution for the crimes of the Nazi era. The German president Richard von Weizsäcker was especially eloquent in reminding Germans of their responsibility "for the unspeakable sorrow that occurred in the name of Germany."

After the Adenauer era, German voters moved politically from the center-right politics of the Christian Democrats to center-left politics, and in 1969 the Social Democrats became the leading party. By forming a ruling coalition with the small Free Democratic Party (FPD), the Social Democrats remained in power until 1982. The first Social Democratic chancellor was Willy Brandt (1913–1992). Brandt was especially successful with his "opening toward the east" (known as *Ostpolitik*), for which he received the Nobel Peace Prize in 1972. On March 19, 1971, Brandt met with Walter Ulbricht, the East German leader, and worked out the details of a Basic Treaty that was signed in 1972. This agreement did not establish full diplomatic relations with East Germany, but did call for "good neighborly" relations. As a result, it led to greater cultural, personal, and economic contacts between West and East Germany. Despite this success, the discovery of an East German spy among Brandt's advisers caused his resignation in 1974.

His successor, Helmut Schmidt (b. 1918), was more of a technocrat than a reform-minded socialist and concentrated on the economic problems brought about largely by high oil prices between 1973 and 1975. Schmidt was successful in eliminating a deficit of 10 billion marks in three years. In 1982, when the coalition of Schmidt's Social Democrats with the Free Democrats fell apart over the reduction of social welfare expenditures, the Free Democrats joined with the Christian Democratic Union of Helmut Kohl (b. 1930) to form a new government.

GREAT BRITAIN: SUNSET OF EMPIRE

The end of World War II left Britain with massive economic problems. In elections held immediately after the war, the Labour Party overwhelmingly defeated Churchill's Conservative Party. The Labour Party promised far-reaching reforms, particularly in the area of social welfare—an appealing platform in a country with a tremendous shortage of consumer goods and housing. Clement Atlee (1883–1967), the new prime minister, was a pragmatic reformer and certainly not the leftist revolutionary that Churchill warned against during the election campaign. His Labour government proceeded to enact the reforms that created a modern welfare state.

The establishment of the British welfare state began with the nationalization of the Bank of England, the coal and steel industries, public transportation, and public utilities such as electricity and gas. In the area of social welfare, the new government enacted the National Insurance Act and the National Health Service Act, both in 1946. The insurance act established a comprehensive social security program and nationalized medical insurance, thereby enabling the state to subsidize the unemployed, the sick, and the aged. The health act created a system of socialized medicine that forced doctors and dentists to work with state hospitals, although private practices could be maintained. This measure was especially costly for the state, but within a few years 90 percent of the medical profession was participating. The British welfare state became the norm for most European countries after the war.

The cost of building a welfare state at home forced the British to reduce expenses abroad. This meant dismantling the British Empire and reducing military aid to such countries as Greece and Turkey, a decision that inspired the enunciation in Washington of the Truman Doctrine (see Chapter 7). It was not only a belief in the morality of self-determination but also economic necessity that brought an end to the British Empire.

Continuing economic problems brought the Conservatives back into power from 1951 to 1964. Although they favored private enterprise, the Conservatives accepted the welfare state and even extended it, undertaking an ambitious construction program to improve British housing. Although the British economy had recovered from the war, it had done so at a slower rate than other European countries. This slow recovery masked a long-term economic decline caused by a variety of factors. Demands by British trade unions for wages that rose faster than productivity were certainly a problem in the 1950s and 1960s. British unwillingness to invest in modern industrial machinery and to adopt new methods also did not help. Underlying the immediate problems, however, was a deeper issue. As a result of World War II, Britain had lost much of its prewar revenue from abroad but was left with a burden of debt from its many international commitments. At the same time, with the rise of the United States and the Soviet Union, Britain's ability to play the role of a world power declined substantially.

Between 1964 and 1979, Conservatives and Labour alternated in power. Both parties faced seemingly intractable problems. Although separatist movements in Scotland and Wales were overcome, fighting between Catholics and Protestants in Northern Ireland was not so easily settled. Violence increased as the Irish Republican Army (IRA) staged a series of dramatic terrorist acts in response to the suspension of Northern Ireland's parliament in 1972 and the establishment of direct rule by London. The problem of Northern Ireland remained unresolved. Nor was either party able to deal with Britain's ailing economy. Failure to modernize made British industry less and less competitive. Britain was also hampered by frequent labor strikes, many of them caused by conflicts between rival labor unions.

In 1979, after five years of Labour government and worsening economic problems, the Conservatives returned to power under Margaret Thatcher (b. 1925), the first woman prime minister in British history. Thatcher pledged to lower taxes, reduce government bureaucracy, limit social welfare, restrict union power, and end inflation. The "Iron Lady," as she was called, did break the power of the labor unions. While she did not eliminate the basic components of the social welfare system, she did use austerity measures to control inflation. "Thatcherism," as her economic policy was termed, improved the British economic situation, but at a price. The south of England, for example, prospered, but the old industrial areas of the Midlands and north declined and were beset by high unemployment, poverty, and even violence. Cutbacks in funding for education seriously undermined the quality of British schools, long regarded as among the world's finest.

In foreign policy, Thatcher took a hard-line approach against communism. She oversaw a large military build-up aimed at replacing older technology and reestablishing Britain as a world policeman. In 1982, when Argentina attempted to take control of the Falkland Islands (one of Britain's few remaining colonial outposts) 300 miles off its coast, the British successfully rebuked the Argentines, although at considerable economic cost and the loss of 255 lives. The Falklands War, however, did generate much popular patriotic support for Thatcher, as many in Britain reveled in memories of the nation's glorious imperial past.

Western Europe: The Search for Unity

As we have seen, the divisions created by the Cold War led the nations of Western Europe to form the North Atlantic Treaty Organization in 1949. But military cooperation was not the only kind of unity fostered in Europe after 1945. The destructiveness of two world wars caused many thoughtful Europeans to consider the need for some form of European integration. National feeling was still too powerful, however, for European nations to give up their political sovereignty. Consequently, the quest for unity focused primarily on the economic arena, not the political one.

In 1951, France, West Germany, the Benelux countries (Belgium, the Netherlands, and Luxembourg), and Italy formed the European Coal and Steel Community (ECSC). Its purpose was to create a common market for coal and steel products among the six nations by eliminating tariffs and other trade barriers. The success of the

✖ Map 10.2   The Economic Division of Europe during the Cold War

ECSC encouraged its members to proceed further, and in 1957 they created the European Atomic Energy Community (EURATOM) to further European research on the peaceful uses of nuclear energy.

In the same year, the same six nations signed the Rome Treaty, which created the European Economic Community (EEC), also known as the Common Market. The EEC eliminated customs barriers among the six member nations and created a large free-trade area protected from the rest of the world by a common external tariff. By promoting free trade, the EEC also encouraged cooperation and standardization in many aspects of the six nations' economies. All the member nations benefited economically.

Europeans moved toward further integration of their economies after 1970. The European Economic Community expanded in 1973 when Great Britain, Ireland, and Denmark gained membership in what its members now began to call the European Community (EC). By 1986, three more members—Spain, Portugal, and Greece—had been added. The economic integration of the members of the EC led to cooperative efforts in international and political affairs as well. The foreign ministers of the twelve members consulted frequently and provided a common front in negotiations on important issues.

Postwar Europe: An Age of Affluence

During the postwar era, Western society witnessed remarkably rapid change. Such products of new technologies as computers, television, jet planes, contraceptive devices, and new surgical techniques all dramatically and quickly altered the pace and nature of human life. The rapid changes in postwar society, fueled by scientific advances and rapid economic growth, led many to view it as a new society. Called variously a technocratic society, an affluent society, or the consumer society, postwar Western society was characterized by a changing social structure and new movements for change.

The structure of European society was altered in major respects after 1945. Especially noticeable were the changes in the nature of the middle class. Such traditional middle-class groups as businesspeople and professionals in law, medicine, and the universities were greatly augmented by a new group of managers and technicians, as large companies and government agencies employed increasing numbers of white-collar supervisory and administrative personnel. Whether in Eastern or Western Europe, the new managers and experts were very much alike. Everywhere, their positions depended upon specialized knowledge acquired from some form of higher education. Everywhere, they focused on the effective administration of their corporations. Since their positions usually depended upon their skills, they took steps to ensure that their children would be similarly educated.

Changes also occurred among the traditional lower classes. Especially noticeable was the dramatic shift of people from rural to urban areas. The number of people in agriculture declined drastically; by the 1950s, the number of peasants throughout most of Europe had dropped by 50 percent. Nor did the size of the industrial working class expand. In West Germany, industrial workers made up 48 percent of the labor force throughout the 1950s and 1960s. Thereafter, the number of industrial workers began to dwindle as the number of white-collar service employees increased. At the same time, a substantial increase in their real wages enabled the working classes to aspire to the consumption patterns of the middle class, leading to what some observers have called the "consumer society." Buying on the installment plan, introduced in the 1930s, became widespread beginning in the 1950s and gave workers a chance to imitate the middle class by buying such products as televisions, washing machines, refrigerators, vacuum cleaners, and stereos. But the most visible symbol of mass consumerism was the automobile. Before World War II, cars were reserved mostly for the European upper classes. In 1948, there were 5 million cars in all of Europe, but by 1957, the number had tripled. By the 1960s, there were almost 45 million cars.

Rising incomes, combined with shorter working hours, created an even greater market for mass leisure activities. Between 1900 and 1980, the workweek was reduced from sixty hours to about forty hours, and the number of paid holidays increased. All aspects of popular culture—music, sports, media—became commercialized and offered opportunities for leisure activities including concerts, sporting events, and television viewing.

Another very visible symbol of mass leisure was the growth of mass tourism. Before World War II, most persons who traveled for pleasure were from the upper and middle classes. After the war, the combination of more vacation time, increased prosperity, and the flexibility provided by package tours with their lower rates and low-budget rooms enabled millions to expand their travel possibilities. By the mid-1960s, 100 million tourists were crossing European boundaries each year.

Social change was also evident in new educational patterns and student revolts. Before World War II, higher education was largely the preserve of Europe's wealthier classes. Even in 1950, only 3 or 4 percent of

West European young people were enrolled in a university. European higher education remained largely centered on the liberal arts, pure science, and preparation for the professions of law and medicine.

Much of this changed after World War II. European states began to foster greater equality of opportunity in higher education by eliminating fees, and universities experienced an influx of students from the middle and lower classes. Enrollments grew dramatically. In France, 4.5 percent of young people went to a university in 1950; by 1965, the figure had increased to 14.5 percent. Enrollments in European universities more than tripled between 1940 and 1960.

But there were problems. Overcrowded classrooms, professors who paid little attention to students, and authoritarian administrators aroused student resentment. In addition, despite changes in the curriculum, students often felt that the universities were not providing an education relevant to the modern age. This discontent led to an outburst of student revolts in the late 1960s. In part, these protests were an extension of the disruptions in American universities in the mid-1960s, which were often sparked by student opposition to the Vietnam War. Perhaps the most famous student revolt occurred in France in 1968. It erupted at the University of Nanterre outside Paris but soon spread to the Sorbonne, the main campus of the University of Paris. French students demanded a greater voice in the administration of the university, took over buildings, and then expanded the scale of their protests by inviting workers to support them. Half of France's workforce went on strike in May 1968. After the Gaullist government instituted a hefty wage hike, the workers returned to work, and the police repressed the remaining student protesters.

Although the student protest movement reached its high point in 1968, scattered incidents lasted into the early 1970s. Student radicalism had several causes. Some students were genuinely motivated by a desire to reform the university. Others were protesting the Vietnam War, which they viewed as a product of Western imperialism. They also attacked other aspects of Western society, such as its materialism, and expressed concern about becoming cogs in the large and impersonal bureaucratic jungles of the modern world. For many students, the calls for democratic decision making within the universities were a reflection of their deeper concerns about the direction of Western society.

One source of anger among the student revolutionaries of the late 1960s was the lingering influence of traditional institutions and values. World War I had seen the first significant crack in the rigid code of manners

and morals of the nineteenth century. The 1920s had witnessed experimentation with drugs, the appearance of hard-core pornography, and a new sexual freedom (police in Berlin, for example, issued cards that permitted female and male homosexual prostitutes to practice their trade). But these indications of a new attitude appeared mostly in major cities and touched only small numbers of people. After World War II, changes in manners and morals were far more extensive and far more noticeable.

Sweden took the lead in the so-called sexual revolution of the 1960s, but the rest of Europe and the United States soon followed. Sex education in the schools and the decriminalization of homosexuality were but two aspects of Sweden's liberal legislation. Introduction of the birth control pill, which became widely available by the mid-1960s, gave people more freedom in sexual behavior. Meanwhile, sexually explicit movies, plays, and books broke new ground in the treatment of once-hidden subjects. Cities such as Amsterdam, which allowed open prostitution and the public sale of hard-core pornography, attracted thousands of curious tourists.

The new standards were evident in the breakdown of the traditional family. Divorce rates increased dramatically, especially in the 1960s, while premarital and extramarital sexual experiences also rose substantially. A survey in the Netherlands in 1968 revealed that 78 percent of men and 86 percent of women had participated in extramarital sex.

The decade of the 1960s also saw the emergence of a drug culture. Marijuana was widely used among college and university students as the recreational drug of choice. For young people more interested in mind expansion into higher levels of consciousness, Timothy Leary, who had done psychedelic research at Harvard on the effects of LSD (lysergic acid diethylamide), became the high priest of hallucinogenic experiences.

New attitudes toward sex and the use of drugs were only two manifestations of a growing youth movement in the 1960s that questioned authority and fostered rebellion against the older generation. Spurred on by the Vietnam War and a growing political consciousness, the youth rebellion became a youth protest movement by the second half of the 1960s.

The Emergence of the United States

At the end of World War II, the United States emerged as one of the world's two superpowers. Reluctantly, the United States remained involved in European affairs and, as its Cold War confrontation with the Soviet Union intensified, directed much of its energy toward combating the spread of communism throughout the world.

The Welfare State, American Style

Between 1945 and 1970, the legacy of Franklin Roosevelt's New Deal largely determined the parameters of American domestic politics. The New Deal gave rise to a distinct pattern that signified a basic transformation in American society. This pattern included a dramatic increase in the role and power of the federal government; the rise of organized labor as a significant force in the economy and politics; a commitment to the welfare state, albeit a restricted one (Americans did not have access to universal health care as most other industrialized societies did); a grudging acceptance of the need to resolve minority problems; and a willingness to experiment with deficit spending as a means of spurring the economy. The influence of New Deal politics was bolstered by the election of Democratic presidents—Harry Truman in 1948, John F. Kennedy in 1960, and Lyndon B. Johnson in 1964. Even the election of a Republican president, Dwight D. Eisenhower, in 1952 and 1956, did not significantly alter the fundamental direction of the New Deal. As Eisenhower conceded in 1954, "Should any political party attempt to abolish Social Security and eliminate labor laws and farm programs, you would not hear of that party again in our political history."

No doubt, the economic boom that took place after World War II fueled public confidence in the new American way of life. A shortage of consumer goods during the war left Americans with both surplus income and the desire to purchase these goods after the war. Then, too, the growing power of organized labor enabled more and more workers to obtain the wage increases that fueled the growth of the domestic market. Increased government expenditures (justified by the theory of the English economist John Maynard Keynes that government spending could stimulate a lagging economy to reach higher levels of productivity) also indirectly subsidized the American private enterprise system. Especially after the Korean War began in 1950, outlays on defense provided money for scientific research in the universities and markets for weapons industries. After 1955, tax dollars built a massive system of interstate highways, while tax deductions for mortgages subsidized homeowners. Between 1945 and 1973, real wages grew at an average rate of 3 percent a year, the most prolonged advance in American history.

The prosperity of the 1950s and 1960s also translated into significant social changes. Work patterns changed as more and more people in the labor force left the factories and fields and moved into white-collar occupations, finding jobs as professional and technical workers, managers, proprietors, officials, and clerical and sales workers. In 1940, blue-collar workers made up 52 percent of the labor force; farmers and farmworkers, 17 percent; and white-collar workers, 31 percent. By 1970, blue-collar workers constituted 50 percent; farmers and farmworkers, 3 percent; and white-collar workers, 47 percent. Many of these white-collar workers now considered themselves middle class, and the growth of this middle class had other repercussions. From rural areas, small towns, and central cities, people moved to the suburbs. In 1940, 19 percent of the American population lived in suburbs, 49 percent in rural areas, and 32 percent in central cities. By 1970, those figures had changed to 38, 31, and 31 percent, respectively. The move to the suburbs also produced an imposing number of shopping malls and reinforced the American passion for the automobile, which provided the means of transport from suburban home to suburban mall and workplace. Finally, the search for prosperity led to new migration patterns. As the West and South experienced rapid economic growth through the development of new industries, especially in the defense field, massive numbers of people made the exodus from the cities of the Northeast and Midwest to the Sunbelt of the South and West. Between 1940 and 1980, cities like Chicago, Philadelphia, Detroit, and Cleveland lost between 13 and 36 percent of their populations, while Los Angeles, Dallas, and San Diego grew between 100 and 300 percent.

A new prosperity was not the only characteristic of the early postwar era. Cold War confrontations abroad had repercussions at home. The takeover of China by Mao Zedong's Communist forces in 1949 and North Korea's invasion of South Korea in 1950 led to fears that Communists had infiltrated the United States. President Truman's attorney general warned that Communists "are everywhere—in factories, offices, butcher stores, on street corners, in private businesses. And each carries in himself the germ of death for society." A demagogic senator from Wisconsin, Joseph McCarthy, helped to intensify a massive "Red Scare" with his (unsubstantiated) allegations that there were hundreds of Communists in high government positions. But McCarthy went too far when he attacked alleged "Communist conspirators" in the U.S. Army, and he was censured by Congress in 1954. Shortly after, his anti-Communist crusade came to an end. The pervasive fear of Communism and the possibility of a nuclear war, however, remained at a peak.

While the 1950s have been characterized (erroneously) as a tranquil age, the period between 1960 and 1973 was clearly a time of upheaval that brought to the fore some of the problems that had been glossed over in the 1950s. The 1960s began on a youthful and optimistic note. At age forty-three, John F. Kennedy (1917–1963) became the youngest elected president in the history of the United States, and the first born in the twentieth century. His own administration, cut short by an assassin's bullet on November 22, 1963, focused primarily on foreign affairs, although it inaugurated an extended period of increased economic growth. Kennedy's successor, Lyndon B. Johnson (1908–1973), who won a new term as president in a landslide in 1964, used his stunning mandate to pursue the growth of the welfare state, first begun in the New Deal. Johnson's programs included health care for the elderly; a War on Poverty to be fought with food stamps and a Job Corps; a new Department of Housing and Urban Development to deal with the problems of the cities; and federal assistance for education.

Lyndon Johnson's other domestic passion was the achievement of equal rights for African Americans. The Civil Rights movement had its beginnings in 1954 when the U.S. Supreme Court took the dramatic step of striking down the practice of racially segregated public schools. According to Chief Justice Earl Warren, "Separate educational facilities are inherently unequal." A year later, during a boycott of segregated buses in Montgomery, Alabama, the eloquent Martin Luther King, Jr. (1929–1968) surfaced as the leader of a growing movement for racial equality.

By the early 1960s, a number of groups, including King's Southern Christian Leadership Conference (SCLC), were organizing demonstrations and sit-ins across the South to end racial segregation. In August 1963, King led a March on Washington for Jobs and Freedom. This march and King's impassioned plea for racial equality had an electrifying effect on the American people. By the end of 1963, 52 percent of the American people called civil rights the most significant national issue; only 4 percent had done so eight months earlier.

President Johnson took up the cause of civil rights. As a result of his initiative, in 1964, Congress enacted a

◆ **The Civil Rights Movement.**
In the early 1960s, Martin Luther King, Jr., and his Southern Christian Leadership Conference organized a variety of activities to pursue the goal of racial equality. He is shown here with his wife, Coretta Scott King (right) as well as Rosa Parks and Ralph Abernathy (far left), leading a march in 1965 against racial discrimination.

Civil Rights Act that created the machinery to end segregation and discrimination in the workplace and all public accommodations. A Voting Rights Act the following year eliminated racial obstacles to voting in southern states. But laws alone could not guarantee a Great Society, and Johnson soon faced bitter social unrest, both from African Americans and from a burgeoning antiwar movement.

In the North and West, African Americans had had voting rights for many years, but local patterns of segregation resulted in considerably higher unemployment rates for blacks (and Hispanics) than for whites and left blacks segregated in huge urban ghettos. In these ghettos, calls for militant action by radical black nationalist leaders, such as Malcolm X of the Black Muslims, attracted more attention than the nonviolent appeals of Martin Luther King. In the summer of 1965, race riots erupted in the Watts district of Los Angeles that led to thirty-four deaths and the destruction of more than 1,000 buildings. Cleveland, San Francisco, Chicago, Newark, and Detroit likewise exploded in the summers of 1966 and 1967. After the assassination of Martin Luther King in 1968, more than 100 cities experienced rioting, including Washington, D.C., the nation's capital. The combination of riots and extremist comments by radical black leaders led to a "white backlash" and a severe division of American society. In 1964, 34 percent of white Americans agreed with the statement that blacks were asking for "too much"; by late 1966, that number had risen to 85 percent, a figure not lost on politicians eager to achieve political office.

Antiwar protests also divided the American people after President Johnson committed American troops to a costly war in Vietnam (see box on p. 216). The antiwar movement arose out of the Free Speech movement that began in 1964 at the University of California at Berkeley as a protest against the impersonality and authoritarianism of the large university (the "multiversity"). As the war progressed and a military draft ensued, protests escalated. Teach-ins, sit-ins, and occupations of university buildings alternated with more radical demonstrations that increasingly led to violence. The killing of four students at Kent State University in 1970 by the Ohio National Guard caused a reaction, and the antiwar movement began to subside. By that time, however, antiwar demonstrations had helped to weaken the willingness of many Americans to continue the war. But the combination of antiwar demonstrations and ghetto riots in the cities also prepared many people to embrace "law and order," an appeal used by Richard Nixon (1913–1995), the Republi-

can presidential candidate in 1968. With Nixon's election in 1968, a shift to the right in American politics had begun.

The United States Moves Right

That shift was only a partial one during the Nixon years. Nixon eventually ended American involvement in Vietnam by gradually withdrawing American troops. Politically, he pursued a "southern strategy," carefully calculating that "law and order" issues and a slowdown in racial desegregation would appeal to southern whites. The South, which had once been a stronghold for the Democrats, began to form a new allegiance to the Republican Party. The Republican strategy, however, also gained support among white Democrats in northern cities, where court-mandated busing to achieve racial integration had produced a white backlash. But Nixon was less conservative on other issues and, breaking with his own strong anti-Communist past, visited China in 1972 and opened the door toward the eventual diplomatic recognition of that Communist state.

As president, Nixon was also paranoid about conspiracies and began to use illegal methods of gaining political intelligence about his political opponents. One of the president's advisers explained that their intention was to "use the available federal machinery to screw our political enemies." "Anyone who opposes us, we'll destroy," said another aide. Nixon's zeal led to the infamous Watergate scandal—the attempted bugging of Democratic National Headquarters. Although Nixon repeatedly lied to the American public about his involvement in the affair, secret tapes of his own conversations in the White House revealed the truth. On August 9, 1974, Nixon resigned in disgrace, an act that saved him from almost certain impeachment and conviction.

After Watergate, American domestic politics focused on economic issues. Gerald Ford (b. 1913) became president when Nixon resigned, only to lose in the 1976 election to the former governor of Georgia, Jimmy Carter (b. 1924), who campaigned as an outsider against the Washington establishment. Both Ford and Carter faced severe economic problems. The period from 1973 to the mid-1980s was one of economic stagnation, which came to be known as stagflation—a combination of high inflation and high unemployment. In 1984, median family income was 6 percent below that of 1973.

In part, the economic downturn stemmed from a dramatic change in oil prices. Oil was considered a cheap and abundant source of energy in the 1950s, and Americans had grown dependent on its importation from the

⇒ *The Age of Aquarius* ⇐

The election of John F. Kennedy to the presidency in the fall of 1960 sparked a vast wave of enthusiasm among young people across the United States. In his inaugural address, the new president dramatically declared that the "torch of liberty" had passed to "a new generation of Americans," who were now admonished to ask not what their country could do for them, but what they could do for their country.

Within a few short years, however, the optimism engendered by the Kennedy presidency had dissipated, to be replaced by an era of discontent marked by antiwar protests on college campuses, urban riots, and a widespread distaste for the shallowness of life in the postwar United States. By the 1970s, many Americans had lost faith in their government and in its ability to adequately service their needs and realize their aspirations.

What had happened to tarnish the dream of the Kennedy years? In part, of course, the disillusionment was a direct consequence of the Vietnam War, a war for which President Kennedy himself bore part of the responsibility and which eventually aroused massive unrest on college campuses across the country. But it is clear that the public discontent over U.S. foreign policy in the 1960s was only one symptom of a deeper current of protest over domestic issues in the United States—over civil rights for racial minorities, over inequalities between men and women, and even over the materialistic lifestyle that characterized the country's capitalist civilization. To one close observer, political scientist Samuel P. Huntington, the "age of protest" actually began in February 1960, months before the Kennedy election, when four young African Americans demanded service at a lunch counter in Greensboro, North Carolina.

What puzzled many Americans was that the discontent of the 1960s and early 1970s took place during a period marked by the greatest material prosperity that the country had ever known. To seasoned observers, however, the ferment was a product of deep-seated cyclical changes that were an integral part of the rhythm of American society. Huntington notes that there has

historically been a serious gap between the nation's ideals of freedom and equality and the degree to which such aspirations have actually been achieved in American society. In that sense, Kennedy may have helped to unleash the era of protest with his campaign pledge to "get this country moving again." That legacy continued to fester after his untimely death in November 1963.

To participants, such periods of intense societal energy may appear to be a permanent feature on the landscape. Rock musician Bob Dylan—whose song "The Times, They Are A-Changin,'" published in 1964, became the anthem of the protest movement—wrote that the old order was rapidly fading, and anyone who was not ready to follow the new road had better get out of the way. In fact, however, such periods of creedal passion cannot be sustained. As historian Arthur F. Schlesinger, Jr., has expressed it, life in America has always been a process of ebb and flow between eras of innovation and conservatism, with each phase bearing the seeds of its own contradiction. Sustained public action is emotionally exhausting, breeding a desire to return to private life. But when social problems begin to fester and people grow weary of selfish motives and a concentration on material pleasures, the process begins again.

So it has happened periodically in American history. And so it was in the 1960s, when a generation of young Americans grew bored with the complacency of the Eisenhower years and welcomed a new "Age of Aquarius," marked by "harmony and understanding, sympathy and trust abounding." All too soon, the dream died, and an exhausted country returned to its private concerns in the self-indulgent years of the 1980s.

Sources: Arthur F. Schlesinger, Jr., *The Cycles of American History* (Boston: Houghton Mifflin, 1986); Samuel P. Huntington, *American Politics: The Promise of Disharmony* (Cambridge, MA: Belknap Press of Harvard University, 1981); Bob Dylan, *Lyrics, 1962–1985* (New York: Alfred A. Knopf, 1992); "Aquarius," from the American rock musical *Hair*, words by James Rado and Gerome Ragni (New York: United Artists, 1968).

Middle East. By the late 1970s, 50 percent of the oil used in the United States came from the Middle East. But an oil embargo imposed by the Organization of Petroleum Exporting Countries (OPEC) as a result of the Arab-Israeli War in 1973 and OPEC's subsequent raising of prices led to a quadrupling of oil prices. As a result of

additional price hikes, oil prices increased twentyfold by the end of the 1970s, no doubt encouraging inflationary tendencies throughout the entire economy. Although the Carter administration produced a plan for reducing oil consumption at home while spurring domestic production, neither Congress nor the American people could be persuaded to follow what they regarded as drastic measures.

By 1980, the Carter administration was facing two devastating problems. High inflation and a noticeable decline in average weekly earnings were causing a perceptible drop in American living standards. At the same time, a crisis abroad had erupted when fifty-three Americans were taken and held hostage by the Iranian government of Ayatollah Khomeini. Although Carter had little control over the situation, his inability to gain the release of the American hostages led to perceptions at home that he was a weak president. His overwhelming loss to Ronald Reagan (b. 1911) in the election of 1980 brought forward the chief exponent of right-wing Republican policies and a new political order.

Canada: In the Shadow of Goliath

Canada experienced many of the same developments as the United States in the postwar years. For twenty-five years after World War II, Canada realized extraordinary economic prosperity as it set out on a new path of industrial development. Canada had always had a strong export economy based on its abundant natural resources. Now it also developed electronic, aircraft, nuclear, and chemical engineering industries on a large scale. Much of the Canadian growth, however, was financed by capital from the United States, which resulted in American ownership of Canadian businesses. While many Canadians welcomed the economic growth, others feared American economic domination of Canada and its resources.

A notable feature of Canada's postwar history has been its close relationship with the United States. In addition to fears of economic domination, Canadians have also worried about playing a subordinate role politically and militarily to the neighboring superpower. Canada agreed to join the North Atlantic Treaty Organization in 1949 and even sent military contingents to fight in Korea the following year. But to avoid subordination to the United States or any other great power, Canada has consistently and actively supported the United Nations. Nevertheless, concerns about the United States have not kept Canada from maintaining a special relationship with its southern neighbor. The North American Air Defense Command (NORAD), formed in 1957, was based on close cooperation between the air forces of the two countries for the defense of North America against missile attack. As another example of their close cooperation, in 1972, Canada and the United States signed the Great Lakes Water Quality Agreement to regulate water quality of the lakes that border both countries.

After 1945, the Liberal Party continued to dominate Canadian politics until 1957, when John Diefenbaker (1895–1979) achieved a Conservative victory. But a major recession returned the Liberals to power, and under Lester Pearson (1897–1972), they created Canada's welfare state by enacting a national social security system (the Canada Pension Plan) and a national health insurance program.

The most prominent Liberal government, however, was that of Pierre Trudeau (b. 1919), who came to power in 1968. Although French in background, Trudeau was dedicated to Canada's federal union. In 1968, his government passed the Official Languages Act, creating a bilingual federal civil service and encouraging the growth of French culture and language in Canada. Although Trudeau's government vigorously pushed an industrialization program, high inflation and Trudeau's efforts to impose the will of the federal government on the powerful provincial governments alienated voters and weakened his government.

Democracy, Dictatorship, and Development in Latin America since 1945

As a result of the Great Depression of the 1930s, many Latin American countries experienced political instability that led to military coups and militaristic regimes (see Chapter 5). But the Great Depression also helped to transform Latin America from a traditional to a modern economy.

Since the nineteenth century, Latin Americans had exported raw materials, especially minerals and foodstuffs, while buying the manufactured goods of the industrialized countries, particularly Europe and the United States. Despite a limited degree of industrialization, Latin America was still dependent on an export-import economy. As a result of the Great Depression, however, exports were cut in half, and the revenues available to buy manufactured goods declined. In response, many Latin American countries encouraged the development of new industries to produce goods that were formerly imported. This process of industrial development, known as "import-substituting industrialization" (ISI), was supposed to achieve greater economic independence for Latin America. With a shortage of capital in the private sector, governments often invested in the new industries, thereby leading, for example, to

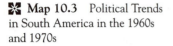 **Map 10.3** Political Trends in South America in the 1960s and 1970s

government-run steel industries in Chile and Brazil and petroleum industries in Argentina and Mexico.

By the 1960s, however, the policy of import substitution had begun to fail. Despite their gains, Latin American countries were still dependent on the United States, Europe, and now Japan for the advanced technology needed for modern industries. To make matters worse, poverty conditions in some Latin American countries limited the size of domestic markets, and many countries were unable to find markets abroad for their products.

The failure of import-substituting industrialization led to instability and a new reliance on military regimes, especially to curb the demands of the new industrial middle class and working class that had increased in size and power as a result of industrialization. Beginning in the 1960s, almost all economically advanced Latin American countries experienced some form of domestic strife and military despotism. In the 1960s, repressive military regimes in Chile, Brazil, and Argentina portrayed themselves as "antipolitical" as they abolished political parties and left few avenues for political opposition. These despotic regimes often returned to export-import economies financed by foreigners, while encouraging multinational corporations to come into their countries. Because these companies were primarily interested in taking advantage of Latin America's raw materials and abundant supply of cheap labor, their presence often offered little benefit to the local economy and only contributed to the ongoing dependency of Latin America on the industrially developed nations.

In the decade of the 1970s, Latin American regimes, struggling to maintain their failing economies, grew even more reliant on borrowing from abroad, especially from banks in Europe and the United States. Between 1970 and 1982, debt to foreigners increased from $27 billion to $315.3 billion. By 1982, a number of governments announced that they could no longer pay interest on their debts to foreign banks, and their economies began to crumble. Wages fell, and unemployment skyrocketed. Governments were forced to undertake fundamental reforms to qualify for additional loans and at the same time were encouraged to reevaluate the strategies they had used in their economic modernization. Many came to believe that the state sector had become too large and had overprotected domestic industries too long. The overly fast pace of industrialization had led to a decline in the rural economy as well, and many hoped that by improving agricultural production for home consumption, they could stem the flow of people from the countryside to the cities and at the same time strengthen the domestic market for Latin American industrial products.

Other factors have also played important roles in the history of Latin America since 1945. The Catholic Church had been a powerful force in Latin America for centuries, but its hold over people diminished as cities and industrial societies developed. By the beginning of the twentieth century, most Latin American governments had separated church and state, although the church remained a potent social and cultural force.

Eventually, the Catholic Church pursued a middle way in Latin American society, advocating a moderate capitalist system that would respect workers' rights, institute land reform, and provide for the poor. This policy led to the formation of Christian Democratic parties that had some success in the 1960s and 1970s. In the 1960s, however, some Catholics in Latin America took a more radical path to change by advocating a theology of liberation. Influenced by Marxist ideas, advocates of liberation theology believed that Christians must fight to free the oppressed, using violence if necessary. Some Catholic clergy recommended armed rebellions and even teamed up with Marxist guerrillas in rural areas. Other radical priests worked in factories alongside workers or carried on social work among the poor in the slums. Although liberation theology attracted much attention, it was by no means the ideology of the majority of Latin American Catholics and was rejected by the church hierarchy. Still, in the 1970s and 1980s, the Catholic Church continued to play an important role in Latin America by becoming the advocate of human rights against authoritarian regimes.

The United States has traditionally cast a large shadow over Latin America. During the 1930s, President Roosevelt renounced U.S. unilateral military action in the Western Hemisphere. In 1948, the nations of the region formed the Organization of American States (OAS), which was intended to eliminate unilateral action by one state in the internal or external affairs of another state. Instead, the OAS encouraged regional cooperation and allowed for group action to maintain peace. It certainly did not end U.S. interference in Latin American affairs, however. Especially after World War II, as the Cold War between the United States and the Soviet Union intensified, U.S. policymakers grew anxious about the possibility of Communist regimes in Central America and the Caribbean. The United States returned to a policy of unilateral action when it believed that Soviet agents were attempting to use local Communists or radical reformers to establish governments hostile to U.S. interests.

Especially after the success of Castro in Cuba (discussed later in this chapter), the goal of preventing "another Cuba" largely determined U.S. policy toward Latin America throughout the Cold War era. In the 1960s, President Kennedy's Alliance for Progress encouraged social reform and economic development by providing private and public funds to elected governments whose reform programs were acceptable to the United States. But the Alliance failed to work, and after the Cubans began to export the Cuban Revolution, starting guerrilla wars in other Latin American countries, the United States responded by providing massive military aid to anti-Communist regimes, regardless of their nature. By 1979, 83,000 military personnel from twenty-one Latin American countries had received U.S.–assisted military training, with special emphasis on antiguerrilla activity to fight social revolutionaries.

The Threat of Marxist Revolutions

Until the 1960s, Marxism played little role in the politics of Latin America. The success of Fidel Castro in Cuba and his espousal of Marxism, however, opened the door for other Marxist movements that aimed to gain the support of peasants and industrial workers and bring radical change to Latin America. The United States portrayed these movements as Communist threats and provided substantial military assistance to fight them.

THE CUBAN REVOLUTION

An authoritarian regime, headed by Fulgencio Batista (1901–1973) and closely tied economically to U.S. investors, had ruled Cuba since 1934. A strong opposition movement to Batista's government developed, led by Fidel Castro (b. 1926) and assisted by Ernesto "Ché" Guevara (1928–1967), an Argentinian who believed that revolutionary upheaval was necessary to change Latin America. Castro maintained that only armed force could overthrow Batista, but when their initial as-

saults on Batista's regime brought little success, Castro's forces, based in the Sierra Maestra mountains, turned to guerrilla warfare. As the rebels gained more support, Batista responded with such brutality that he alienated his own supporters. The dictator fled in December 1958, and Castro's revolutionaries seized Havana on January 1, 1959.

The new government proceeded cautiously, but relations between Cuba and the United States quickly deteriorated. An agrarian reform law in May 1959 nationalized all landholdings over 1,000 acres, and in December 1961, Castro declared himself a Marxist-Leninist. A new level of antagonism arose early in 1960 when the Soviet Union agreed to buy Cuban sugar and provide $100 million in credits. On March 17, 1960, President Eisenhower directed the Central Intelligence Agency (CIA) to "organize the training of Cuban exiles, mainly in Guatemala, against a possible future day when they might return to their homeland."[1] Arms from Eastern Europe began to arrive in Cuba, the United States cut its purchases of Cuban sugar, and the Cuban government nationalized U.S. companies and banks. In October 1960, the United States declared a trade embargo of Cuba, driving Castro closer to the Soviet Union.

On January 3, 1961, the United States broke diplomatic relations with Cuba. The new U.S. president, John

◆ **Fidel Castro.** On January 1, 1959, a band of revolutionaries led by Fidel Castro overthrew the authoritarian government of Fulgencio Batista. Castro is shown here in 1957 with some of his followers at a secret base near the Cuban coast.

F. Kennedy, supported a coup attempt against Castro's government, but the landing of 1,400 CIA-assisted Cubans in Cuba on April 17, 1961, turned into a total military disaster (the infamous Bay of Pigs). This fiasco encouraged the Soviets to make an even greater commitment to Cuban independence by placing nuclear missiles in the country, an act that led to a showdown with the United States (see Chapter 7). As its part of the bargain to defuse the missile crisis, the United States agreed not to invade Cuba.

But the missile crisis affected Cuba in another way as well. Castro, who had urged Khrushchev to stand firm even at the risk of nuclear war with the United States, now realized that the Soviet Union was unreliable. If revolutionary Cuba was to be secure and no longer encircled by hostile states tied to U.S. interests, the Cubans would have to instigate social revolution in the rest of Latin America. Castro judged Bolivia, Haiti, Venezuela, Colombia, Paraguay, and a number of Central American states as especially vulnerable to radical revolution. He believed that once guerrilla wars were launched, peasants would flock to the movement and overthrow the old regimes. Guevara attempted to instigate a guerrilla war in Bolivia but was caught and killed by the Bolivian army in the fall of 1967. The Cuban strategy had failed.

Within Cuba, however, Castro's socialist revolution proceeded, although with mixed results. The Cuban Revolution did secure some social gains for its people, especially in health care and education. The regime provided free medical services for all citizens, and the population's health improved noticeably. Illiteracy was wiped out by developing new schools and establishing teacher-training institutes that tripled the number of teachers within ten years. Eschewing the path of rapid industrialization, Castro encouraged agricultural diversification. But the Cuban economy continued to rely on the production and sale of sugar. Economic problems forced the Castro regime to depend on Soviet subsidies and the purchase of Cuban sugar by Soviet bloc countries.

CHILE

Another challenge to U.S. influence in Latin America appeared in 1970 when the Marxist Salvador Allende (1908–1973) was elected president of Chile and attempted to create a socialist society by constitutional means. Chile suffered from a number of economic problems. Wealth was concentrated in the hands of large landowners and a few large corporations. Inflation, foreign debts, and a decline in the mining industry (copper exports accounted for 80 percent of Chile's export income) caused untold difficulties. Right-wing control of the government failed to achieve any solutions, especially since foreign investments were allowed to expand. There was growing resentment of U.S. corporations, especially Anaconda and Kennecott, which controlled the copper industry.

In the 1970 elections, a split in the moderate forces enabled Allende to become president of Chile as head of a coalition of Socialists, Communists, and Catholic radicals. A number of labor leaders, who represented the interests of the working classes, were given the ministries of labor, finance, public works, and interior in the new government. Allende increased the wages of industrial workers and began to move toward socialism by nationalizing the largest domestic and foreign-owned corporations. Nationalization of the copper industry—essentially without compensation for the owners—caused the Nixon administration to cut off all aid to Chile, creating serious problems for the Chilean economy. At the same time, the government offered only halfhearted resistance to radical workers who were beginning to take control of the landed estates.

These actions brought growing opposition from the upper and middle classes, who began to organize strikes against the government (with support from the CIA). Allende attempted to stop the disorder by bringing three military officers into his cabinet. They succeeded in ending the strikes, but when Allende's coalition increased its vote in the congressional elections of March 1973, the Chilean army, under the direction of General Augusto Pinochet, decided on a coup d'etat. In September 1973, Allende and thousands of his supporters were killed. Contrary to the expectations of many right-wing politicians, the military remained in power and set up a dictatorship. The regime moved quickly to outlaw all political parties, remove the congress, and restore many nationalized industries and landed estates to their original owners. The copper industry, however, remained in government hands. Although Pinochet's regime liberalized the economy, its flagrant abuse of human rights led to growing unrest against the government in the mid-1980s. In 1989, free elections produced a Christian Democratic president who advocated free-market economics.

NICARAGUA

The United States intervened in Nicaraguan domestic affairs in the early twentieth century, and U.S. marines actually remained there for long periods of time. The leader of the U.S.-supported National Guard, Anastasio

Somoza, seized control of the government in 1937, and his family remained in power for the next forty-three years. U.S. support for the Somoza military regime enabled the family to overcome any opponents while enriching themselves at the expense of the state.

Opposition to the regime finally arose from Marxist guerrilla forces known as the Sandinista National Liberation Front. By mid-1979, military victories by the Sandinistas left them in virtual control of the country. Inheriting a poverty-stricken nation, the Sandinistas organized a provisional government and aligned themselves with the Soviet Union. The Reagan and Bush administrations, believing that Central America faced the danger of another Communist state, financed the counterrevolutionary Contra rebels in a guerrilla war against the Sandinista government.

Nationalism and the Military: The Examples of Argentina and Brazil

The military became the power brokers of twentieth-century Latin America. Especially in the 1960s and 1970s, Latin American armies portrayed themselves as the guardians of national honor and orderly progress.

ARGENTINA

Fearful of the forces unleashed by the development of industry, the military intervened in Argentinian politics in 1930 and propped up the cattle and wheat oligarchy that had controlled politics since the beginning of the twentieth century. By this policy, the military hoped to continue the old import-export economy and thus avoid the growth of working-class power that would come with more industrialization.

During World War II, restless military officers formed a new organization, known as the Group of United Officers (GOU). Unhappy with the civilian oligarchy, they overthrew it in June 1943. But the new military regime was not sure how to deal with the working classes. One of its members, Juan Perón (1895–1974), thought that he could manage the workers and used his position as labor secretary in the military government to curry favor with them. He encouraged workers to join labor unions and increased job benefits as well as the number of paid holidays and vacations. In 1944, Perón became vice president of the military government and made sure that people knew he was responsible for the social welfare measures. But as Perón grew more popular, other army officers began to fear his power and arrested him. An up-

rising by workers forced the officers to back down, and in 1946, Perón was elected president.

Perón pursued a policy of increased industrialization in order to please his chief supporters—labor and the urban middle class. At the same time, he sought to free Argentina from foreign investors. The government bought the railways; took over the banking, insurance, shipping, and communications industries; and assumed regulation of imports and exports. But Perón's regime was also authoritarian. His wife, Eva Perón , organized women's groups to support the government while Perón created fascist gangs, modeled after Hitler's Brown Shirts, that used violence to overawe his opponents. But growing corruption in the Perón government and the alienation of more and more people by the regime's excesses encouraged the military to overthrow him in September 1955. Perón went into exile in Spain.

It had been easy for the military to seize power, but it was harder to rule, especially now that Argentina had a party of Peronistas clamoring for the return of the exiled leader. In the 1960s and 1970s, military and civilian governments (the latter closely watched by the military) alternated in power. When both failed to provide economic stability, military leaders decided to allow Juan Perón to return. Reelected president in September 1973, Perón died one year later. In 1976, the military installed a new regime, using the occasion to kill more than 6,000 leftists. With the economic problems still unsolved, the regime tried to divert people's attention by invading the Falkland Islands in April 1982. Great Britain, which had controlled the islands since the nineteenth century, decisively defeated the Argentine forces. The loss discredited the military and opened the door once again to civilian rule. In 1983, Raúl Alfonsín was elected president and sought to reestablish democratic processes.

BRAZIL

In 1889, a bloodless coup overthrew the Brazilian monarchy and established a republic controlled primarily by the landed elites, especially the coffee barons. In 1930, Getúlio Vargas (1883–1954), a wealthy rancher, became president of Brazil with the full support of the Brazilian military. Vargas ruled Brazil from 1930 to 1945, during which time Brazil made the shift from an export-import economy to one of state-supported import-substituting industrialization. Between 1938 and 1945, Vargas established his New State, basically an authoritarian, fascist-like state that outlawed political parties, restricted civil rights, and actively stimulated new industries. In 1945, the army, fearing that Vargas might prolong his power illegally after calling for new elections, forced him to resign.

A second Brazilian republic came into being in 1946; three years later, Vargas was elected to the presidency. But he was unable to solve Brazil's economic problems, especially its soaring inflation, and in 1954, after the armed forces called upon him to resign, Vargas committed suicide. Subsequent democratically elected presidents had no better success in controlling inflation while trying to push rapid industrialization. In the spring of 1964, the military decided to intervene and took over the government.

Unlike previous interventions in politics by Brazil's military leaders, this time the armed forces remained in direct control of the country for twenty years. The military set the country on a new economic course, cutting back somewhat on state control of the economy and emphasizing market forces. Beginning in 1968, the new policies seemed to work, and Brazil experienced an "economic miracle" as it moved into self-sustaining economic growth, generally the hallmark of a modern economy. Economic growth also included the economic exploitation of the Amazon basin, which the regime opened to farming. Some people believe the corresponding destruction of the extensive Amazon rain forests, which is still going on, poses a threat to the ecological balance not only of Brazil but of the earth itself.

Rapid economic growth had additional drawbacks. Ordinary Brazilians hardly benefited as the gulf between rich and poor, always wide, grew even wider. In 1960, the wealthiest 10 percent of Brazil's population received 40 percent of the nation's income; in 1980, they received 51 percent. At the same time, rapid development led to an inflation rate of 100 percent a year, while an enormous foreign debt added to the problems. By the early 1980s, the economic miracle was turning into an economic nightmare. Overwhelmed, the generals retreated and opened the door for a return to democracy in 1985.

The Mexican Way

The Mexican Revolution at the beginning of the twentieth century was the first significant effort in Latin American history to overturn the system of large landed estates, limit foreign control over the country's resources, and increase the living standards of the masses (see Chapter 5). Out of this revolution emerged a political order that long remained the most stable in Latin America. A new wave of change began with Lázaro Cárdenas (1895–1970), who was president from 1934 to 1940. He returned to some of the original revolutionary goals by distributing 44 million acres of land to landless Mexican peasants, thereby appealing to the rural poor. He reorganized the official political party of the Mexican Revolution (known as the Institutional Revolutionary Party, or PRI) to include separate divisions for the peasants, labor, the military, and the middle class. The Revolutionary Party thus became an umbrella organization that contained and controlled the major groups within Mexican society. Every six years, party bosses of the PRI chose the party's presidential candidate, who was then dutifully elected by the people. Cárdenas also gained support by nationalizing U.S.–owned oil companies. He was viewed as the president who stood up to the Yankees.

During the 1950s and 1960s, Mexico's ruling party focused on a balanced industrial program. Fifteen years of steady economic growth combined with low inflation and real gains in wages for more and more people made those years appear to be a "golden age" in Mexico's economic development. But at the end of the 1960s, one implication of Mexico's domination by one party became apparent with the rise of the student protest movement. On October 2, 1968, a demonstration by university students in Tlaltelolco Square in Mexico City was met by police, who opened fire and killed hundreds of students. Leaders of the PRI became concerned about the need to change the system.

The next two presidents, Luis Echeverría (b. 1922) and José López Portillo (b. 1920), introduced political reforms. The government eased rules for the registration of political parties and allowed greater freedom of debate in the press and universities. But economic problems continued to trouble Mexico.

Aspects of Society and Culture in the Western World

Socially, intellectually, and culturally, the Western world changed significantly during the first four decades following the end of World War II. Although many trends represented a continuation of prewar developments, in other cases the changes were quite dramatic, leading some observers in the 1980s to begin speaking of the gradual emergence of a postmodern age.

Expanding Roles for Women

One area of Western society in which the changes have been significant is in the role of women. Although women were to be found in professional careers and a number of other vocations in the 1920s and 1930s, the place for most women was in the home. Half a century later, there were almost as many women as men in the workplace, many of them in professions hitherto reserved for men.

One consequence of the trend toward greater employment outside the home for women has been a drop in the birthrate. In many European countries, the population stopped growing in the 1960s, and the trend has continued since then. The situation was somewhat different in the United States, where a high level of immigration, primarily from Latin America and Asia, boosted the rate of population increase.

One important development was the increased number of married women in the workforce. At the beginning of the twentieth century, even working-class wives tended to stay at home if they could afford to do so. In the postwar period, this was no longer the case. In the United States, for example, married women made up about 15 percent of the female labor force in 1900; by 1970, their number had increased to 62 percent. The percentage of married women in the female labor force in Sweden increased from 47 to 66 percent between 1963 and 1975.

But the increased number of women in the workforce has not changed some old patterns. Working-class women in particular still earn salaries lower than those paid to men for equal work. Women still tend to enter traditionally female jobs. As one Swedish woman guidance counselor remarked in 1975, "Every girl now thinks in terms of a job. This is progress. They want children, but they don't pin their hopes on marriage. They don't intend to be housewives for some future husband. But there has been no change in their vocational choices."[2] A 1980 study of twenty-five European nations revealed that women still made up more than 80 percent of the typists, nurses, tailors, and dressmakers in those countries. Many European women (like their American counterparts) also still faced the double burden of earning income on the one hand and raising a family and maintaining the household on the other. Such inequalities led increasing numbers of women to rebel against their conditions.

The participation of women in World Wars I and II helped them achieve one of the major aims of the nineteenth-century feminist movement—the right to vote. After World War I, many governments acknowledged the contributions of women to the war effort by granting them the vote—Sweden, Great Britain, Germany, Poland, Hungary, Austria, and Czechoslovakia in 1918, followed by the United States in 1920. Women in France and Italy finally gained the right to vote in 1945.

After World War II, European women tended to fall back into the traditional roles expected of them, and little was heard of feminist concerns. A similar phenomenon was evident during the Eisenhower years in the United States. But by the late 1960s, women began to assert their rights again and speak as feminists. Along with the student upheavals of the late 1960s came renewed interest in feminism, or the Women's Liberation movement as it was now called. Increasingly, women protested that the acquisition of political and legal equality had not brought true equality with men.

> We are economically oppressed: in jobs we do full work for half pay, in the home we do unpaid work full time. We are commercially exploited by advertisement, television and the press; legally we often have only the status of children. We are brought up to feel inadequate, educated to narrower horizons than men. This is our specific oppression as women. It is as women that we are, therefore, organizing.[3]

These were the words of a British Women's Liberation Workshop in 1969.

Leading advocates of women's rights in the United States were Betty Friedan and Gloria Steinem. In Western Europe, a leading role in the movement was played by Simone de Beauvoir (1908–1986). Born into a Catholic middle-class family and educated at the Sorbonne in Paris, she supported herself as a teacher and later as a novelist and writer. She maintained a lifelong relationship (but not marriage) with the philosopher Jean-Paul Sartre. Her involvement in the existentialist movement—the leading intellectual movement of its time—led her to become active in political causes. De Beauvoir believed that she lived a "liberated" life for a twentieth-century European woman, but for all her freedom, she still came to perceive that as a woman she faced limits that men did not. In 1949, she published her highly influential work, *The Second Sex*, in which she argued that living in male-dominated societies, women had been defined by their differences from men and consequently received second-class status. "What particularly signalizes the situation of woman is that she—a free autonomous being like all human creatures—nevertheless finds herself in a world where men compel her to assume the status of the Other."[4] De Beauvoir played an active role in the French women's movement of the 1970s, and her book was a major influence on both the American and European women's movements.

Feminists in the Women's Liberation movement came to believe that women themselves must transform the fundamental conditions of their lives. They did so in a variety of ways. First, in the 1960s and 1970s, they formed numerous "consciousness-raising" groups to further awareness of women's issues. Women also sought and gained a measure of control over their own bodies by working to legalize both contraception and abortion. A French law in 1968 legalized the sale of contraceptive devices. In 1979, abortion became legal in France. Even in Catholic countries, where the Church remained strongly opposed to legalizing abortion, legislation allowing contraception and abortion was passed in the 1970s and 1980s.

The Environment and the Green Movements

Beginning in the 1970s, environmentalism became a serious item on the political agenda throughout the Western world. By that time, serious ecological problems had become all too apparent. Air pollution, produced by nitrogen oxide and sulfur dioxide emissions from road vehicles, power plants, and industrial factories, was causing respiratory illnesses and having corrosive effects on buildings and monuments. Many rivers, lakes, and seas had become so polluted that they posed serious health risks. Dying forests and disappearing wildlife alarmed more and more people.

The movement first began to earn broad public attention in the United States when high pollution levels in major cities such as Los Angeles, Chicago, and Pittsburgh, combined with the popularity of Rachel Carson's book, *The Silent Spring,* aroused concerns over the impact that unfettered industrialization was having on the quality of life and the health of the American people. If anything, however, the problem was more serious in Europe, with its higher population density and high levels of industrial production in countries such as Great Britain and West Germany.

Growing ecological awareness gave rise to Green movements and Green parties throughout Europe in the 1970s. The origins of these movements were by no means uniform. Some came from the antinuclear movement; others arose out of such causes as women's liberation and concerns for foreign workers. Most started at the local level and then gradually extended their activities to the national level, where they became formally organized as political parties. Most visible was the Green Party in Germany, which was officially organized in 1979 and eventually elected forty-one delegates to the West German parliament, but Green parties also competed successfully in Sweden, Austria, and Switzerland.

As in the United States, however, concerns that strict environmental regulations could hinder economic growth and raise the level of unemployment undermined the movement's effectiveness. National rivalries and disagreements over how to deal with rising levels of pollution along international waterways such as the Rhine River also hindered cooperation. As the 1980s dawned, the problem was growing worse, with no solution in sight.

Recent Trends in Art and Literature

After World War II, the capital of the Western art world shifted from Paris to New York. Continuing the avant-garde quest to express reality in new ways, a group of New York artists known as abstract expressionists began to paint large abstract canvases in an effort to express a spiritual essence beyond the material world. Among the first was Jackson Pollock (1912–1956), who developed the technique of dripping and swinging paint onto a canvas spread out on the floor. Pollock's large paintings of interlocking colors expressed the energy of primal forces as well as the vast Western landscapes of his native Wyoming.

During the 1960s, many American artists began to reject the emotional style of the previous decade and chose to deal with familiar objects from everyday experience. Some feared that art was being drowned out by popular culture, which bombarded Americans with the images of mass culture in newspapers, in the movies, or on television. In the hope of making art more relevant and accessible to the public, artists sought to pattern their work on contemporary advertisements to reach and manipulate mass taste. Works such as those by Andy Warhol (1930–1987), which repeated images such as soup cans, dollar bills, and the faces of the Mona Lisa and Marilyn Monroe, often left the viewer with a detached numbness and a sense of being trapped in an impersonal, mechanized world. Repetitious and boring, most such paintings did little to close the gap between popular culture and serious art.

Perhaps the most influential American artist of the postwar era was Robert Rauschenberg (b. 1926), whose works broke through the distinctions between painting and other art forms such as sculpture, photography, dance, and theater. In his "collages" or "combines," he juxtaposed disparate images and everyday objects—photographs, clothing, letters, even dirt and cigarette butts—to reflect the energy and disorder of the world around us. He sought to reproduce the stream of images

◆ **Jackson Pollock Does a Painting.** One of the best-known practitioners of abstract expressionism, which remained at the center of the artistic mainstream after World War II, was the American Jackson Pollock, who achieved his ideal of total abstraction in his drip paintings. He is shown here at work in his Long Island studio. Pollock found it easier to cover his large canvases with exploding patterns of color when he put them on the floor.

projected by flicking the channels on a TV set. His works represented an encapsulated documentary of American life in the 1960s, filled with news events, celebrities, war, sports, and advertisements.

Rauschenberg's work helped to free future artists to find art in anything under the sun. Beginning in the late 1960s, a new school, of conceptual art, began to reject the commercial marketability of an art object and seek the meaning of art in ideas. Art as idea could be philosophy, linguistics, mathematics, or social criticism, existing solely in the mind of the artist and the audience. In a related attempt to free art from the shackles of tradi-

tion, a school of performance art used the body as a means of living sculpture. Often discomfiting or shocking in its intimate revelations, performance art offended many viewers. Such works expanded the horizons of modern creativity, but also widened the gap between modern art and the public, many of whom now considered art as socially dysfunctional and totally lacking in relevance to their daily fives.

Since the end of World War II, serious music, like art, has witnessed a wide diversity of experimental movements, each searching for new tonal and rhythmic structures. Striving to go beyond Schoenberg's atonality, European composers in the 1950s set out to free their music from the traditional constraints of meter, form, and dynamics. They devised a new procedure called serialism—a mathematical ordering of musical components that, once set in motion, essentially wrote itself automatically. Another experimental music, developed in the 1950s by the American John Cage (1912–1992) was indeterminacy, which called upon chance and the performer to determine the work, thereby minimizing the role of the composer as organizer of the piece.

In the 1960s, minimalism took hold in the United States. Largely influenced by Indian music, minimalist composers such as Philip Glass (b. 1937) focus on the subtle nuances in the continuous repetitions of a melodic or rhythmic pattern. Yet another musical development is microtonality, which expands the traditional twelve-tone chromatic scale to include quarter tones and even smaller intervals. Since the 1960s there has also been much experimental electronic and computer music. However, despite the excitement of such musical exploration, much of it is considered too cerebral and alien, even by the educated public.

Of all the arts, architecture best reflects the extraordinary global economic expansion of the second half of the twentieth century, from the rapid postwar reconstruction of Japan and Europe, to the phenomenal prosperity of the West, to the newfound affluence of emerging Third World nations. No matter where one travels today, from Kuala Lumpur to Johannesburg, from Buenos Aires to Shanghai, the world's cities boast the identical monolithic rectangular skyscraper—the international symbol of modernization, money, and power.

A major failure of modernist architecture, inspired by the utopian schemes of the 1920s and built in the 1960s, was the creation of a new capital in Brazil. Brasília, a glistening but sterile city of glass and steel erected as a futuristic ideal, totally ignored the human factor and, as a consequence, has suffered from its impractical limitations. A more realistic example of city planning is to be found in Singapore, which since the 1980s has housed 80 percent of its 3 million inhabitants in government-built high-rise buildings grouped together in independent communities called estates. These estates have been adapted to local conditions on a human scale and include schools, places of worship, stores, metro system, day care, and entertainment.

Along with the visual arts and music, the literature of this era experimented with radically new narrative techniques. In Europe, the postwar period's disillusionment found expression in the existential works of Jean-Paul Sartre (1905–1980) and Albert Camus (1913–1960). The fundamental premise of existentialism was the absence of a god in the universe, thereby denying any preordained destiny to mankind. Humans were thus deprived of any absolute purpose or meaning, set adrift in an absurd world. Often reduced to despair and depression, the protagonists of these existential works were left with only one hope—themselves, voluntarily reaching out and becoming involved in their community.

This elemental worldview found expression in the Paris of the 1950s in the "theater of the absurd." One of its foremost proponents was the Irish dramatist Samuel Beckett (1906–1990), who lived in France. In his trailblazing, seminal play *Waitng for Godot* (1952), two nondescript men eagerly await the appearance of someone who never arrives. While they wait, they pass the time exchanging hopes and fears, with humor, courage, and touching friendship. This waiting represents the existential meaning of life, which is found in the daily activities and fellowship of the here and now, despite the absence of any absolute salvation to the human condition.

In the 1960s, Beckett and other French authors experimented so radically with literary form and language that they pushed fiction well beyond its traditional limits of rational understanding, provoking shocked critics to label it "verbal nonsense." In the "new novel," for example, many authors abolished plot, chronology, character development, or coherent sentence structure, altogether emancipating the novel to an imaginatively new realm of possibilities and meaning (see box on p. 228).

Popular Culture

Popular culture in the twentieth century, especially since World War II, has played an important role in helping Western people define themselves. It also reflects the economic system that supports it, for it is this system that manufactures, distributes, and sells the images that people consume as popular culture. As popular culture and its economic support system have become increasingly intertwined, leisure industries have emerged. Modern popular culture is thus inextricably tied to the mass consumer society in which it has emerged. This consumer-oriented aspect of popular culture delineates it clearly from the folk culture of preceding centuries; folk culture is something people make, while popular culture is something people buy.

The United States has been the most influential force in shaping popular culture in the West and, to a lesser degree, throughout the world. Through movies, music, advertising, and television, the United States has spread its particular form of consumerism and the American Dream to millions around the world.

Motion pictures were the primary vehicle for the diffusion of American popular culture in the years immediately following the war and continued to dominate both European and American markets in the next decades. Although developed in the 1930s, television did not become readily available until the late 1940s. By 1954, there were 32 million sets in the United States as television became the centerpiece of middle-class life. In the 1960s, as television spread around the world, American networks unloaded their products on Europe and developing countries at extraordinarily low prices. Only the establishment of quota systems prevented American television from completely inundating these countries.

The United States has also dominated popular music since the end of World War II. Jazz, blues, rhythm and blues, rap, and rock and roll have been by far the most popular music forms in the Western world—and much of the non-Western world—during this time. All of them originated in the United States, and all are rooted in African American musical innovations. These forms later spread to the rest of the world, inspiring local artists who then transformed the music in their own way.

In the postwar years, sports became a major product of both popular culture and the leisure industry. The development of satellite television and various electronic breakthroughs helped make spectator sports a global phenomenon. The Olympic Games could now be broadcast around the world from anywhere on earth. Sports became a cheap form of entertainment for consumers, as fans did not have to leave their homes to enjoy athletic competitions. In fact, some sports organizations initially resisted television, fearing that it would hurt ticket sales. However, the tremendous revenues possible from television contracts overcame this hesitation. As sports television revenue escalated, many sports came to receive the bulk of their yearly revenue from television contracts.

Sports became big politics as well as big business. Politicization has been one of the most significant trends

The Search for a New Literature

Ever since James Joyce at the beginning of the twentieth century, Western authors have been searching for new literary means of expressing the complexities of modern life. Their often radical experiments culminated in the years after World War II. In this process, American literature has followed its own independent path, led by two authors, William Faulkner (1897–1962) and Ernest Hemingway (1899–1961). Although both wrote masterpieces before the war, they continued to write important works in the 1950s and influenced subsequent generations of authors with their unique styles. Under the impact of these two masters, postwar writing in the United States omitted authorial explanation and commentary and made its point by suggestion rather than assertion, by prying coherence and meaning from the text.

Faulkner's world was the Old South. Admired for their stylistic innovations regarding chronology and inner monologue, Faulkner's novels chronicled the history of an imaginary county in Mississippi from its early settlers to his own day. In novels such as *The Sound and the Fury* (1929), *Absalom, Absalom* (1936), and *Intruder in the Dust* (1948), he expressed his outrage at the moral decay of the modern-day South and its failure to solve its social problems.

Hemingway's world was that of the American expatriate, roaming the world to find purpose and identity in a larger global culture. Using his patented laconic style (he once explained his striped-down prose by referring to the principle of an iceberg, that "there is seven-eighths of it underwater for every part that shows"), his works—including *The Sun Also Rises*(1926), *For Whom the Bell Tolls* (1940), and *The Old Man and the Sea* (1952)—explored the psychological meaning of masculinity under the pressures of different aspects of modern life. Injured in a plan crash on safari in Africa, he committed suicide in 1961.

Fictional writing in the 1960s reflected growing concerns about the materialism and superficiality of American culture and often took the form of exuberant and comic verbal fantasies. As the decade intensified with the pain of the Vietnam War and the ensuing social and political turmoil, authors turned to satire, using "black humor" and cruelty, hoping to shock the American public into a recognition of its social ills. Many of these novels—such as Thomas Pynchon's *V* (1953), Joseph Heller's *Catch 22* (1961), and John Barth's *The Sotweed Factor* (1961)—were wildly imaginative, highly entertaining, and very different from the writing of the first half of the century, which had detailed the "real" daily lives of small-town or big-city America.

In the 1970s and 1980s, American fiction relinquished the extravagant verbal displays of the 1960s, returning to a more sober exposition of social problems, this time related to race, gender, and sexual preference. Much of the best fiction explored the moral dimensions of contemporary life from Jewish, African American, feminist, or gay perspectives. Some outstanding women's fiction was authored by foreign-born writers from Asia and Latin America, who examined the problems of immigrants, such as cultural identity and assimilation into the American mainstream.

Postwar writing in Latin American has been equally vibrant. Nobel Prize–winning writers such as Mario Vargas Llosa, Gabriel García Márquez, José Luis Borges, and Carlos Fuentes are among the most respected literary names of the past half century. These authors often use dazzling language and daring narrative experimentation to make their point. Master of this new style is the Colombian Gabriel García Márquez (b. 1938). In *One Hundred Years of Solitude* (1967), he explores the transformation of a small town under the impact of political violence, industrialization, and the arrival of a U.S. banana company. Especially noteworthy is his use of magical realism, relating the outrageous events that assail the town in a matter-of-fact voice, thus transforming the fantastic into the commonplace.

Unlike novelists in the United States and Western Europe, who tend to focus their attention on the interior landscape within the modern personality in an industrial society, fictional writers in Latin America, like their counterparts in Africa and much of Asia, have sought to project an underlying political message. Many have been inspired by a sense of social and political injustice, a consequence of the economic inequality and authoritarian politics that have marked the local scene throughout much of the century. Some, like the Peruvian José Maria Arguedas, have championed the cause of the Amerindian and lauded the diversity that marks the ethnic mix throughout the continent. Others have run for high political office as a means of remedying social problems. Some have been women, reflecting the rising demand for sexual equality in a society traditionally marked by male domination. The memorable phrase of the Chilean poet Gabriela Mistral—"I have chewed stones with woman's gums"—encapsulates the plight of Latin American women.

Sources: *The Norton Anthology of American Literature*, 4th ed. (New York: W. W. Norton, 1995); Naomi Lindstrom, *Twentieth Century Spanish American Fiction* (Austin: University of Texas Press, 1994).

in sports during the second half of the twentieth century. Football (soccer) remains the dominant world sport and more than ever has become a vehicle for nationalist sentiment and expression. The World Cup is the most watched event on television. Although the sport can be a positive outlet for national and local pride, all too often it has been marred by violence as nationalistic fervor has overcome rational behavior.

Science and Technology

Since the Scientific Revolution of the seventeenth century and the Industrial Revolution of the nineteenth century, science and technology have played increasingly important roles in world civilization. Many of the scientific and technological achievements since World War II have revolutionized people's lives. When American astronauts walked on the moon, millions watched the event on their television sets in the privacy of their living rooms.

Before World War II, theoretical science and technology were largely separated. Pure science was the domain of university professors, far removed from the practical technological matters of technicians and engineers. But during World War II, university scientists were recruited to work for their governments to develop new weapons and practical instruments of war. British physicists played a crucial role in developing an improved radar system in 1940 that helped to defeat the German air force in the Battle of Britain. The computer, too, was a wartime creation. The British mathematician Alan Turing designed a primitive computer to assist British intelligence in breaking the secret codes of German ciphering machines. The most famous product of wartime scientific research was the atomic bomb, created by a team of American and European scientists under the guidance of physicist J. Robert Oppenheimer. Obviously, most wartime devices were created for destructive purposes, but computers and breakthrough technologies such as nuclear energy were soon adapted for peacetime uses.

The sponsorship of research by governments and the military during World War II led to a new scientific model. Science had become very complex, and only large organizations with teams of scientists, huge laboratories, and complicated equipment could undertake such large-scale projects. Such facilities were so expensive, however, that only governments and large corporations could support them. Because of its postwar prosperity, the United States was able to lead in the development of the new science. Almost 75 percent of all scientific research funds in the United States came from the gov-

ernment in 1965. Unwilling to lag behind, especially in military development, the Soviet Union was also forced to provide large outlays for scientific and technological research and development. In fact, the defense establishments of the United States and the Soviet Union generated much of the scientific research of the postwar era. One-fourth of the trained scientists and engineers after 1945 were engaged in the creation of new weapons systems. Universities found their research agendas increasingly determined by government funding for military-related projects.

There was no more stunning example of how the new scientific establishment operated than the space race of the 1960s. In 1957, the Soviets announced that they had sent the first space satellite, *Sputnik I*, into orbit around the earth. In response, the United States launched a gigantic project to land a manned spacecraft on the moon within a decade. Massive government funds financed the scientific research and technological advances that attained this goal in 1969.

The postwar alliance of science and technology led to an accelerated rate of change that became a fact of life in Western society. But the underlying assumption of this alliance—that scientific knowledge gave human beings the ability to manipulate the environment for their benefit—was questioned in the 1960s and 1970s by some who were concerned with potentially far-reaching side effects damaging to the environment. The chemical fertilizers that were touted for producing larger crops, for example, wreaked havoc with the ecological balance of streams, rivers, and woodlands. *Small Is Beautiful*, written by the British economist E. F. Schumacher (1911–1977), is a fundamental critique of the dangers of the new science and technology. The widespread proliferation of fouled beaches and dying forests and lakes made environmentalism an issue of growing importance in the postwar era.

Conclusion

During the immediate postwar era, Western Europe emerged from the ashes of World War II and achieved a level of political stability and economic prosperity unprecedented in its long history. By the 1970s, European leaders were beginning to turn their attention to bringing about further economic unity among the nations in the region. In the Western Hemisphere, the two North American giants—the United States and Canada—followed a similar path, raising the standard of living for their citizens and maintaining their democratic institutions. To the south, some Latin American nations were able to share in the economic growth of the 1950s and 1960s, although political stability was elusive until the early 1980s, when democratic governments begin to replace oppressive military regimes with some consistency.

With all these signs of progress, however, there were signs of trouble in Camelot. During the 1960s, massive protest movements arose to protest the Vietnam War and the growing materialism and impersonality of mod-ern-day living. In the meantime, continuing problems with race relations in both Europe and the Western Hemisphere raised troubling questions about the ability of modern states to create diverse societies based on equal opportunity and the protection of human rights. For many observers in the modern West, the relentless drive for economic well-being and the creation of a consumer society betrayed a spiritual malaise and the absence of a sense of purpose and identity in modern life.

NOTES

1. Dwight Eisenhower, *The White House Years: Waging Peace, 1956–1961* (Garden City, NY, 1965), p. 533.
2. Quoted in Hilda Scott, *Sweden's "Right to Be Human"— Sex-Role Equality: The Goal and the Reality* (London, 1982), p. 125.
3. Quoted in Marsha Rowe et al., eds., *Spare Rib Reader* (Harmondsworth, 1982), p. 574.
4. Simone de Beauvoir, *The Second Sex*, trans. H. M. Parshley (New York, 1961), p. xxviii.

Reflections

As World War II came to an end, the survivors of that bloody struggle could afford to face the future with at least a measure of cautious optimism. With the death of Adolf Hitler in his bunker in Berlin, there were reasons to hope that the bitter rivalry that had marked relations among the Western powers would finally be put to an end, and that the wartime alliance of the United States, Great Britain, and the Soviet Union could be maintained into the postwar era. In the meantime, the peoples of Asia and Africa saw the end of the war as a gratifying sign that the colonial system would soon come to an end, ushering in a new era of political stability and economic development on a global scale.

With the perspective of half a century, we can see that these hopes have been only partly realized. In the decades following the war, the capitalist nations managed to recover from the extended economic depression that had contributed to the start of World War II and advanced to a level of economic prosperity never before seen throughout world history. The bloody conflicts that had erupted among European nations during the first half of the twentieth century came to an end, and Germany and Japan were fully integrated into the world community.

On the other hand, the prospects for a stable, peaceful world and an end to balance-of-power politics were hampered by the emergence of the grueling and sometimes tense ideological struggle between the socialist and capitalist camps, a competition headed by the only remaining great powers, the Soviet Union and the United States. While the two superpowers were able to avoid an open nuclear confrontation, the postwar world was divided into two heavily armed camps in a balance of terror that on one occasion—the Cuban Missile Crisis—brought the world briefly to the brink of nuclear holocaust.

Once again, Europe became divided into hostile camps as the Cold War rivalry between the United States and the Soviet Union forced the European nations to become dependent upon one or the other of the superpowers. The creation of two mutually antagonistic

military alliances—NATO in 1949 and the Warsaw Pact in 1955—confirmed the new division of Europe, while a divided Germany, and, within it, a divided Berlin, remained its most visible symbols. Repeated crises over the status of Berlin only intensified the fears in both camps.

In the midst of this rivalry, the Western European states, with the assistance of the United States, made a remarkable economic recovery and reached new levels of prosperity. In Eastern Europe, Soviet domination, both politically and economically, seemed so complete that many doubted it could ever be undone. Soviet military intervention, as in Hungary in 1956 and Czechoslovakia in 1968, reminded the Soviet satellites of their real condition; Communism appeared, at least for the time being, to be too powerful to be dislodged. The Helsinki Agreement, signed in 1975, appeared to be a tacit admission by the West that the Iron Curtain had taken on a near-permanent status.

In the meantime, behind a shield of Soviet troops and tanks, the USSR and its Eastern European satellites acted to stabilize the socialist system and realize the promise of a better society. Although Nikita Khrushchev appeared to harbor a sincere belief in the superiority of Marxist-Leninist ideas over those of the capitalist West, by the 1960s for the average citizen in the socialist bloc countries, the dream of a utopian society had long since begun to fade, while party leaders cynically manipulated the system for their own benefit.

Only in China was the dream still alive, actively promoted by Mao Zedong and his radical disciples during the frenetic years between the Great Leap Forward and Mao's death at the end of the Cultural Revolution. Whether or not his "uninterrupted revolution" was simply a last-ditch effort to retain power, Mao appeared to have a real awareness that even in China there lurked the danger of creeping bourgeoisification. His failure is a striking testimonial to the difficulties of continually stoking the fires of social revolution.

In the West, economic affluence appeared to give birth to its own set of problems. The voracious focus on material possessions, an intrinsic characteristic of the capitalist ethos, helped to promote high levels of productivity in office and factory, but at the same time produced a spiritual malaise in individual members of society, who increasingly began to question the meaning and purpose of life beyond the sheer accumulation of things. As the spread of scientific knowledge eroded religious belief, increasing social mobility undermined the traditional base-level structural units of human society—the family and the community. Modernity, as postwar society in the West was now commonly described, appeared to have no answer to the search for meaning in life beyond an unconfirmed and complacent belief in the Enlightenment doctrine of progress.

For the have-nots of capitalist society, the sources of discontent were more immediate, focusing on a lack of equal access to the cornucopia of goods produced by the capitalist machine. To their credit, political leaders in many countries sought ways to extend the benefits of an affluent society to their disadvantaged constituents, but success was limited, while experts searched without result for the ultimate cause.

The driving force behind many of these changes in the postwar world was the Industrial Revolution, which continued to undermine the political, social, and economic foundations of traditional society, without disclosing the final destination. Human beings could only hope that as old ways were inexorably ground up and chucked aside in the new industrial world, the expanding power of scientific knowledge would provide them with clues on how to manipulate the situation to their ultimate benefit.

PART

IV

Third World Rising

CHAPTER

11

A House Divided: The Emergence of Independent States in South Asia

*I*n a letter to his friend and colleague Jawaharlal Nehru in October 1945, the Indian spiritual leader Mahatma Gandhi argued passionately against Nehru's dream of building a modern industrialized society in India. "I believe," Gandhi said, "that if India, and through India the world, is to achieve real freedom, then sooner or later we shall have to go and live in the villages—in huts, not in palaces."[1] Truth and nonviolence, he insisted, could only be found in the simplicity of village life, not in modern industrialized cities patterned after those in the West. Nehru did not agree, and after independence in 1947, he set his country on the path of industrial revolution. As we shall see, Nehru's decision did not end the debate, which continues today, as Indians seek to reconcile their traditional values with the demands of modern life.

For more than a century, the resources of South Asia were systematically plundered by the Western colonial powers. In the process, the region was linked ever more closely to the global capitalist economy. Yet, as in other areas of Asia and Africa, the experience brought only limited benefits to the local peoples,

as little industrial development took place and the bulk of the profits went into the pockets of Western entrepreneurs.

Early in the twentieth century, nationalist forces began to seek reforms in colonial policy and the eventual overthrow of colonial power. But the peoples of South Asia did not regain their national independence until after World War II, when the British agreed to the creation of the new states of India, Pakistan, and Ceylon.

The leaders of these new nations were generally dedicated to building modern societies on the Western model. But escaping the legacy of the past was not easy. Most of the new states were weak and inexperienced and struggled with only limited success to develop advanced economies, establish stable political systems, and foster a sense of common identity among their diverse populations. Old animosities among the various ethnic groups reemerged and led to mutual suspicion and strife within the region. Half a century after independence, peace and prosperity are still more a dream than a reality for many peoples of the area.

. . . .

*T*he End of the British Raj

During the 1930s, the nationalist movement in India was severely shaken by factional disagreements between Hindus and Muslims within its own ranks. The outbreak

of World War II interrupted these sectarian clashes and brought new problems. To the dismay of the leaders of the Indian National Congress, the British government committed India to the war without consulting its people or its elected leaders (the same thing had occurred during Would War I). At the news, a number of Congress legislators resigned, and Mohammed Ali Jinnah, leader of the Muslim League, demanded the creation of a separate state. Mahatma Gandhi started a new disobedience movement and demanded that the British "quit India." Jawaharlal Nehru was arrested. To dampen the protests, the British offered India dominion status after the war and the right of secession for individual states, but the offer was rejected by the Congress.

When the war ended in 1945, the British sent a three-man commission to India to study the situation and make recommendations. The British government offered a complicated union arrangement with divided powers and continued British presence, but Congress leaders were dubious. When clashes between Hindus and Muslims broke out in several cities, Jinnah called for "direct action," while British Prime Minister Clement Attlee announced that power would be transferred to "responsible Indian hands" by June 1948. To bring about the transfer of power, Lord Louis Mountbatten, a member of the British royal family, was appointed viceroy.

But the imminence of independence did not dampen communal strife. As riots escalated, Mountbatten reluctantly accepted the inevitability of partition, while the Congress and the Muslim League were reconciled to the division of Bengal and the Punjab, two provinces with Hindu and Muslim populations. Pakistan itself would be divided between the main area of Muslim habitation in the Indus River valley in the west and a separate territory in east Bengal 2,000 miles to the east. Among Congress leaders, Gandhi alone objected to the division of India. A Muslim woman criticized him for his opposition to partition, asking him, "If two brothers were living together in the same house and wanted to separate and live in two different houses, would you object?" "Ah," Gandhi replied, "if only we could separate as two brothers. But we will not. It will be an orgy of blood. We shall tear ourselves asunder in the womb of the mother who bears us."[2]

But Gandhi was increasingly regarded as a figure of the past by many Indian leaders, and his views were ignored. On July 15, 1947, the British declared that one month later, two independent nations—India and Pakistan—would be established. A boundary commission was formed, and Mountbatten instructed the rulers in the princely states to choose which state they would join by August 15. But problems arose in predominantly Hindu Hyderabad, where the maharaja was a Muslim, and the mountainous Kashmir, where a Hindu prince ruled over a Muslim population. Independence

was declared on August 15, but the auguries were ominous. The flight of millions of Hindus and Muslims across the borders in Bengal and the Punjab led to violence and the death of more than a million people. One of the casualties evoked widespread mourning. On January 30, 1948, a Hindu militant assassinated Gandhi as he was going to morning prayer. The assassin was apparently motivated by Gandhi's opposition to a Hindu India.

Independent India

With independence, the Indian National Congress, now renamed the Congress Party, moved from opposition to the responsibility of power. The prospect must have been intimidating. The vast majority of India's nearly 400 million people were poor and illiterate. The new nation encompassed a bewildering number of language and ethnic groups and fourteen major languages. Although Congress leaders spoke bravely of building a new nation, Indian society still bore many of the scars of past wars and divisions.

One advantage that India possessed was an intelligent, self-confident, and reasonably united leadership. In the crucible years of colonialism, the Congress Party had gained experience in government, while the Indian Civil Service provided solid expertise in the arcane art of bureaucracy. Jawaharlal Nehru, the new prime minister, was a charismatic figure respected and even revered by millions of Indians.

The government's first problem was to resolve the border disputes left over from the transition period. The rulers of Hyderabad and Kashmir had both followed their own preferences rather than the wishes of their subject populations. Nehru was determined to include both states within India. In 1948, Indian troops invaded Hyderabad and annexed the area. India was also able to seize most of Kashmir, but at the cost of incurring the hostility of Pakistan's new leaders. An intractable problem had been created that poisoned relations between the two countries for the next generation.

An Experiment in Democratic Socialism

India's new leaders had strong ideas on the future of Indian society. Nehru was an admirer of British political institutions, but had also been influenced by the Fabian socialist movement in England. With his dominating personality, he imposed his vision of an India with democratic political institutions but a moderately socialist economic structure and, in doing so, put a personal stamp on the country that would last long after his death.

Under Nehru's leadership, the new Republic of India adopted a political system on the British model with a figurehead president and a parliamentary form of government. A number of political parties operated legally, from the Indian Communist Party on the left to capitalist and religious parties on the right. But the Congress Party, with its enormous prestige and charismatic leadership, was dominant at both the central and the local levels. The Congress Party aspired to represent all Indians, from rich to poor, *brahmins* to *harijans* (untouchability was legally abolished by the new government), and Hindus to Muslims and other minority religious groups.

Economic policy was patterned roughly after the program of the British Labour Party with adjustments for local circumstances. The state took over ownership of the "commanding heights" of the economy, such as major industries and resources, transportation, and utilities, while private enterprise was permitted at the local and retail levels. Farmland remained in private hands, but rural cooperatives were officially encouraged.

In other respects, Nehru was a devotee of Western materialism. He was fully convinced that to succeed, India must industrialize. In advocating industrialization, Nehru departed sharply from Gandhi. Gandhi believed firmly that materialism was morally corrupting and that only simplicity and nonviolence (as represented by the traditional Indian village and the symbolic spinning wheel) could save India, and the world itself, from self-destruction (see box on p. 237). Nehru, however, had little fear of the corrupting consequences of material wealth and complained that Gandhi "just wants to spin and weave."

Accordingly, Nehru actively pursued industrialization, although he recognized that a more efficient agricultural sector was a prerequisite for success. He attempted to bring about agricultural reforms through voluntary cooperatives and government assistance. Reflecting the strong anticolonial views of the Congress leadership, the Indian government also sought to avoid excessive dependence upon foreign investment and technological assistance. All business enterprises were required by law to have majority Indian ownership.

Nehru's staunch sense of morality was also apparent in his foreign policy. Under his guidance, India adopted a neutral posture in the Cold War and sought to provide leadership to all newly independent nations in Asia, Africa, and Latin America. The primary themes of Indian foreign policy were anticolonialism and antiracism. This neutral and independent stance quickly placed India in opposition to the United States, which during the 1950s was trying to mobilize all nations against what it viewed as the menace of international communism. India stood equidistant between the two superpowers and tried to establish good relations with the new People's Republic of China.

Although India sought to represent the needs and aspirations of all developing nations, Indian leaders also looked out for their country's own self-interest. In fact, like many other modern governments, India often used morality for its own purposes. Thus, India's opposition to the remnants of colonialism became a justification for resorting to force to evict the Portuguese from their tiny enclave in Goa in 1960. India also refused to consider Pakistan's claim to Kashmir, even though the majority of the population there was Muslim. Tension between the two countries increased during the early 1960s, leading to war in 1965. India won a quick victory, and a cease-fire was signed in the Soviet city of Tashkent. Nevertheless, the sources of mutual hostility were not resolved, and when riots against the Pakistani government broke out in East Pakistan in 1971, India intervened on the side of East Pakistan, which declared its independence as the new nation of Bangladesh.

India also encountered difficulties with China. Nehru attempted to conciliate the Chinese government by supporting its demand for admission into the United Nations and recognizing Chinese sovereignty over the province of Tibet. But when China cracked down on Tibetan autonomy in the late 1950s, India was severely critical. Shortly after, Nehru became aware that China was constructing a road in an area of Tibet claimed by India. When India sent troops to the area in the late summer of 1962, Chinese forces crossed the border and drove them back. A cease-fire was reached, but the border dispute, a consequence of boundaries drawn by a British surveying team at the beginning of the century, was not resolved.

The Post-Nehru Era

Nehru's death in 1964 aroused widespread anxiety; many observers speculated that Indian democracy was dependent upon the Nehru mystique. When his successor, the soft-spoken Congress Party veteran Lal Bahadur Shastri, died in 1966, Congress leaders selected Nehru's daughter, Indira Gandhi (no relation to Mahatma Gandhi), as the new prime minister. Gandhi was inexperienced in politics, and many thought the party bosses had chosen her because she would be easy to dominate, but she quickly showed the steely determination of her father.

❧ Two Visions for India ❧

Before World War II, Jawaharlal Nehru was a leading member of the Indian National Congress and an outspoken advocate of independence from British colonial rule. Mohandas Gandhi was the spiritual leader of the movement and had called on the British to "quit India." But although the two agreed on their desire for an independent India, their visions of the future of their homeland were dramatically different.

Nehru rejected not only Western imperialism, but also the capitalist system that underlay the drive for empire. Nehru saw socialism as the answer for India, but he rejected the Soviet form in favor of a more moderate version that respected Western democratic principles and the concept of private property. At the same time, he was convinced that India must industrialize. As he declared in a speech to members of the Indian National Congress in 1936, only by carrying out an industrial revolution based on socialist principles could India bring an end to "the poverty, the vast unemployment, the degradation and the subjection of the Indian people." Although he conceded that he disagreed with much that had happened in the USSR, if the future was full of hope, "it is largely because of Soviet Russia and what it has done, and I am convinced that if some world catastrophe does not intervene, this new civilization will spread to other lands and put an end to the wars and conflicts which capitalism feeds."

While Nehru saw socialism as the answer to India's ills, Gandhi found it in the traditional village. Whereas Nehru favored industrialization to achieve material affluence, Gandhi praised the simple virtues of manual labor. In a letter to Nehru in October 1945, Gandhi set forth his own vision for the future India. "I believe," he said, "that if India, and through India the world, is to achieve real freedom, then sooner or later we shall have to go and live in the villages—mud huts, not in palaces." Whereas Nehru saw the future of India in factories, Gandhi saw it in "the simplicity of the villages." In the village of his dreams, the Indian

> will not live like an animal in filth and darkness. Men and women will live in freedom, prepared to face the whole world. There will be no plague, no cholera and no smallpox. Nobody will be allowed to be idle or to wallow in luxury. Everyone will have to do body labour.

Gandhi conceded that "the world seems to be going in the opposite direction," but he feared that humankind was like a moth that whirled around a flame faster and faster until it was burnt up. He saw it as his duty to try, until his last breath, to save India and through India the world from such a fate.

Although millions of Indians revered Mahatma (Great Soul) Gandhi for his saintliness, they did not follow his advice. Two years after his letter to Nehru, he was dead of an assassin's bullet. Nehru became the country's first prime minister and launched a program to create a modern India based on socialist principles.

Sources: Stephen Hay, ed., *Sources of Indian Tradition* (New York: Columbia University Press, 1988); Martin Green, ed., *Gandhi in India: In His Own Words* (Hanover, NH: University Press of New England, 1987).

In a number of respects, Gandhi followed in her father's footsteps, embracing democratic socialism and a policy of neutrality in foreign affairs. If anything, she was more activist than her father. Concerned that rural poverty had become chronic, she launched major programs, including nationalizing banks, providing loans to peasants on easy terms, building low-cost housing, and distributing land to the landless. As part of the land redistribution program, she attempted to lower the ceiling on landholdings to 100 acres per family. She also introduced electoral reforms to enfranchise the poor.

Gandhi was especially worried by India's growing population, which was increasing at an annual rate of more than 2 percent. To curb the rate of growth, she adopted a policy of enforced sterilization. This policy proved unpopular, however, and along with growing official corruption and Gandhi's authoritarian tactics and intolerance of opposition, led to her defeat in the general election of 1975, the first time the Congress Party had failed to win a majority at the national level since independence. Congress also lost control of a number of state governments, where regional and ethnic parties were gaining strength.

A minority government of procapitalist parties was formed under Prime Minister Morarji Desai, who attempted to reverse India's steady drift toward socialism. But India's first non-Congress government lacked the competence and experience to handle the country's enormous problems, and within two years Gandhi was back in power with an increased electoral mandate. She now faced a new challenge, however, in the rise of ethnic and religious strife. The most dangerous situation

 **Map 11.1**   Modern South Asia

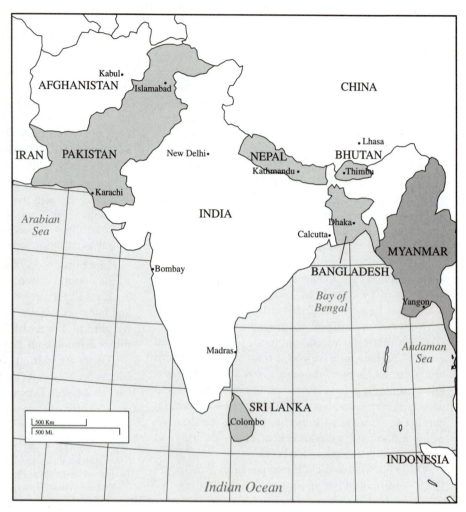

was in the Punjab, where militant Sikhs were demanding provincial autonomy or even independence from India. Gandhi did not shrink from a confrontation and attacked Sikh rebels hiding in their Golden Temple in the city of Amritsar. The incident aroused widespread anger among the Sikh community, and in 1984, Sikh members of Gandhi's personal bodyguard assassinated her.

By now, Congress politicians were convinced that the party could not remain in power without a member of the Nehru family at the helm. Gandhi's son Sanjay, the original heir apparent, had been killed in a plane crash. Now her elder son, Rajiv, a commercial airline pilot with little apparent interest in politics, was persuaded to replace his mother as prime minister. As a politician, Rajiv lacked the strong ideological and political convictions of his mother and grandfather and proceeded to allow a greater role for private enterprise. But his government was harshly criticized for cronyism, inefficiency,

and corruption, as well as insensitivity to the poor. It steadily lost its political dominance over India, particularly at the local level.

In the late 1980s, India faced a new problem. The neighboring island of Sri Lanka (previously known as Ceylon) was torn by violence between the majority Sinhalese, who are Buddhist, and the Tamils, a racial and religious minority (most Tamils are Hindus) living primarily in the northern part of the island. The leading Tamil rebel organization, which called itself the Elam Tigers of Tamil Elam, sought support and sanctuary in the southern Indian province of Tamil Nadu, where the population was ethnically related. In an effort to reduce the violence, India sent troops to Sri Lanka to suppress the rebels. While campaigning for reelection in the spring of 1991, Rajiv Gandhi was assassinated, reportedly by a member of the Tiger organization. For almost the first time since independence,

India faced the future without a member of the Nehru family as prime minister. Desperate, Congress leaders even considered conferring the premiership on Rajiv's Italian widow.

In the years immediately following the assassination of Rajiv Gandhi, Congress remained the leading party, but the powerful hold it had once enjoyed over the Indian electorate was gone. Rising new parties, such as the militantly Hindu Bharata Janata Party (BJP), actively vied with Congress for control of the central and state governments. Growing political instability at the center was accompanied by rising ethnic tensions between Hindus and Muslims. In the city of Bombay, the militantly Hindu Shiv Sena (Army of Siva) Party bluntly rejected the Gandhian vision of ethnic and racial harmony and attacked Muslim and foreign interests in the country.

In national elections held in May 1996, the Congress Party was badly defeated, and Prime Minister Narasimha Rao resigned from office. But the BJP, which lacked a majority of seats in the new legislature, was unable to form a government, and in the end a coalition of left and center political groups was formed. Bickering within the coalition government was intense, however, while the Congress Party, with its own president, Narasimha Rao, under investigation for corruption, tried to get its own house in order. Although economic growth continued at a gratifying pace, the growing signs of political and religious strife were disturbing.

The Land of the Pure: Pakistan since Independence

In August 1947, the new nation of Pakistan declared its independence. Unlike its neighbor India, Pakistan was in all respects a new nation, based on religious conviction rather than historical or ethnic tradition. Comprising two separate territories 2,000 miles apart, Pakistan by its very nature was unique and distinctive. West Pakistan, including the basin of the Indus River and the West Punjab, was perennially short of water and was populated by dry crop farmers and peoples of the steppe. East Pakistan, comprising the eastern parts of the old Indian province of Bengal, was made up of the marshy deltas of the Ganges and Brahmaputra rivers. Densely populated with rice farmers, it was the home of the artistic and intellectual Bengalis.

From its very origins, the new state was a product of the Muslims' wish to have their own state. Among the first to express this desire was Mohammad Iqbal (1873–1938), who founded the Muslim League in 1907 and became one of South Asia's greatest poets. He helped keep the dream alive during the final years of colonial rule.

Yet from the start, Pakistan's leaders made it clear that they did not intend to carry the logic of the Muslim League's demand for an Islamic state to extremes. Mohammad Ali Jinnah set the tone in a speech that he gave in August 1947 before a constitutional assembly

✦ **Independence Monument at Lahore.** In a speech given in a public park in Lahore in 1930, the poet Mohammad Iqbal proposed that a separate federation of Muslim provinces be created within colonial India. Iqbal's dream of creating a distinct political unit to realize the spiritual aspirations of Indian Islam was finally realized with the establishment of Pakistan in 1947. A monument erected on the spot was dedicated to Iqbal's role in the process.

convened to prepare for the transition to independence. Conceding that many had opposed the division of British India into two separate states, he argued that no other solution was possible. A united India, he maintained, would have been a "terrific disaster." Yet Jinnah insisted that now that the independence of Pakistan had been secured, it must "bury the hatchet" with the new Indian republic and concentrate on the well-being of the people. India had been conquered, he warned, because the Indian people had allowed themselves to be divided. Now Pakistan must assure freedom of religion and equal treatment for all.[3]

Mohammad Ali Jinnah's vision of a democratic society based on equal treatment for all citizens was only partly realized. The bitter division between advocates of a state based on Islamic principles and supporters of a Western-style democracy resulted in a compromise. The Constitution of 1956 described Pakistan as an "Islamic Republic, under the sovereignty of Allah," where Muslims could live their lives in accordance with "the Holy Qur'an and the Sunnah." Even though Pakistan was an essentially Muslim society, its first years were marked by intense internal conflicts over linguistic, religious, and regional issues. Most dangerous was the growing division between east and west. Many in East Pakistan felt that the government, based in the west, ignored the needs of the eastern section of the country. In 1952, riots erupted in East Pakistan over the government's decision to adopt Urdu (a Muslim version of Hindi) as the national language of the entire country. Most East Pakistanis spoke Bengali, an unrelated language. In 1958, the civilian government was overthrown by a military coup by General Ayub Khan. He expressed his views as follows:

> My task, as I saw it, was to set up institutions which should enable the people of Pakistan to develop their material, moral and intellectual resources and capacities to the maximum extent. . . . I could not convince myself that we had become a nation in the real sense of the word; the whole spectacle was one of disunity and disintegration. We were divided in two halves, each half dominated by a distinct linguistic and cultural pattern. . . . We had inherited a deep antagonism which separated the people in the countryside from the urban class. The latter represented a small minority in the total population, but it was a vocal minority and the people in the villages suffered from a sense of domination and exploitation by the elite of the towns. Then there were the regional identities, which often asserted themselves to the exclusion of the national identity. But more than anything else it was the irreconcilable nature of the forces of science and reason and the forces of dogmatism and revivalism which was operating against the unification of the people. In more precise terms the essential conflict was between the *ulema* and the educated classes.[4]

Khan believed the answer to the disunity lay in a greater emphasis on law and order and less on Western-style democratic procedures. His regime dissolved the constitution and set up a new system called "Basic Democracy" with a strong central government and a limited franchise of fewer than 100,000 voters. But the new military government was unable to curb the religious and ethnic tensions, and in 1969 Khan stepped down in favor of one of his key supporters, General Mohammad Yahya Khan.

In elections for the National Assembly in 1970, supporters of autonomy led by Sheikh Mujibur Rahman of the Awami League won a majority in East Pakistan. The Pakistani People's Party led by the populist Zulfikar Ali Bhutto won a similar majority in the west, but the military government refused to step down and declared martial law. In March 1971, negotiations between representatives of east and west broke down and East Pakistan declared its independence as the new nation of Bangladesh. Pakistani troops arrested Mujibur Rahman and attempted to restore central government authority in the capital of Dhaka, but rebel forces supported by India went on the offensive, and General Yahya Khan, who had earlier declared that "no power on earth" could separate East and West Pakistan, bowed to the inevitable. Sheikh Mujibur Rahman was released and soon became the first prime minister of the new nation of Bangladesh.

The breakup of the union between East and West Pakistan undermined the fragile authority of the military regime and led to its replacement by a civilian government under Zulfikar Ali Bhutto. But the religious tensions persisted despite a new constitution that made a number of key concessions to conservative Muslims. In 1977, a new military government under General Zia Ul Ha'q came to power with a commitment to make Pakistan a truly Islamic state. Islamic law became the basis for social behavior as well as for the legal system. Laws governing the consumption of alcohol and the position of women were tightened in accordance with strict Muslim beliefs, and Zia promised a government that would conform to Islamic principles. But after Zia was killed in a plane crash, Pakistanis elected Benazir Bhutto, the daughter of Zulfikar Ali Bhutto and a supporter of secularism who had been educated in the United States. She too was removed from power by a military regime in 1990 on charges of incompetence and corruption. Reelected in 1993, she attempted to crack down on opposition forces, but was removed once again by President Farooq Leghari amidst widespread jubilation and renewed charges of official corruption.

Problems of Poverty and Pluralism in South Asia

The leaders of the new states that emerged in South Asia after World War II all hoped that with independence their peoples would enjoy prosperity, popular participation, and national unity. Although their approaches varied, all declared their intention to build modern states based on some adaptation of the Western model. They faced a number of problems distinctive to their part of the world, however. A century of British rule had changed the subcontinent in many ways, but some basic historical realities remained. The peoples of South Asia were still overwhelmingly poor and illiterate, while the sectarian, ethnic, and cultural divisions that had plagued Indian society for centuries had not dissipated. It was a daunting challenge for even the most self-confident of political leaders.

The Politics of Communalism

Like most leaders throughout Asia and Africa, South Asian leaders tried to broaden popular participation in government and establish democratic institutions and values. Perhaps the most sincere effort was in India, where Nehru's government enacted a new constitution in 1950 that called for social justice, liberty, equality of status and opportunity, and fraternity.

The new Indian government followed the British parliamentary model. At the pinnacle was a president whose power, like that of the British monarch, was ceremonial. Executive authority was lodged in a prime minister operating through a cabinet called the Council of Ministers. Sovereignty was located in the lower house of Parliament, called the Lok Sabha, or House of the Peoples. India became a federation with power divided between the central government and fifteen separate states; in addition, a number of "union territories" were administered by the central government. Residual powers were assigned to the central government. The one-time princely states remained under the authority of their maharajas, while the president appointed governors for the other states for five-year terms. Regardless of population, all states had the same number of representatives in the Council of States, the upper chamber of Parliament.

The constitution also reflected Western models in its protection of human rights. All citizens were guaranteed protection from discrimination on the grounds of religious belief, race, caste, sex, or place of birth. The curse of untouchability was expressly forbidden (the constitution had been drafted under the direction of an untouchable, Bhimrao Ambedkar). Another clause em-bodied an early form of affirmative action: if any group was inadequately represented in public service positions, the government was empowered to enact legislation that would allow citizens of that group to be favored in future appointments.

In theory, then, India became a full-fledged democracy on the Western model. In actuality, a number of distinctive characteristics may have made the system less than fully democratic (at least in the Western sense) but may also have enabled it to survive. Though pluralist in design, India became in essence a one-party state for several years. By leading the independence movement, the Congress Party had amassed massive public support, and in the first general elections in 1951, it won a smashing victory, securing three-quarters of the seats in the Lok Sabha as well as control of the legislative assemblies in all the states.

The party retained its preeminent position in Indian politics over the next three decades, although the percentage of Congress representation in the Lok Sabha gradually began to decline. The party benefited from Nehru's personal popularity and from his ability to position the party in the middle of the political spectrum, while rivals like the Communist Party of India (CPI) on the left and the Swatantra Freedom Party on the right moved to the extremes. Congress also avoided being identified as a party exclusively for the Hindu majority by including prominent non-Hindus among its leaders and favoring measures to protect minority groups such as Sikhs and Muslims from discrimination.

Through such adept maneuvering, Nehru kept his party in power through three general elections until his death in 1964; he also lost only one state election—to the Communists in the southern state of Kerala. But Nehru's success disguised the weakening of his party and the entire democratic political system that took place under his rule. Part of the problem was the familiar one of a party too long in power. Entering office with enthusiasm and high ideals, party officials became complacent in their secure positions and all too easily fell prey to the temptations of corruption and pork-barrel politics. Although the Congress Party sincerely sought to speak for all people, especially the poor and disadvantaged, many party deputies came from privileged backgrounds and had little in common with their constituents.

Another problem was communalism. Beneath the surface unity of the new republic lay age-old ethnic, linguistic, and religious divisions. Although the government was reasonably successful in avoiding internecine religious conflict, regional and linguistic tensions were more difficult to surmount. Because of India's vast size and complex history, no national language had ever emerged from the plethora of tongues and dialects scattered throughout the subcontinent. Hindi, spoken mainly in the upper Ganges valley, was the most prevalent, but it was the native language of less than one-third of the population. During the colonial period, English had served as the official language of government, and many non-Hindi speakers in Bengal and the southern states preferred making it the official language of independent India to avoid favoring some Indians over others. But English had its own difficulties. It was spoken only by the educated elite, and it represented an affront to national pride. Eventually, India recognized fourteen official tongues, making the Lok Sabha sometimes sound like the proverbial Tower of Babel.

These problems increased after Nehru's death in 1964. Under his successors, official corruption grew, and Congress began to look like a tired party that had forgotten its ideals. Only the limited appeal of its rivals and the magic of the Nehru name carried on by his daughter Indira Gandhi kept the party in power. But Gandhi was unable to prevent the progressive disintegration of the party's power base at the state level, where regional parties (such as in Tamil Nadu in the south) or ideological ones (such as the Communists in Bengal) won the allegiance of the local population by exploiting ethnic or social revolutionary themes.

During the 1980s, religious tensions began to intensify, not only among Sikhs in the northwest but also between Hindus and Muslims. As we have seen, Gandhi's uncompromising approach to Sikh separatism led to her assassination in 1987. Under her son and successor, Rajiv Gandhi, Hindu militants at Ayodhya in northern India demanded the destruction of a mosque built on the alleged site of King Rama's birthplace, where a Hindu temple had previously existed. The mosque had reportedly been built at the order of Emperor Babur, but was now little used. Eventually, the dispute became involved in national politics, as both the Congress Party and its rivals, hoping to cultivate support among the Muslim minority, leaned to the Muslim side. In 1992, Hindu demonstrators destroyed the mosque and erected a temporary temple at the site, provoking widespread clashes between Hindus and Muslims throughout the country and shaking the Congress government of Narasimha Rao. In protest, rioters in neighboring Pakistan destroyed a number of Hindu shrines in that country. As we have seen, India's involvement in similar ethnic strife in Sri Lanka may have led to the assassination of Rajiv Gandhi in 1991.

During the mid-1990s, communal divisions have continued to intensify. As we have seen, one element in the debate is ethnic and religious, as militant Hindu groups centered around the figure of Shiv Sena leader Balasaheb Thackeray, the self-styled "Hitler of Bombay," agitate for a state that caters to the interests and aspirations of the Hindu majority, now numbering more than 700 million people. During the parliamentary debate over the formation of a new government in May 1996, opposition figures criticized the BJP for its role in fomenting anti-Muslim riots during the incident at Ayodhya, as well as for its demand that all education throughout the country take place in Hindi, a language that is widely spoken only in Hindu-majority areas in the north.

In recent years, an equally serious source of tension in Indian politics has begun to emerge around the issue of caste. Inspired by political figures such as Phoolan Devi, low-caste Indians are beginning to use the political process to struggle against the legacy of restrictions limiting their activities in Indian society. Phoolan Devi, known as the "bandit queen," spent several years in jail on the charge of taking part in the murder of twenty men from a landowning caste in the early 1980s. Members of the caste had allegedly gang-raped her while she was an adolescent. Her campaign for office during the 1996 elections was the occasion of violent arguments between supporters and opponents.

One of Phoolan Devi's sponsors is Laloo Prasad Yadav, onetime chief minister of the state of Bihar in the Ganges River valley. Yadav openly cites the memory of Mahatma Gandhi to promote the interests of the poor in his province. "I am fighting against evil," he remarked in a recent interview, "the evil of upper-caste domination of the backward and the downtrodden. And of course, the upper-caste people hate me. Now, they are thinking, he will be Prime Minister, and we will be slaves."[5]

Indian politics is thus assuming an increasingly class-based character, as members of the lower castes, representing more than 80 percent of the voting public, begin to demand affirmative action to relieve their disabilities and give them a more equal share in the national wealth. Officials at U.S. consulates in India have reportedly noticed an increase in applications for visas from members of the *brahmin* caste, who claim that they have "no future" in the new India.

The Economy

India's new leaders also realized the necessity of eliminating the social and economic inequality that had afflicted the subcontinent for centuries. Nehru's answer was socialism. Like many leaders of the Indian National Congress, he had been repelled by the excesses of European capitalism and impressed with the egalitarian principles of Marxism. Mahatma Gandhi had tapped similar sources of human idealism when he appealed for an end to the materialism, greed, and social inequality that plagued modern society. Gandhi, however, did not find the answer in Marx. In a letter to a friend in 1944, he remarked that during a recent stay in jail he had read about Marx and the Soviet experiment in Russia: "What a difference between our spinning-wheel and their machines driven by steam or electricity." Nevertheless, he added, "I prefer the snail-like speed of the spinning-wheel. The spinning-wheel is a symbol of *ahimsa* [nonviolence], and ultimately it is ahimsa that will triumph."[6]

As we have seen, Nehru did not share Gandhi's glorification of poverty. He wanted equality at a higher level of material affluence and was attracted by Lenin's effort to combine socialist ownership with industrialization. Nehru therefore instituted a series of five-year plans, which achieved some success. During the first decades of independence, India developed a relatively large and reasonably efficient industrial sector, centered on steel, vehicles, and textiles. Industrial production almost tripled between 1950 and 1965, and per capita income rose by 50 percent between 1950 and 1980, although it was still less than US$300.

By the 1970s, however, industrial growth had slowed. The lack of a modern, efficient infrastructure (transportation and communications, for example) was a problem, as was the rising price of oil, most of which had to be imported. Another problem was the relative weakness of the state-owned sector, which grew at an annual rate of only about 2 percent in the 1950s and 1960s while the private sector averaged rates of more than 5 percent. By the 1980s, many Indian officials and economists began to recommend returning some state-owned enterprises to the private sector.

India's major economic weakness, however, was in agriculture. At independence, rural production techniques were still overwhelmingly primitive. Mechanization was almost unknown, fertilizer was rarely used, and most farms were small and uneconomical because of the Hindu tradition of dividing the land equally among all male children. As a result, the vast majority of the Indian people lived in conditions of abject poverty. Landless laborers outnumbered landowners by almost two to one.

The government attempted to relieve the problem by limiting the size of landholdings, thereby forcing a redistribution of land to the poor, while encouraging farmers to form voluntary cooperatives. But both programs ran into widespread opposition and apathy. The government encouraged the states to enact legislation restricting the maximum amount of land that an individual could possess, but many landlords evaded the law by distributing their land among family members. As a result, in many instances tenants were evicted from lands they had farmed for years. In one village, the sociologist Kusum Nair found 200 families who had been deprived of their tenancy rights and reduced to working as coolies. Nor was legal action a remedy. In *Blossoms in the Dust*, Nair quotes one man as saying:

> Not a single man in this village has or will benefit by the land reforms. The tenants were so convinced that even if they went to court or to the tribunal the case would be decided in favour of the landowner that they thought it wiser to negotiate and come to terms with the landowner. So they got as much cash as they could out of him and surrendered their tenancy.[7]

Farmers were equally skeptical of the cooperatives. As one farmer said, many feared that "everyone will leave it to the other to do the work and shirk his own responsibility." Some complained that the government had attempted to consolidate landholdings by compulsory measures, and that cooperatives were always tied up in red tape and litigation. Better, they said, to return to the old system of *zamindars*, who were at least considerate of the needs of the individual farmer. To a considerable extent, these attitudes simply reflected the conservation and suspicion of change that is sometimes characteristic of farmers, but they also reveal the difficulty that the government encountered in changing attitudes in rural India.

Another crucial problem India faced was overpopulation. Even before independence, drought, soil erosion, and primitive mechanization made it difficult for the country to support its population of nearly 400 million. In the 1950s and 1960s, the population increased at a rate of more than 2 percent annually. The annual rate of population growth increased from nine per thousand in the nineteenth century to more than twenty per thousand in the 1960s. The fundamental problem, according to economist Gunnar Myrdal, was not governmental indifference; rather, conditions in South Asian villages were not conducive to birth control.

> Up to a point, bearing and rearing children can even be looked on as an investment; they offer a measure of security in illness and old age, and frequently begin to lighten their parents' work load while still in early childhood. Comparatively speaking, the setting of South Asian life is such that children are expected to fulfill obligations to parents more than parents to children.

Furthermore, in Hindu society, it is important to have male offspring.

> A young man does not acquire the status of full manhood in these societies before a son is born to him, and the Hindus believe it essential that a man's skull, after his death, be opened by a son. There is thus an urge to have a son and in view of high mortality, preferably two or three.[8]

Beginning in the 1960s, the Indian government began to adopt stiff measures to curb population growth. Indira Gandhi instituted a program combining monetary rewards and compulsory sterilization. Males who had fathered too many children were sometimes forced to undergo a vasectomy. Popular resistance undermined the program, however, and the goals were scaled back in the 1970s. Despite such efforts, India has made little progress in holding down its burgeoning population, now estimated at more than 800 million. One factor is the decline in the death rate, especially the rate of infant mortality. Whereas life expectancy for the average Indian was less than thirty years in 1947, by the 1990s it had risen to nearly fifty.

The "Green Revolution" of the 1970s at least reduced the severity of the population problem. The introduction of new strains of rice and wheat that were more productive and more disease-resistant significantly increased grain production, from about 50 million tons per year in 1950 to 100 million in 1970. But the Green Revolution exacted its own cost in the form of increased rural inequality. Only the wealthy and more enterprising peasants were able to master the new techniques and purchase the necessary fertilizer, while poor peasants were often driven off the land. Millions fled to the cities, where they live in vast slums, working at menial jobs or even begging for a living. After the death of Indira Gandhi in 1984, her son Rajiv proved more receptive to foreign investment and a greater role for the private sector in the economy. Limitations on imports of consumer goods from abroad were loosened, and beggars were driven away from the downtown streets of major cities. The results were quickly apparent. In urban areas, the pace of manufacturing and commercial activity quickened, and a newly affluent middle class began to take on the characteristics of a consumer society. India began to export more manufactured goods, such as computer software, and produced more motor scooters than any other country in the world.

The pace of change has accelerated under Rajiv Gandhi's successors, who have continued to transfer state-run industries to private hands and rely on the free market for the allocation of resources. These policies have stimulated the growth of India's prosperous new middle class, now estimated at more than 100 million, or 12 percent of the entire population. Consumerism—which was reflected in Rajiv Gandhi's abandoning the traditional *dhoti* and sporting designer loafers and sunglasses—has soared, and the sale of television sets, automobiles, videocassette recorders, and telephones has increased dramatically in recent years. Equally important, Western imports are being replaced by new products manufactured in India with Indian brand names.

The trend toward privatization and the increase in foreign investment probably played a role in stimulating the growth of the industrial sector, estimated at more than 8 percent annually in 1994 and 1995. But the pull of Nehru's dream of a socialist society remains strong. The state-owned enterprises still produce about one-half of all goods produced in the country, while high tariffs continue to stifle imports. There is a widespread fear of foreign influence over the economy, a fact eagerly played on by nationalist parties, who have brought about the cancellation of some contracts and forced some foreign firms to relocate. In one celebrated case, a combination of religious and environmental groups attempted unsuccessfully to prevent Kentucky Fried Chicken from establishing outlets in major Indian cities (see box on p. 245).

As in the industrialized countries of the West, economic growth has been accompanied by environmental damage. Water and air pollution, as well as the leakage of chemicals in industrial zones, has led to illness and death for many people living in the vicinity, and a new environmental movement has emerged, taking its cue and its tactics from similar movements in Europe and the United States. Some critics, reflecting the traditional anti-imperialist attitude of Indian intellectuals, blame Western capitalist corporations for the problem, as in the highly publicized case of leakage from the foreign-owned chemical plant at Bhopal. Much of the problem, however, comes from state-owned factories erected with Soviet aid. A recent "Citizen's Report" from the southeastern state of Andhra Pradesh charged that local developers were part of "an international network of capitalists, capitalist governments, military power and bureaucratic steel frame [an apparent reference to the entrenched power of Indian officialdom]." But not all the environmental damage can be ascribed to industrialization. The river Ganges is so polluted by human overuse that it is risky for Hindu believers to bathe in it.[9]

Moreover, many Indians have not benefited from the new prosperity. The average annual income remains under $300 per person (in U.S. dollars), and nearly one-

➤ Say No to McDonald's! ➤

One of the consequences of Prime Minister Rajiv Gandhi's decision to deregulate the Indian economy has been an increase in the presence of foreign corporations. Among them are the U.S. fast-food restaurants Pizza Hut and Kentucky Fried Chicken. Their arrival set off a storm of protest in India—from environmentalists concerned about pastures as an inefficient use of land, from religious activists angry at the killing of animals for food, and from nationalists anxious to protect the domestic market from foreign competition. In June 1995, Maneka Gandhi, daughter-in-law of Indira Gandhi and a one-time minister of the environment, took up the issue in an article in the newspaper Hindustan Times.

The great danger of such junk-food chains, she said, was their potential impact on the health of the Indian people. The food served at Kentucky Fried Chicken, she noted, was chicken-based and fried. This was "the worst combination possible for the body and can create a host of health problems, including obesity, high cholesterol, heart ailments, and many kinds of cancer." Citing a recent survey by the British Broadcasting Corporation, she said that 80 million Americans suffered from obesity and were thus prone to heart disease. What was the culprit? According to a U.S. Senate report in 1992, it was the junk-food industry.

Maneka Gandhi also criticized the environmental impact of allowing junk-food chains into the country. Modern meat production, she charged, "involves misuse of crops, water, energy, and grazing areas," resources that are badly needed in densely populated India. Animal farms, she pointed out, use enormous amounts of grain. Can India afford to use its grain to feed animals? India already diverts nearly 40 percent of its arable land to growing animal fodder. Were that grain to be consumed directly by humans, it "would nourish five times as many people as it does after being converted into meat, milk, and eggs." Each city in the United States, she concluded, has an average of 5,000 junk-food restaurants. "Is that what we want for India?"

Maneka Gandhi's arguments may have considerable merit, but like those of Mahatma Gandhi half a century earlier, the world "seems to be going in the opposite direction." Two-thirds of the annual profits from McDonald's today comes from restaurants outside the United States. Even in India, with the growth of a large middle class, the popularity of junk-food restaurants is on the rise. India, like much of the developing world, is discovering that in advanced industrial societies, "needs" become transferred to "wants," whatever the impact on the environment.

Source: *World Press Review* (September 1995), p. 47

---

third of the population lives below the national poverty line. Millions continue to live in rural slums, such as the famous "City of Joy" in Calcutta, where thousands of families live in primitive shacks and lean-tos, sharing water and toilet facilities. And while a leisured class has begun to appear in the countryside, most farm families remain desperately poor. Despite the socialist rhetoric of Indira Gandhi and other national leaders, the inequality of wealth in India is as pronounced as it is in capitalist nations like the United States. Indeed, India has been described as two nations: an educated urban India of 100 million people surrounded by 700 million impoverished peasants in the countryside.

Caste, Class, and Gender

Drawing generalizations about the effect of these changes on the life of the average Indian is difficult because of the ethnic, religious, and caste differences among Indians.

Furthermore, these differences are compounded by the vast gulf between town and country.

The major lines of division in traditional Indian society were those of class and caste. Caste membership determined all the crucial issues in life, including marriage, occupation, moral and social obligations, social status, and even eating habits. During the colonial period, the British government sporadically attempted to reduce the tyrannical hold of class restrictions on Indian society, but for the most part, it took an attitude of benign indifference. Efforts by high-class Hindus to bring about social reforms or help untouchables sometimes led to excommunication from their own caste.

The Constitution of 1950 accepted the reality of caste distinctions, but tried to eliminate their worst consequences. It guaranteed equal treatment and opportunity for all, regardless of caste, and prohibited discrimination based on untouchability, such as barring *harijans* from the village well or local restaurants. It set quotas for

◆ **Poverty and Affluence.** India is a society of blatant wealth surrounded by grinding poverty. In this photograph, the lean-to shacks of a slum present a sharp contrast to the high-rise apartments of the well-to-do in the commercial city of Bombay.

government service and membership in legislative assemblies as well as admission to institutions of higher learning.

But prejudice is hard to eliminate. Untouchability still persists, particularly in the villages, where *harijans* still perform menial tasks and are often denied fundamental human rights. Mistreatment and exploitation by landlords or government officials have led to protests and even violence in the countryside and have become a major issue in national politics. In 1990, the prime minister, V. P. Singh, attempted to woo untouchables from their traditional support for the Congress Party by acceding to their demands for higher quotas for entrance into bureaucracy and the universities. The measure led to widespread protests by members of higher castes, who claimed to be victims of reverse discrimination.

In the cities, there appears to be more reason for cautious optimism. In general, urban Indians appear less conscious of caste distinctions. Material wealth rather than caste identity is increasingly beginning to define status. The days when high-class Indians refused to eat in a restaurant unless assured that the cook was a *brahmin* are gone. Marriage and choice of occupation are more subject to individual preference than in the past. Still, the legacy of tradition is difficult to shake. Color consciousness based on the age-old distinctions between upper-class Aryans and lower-class Dravidians remains strong. Class-conscious Hindus still express a distinct preference for light-skinned marital partners. Young Indians looking for a wife or husband sometimes place detailed advertisements in the newspapers. Among the attributes most often mentioned is a light skin.

For most Indians, then, caste is simply the reality of the world they live in. Many do not question it and assume that it is the consequence of behavior in a past incarnation. As one farmer said, "How can we get other people's lands? If we are destined to be landless we must remain so."[10]

◆ **An Indian Village.** Nearly 80 percent of the Indian people still live in traditional rural villages such as the one shown here. Note the thatched roofs and the mud and straw walls plastered with dung. Housing styles, village customs, and methods of farming have changed little since they were first described by Portuguese travelers in the sixteenth century.

In economic terms, life has changed for the urban middle class, though not necessarily for the better. More income, combined with the presence of more foreign goods on the shelves, means refrigerators, color television sets, and videocassette recorders—leading, in turn, to a consumer-oriented society and greater homogenization of culture. Young Indians, like their counterparts elsewhere, are increasingly interested in rock music and new clothing styles. In that sense, the traditional ways are being steadily eroded.

Such changes have had less impact in the villages. While the newly affluent have become active consumers and often send their children to the cities to study and live, the rural poor appear to live in conditions little changed form past generations. Although some progress has been made in education since independence, rural education has been neglected, and thousands of villages remain without schools; the graduation rate from primary school in India is only 37 percent compared to more than 60 percent for all Asia. According to recent statistics, nearly 40 percent of the rural population lives below the poverty level; the vast majority live in mud-and-thatch dwellings without running water or electricity, without education, and frequently without hope. Their lives have been affected only minimally by the changes taking place in the cities or the world beyond. A visitor described one such village in the state of Uttar Pradesh in the upper Ganges valley:

I went inside every single cottage in the village. They are small mud huts with tiled roofs. The entrance is very low and many have no doors. Inside is a small walled-in yard, lined on one side with a little verandah, and one or at the most two rooms. In each room lives a whole family. Inside the room there is usually an earthen silo for storing grain, but no other furniture. The *chula* [a brick or earthen stove used for cooking] is in the verandah; straw lies scattered in the yard; in some a little grain is drying on the floor. . . . In the corner near the *chula* are piled neatly, face downward, the cooking utensils, earthen pots and a rare piece of brass.[11]

That description was written in 1961. It could easily apply to thousands of Indian villages today.

In few societies was the life of women more restricted than in traditional India. Hindu favoritism toward men was compounded by the Muslim custom of *purdah* to create a society in which males were dominant in virtually all aspects of life. Females received no education and had no inheritance rights. They were restricted to the home and tied to their husbands for life. Widows were expected to shave their heads and engage in a life of religious meditation or even to immolate themselves on their husband's funeral pyre.

Stimulated in part by Mahatma Gandhi's efforts to improve the lot of Indian women and involve them in national affairs, many women took part in the anti-colonialist activities that led to the British departure in 1947. After independence, India's leaders sought to equalize treatment of the sexes. The constitution expressly forbade discrimination based on sex and called for equal pay for equal work. Laws prohibited child marriage, *sati*, and the payment of a dowry by the bride's family. Women were encouraged to attend school and enter the labor market.

Such laws, along with the dynamics of economic and social change, have had a major impact on the lives of many Indian women. Middle-class women in urban areas are much more likely to accept employment outside the home, and many hold managerial and professional positions. Before independence, a man's pride might have been offended if his wife were employed, but now the increasing demands of the consumer society lead many families to put their creature comforts first.

The sexual attitudes and practices of urban women have changed as well. While premarital sex is probably much less common than in most Western societies, it is becoming more frequent, and the mingling of the sexes in social situations is much more acceptable than in the past, even in high-class families. On the other hand, surveys suggest that many if not most young Indians still accept the idea of arranged marriages and will ultimately accede to their parents' wishes in the choice of a spouse.

In fact, Indian women, like some Western women, tend to play a modern role in their work and in the marketplace and a more submissive, traditional one at home. The dichotomy is especially apparent in a country like India, where the choice is not simply between the traditional and the modern, but the native and the foreign. An Indian woman is often expected to be a professional executive at work and a loving, dutiful wife and mother at home (see box on p. 249)

(see box on p. 249)

Such attitudes are also reflected in the Indian movie industry, where aspiring actresses must often brave family disapproval to enter the entertainment world. Before World War II, female actors were routinely viewed as prostitutes or "loose women," and even now, such views are prevalent among conservative Indian families. Even Karisma Kapoor, one of India's current film stars and a

◆ **Bombay, Hollywood of the East.** India produces more movies than any other country in the world, including the United States. The capital of the Indian film industry is Bombay, which is sometimes dubbed India's "Bollywood." Shown here is a billboard in downtown Bombay.

➤ An Indian Critique of Feminism ⬅

Organized efforts to protect the rights of women have been under way in India since the 1970s, when the Progressive Organization for Women (POW) instituted a campaign against sexual harassment and other forms of discrimination against women in Indian society. Since then, women have been active in attacking many social problems, including alcoholism, family violence, the dowry, and poor education and sanitation, and have become a vital force in the political process. Like many of their counterparts in other parts of Asia and Africa, however, many activists for women's rights in India are critical of Western feminism, charging that it is irrelevant to their own realities. Although Indian feminists feel a bond with their sisters all over the world, they insist upon resolving Indian problems with Indian solutions.

One of the more outspoken advocates of an Indian approach to women's rights is Madhu Kishwar, founder and editor of a women's journal in the capital, New Delhi. In a recent article in the journal, she declares that Western feminism has brought a number of problems with it when applied in India. Feminists from Western countries, she explains, apply the Western concept of individualism to their analysis of gender issues. But in societies like India, "most of us find it difficult to tune in to this extreme individualism. For instance, most Indian women are unwilling to assert rights in a way that estranges them not just from their family but also from their larger community."

Anticipating the criticism that such views represent "slavery to public opinion," or the product of a worldview based on "low self-esteem," she counters that many Indian women believe that life is "a poor thing" if it serves to cut them off from others. They prefer to ensure that their own rights are protected without isolating themselves from other members of the family.

The author's second criticism of Western feminism is that it follow the statist authoritarian route to achieve social reform. "The characteristic feminist response to most social issues affecting women," she declares, "is to demand more and more stringent laws." In most cases, the result is not an improvement in women's lives, but rather "a whole spate of vicious and harmful legislation which has put even more arbitrary powers in the hands of the police and the government—powers that are routinely abused." In fact, she argues, deep-seated cultural attitudes "cannot be changed simply by applying the instruments of state repression through legal punishment." The best of laws cannot work if social opinion runs counter to them.

In her article, Madhu Kishwar has effectively pointed out that efforts to improve the rights of women must be carried out within the framework of conditions in individual societies. In fact, in some respects, conditions for women in India have vastly improved in recent decades. Yet the legacy of the past sometimes dies hard, especially in rural areas, where spousal abuse is still common and *sati*—the immolation of a widow on her husband's pyre—is still occasionally practiced. Here the government has no choice but to step in.

Source: *Far Eastern Economic Review* (May 16, 1996), p. 30

---

member of the Kapoor clan, which has produced several generations of actors, had to defy her family's ban on the family women entering show business.

Nothing more strikingly indicates the changing role of women in South Asia than the fact that in recent years, three of the major countries in the area—India, Pakistan, and Sri Lanka—have had women as prime ministers. It is worthy of mention, however, that all three—Indira Gandhi, Benazir Bhutto, and Srimivao Bandaranaike—came from prominent political families and probably owed their initial success to a husband or a father who had served as a prime minister before them.

Like other aspects of life, the role of women has changed much less in rural areas. In the early 1960s, many villagers still practiced and believed in the institution of *purdah*. A woman who went about freely in society would get a bad reputation. Female children are still much less likely to receive an education. The overall literacy rate in India today is less than 40 percent, but it is undoubtedly much lower among women. Laws relating to dowry, child marriage, and inheritance are routinely ignored in the countryside. Dowry costs have escalated rapidly in recent years and often take the form of bargaining between the families of the bride and groom. All too often, families allow female children to die in the hope of later having a son. There have been a few highly publicized cases of *sati*, although undoubtedly more women die of mistreatment or in kitchen fires. In a few instances, widows have been forcibly thrown on the funeral pyre by their in-laws.

Perhaps the most tragic aspect of continued sexual discrimination in India is the high mortality rate among girls. According to a recent UNICEF study, one-quarter of the female children born in India die before the age of fifteen as a result of neglect or even infanticide. Others are aborted before birth after gender-detection examinations. Statistically, the results are striking. Whereas in most societies the number of women equals or exceeds that of men, in India, according to a 1981 estimate, the ratio was only 933 females to 1,000 males.

Indian Art and Literature since Independence

Recent decades have witnessed a prodigious outpouring of literature in India. Most works have been written in one of the Indian languages and have not been translated into a foreign tongue. Fortunately, however, many authors choose to write in English. Known as Indo-Anglian literature, such works are written primarily for the Indian elite, or for foreign audiences. For that reason, some charge that Indo-Anglian literature lacks authenticity and is polluted by market concerns and secular attitudes. Defenders respond that the English language is sufficiently flexible to express Indian idioms, style, and temperament. As the Indo-Anglian author Salman Rushdie wrote in 1982, the English language "now grows from many roots; and those whom it once colonized are carving out large territories within the language for themselves."[12]

Because of the vast quantity of works published (India is currently the third largest publisher of English-language books in the world), only a few of the most prominent fictional writers can be mentioned here. One of the most popular is R. K. Narayan (b. 1907). Born of a *brahmin* family in Madras, Narayan is a prolific writer who appeals to readers by his use of traditional themes and the vivid descriptions of his characters.

Another popular writer today is Anita Desai. Born in New Delhi in 1937, Desai was one of the first prominent female writers in contemporary India. Her writings focus on the struggle of Indian women of all classes and ages to achieve a degree of independence from the suffocating bondage imposed on them by traditional society. In her first novel, *Cry, the Peacock*, the heroine finally seeks liberation from the surrounding male-dominated society by murdering her husband, preferring freedom at any cost to remaining a captive of traditional society.

In recent years, many female writers have taken up the cause. In *The Stars Are Trembling*, for example, the

Urdu writer Siddiqa Begum Sevharri (b. 1925) relates the story of a man who forbids his sister to teach his young wife to read. The next thing you know, he grumbles, she will want to take up tennis. But the best-known female writer in South Asia today is Taslima Nasrin of Bangladesh. She first became famous when she was sentenced to death for criticizing the Koran in one of her novels. Islam, she declared, obstructs human progress and women's equality. She now lives in exile in Europe.

Unquestionably the most controversial of modern writers in India today is Salman Rushdie (b. 1947). In *Midnight's Children*, published in 1980, the author linked his protagonist, born on the night of independence, to the history of modern India, its achievements and its frustrations. Like his contemporaries Günter Grass and the Gabriel García Márques, Rushdie used the technique of magical realism to jolt his audience into a recognition of the inhumanity of modern society and the need to develop a sense of moral concern for the fate of the Indian people, and for the world as a whole.

Rushdie's later novels have continued to attack such problems as religious intolerance, political tyranny, social injustice, and greed and corruption. His attack on Islamic fundamentalism in *The Satanic Verses* (1988) won plaudits from literary critics, but provoked widespread criticism among Muslims, including a death sentence by the Ayatollah Khomeini in Iran. His latest novel, *The Moor's Last Sigh*, turns its attention to the alleged excesses of Hindu nationalism and has been banned in India.

Indian art has also been affected by the colonial experience. Like Chinese and Japanese artists, Indian artists have agonized for more than a century over how best to paint with a modern yet indigenous mode of expression. Indeed, India's cultural schizophrenia was perhaps more poignant because its artists had to search for identity and artistic expression while living under colonial domination.

During the colonial period, Indian art went in several directions at once. One school of painters favored sentimental renderings of traditional themes; another experimented with a colorful primitivism founded on folk art. Many Indian artists painted representational social art extolling the suffering and silent dignity of India's impoverished millions. After 1960, however, most Indian artists adopted abstract art as their medium. Surrealism in particular, with its emphasis on spontaneity and the unconscious, appeared closer to the Hindu tradition of favoring intuition over reason. Yet Indian artists are still struggling to find the ideal way to be both modern and Indian.

Because of its representational character, sculpture was in eclipse during the centuries of Muslim rule. Since independence, however, sculpture and other forms of handicrafts have revived. The government has vigorously supported the revival, sponsoring local handicrafts and encouraging each village to produce its own unique artifacts in textiles, wood, clay, or metal. It is hardly surprising that India boasts an exceptional variety of folk art of high quality today.

Conclusion: The Vision of Mahatma Gandhi

India, like other non-Western countries, is clearly changing. Traditional ways are giving way to modern ones, and often the result is a society that looks increasingly Western in form, if not in content. In India, as in a number of other Asian and African societies, the distinction between traditional and modern, or native and Westernized, sometimes appears to be a simple dichotomy between rural and urban areas. Downtown areas in the major cites are modern and Westernized in appearance, but the villages have changed little since precolonial days.

Yet it would be a mistake to draw simple comparisons between what is taking place in India and what is happening in other countries undergoing a similar transition into the industrial and technological age. In India, the past appears to be more resilient, and the result is often a synthesis rather than a frontal clash between conflicting institutions and values. Unlike China, India has not rejected its past, but merely adjusted it to meet the needs of the present. Clothing styles in the streets, where the *sari* and *dhoti* continue to be popular, religious practices in the temples, and social relationships in the home all testify to the greater role of tradition in India than in China or many other societies in the region.

One disadvantage of the eclectic approach that seeks to blend the old and the new rather than choosing one over the other is that sometimes contrasting traditions and customs cannot be reconciled. Such was the lesson of the failed experiment of self-strengthening in late nineteenth-century China (see Chapter 3). In his book *India: A Wounded Civilization,* author V. S. Naipaul, a West Indian of Indian descent, charged that Mahatma Gandhi's legacy of glorifying poverty and the simple Indian village was a severe obstacle to Indian efforts to overcome the poverty, ignorance, and degradation of its past and build a prosperous modern society. Gandhi's vision of a spiritual India, Naipaul complained, was a balm for defeatism and an excuse for failure.

Certainly, India faces a difficult and sometimes painful dilemma. Some of India's problems are undoubtedly a consequence of the colonial era, but the British cannot be blamed for all of the country's economic and social ills. To build a democratic, prosperous society, the Indian people must discard many of their traditional convictions and customs. Belief in karma and inherent caste distinctions are incompatible with the democratic belief in equality before the law. These traditional beliefs also undercut the work ethic and the assumption, basic to modern Western society, that hard work earns concrete rewards. Identification with class or caste undermines the modern sentiment of nationalism.

So long as Indians accept their fate as predetermined, they will find it difficult to change their environment and create a new society. Yet their traditional beliefs provide a measure of identity and solace often lacking in other societies where such traditional spiritual underpinnings have eroded. Despite the difficulties the Indian people must surmount daily, they appear, at least on the surface, to be reasonably happy and content with their lot. Destroying India's traditional means of coping with a disagreeable reality without changing that reality would be cruel indeed. That, in a nutshell, is the cruel dilemma that India faces.

There is, of course, a final question that cannot be answered here. The vision of Mahatma Gandhi, maligned by some and treated with condescending amusement by others, was that materialism is ultimately a dead end. In light of contemporary concerns about the emptiness of life in the West and the self-destructiveness of material culture, can the Mahatma's message be ignored?

NOTES

1. Martin Green, ed., *Gandhi in India: In His Own Words* (Hanover, NH, 1987), p. 329.

2. Quoted in Larry Collins and Dominique Lapierre, *Freedom at Midnight* (New York, 1975), p. 252

3. Stephen Hay, ed., *Sources of Indian Tradition*, vol.2 (New York, 1988), p. 386

4. Quoted in ibid., pp. 399–400.

5. *New York Times*, April 26, 1996.

6. Letter to Narandas Gandhi, May 20, 1944, in Green, *Gandhi in India*, p. 309.

7. Kusum Nair, *Blossoms in the Dust: The Human Factor in Indian Development* (New York, 1961), p. 76.

8. Gunnar Myrdal, *Asian Drama: An Inquiry into the Poverty of Nations*, abridged version (New York, 1971), p. 345.

9. *New York Times*, February 6, 1991.

10. Nair, *Blossoms in the Dust*, p. 66.

11. Ibid., p. 82.

12. Salman Rushdie, "The Empire Writes Back with a Vengeance," *London Times*, July 3, 1982.

CHAPTER
12

Nationalism Triumphant: The Emergence of Independent States in Southeast Asia

First-time visitors to the Malaysian capital of Kuala Lumpur are astonished to observe on the skyline a pair of twin towers thrusting up from the surrounding buildings into the scudding monsoon clouds passing over the city. The Petronas Towers, as they are known, rise 1,483 feet from ground level and are officially recognized as the world's tallest building, 33 feet higher than the Sears Tower in Chicago.

The new building is more than an architectural achievement; it is a deliberate statement regarding the emergence of Southeast Asia as a major player on the international scene, and of the state of Malaysia as an aspiring member of the world's advanced nations. It is probably no accident that the foundations were laid on the site of the Selangor Cricket Club, symbol

of colonial hegemony in Southeast Asia. "These towers," commented one local official, "will do wonders for Asia's self-esteem and confidence, which I think is very important, and which I think at this moment are at the point of takeoff."[1]

Slightly more than a year after that remark, Malaysia and several of its neighbors were suddenly mired in a financial crisis that threatened to derail the rapid advance to economic affluence and severely undermined the "self-esteem" that the Petronas Towers were meant to symbolize. That ironic reality serves as a warning to the region's leaders that the road to industrialized status is often strewn with hidden obstacles. At the moment, the building serves as testament to the danger of excessive hubris.

The Dismantling of Colonialism in Southeast Asia

As we have seen, Japanese wartime occupation had a great impact on attitudes among the peoples of Southeast Asia. It demonstrated the vulnerability of colonial rule in the region and showed that an Asian power could defeat Europeans. The Allied governments themselves also contributed—sometimes unwittingly—to rising aspirations for independence by promising self-determination for all peoples at the end of the war. Although British Prime Minister Winston Churchill later said that the Atlantic Charter he and President Franklin D. Roosevelt had signed in August 1941 did not apply to the colonial

peoples, it would be difficult to put the genie back in the bottle again.

Some did not try. In July 1946, the United States lived up to the promise that it had made nearly ten years earlier and granted total independence to the Philippines. The Americans insisted on maintaining a military presence on the islands, however, and U.S. citizens were able to retain economic and commercial interests in the new country, a decision that would later spur charges of neocoloniallism.

The British were equally willing to bring an end to a century of imperialism in the region. As prime minister, Churchill had made it clear that he did not intend to preside over the dissolution of the British Empire. But his successor from the Labour Party, Clement Attlee, had different views. The Labour Party had long been critical of the British colonial legacy on both moral and economic grounds and, once in power, moved rapidly to grant independence to those colonies prepared to accept it. In 1948, the Union of Burma received its independence. Malaya's turn came in 1957 after a Communist guerrilla movement had been suppressed.

Other European nations were less willing to abandon their colonial possessions in Southeast Asia. The French and the Dutch both regarded their colonies in the region as economic necessities as well as symbols of national grandeur and refused to turn them over to nationalist movements at the end of the war. The Dutch returned to the East Indies and attempted to suppress a new Indonesian republic established by Sukarno, leader of the Indonesian Nationalist Party (PNI). The PNI faced internal dissension within its own ranks as the Indonesian Communist Party (PKI) broke off its wartime alliance with the nationalist movement and launched its own abortive rebellion in central Java in 1948. But the United States, which feared a Communist victory in Indonesia, pressured the Dutch to grant independence to Sukarno and his non-Communist forces, and in 1950 the Dutch finally agreed to withdraw and recognize the new Republic of Indonesia.

The situation was somewhat different in Vietnam, where the leading force in the anticolonial movement was the local Indochinese Communist Party (ICP) led by the veteran Moscow-trained revolutionary Ho Chi Minh. In August 1945, virtually at the moment of the Japanese surrender, the Vietminh Front, an alliance of

Map 12.1 Modern Southeast Asia

patriotic forces under secret ICP leadership that had been founded to fight the Japanese in 1941, launched a general uprising and seized power throughout most of Vietnam. In early September, Ho Chi Minh was elected president of a new provisional republic in Hanoi. The new government appealed to the victorious Allies for recognition but received no response, and by late fall the southern part of the country was back under French rule. Ho signed a preliminary agreement with the French recognizing Vietnam as a "free state" within the French Union, but negotiations in France broke down in July 1946, and war broke out in December. At the time it was only an anticolonial war, but it would soon become much more (see Chapter 7).

The Era of Independent States

The leaders of the newly independent states in Southeast Asia had been members of nationalist movements before the war. Although many of them had dedicated their lives to ending colonial rule, in general they admired Western political principles and institutions and hoped to apply them, subject to historical and cultural differences, in their own countries. New constitutions were patterned on Western democratic models, and multiparty political systems quickly sprang into operation.

The Search for Native Political Traditions: Guided Democracy

By the end of the 1950s, most of these budding experiments in pluralist democracy had been abandoned or were under serious threat. Some had been replaced by military or one-party autocratic regimes. In Burma, a moderate government based on the British parliamentary system and dedicated to Buddhism and nonviolent Marxism had given way to a military government under General Ne Win. In Thailand, too, where traditional kingship had been replaced by a constitutional monarchy, the military now ruled. In the Philippines, an American-style two-party presidential system survived, but democratic practices were undermined by the dominating presence of an influential landed elite.

Perhaps the most publicized example of a failed experiment in democracy was in Indonesia. When national independence was finally established in 1950, the new leaders from the PNI drew up a new constitution creating a parliamentary system of government under a titular presidency, and a central government with limited powers. The first elected president was Sukarno, one of the leading members of the PNI before World War II.

A spellbinding orator, Sukarno became widely popular among the Indonesian people and undoubtedly played a major role in creating a new sense of national identity among the disparate peoples of the Indonesian archipelago. As he stated in one fiery speech:

What was Indonesia in 1945? What was our nation then? It was only two things, only two things. A flag and a song. That is all. (Pause, finger held up as after thought) But no, I have omitted the main ingredient. I have missed the most important thing of all. I have left out the burning fire of freedom and independence in the breast and heart of every Indonesian. That is the most important thing—this is the vital chord—the spirit of our people, the spirit and determination to be free. This was our nation in 1945—the spirit of our people!

And what are we today? We are a great nation. We are bigger than Poland. We are bigger than Turkey. We have more people than Australia, than Canada; we are bigger in area and have more people than Japan. In population now we are the fifth largest country in the world. In area, we are even bigger than the United States of America. The American Ambassador, who is here with us, admits this. Of course, he points out that we have a lot of water in between our thousands of islands. But I say to him—America has a lot of mountains and deserts, too![2]

In the late 1950s, President Sukarno, exasperated at the incessant maneuvering among conservative Muslims, Communists, and the army, which had led to the overthrow of several cabinets and made long-term planning difficult if not impossible, dissolved the constitution and the pluralist political system that had functioned since independence and attempted to rule on his own through what he called "Guided Democracy." Highly suspicious of the West, Sukarno nationalized foreign-owned enterprises and sought economic aid from China and the Soviet Union, while relying for domestic support on the Indonesian Communist Party (PKI). His suspicions of the West had been sharpened by reports that an abortive rebellion against his rule launched by military forces in Sumatra had been assisted by operatives of the U.S. Central Intelligence Agency (CIA).

In turning away from the Western concept of democracy, Sukarno explained to his people that his Guided Democracy was closer to Indonesian traditions and superior to the Western variety. Indonesian democracy, in his eyes, was neither Western liberal democracy nor Soviet socialist democracy. The weakness of Western democracy was that it provided for the domination of the majority over the minority:

Indonesia's democracy is not liberal democracy. Indonesian democracy is not the democracy of the world of Montaigne or Voltaire. Indonesia's democracy is not à la America, Indonesia's democracy is not the Soviet—NO! Indonesia's democracy is the democracy which is implanted in the breasts of the Indonesian people and it is that which I have tried to dig up again, and have put forward as an offering to you. . . . If you, especially the undergraduates, are still clinging to, and being borne along the democracy made in England, or democracy made in France, or democracy made in America, or democracy made in Russia, you will become a nation of copyists.[3]

Sukarno's concept of Guided Democracy, on the other hand, would attempt to reconcile different opinions and points of view in a government operated by consensus. Guided Democracy, he asserted,

is the genuine reflection of the identity of the Indonesian nation, who since ancient times based their system of government on *musjawarah* [deliberation] and *mufakat* [consensus] with the leadership of one central authority in the hands of a *"sesepuh"*—an elder—who did not dictate, but led, and protected. Indonesian democracy since ancient times has been Guided Democracy, and this is characteristic of all original democracies in Asia.[4]

That *sesepuh*, of course, would be Sukarno himself.

The Maoist Model: New Democracy in North Vietnam

The one country in Southeast Asia that explicitly rejected the Western model was the Democratic Republic of Vietnam (DRV), or North Vietnam. On their return to Hanoi after the Geneva Conference in 1954, DRV leaders under President Ho Chi Minh opted for the Stalinist pattern of national development, based on Communist Party rule and socialist forms of ownership. Ho and his colleagues recognized, however, that the Communist utopia could not be built in a day. Following the Chinese pattern of "New Democracy" (see Chapter 9), the Vietnamese Workers' Party (the new name for the Indochinese Communist Party) declared that it would rule behind a united front composed of all progressive forces in the country, while the nationalization of industry and collectivization of agriculture were to be delayed until "mass line" policies had earned broad popular support and restored a measure of dynamism to the stagnant national economy.

Behind the facade of Ho Chi Minh's immense popularity, however, the iron hand of the party periodically showed through. A land reform program designed to distribute the land of wealthy landlords to poor peasants was implemented by brutal measures that resulted in the death of thousands of alleged "reactionaries," many of whom had loyally supported the Vietminh Front in its struggle against the French (see box on p. 257). In 1957, a brief era of political tolerance came to an end when the regime arrested a number of writers and intellectuals who had dared to criticize the party for its shortcomings. Opposition publications were closed down, and all criticism of the ruling elite was brutally suppressed.

In 1958, probably stimulated to action by the success of collectivization policies in neighboring China, the government launched a three-year plan to lay the foundation for a socialist society in North Vietnam. Collective farms were established throughout the country, and all industry and commerce above the family level were nationalized. Two years later, the regime launched a five-year plan to carry out the first stage in building a highly industrialized socialist society, but by the mid-1960s the demands of the war in the south intervened, and the plan remained a dead letter.

Problems of National Development

During the early post–World War II era, many Western social scientists assumed that Southeast Asia would pass inevitably through a predetermined process of political and economic evolution from traditional preindustrial societies to modern societies of the Western capitalist democratic model. They thought the transitional period would be difficult, but believed Western advice and technological assistance could make it easier.

As we have seen, many Southeast Asian political leaders initially accepted this assessment. New political systems incorporating Western-style institutions were established, and governments spoke bravely of a new era of growth and material prosperity. By the end of the first decade of independence, however, it was apparent that they had been overoptimistic. Fragile experiments in Western-style democracy came to an end, ethnic and ideological tensions rose to the surface, and deep-rooted economic problems set back plans for rapid economic growth.

One problem was that independence had not brought material prosperity or ended economic inequality and the domination of the local economies by foreign interests. Underdevelopment was not automatically solved by the end of colonial rule, even though foreign domination had been one of its causes. Most economies in the region were still characterized by tiny industrial sectors based on

⇒ Apologies from President Ho ⇐

After settling in Hanoi following the Geneva Agreement of 1954, the Communist government in North Vietnam decided to carry out a vast land reform campaign to confiscate the landholdings of wealthy landlords and distribute them to poor peasants. By 1965, more than half the total amount of farmland in the northern provinces had changed hands. Unfortunately, in the process, many individuals who had served in the resistance movement were criticized and attacked by overzealous land reform cadres. After a stormy meeting of the Central Committee in the summer of 1956, President Ho Chi Minh apologized to the people, while justifying the program in its main outlines. Land reform, he explained, "is an anti-feudal class struggle, and a bitter, fierce, and earth-shaking revolution." For this reason, some party cadres (party officials or land reform workers) "have not correctly grasped our policies and have not correctly followed the mass line." Moreover, he conceded, "the leadership by the party Central Committee and the government has sometimes lacked in concreteness, inspection and oversight." As a result, the land reform program was accompanied by "some errors and shortcomings—in bringing about unity in the rural villages, in defeating the enemy, in the process of reorganization, in the policy of assigning agricultural taxes and so forth."

The party leadership, he assured his compatriots, had carefully reviewed the errors that had been committed and "have already adopted measures to correct them." Those "who have been incorrectly classified as landlords and rich peasants" would have their records reviewed, and if necessary, their rights restored. In cases where statistical errors had been made in registering the amount of land under individual ownership, that mistake, too, "must be rectified."

President Ho's speech was an unprecedented admission that party leaders had erred in carrying out the Vietnamese Revolution. Yet it is clear from his words that the error, in their view, was not in the program per se, but in the way it was carried out at the local level. The basic goal of confiscating the land of the wealthy and distributing it to the poor was correct, and would continue to be carried out. But in a tacit recognition that the party leadership had been overly zealous in drafting the program, General Secretary Truong Chinh and other bureaucrats directly connected with carrying out the program were dismissed from office.

Source: "Letter to Villages and Cadres on the Occasion of the Completion in the Main of Land Reform," in Ho Chi Minh, *Toan Tap* [Complete Works] (Hanoi: Su That, 1987), pp. 506–510.

---

light industry and the processing of raw materials for export, backward agricultural sectors, and burgeoning populations; they lacked technology, educational resources, capital investment, and leaders trained in developmental skills. It is not surprising, then, that independence did not immediately bring rapid economic growth and an improvement in the standard of living.

The presence of widespread ethnic, linguistic, cultural, and economic differences also made the transition difficult. In Burma, for example, one-third of the population was composed of a variety of ethnic groups not directly related to the majority Burmese population. Some were Christians; others were Muslims or held shamanistic beliefs. Many of them resented the efforts of the devout Buddhist prime minister U Nu to impose his unique combination of Marxist and Theravada Buddhist values on the entire population. Some ethnic groups allied with the local Burmese Communist Party to launch a rebellion against the government.

Ethnic differences also caused problems in Malaya. The majority Malays—most of whom were farmers—feared economic and political domination by the local Chinese minority, who were much more active and experienced in industry and commerce. When the British controlled the area, colonial officials had kept the two communities apart, while recognizing the suzerain political power of the local Malay sultanates. With independence, however, many Malays feared that Chinese economic dominance would intensify and extend into politics. These Malay fears were expressed in a provocative book by Mahathir Mohamad (currently Malaysia's prime minister) published in 1970. Mahathir cited numerous cases of discrimination in the employment of Malays by Chinese or other non-Malays and concluded that

> from these inequalities of opportunity spring other inequalities, such as the miserable houses of the Malays compared to the houses of the non-Malays, the poor health of the Malays against the vigor of the non-Malays, the high death and infant mortality rates of the Malays compared to non-Malays, the lack of savings and capital of the Malays when compared to the non-Malays.[5]

In 1961, the Federation of Malaya, whose ruling party, the United Malays National Organization (UMNO), was dominated by Malays, integrated former British possessions on the island of Borneo into a new Union of Malaysia in a patent move to increase the non-Chinese proportion of the country's population. Similar reasons dictated the expulsion of the island of Singapore three years later. (Once a British Crown colony and a major naval base to maintain a British military present in Southeast Asia, the tiny island of Singapore—three-quarters of whose population were ethnic Chinese—had been attached to the new Federation of Malaya in 1959.) Yet periodic conflicts persisted as the Malaysian government adopted a program to guarantee the Malay peoples control over politics and a larger role in the economy. In 1969, tensions between Malays and Chinese erupted into violent confrontations on the streets of Malaysian cities.

In some cases, the tensions were economic or regional rather than ethnic. In Indonesia, for example, many urban intellectuals, supported by poor rice farmers on the inner islands of Java and southern Sumatra, advocated a socialist approach that would limit Western investment and equalize income among the Indonesian people. Prosperous planters and merchants on the outer island of Sumatra, on the other hand, preferred more free enterprise and a good relationship with the West, their primary market for exports. Such tensions contributed to the collapse of Indonesian democracy and the institution of Sukarno's experiment with Guided Democracy in 1959.

Some of these problems are common to developing societies everywhere and were experienced by many European countries during the early stages of industrialization. Many Southeast Asians, however, experienced lingering doubts about whether Western-style democracy and materialistic culture were relevant to their region. They questioned whether Western secular institutions and values were appropriate in societies that traditionally ascribed a charismatic or semireligious character to their leaders (in Burma, for example, the ruler was viewed by his subjects as an incipient Buddha-to-be). Similar doubts were expressed about the introduction of capitalism into Southeast Asian societies. In Burma, Prime Minister U Nu said that Marxist ideas of economic equality were more appropriate to a Buddhist society than the capitalist search for profit and launched what he called a "Burmese Way to Socialism."

In the initial enthusiasm after independence, many Southeast Asian political leaders submerged their doubts as they tried to imitate the West. But as disillusion set in, some began to search for a more eclectic approach

◆ **The Freedom Monument in Jakarta.** President Sukarno ordered the erection of a massive monument to freedom (*Merdeka*) in downtown Jakarta. At the base of the obelisk is a museum portraying the key events in the Indonesian struggle for independence from the Dutch. Many Indonesians have criticized Sukarno for spending precious funds on a monument while the country's many social and economic needs were neglected.

that would combine native and foreign elements. A prime example we have seen was Sukarno's concept of Guided Democracy in Indonesia.

The main opposition to Sukarno and his plans came from the army and conservative Muslims. Both resented Sukarno's increasing reliance on the PKI. The Muslims were further upset by his refusal to consider a state based on Islamic principles. One of the so-called five principles (*pantja sila*) popularized by Sukarno as the basic goals of the Republic of Indonesia was religious freedom. As a representative of the Muslim community stated in 1957, the heroes and patriots of the Indonesian Revolution sacrificed their lives not only for independence

> but for one idealism, for one ideal inspired by the goal and purpose of their lives: to devote themselves to God, praise be Him the Most High, by upholding His Word and by expecting merely His grace. They fought to place Islam in the life of our society and state. They fought to establish the Sovereignty and the Law of Islam.[6]

The combined opposition of the army and the orthodox Muslims proved too much for Sukarno to surmount. In 1965, military officers launched a coup d'etat that severely restricted his authority. The coup, whose origins are still widely debated, provoked a mass popular uprising that resulted in the slaughter of several hundred thousand suspected Communists, many of whom were overseas Chinese, long distrusted by the Muslim majority. In 1967, Sukarno was forced from office and replaced by a military government under General Suharto.

The new government made no pretensions of reverting to democratic rule, but it did restore good relations with the West and sought foreign investment to repair the country's ravaged economy. But it also found it difficult to placate Muslim demands for an Islamic state. As in Pakistan, pressure for the strict application of Islamic law continued in Indonesia despite efforts by the government to repress it. In a few areas, including western Sumatra, militant Muslims took up arms against the state.

Indonesia was not the only country in the region to abandon democratic institutions for centralized power. In Burma and Thailand, the military seized control from civilian governments in the interest of law and order. Both promised to return the government to civilian authorities but failed to do so. In the Philippines, President Ferdinand Marcos discarded democratic restraints that had been widely abused by traditional landed elites, who manipulated the system for their own political and economic benefit, and established his own centralized control under a program called the "New Order." In South Vietnam, Ngo Dinh Diem and his successors paid lip service to the Western democratic model, but ruled by authoritarian means.

In recent years, many Southeast Asian societies have shown signs of evolving toward more democratic forms. One example is the Philippines, where the dictatorial Marcos regime was overthrown by a massive public uprising in 1986 and replaced by a democratically elected government under President Corazon Aquino, the widow of a popular politician assassinated under mysterious circumstances a few years earlier. Although Aquino showed few political skills and was unable to resolve many of the country's chronic economic and social difficulties, her successor, Fidel Ramos, has had somewhat more success, and the Philippines is exhibiting a few promising signs of entering a period of political stability. Here, too, however, ethnic tensions roil the waters as Muslim elements in the southern island of Mindanao have mounted a terrorist campaign in their effort to obtain autonomy or independence.

In other areas, the results have been mixed. Although Malaysia is a practicing democracy, tensions persist between Malays and Chinese as well as between secular and orthodox Muslims. In neighboring Thailand, to prevent political unrest, the military has found it expedient to hold national elections for civilian governments, but the danger of a military takeover is never far beneath the surface. Meanwhile, widespread corruption has poisoned the political system to such an extent that aspiring candidates purchase not only the votes of individuals, but of families and entire polling districts as well.

During the mid-1990s, tensions between authoritarian traditions and rising demands for democratic government have been especially sharp in Indonesia. In the spring and summer of 1996, violent protests by students demanding increased freedoms and by Muslims demanding a larger role for Islam in society prompted the Suharto government to arrest many dissidents and warn against the possibility of the revival of the Communist Party. One of the leaders of the student movement was a daughter of onetime president Sukarno. In elections held a few months later, President Suharto and the government party, called the Golkar, were reelected to power with relatively little difficulty, but popular anger at Suharto's family (many of whom have reportedly used their position to amass considerable wealth) and the regime's close ties with wealthy businessmen of Chinese extraction have exacerbated traditional suspicions between native Indonesians and the minority population and provoked demands for drastic political change.

Even in Vietnam, where the Communist Party has long staked out its exclusive claim to power, the trend in recent years has been toward a greater popular role in the governing process. In December 1986, the party launched a new program labeled *Doi Moi* (Renovation), marked by a promise to reduce the power of the party over all aspects of society while encouraging greater popular participation in the governing process. Elections for the unicameral parliament are more open than in the past, and local authorities lobby effectively in Hanoi for

◆ The Ho Chi Minh Mausoleum.
President Ho Chi Minh died in 1969, six years before the end of the Vietnam War, but his legacy as father of his country and its leading revolutionary continues to serve as a vital symbol of the Vietnamese people. A mausoleum was erected in his honor in the Vietnamese capital of Hanoi.

the interests of their constituents. As in neighboring China, however, the government is suspicious of Western forms of democracy, and represses all forms of criticism aimed at the party's guiding role over society and the state.

Only in Myanmar (formerly Burma), where the military has been in complete control since the early 1960s, have the forces of greater popular participation been virtually silenced. Even there, however, the power of the ruling regime of General Ne Win, known as SLORC, has been vocally challenged by Aung San Huu Kyi, the daughter of one of the heroes of the country's struggle for national liberation after World War II.

The trend toward more representative systems of government, however halting and imperfect, is due in part to increasing affluence and the growth of an affluent and educated middle class. Although Indonesia, Myanmar, and the three Indochinese states are still overwhelmingly agrarian, Malaysia and Thailand have been undergoing relatively rapid economic development, and tiny Singapore with its educated and industrious workforce has become a leading exporter of manufactured goods and a major oil-refining center for oil-producing nations throughout the region. Malaysia has benefited from exports of rubber, tin, and palm oil, Thailand from tourism

and a major U.S. military presence during the Vietnam War, and Singapore from strong leadership and the absence of an impoverished hinterland. Indonesia, although still hindered by a large urban and rural proletariat, has vast economic resources and may be able to enter the traditional stage to an advanced industrial society. Yet here, too, traditional inhibitions often hamper efforts to foster the entrepreneurial spirit. According to an Indonesian author,

> some years back, Indonesian shopkeepers in Jakarta . . . unblushingly protested to the government about "unfair practices" by a Chinese shopkeeper, who tried to boost his sales by giving away prizes (including motorbikes) to people who came to buy at his store. When the government-owned enterprises lost money, the first reaction was always to increase the price of their services. No attempt was made to look into their own inefficiency and mismanagement.[7]

Economic growth will undoubtedly lead to political and social changes. Yet the nations of the region likely will continue to avoid a crude imitation of Western models of development. All show a distinct preference for strong centralized leadership and the fostering of community spirit rather than Western individualism. Former prime minister Lee Kuan-yew, longtime leader of Singapore, for example, has rejected the Western liberal

⇒ An Asia That Can Say No ⇐

In recent years, many Asian leaders have become increasingly unhappy at Western criticisms of Asia's record in the area of human rights. One of the most vocal spokespersons for this point of view is Mahathir Mohamad, currently prime minister of Malaysia. In a book titled The Asia That Can Say No, *authored jointly with the Japanese politician Shintaro Ishiwara (see Chapter 15), Mahathir voices the suspicion that the United States and other Western countries have deliberately used the issue of human rights as a means of slowing economic growth in competing countries in East and Southeast Asia. As one Japanese journalist remarked, "Mahathir goes over well in Japan because he says what a lot of us think but don't dare to say openly."*

In a recent essay, Vietnamese Vice Foreign Minister Tran Quang Co argued that developing countries like Vietnam should not be held to the same standard on this issue as the advanced countries of the West. In principle, he said, human rights should become "a field for cooperation rather than a battleground of confrontation." But for this to happen, it is necessary to keep in mind that human rights "are a product of human evolution and as such evolve with time, being nei-

ther absolute nor immutable." History shows, for example, that "economic rights have always been as important as, if not more than, civil and political rights." Nor are human rights mere "individual rights." They also include "the collective right of communities and nations to self-determination; the right to sovereign use of national natural resources, the right to development, the right to equality of status among nations."

To many Western observers, such comments too easily ignore that some rights are universal to all societies and are thus not subject to the laws of evolution. Critics also argue that only in societies where individual human rights are recognized can a technologically advanced economic sector be stabilized. Still, Tran Quang Co's comments echo the feelings of many other Asians, who resent preaching on the issue of human rights from countries whose own performance during the colonial era, and indeed within their own borders today, is hardly unblemished.

Source: *Far Eastern Economic Review*, February 24, 1994, p. 18; August 4, 1994, p. 17.

---

democratic and individualist model. He has persistently urged his people to follow the more communitarian Japanese model and to rely on their inherited Confucian traditions to foster community spirit, a work ethic, and high moral fiber. The authoritarianism inherent in Lee's interpretation of these values has aroused criticism in the West and even within Singapore itself. But for the most part, Singaporeans appear willing to accept the bargain as the necessary price for political stability and economic prosperity.

Lee Kuan-yew's cue has been taken up by other leaders in the region. Malaysian Prime Minister Mahathir Mohamad is a prominent critic of the Western tendency to sermonize about the virtue of democracy and human rights to Asians. In a recent book titled *The Asia That Can Say No*, coauthored with Shintaro Ishihara, Mahathir counsels his Asian readers to resist U.S. efforts to promote American values, warning them that the United States is trying to hold back economic growth in the region for its own benefit. He even questions the value of the U.S. security shield, arguing that Japan should step in to fill the gap (see box above).

In the late summer of 1997, the assumption of many observers that the rapid pace of economic development would continue into the indefinite future, thus bringing about liberalization in the political arena, was suddenly shaken when a financial crisis swept through the region. The problem was triggered by a number of factors, including excessive government expenditures on ambitious developmental projects leading to growing budget deficits, irresponsible lending and investment practices by financial institutions, and an overvaluation of local currency relative to the U.S. dollar. One underlying cause of these problems was the prevalence of back room deals between politicians and business leaders that temporarily enriched both groups at the cost of eventual economic dislocation.

As local currencies plummeted in value, the International Monetary Fund (IMF) agreed to step in to provide assistance but only on the condition that the governments concerned permit greater transparency in their economic systems and allow market forces to operate more freely, even at the price of bankruptcies and the loss of jobs. While there were signs that some political leaders recognized the serious nature of their problems and were willing to take steps to resolve them, the political cost of such changes remained uncertain. The first casualty was President Suharto, who was forced to step down after a popular uprising in the spring of 1998.

Daily Life: Town and Country in Contemporary Southeast Asia

Like much of the non-Western world, most Southeast Asian countries today can still be classified as dual societies. Their modern cities resemble those in the West while the villages in the countryside often appear little changed from precolonial days.

The contrast between town and country in modern Southeast Asia has been eloquently described by the Thai author Phya Anuman Rajadhon in *Life and Ritual in Old Siam*. The cities, he writes (almost certainly referring to Bangkok), are crowded with thronging humans. There is a deafening din of people and of cars almost all the time. One cannot see anything at a distance, for buildings and shops and houses intervene almost everywhere. The atmosphere is hot and oppressive and impure; one breathes with difficulty. Foul and rotten odors assail the nose frequently. Some places are disgustingly dirty and cluttered. What a sharp contrast to life in the country:

> Not too far out from the city, one sees great vacant space as far as the eye can reach; clumps of trees rise at regular intervals. In the extreme distance one sees the treetops looking as if placed in orderly rows. The sky is clear to the distant horizon. . . . At long intervals one sees a few people in the distance. The air one breathes feels pure and fresh. This is the conditions of the meadows and fields outside of town.[8]

No one who has traveled in contemporary Southeast Asia can fail to be affected by the difference between the peaceful rural scenes of palm trees and rice paddies stretching as far as the eye can see and the congested and polluted atmosphere of the region's modern cities. In Bangkok, Manila, and Jakarta, broad boulevards lined with shiny white and silver skyscrapers alternate with muddy lanes passing through neighborhoods packed with wooden shacks topped by thatch or rusty tin roofs. Soft drink cans and coconut shells are scattered along the roadway, and there is a pervasive smell of urine, rotting fruit, and frying meat.

Nevertheless, millions of Southeast Asians in recent decades have fled from the peaceful rice fields to the urban slums. To many Southeast Asians, especially the young, the village represents boredom and poverty, while the city represents excitement and opportunity. Although most urban jobs are menial, such as selling cheap clothing or fruit at a roadside stall or driving a pedicab or (for the fortunate) a taxicab, the earnings are better than they can get in their villages. A few urban migrants become even more affluent, and their success inspires others to come to the cities.

In recent years, a number of manufacturing companies in the advanced countries have taken advantage of these conditions to establish factories in Indonesia and other states in the region. The practice has provoked criticism in the United States, where labor groups and human rights activists charge that workers in such factories—mostly young women—are underpaid and forced to labor in substandard conditions. It is true that daily wages are often less than US$2.50 a day, and that fires and other accidents have taken the lives of workers in a few celebrated cases. For many employees, however, these jobs represent opportunity. "Thanks to God, it's enough money for me," said one young women at a Nike factory in Serang. She claims to be able to save more than half her salary and send it back to her family. Her father is a schoolteacher.[9]

The urban migrants change not only their physical surroundings but their attitudes and values as well. Many experience feelings of deracination—a sense of being uprooted from their family and village. Sometimes the move leads to a decline in traditional beliefs. Surveys suggest, for example, that belief in the existence of nature and ancestral spirits tends to decline among the urban populations of Southeast Asia, although it has not disappeared. Even major religions like Buddhism and Islam sometimes suffer from the secular focus of urban living.

In Thailand, for example, Buddhism has recently come under heavy pressure from the rising influence of materialism. Although temple schools still provide a ladder to upward mobility for thousands of rural youths whose families cannot afford the cost of public education, the behavior of Buddhist monks—many of whom chafe under the vows of chastity and fasting—has aroused deep concern among many observers. In one highly publicized recent case, a handsome young monk, whose popular appeal is reminiscent of the TV evangelists in the United States, was involved in a sex scandal with some of his female followers. The case aroused a major controversy, in part because the church leadership had made use of his charismatic personality as a means of raising funds for Buddhist causes.

The increasingly secular attitude in Thailand and other Southeast Asian societies has also been linked to

the rising incidence of drugs, pornography, and crime throughout the region. Family values appear to be eroding. Surveys indicate that many parents spend less than fifteen minutes a day with their preschool children, compared with an average of about forty-five minutes in the United States. Care for the elderly has also suffered. As one observer complained, "Times have changed. Just ten years ago, people used to live under the same roof and work in nearby fields. Today, people work in the city or in factories. Either they have moved away entirely or don't spend as much time at home"[10] Some countries have attempted to reverse such trends. In Malaysia, an Islamic revival among ethnic Malays has led to a greater acceptance of the traditional Muslim code of behavior.

Perhaps the greatest changes in lifestyle have taken place within the middle class and the small but influential financial and professional elites. Western values, tastes, and customs have deeply penetrated the lives of the affluent urban minority throughout Southeast Asia. A taste for Western films, novels, food, and alcohol and the conspicuous consumption of luxury goods like expensive automobiles, clothing, and household appliances have become common among the wealthy throughout the region. Most speak English or another Western language, and many have been educated abroad.

The urban elites have not lost their cultural roots entirely, however. Buddhist, Muslim, and even Confucian beliefs remain strong, even in cosmopolitan cities such as Bangkok, Jakarta, and Singapore. According to unconfirmed reports, when new buildings are erected, local shamans are consulted to avoid irritating the nature spirits of the earth. As the Indonesian intellectual and journalist Mochtar Lubis observes, "deep in the subconscious of the Indonesian—even in that of someone who is Western-educated and has attended a university in Europe or America—is a belief in mystical, supernatural powers, in spirits that possess the power to aid and hurt man."[11] According to Lubis, Sukarno himself believed in supernatural powers and carried a sacred kris (dagger) as a charm to ward off evil spirits. At the same time, Lubis points out, Sukarno took no chances and rode in a bulletproof car built in the United States.

This preference for the traditional also shows up in lifestyle. Native dress, or at least an eclectic blend of Asian and Western dress like the leisure suit, is still common. Traditional music, art, theater, and dance remain popular, although Western rock music has become fashionable among the young and Indonesian filmmakers complain that Western films are beginning to dominate the market. Southeast Asian novels and short stories, although Western in form, still focus on local problems or political issues. Sometimes, as in Indonesia, books and plays carry an implicit political message, as authors express their discontent with the current political leader.

This Western veneer is less readily apparent among the less affluent urban dwellers. Yet their lifestyles are changing as well, stimulated by widespread access to television (including, in many countries, old American television programs like *Dallas, Kojak,* and *All in the Family*) and the rapid expansion of the educational system. Indeed, the spread of literacy is one of the most impressive aspects of the social changes taking place in Southeast Asia. The literacy rate is well above 80 percent in Singapore, Thailand, and the Philippines, and more than 75 percent even in such predominantly rural societies as Myanmar and Indonesia.

This superficially Westernized way of life is less prevalent in the three states of Indochina. Isolated from much of the capitalist world since the end of the Vietnam War in 1975, most cities in Vietnam, Laos, and Cambodia lack the visible evidence of Western influence—the skyscrapers, expensive automobiles, and traffic jams and pollution found elsewhere in the region. Automobiles are scarce, and most residents travel by bicycle or motor bus (mostly of Soviet manufacture, and often a generation old). Yet even such cities as Hanoi and Phnom Penh are not beyond the reach of the all-pervasive influence of Western culture. Coca-Cola, fashionable sneakers, and sweatshirts (or at least a facsimile thereof) are for sale in the shops, and a concert featuring the music of the Beatles or the Rolling Stones gathers immense crowds of adolescents.

The integration of Southeast Asia into the emerging world culture is less advanced, of course, in rural areas, where little has changed since precolonial days. Most peasants still live in traditional housing and adjust their lives to the annual harvest cycle. Travel is by cart or bicycle or on foot. Telephones are rare—one for every fifty people in Thailand, and for nearly two hundred in Indonesia. Only rarely does the average rural Southeast Asian visit the major cities. Yet through the spread of electricity, radio and television (although relatively few peasants can as yet afford to buy their own set), and newspapers, changes are coming to the countryside as well.

Understandably, traditional beliefs are more persistent in the villages than in the big cities. A survey taken in a Thai village in the early 1970s found that two-thirds of the respondents believed in the existence of nature spirits, although only one-third had actually seen one. An anthropologist in the same country discovered that some villagers were using Coca-Cola bottles as a religious offering. The Buddhist temple or the mosque remains the center of everyday life. Although public education has replaced temple schools in some countries, in others they continue to attract students as does the *pesantren* (the traditional Muslim school) in Muslim Indonesian and Malaysia.

The increasing inroads made by Western culture have caused anxiety in some countries. In Malaysia, for example, fundamentalist Muslims criticize the prevalence of pornography, hedonism, drugs, and alcohol in Western culture and have tried to limit their presence in their own country. Signs stating "Dada means Death" (death to drugs) are a graphic illustration of what happens to drug pushers, whether native or foreign. The Malaysian government has attempted to limit the number of U.S. entertainment programs shown on local television stations and has replaced them with shows on traditional themes.

Neighboring countries have adopted similar measures. Pornography, long hair, and even chewing gum have been forbidden in Singapore. In Myanmar, where the military government has been suspicious of all foreigners, until recently tourists were allowed to remain inside the country for only seven days and were not permitted to walk unescorted on the streets of the capital, Rangoon. Even in easygoing Thailand, concern has been expressed that Christian missionaries have been undermining the Buddhist character of Thai society. A more immediate problem, however, is the rapid spread of AIDS, a consequence of the Thai government's tolerance of widespread prostitution as a means of encouraging tourism.

One of the most significant changes that has taken place in Southeast Asia in recent decades is in the role of women in society. In general, women in the region have historically faced fewer restrictions on their activities and enjoyed a higher status than women elsewhere in Asia. Nevertheless, they were not the equal of men in every respect. In Vietnam, Confucian precepts imported from China limited women's legal rights and occupational opportunities. In Buddhist and Muslim societies, women ranked lower on the social scale than men and generally did not play an active role in religious ritual. But women did not suffer from the extreme policies of seclusion, social degradation, and even physical mutilation, such as the foot-binding practiced in many other societies in precolonial times. In that sense, it is clear that the relatively egalitarian traditions of early Southeast Asian societies moderated the rigid sexual discrimination practiced in other Confucian and Muslim societies.

The advent of colonial rule brought some minor improvements in the status of women in Southeast Asia. With the opening of government-supported public schools, females for the first time began to be educated alongside males. Colonial rule also opened up new career opportunities for women. The vast majority of women remained in the home or in the rice fields, but some found jobs as maids or cooks in the homes of the wealthy or worked in the factories in the growing colonial cities. Daughters of elite families occasionally even went abroad for higher education.

But perhaps the most striking effect of the colonial period was the arousing of women's consciousness. In the 1910s, for example, a magazine specifically for women appeared in French Indochina. Though it tended to concentrate on the woman's role as wife, mother, and homemaker, its very existence focused attention on the fact that women were expected to become educated and to play an active role in modern society. In the 1920s, the publication of a second magazine, called *Women's News*, revealed the attitudinal changes that had taken place in a few short years. Articles in *Women's News* reflected the growing demand for equality of status, education, and occupation that was occurring in many Western countries. The magazine catered to the small but vocal elites in Hanoi and Saigon, and its advertisements were similar to those in magazines aimed at the sophisticated and the affluent in Europe and the United States.

Such direct attacks on traditional gender inequality were somewhat less common elsewhere in Southeast Asia, because outside Vietnam, rigid Confucian social ethics were found only in local Chinese communities and women in general were less restricted than in Vietnam. In the Dutch East Indies, women benefited from the modernist movement among many Western-educated Muslims, which attempted to reconcile traditional fundamentalist beliefs with contemporary Western notions of social equality. Women were not cloistered from males as in many other Islamic societies, and young women were sometimes permitted to attend the religious schools set up by modernist elements to introduce young Indonesians to Muslim teachings. In some cases, they even attended coeducational classes.

With independence, the trend toward liberating Southeast Asian women continued. Virtually all of the constitutions adopted by the newly independent states granted women full legal and political rights, including the right to work. In some respects, that promise has been fulfilled. In countries throughout the region, women have increased opportunities for education and have entered new careers previously reserved for men. Social restrictions on female behavior and activities have been substantially reduced, if not entirely eliminated. Women have become more active in politics, and in 1986, Corazon Aquino became the first woman to be elected president of a country in Southeast Asia. The wife of her predecessor, Imelda Marcos, was influential in Filipino politics in her own right.

Yet women are not truly equal to men in any country in Southeast Asia. Sometimes the distinction is simply a matter of custom. In Thailand, women are not permitted to enter monkhood. In Vietnam, women are legally equal to men, yet until recently no women had served on the Communist Party's ruling Politburo. In Thailand, Malaysia, and Indonesia, women rarely hold senior positions in government service or in the boardrooms of major corporations. Similar restrictions apply in Myanmar, although Aung San Huu Kyi is the leading figure in the democratic opposition movement.

Sometimes, too, women's rights have been undermined by a social or religious backlash. The revival of Islamic fundamentalism stemming from the Iranian Revolution has had an especially strong impact in Malaysia, where Malay women are expected to cover their bodies and wear the traditional Muslim headdress. Women who dress in skimpy bathing suits at the beach have been criticized or even physically attacked by conservative Muslims. A local consumer group has called for a ban on the sale of Barbie dolls, on the grounds that they give a warped idea of female beauty and attractiveness. Even in non-Muslim countries, women are still expected to behave demurely and exercise discretion in all contacts with the opposite sex. Yet the signs of change are everywhere. In predominantly Muslim Indonesia, talk radio programs provide advice to their listeners on how to gain greater sexual satisfaction from their marriage.

Cultural Trends

Culture is flourishing today in most countries in Southeast Asia, as writers, artists, and composers attempt to synthesize international styles and themes with local tradition and experience. In the field of literature, the novel has become increasingly popular, as writers seek to find the best medium to encapsulate the national experience in coping with the dramatic changes that have taken place in the region in recent decades. Although many contemporary novels reflect trends taking place in the West, some of the best writers from the region adopt a strong political orientation, as they take their stand on key issues relevant to the lives of their compatriots.

The best-known writer in postwar Indonesia—at least to readers abroad—is Pramoedya Toer. Born in 1925 in eastern Java, he joined the Indonesian nationalist movement in his early twenties while serving as an editor of a PNI newspaper. Arrested in 1965 on the charge of being a Communist, he spent the next several years in prison. While under incarceration he began writing his four-volume *Buru Quartet*, which recounts in fictional form the story of the struggle of the Indonesian people for freedom from colonial rule and the autocratic regimes of the independence period. He remains under house arrest in Java today, and his novels are forbidden to circulate in Indonesia. In a recent interview with a foreign journalist, he praised the Indonesian youth of today, but called on them to avoid violence and to struggle for freedom by democratic means. "Without democracy," he contends, "all institutions that exercise power are nothing but mafia."[12]

As in Indonesia, novelists in contemporary Vietnam seek to play the dual role of writing good fiction and expressing the sometimes brutal realities of life in their country. During the Vietnam War, writers were expected to follow the tradition of socialist realism, praising the firm leadership of the Communist Party and the heroism and self-sacrifice of the people in their struggle for independence and socialism. In recent years, many fiction writers have braved the displeasure of the regime by presenting a realistic portrayal of individual Vietnamese living under the strain of war and socialist transformation. Among the most talented of contemporary Vietnamese novelists is Duong Thu Huong (b. 1947).

A member of the Vietnamese Communist Party who served on the front lines during the Sino-Vietnamese war in 1979, she later became outspoken in her criticism of the party's failure to carry out democratic reforms and was briefly imprisoned in 1991. Undaunted by official pressure, she has written several novels that express the horrors experienced by guerrilla fighters during the Vietnam War and the cruel injustices perpetrated by the regime in the cause of building socialism. In *Paradise of the Blind*, published in 1988, she portrays the trials of a family buffeted by war, poverty, and the injustices committed by the party during the land reform program in the 1950s. Repulsed by the corrupt habits of her uncle, a onetime party cadre with a fanatical belief in Marxist utopia, the young woman is reassured by a male friend:

> He swept a strand of hair off his face. "Little Sister, you must understand, even if it hurts. Your uncle is like a lot of people I've known. They've worn themselves out trying to

recreate heaven on earth. But their intelligence wasn't up to it. They don't know what their heaven is made of, let alone how to get there. When they woke up, they had just enough time to grab a few crumbs of real life, to scramble for it in the mud, to make a profit—at any price. They are their own tragedy. Ours, as well."[13]

Although music and art in Southeast Asia are less imbued with political themes, they too display the effort to meld East and West in a fruitful synthesis for local consumption. In Indonesia, for example, traditional gamelan music remains popular, although it has changed considerably under the impact of modern ways. Other popular musical styles have evolved out of Indonesia's growing familiarity with the West. Some reflect a "dreamy" style of music popular in the immediate postwar period; others mix Western rock with Indian film music or Middle Eastern styles.

Many artists have become obsessed with how to project their own cultural and national identity in their paintings and artworks. In Thailand, for example, some artists have remained faithful to traditional Buddhist forms, while others have experimented with surrealist or semiabstract representations of the Buddha. Although shocking to many purists, the latter style is quite popular today among Bangkok's affluent elites. Still others opt for political or socially activist art. One such example is the portrayal of a vendor's cart selling (via video screen) prostitution to foreigners, an obvious reference to the sex market in present-day Bangkok. Another artist painted a self-portrait in traditional Buddhist pose, but instead of radiating inner peace, the subject displays a ferocious grin, mocking the inner turmoil and inhumanity of contemporary Thailand.

Tourism has had a tremendous but mixed impact on the revitalization of art and music throughout the region. In Vietnam, traditional drama and water puppetry have been revived at least in part to please tourists and earn precious foreign exchange. A similar process is under way in Indonesia, where woodworking, metalworking, and the textile industry have benefited from a large foreign presence. The island of Bali, however, demonstrates the risks involved in promoting tourism. Once the site of a unique and beautiful culture, parts of the island now reflect many of the more tawdry aspects of Western commercialism. Beyond the tourists, however, traditional culture in Bali, as elsewhere in Southeast Asia, still serves a purpose. On the island of Java, for example, traditional shadow puppet theater has been used by the government to promote its population control program, and in 1997 to assuage the fears of Indonesia farmers during a terrible drought.

Regional Conflict and Cooperation: The Rise of ASEAN

In addition to their continuing internal challenges, Southeast Asian states have been sporadically hampered by serious tensions among themselves. Some of these tensions were a consequence of historical rivalries and territorial disputes that had been submerged during the long era of colonial rule. Cambodia, for example, bickered with both of its neighbors, Thailand and Vietnam, over mutual frontiers drawn up originally by the French for their own convenience. A similar dispute erupted further to the south in the early 1960s, when Sukarno of Indonesia unleashed a policy of *konfrontasi* (confrontation) against nearby Malaysia. Sukarno contended that the Malayan peninsula was populated by Malay peoples who had once been part of the traditional greater Indonesian empires of Sailendra and Srivijaya and had only been separated from Indonesia as a result of colonial policies.

Sukarno's contention had some historical validity; the political separation of Malaysia from the Indonesian archipelago was in effect the result of a bargain between the British and the Dutch after the Napoleonic Wars. But it made little sense to the people of the resource-rich Malayan peninsula, who saw no advantage in the creation of a Greater Indonesia dominated by the charismatic but demagogic Sukarno, who might be inclined to redistribute their wealth to the poorer Indonesian islands. In the end, Indonesia dropped its claim after Sukarno's fall from power in the mid-1960s.

The territorial disputes between Cambodia and its neighbors were more difficult to resolve. During the Vietnam War, the country's ruler, Norodom Sihanouk, sought close relations with China and North Vietnam at least partly because he feared that the United States would support claims by Thailand and South Vietnam for territories inside Cambodia. Beijing agreed to support Cambodian national sovereignty inside its existing boundaries.

The reunification of Vietnam under Communist rule in 1975 had an immediate impact on the region. By the end of the year, both Laos and Cambodia had Communist governments. In Cambodia, a brutal revolutionary regime under the leadership of the Khmer Rouge (Red Khmer) dictator Pol Pot carried out the massacre of more than 1 million Cambodians. But the Communist triumph in Indochina did not lead to the falling dominoes that many U.S. policymakers had feared. One reason was that the political and economic situation within the region had gradually stabilized during the 1960s and 1970s.

Another was that the Communist governments in China, Vietnam, and Cambodia immediately began to squabble among themselves. A key aspect of the problem was a lingering border dispute between Vietnam and Cambodia. The new Khmer Rouge regime in Phnom Penh claimed that vast territories in the Mekong Delta had been seized from Cambodia by the Vietnamese in previous centuries, and in the weeks following the end of the Vietnam War, Cambodia launched attacks across the common border to punctuate its demand. It also rejected Hanoi's offer to join with Vietnam and Laos in a new "special relationship" to oppose the influence of "imperialist" forces in the region.

The growing tension in relations between Cambodia and Vietnam soon attracted the concern of leaders in China. Beijing had provided military and diplomatic support to both North Vietnam and the Khmer Rouge during the Vietnam War, but its actions were motivated at least in part by a desire to restore a degree of influence in the area that it had exercised prior to the colonial period. Suspecting that the "special relationship" was simply a Vietnamese ploy to establish its domination over all of Indochina, China provided strong diplomatic support to the government in Phnom Penh and warned that any Vietnamese aggression against Cambodia would meet with a strong Chinese response. Hanoi responded by signing a treaty of military cooperation with China's bitter rival, the USSR. When Vietnamese forces invaded Cambodia in December 1978 to install a new, pro-Hanoi regime in Phnom Penh, Beijing responded by launching a short but bitter attack across the border into northern Vietnam.

The outbreak of war among the erstwhile Communist allies in the region—which outside analysts quickly recognized as a resumption of historical rivalries predating the colonial era—aroused the concern of other countries in the neighborhood. In 1967, several non-Communist countries had established the Association of Southeast Asian Nations (ASEAN). Composed of Indonesia, Malaysia, Thailand, Singapore, and the Philippines, ASEAN at first concentrated on cooperative social and economic endeavors, but after the end of the Vietnam War, it began to seek a greater degree of political and military cohesion to resist further Communist encroachment in the region. When renewed territorial and ethnic rivalry between the Communist governments in Vietnam and Cambodia led the Vietnamese to invade Cambodia and install a pro-Hanoi regime in December 1978, ASEAN cooperated with other states in supporting a loose coalition of non-Communist groups with the ultimate purpose of forcing the Vietnamese to remove their occupational forces. In 1991, an agreement was finally reached in Paris whereby Hanoi agreed to withdraw its remaining troops from Cambodia, while a coalition government led by the non-Communist leader Norodom Ranarridh (son of Norodom Sihanouk) and Hun Sen, prime minister of the pro-Vietnamese regime, was formed in Phnom Penh. In 1997, however, the arrangement collapsed when Hun Sen deposed his rival and assumed sole power. The Khmer Rouge, now divided into hostile factions, remains in its jungle lair.

Although the continuing crisis in Cambodia is a source of concern to all nations in the region, the relationship between the Indochinese states and their neighbors has been improving. Vietnam was invited to join ASEAN in 1995, and Myanmar and Laos became members two years later. The addition of Myanmar, still under autocratic rule, aroused criticism in the West, but ASEAN officials argue that a policy of constructive engagement is the most effective means to bring about change in that isolated country. The addition of Cambodia has been postponed as a result of the recent coup d'etat.

The emergence of ASEAN from its previous status as a weak collection of diverse states into a stronger organization involving military cooperation and a degree of political consensus among its members has helped to provide the nations of Southeast Asia with a more cohesive voice to represent their interests on the world stage. They will need it, for disagreements with Western countries over global economic issues and the rising power of China to the north will present major challenges to the region in coming years. Concern over China today is focused primarily on the dispute over ownership of the Spratly and Paracel Islands in the South China Sea. Most of the states in the region have staked claims to one or more of the islands, which are reportedly located over substantial oil reserves, but it is Beijing's insistence that both island groups are historically Chinese that has made a compromise settlement difficult. The admission of Vietnam into ASEAN should provide both Hanoi and its neighbors with greater leverage in dealing with their powerful neighbor to the north.

Conclusion

Today, the Western image of a Southeast Asia mired in the Vietnam conflict and the tensions of the Cold War has become a memory. In ASEAN the states in the region have created the framework for a regional organization that can serve their common political, economic, technological, and security interests. A few members of ASEAN are already on the road to advanced development. The remainder are showing signs of undergoing a similar process within the next generation. While ethnic and religious tensions continue to exist in most ASEAN states, there are promising signs of increasing political stability and pluralism throughout the region.

To be sure, there are continuing signs of trouble. The recent financial crisis has aroused serious political unrest in Indonesia and has the potential to create similar problems elsewhere. Myanmar remains isolated from trends in the region and appears mired in a state of chronic underdevelopment and brutal military rule. The three states of Indochina remain potentially unstable and have not yet been fully integrated into the region as a whole. All three are among the poorest nations of Asia, and the political situation in Cambodia remains especially perilous.

All things considered, however, the situation is more promising today than would have appeared possible a generation ago. The nations of Southeast Asia appear capable of coordinating their efforts to erase the internal divisions and conflicts that have brought so much tragedy to the peoples of the region for centuries. If the original purpose of the U.S. intervention in the Indochina conflict was to buy time for the other nations of the region to develop, the gamble may have paid off. Although the war in Vietnam was lost at considerable cost and bloodshed to the participants, the dire predictions in Washington of a revolutionary reign of terror and falling dominoes were not fulfilled, and some countries in the region appear ready to join the steadily growing ranks of developing nations.

To some observers, economic success in the region has come at a high price, in the form of political authoritarianism and a lack of attention to human rights. Indeed, proponents of the view that Asian values are different from those of the West should not be too complacent in their conviction that there is no correlation between economic prosperity and democracy. Still, a look at the historical record suggests that political pluralism is often a by-product of economic advancement, and that political values and institutions evolve in response to changing societal conditions. In the end, the current growing pains in Southeast Asia may prove to be beneficial in their overall impact on societies in the region.

NOTES

1. *New York Times*, May 2, 1996.
2. Quoted in Howard Jones, *Indonesia: The Possible Dream* (New York, 1971), p. 223.
3. Ibid., p. 237.
4. Quoted in Harry J. Benda and John A. Larkin, eds., *The World of Southeast Asia: Selected Historical Readings* (New York, 1967), p. 250. The Indonesian word *musjawarah* derives from the Arabic word *mashwara*, which carries a connotation of "consultation."
5. Mahathir Bin Mohamad, *The Malay Dilemma* (Kuala Lumpur, 1970), p. 94.
6. Quoted in Benda and Larkin, *World of Southeast Asia*, p. 252.
7. Mochtar Lubis, "Mysticism in Indonesian Politics," in *Man, State and Society in Contemporary Southeast Asia*, ed. Robert O. Tilman, (New York, 1969), p. 185.
8. Benda and Larkin, *World of Southeast Asia*, pp. 289–290.
9. *New York Times*, July 28, 1996.
10. *Far Eastern Economic Review*, August 1, 1996.
11. Lubis, *Mysticism*, p. 180.
12. *Far Eastern Economic Review*, October 10, 1996, p. 57.
13. Duong Thu Huong, *Paradise of the Blind* (New York, 1993), p. 225.

CHAPTER
13

Emerging Africa

In the three decades following the end of World War II, the peoples of Africa were gradually liberated from the formal trappings of European colonialism. The creation of independent states in Africa began in the late 1950s and proceeded gradually over the next thirty years until the last colonial regimes were finally dismantled. But the transition to independence has not been an unalloyed success. The legacy of colonialism in the form of political inexperience and continued European economic domination has combined with overpopulation and climatic disasters to frustrate

the new states' ability to achieve political stability and economic prosperity. At the same time, arbitrary boundaries imposed by the colonial powers and ethnic and religious divisions within the African countries have led to bitter conflicts that have posed a severe obstacle to the dream of continental solidarity and cooperation in forging a common destiny. Today, the continent of Africa, although blessed with enormous potential, is one of the most volatile and conflict-ridden areas of the world.

*U*huru: The Struggle for Independence

After World War II, Europeans reluctantly recognized that the end result of colonial rule in Africa would be African self-government, if not full independence. Accordingly, the African population would have to be trained to handle the responsibilities of representative government. In many cases, however, relatively little had been done to prepare the local population for self-rule. Early in the colonial era, during the late nineteenth century, African administrators had held influential positions in several British colonies, and one even served as governor of the Gold Coast. Several colonies had legislative councils with limited African participation, although their functions were solely advisory. But with the formal institution of colonial rule, senior positions were reserved for the British, although local authority remained in the hands of native rulers.

After World War II, most British colonies introduced reforms that increased the representation of the local

population. Members of legislative and executive councils were increasingly chosen through elections, and Africans came to constitute a majority of these bodies. Elected councils at the local level were introduced in the 1950s to reduce the power of the tribal chiefs and clan heads, who had controlled local government under indirect rule. An exception was South Africa, where European domination continued. In the Union of South Africa, the franchise was restricted to whites except in the former territory of the Cape Colony, where persons of mixed ancestry had enjoyed the right to vote since the mid-nineteenth century. Black Africans did win some limited electoral rights in Northern and Southern Rhodesia (now Zambia and Zimbabwe), although whites generally dominated the political scene.

A similar process of political liberalization was taking place in the French colonies. At first, as we have seen, the French tried to assimilate the African peoples into French culture. By the 1920s, however, racist beliefs in

Western cultural superiority and the tenacity of traditional beliefs and practices among Africans had somewhat discredited this ideal. The French therefore substituted a more limited program of assimilating African elites into Western culture and using them as administrators at the local level as a link to the remainder of the population. This policy resembled the British policy of indirect rule, although it placed more emphasis on French culture in training local administrators. It had only limited success, however, because many Western-educated Africans refused to leave the urban centers to live in the countryside. Others, who were exposed to radical ideas while studying abroad, rejected the prevailing forms of Western civilization and called for the restoration of national independence.

The Nazi occupation of northern France had an effect on black Africans somewhat like that of the Japanese occupation of Southeast Asia on Asians. In 1944, the Free French movement under General Charles de Gaulle issued the Brazzaville Declaration, which promised equal rights, though not self-government, in a projected French Union composed of France and its overseas possessions. After the war, a legislative assembly for the new organization was created, although its political powers were limited. At the same time, African representatives were elected to the French National Assembly in Paris. But even this new community of nations had separate categories of citizenship based on education and ethnic background, and decisions on major issues were still made in France or by French officials in French Africa.

The Colonial Legacy

As in Asia, colonial rule had a mixed impact on the societies and peoples of Africa. The Western presence brought a number of short-term and long-term benefits to Africa, such as improved transportation and communication facilities, and in a few areas laid the foundation for a modern industrial and commercial sector. Improved sanitation and medical care in all probability increased life expectancy. The introduction of selective elements of Western political systems laid the basis for the gradual creation of democratic societies.

Yet the benefits of Westernization were distributed highly unequally, and the vast majority of Africans found their lives little improved, if at all. Only South Africa and French-held Algeria, for example, developed modern industrial sectors, extensive railroad networks, and modern communications systems. In both countries, European settlers were numerous, most investment capital for industrial ventures was European, and whites comprised almost the entire professional and managerial class. Members of the native population were generally restricted to unskilled or semiskilled jobs at wages less than one-fifth of those enjoyed by Europeans. Those who worked in industry or on infrastructure projects often suffered from inhuman working conditions. Several thousand African conscripts reportedly died on press gangs building the new railroad system.

Many colonies concentrated on export crops—peanuts from Senegal and Gambia, cotton from Egypt and Uganda, coffee from Kenya, and palm oil and cocoa products from the Gold Coast. Here the benefits of development were somewhat more widespread. In some cases, the crops were grown on plantations, which were usually owned by Europeans. But plantation agriculture was not always suitable in Africa, and much farming was done by free or tenant farmers. In some areas, where land ownership was traditionally vested in the community, the land was owned and leased by the corporate village.

Even here, however, the vast majority of the profits from the export of tropical products accrued to Europeans or to merchants from other foreign countries, such as India and the Arab emirates. While a fortunate few benefited from the increase in exports, the vast majority of Africans continued to be subsistence farmers growing food for their own consumption. The gap was particularly wide in places like Kenya, where the best lands had been reserved for European settlers to make the colony self-sufficient. As in other parts of the world, the early stages of the Industrial Revolution were especially painful for the rural population, and ordinary subsistence farmers reaped few benefits from colonial rule.

The Rise of Nationalism

The African response to the loss of independence can be traced through several stages, beginning with resistance. In some cases, the opposition came from an organized state, such as Ashanti, which fought against the British takeover of the Gold Coast in the 1860s. Where formal states did not exist, the colonial takeover was often easier and more gradual; in a few instances, however, such as the Zulu tribesmen in South Africa in the 1880s and Abdel Qadir's rebellion against the French in Algeria, resistance to white rule was quite fierce.

But formal nationalist movements and parties generally arose later in Africa than in Asia. The first nationalist groups were formed in urban areas, primarily among people who had been exposed to Western civilization. The first Afro-Europeans, as such people are sometimes called, often benefited from the European presence, and some, as we have seen, held responsible positions in the colonial bureaucracy. But as the system became more formalized in the early twentieth century, more emphasis was placed on racial distinctions, and opportunities in government and other professional positions diminished, especially in the British colonies, where indirect rule was based on collaboration with the local tribal aristocracy. The result was a dissatisfied urban educated elite, who were all the more angry when they realized they would not benefit from the improved conditions.

Political organizations for African rights did not arise until after World War I, and then only in a few areas, such as British-ruled Kenya and the Gold Coast. At first, organizations such as the National Congress of British West Africa (formed in 1919 in the Gold Coast) and Jomo Kenyatta's Kikuyu Central Association focused on improving African living conditions in the colonies rather than on national independence. After World War II, however, following the example of independence movements elsewhere, these groups became organized political parties with independence as their objective. In the Gold Coast, Kwame Nkrumah (1909–1972) led the Convention People's Party, the first formal political party in black Africa. In the late 1940s, Jomo Kenyatta (1894–1978) founded the Kenya African National Union (KANU), which focused on economic issues but had an implied political agenda as well.

For the most part, these political activities were basically nonviolent and were led by Western-educated African intellectuals. Their constituents were primarily urban professionals, merchants, and members of labor unions. But the demand for independence was not entirely restricted to the cities. In Kenya, for example, the widely publicized Mau Mau movement among the Kikuyu people used terrorism as an essential element of its program to achieve *uhuru* (Swahili for "freedom") from the British. Although most of the violence was directed against other Africans—only about 100 Europeans were killed in the violence, compared with an estimated 1,700 Africans who lost their lives at the hands of the rebels—the specter of Mau Mau terrorism alarmed the European population and convinced the British government in 1959 to promise eventual independence.

A similar process was occurring in Egypt, which had been a protectorate of Great Britain (and under loose Turkish suzerainty until the breakup of the Ottoman Empire) since the 1880s. National consciousness had existed in Egypt since well before the colonial takeover, and members of the legislative council were calling for

independence even before World War I. In 1918, a formal political party called the Wafd was formed to promote Egyptian independence. The intellectuals were opposed as much to the local palace government as to the British, however, and in 1952 an army coup overthrew King Farouk, the grandson of Khedive Ismail, and established an independent republic.

In areas such as South Africa and Algeria, where the political system was dominated by European settlers, the transition to independence was more complicated. In South Africa, political activity by local Africans began with the formation of the African National Congress (ANC) in 1912. Initially, the ANC was dominated by Western-oriented intellectuals and had little mass support. Its goal was to achieve economic and political reforms, including full equality for educated Africans, within the framework of the existing system. But the ANC's efforts met with little success, while conservative white parties managed to stiffen the segregation laws. In response, the ANC became increasingly radicalized, and by the 1950s, the prospects for a violent confrontation were growing.

In Algeria, resistance to French rule by Berbers and Arabs in rural areas had never ceased. After World War II, urban agitation intensified, leading to a widespread rebellion against colonial rule in the mid-1950s. At first, the French government tried to maintain its authority in Algeria, which was considered an integral part of metropolitan France. But when Charles de Gaulle became president in 1958, he reversed French policy, and Algeria became independent under President Ahmad Ben Bella (b. 1918) in 1962. The armed struggle in Algeria hastened the transition to statehood in its neighbors as well. Tunisia won its independence in 1956 after some urban agitation and rural unrest, but retained close ties with Paris. The French attempted to suppress the nationalist movement in Morocco by sending Sultan Muhammad V into exile, but the effort failed, and in 1956 he returned as the ruler of the independent state of Morocco.

Most black African nations achieved their independence in the late 1950s and 1960s, beginning with the Gold Coast, now renamed Ghana, in 1957. Nigeria, the Belgian Congo (renamed Zaire), Kenya, Tanganyika (later, when joined with Zanzibar, renamed Tanzania), and several other countries soon followed. Most of the French colonies agreed to accept independence within the framework of de Gaulle's French Community. By the late 1960s, only parts of southern Africa and the Portuguese possessions of Mozambique and Angola remained under European rule.

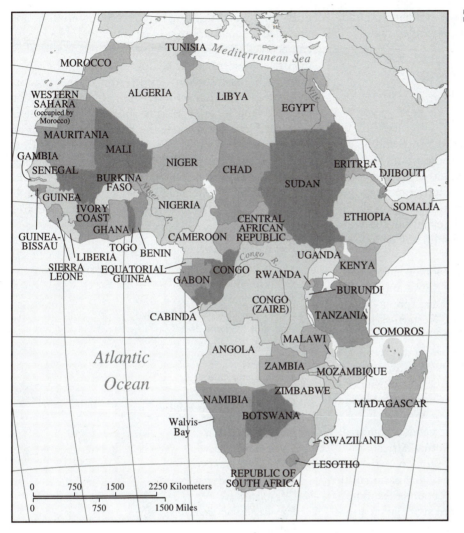

Map 13.1   Modern Africa

Independence came later to Africa than to most of Asia. Several factors help explain the delay. For one thing, colonialism was established in Africa somewhat later than in most areas of Asia, and the inevitable reaction from the local population was consequently delayed. Furthermore, with the exception of a few areas in West Africa and along the Mediterranean, coherent states with a strong sense of cultural, ethnic, and linguistic unity did not exist in most of Africa. Most traditional states, such as Ashanti in West Africa, Songhai in the southern Sahara, and Bakongo in the Congo Basin, were collections of heterogeneous peoples with little sense of national or cultural identity. Even after colonies were established, the European powers often practiced a policy of "divide and rule," while the British encouraged political decentralization by retaining the authority of the tra-

ditional native chieftains. It is hardly surprising that when opposition to colonial rule emerged, unity was difficult to achieve.

The Era of Independence

The newly independent African states faced intimidating challenges. Like the new states in South and Southeast Asia, they had been profoundly affected by colonial rule. Yet the experience had been highly unsatisfactory in most respects. Although Western political institutions, values, and technology had been introduced, at least into the cities, the exposure to European civilization had been superficial at best for most Africans and tragic for many. At the outset of independence, most

African societies were still primarily agrarian and traditional, and their modern sectors depended mainly on imports from the West.

Pan-Africanism and Nationalism: The Destiny of Africa

Like the leaders of the new states in South and Southeast Asia, most African leaders came from the urban middle class. They had studied in either Europe or the United States and spoke and read European languages. Although most were profoundly critical of colonial policies, they appeared to accept the relevance of the Western model to Africa and gave at least lip service to Western democratic values.

Their views on economics were somewhat more diverse. Some, like Jomo Kenyatta of Kenya and General Mobutu Sese Seko (1930–1998) of Zaire (previously the Belgian Congo), were advocates of Western-style capitalism. Others, like Julius Nyerere (b. 1922) of Tanzania, Kwame Nkrumah of Ghana, and Sékou Touré (1922–1984) of Guinea, preferred an "African form of socialism," which bore slight resemblance to the Marxist-Leninist socialism practiced in the Soviet Union and more to the syndicalist movement in Western Europe. According to its advocates, it was descended from traditional communal practices in precolonial Africa.

Like the leaders of other developing countries, the new political leaders in Africa were highly nationalistic and generally accepted the colonial boundaries. But, as we have seen, these boundaries were artificial creations of the colonial powers. Virtually all of the new states included widely diverse ethnic, linguistic, and territorial groups. Zaire, for example, was composed of more than 200 different territorial groups speaking seventy-five different languages.

Some African leaders themselves harbored attitudes that undermined the fragile sense of common identity needed to knit together these diverse groups. A number of leaders—including Nkrumah of Ghana, Touré of Guinea, and Kenyatta of Kenya—were enticed by the dream of pan-Africanism, a concept of continental unity that transcended national boundaries and was to find its concrete manifestation in the Organization of African Unity (OAU), which was founded in Addis Ababa in 1963 (see box on p. 275)

Pan-Africanism originated among African intellectuals during the first half of the twentieth century. A basic element was the belief in negritude (blackness)—the conviction that there was a distinctive "African person-

ality" that owed nothing to Western materialism and provided a common sense of destiny for all black African peoples. According to Aimé Césaire, a West Indian of African descent and a leading ideologist of the movement, whereas Western civilization prized rational thought and material achievement, African culture emphasized emotional expression and a common sense of humanity. In a world where the Western drive for profit and political hegemony threatened to destroy civilization, Africans had an obligation to use their humanistic and spiritual qualities to help save the human race. The Ghanaian official Michael Francis Dei-Anang agreed. In *Whither Bound Africa*, written in 1946, he declared scathingly,

> Forward! To What?
> The Slums, where man is dumped upon man,
> Where penury
> And misery
> Have made their hapless homes,
> And all is dark and drear?
> Forward! To what?
> The factory
> To grind hard hours
> In an inhuman mill,
> In one long ceaseless spell?
>
> Forward! To what?
> To the reeking round
> Of medieval crimes,
> Where the greedy hawks
> Of Aryan stock
> Prey with bombs and guns
> On men of lesser breed?
> Forward to CIVILIZATION[1]

The concept of negritude was in part a natural defensive response to the social Darwinist concepts of Western racial superiority and African inferiority that were popular in Europe and the United States during the early years of the twentieth century. At the same time, it was stimulated by growing self-doubt among many European intellectuals after World War I, who feared that Western civilization was on a path of self-destruction. Aimé Césaire compared the white world,

> appalling weary from its immense effort
> the crack of its joints rebelling under the hardness of the
>   stars

with that of the Africans,

> Those who invented neither gunpowder nor compass
> those who tamed neither steam nor electricity

≽ The African Dream ≼

In May 1963, the leaders of thirty-two African states met in Addis Ababa, the capital of Ethiopia, to discuss the creation of an organization that would represent the interests of all the peoples of Africa. The result was the Organization of African Unity (OAU). The goals of the new organization were contained in a charter approved by the conference.

The group's aspirations reflected the optimism engendered by the restoration of independence, and confidence that the peoples and nations of Africa could avoid the bitter struggles that had taken place in Europe and other areas around the world. Affirming "the inalienable right of all people to control their own destiny," and that "freedom, equality, justice, and dignity" were "essential objectives" in realizing the aspirations of all Africans, the signatories called for cooperative efforts to harness the immense resources of the continent for the common good and to promote understanding among all African states "in a larger unity transcending ethnic and national differences."

In the years since these objectives were first enunciated, the peoples of Africa have endured many disappointments—not the least of which has been the failure to realize the dream of African unity and cooperation. Territorial disputes and internal conflicts have erupted throughout the continent, just as they have in other parts of the world. Some were undoubtedly triggered by external forces, including competition between the superpowers, but others were provoked by internal conditions and the legacy of boundaries drawn at the whim of European states during the colonial era.

Yet the dream of African cooperation is not dead. In 1991, the OAU created a new African Economic Community, and a few years later, several West African states set up a multinational peacekeeping force to monitor a fragile truce in Liberia, which had been rent by a fractious civil war. Out of the germ of such organizations, the dream may yet reach fruition.

Source: Jon Woronoff, *Organizing African Unity* (Lanham, MD: Scarecrow Press, 1980).

> *those who explored neither sea nor sky*
> *but those who know the humblest corners of the country*
>   *suffering*
> *those whose only journeys were uprooting*
> *those who went to sleep on their knees*
> *those who were domesticated and christianized*
> *those who were inoculated with degeneration.*[2]

Negritude had more appeal to Africans from French colonies than to those from British possessions. Yet it also found adherents in the British colonies, as well as in the United States and elsewhere in the Americas. African American intellectuals such as W. E. B. Dubois and George Padmore and the West Indian politician Marcus Garvey attempted to promote a "black renaissance" by popularizing the idea of a distinct African personality. Their views were shared by several of the new African leaders, including Leopold Senghor (b. 1906) of Senegal, Kwame Nkrumah of Ghana, and Jomo Kenyatta of Kenya. Nkrumah in particular appeared to hope that a pan-African union could be established that would unite all of the new countries of the continent in a broader community.

Dream and Reality: Political and Economic Conditions in Contemporary Africa

The program of the OAU had forecast a future Africa based on freedom, equality, justice, and dignity, and on the unity, solidarity, and territorial integrity of African states. It did not take long for reality to set in. Vast disparities in education and income made it hard to establish democracy in much of Africa. Expectations that independence would lead to stable political structures based on "one person, one vote" were soon disappointed, as the initial phase of pluralistic governments gave way to a series of military regimes and one-party states. Between 1957 and 1982, more than seventy leaders of African countries were overthrown by violence, and in recent years, the pace has increased. In 1984, *Time* magazine reported that only seven of the forty-one major African states permitted opposition parties to operate legally. The remainder were under single-party regimes or were ruled by the military.[3]

Hopes that independence would inaugurate an era of economic prosperity and equality were similarly dashed. Part of the problem could be (and was) ascribed to the

◆ **Urban Affluence in Nigeria.**
In Africa, as in many countries of Asia and Latin America, affluent cities have emerged as a result of economic modernization and contact with the West. In this photograph, two wealthy aristocrats from Nigeria, protected from the sun by a parasol, are emerging from their new Mercedes.

lingering effects of colonialism. Most newly independent countries in Africa were dependent upon the export of a single crop or natural resource. When prices fluctuated or dropped, they were at the mercy of the vagaries of the international market. In several cases, the resources were still controlled by foreigners, leading to the charge that colonialism had been succeeded by "neocolonialism," in which Western domination was maintained by economic rather than by political or military means. To make matters worse, most African states had to import technology and manufactured goods from the West, and the prices of those goods rose more rapidly than those of the export products.

The new states also contributed to their own problems. Scarce national resources were squandered on military equipment or expensive consumer goods rather than on building up their infrastructure to provide the foundation for an industrial economy. Corruption, a painful reality throughout the modern world, became almost a way of life in Africa, as bribery (known variously as *dash*, *chai*, or *bonsella*) became necessary to obtain even the most basic services. The Nigerian author Cyprian Ekwensi expressed his disillusionment with African politics in his novel *Jagua Nana*. When the heroine's boyfriend Freddie states, "I wan' money quick-quick; an' politics is de only hope," she replies, "No Freddie. I no wan' you to win. . . . Politics not for you, Freddie. You got education. You got culture. You're a gentleman an' proud. Politics be a game

for dog. And in dis Lagos, is a rough game. De roughest game in de whole worl'. Is smell an' dirty an' you too clean an' sweet."[4]

Finally, population growth, which more than anything else has hindered economic growth in the new nations of Asia and Africa, became a serious problem and crippled efforts to create modern economies. By the mid-1980s, annual population growth averaged nearly 3 percent throughout Africa, the highest rate of any continent. Drought conditions and the inexorable spread of the Sahara (usually known as desertification, a condition caused partly by overpopulation) have led to widespread hunger and starvation, first in West African countries such as Niger and Mali and then in Ethiopia, Somalia, and the Sudan. Despite global efforts to provide food, millions are in danger of starvation and malnutrition, and countless others have fled to neighboring countries in search of sustenance.

In recent years, the spread of AIDS in Africa has reached epidemic proportions. According to one estimate, one-third of the entire population of sub-Saharan Africa is infected with the virus, including a high percentage of the urban middle class. Some observers estimate that without measures to curtail the effects of the disease, it will have a significant impact on several African countries by reducing population growth, which is presently predicted to increase throughout the continent by at least 300 million in the next fifteen years.

Poverty is endemic in Africa, particularly among the three-quarters of the population still living off the land. Urban areas have grown tremendously, but as in much of Asia, most are surrounded by massive squatter settlements of rural peoples who had fled to the cities in search of a better life. The expansion of the cities has overwhelmed fragile transportation and sanitation systems and led to rising pollution and perpetual traffic jams, while millions are forced to live without water and electricity. Meanwhile, the fortunate few (all too often government officials on the take) live the high life and emulate the consumerism of the West (in a particularly expressive phrase, the rich in many East African countries are know as *wabenzi*, or Mercedes-Benz people).

In "Pedestrian, to Passing Benz-man," the Kenyan poet Albert Ojuka voices the popular discontent with economic inequality:

You man, lifted gently
out of the poverty and suffering
we so recently shared; I say—
why splash the muddy puddle on to
my bare legs, as if, still unsatisfied
with your seated opulence
you must sully the unwashed
with your diesel-smoke and mud-water
and force him to buy, beyond his means
a bar of soap from your shop?
a few years back we shared a master
today you have none, while I have
exchanged a parasite for something worse.
But maybe a few years is too long a time.[5]

THE SEARCH FOR SOLUTIONS

Concern over the dangers of economic inequality inspired a number of African leaders—including Nkrumah in Ghana, Nyerere in Tanzania, and Samora Michel of Mozambique—to restrict foreign investment and nationalize the major industries and utilities while promoting social ideals and values. Nyerere was the most consistent, promoting the ideals of socialism and self-reliance through his Arusha Declaration of 1967. Taking advantage of his powerful political influence, Nyerere placed limitations on income and established village collectives to avoid the corrosive effects of economic inequality and government corruption. Sympathetic foreign countries provided considerable economic aid to assist the experiment, and many observers noted that levels of corruption, political instability, and ethnic strife were lower in

Tanzania than in many other African countries. Unfortunately, corruption has increased in recent years, while political elements in Zanzibar, citing the stagnation brought by two decades of socialism, are agitating for autonomy or even total separation from the mainland. Tanzania also has poor soil, inadequate rainfall, and limited resources, all of which have contributed to its slow growth and continuing rural and urban poverty.

In 1985, Julius Nyerere voluntarily retired from the presidency. In his farewell speech, he confessed that he had failed to achieve many of his ambitious goals to create a socialist society in Africa. In particular, he admitted that his plan to collectivize the traditional private farm (*shamba*) had run into strong resistance from conservative peasants. "You can socialize what is not traditional," he remarked. "The *shamba* can't be socialized." But Nyerere insisted that many of his policies had succeeded in improving social and economic conditions, and he argued that the only real solution was to consolidate the multitude of small countries in the region into a larger East African Federation.[6]

The countries that opted for capitalism faced their own dilemmas. Neighboring Kenya, blessed with better soil in the highlands, a local tradition of aggressive commerce, and a residue of European settlers, welcomed foreign investment and profit incentives. The results have been mixed. Kenya has a strong current of indigenous African capitalism and a substantial middle class, mostly based in the capital, Nairobi. But landlessness, unemployment, and income inequities are high, even by African standards, and the rate of population growth—more than 4 percent annually—is one of the highest in the world. Eighty percent of the population remains rural, and 40 percent live below the poverty line. The result has been widespread unrest in a country formerly admired for its successful development.

Beginning in the mid-1970s, a few African nations decided to adopt Soviet-style Marxism-Leninism. In Angola and Ethiopia, Marxist parties followed the Soviet model and attempted to create fully socialist societies with the assistance of Soviet experts and Cuban troops and advisors. Economically, the results were disappointing, and both countries faced severe internal opposition. In Ethiopia, the revolt by Muslim tribal peoples in the province of Eritrea led to the fall of the Marxist leader Mengistu and his regime in 1990. A similar revolt erupted against the government in Angola, with the rebel group UNITA controlling much of the rural population and for a time threatening the capital city, Luanda.

THE SEARCH FOR COMMUNITY

Finally, Africans have been disappointed that the dream of a united Africa has not been realized. No one skewered the pretensions of the apostles of negritude better than the Ugandan poet Taban Lo Liyong. In his poem "Negritude Is Crying over Spilt Milk," he observed:

Strange mules called Negritude
and African Personality
Overran the terrain
And kicked wisdom down
Or above our heads.

Politicians quite unaware
How low we are
On the ladder universal
Decided to halt the race
And embrace the niches sure
Where we were stuck for the moment.[7]

But while some criticize the tendency to pursue what Taban called the "vanishing exotica" of the past, most Africans feel a shared sense of continuing victimization at the hands of the West and are convinced that independence has not ended Western interference in and domination of African affairs. Many African leaders were angered when Western powers led by the United States conspired to overthrow the radical Congolese politician Patrice Lumumba in Zaire in the early 1960s. The episode reinforced their desire to form the Organization of African Unity as a means of reducing Western influence. But aside from agreeing to adopt a neutral stance during the Cold War, African states have had difficulty achieving a united position on many issues, and their disagreements have left the region vulnerable to external influence and even led to conflict. During the late 1980s and early 1990s, border disputes festered in many areas of the continent and in some cases—as with Morocco and a rebel movement in the western Sahara, and between Kenya and Uganda—flared into outright war.

Even within many African nations, the concept of nationhood has been undermined by the renascent force of regionalism or tribalism. Nigeria, with the largest population on the continent, was rent by civil strife during the late 1960s, when dissident Ibo groups in the southeast attempted unsuccessfully to form an independent state of Biafra. Ethnic conflicts broke out among hostile territorial groups in Zimbabwe (the new name for Southern Rhodesia) and in several nations in Central Africa. In Kenya, the Luo tribal leader Tom Mboya was assassinated, presumably because rival groups feared that

he would be selected to succeed the charismatic Kikuyu president Jomo Kenyatta.

Another force undermining nationalism in Africa has been pan-Islamism. Its prime exponent in Africa was the Egyptian president Gamal Abdul Nasser. After Nasser's death in 1970, the torch of Islamic unity in Africa was carried by the Libyan president Muammar Qadhafi, whose ambitions to create a greater Muslim nation in the Sahara under his authority led to conflict with neighboring Chad. The Islamic resurgence also surfaced in Ethiopia, where Muslim tribesmen in Eritrea (the former Italian colony of Eritrea had been joined with Ethiopia in 1952) rebelled against the Marxist regime of Colonel Mengistu in Addis Ababa.

RECENT TRENDS

Not all the news in Africa has been bad. In recent years, popular demonstrations, fueled by stagnant economies, have led to the collapse of one-party regimes and the emergence of fragile democracies in several countries. Dictatorships were brought to an end in Ethiopia, Liberia, and Somalia, although in each case the fall of the regime was later followed by political instability or, in the latter two instances, by a bloody civil war. Perhaps the most notorious case was that of Idi Amin of Uganda. Colonel Amin led a coup against Prime Minister Milton Obote in 1971. After ruling by terror and brutal repression of dissident elements, he was finally deposed in 1979. In recent years, stability has returned to the country, which in May 1996 had its first presidential election in more than fifteen years. In Eritrea, a popular Islamic government is gradually rebuilding the country and planning for the creation of a parliamentary system.

Africa has also benefited from the end of the Cold War, as the superpowers have virtually ceased to compete for power and influence in Africa. When the Soviet Union withdrew its support from the Marxist government in Ethiopia, the United States allowed its right to maintain military bases in neighboring Somalia to lapse, resulting in the overthrow of the authoritarian government there. Unfortunately, clan rivalries led to such turbulence that many inhabitants were in imminent danger of starvation, and in the winter of 1992, U.S. military forces occupied the country in an effort to provide food to the starving population. Since the departure of foreign troops in 1993, the country has been divided into clan fiefdoms, while Islamic groups attempt to bring a return to law and order.

Yet foreign intervention into the internal affairs of the African countries has by no means come to an end.

◆ From Rebel to Statesman. After spending more than twenty-five years in prison after conviction for terrorist activities, African National Congress leader Nelson Mandela was finally released in 1990. Shortly after, he signed an agreement with South African President F. W. de Klerk to bring an end to apartheid and create a multiracial state. The historic moment is shown here.

This is particularly the case in the ex-French colonies in central and western Africa. French troops have been stationed in a number of these countries for several years at the request of local governments. But opposition groups now contend that French forces are being used to uphold dictatorial regimes, and should be withdrawn.

Perhaps Africa's greatest success story is in South Africa, where the white government—which long maintained a policy of racial segregation (apartheid) and restricted black sovereignty to a series of small "Bantustans" in relatively infertile areas of the country—finally accepted the inevitability of African involvement in the political process and the national economy. In 1990, the government of President F. W. de Klerk (b. 1936) released ANC leader Nelson Mandela (b. 1918) from prison, where he had been held since 1964. In 1993, the two leaders agreed to hold democratic national elections the following spring. In the meantime, ANC representatives agreed to take part in a transitional coalition government with de Klerk's National Party. Those elections resulted in a substantial majority for the ANC, and Mandela became president.

In May 1996, a new constitution was approved, calling for a multiracial state (see box on p. 280). The National Party immediately went into opposition, claiming that the new charter did not adequately provide for joint decision making by members of the coalition. The third group in the coalition government, the Zulu-based Inkatha Freedom Party, agreed to remain within the government, but rivalry between the ANC and Zulu elites intensified. Zulu chief Mangosuthu Buthelezi, drawing on the growing force of Zulu nationalism, has begun to invoke the memory of the great nineteenth-century Zulu ruler Shaka in a possible bid at future independence. Although many Zulus currently support the ANC, the future of a multiracial society in the Republic of South Africa remains in doubt. With all its problems, however, South Africa remains the wealthiest and most industrialized state on the continent.

If the situation in South Africa provides grounds for modest optimism, the situation in Nigeria provides reason for serious concern. Africa's largest country in terms of population, and one of its wealthiest because of substantial oil reserves, Nigeria in recent years has been in the grip of military rulers. During his rule, General Sani Abacha ruthlessly suppressed all opposition, and in late 1995 ordered the execution of author Ken Saro-Wiwa despite widespread protests from human rights groups abroad. Saro-Wiwa had vocally criticized environmental damage caused by foreign interests in southern Nigeria, but the regime's major concern was his support for separatist activities in an area that had previously launched the Biafran insurrection in the late 1960s. In a protest against the brutality of the Abacha regime, Nobel prize–winning author Wole Soyinka published from exile a harsh exposé of the crisis inside the country. His book, *The Open Sore of a Continent*, places the primary responsibility for failure not on Nigeria's long list of dictators, but on the very concept of the modern nation-state, which was introduced into Africa arbitrarily by Europeans during the later stages of the colonial era. A nation, he contends, can only emerge from below, as the expression of the moral and political will of the local inhabitants, not be imposed artificially from above, as was the case throughout Africa. Abacha died in 1998, but the army remains in power.

Currently, the most tragic situation is in the central African states of Rwanda and Burundi, where a chronic conflict between the minority Tutsis and the Hutu majority has led to a bitter civil war, with thousands of refugees fleeing to neighboring Zaire. In a classic

❧ A New Constitution for South Africa ❦

The long and painful transition from apartheid to a multiparty democracy in South Africa was finally completed with the promulgation of a new constitution in the spring of 1996. The 140-page document explicitly renounces the racist policies that marked the past and guarantees freedom of speech, freedom of movement, and freedom of political activity. "The Republic of South Africa," it declares,

is one sovereign democratic state founded on the following values: a) human dignity, the achievement of equality and advancement of human rights and freedoms, b) non-racialism and non-sexism, c) supremacy of the Constitution and the rule of law, d) universal adult suffrage, a national common voters roll, regular elections, and a multi-party system of democratic government, to ensure accountability, responsiveness and openness.

The charter calls for a federal system with a strong presidency, similar to that of the United States, and a bicameral legislature. The lower house is a National Assembly composed of nearly 400 delegates elected by proportional representation; the upper chamber, the National Council of Provinces, is to be composed of 10 delegates selected by the legislative bodies from each of the country's nine provinces. A bill of rights prohibits discrimination on the basis of race, gender, age, or sexual orientation, and also guarantees the right to housing, health care, food, and education for all citizens. It calls for an independent judicial branch headed by a Constitutional Court composed of eleven judges, to be appointed by the president after consultation with leading figures in all political parties and a judicial review commission. According to the constitution, the composition of appointments to the judiciary must "reflect broadly the racial and gender composition of South Africa."

The establishment of the new constitution was the result of cooperation between F. W. de Klerk, president of the republic and head of the National Party, and Nelson Mandela's African National Congress, which had recently won a majority vote in national elections. Shortly after, de Klerk's party unilaterally left Mandela's coalition government and declared itself in opposition. A third member of the coalition, the Zulu-based Inkatha Freedom Party, remained within the government, but its members boycotted the vote on the constitution to signal their anger that the party's demand for greater provincial autonomy had been rejected.

Source: *New York Times*, May 9 and 10, 1996.

---

example of conflict between pastoral and farming peoples, the nomadic Tutsis had long dominated the sedentary Hutu population. It was the attempt of the Bantu-speaking Hutus to bring an end to Tutsi domination that initiated the recent conflict, marked by massacres on both sides. In the meantime, the presence of large numbers of foreign troops and refugees intensified centrifugal forces inside Zaire, where General Mobutu Sese Seko had long ruled with an iron hand. In 1997, military forces led by Mobutu's longtime opponent Lauren Kabila managed to topple the general's corrupt government in Kinshasa. Once in power, Kabila renamed the country the Democratic Republic of the Congo and promised a return to democratic practices. Outside observers, however, have charged that the rebels committed numerous atrocities en route to power, and that the new government in Kinshasa is systematically suppressing political dissent.

It is clear that African societies have not yet begun to surmount the challenges they have faced since independence. Most African states are still poor and their populations illiterate. But as Tanzania's former president Julius Nyerere and the Nigerian author Wole Soyinka have pointed out, a significant part of the problem is related to the current inapplicability of the nation-state system to the African continent. Africans must find better ways to cooperate with each other and to protect and promote their own interests. A first step in that direction was taken in 1991, when the Organization for African Unity agreed to establish a new African Economic Community (AEC). More recently, West African states have set up a peacekeeping force to monitor the fragile cease-fire in Liberia.

As Africa evolves, it is useful to remember that economic and political change is often an agonizingly slow and painful process. Introduced to industrialization and concepts of Western democracy only a century ago, African societies are still groping for ways to graft Western political institutions and economic practices onto a native structure still significantly influenced by traditional values and attitudes. As one African writer recently observed, it is easy to be cynical in Africa, because changes in political regimes have had little effect on people's livelihood. Still, he said, "let us welcome the wind of change. This, after all, is a continent of winds. The trick is to keep hope burning, like a candle protected from the wind."[8]

Continuity and Change in Modern African Societies

In general, the impact of the West has been greater on urban and educated Africans and more limited on their rural and illiterate compatriots. After all, the colonial presence was first and most firmly established in the cities. Many cities, including Dakar, Lagos, Johannesburg, Capetown, Brazzaville, and Nairobi, are direct products of the colonial experience. Most African cities today look like their counterparts elsewhere in the world. They have high-rise buildings, blocks of residential apartments, wide boulevards, neon lights, movie theaters, and traffic jams.

The cities are also where the African elites live and work. Affluent Africans, like their contemporaries in other developing countries, have been strongly attracted to the glittering material aspects of Western culture. They live in Western-style homes or flats and eat Western foods stored in Western refrigerators, and those who can afford it drive Western cars. It has been said, not wholly in praise, that there are more Mercedes-Benzes in Nigeria than in Germany, where they are manufactured.

The furniture of their minds has become increasingly Western as well, in part because of the educational system. In the precolonial era, education as we know it did not really exist in Africa except for parochial schools in Christian Ethiopia and academies to train young males in Islamic doctrine and law in Muslim societies in North and West Africa. For the average African, education took place at the home or in the village courtyard and stressed socialization and vocational training.

Traditional education in Africa was not necessarily inferior to that in Europe. Social values and customs were transmitted to the young by storytellers, often village elders who could gain considerable prestige through their performance. Among the Luo people in Kenya, for example, children were taught in a *siwindhe,* or the house of a widowed grandmother. Here they would be instructed in the ways and thinking of their people. A favorite saying for those who behaved stupidly was "you are uneducated, like one who never slept in a *siwindhe.*"[9]

Europeans introduced modern Western education into Africa in the nineteenth century, although some Africans had already become literate in one or more Western languages by taking part in commerce. The French set up the first state-run schools in Senegal in 1818. In British colonies and protectorates, the earliest schools were established by missionaries. At first, these schools concentrated on vocational training with some instruction in European languages and Western civilization. Most courses were taught in the vernacular, although later many schools switched to English or French. Eventually, pressure from Africans led to the introduction of professional training, and the first institutes of higher learning were established in the early twentieth century. Most college-educated Africans, called "been-to's," however, received their higher training abroad.

With independence, African countries established their own state-run schools. The emphasis was on the primary level, but high schools and universities were established in major cities. The basic objectives have been to introduce vocational training and improve literacy rates. Unfortunately, both funding and trained teachers are scarce in most countries, and few rural areas have schools. As a result, illiteracy remains high, estimated at about 70 percent of the population across the continent. There has been a perceptible shift toward education in the vernacular languages. In West Africa, only about one in four adults is conversant in a Western language.

One interesting vehicle for popular education that emerged during the transition to independence in Nigeria was the Onitsha Market pamphlet. Produced primarily by the Ibo people in the southeast, who traditionally valued egalitarianism and individual achievement, the pamphlets were "how-to" books advising readers on how to succeed in a rapidly changing Africa. They tended to be short, inexpensive in price, and humorous in content, with flashy covers to attract the potential buyer's attention. One, titled "The Nigerian Bachelor's Guide," sold 40,000 copies. Unfortunately, the Onitsha Market and the pamphlet tradition were destroyed during the Nigerian civil war of the late 1960s, but it undoubtedly played an important role during a crucial period in the country's history.

Christianity has also been a conduit for the introduction of Western ideas. Assisted by the strenuous efforts of missionaries, Christianity spread rapidly during the nineteenth century among the urban elites and in rural areas as well. By 1950, an estimated 50 million Africans, or about half the population outside the Muslim areas, were Christians. Although many accepted Western religious beliefs to advance their careers, sincere conversions were by no means uncommon.

✦ **Home Sweet Home.** Although many large African cities have taken on a modern character, with skyscrapers, environmental pollution, fashionable shops, and traffic jams, the African village has been relatively little affected by the winds of change sweeping parts of the continent. Shown here is a traditional thatched-roof hut in a village south of Dar es Salaam in Tanzania.

Outside the major cities, where about three-quarters of the continent's inhabitants live, Western influence has had less of an impact. Millions of people throughout Africa (as in Asia) live much as their ancestors did, in thatch huts without modern plumbing and electricity; they farm or hunt by traditional methods, practice time-honored family rituals, and believe in the traditional deities. Even here, however, change is taking place. Slavery has been eliminated, for the most part, although there have been persistent reports of raids by slave traders on defenseless villages in the southern Sudan. Economic need, though, has brought about massive migrations, as some leave to work on plantations, others move to the cities, and still others flee to refugee camps to escape starvation. Migration itself is a wrenching experience, disrupting familiar family and village ties and enforcing new social relationships.

Nowhere, in fact, is the dichotomy between the old and the new, the native and the foreign, the rural and the urban, so clear and painful as in Africa. Urban dwellers regard the village as the repository of all that is backward in the African past, while rural peoples view the growing urban areas as a source of corruption, prostitution, hedonism, and the destruction of time-honored communal customs and values. The tension between traditional ways and Western culture is particularly strong among African intellectuals, many of whom are torn between their admiration for things Western and their desire to retain an African identity. "Here we stand," wrote one Nigerian,

infants overblown
poised between two civilizations
finding the balancing irksome,

itching for something to happen,
to tip us one way or the other,
groping in the dark for a helping hand
and finding none.[10]

African Women

One of the consequences of colonialism and independence has been a change in the relationship between men and women. In precolonial Africa, as in traditional societies in Asia, men and women had distinctly different roles. Women in sub-Saharan Africa, however, generally did not live under the severe legal and social disabilities that we have seen in such societies as China and India. Their role, it has been said, was "complimentary rather than subordinate to that of men."[11]

This complementary relationship existed at various levels. Within the family, wives normally showed a degree of deference to their husbands, and polygamy was not uncommon. But because society was usually arranged on communal lines, property was often held in common, and production tasks were divided on a cooperative rather than hierarchical basis. The status of women tended to rise as they moved through the life cycle. Women became more important as they reared children; in old age, they often became eligible to serve in senior roles within the family, lineage, or village. In some societies, such as the Ashanti kingdom in West Africa, women such as the queen mother were eligible to hold senior political positions. Some observers argue that polygamy was beneficial for women because it promoted communal and cooperative attitudes within the community and divided up the task of motherhood among several wives.

Sexual relationships changed profoundly during the colonial era, sometimes in ways that could justly be described as beneficial. Colonial governments attempted to bring an end to forced marriage, bodily mutilation such as clitoridectomy, and polygamy. Missionaries introduced women to Western education and encouraged them to organize themselves to defend their interests.

But the new system had some unfavorable consequences as well. Like men, women now became a labor resource. As African males were taken from the villages to serve as forced labor on construction projects, the traditional division of labor was disrupted, and women were forced to play a more prominent role in the economy. At the same time, their role in the broader society was constricted. In British colonies, Victorian attitudes of sexual repression and female subordination led to restrictions on women's freedom, and the positions in government they had formerly held were closed to them.

Independence also had a significant impact on gender roles in African society. Almost without exception, the new governments established the principle of sexual equality and permitted women to vote and run for political office. Yet, as elsewhere, women continue to operate at a disability in a world dominated by males. Politics remains a male preserve, and although a few professions, such as teaching, child care, and clerical work, are dominated by women, most African women are employed in menial positions such as agricultural labor, factory work, and retail trade, or as domestics. Education is open to all at the elementary level, but women comprise less than 20 percent of students at the upper levels in most African societies today.

Not surprisingly, women have made the greatest strides in the cities. Most urban women, like men, now marry on the basis of personal choice, although a significant minority are still willing to accept their parents' choice. After marriage, African women appear to occupy a more equal position than their counterparts in most Asian countries. Each marriage partner tends to maintain a separate income, and women often have the right to possess property separate from their husbands. While many wives still defer to their husbands in the traditional manner, others are like the woman in Abioseh Nicol's story "A Truly Married Woman," who, after years as living as a common-law wife with her husband, is finally able to provide the price and finalize the marriage. After the wedding, she declares, "For twelve years I have got up every morning at five to make tea for you and breakfast. Now I am a truly married woman [and] you must treat me with a little more respect. You are now my husband and not a lover. Get up and make yourself a cup of tea."[12]

Sexual relationships between men and women in contemporary Africa are relatively relaxed, as they were in traditional society. Sexual activity among adolescents is customary in most societies, and only a minority of women are still virgins at the time of marriage. Most marriages are monogamous. Males seem to be more likely to have extramarital relationships, often with bar girls or prostitutes (sometimes known as "walk-about women"), but adultery on the part of women is not rare.

There is a growing feminist movement in Africa, but it is firmly based on conditions in the local environment. Many African women writers, for example, refuse to be defined by Western dogma and opt instead for a brand of African feminism much like that of Ama Ata Aidoo, a Ghanaian novelist, whose ultimate objective is to free

African society as a whole, not just its female inhabitants. After receiving her education at a girls' school in the Gold Coast and attending classes at Stanford University in the United States, she embarked on a writing career in which, as she notes, she has committed herself to the betterment of the African people. Every African women and every man, she insists, "should be a feminist, especially if they believe that Africans should take charge of our land, its wealth, our lives, and the burden of our development. Because it is not possible to advocate independence for our continent without also believing that African women must have the best that the environment can offer."[13]

In a few cases, women are even going into politics. One example is Margaret Dongo of Zimbabwe, where a black African government under Robert Mugabe succeeded white rule in onetime Southern Rhodesia in 1980. Now an independent member of Zimbabwe's Parliament, she is labeled "the ant in the elephant's trunk" for her determined effort to root out corruption and bring about social and economic reforms to improve the lot of the general population. "We didn't fight to remove white skins," she remarks. "We fought discrimination against blacks in land distribution, education, employment. If we are being exploited again by our black leaders, then what did we fight for?"[14]

In general, then, women in urban areas in contemporary Africa have been able to hold their own. Although they are still sometimes held to different standards than men (African men often expect their wives to be both modern and traditional, fashionable and demure, wage earners and housekeepers) and do not possess the full range of career opportunities that men do, they are manifestly better off than women in many Asian societies.

The same cannot necessarily be said about women in rural areas, where traditional attitudes continue to exert a strong influence and individuals may still be subordinated to communalism. In some societies, clitoridectomy is still widely practiced. Polygamy is also not uncommon, and arranged marriages are still the rule rather than the exception. As a father tells his son in Cyprian Ekwensi's *Iska:*

> We have our pride and must do as our fathers did. You see your mother? I did not pick her in the streets. When I wanted a woman I went to my father and told him about my need of her and he went to her father. . . . Marriage is a family affair. You young people of today may think you are clever. But marriage is still a family affair.[15]

To a villager in Africa as elsewhere, an African city often looks like the fount of evil, decadence, and corruption. Women in particular have suffered from the tension between the pull of the city and the village. As men are drawn to the cities in search of employment and excitement, their wives and girlfriends are left behind, both literally and figuratively, in the native village. Nowhere has this been more vividly described than in the anguished cry of Lawino, the abandoned wife in Ugandan author p'Bitek Okot's *Song of Lawino.* Lawino laments not just her husband's decision to take a modern urban wife, who dusts powder over her face to look like a white woman and has red-hot lips like glowing charcoal, but his rejection of his roots. He in turn lashes out in frustration at what he considers the poverty, backwardness, and ignorance of the rural environment.

African Culture

Inevitably, the tension between traditional and modern, native and foreign, and individual and communal that has permeated contemporary African society has spilled over into culture. In general, in the visual arts and music, utility and ritual have given way to pleasure and decoration. In the process, Africans have been affected to a certain extent by foreign influences, but have retained their distinctive characteristics. Wood carving, metalwork, painting, and sculpture, for example, have preserved their traditional forms, but are now increasingly adapted to serve the tourist industry and the export market. Some African art retains its traditional purpose, however. Reportedly, a foreign tourist displayed to a customs agent a wood carving he had purchased in an African country, only to find that an African woman standing nearby had knelt down to pay homage and address praise songs to the carving. The carving turned out to be a sacred headpiece that had been stolen from the woman's hometown a few days earlier.

Similar developments have taken place in music and dance. They retain their traditional popularity, but the earlier emphasis on religious ritual and the experience of the performer has been replaced to some degree by a new interest in the spectator. In the process, some of the social functions of traditional music and dance—to express grief or other emotions, to exorcise evil spirits, or to express community solidarity—have eroded, sometimes to the detriment of the society. To restore such activity to its traditional vigor, or to take advantage of the growing popularity of African dancing, several governments have sponsored traveling folk dance companies. African music has been exported to Europe and the Americas and has returned to Africa in a new synthesis with foreign styles, as in the cha cha and the samba.

No area of African culture has been so strongly affected by political and social events as literature. Except for Muslim areas in North and East Africa, precolonial Africans did not have a written literature, although their tradition of oral storytelling served as a rich repository of history, custom, and folk culture. The absence of written languages, of course, means a lack of a traditional African literature. The first written literature in the vernacular or in European languages emerged during the nineteenth century in the form of novels, poetry, and drama.

Angry at the negative portrayal of Africa in Western literature, African authors initially wrote primarily for a European audience as a means of establishing black dignity and purpose. Embracing the ideals of negritude, many glorified the emotional and communal aspects of the traditional African experience.

One of the first was the Guinean author Camara Lay (1928–1980), who in 1953 published *The Dark Child*, a touching and intimate initiation into village life in precolonial Africa. In the novel, which admitted the reader to the secret rituals and practices of daily life behind the protective hedges of an African village compound, the author openly regretted the lost ways of the African past, while conceding that they were not appropriate to the Guinea of tomorrow.

Another Francophone writer is Ousmane Sembène of Senegal. Not a member of the educated African elite, Sembène enlisted in the French army at the age of fifteen and fought in Europe during World War II. Afterwards he participated in a rail workers' strike and later served as a dockworker and leader of a longshoremen's union in Marseilles. His novels, such as the renowned *God's Bits of Wood*, have often been compared to André Malraux's *Man's Fate* in their use of Marxist themes to promote the struggle of African workers against capitalist exploitation. Eventually, Sembène became one of Africa's first native film producers.

The Nigerian Chinua Achebe is considered the first major African novelist to write in the English language. In his writings, he attempts to interpret African history from a native perspective and to forge a new sense of African identity. In his most famous novel, *Things Fall Apart* (1958), he recounts the story of a Nigerian who refuses to submit to the new British order and eventually commits suicide. Criticizing those of his contemporaries who have accepted foreign rule, the protagonist laments that the white man "has put a knife on the things that held us together and we have fallen apart."

After 1965, the African novel took a dramatic turn, shifting its focus from the brutality of the foreign oppressor to the shortcomings of the new native leadership. Having gained independence, African politicians were now portrayed as mimicking and even outdoing the injustices committed by their colonial predecessors. A prominent example of this genre is the work of the Kenyan Ngugi Wa Thiong'o (b. 1938). His first novel, *A Grain of Wheat*, takes place on the eve of *Uhuru*, or independence. Although it mocks local British society for its racism, snobbishness, and superficiality, its chief interest lies in its unsentimental and even unflattering portrayal of ordinary Kenyans in their daily struggle for survival.

Like most of his predecessors, Ngugi initially wrote in English, but he eventually decided to write in his native Kikuyu as a means of broadening his readership. For that reason, perhaps, in the late 1970s, he was placed under house arrest for writing subversive literature. From prison he secretly wrote *Devil on the Cross*, which urged his compatriots to overthrow the government of Daniel Arap Moi. Published in 1980, the book sold widely and was eventually read aloud by storytellers throughout Kenyan society. Fearing an attempt on his life, in recent years Ngugi has lived abroad.

Many of Ngugi's contemporaries have followed his lead and focused their frustration on the failure of the continent's new leadership to carry out the goals of independence. One of the most outstanding is the Nigerian Wole Soyinka (b. 1932). His novel *The Interpreters* (1965) lambasted the corruption and hypocrisy of Nigerian politics. Succeeding novels and plays have continued that tradition, resulting in a Nobel Prize for Literature in 1986. Like other contemporary writers, he has also directed his attention to the problems of daily life in Africa, including the alienation and estrangement that often characterize the shift from the traditional rural village to the impersonal modern cities. In 1994, however, he barely managed to escape arrest, and now lives abroad, from whence he has directed his satire at the inhumanity of the Abacha regime (discussed earlier in this chapter).

Among Africa's most prominent writers today, a number are women. Traditionally, African women were valued for their talents as storytellers, but writing was strongly discouraged by both traditional and colonial authorities on the grounds that women should occupy themselves with their domestic obligations. In recent years, however, a number of women have emerged as prominent writers of African fiction. Two examples are Buchi Emecheta (b. 1940) of Nigeria and Ama Ata Aidoo (b. 1942) of Ghana. Beginning with *Second Class Citizen* (1975), which chronicled the breakdown of her own marriage, Emecheta has published numerous works exploring the role of women in contemporary African society and decrying the practice of polygamy. In her own writings, Ama Ata Aidoo has focused on the identity of today's African women and the changing relations between men and women in society. In her recent novel *Changes: A Love Story* (1991), she chronicles the lives of three women, none presented as a victim, but all caught up in the struggle for survival and happiness. Sadly, the one who strays the furthest from traditional African values finds herself free but isolated and lonely.

One of the overriding concerns confronting African intellectuals since independence has been the problem of language. Unlike Asian societies, Africans have not inherited a long written tradition from the precolonial era. As a result, many intellectuals have written in the colonial language, a practice that sometimes results in guilt and anxiety. As we have seen, some have reacted by writing in their local languages to reach a native audience. The market for such work is limited, however, because of the high illiteracy rate, and also because novels written in African languages have no market abroad. Moreover, because of the deep financial crisis throughout the continent, there is little money for the publication of serious books. Many of Africa's libraries and universities are almost literally without books. It is little wonder that many African authors, to their discomfort, continue to write and publish in foreign languages.

Conclusion: Gathered at the Beach

Nowhere in the developing world is the dilemma of continuity and change more agonizing than in contemporary Africa. Mesmerized by the spectacle of Western affluence, yet repulsed by the bloody trail from slavery to World War II and the atomic bombs over Hiroshima and Nagasaki, African intellectuals have been torn between the dual images of Western materialism and African negritude.

What is the destiny of Africa? Some still yearn for the dreams embodied in the program of the OAU. Novelist Ngugi Wa Thiong'o argues that for his country, the starting point is a democratic Kenya. More broadly, he calls for "an internationalization of all the democratic and social struggles for human equality, justice, peace, and progress."[16] Some African political leaders, however, have apparently discarded the democratic ideal and turned their attention to what is sometimes called the "East Asian model," based on the Confucian tenet of subordination of the individual to the community as the guiding principle of national development (see Chapter 15). Whether African political culture today is well placed to imitate the strategy adopted by the fast-growing nations of East Asia—who in any event are now encountering problems of their own—is questionable. Like all peoples, Africans must ultimately find their own solutions within the context of their own traditions, and not by seeking to imitate the example of others.

For the average African, of course, such intellectual dilemmas pale before the daily challenge of survival. But the fundamental gap between the traditional village and the modern metropolis is perhaps wider in Africa than anywhere else in the world and may well be harder to bridge. The solution is not yet visible. In the meantime, writes Ghanaian author George Awoonor-Williams, all Africans are exiles:

The return is tedious
And the exiled souls gathered at the beach
Arguing and deciding their future
Should they return home
And face the fences the termites had eaten
And see the dunghill that has mounted their birthplace?
. . . The final strokes will land them on forgotten shores
They committed to the impiety of self-deceit
Slashed, cut and wounded their souls
And left the mangled remainder in manacles.

The moon, the moon is our father's spirit
At the stars entrance the night revellers gather
To sell their chatter and inhuman sweat to the gateman
And shuffle their feet in agonies of birth.
Lost souls, lost souls, lost souls, that are
still at the gate.[17]

NOTES

1. Quoted in G.-C. M. Mutiso, *Socio-Political Thought in African Literature* (New York, 1974), p. 117.
2. Aimé Césaire, *Cahier d'un retour du pays natal*, trans. John Berger and Anna Bostock (Harmondsworth, 1969), p. 10, quoted in Emmanuel N. Obiechina, *Language and Theme: Essays on African Literature* (Washington, DC, 1990), pp. 78–79.
3. *Time*, January 16, 1984.
4. Cyprian Ekwensi, *Jagua Nana* (Greenwich, 1961), pp. 146–47.
5. Albert Ojuka, "Pedestrian, to Passing Benz-man," quoted in Adrian Roscoe, *Uhuru's Fire: African Literature East to South* (Cambridge, 1977), p. 103.
6. *New York Times*, September 1, 1996.
7. Taban Lo Liyong, "Student's Lament," quoted in Roscoe, *Uhuru's Fire*, pp. 120–21.
8. Dan Agbee, in *Newswatch* (Lagos), quoted in *World Press Review*, August 1991, p. 16.
9. Roscoe, *Uhuru's Fire*, p. 23.
10. Francis Ademola, *Reflections: Nigerian Prose and Verse* (Lagos, 1962), p. 65, quoted in Mutiso, *Socio-Political Thought in African Literature*, p. 117.
11. Kenneth Little, *African Women in Towns: An Aspect of Africa's Social Revolution* (Cambridge, 1973), p. 6.
12. Abioseh Nicol, *A Truly Married Woman and Other Stories* (London, 1965), p. 12.
13. Ama Ata Aidoo, *No Sweetness Here* (New York, 1995), p. 136.
14. Quoted in the *New York Times*, May 13, 1996.
15. Cyprian Ekwensi, *Iska* (London, 1966), p. 21.
16. Ngugi Wa Thiong'o, *Decolonising the Mind: The Politics of Language in African Literature* (Portsmouth, NH, 1986), p. 103.
17. George Awoonor-Williams, *Rediscovery and Other Poems* (Ibadan, 1964), p. 11, quoted in Mutiso, *Socio-Political Thought in African Literature*, pp. 81–82.

CHAPTER
14

Ferment in the Middle East

"We Muslims are of one family even though we live under different governments and in various regions."[1] So said the Ayatollah Ruholla Khomeini, the Islamic religious figure and leader of the 1979 revolution that overthrew the shah in Iran. The Ayatollah's remark was not just a pious wish by a religious mystic, but an accurate reflection of one crucial aspect of the political dynamics in the region.

If the concept of negritude represents an alternative to the system of nation-states in Africa, in the Middle East a similar role has been played by the forces of militant Islam. In both regions, a yearning for a sense of community beyond national borders tugs at the emotions and intellect of their inhabitants and counteracts the dynamic pull of nationalism that has provoked political turmoil and conflict in much of the rest of the world.

Crescent of Conflict

For the Middle East, the period between the two world wars was an era of transition. With the fall of the Ottoman and the Persian empires, new modernizing regimes emerged in Turkey and Iran, and a more traditionalist but fiercely independent government was established in Saudi Arabia. Elsewhere, European influence continued to be strong; the British and French had mandates in Syria, Lebanon, Jordan, and Palestine, and British influence persisted in Iraq, southern Arabia, and throughout the Nile valley. Pan-Arabism was on the rise, but it lacked focus and coherence.

During World War II, the region became the cockpit of European rivalries, as it had been during World War I. Germany no longer had a physical presence in the area. With Turkey remaining neutral, but with the Italian occupation of Libya and Vichy control over French colonies in North Africa, it had a strong potential presence along the southern coast of the Mediterranean. The region was more significant to the warring powers than previously because of the growing importance of oil and the Suez Canal's position as a vital sea route.

During the war, the primary theater of Axis activity was along the Mediterranean coast rather than in the Middle East itself. For a brief period, the Afrika Korps, under the command of the brilliant German general Erwin Rommel, threatened to seize Egypt and the Suez Canal. Rommel's campaign benefited from widespread sympathy for the Axis cause in Egypt, where nationalist forces in the Wafd Party agitated for complete independence and an end to the informal British protectorate. But British troops defeated the German forces at El Alamein, west of Alexandria, and gradually drove them westward until their final defeat after the arrival of U.S. troops in Morocco under the field command of General George S. Patton. From that time until the end of the war, the entire region from the Mediterranean Sea eastward was under secure Allied occupation.

The Question of Palestine

As in other areas of Asia, the end of World Was II led to the emergence of a number of independent states. Jordan, Lebanon, and Syria, all European mandates before the war, became independent. Egypt, Iran, and Iraq, though still under a degree of Western influence, became increasingly autonomous. Sympathy for the idea of Arab unity led to the formation of an Arab League in 1945, but different points of view among its members prevented it from achieving anything of substance.

The one issue on which all Arab states in the area could agree was the question of Palestine. As tensions between Jews and Arabs in that mandate intensified during the 1930s, the British reduced Jewish immigration into the area and firmly rejected proposals for independence. After World War II, the Zionists turned for support to the United States, and in March 1948, the Truman administration approved the concept of an independent Jewish state, despite the fact that only about one-third of the local population were Jews. In May, the new state of Israel was formally established.

To its Arab neighbors, the new state represented a betrayal of the interests of the Palestinian people, 90 percent of whom were Muslim, and a flagrant disregard for the conditions set out in the Balfour Declaration of 1917. Outraged at the lack of Western support for Muslim interests in the area, several Arab countries invaded the new Jewish state. The invasion did not succeed because of internal divisions among the Arabs, but both sides remained bitter, and the Arab states refused to recognize Israel.

The war had other lasting consequences as well, because it led to the exodus of thousands of Palestinian refugees into neighboring Muslim states. Jordan, which had become independent under its Hashemite ruler, was now flooded by the arrival of 1 million urban Palestinians in a country occupied by half a million Bedouins. To the north, the state of Lebanon had been created to provide the local Christian community with a country of their own, but the arrival of the Palestinian refugees upset the delicate balance between Christians and Muslims. In any event, the creation of Lebanon had angered the Syrians, who had lost it as well as other territories to Turkey as a result of European decisions before and after the war.

Nasser and Pan-Arabism

The dispute over Palestine placed Egypt in an uncomfortable position. Technically, Egypt was not an Arab state. King Farouk, who had acceded to power in 1936, had frequently declared support for the Arab cause, but the Egyptian people were not Bedouins and shared little of the culture of the peoples across the Red Sea. Nevertheless, Farouk committed Egyptian armies to the disastrous war against Israel.

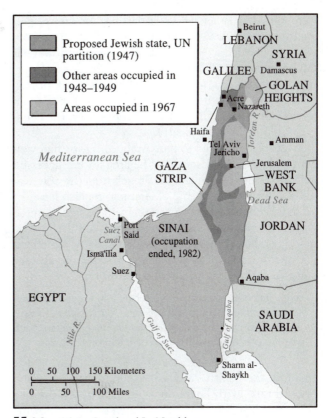

Map 14.1   Israel and Its Neighbors

In 1952, King Farouk, whose corrupt habits had severely eroded his early popularity, was overthrown by a military coup engineered by young military officers ostensibly under the leadership of Colonel Muhammad Nagib. The real force behind the scenes was Colonel Gamal Abdul Nasser (1918–1970), the son of a minor government functionary who, like many of his fellow officers, had been angered by the army's inadequate preparation for the war against Israel four years earlier. In 1953, the monarchy was replaced by a republic.

In 1954, Nasser seized power in his own right and immediately instituted a land reform program. He also adopted a policy of neutrality in foreign affairs and expressed sympathy for the Arab cause. The British presence had rankled many Egyptians for years, for even after granting Egypt independence, Britain had retained control over the Suez Canal to protect its route to the Indian Ocean. In 1956, Nasser suddenly nationalized the Suez Canal Company, which had been under British and French administration. Seeing a threat to their route to the Indian Ocean, the British and the French launched a joint attack on Egypt to protect their investment. They were joined by Israel, whose leaders had grown exasperated at sporadic Arab commando raids on Israeli territory and now decided to strike back. But the Eisenhower administration in the United States, concerned that the attack smacked of a revival of colonialism, supported Nasser and brought about the withdrawal of foreign forces from Egypt and of Israeli troops from the Sinai Peninsula (see box on p. 291).

Nasser now turned to pan-Arabism. Egypt had won approval from other states in the area for its successful eviction of the British and the French from the Suez Canal and for its sponsorship of efforts to replace Israel by an independent Palestinian state. In 1958, Egypt united with Syria in a new United Arab Republic (UAR). The union had been proposed by the Ba'ath Party, which advocated the unity of all Arab states in a new socialist society. According to the party's constitution,

> The Arab nation has an immortal mission which has manifested itself in renewed and complete forms in the different stages of history and which aims at reviving human values, encouraging human development, and promoting harmony and cooperation among the nations of the world.[2]

In 1957, the Ba'ath Party assumed power in Syria and opened talks with Egypt on a union between the two countries, which took place in March of 1958 following a plebiscite. Nasser, despite his reported ambivalence about the union, was named president of the new state.

Egypt and Syria hoped that the union would eventually include all Arab states, but other Arab leaders, including young King Hussein of Jordan and the kings of Iraq and Saudi Arabia, were suspicious. The latter two in particular feared pan-Arabism on the reasonable assumption that they would be asked to share their vast oil revenues with the poorer states of the Middle East.

Nasser's concept of Arab socialism and his hopes for the union are more easily explained in terms of what he did not want than what he did. Nasser opposed existing relationships in which the world was dominated by two competing blocs, while much of the wealth of the Middle East flowed into the treasuries of a handful of wealthy feudal states or, even worse, the pockets of foreign oil interests. In Nasser's view, through Arab unity, this wealth could be put to better use to improve the standard of living in the area. To achieve a more equitable division of the wealth of the region, natural resources and major industries would be nationalized; central planning would guarantee that resources were exploited efficiently, but private enterprise would continue at the local level.

In the end, however, Nasser's determination to extend state control over the economy brought an end to

◆ **Gamal Abdul Nasser.** Gamal Abdul Nasser was a leading figure in the overthrow of King Farouk in 1953. Nasser's integrity, charisma, and program for government reform endeared him to the Egyptian people. In 1956, Nasser seized the Suez Canal from the British and the French, who in turn mounted a joint attack on Egypt. They withdrew, however, when the United States supported Nasser. During his sixteen years as president, Nasser was an articulate spokesman for the Arab cause in the Middle East.

the UAR. When the government announced the nationalization of a large number of industries and utilities in 1961, a military coup overthrew the Ba'ath leaders in Damascus, and the new authorities declared that Syria would end its relationship with Egypt.

The breakup of the UAR did not necessarily end Nasser's dream of pan-Arabism. In 1962, Algeria finally received its independence from France and, under its new president, Ahmad Ben Bella, established close relations with Egypt, as did a new republic in Yemen. During the mid-1960s, Egypt took the lead in promoting Arab unity against Israel. At a meeting of Arab leaders held in Jerusalem in 1964, the Palestine Liberation Organization (PLO) was set up under Egyptian sponsorship to

❧ The Suez Canal Belongs to Egypt ❧

The Suez Canal was built between 1854 and 1869, using mainly French capital and Egyptian labor, under the direction of the French promoter Ferdinand de Lesseps. It was managed by a Paris-based limited liability corporation, called the Suez Canal Company, under a ninety-nine-year lease. Over time, the canal came to symbolize colonial exploitation in the minds of many Egyptians. In a speech in July 1956, President Nasser declared that it was time for the canal to be owned and managed by Egyptians. "The Suez Canal," he declared, "is an Egyptian canal built as a result of great sacrifices." It was built by an Egyptian company, he explained, but was later expropriated by the British, who ever since had kept the lion's share of the profits for themselves. The Suez Canal Company was "a state within a state, depending on the conspiracies of imperialism and its supporters." Today, he promised, Egypt had decided to restore its rights over the canal, and the profits from its operations would be used to benefit the Egyptian people. "We have taken this decision," he concluded, "to restore part of the glories of the past and to safeguard our national dignity and pride."

Nasser's decision to seize the canal led to a brief invasion of Egypt by the military forces of Great Britain and France, but the United States, fearing that the invasion would drive Egypt and other countries in the region into the arms of the Soviet Union, put enormous pressure on its European allies, and in the end Nasser got his way. Funds from the canal now went into the hands of the Egyptian government and were eventually put to use in constructing the High Dam at Aswan, a project built ironically with the assistance of the USSR. The dam was intended to open up thousands of acres along the Nile River for cultivation, but environmental side effects have plagued the project in recent decades.

Today the Suez Canal remains under Egyptian administration, but inadequate conditions (many of today's supertankers are too wide to use the canal) and high fees imposed by Cairo on ships passing through the canal have persuaded many shipping companies to abandon the Red Sea route in favor of a voyage around the Cape of Good Hope.

Source: *The Egyptian Gazette,* July 27, 1956, p. 12.

---

represent the interests of the Palestinians. According to the charter of the PLO, only the Palestinian people (and thus not Jewish immigrants from abroad) had the right to form a state in the old British mandate. A guerrilla movement called al-Fatah, led by the dissident PLO figure Yasir Arafat (b. 1929), began to launch terrorist attacks on Israeli territory, prompting the Israeli government to raid PLO bases in Jordan in 1966.

The Arab-Israeli Dispute

The growing Arab hostility was a constant threat to the security of Israel. In the years after independence, Israeli leaders dedicated themselves to creating a Jewish homeland. Aided by reparations paid by the postwar German government of Chancellor Konrad Adenauer and private funds provided by Jews living abroad, notably in the United States, the government attempted to build a democratic and modern state that would be a magnet for Jews throughout the world and a symbol of Jewish achievement.

Ensuring the survival of the tiny state surrounded by antagonistic Arab neighbors was a considerable chal-lenge, made more difficult by divisions within the Israeli population. Some were immigrants from Europe, while others came from the countries of Middle East. Some were secular and even socialist in their views, while others were politically conservative and stressed religious orthodoxy. There were also Christians as well as many Muslim Palestinians who had not fled to other countries. To balance these diverse interests, Israel established a parliament, called the Knesset, on the European model, with proportional representation based on the number of votes each party received in the general election. The parties were so numerous that none ever received a majority of votes, and all governments had to be formed from a coalition of several parties. As a result, moderate secular leaders such as longtime prime minister David Ben Gurion had to cater to more marginal parties composed of conservative religious groups.

During the late 1950s and 1960s, the dispute between Israel and other states in the Middle East escalated in intensity. Essentially alone except for the sympathy of the United States and several Western European countries, Israel adopted a policy of determined resistance to and immediate retaliation against alleged

PLO and Arab provocations. By the spring of 1967, relations between Israel and its Arab neighbors had deteriorated, as Nasser attempted to improve his standing in the Arab world by intensifying military activities and imposing a blockade against Israeli commerce through the Gulf of Aqaba. In a speech before the Egyptian Popular Assembly, he declared:

> Israel used to boast a great deal, and the Western powers, headed by the United States and Britain, used to ignore and even despise us and consider us of no value. But now that the time has come—and I have already said in the past that we will decide the time and place and not allow them to decide—we must be ready for triumph and not for a recurrence of the 1948 comedies. We shall triumph, God willing.
>
> Preparations have already been made. We are now ready to confront Israel. . . . Now we are ready for the confrontation. We are now ready to deal with the entire Palestine question.[3]

Concerned that it might be isolated, and lacking firm support from Western powers (who had originally guaranteed Israel the freedom to use the Gulf of Aqaba), in June 1967, Israel suddenly launched air strikes against Egypt and several of its Arab neighbors. Israeli armies then broke the blockade at the head of the Gulf of Aqaba and occupied the Sinai Peninsula. Other Israeli forces attacked Jordanian territory on the West Bank of the Jordan River (Jordan's King Hussein had recently signed an alliance with Egypt and placed his army under Egyptian command), occupied the whole of Jerusalem, and seized Syrian military positions in the Golan Heights along the Israeli-Syrian border.

Despite limited Soviet support for Egypt and Syria, in a brief, six-day war, Israel had mocked Nasser's pretensions of Arab unity and tripled the size of its territory, thus enhancing its precarious security. Yet the new Israel also aroused even more bitter hostility among the Arabs and included an additional million Palestinians inside its borders, most of them living on the West Bank (see box on p. 293).

During the next few years, the focus of the Arab-Israeli dispute shifted, as Arab states demanded the return of the occupied territories. Meanwhile, many Israelis argued that the new lands improved the security of the beleaguered state and should be retained. Concerned that the dispute might lead to a confrontation between the superpowers, the Nixon administration tried to achieve a peace settlement. The peace effort received a mild stimulus when Nasser died of a heart attack in September 1970 and was succeeded by his vice president, ex-general Anwar al-Sadat (1918–1981).

Sadat soon showed himself to be more pragmatic than his predecessor, dropping the now irrelevant name United Arab Republic in favor of the Arab Republic of Egypt and replacing Nasser's socialist policies with a new strategy based on free enterprise and encouragement of Western investment. He also agreed to sign a peace treaty with Israel on condition that Israel retire to its pre-1967 frontiers. Concerned that other Arab countries would refuse to make peace and take advantage of its presumed weakness, Israel refused.

Rebuffed in his offer of peace, smarting from criticism of his moderate stand from other Arab leaders, and increasingly concerned over Israeli plans to build permanent Jewish settlements in the occupied territories, Sadat attempted once again to renew Arab unity through a new confrontation with Israel. On Yom Kippur (the Jewish Day of Atonement), an Israeli national holiday, Egyptian forces suddenly launched an air and artillery attack on Israeli positions in the Sinai just east of the Suez Canal. Syrian armies attacked Israeli positions in the Golan Heights. After early Arab successes, the Israelis managed to recoup some of their losses on both fronts. As a superpower confrontation between the United States and the Soviet Union loomed, a cease-fire was finally reached.

In the next years, a fragile peace was maintained, marked by U.S. "shuttle diplomacy" (carried out by U.S. Secretary of State Henry Kissinger) and the rise to power in Israel of the militant Likud Party under Prime Minister Menachem Begin (1913–1992). The conflict now spread to Lebanon, where many Palestinians had found refuge and the PLO had set up its headquarters. Rising tension along the border was compounded by increasingly hostile disputes between Christians and Muslims over control of the capital, Beirut.

After his election as president in 1976, Jimmy Carter began to press for a compromise peace based on Israel's return of occupied Arab territories and Arab recognition of the state of Israel (an idea originally proposed by Henry Kissinger). By now, Sadat was anxious to reduce his military expenses and announced his willingness to visit Jerusalem to seek peace. The meeting took place in November 1977, with no concrete results, but Sadat persisted. In September 1978, he and Begin met with Carter at Camp David in the United States. Israel agreed to withdraw from the Sinai, but not from other occupied territories unless it was recognized by other Arab countries.

The promise of the Camp David agreement was not fulfilled. One reason was the assassination of Sadat by Islamic militants in October 1981. But there were deeper

⟫ *The Plight of Palestine* ⟪

For many Arabs in the Middle East, the very existence of the state of Israel and its occupation of the West Bank after the 1967 War was an affront. It not only represented an injustice to the Palestinian population forced to live under Israeli rule, but was a direct security threat to all Islamic states in the region and a challenge to the very existence of the pan-Arab ideal. In an article published in the U.S. periodical Foreign Affairs *in 1978, Walid Khalidi, a professor of political studies at the American University in Beirut, Lebanon, expressed the Arab point of view. The Palestinian problem, he declared, "encapsulates the concepts of pan-Arabism." Because the Palestinian people, the vast majority of whom are Muslims, were viewed as an integral part of the Arab nation, by definition their injustice was an injustice to the entire nation. The creation of Israel was viewed as "a violation of the principles of the unity and integrity of Arab soil, an affront to the dignity of the Nation."*

Added to the emotional issue were security considerations. By controlling Palestine, the state of Israel separated the Muslim societies of Northern Africa from their counterparts in the Middle East. Israel was all the more feared, he added, "because of its territorial dynamism and seemingly inexhaustible reservoir of Western and particularly American support it commanded." In a word, Israel was "a beachhead of American imperialism in the Middle East and its executioner."

For many Muslims in the region, then, the very existence of Israel represented a betrayal of the sacred cause of pan-Arab unity, and that sentiment fueled three decades of hostility to the Jewish state in their midst. By the late 1970s, however, some moderate states in the region, led by Egypt, became increasingly willing to accept the presence of Israel, provided that territories on the West Bank, occupied since the 1967 War, were returned to Palestinian authority. Negotiations between Israel and moderate states in the region led eventually to a tentative agreement for the establishment of Palestinian authority on the West Bank in return for Arab recognition of Israel's legitimacy. Militants on both sides, however, have resisted compromise. As terrorist incidents perpetrated by Arab militants inflame Israeli public opinion and make Israelis less willing to turn territories on the West Bank over to Palestinian administration, so the establishment of Jewish settlements in the area with official support angers Palestinians and drives many of them into the arms of militants. Whether a compromise peace can be achieved remains uncertain.

Source: Walid Khalidi, "Thinking the Unthinkable: A Sovereign Palestinian State," *Foreign Affairs*, July 1978, pp. 696–97.

---

causes, including the continued unwillingness of many Arab governments to recognize Israel and the Israeli government's encouragement of Jewish settlements on the occupied West Bank.

During the early 1980s, the militance of the Palestinians increased, leading to rising unrest, popularly labeled the *intifada* (uprising) among PLO supporters living inside Israel. To control the situation, a new Israeli government under Prime Minister Itzhak Shamir invaded southern Lebanon to destroy PLO commando bases near the Israeli border. The invasion provoked international condemnation and further destabilized the perilous balance between Muslims and Christians in Lebanon. As the 1990s began, U.S. sponsored peace talks opened between Israel and a number of its neighbors. The first major breakthrough came in 1993, when Israel and the PLO reached an agreement calling for Palestinian autonomy in selected areas of Israel in return for PLO recognition of the legitimacy of the Israeli state.

Progress in implementing the agreement, however, has been slow. Terrorist attacks by Palestinian militants have resulted in heavy casualties and shaken the confidence of many Jewish citizens that their security needs can be protected under the agreement. At the same time, Jewish residents of the West Bank have resisted the extension of Palestinian authority in the area. In November 1995, Prime Minister Yitzhak Rabin was assassinated by an Israeli opponent of the accords. National elections held a few months later led to the formation of a new government under Benjamin Netanyahu, which has adopted a tougher stance in negotiations with the Palestinian Authority under Yasir Arafat. For the moment, future progress in implementing the agreement is in doubt.

Revolution in Iran

The Arab-Israeli dispute also provoked an international oil crisis. In 1960, a number of oil-producing states formed the Organization of Petroleum Exporting

◆ Bone of Contention. The Golan Heights, a range of mountains to the east of the Sea of Galilee in northern Israel, has become a major bone of contention between the state of Israel and its neighbor Syria. Israeli forces seized the area during the brief Arab-Israeli conflict in 1967 and continue to occupy it today. As the photo clearly shows, whoever controls the heights is in a position to dominate the Israeli lowlands below.

Countries (OPEC) to gain control over oil prices, but the organization was not recognized by the foreign oil companies. In the 1970s, a group of Arab oil states established the Organization of Arab Petroleum Exporting Countries (OAPEC) to use as a weapon to force Western governments to abandon pro-Israeli policies. During the 1973 Yom Kippur War, some OPEC nations announced significant increases in the price of oil to foreign countries. The price hikes were accompanied by an apparent oil shortage and created serious economic problems in the United States and Europe as well as in the Third World. They also proved to be a boon to oil-exporting countries, such as Libya, now under the leadership of the militantly anti-Western Colonel Muammar Qadhafi (b. 1942).

One of the key oil-exporting countries was Iran. Under the leadership of Shah Mohammad Reza Pahlavi (1919–1980), who had taken over from his father in 1941, Iran had become one of the richest countries in the Middle East. Although relations with the West had occasionally been fragile (especially after Prime Minister Mossadeq had briefly attempted to nationalize the oil industry in 1951), during the next twenty years Iran became a prime ally of the United States in the Middle East. With encouragement from the United States, which hoped that Iran could become a force for stability in the Persian Gulf, the shah attempted to carry through a series of social and economic reforms to transform the country into the most advanced in the region.

Statistical evidence suggests that his efforts were succeeding. Per capita income increased dramatically, literacy rates improved, a modern communications infrastructure took shape, and an affluent middle class emerged in the capital of Tehran. Under the surface, however, trouble was brewing. Despite an ambitious land reform program, many peasants were still landless, unemployment among intellectuals was dangerously high, and the urban middle class was squeezed by high inflation. Housing costs had skyrocketed, provoked in part by the massive influx of foreigners attracted by oil money.

Some of the unrest took the form of religious discontent, as millions of devout Muslims looked with distaste at a new Iranian civilization based on greed, sexual license, and material accumulation. Conservative *ulama* opposed rampant government corruption, the ostentation of the shah's court, and the extension of voting rights to women. Some opposition elements took to terrorism against wealthy Iranians or foreign residents in an attempt to provoke social and political disorder. In response, the shah's U.S.–trained security police, the *Savak*, imprisoned and sometimes tortured thousands of dissidents.

Leading the opposition was the Ayatollah Ruholla Khomeini (1900–1989), an austere Shi'ite cleric who had been exiled to Iraq and then to France because of his outspoken opposition to the shah's regime. From Paris, Khomeini continued his attacks in print, on television, and in radio broadcasts. By the late 1970s, large numbers of Iranians—students, peasants,, and townspeople—began to respond to Khomeini's diatribes against the "satanic regime," and demonstrations by his supporters were repressed with ferocity by the police. But workers' strikes (some of them in the oil fields, which reduced government revenue) grew in intensity. In January 1979, the shah appointed a moderate, Shapur Bakhtiar, as prime minister and then left the country for medical treatment.

Bakhtiar attempted to conciliate the rising opposition and permitted Khomeini to return to Iran, where he presided over a new Islamic Revolutionary Council and demanded the government's resignation. With rising public unrest and incipient revolt within the army, the government collapsed and was replaced by a hastily formed Islamic Republic. The new government, which was dominated by Shi'ite *ulama* under the guidance of Ayatollah Khomeini, immediately began to introduce and restore traditional Islamic law. A new reign of terror ensued, as supporters of the shah were rounded up and executed. Along the borders, ethnic groups such as the Kurds and the Azerbaijanis rose in rebellion.

Though much of the outside world focused on the U.S. Embassy in Tehran, where militants held a number of foreign hostages, the Iranian Revolution involved much more. In the eyes of the ayatollah and his followers, the United States was "the great Satan," the powerful protector of Israel, and the enemy of Muslim peoples everywhere. Furthermore, it was responsible for the cor-

ruption of Iranian society under the shah. Now Khomeini demanded that the shah be returned to Iran for trial and that the United States apologize for its acts against the Iranian people. In response, the Carter administration stopped buying Iranian oil and froze Iranian assets in the United States.

The effects of the disturbances in Iran quickly spread beyond its borders. Sunni militants briefly seized the holy places in Mecca and began to appeal to their brothers to launch similar revolutions in Islamic countries around the world, including far-off Malaysia and Indonesia. At the same time, the ethnic unrest among the Kurdish minorities along the border continued. In July 1980, the shah died of cancer in Cairo. Two months later, Iraq and Iran went to war (see the next section). With economic conditions in Iran rapidly deteriorating, the Islamic revolutionary government finally agreed to free the hostages in return for the release of Iranian assets in the United States. During the next few years, the intensity of the Iranian Revolution moderated slightly, and the government of President Hashemi Rafsanjani displayed a modest tolerance for a loosening of clerical control over freedom of expression and social activities. But rising criticism of rampant official corruption and a high rate of inflation sparked a new wave of government repression in the mid-1990s; newspapers were censored, the universities were purged of disloyal or "un-Islamic" elements, and religious militants raided private homes in search of blasphemous activities. "There is deep fear and absolutely no freedom of expression," remarked one Iranian journalist.

Crisis in the Gulf

Although much of the Iranians' anger was directed against the United States during the early phases of the revolution, Iran had equally hated enemies closer to home. To the north, the immense power of the Soviet Union, driven by atheistic communism, was viewed as a modern-day version of the Russian threat of previous centuries. To the west was a militant and hostile Iraq, now under the leadership of the ambitious Saddam Hussein (b. 1937). Problems from both directions appeared shortly after Khomeini's rise to power. Soviet military forces occupied Afghanistan to prop up a weak Marxist regime there. The following year, Iraqi forces suddenly attacked along the Iranian border.

Iraq and Iran had long had an uneasy relationship, fueled by religious differences (Iranian Islam is predominantly Shi'ite, while the ruling caste in Iraq is Sunni), and a perennial dispute over borderlands adjacent to the

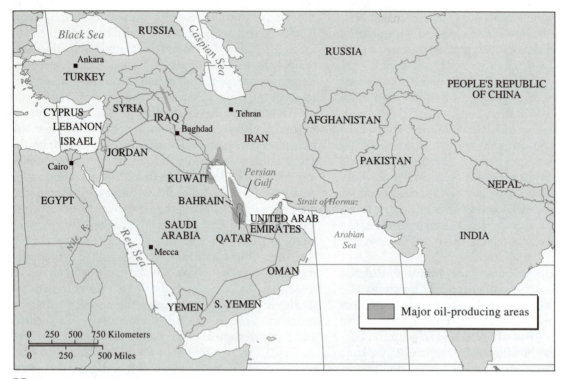

Black Sea
RUSSIA
RUSSIA
Caspian Sea
Ankara ■
TURKEY
PEOPLE'S REPUBLIC
OF CHINA
CYPRUS
LEBANON
SYRIA
IRAQ
Tehran ■
AFGHANISTAN
Baghdad ■
ISRAEL
IRAN
PAKISTAN
JORDAN
Cairo ■
KUWAIT
Persian
Gulf
NEPAL
EGYPT
BAHRAIN
Strait of Hormuz
Nile R.
SAUDI
ARABIA
QATAR
UNITED ARAB
EMIRATES
Arabian
Sea
INDIA
Red Sea
Mecca ■
OMAN
0 250 500 750 Kilometers
0   250   500 Miles
YEMEN   S. YEMEN
Major oil-producing areas

Map 14.2   The Modern Middle East

Persian Gulf, the vital waterway for the export of oil from both countries. Like several of its neighbors, Iraq had long dreamed of unifying the Arabs, but had been hindered by internal factions and suspicion among its neighbors.

During the mid-1970s, Iran gave some support to a Kurdish rebellion in the mountains of Iraq. In 1975, the government of the shah agreed to stop aiding the rebels in return for territorial concessions at the head of the Gulf. Five years later, however, the Kurdish revolt had been suppressed, and President Saddam Hussein, who had assumed power in Baghdad in 1979, accused Iran of violating the territorial agreement and launched an attack on his neighbor. The war was a bloody one, involving the use of poison gas against civilians and the employment of children to clear minefields, and lasted for nearly ten years. Other countries, including the two superpowers, watched nervously in case the conflict should spread throughout the region. Finally, with both sides virtually exhausted, a cease-fire was arranged in the fall of 1988.

The bitter conflict with Iran had not slaked Saddam Hussein's appetite for territorial expansion. In early Au-

gust 1990, Iraqi military forces suddenly moved across the border and occupied the small neighboring country of Kuwait at the head of the Gulf. The immediate pretext was the claim that Kuwait was pumping oil from fields inside Iraqi territory. Baghdad was also angry over the Kuwaiti government's demand for repayment of loans it had made to Iraq during the war with Iran. But the underlying reason was Iraq's contention that Kuwait was legally a part of Iraq. Kuwait had been part of the Ottoman Empire until the opening of the twentieth century, when the local prince had agreed to place his patrimony under British protection. When Iraq became independent in 1932, it claimed the area on the grounds that the state of Kuwait had been created by British imperialism, but opposition from major Western powers and other countries in the region, who feared the consequences of a "greater Iraq," prevented an Iraqi takeover.

The Iraqi invasion of Kuwait in 1990 sparked an international outcry, and the United States amassed an international force that liberated the country and destroyed a substantial part of Iraq's armed forces. President George Bush had promised the American people that U.S. troops would not fight with one hand tied behind their backs (a clear reference to the Vietnam War), but the allied forces did not occupy Baghdad at the end of the war because the allies feared that doing so would cause a total breakup of the country, an eventuality that would operate to the benefit of Iran. The allies hoped instead that the Hussein regime would be ousted by an internal revolt. In the meantime, harsh economic sanctions were imposed on the Iraqi government as the condition for peace. The anticipated overthrow of Saddam Hussein did not materialize, however, and his tireless efforts to evade the conditions of the cease-fire continued to bedevil the administration of President Bill Clinton, which came into office in January 1993.

The dilemma for the leaders of the anti-Iraqi coalition is clear. They view Saddam Hussein as a dangerous and power-crazed dictator who oppresses his own people and threatens to seek dominance over the entire region, the world's chief source of oil. But a total collapse of Iraq would open the door for Iranian militants to move into the vacuum. The Shi'ite majority might also seek to set up an "Islamic Republic" similar to that in neighboring Iran.

Recent statements by the newly elected president of Iran, Mohammed Khatemi, signal the tantalizing possibility that relations between the United States and Iran might begin to improve. Such a development could strengthen efforts to maintain a balance among competing states to prevent a single power from dominating the region. The struggle for political and economic dominance in the Middle East has been going on for centuries, however, and a lasting peace seems unlikely.

Politics in the Contemporary Middle East

Unlike the newly independent states of South and Southeast Asia, which generally attempted to set up Western-style governments, the Middle Eastern states that became independent after World War II exhibited a variety of forms of government.

In some cases, the traditional leaders survived into the postwar period—notably on the Arabian peninsula, where feudal rulers remain in power. The kings of Saudi Arabia, for example, continue to rule by traditional precepts and, citing the distinctive character of Muslim political institutions, have been reluctant to establish representative political institutions. As a general rule, these rulers maintain and even enforce the strict observance of traditional customs. Religious police in Saudi Arabia

are responsible for enforcing the Muslim dress code, maintaining the prohibition against alcohol, and making sure offices close during the time for prayer. Reportedly, the government even forbade airing "The Muppet Show" on local television because its characters included a pig, which was considered offensive to Islamic strictures against eating pork.

In other societies, traditional authority has been replaced by charismatic one-party rule or military dictatorships. Nasser's regime in Egypt is a good example of a single-party state. Nasser clearly had immense appeal to the Egyptian people, as a French observer explained:

> What first impresses you is his massive, thick-set build, the dazzlingly white smile in his dark face. He is tall, tough, African. As he comes toward you on the steps of his small villa on the outskirts of the city, or strides across his huge office at the presidency, he has the emphatic gait of some Covent Garden porter or some heavy feline creature, while he stretches his brawny hand out with the wide gesture of a reaper, completely sure of himself.[4]

Nasser was only the first of several Middle Eastern leaders who won political power by the force of their presence or personality. The Ayatollah Khomeini in Iran, Muammar Qadhafi in Libya, and Saddam Hussein in Iraq are other examples. Although their personal characteristics and images differ, they all have ruled by the force of their personalities.

In other instances, charismatic rule has given way to modernizing bureaucratic regimes. Examples include the governments of Syria, Yemen, Turkey, and Egypt since Nasser, where Anwar al-Sadat and his successor, Hosni Mubarak, have avoided dramatic personal appeal in favor of a regime focused on performance. Sometimes the authoritarian character of the regimes has been modified by some democratic tendencies, especially in Turkey, where free elections and the sharing of power have become more prevalent in recent years.

Only in Israel, however, are democratic institutions firmly established. The Israeli system suffers from the proliferation of minor parties, some of which are able to dictate policy because their support is essential to keeping a government in power. In recent years, divisions between religious conservatives and secular elements within the Jewish community have become increasingly sharp, resulting in bitter disagreements over social policy and the negotiating process with the Palestinians. Nevertheless, the government generally reflects the popular will, and power is transferred by peaceful and constitutional means.

The Economics of Oil

Few areas exhibit a greater disparity of individual and national wealth than the Middle East. While millions live in abject poverty, a fortunate few rank among the wealthiest people in the world. While the annual per capita income in Egypt is about $600 (in U.S. dollars), in the tiny states of Kuwait and United Arab Emirates, it is nearly $20,000. Some of that disparity can be explained by the uneven distribution of fertile and barren land, but the primary reason, of course, is oil. Unfortunately for most of the peoples of the region, oil reserves are distributed unevenly and all too often are located in areas where the population density is low. Egypt and Turkey, with more than 50 million inhabitants apiece, have almost no oil reserves. The combined population of Kuwait, the United Arab Emirates, and Saudi Arabia is well under 10 million people. This disparity in wealth inspired Nasser's quest for Arab unity (and perhaps Saddam Hussein's as well), but it has also posed a major obstacle to that unity.

The growing importance of petroleum has obviously been a boon to several of the states in the region, but it has been an unreliable one. Because of the violent fluctuations in the price of oil during the past twenty-five years, the income of oil-producing states has varied considerably. The spectacular increase in oil prices during the 1970s, when members of OPEC were able to raise the price of a barrel of oil from about $3 to $30, has not been sustained, forcing a number of oil-producing countries to scale back their economic development plans.

Not surprisingly, considering their different resources and political systems, the states of the Middle East have adopted diverse approaches to the problem of developing strong and stable economies. Some, like Nasser in Egypt and the leaders of the Ba'ath Party in Syria, attempted to create a form of Arab socialism, favoring a high level of government involvement in the economy to relieve the inequities of the free enterprise system. Others turned to the Western capitalist model to maximize growth, while using taxes or massive development projects to build a modern infrastructure, redistribute wealth, and maintain political stability and economic opportunity for all.

Whatever their approach, all the states have attempted to develop their economies in accordance with Islamic beliefs. Although the Koran has little to say about economics and can be variously interpreted as capitalist or socialist, it is clear in its opposition to charging interest and in its concern for the material welfare of the Muslim community, the *umma*. How these goals are to be achieved, however, is a matter of interpretation.

Socialist theories of economic development such as Nasser's were often suggested as a way to promote economic growth while meeting the requirements of Islamic doctrine. State intervention in the economic sector would bring about rapid development, while land redistribution and the nationalization or regulation of industry would prevent or minimize the harsh inequities of the marketplace. In general, however, the socialist approach has had little success, and most governments, including those of Egypt and Syria, have recently shifted to a more free enterprise approach while encouraging foreign investment to compensate for a lack of capital or technology.

Although the amount of arable land is relatively small, most countries in the Middle East rely to a certain degree on farming to supply food for their growing populations. In some cases, as in Egypt, Iran, Iraq, and Turkey, farmers have until recently been a majority of the population. Often, much of the fertile land was owned by wealthy absentee landlords, but land reform programs in several countries have attempted to alleviate this problem.

The most comprehensive, and probably the most successful, land reform program was instituted in Egypt, where Nasser and his successors managed to reassign nearly a quarter of all cultivable lands by limiting the amount a single individual could hold. Similar programs in Iran, Iraq, Libya, and Syria generally had less effect. In Iran, large landlords at the local and national level managed to limit the effects of the shah's reform program. After the 1979 revolution, many farmers seized lands forcibly from the landlords, creating questions of ownership that the revolutionary government has tried with minimal success to resolve.

Agricultural productivity throughout the region has been plagued by the lack of water resources. With populations growing at more than 2 percent annually on average in the Middle East (more than 3 percent in some countries), several governments have tried to increase the amount of water available for irrigation. Many attempts have been sabotaged by government ineptitude, political disagreements, and territorial conflicts, however. The best-known example is the Aswan Dam, which was built by Soviet engineers in the 1950s. The project was designed to control the flow of water throughout the Nile valley, but it has had a number of undesirable environmental consequences. Today, the dearth of water in the region is reaching crisis proportions.

Another way in which governments have attempted to deal with rapid population growth is to encourage emigration. Oil-producing states with small populations, such as Saudi Arabia and the United Arab Emirates, have imported labor from other countries in the region, mostly to work in the oil fields. By the mid-1980s, more than 40 percent of the population in those states was composed of foreign nationals, who often sent the bulk of their salaries back to their families in their home countries. The decline in oil revenues since the mid-1980s, however, has forced several governments to take measures to stabilize or reduce the migrant population. Since the Iraqi invasion, Kuwait, for example, has expelled all Palestinians and restricted migrant workers from other countries to three-year stays.

The economies of the Middle Eastern countries, then, are in a state of rapid flux. Political and military conflicts have exacerbated economic problems such as water use, which in turn have compounded political issues. For example, disputes between Israel and its neighbors over water rights and between Iraq and its neighbors over the exploitation of the Tigris and the Euphrates have caused serious tensions in recent years. In Saudi Arabia, declining oil revenues combined with the evidence of corruption among Saudi elites have aroused a deep sense of anger and support for radical politics among some segments of the populace.

The Islamic Revival

In recent years, many developments in the Middle East have been described in terms of a resurgence of traditional values and customs in response to the pressure of Western influence. Indeed, some conservative religious forces in the area have consciously attempted to replace foreign culture and values with allegedly "pure" Islamic forms of belief and behavior.

But the Islamic revival that has taken place in the contemporary Middle East is not a simple dichotomy between traditional and modern, native and foreign, or irrational and rational. In the first place, many Muslims in the Middle East believe that Islamic values and modern ways are not incompatible and may even be mutually reinforcing in some ways. Second, the resurgence of what are sometimes called "fundamentalist" Islamic groups may, in a Middle Eastern context, be a rational and practical response to destabilizing forces, such as corruption and hedonism, and self-destructive practices, such as drunkenness, prostitution, and the use of drugs. Finally, the reassertion of Islamic values can be a means of estab-

lishing cultural identity and fighting off the overwhelming impact of Western ideas.

Initially, many Muslim intellectuals responded to Western influence by trying to reconcile the perceived differences between tradition and modernity and by creating a "modernized" set of Islamic beliefs and practices that would not clash with the demands of the twentieth century. This process took place to some degree in most Islamic societies, but it was especially prevalent in Turkey, Egypt, and Iran. Mustapha Kemal Ataturk embraced the strategy when he attempted to secularize the Islamic religion in the new Turkish republic. The Turkish model was followed by Shah Reza Khan and his son Mohammad Reza Pahlavi in Iran and then by Nasser in postwar Egypt, all of whom attempted to make use of Islamic values while asserting the primacy of other issues such as political and economic development. Religion, in effect, had become the handmaiden of political power, national identity, and economic prosperity.

For obvious reasons, these secularizing trends were particularly noticeable among the political, intellectual, and economic elites in urban areas. They had less influence in the countryside, among the poor, and among devout elements within the *ulama*. Many of the latter believed that Western secular trends in the major cities had given birth to regrettable and even repugnant social attitudes and behavioral patterns, such as political and economic corruption, sexual promiscuity, hedonism, individualism, and the prevalence of alcohol, pornography, and drugs. Although such practices had long existed in the Middle East, they were now far more visible and socially acceptable.

This reaction began early in the century and intensified after World War I, when the Western presence increased. In 1928, devout Muslims in Egypt formed the Muslim Brotherhood as a means of promoting personal piety. Later the movement began to take a more activist approach, including eventually the use of terrorism by a radical minority. Despite Nasser's surface commitment to Islamic ideals and Arab unity, some Egyptians were fiercely opposed to his policies and regarded his vision of Arab socialism as a betrayal of Islamic principles. Nasser reacted harshly and executed a number of his leading opponents.

The movement to return to Islamic purity reached its zenith in Iran. It is not surprising that Iran took the lead in light of its long tradition of ideological purity within the Shi'ite sect as well as the uncompromisingly secular character of the shah's reforms in the postwar era. In revolutionary Iran, traditional Islamic beliefs are all-pervasive and extend into education, clothing styles, social practices, and the legal system. In recent years, for example, Iranian women have been heavily fined or even flogged for violating the Islamic dress code.

While the political aspects of the Iranian Revolution inspired distrust and suspicion among political elites elsewhere in the region, its cultural and social effects were profound. Although no other state in the Middle East adopted the violent approach to cultural reform applied in Iran, Iranian ideas have spread throughout the area and affected social and cultural behavior in many ways. In Algeria, the political influence of fundamentalist Islamic groups has grown substantially and enabled them to win a stunning victory in the national elections in 1992. When the military stepped in to cancel the second round of elections and crack down on the militants, the latter responded with a campaign of terrorism against moderates that has claimed thousands of lives.

A similar trend has emerged in Egypt, where militant groups such as the Muslim Brotherhood have engaged in terrorism, including the assassination of Sadat and more recent attacks on foreign tourists, who are considered carriers of corrupt Western influence. In 1994, the prominent novelist Naguid Mahfouz was stabbed outside his home, apparently in response to earlier writings that were deemed blasphemous of Muslim belief.

Even in Turkey, generally considered the most secular of Islamic societies, a militant political group, known as the Islamic Welfare Party, took power in a coalition government formed in 1996. The new prime minister, Necmettin Erbakan, adopted a pro-Arab stance in foreign affairs and threatened to reduce the country's economic and political ties to Europe. Worried moderates voiced their concern that the secular legacy of Kemal Ataturk was being eroded, and eventually Erbakan agreed to resign under heavy pressure from the military. Rejected in its application for membership in the European Union and uncomfortable with the militancy of Arab neighbors, Turkey has established a security relationship with Israel and seeks close ties with the United States. But religious and economic discontent lies just beneath the surface.

Throughout the Middle East, even governments and individuals who do not support efforts to return to pure Islamic principles have adjusted their behavior and beliefs in subtle ways. In Egypt, for example, the government now encourages television programs devoted to religion in preference to comedies and adventure shows imported from the West. Middle-class women in Cairo tend to dress more modestly than in the past, and alcohol is discouraged or at least consumed more discreetly.

The Role of Women

Nowhere have the fault lines between tradition and modernity within Muslim societies in the Middle East been so sharp as in the ongoing debate over the role of women. At the beginning of the twentieth century, women's place in Middle Eastern society had changed little since the death of the Prophet Muhammad. Women were secluded in their homes and had few legal, political, or social rights.

Early in the twentieth century, inspired in part by the Western presence, a "modernist" movement arose in several countries in the Middle East with the aim of bringing Islamic social values and legal doctrine into line with Western values and attitudes. Advocates of modernist views contended that Islamic doctrine was not inherently opposed to women's rights and that the teachings of Muhammad and his successors had actually broadened them in significant ways. To modernists, Islamic traditions such as female seclusion, wearing the veil, and even polygamy were pre-Islamic folk traditions that had been tolerated in the early Islamic era and continued to be practiced in later centuries.

During the first decades of the twentieth century, such views had considerable impact on a number of Middle Eastern societies, including Turkey and Iran. As we have seen, greater rights for women was a crucial element in the social revolution promoted by Mustapha Kemal Ataturk in Turkey. In Iran, Shah Reza Khan and his son granted female suffrage and encouraged the education of women. In Egypt, a vocal feminist movement arose in educated women's circles in Cairo as early as the 1920s.

Modernist views had somewhat less effect in other Islamic states, such as Iraq, Jordan, Morocco, and Algeria, where traditional views of women continued to prevail in varying degrees. Particularly in rural areas, notions of women's liberation made little headway. Most conservative by far was Saudi Arabia, where women were not only segregated and expected to wear the veil in public, but were also restricted in education and forbidden to drive automobiles.

Until recently, the general trend in urban areas of the Middle East was toward a greater role for women. With the exception of conservative religious communities, women in Israel have achieved substantial equality with men and are active in politics, the professions, and even the armed forces. Golda Meir (1898–1978), prime minister of Israel from 1969 to 1974, became an international symbol of the ability of women to be world leaders. But beginning in the 1970s, there was a noticeable

◆ Golda Meir. Golda Meir was one of the most beloved leaders of the new state of Israel. Born in Russia and raised in the United States, she became an ardent Zionist and immigrated to Palestine in the 1920s. An energetic pioneer with a dream and determination, Meir became Israel's fourth prime minister in 1969 and led her nation through a period of tension in Arab-Israeli relations.

shift toward a more traditional approach to gender roles in many Middle Eastern societies. It was accompanied by attacks on the growing Western influence within the media and on the social habits of young people. The re-actions were especially strong in Iran, where attacks by religious conservatives on the growing role of women contributed to the emotions underlying the Iranian Revolution of 1979.

The revolution caused Iranian women to return to more traditional forms of behavior. They were in-structed to wear the veil and to dress modestly in pub-lic. Films produced in postrevolutionary Iran expressed the new morality. They rarely featured women, and when they did, physical contact between men and women was prohibited. Still, Iranian women have many freedoms that they lacked before the twentieth century; for example, they can attend a university, re-ceive military training, vote, practice birth control, and write fiction.

The Iranian Revolution helped to promote a revival of traditional attitudes toward women in other Islamic societies. Women in secular countries such as Egypt,

Turkey, and far-off Malaysia have begun to dress more modestly in public, while public attacks on open sexual-ity in the media have become increasingly frequent.

Contemporary Literature and Art in the Middle East

As in other areas of Asia and Africa, the encounter with the West in the nineteenth and twentieth centu-ries stimulated a cultural renaissance in the Middle East. Muslim authors translated Western works into Arabic and Persian and began to experiment with new literary forms. The advent of modern newspapers and magazines eliminated the traditional differences be-tween the oral and written languages. The resulting fused language included colloquial speech, borrowed Western words, and ancient words resurrected from in-digenous languages. Turkish, however, was cleansed of its foreign borrowings by lexicographers who attempted to return it to its original pure form. Whereas in 1920 nearly three-quarters of all Turkish words had their roots in foreign languages, by 1970 the proportion had dropped to one-fifth.

The new literature dealt with a number of new themes. The rise in national consciousness stimulated interest in historical traditions. Writers also switched from religious to secular themes and addressed the prob-lems of this world and the means of rectifying them. Fur-thermore, literature was no longer the exclusive domain of the elite, but was increasingly written for the broader mass of the population.

Iran has produced one of the most prominent na-tional literatures in the contemporary Middle East. Since World War II, Iranian literature has been ham-pered somewhat by political considerations, since it has been expected to serve first the Pahlavi monarchy and more recently the Islamic Republic. Nevertheless, Ira-nian writers are among the most prolific in the region and often write in prose, which has finally been ac-cepted as the equal of poetry. Perhaps the most out-standing Iranian author of the twentieth century was the short-story writer Sadeq Hedayat. Hedayat was obsessed with the frailty and absurdity of life and wrote with com-passion about the problems of ordinary human beings. Frustrated and disillusioned at the government's suppres-sion of individual liberties, he committed suicide in 1951. Like Japan's Mishima Yukio, Hedayat later be-came a cult figure among his country's youth.

Sadeq Hedayat had a number of imitators, many of whom continued to write stories of everyday Iranian life. Some, like Junichiro Tanazaki in Japan, were pre-occupied with the destructive effects of change on Iranian society and produced nostalgic works, concentrating on the corrosive effects of contemporary ways on the family and other traditional institutions. Despite the male-oriented character of Iranian society, many of the new writers were women. One book by a woman writer was the best-selling Iranian novel in the 1970s. Many women understandably focused on the condition of women in Iran, with some favoring an extension of women's rights and others expressing more traditional views.

Since the revolution, the veil has become the central metaphor in Iranian women's writing. Those who favor the veil praise it as the last bastion of defense against Western cultural imperialism. Behind the veil, the Islamic woman can breathe freely, unpolluted by foreign exploitation and moral corruption. They see the veil as the courageous woman's weapon against Western efforts to dominate the Iranian soul. Other Iranian women, however, consider the veil a "mobile prison" or an oppressive anachronism from the Dark Ages. A few use the pen as a weapon in a crusade to liberate their sisters and enable them to make their own choices. As one recent writer expressed it:

> As I pulled the chador [the veil] over me, I felt a heaviness descending over me. I was hidden and in hiding. There was nothing visible left of Sousan Azadi. I felt like an animal of the light suddenly trapped in a cave. I was just another faceless Moslem woman carrying a whole inner world hidden inside the chador.[5]

Whether or not they accept the veil, women writers are a vital part of contemporary Iranian literature.

Like Iran, Egypt in the twentieth century has experienced a flowering of literature accelerated by the establishment of the Egyptian republic in the early 1950s. As in Iran, the trend has been toward prose. Poetry is still composed, but classical meter and rhyme have been discarded for free verse and prose poetry.

The most illustrious contemporary Egyptian writer is Naguib Mahfouz, who won the Nobel Prize for literature in 1988. His *Cairo Trilogy*, published in 1952, is considered the finest writing in Arabic since World War II. The novel chronicles three generations of a merchant family in Cairo during the tumultuous years between the two world wars. Mahfouz is particularly adept at blending panoramic historical events with the intimate lives of ordinary human beings with great compassion and energy. Unlike many other modern writers, his message is essentially optimistic and reflects his hope that religion

and science can work together for the overall betterment of humankind.

The emergence of a modern Turkish literature can be traced to the establishment of the republic in 1923. As a national state replaced the multinational empire, writers began to return to Turkish folklore for inspiration. Turkish authors, both male and female, began to create a new "village literature" dealing with the lives of ordinary people in rural areas. One of the most popular and prolific was Aziz Nesin, who was born in 1915. Determined to free the common people from oppression, Nesin used humor and satire to ridicule bureaucratic inefficiency and corruption. His short stories have been translated into twenty-four languages and will bring a smile to anyone familiar with the frustrations of red tape and bureaucratic stupidity.

Although Israeli literature arises from a totally different tradition from that of its neighbors, it shares with them certain contemporary characteristics and a concern for ordinary human beings. Israeli writers have inherited not only a long tradition of Hebrew literature but also the various traditions of the country's multinational population. As they identify with the aspirations of the new nation, many Israeli writers try to find a sense of order in the new reality, voicing terrors from the past and hopes for the future.

Some contemporary Israeli authors, however, have refused to serve as spokespersons for Zionism and are speaking out on sensitive national issues. The internationally renowned novelist Amos Oz, for example, has examined the problems inherent in the kibbutz, one of Israel's most hallowed institutions. Other novels explore the psychological and sexual complexities of his characters, such as the emotional disintegration of a housewife in *My Michael*, or the dissection of a marriage in *To Know a Woman*. A vocal supporter of peace with the Palestinians, Oz is a member of Peace Now and the author of a political tract titled *Israel, Palestine, and Peace*. Another of Israel's best-known novelists and poets is A. B. Yehoshua. Yehoshua explores with psychological insight the way Israelis live their daily lives surrounded by the threat of war, terrorism, and political turmoil.

The novels of David Grossman, another Israeli author strongly committed to peace in the region, have been made into films, bringing him international attention. In his nonfiction work *The Yellow Wind*, he attempted to understand the feelings of the Palestinian people living in the occupied territories, presenting them empathetically as the reverse image of the Israelis, dreaming of their own homeland. Although he was criticized for such views by ultra conservative Jewish religious groups, Grossman wrote a sequel focusing on the many questions of identity, land, and language that Palestinians share with Israelis. Praising the 1993 peace agreement over Palestine, Grossman remarked that it would eventually bring the Palestinians "back into history, into time with all the clumsiness of reality." As for the Israelis, "peace will cure us from this profound disease of not trusting our own existence. So finally this unbearable lightness of death will be over—not soon, but in fifty years it will be over."[6]

Like literature, the art of the modern Middle East has been profoundly influenced by its exposure to Western culture. At first artists tended to imitate Western models, but later they began to experiment with national styles, returning to earlier forms for inspiration. Some emulated the writers in returning to the village to depict peasants and shepherds, but others followed international trends and attempted to express the alienation and disillusionment that characterize so much of modern life.

Reflecting their hopes for the new nation, Israeli painters sought to bring to life the sentiments of pioneers arriving in a promised land. Many attempted to capture the longing for community expressed in the Israeli commune, or kibbutz. Others searched for the roots of Israeli culture in the history of the Jewish people or in the horrors of the Holocaust. The experience of the Holocaust has attracted particular attention from sculptors, who work in wood and metal as well as stone.

The popular music of the contemporary Middle East has also been strongly influenced by that of the modern West, but to different degrees in different countries. In Israel, many contemporary young rock stars voice lyrics as irreverent toward the traditions of their elders as do those of Europe and the United States. One idol of many Israeli young people, the rock star Aviv Ghefen, declares himself to be "a person of no values," and his music carries a shock value that attacks the country's political and social shibboleths with abandon. The rock music popular among Palestinians, on the other hand, makes greater use of Arab musical motifs and is closely tied to a political message. One recent recording, "The Song of the Engineer," lauds Yehia Ayash, a Palestinian accused of manufacturing many of the explosive devices used in recent terrorist attacks on Israeli citizens. The lyrics have their own shock value: "Spread the flame of revolution. Your explosive will wipe the enemy out, like a volcano, a torch, a banner." When one Palestinian rock leader from the Gaza Strip was asked why his group employed a musical style that originated in the West, he explained, "For us, this is a tool like any other. Young people in Gaza like our music, they listen to us, they buy our cassettes, and so they spread our message."

Conclusion

The Middle East, like the continent of Africa, is one of the most unstable regions in the world today. In part, this turbulence is due to the continued interference of outsiders attracted by the massive oil reserves under the parched wastes of the Arabian peninsula and in the vicinity of the Persian Gulf. Oil indeed is both a blessing and a curse to the peoples of the region.

Another factor contributing to the volatility of the Middle East is the tug-of-war between the sense of ethnic identity in the form of nationalism and the intense longing to be part of a broader Islamic community, a dream that dates back to the time of the Prophet Muhammad. The desire to create that community—a vision threatened by the presence of the alien state of Israel—inspired Gamal Abdul Nasser in the 1950s and the Ayatollah Khomeini in the 1970s and 1980s and probably motivates many of the actions of Saddam Hussein today.

A final reason for the turmoil currently affecting the Middle East is the intense debate over the role of religion in civil society. It has been customary in recent years for Western commentators to label Muslim efforts to return to a purer form of Islam as fanatical and extremist, reflecting a misguided attempt to reverse the course of history, and there is no doubt that many of the legal and social restrictions now being enforced in various Muslim countries in the Middle East appear excessively harsh and often repugnant to outside observers. But it is important to remember that Muslim societies are not alone in deploring the sense of moral decline that is now allegedly taking place in societies throughout the world. Nor are they alone in advocating a restoration of traditional religious values as a means of reversing the trend. Movements dedicated to such purposes are appearing in many other societies (including, among others, Israel and the United States) and can be viewed as an understandable reaction to the rapid and often bewildering changes that are now taking place in the contemporary world. Not infrequently, members of such groups turn to violence as a means of making their point. While the tensions between tradition and modernity appear to be strongest in the contemporary Middle East, then, they are hardly unique to that region. The consequences as yet cannot be foreseen.

NOTES

1. Quoted in Roy R. Andersen, Robert F. Seibert, and Jon G. Wagner, *Politics and Change in the Middle East: Sources of Conflict and Accommodation,* 4th ed. (Englewood Cliffs, NJ, 1982), p. 51.
2. Quoted in Arthur Goldschmidt, Jr., *A Concise History of the Middle East,* 4th ed. (Boulder, CO, 1991), p. 280.
3. Walter Laqueur and Barry Rubin, eds., *The Israel-Arab Reader* (New York, 1984), pp. 186–89.
4. Andersen, Seibert, and Wagner, *Politics and Change,* p. 200.
5. Sousan Azadi, with Angela Ferrante, *Out of Iran* (London, 1987), p. 223, quoted in *Stories by Iranian Women since the Revolution,* ed. S. Sullivan (Austin, TX, 1991), p. 13.
6. *New York Times,* February 7, 1996.

CHAPTER
15

Toward the Pacific Century?

In August of 1945, Japan was in ruins, its cities destroyed, its vast Asian empire in ashes, its land occupied by a foreign army. A decade earlier, Japanese leaders had proclaimed their national path to development as a model for other Asian nations to follow. A few years later, they had attempted to construct their vast Greater East Asia Co-prosperity Sphere under Japanese tutelage. The result had been a bloody war and ultimate defeat.

Half a century later, Japan had emerged as the second greatest industrial power in the world, democratic in form and content and a source of stability throughout the region. Japan's achievement spawned a number of Asian imitators. Known as the "little tigers," the four industrializing societies of Taiwan, Hong Kong, Singapore, and South Korea achieved considerable success by following the path originally charted by Japan. Along with Japan, they became economic powerhouses and ranked among the world's top seventeen trading nations. Other nations in Asia and elsewhere took note and began to adopt the Japanese

formula. It is no wonder that observers relentlessly heralded the coming of the "Pacific Century."

The impressive success of some countries in East and Southeast Asia prompted some commentators in the region to declare that the global balance of power had shifted away from Europe and the United States toward the lands of the Pacific. Some Western critics retorted that eastern Asia's achievements had taken place at great cost, as authoritarian governments in the region trampled on human rights and denied their citizens the freedoms that they required to fulfill their own destiny. Asian observers argued that freedom is not simply a matter of individuals' doing what they please but, in the words of the Singaporean diplomat Kishore Mahbubani, "can also result from greater social order and discipline."[1] Such views not only reflected the growing self-confidence of many societies in East and Southeast Asia but also their growing inclination to defend Asian values and traditions against critics in the West.

Japan: Asian Giant

For five years after the end of the war in the Pacific, Japan was governed by an Allied administration under the command of U.S. General Douglas MacArthur. The occupation regime, which consisted of a Far Eastern Commission in Washington, D.C., and a four-power Allied Council in Tokyo, was dominated by the United States,

although the country was technically administered by a new Japanese government. As commander of the occupation administration, MacArthur was responsible for demilitarizing Japanese society, destroying the Japanese war machine, trying Japanese civilian and military officials charged with war crimes, and laying the foundations of postwar Japanese society.

During the war, senior U.S. officials had discussed whether to insist on the abdication of the emperor as the symbol of Japanese imperial expansion. During the summer of 1945, the United States rejected a Japanese request to guarantee that the position of the emperor would be retained in any future peace settlement and reiterated its demand for unconditional surrender. After the war, however, the United States agreed to the retention of the emperor after he agreed publicly to renounce his divinity. Although many historians have suggested that Emperor Hirohito opposed the war policy of his senior advisers, some recent studies have contended that he fully supported it.

Under MacArthur's firm tutelage, Japanese society was remodeled along Western lines. The centerpiece of occupation policy was the promulgation of a new constitution to replace the Meiji Constitution of 1889. The new charter, which was drafted by U.S. planners and imposed on the Japanese despite their objections to some of its provisions, was designed to transform Japan into a peaceful and pluralistic society that would no longer be capable of waging offensive war. The Constitution specifically renounced war as a national policy, and Japan unilaterally agreed to maintain armed forces only sufficient for self-defense. Perhaps most important, the Constitution established a parliamentary form of government based on a bicameral legislature, an independent judiciary, and a universal franchise; it also reduced the power of the emperor and guaranteed human rights.

❈ Map 15.1   Modern Japan

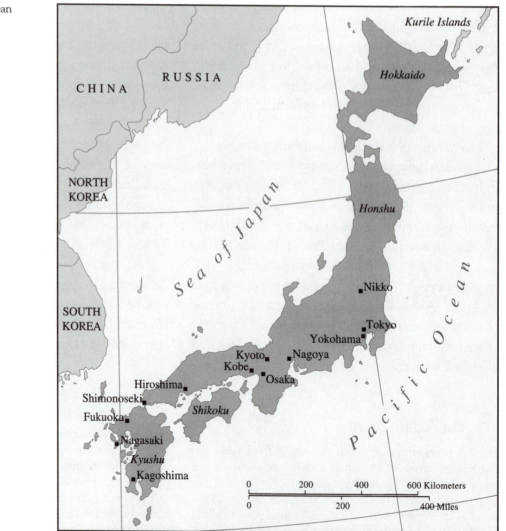

But more than a written constitution was needed to demilitarize Japan and place it on a new course. Like the Meiji leaders in the late nineteenth century, occupation administrators wished to transform Japanese social institutions and hoped their policies would be accepted by the Japanese people as readily as those of the Meiji period had been. The Meiji reforms, however, had been crafted to reflect native traditions and had set Japan on a path quite different from that of the modern West. Some Japanese observers believed that a fundamental reversal of trends begun with the Meiji Restoration would be needed before Japan would be ready to adopt the Western capitalist, democratic model.

One of the sturdy pillars of Japanese militarism had been the giant business cartels, known as *zaibatsu*. Allied policy was designed to break up the *zaibatsu* into smaller units in the belief that corporate concentration, in Japan as in the United States, not only hindered competition but was inherently undemocratic and conducive to political authoritarianism. Occupation planners also intended to promote the formation of independent labor unions, to lessen the power of the state over the economy, and to provide a mouthpiece for downtrodden Japanese workers. Economic inequality in rural areas was to be reduced by a comprehensive land reform program that would turn the land over to those who farmed it. Finally, the educational system was to be remodeled along American lines, so that it would turn out independent individuals rather than automatons subject to manipulation by the state.

The Allied program was an ambitious and even audacious plan to remake Japan society and has been justly praised for its clear-sighted vision and altruistic motives. Parts of the program, such as the Constitution, the land reform program, and the educational system, succeeded brilliantly. But as other concerns began to intervene, changes or compromises were made that were not always successful. In particular, with the rise of Cold War sentiment in the United States in the late 1940s, the goal of decentralizing the Japanese economy gave way to the desire to make Japan a key partner in the effort to defend East Asia against international communism. Convinced of the need to promote economic recovery in Japan, U.S. policymakers began to show more tolerance for the *zaibatsu*. Concerned at growing radicalism within the new labor movement, where left-wing elements were gaining strength, U.S. occupation authorities placed less emphasis on the independence of the labor unions.

Cold War concerns also affected U.S. foreign relations with Japan. On September 8, 1951, the United States and other former belligerent nations signed a peace treaty restoring Japanese independence. In turn, Japan renounced any claim to such former colonies or territories as Taiwan (which had been returned to the Republic of China), Korea (which, after a period of joint Soviet and U.S. occupation, had become two independent states), and southern Sakhalin and the Kurile Islands (which had been ceded to the Soviet Union). The Soviet Union refused to sign the treaty on the grounds that it had not been permitted to play an active role in the occupation. On the same day, the Japanese and Americans signed a defensive alliance and agreed that the United States could maintain military bases on the Japanese islands. Japan was now formally independent, but in a new dependency relationship with the United States.

The Japanese Miracle: The Transformation of Society in Modern Japan

By the early 1950s, then, Japan had regained at least partial control over its own destiny. Although it was linked closely to the United States through the new security treaty and the new American-drafted constitution, Japan was now essentially free to move out on its own. As the world would soon discover, the Japanese adapted quickly to the new conditions. From a semifeudal society with autocratic leanings, Japan has progressed into one of the most stable and advanced democracies in the world today. It has risen from the ashes of total destruction in 1945 to become the second largest and in many ways the most advanced economy in the world.

Japan's achievements in the area of human services are especially noteworthy. Its record on health is impressive, even though it has one-third more people per doctor than in the United States. Life expectancy is high, and the infant mortality rate is only 5 per 1000, the lowest in the world. The literacy rate is almost 100 percent, and a significantly higher proportion of the population graduates from high school than in most advanced nations of the West. Crime rates are low (on an average day, according to a recent statistic, 4,584 crimes are committed in Japan compared to 93,474 in the United States), and although Japan suffered badly from environmental pollution during the 1950s and 1960s, it has moved rapidly to improve its urban environments. Despite its near-total lack of domestic sources of oil, Japan today is less dependent on oil imports than is the oil-rich United States.

Japan appears equally blessed in the area of foreign affairs. Under the umbrella of U.S. nuclear protection, Japan has been able to avoid conflicts with foreign countries and has adhered to its constitutional restriction of staying out of foreign wars. Though linked to the United States through the 1951 security treaty, Japan has carried out an increasingly independent foreign policy in recent years and has succeeded in maintaining amicable relations with virtually all nations. Its only serious dispute is with Russia, which has consistently refused Japan's request for the return of four islands in the Kurile chain near the northern Japanese island of Hokkaido.

In recent years, Japan's rapid emergence as an economic giant has often been described as the "Japanese miracle." Whether or not this description is justified (its recent economic performance raises some doubts on that score), Japan has made a dramatic recovery from the war. Although the "miracle" is often described as beginning after the war as a result of the Allied reforms—a chronology that ascribes most of the credit to U.S. postwar policies—in fact, as we have seen, Japanese economic growth began much earlier with the Meiji reforms, which helped to transform Japan from an autocratic society based on semifeudal institutions into an advanced capitalist democracy. The seeds of the Japanese miracle were sown in the Meiji period, or even in the late Tokugawa era, well over a century ago. Although we tend to think of Japanese achievements primarily in economic terms, a modern economic sector can only be developed where changes are taking place in politics, social institutions, culture, and human values as well. It is in these areas that the Allied occupation may have had its most salutary effects. To fully understand modern Japan, then, we must examine not just the economy but the multifaceted changes that have occurred in recent decades throughout Japanese society.

Politics and Government

The Allied occupation administrators started with the conviction that Japanese expansionism was directly linked to the institutional and ideological foundations of the Meiji Constitution. Accordingly, they set out to change Japanese politics into something closer to the pluralistic approach used in most Western nations. The concepts of universal suffrage, governmental accountability, and a balance of power among the executive, legislative, and judicial branches that were embodied in the Constitution of 1947 have held firm, and Japan today is a stable and mature democratic society with a literate and politically active electorate and a government that actively seeks to meet the needs of its citizens.

Yet a number of characteristics of the current Japanese political system reflect the tenacity of the traditional political culture. Although Japan had a multiparty system with two major parties, the Liberal Democrats and the Socialists, in practice there was a "government party" and a permanent opposition—the Liberal Democrats were not voted out of office for thirty years. The ruling Liberal Democratic Party included several factions, but disputes were usually based on personalities rather than substantive issues. Many of the leading Liberal Democrats controlled factions on a patron-client basis, and decisions on key issues, such as who should assume the prime ministership, were decided by a modern equivalent of the *genro* oligarchs.

That tradition changed suddenly in 1993, when the "ruling" Liberal Democrats, shaken by persistent reports of corruption and "cronyism" between politicians and business interests, failed to win a majority of seats in parliamentary elections. Mirohiro Hosokawa, the leader of one of several newly created parties in the Japanese political spectrum, was elected prime minister. He promised to launch a number of reforms to clean up the political system. The new coalition government, however, quickly split into feuding factions, and in 1995 the Liberal Democratic Party returned to power under a new cabinet led by Prime Minister Ryutaro Hashimoto. Hashimoto promised to carry out a series of reforms to make the government more efficient and less prone to corruption.

One of the problems has been that the current system continues the centralizing tendencies of the Meiji period. The government is organized on a unitary rather than a federal basis; the local administrative units, called prefectures, have few of the powers of states in the United States. Moreover, the central government plays an active and sometimes intrusive role in various aspects of the economy, mediating management-labor disputes, establishing price and wage policies, and subsidizing vital industries and enterprises producing goods for export. This government intervention in the economy has traditionally been widely accepted and is often cited as a key reason for the efficiency of Japanese industry and the emergence of the country as an industrial giant. The Japanese term for this process is *nemawashi*, or "root-binding," which "originally comes from gardening, where it designates the careful untangling and binding of each of the roots of the tree before it is moved." The government plays an active role in resolving major issues and consults all relevant groups before a decision is reached. If the decision works to the disadvantage of any group, "it is understood that they will be given special consideration now or in the future." Thus, the roots of the disadvantaged group are bound and "do not impede the effective moving of the tree."[2]

In recent years, the tradition of active government involvement in the economy has increasingly come under fire. Japanese business, which previously sought government protection from imports, now argues that deregulation is needed to enable Japanese firms to innovate as a means of keeping up with the competition. Such reforms, however, have been resisted by powerful government ministries in Tokyo, which are accustomed to playing an active role in national affairs.

Another problem that has shaken Japanese self-confidence in recent years has been corruption in government. A number of senior politicians, including two recent prime ministers, have been forced to resign because of serious questions about improper financial dealings with business associates. Concern over political corruption was undoubtedly a major factor in the defeat suffered by the Liberal Democrats in the summer of 1993, and the issue continues to plague the political scene.

Japan is also experiencing a rise in nationalist sentiment and growing demands for a more assertive stance toward the United States (see box on p. 310). Although the Japanese government has generally resisted such demands, some officials share these attitudes and quietly applauded Malaysian Prime Minister Mahathir Mohamad when he recently called on Japan to play a larger role in Asian affairs.

Last, but certainly not least, minorities such as the *eta* (now known as the Burakumin) and Korean residents in Japan continue to be subjected to legal and social discrimination. In recent years, official sources have been reluctant to divulge growing evidence that thousands of Korean women were conscripted to serve as prostitutes (euphemistically, "comfort women") for Japanese soldiers during the war, and many Koreans living in Japan contend that such prejudicial attitudes continue to exist. Representatives of the "comfort women" have demanded both financial compensation and a formal letter of apology from the Japanese government for the treatment they received during the Pacific War.

The issue of Japan's behavior during World War II has been especially sensitive. An American political scientist teaching for a year at Kobe University reports that many of his students said they had learned about Pearl Harbor, the invasion of China, and the massacre of Chinese civilians in Nanjing "from my uncle, from my grandfather, from TV, from books, from family talk," but not from their classes. Several students told him that they knew of teachers who had been disciplined for teaching about the war. Asked why such things were not taught in school, they always answered, "Because the government, or the Education Ministry, does not want us to know."[3]

There is ample evidence that such is the case. Critics at home and abroad have charged that textbooks printed under the guidance of the Ministry of Education do not adequately discuss the atrocities committed by the Japanese government and armed forces during World War II. Other Asian governments have been particularly incensed at Tokyo's failure to accept responsibility for such behavior and have demanded a formal apology. The current government of Prime Minister Hashimoto has responded with a statement that expresses remorse, but only in the context of the aggressive actions of all colonial powers during the imperialist era. In the view of many Japanese, the actions of their government during the Pacific War were a form of self-defense. Fear of the potential revival of Japanese militarism, however, is still strong elsewhere in the region.

Still, such problems pale before the impressive achievements realized by Japan since the dark days at the end of World War II. The nation's postwar leaders dedicated themselves to realizing Japan's national aspirations within a democratic and pluralistic framework. Although the recurrent fragility of the party system raises questions about future trends in Japanese politics, few countries today possess a political system as stable and respecting of human values as that of Japan.

The Economy

Nowhere are the changes in postwar Japan so visible as in the economic sector, where Japan has developed into a major industrial and technological power in the space of a century, surpassing such advanced Western societies as Germany, France, and Great Britain. Here, indeed, is the Japanese miracle in its most concrete manifestation.

The process began a century ago in the single-minded determination of the Meiji modernizers to create a "rich country and strong state" (*fukoku kyohei*). Their initial motive was to guarantee Japan's survival against Western imperialism, but this defensive urge evolved into a desire to excel and, during the years before World War II, to dominate. That desire led to the war in the Pacific and, in the eyes of some, still contributes to Japan's problems with its trading partners in the world today.

⇒ *Americans! Look in the Mirror* ⇐

The rapid emergence of Japan as the second largest indus-trial power took the world by surprise and inspired con-siderable comment in Japan and abroad as to the factors behind the Japanese success. By the 1980s, when Japanese achievements began to threaten the long supremacy of the United States over the global economy, many American ob-servers began to criticize Japan for increasing its exports to the United States while keeping its own markets closed to for-eign goods. Others pointed out that Tokyo had benefited from minuscule defense budgets while the United States took prime responsibility for the security of the entire region.

Criticism from the United States eventually pro-voked a response in Japan. In the late 1980s, the writer and movie director Shintaro Ishiwara wrote a book, *The Japan That Can Say No*, which bluntly declared that the problems of the United States were of its own making. Let's be candid, he declared. Although it was true that there were some impediments to free trade in Japan, America's problem "is not Japan's economic strength but its own industrial weakness." Before pointing their finger at policies adopted in Tokyo or Osaka, Americans "should deal first with the host of problems in their own backyard."

Ishiwara's criticisms were primarily directed at what he termed "endemic shortsightedness in U.S. board-rooms." In Japan, he noted, companies are either family owned and managed or there is a "psychological solidar-ity between shareholders and management." In the United States, professional managers run their compa-nies for immediate profit rather than long-term growth. If earnings drop, they unload their stock and move on, thus damaging the company's long-term prospects.

Other Asian critics pointed out that U.S. economic growth had been hindered by a variety of social factors, including low productivity, declining educational stan-dards, and a general tendency to emphasize consumption and pleasure rather than hard work. In East Asian coun-tries, they observed, savings rates were much higher than in the Unites States, management-labor differences were usually resolved without costly work stoppages, and edu-cation received greater emphasis on the scale of social priorities.

Such criticisms of economic conditions in the United States were well taken and often echoed concerns voiced by American observers. But events since the publication of his book suggest that commentators like Ishiwara were probably being too complacent about the factors behind their own "Asian miracle." By the mid-1990s, Japan was mired in its own long-term economic recession, and growth rates throughout the region had declined. In the meantime, corporate downsizing and a variety of other factors had boosted economic vitality in the United States and restored its position as the single dominant economic power on earth. The financial crisis of 1997 (see Chapter 17) demonstrated clearly that Asian societ-ies were not immune to the problems afflicting capitalist economies elsewhere, and indeed suffered from some shortcomings of their own making. There is no little irony in the fact that Japan and many of its neighbors are now being urged to adopt policies practiced in the United States and other Western countries as a means of recovering from their own economic slump.

Source: Shintaro Ishiwara, *The Japan That Can Say No* (New York: Simon & Schuster, 1989).

As we have seen, the officials of the Allied occupa-tion identified the Meiji economic system with central-ized power and the rise of Japanese militarism. Accord-ingly, MacArthur's planners set out to break up the *zaibatsu* and decentralize Japanese industry and com-merce. But with the rise of Cold War tensions, the policy was scaled back in the late 1940s, and only the nineteen largest conglomerates were affected. In any event, the new antimonopoly law did not hinder the for-mation of looser ties between Japanese companies, and as a result, a new type of informal relationship, some-times called the *keiretsu* or "interlocking arrangement,"

began to take shape after World War II. Through such arrangements among suppliers, wholesalers, retailers, and financial institutions, the *zaibatsu* system was recon-stituted under a new name.

The occupation administration had more success with its program to reform the agricultural system. Half of the population still lived on farms, and half of all farmers were still tenants. Under a stringent land reform program in the late 1940s, all lands owned by absentee landlords and all cultivated landholdings over an estab-lished maximum were sold on easy credit terms to the tenants. The maximum size of an individual farm was set at 7.5 acres, while an additional 2.5 acres could be leased to tenants. The reform program created a strong class of yeoman farmers, and tenants declined to about 10 percent of the rural population.

During the past fifty years, Japan has re-created the stunning results of the Meiji era. At the end of the Allied occupation in 1950, the Japanese gross national product was about one-third that of Great Britain or France. Today, it is larger than both put together and well over half that of the United States. Japan is the greatest exporting nation in the world, and its per capita income equals or surpasses that of most advanced Western states. In terms of education, mortality rates, and health care, the quality of life in Japan is superior to that in the United States or the advanced nations of Western Europe.

By the mid-1980s, the economic challenge presented by Japan had begun to arouse increasing concern in both official and private circles in Europe and the United States. Explanations for the phenomenon tended to fall into two major categories. Some pointed to cultural factors: The Japanese are naturally group-oriented and find it easy to cooperate with one another. Traditionally hardworking and frugal, they are more inclined to save than to consume, a trait that boosts the savings rate and labor productivity. The Japanese are family-oriented and therefore spend less on welfare for the elderly, who normally live with their children. Like all Confucian societies, the Japanese value education, and consequently the labor force is highly skilled. Finally, Japan is a homogeneous society, in which people share common values and respond in similar ways to the challenges of the modern world.

Others cited more practical reasons for Japanese success. Paradoxically, Japan benefited from the total destruction of its industrial base during World War II because it did not face the problem of antiquated plants that plagued many industries in the United States. Under the terms of its Constitution and the security treaty with the United States, Japan spends less than 1 percent of its gross national product on national defense, whereas the United States spends more than 5 percent. Labor productivity is high, not only because the Japanese are hard workers (according to statistics, Japanese workers spend a substantially longer period of time at their job than do workers in other advanced societies), but also because corporations reward innovation and maintain good management-labor relations. Consequently, employee mobility and the number of days lost to labor stoppages are minimized (on an average day, according to one estimate, 603 Japanese workers are on strike compared to 11,956 Americans). Just as it did before World War II, the Japanese government promotes business interests rather than hindering them. Finally, some charge that Japan uses unfair trade practices, subsidizing exports through the Ministry of International Trade and Industry (MITI), dumping goods at prices below cost to break into a foreign market, maintaining an artificially low standard of living at home to encourage exports, and unduly restricting imports from other countries.

The truth in this case is probably a little of both. Undoubtedly, Japan benefited from its privileged position beneath the U.S. nuclear umbrella as well as from its ability to operate in a free trade environment that provided both export markets and access to Western technology. The Japanese also took a number of practical steps to improve their competitive position in the world and the effectiveness of their economic system at home.

Yet many of these steps were possible precisely because of the cultural factors described here. The concept of "root-binding" and the tradition of loyalty to the firm, for example, derive from the communal tradition in Japanese society. The concept of sacrificing one's personal interests to those of the state, though not necessarily rooted in the traditional period, was certainly fostered by the *genro* oligarchy during the Meiji era.

In recent years, the cacophony of concern that Japan might overtake the United States and reduce it to a second-rank economic power has abated somewhat. One reason is the increasingly competitive position of U.S. firms in the global marketplace (see Chapter 16). Another is the economic downturn in the Japanese economy in the 1990s and the realization that Japan, too, is encountering some of the problems that have afflicted the United States, as well as others that may be the result of factors unique to Japan. A rise in the value of the yen hurt exports and burst the bubble of investment by Japanese banks that had taken place under the umbrella of government protection. Lacking a domestic market equivalent in size to the United States, the Japanese economy slipped into a long-term recession.

These economic difficulties have placed heavy pressure on some of the vaunted features of the Japanese economy. The tradition of lifetime employment created a bloated white-collar workforce and has made downsizing difficult. Today, job security is on

◆ **KFC in Japan.** Although Japan has been widely criticized for its reluctance to import goods from other countries, the Japanese people display a strong interest in many aspects of Western culture. Items of American culture, including Mickey Mouse, fashionable sneakers, and Kentucky Fried Chicken, are especially prized. This outlet, complete with a statue of Colonel Sanders, is on a downtown street in Kobe.

concerned at the prospect of growing food shortages—has committed itself to facilitating the importation of rice from abroad. This last move was especially sensitive, given the almost sacred role that rice farming holds in the Japanese mindset.

A Society in Transition

Although the Meiji Restoration resulted in significant changes in Japanese customs and attitudes, the essentially hierarchical character of traditional society persisted. Japanese farmers, miners, and factory workers were ruthlessly exploited to provide the sinews of state power, while the male-oriented character of pre-Meiji Japan remained substantially unchanged.

Allied planners during the occupation set out to change social characteristics that they believed had contributed to Japanese aggressiveness before and during World War II. The new educational system removed all references to filial piety, patriotism, and loyalty to the emperor, while emphasizing the individualistic values of Western civilization. The new Constitution and a revised civil code attempted to achieve true sexual equality by removing remaining legal restrictions on women's rights to obtain a divorce, hold a job, or change their domicile. Women were guaranteed the right to vote and were encouraged to enter politics.

Such efforts to remake Japanese behavior through legislation were only partially successful. During the past fifty years, Japan has unquestionably become a more individualistic and egalitarian society. Freedom of choice in marriage and occupation is taken for granted, and social mobility, though not so extensive as in the United States, has increased considerably beyond prewar levels. Although Allied occupation policy established the legal framework for these developments, the primary credit undoubtedly can be assigned to the evolution of Japan into an urbanized and technologically advanced industrial society.

At the same time, many of the distinctive characteristics of traditional Japanese society have persisted into the present day, although in somewhat altered form. The emphasis on loyalty to the group and community relationships, for example, known in Japanese as *amae*, is reflected in the strength of corporate loyalties in contemporary Japan. While competition among enterprises in a particular industry is often quite vigorous, social cohesiveness among both management and labor personnel is exceptionally strong within each individual corporation, although, as we have seen, the attitude has eroded somewhat in recent years.

the decline as increasing numbers of workers are being laid off. Unfortunately, a disproportionate burden has fallen on women, who lack seniority and continue to suffer from various forms of discrimination in the workplace. A positive consequence is that job satisfaction is beginning to take precedence over security in the minds of many Japanese workers, while salary is beginning to reflect performance more than time on the job.

A final factor is that slowly but inexorably, the Japanese market is beginning to open up to international competition. Foreign automakers are winning a growing share of the domestic market, while the government—

One possible product of this attitude may be the relatively egalitarian character of Japanese society in terms of income. A chief executive officer in Japan receives, on average, seventeen times the salary of the average worker, compared with eighty-five times in the United States. The disparity between wealth and poverty is also generally less in Japan than in most European countries and certainly less than in the United States. In Japan, the poorest 20 percent of the population possesses about 9 percent of the wealth, while the richest 20 percent owns 37 percent. In the United States, the poorest 20 percent possesses only 4 percent of the wealth, while the richest 20 percent owns 46 percent.[4]

Emphasis on the work ethic also remains strong. The tradition of hard work is implanted at a young age within the educational system. The Japanese school year runs for 240 days a year, compared to 180 days in the United States, and work assignments outside class tend to be more extensive (according to one source, a Japanese student averages about five hours of homework per day). Competition for acceptance into universities is intense, and many young Japanese take cram courses to prepare for the "examination hell" that lies ahead. The results are impressive: the literacy rate in Japanese schools is almost 100 percent, and Japanese schoolchildren consistently earn higher scores on achievement tests than children in other advanced countries.

At the same time, this devotion to success has often been accompanied by bullying by teachers and what Americans might consider an oppressive sense of conformity. One Japanese writer who specializes in educational matters has observed:

> Many Japanese incorrectly believe that our education has been a success because there aren't as many dropouts or drug abuse cases as in the United States. But in fact Japanese schools are akin to prisons ruled by fear, where kids must constantly be looking around to make sure they're behaving exactly like everyone else.[5]

Bullying of nonconforming students by their peers has become endemic and arouses serious concern among educators and political leaders alike.

Some young Japanese find suicide the only escape from the pressures emanating from society, school, and family. Parental pride often becomes a factor, with "education mothers" pressuring their children to work hard and succeed for the honor of the family. Ironically, once the student is accepted into college, the amount of work assigned tends to decrease, because graduates of the best universities are virtually guaranteed lucrative employment offers. Nevertheless, the early training instills an attitude of deference to group interests that persists throughout life. Some outside observers, however, believe such attitudes can have a detrimental effect on individual initiative. To give one example, the Japanese professional tennis player Kimiko Date played tennis with her right hand, at the insistence of her father, even though she was naturally left-handed. As a child she made no protest, she explains, "because I thought everybody played that way."[6]

The tension between the Japanese way and the foreign approach is especially noticeable in Japanese baseball, where major league teams frequently hire U.S. players. One American noted the case of Tatsunori Hara, one of the best Japanese players in the league. "He had so many different people telling him what to do," remarked Warren Cromartie, a teammate, "it's a wonder he could still swing the bat. They turned him into a robot, instead of just letting him play naturally and expressing his natural talent." To his Japanese coach, however, conformity brought teamwork, and teamwork in Japan is the road to success.[7]

By all accounts, independent thinking is on the increase in Japan. In some cases, it leads to antisocial behavior, such as crime or membership in a teenage gang. Usually it is expressed in more indirect ways, such as the recent fashion among young people of dyeing their hair brown (known in Japanese as "tea hair"). Because the practice is banned in many schools and generally frowned upon by the older generation (one police chief dumped a pitcher of beer on a student with brown hair whom he noticed in a bar), many young Japanese dye their hair as a gesture of independence and a means of gaining acceptance among their peers. When seeking employment or getting married, however, they return their hair to its natural color.

One of the more tenacious legacies of the past in Japanese society is sexual inequality (see box on p. 314). Although women are now legally protected against discrimination in employment, very few have reached senior levels in business, education, or politics, and, in the words of one Western scholar, they remain "acutely disadvantaged"—though ironically, in a recent survey of business executives in Japan, a majority declared that women were smarter than men. Women now comprise nearly 50 percent of the workforce, but most are in retail or service occupations, and their average salary is only about half that of men. There is a feminist movement in Japan, but it has none of the vigor and mass support of its counterpart in the United States.

Most women in Japan consider being a homemaker the ideal position; a poll taken during the 1980s found

⟫ Breaking the Glass Ceiling in Japan ⟪

Although social conditions in contemporary Japan are in general the envy of the rest of the world, many foreign observers remain critical of Japanese society for its failure to accord equal rights to women. In many respects, Japan remains a male-oriented society, with women expected to remain in the home and provide for the education of their children. Compared to advanced countries in the West, relatively few Japanese women enter politics or sit in the boardrooms of giant corporations. They are Japan's "silent majority."

Nevertheless, there are numerous signs that the role of women in Japan is changing rapidly, much as it did in other industrializing countries earlier in the century. In a recent collection of essays by Japanese women writers, Kumiko Fujimura-Fanselow, a professor of education and women's studies at a leading Japanese university, presents an overview of the status of Japanese women today.

On the political front, she notes, women are becoming more active in local and national politics. In 1986, a woman was named leader of Japan's largest opposition party, the Socialist Party. Three years later, a record number of female candidates won election to the lower house of the Japanese legislature, the National Diet. At the local level, representation of women in local offices increased from about 1 percent in 1976 to more than 3 percent in 1992. The first female mayor of a Japanese city was elected in 1991.

One clear sign of the emergence of women in Japanese society can be found in educational statistics. By the mid-1990s, more female than male high school graduates were entering Japanese colleges and universities, and more than 80 percent of female college graduates were entering the workforce. In 1992, more than 56 percent of female college graduates between the ages of 25 and 29 were employed, compared to only 41 percent in 1980. Legislation passed in the 1980s has opened up career opportunities for women in several previously all-male careers, while a Child Care Leave Law passed in 1991 requires companies to grant unpaid leave to either parent until a child reaches the age of one. In the most visible professional position in most advanced countries today, female newscasters have become a familiar presence on nearly all television news programs.

The emergence of Japanese women from the legacy of the imperial past has not been without problems. Social pressures on women to adopt the role of homemaker and mother are still strong, and women are often the first to be dismissed during a period of corporate downsizing. But the statistical evidence makes it clear that the transition to a society based on true equality of the sexes is taking place today in Japan, much as it is in other advanced countries around the world.

Source: Kumiko Fujimura-Fanselow et al., *Japanese Women: New Feminist Perspectives on the Past* (New York: The Feminist Press at the City University of New York, 1995).

---

that only 15 percent of Japanese women wanted a full-time job.[8] In the home, a Japanese woman has considerable responsibility. She is expected to be a "good wife and wise mother" and has the primary responsibility for managing the family finances and raising the children. Japanese husbands carry little of the workload around the house, spending an average of nine minutes a day on housework, compared to twenty-six minutes for American husbands. At the same time, Japanese divorce rates are well below those of the United States, and only 1.4 million elderly Japanese (most of them undoubtedly women) live alone, compared to 8.6 million in the United States.

Japan's welfare system also differs profoundly from its Western counterparts. Applicants are required to seek assistance first from their own families, and the physically able are ineligible for government aid. As a result,

less than 1 percent of the population receives welfare benefits, compared with more than 10 percent who receive some form of assistance in the United States. Outside observers interpret the difference as the product of several factors, including low levels of drug addiction and illegitimacy, as well as the importance in Japan of the work ethic and family responsibility.

No one is more conscious of Japanese distinctiveness than are the Japanese themselves. Although the old Meiji concept of *kokutai* (national polity) has been officially disavowed, the feeling that Japan is a unique and indeed a superior culture survives. Both the self-confidence that comes from Japan's economic achievements and the sense of ethnic and cultural homogeneity that is a product of Japanese history contribute to this sense of uniqueness. The Japanese are proud of what they have achieved and are convinced that it is a direct product of their hard work, community spirit, and common sense of destiny.

Whether the unique character of modern Japan will endure is unclear. Confidence in the Japanese "economic miracle" has been shaken because of the recent downturn, and there are indications of a growing tendency toward hedonism and individualism among Japanese youth. Older Japanese frequently complain that the younger generation lacks their sense of loyalty and willingness to sacrifice. Some have also discerned signs that the concept of loyalty to one's employer may be beginning to erode among Japanese youth. Some observers have predicted that with increasing affluence, Japan will become more like the industrialized societies in the West. Nevertheless, Japan is unlikely to evolve into a carbon copy of the United States. Not only is Japan a much more homogeneous society, but its small size and dearth of natural resources encourage a strong work ethic and a sense of togetherness that have long since begun to dissipate in American society.

Religion and Culture

The sense of racial and cultural pride that characterizes contemporary Japan is rather different from Japanese attitudes at the beginning of the Meiji era. When Japan was opened to the West in the nineteenth century, many Japanese became convinced of the superiority of foreign ideas and institutions and were especially interested in Western religion and culture. Although Christian converts were few, numbering less than 1 percent of the population, the influence of Christianity was out of proportion to the size of the community. Many intellectuals during the Meiji era were impressed by the emotional commitment shown by missionaries in Japan and viewed Christianity as a contemporary version of Confucianism.

Today, Japan includes almost 1.5 million Christians along with 93 million Buddhists and 111 million who follow Shintoism; these figures are large because they include the many Japanese who believe in both Buddhism and Shintoism. Shintoism has not been identified with reverence for the emperor and the state since the occupation period. As in the West, increasing urbanization has led to a decline in the practice of organized religion, although evangelical sects have proliferated in recent years. In all likelihood, their members, like those belonging to similar sects elsewhere, are seeking spiritual underpinnings in an increasingly secular and complex world. The largest and best-known sect is the Soka Gakkai, a lay Buddhist organization that has attracted millions of followers and formed its own political party called the Komeito.

As we have seen, Western literature, art, and music also had a major impact on Japanese society. Western influence led to the rapid decline of traditional forms of drama and poetry and the growth in popularity of the prose novel. After the Japanese defeat in World War II, many of the writers who had been active before the war resurfaced, but now their writing reflected their demoralization, echoing the spiritual vacuum of the times. Labeled "apure" from the French *après-guerre* (postwar), these disillusioned authors were attracted to existentialism, and some turned to hedonism and nihilism. This "lost generation" described its anguish with piercing despair; several committed suicide. For them, defeat was compounded by fear of the Americanization of postwar Japan.

One of the best examples of this attitude was the novelist Yukio Mishima, who led a crusade to stem the tide of what he described as America's "universal and uniform 'Coca-colonization'" of the world in general and Japan in particular.[9] In *Confessions of a Mask*, written in 1949, Mishima describes the awakening of a young man to his own homosexuality. His later novels, *The Thirst for Love* and *The Temple of the Golden Pavilion*, are riveting narratives about disturbed characters. Mishima's ritual suicide in 1970 was the subject of widespread speculation and transformed him into a cult figure.

One of Japan's most serious-minded contemporary authors is Kenzaburo Oe (b. 1935). His work, which was rewarded with a Nobel Prize for Literature in 1994, presents Japan's ongoing quest for modern identity and purpose. His characters reflect the spiritual anguish precipitated by the collapse of the imperial Japanese tradition and the subsequent adoption of Western culture—a trend which, according to Oe, has culminated in unabashed materialism, cultural decline, and a moral void. Yet, unlike Mishima, he does not seek to reinstill the imperial traditions of the past, but rather to regain spiritual meaning by retrieving the sense of communality and innocence found in rural Japan.

One of Oe's best-known novels is *A Personal Matter* (1964), in which the author recounts in fictionalized form his own experience in raising a brain-damaged son, leading him from despair to a final sense of transcendent humanism. In *Teach Us to Outgrow Our Madness*, a collection of four novellas, he describes the fascination of Japanese children when they first saw a black American soldier held in captivity at the end of World War II. Initially viewing him as an intimidating oddity, the children eventually accept him as a human being, admiring his powerful body and sense of joy in being alive.

Haruki Marakami, one of Japan's most popular authors today, was one of the first to discard the introspective and somber style of the earlier postwar period and speak a more contemporary language. *A Wild Sheep Chase*, published in 1982, is an excellent example of his gripping yet humorous writing.

Since the 1970s, increasing affluence and a high literacy rate have contributed to a massive quantity of publications, ranging from popular potboilers to first-rate fiction. By 1975, Japan already produced twice as much fiction as the United States, a trend that has continued into the 1990s. Much of this new literature deals with the common concerns of all affluent industrialized nations, including the effects of urbanization, advanced technology, and mass consumption. One recent phenomenon is the so-called "industrial novel," which seeks to lay bare the vicious infighting and pressure tactics that characterize Japanese business today. In the novel *Keiretsu*, author Ikko Shimizu describes the abortive efforts of the owner of Taisei Lighting, a headlight supplier, to cope with the pressure imposed by one of his main customers, the giant affiliate Tokyo Motors. Another popular genre is the "art-manga," or literary cartoon. Michio Hisauchi presents serious subjects, such as Japanese soldiers marooned after the war on an island in the South Pacific, in *Japan's Junglest Day*, a full-length novel in comic book form with cartoon characters posing philosophical questions.

The theater has gone through a similar process of growth. Some traditional forms, such as *Kabuki* drama, have survived by adopting new subject matter. Japanese drama has sometimes been a showcase for radical political views, which has limited its popular appeal and led to official efforts to suppress it before World War II. A new type of play influenced by the "theater of the absurd" of Samuel Beckett and Eugene Ionesco and reflecting the search for personal and national identity became popular in the 1960s.

There were many women writers during early Japanese history. With the rise of the samurai class, however, works by women vanished until the Meiji Restoration, when a few courageous women wrote of their struggle for self-fulfillment in a male-dominated society. Japanese literary critics, who were invariably men, accepted "female" literature as long as it dealt exclusively with what they viewed as appropriately "female" subjects, such as the "mysteries" of the female psyche and motherhood. Even today, Japan has separate literary awards for men and women, and women are not considered capable of abstract or objective writing. Nevertheless, many contemporary women authors are daring to broach "male" subjects and are producing works of considerable merit.

Other aspects of Japanese culture have also been influenced by Western ideas, although without the intense preoccupation with synthesis that is evident in literature. Western art had begun to influence Japanese artists prior to the Meiji period, a process that accelerated in the late nineteenth and early twentieth centuries, when impressionists, cubists, and surrealists, among others, jockeyed for preeminence. Western music is highly popular in Japan, and scores of Japanese classical musicians have succeeded in the West. Even rap music has gained a foothold among Japanese youth, although without its association in the United States with sex, drugs, and violence. Although some of the lyrics betray an attitude of modest revolt against the uptight world of Japanese society, most lack any such connotations. An example is the rap song "Street Life":

> Now's the time to hip-hop,
> Everybody's crazy about rap,
> Hey, hey, you all, listen up,
> Listen to my rap and cheer up.

As one singer remarked, "We've been very fortunate, and we don't want to bother our Moms and Dads. So we don't sing songs that would disturb parents."[10]

No longer are Japanese authors seeking to revive the old Japan of the tea ceremony and falling plum blossoms. Raised in the crowded cities of postwar Japan, soaking up movies and television, rock music and jeans, Coca-Cola and McDonald's, many contemporary Japanese authors speak the universal language of today's world.

Many English words have entered the Japanese vocabulary, although with Japanese pronunciations. Corporate downsizing is known as *kosutu daun* (cost down), while a student who cuts class is engaging in *esukeepu* (escape). Even rice, the very symbol of Japanese uniqueness, is sometimes known as *raisu* when sold in a restaurant. Yet even as the Japanese enter the global marketplace, they retain ties to their own traditions. Businesspeople sometimes use traditional Daoist forms of physical and mental training to reduce the stress inherent in their jobs, while others retreat to a Zen monastery to learn to focus their willpower as a means of besting a competitor.

There are some signs that under the surface, the tension between traditional and modern is exacting a price. As novelists such as Yukio Mishima and Kenzaburo Oe feared, the growing focus on material possessions and the decline of traditional religious beliefs have left a spiritual void that cannot but undermine the sense of community and purpose that have motivated the country since the Meiji era. Some young people have reacted to the emptiness of their lives by joining religious cults such as Aum Shinri Kyo, which came to widespread world attention in 1995 when members of the organization, inspired by their leader Asahara Shoko, carried out a poison gas attack on the Tokyo subway that killed several people. Such incidents serve as a warning that Japan is not immune to the social ills that currently plague many Western countries.

South Korea: A Peninsula Divided

While the world was focused on the economic miracle occurring on the Japanese islands, another miracle of sorts was taking place across the Sea of Japan on the Asian mainland. In 1953, the Korean peninsula was exhausted from three years of bitter fraternal war, a conflict that took the lives of an estimated 4 million Koreans on both sides of the 38th parallel and turned as much as one-quarter of the population into refugees. Although a cease-fire was signed at Panmunjom in July 1953, it was a fragile peace that left two heavily armed and mutually hostile countries facing each other suspiciously.

North of the truce line was the People's Republic of Korea (PRK), a police state under the dictatorial rule of the Communist leader Kim Il Sung (1912–1994). To the south was the Republic of Korea under the equally autocratic President Syngman Rhee (1875–1965), a fierce anti-Communist who had led the resistance to the northern invasion and now placed his country under U.S. military protection. But U.S. troops could not protect Syngman Rhee from his own people, many of whom resented his reliance on the political power of the wealthy landlord class. After several years of harsh rule, marked by government corruption, fraudulent elections, and police brutality, demonstrations broke out in the capital city of Seoul in the spring of 1960 and forced him into retirement.

The Rhee era was followed by a brief period of multiparty democratic government, but in 1961, a coup d'état placed General Chung Hee Park (1917–1979) in power. The new regime promulgated a new constitution, and in 1963, Park was elected president of a civilian government. He set out to foster recovery of the economy from decades of foreign occupation and civil war. Adopting the nineteenth-century Japanese slogan "rich country and strong state," Park built up a strong military while

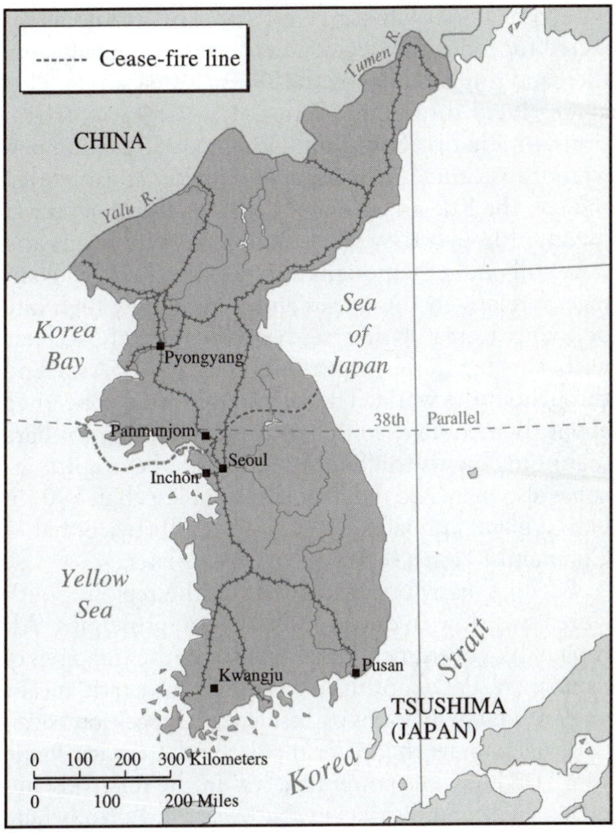

Map 15.2 Modern Korea

relying on U.S. and later Japanese assistance to help build a strong manufacturing base in what had been a predominantly agricultural society (in 1961, about 40 percent of the gross national product came from agriculture). Because the private sector had been relatively weak under Japanese rule, the government played an active role in the process, creating a super ministry called the Economic Planning Board that instituted a series of five-year plans. These plans targeted specific industries for development, promoted exports, and funded infrastructure development. Under a land reform program, large landowners were required to sell all their farmland above 7.4 acres to their tenants at low prices.

The program was a solid success. Benefiting from the Confucian principles of thrift, respect for education, and hard work (during the 1960s and 1970s, Korean workers spent an average of sixty hours a week at their jobs), as well as from Japanese capital and technology, Korea gradually emerged as a major industrial power in East Asia. The economic growth rate rose from less than 5 percent annually in the 1950s to an average of

9 percent under Chung Hee Park. The key areas selected for industrial development were chemicals, textiles, and shipbuilding. By the 1980s, Korea was moving aggressively into automobiles. The largest corporations—including Samsung, Daewoo, and Hyundai—were transformed into massive conglomerates called *chaebol*, the Korean equivalent of the *zaibatsu* of prewar Japan, although they were more recent in origin and were still under their original ownership. Taking advantage of relatively low wages and a stunningly high rate of saving, Korean businesses began to compete actively with the Japanese for export markets in Asia and throughout the world. The Japanese became concerned about their "hungry spirit" and began refusing to share technology with the South Koreans.[11] Per capita income also increased dramatically, from less than $90 (in U.S. dollars) annually in 1960 to $1,560 (twice that of Communist North Korea) twenty years later.

But like many other countries in the region, South Korea was slow to develop democratic principles. Although his government functioned with the trappings of democracy, Park continued to rule by autocratic means and suppressed all forms of dissidence. Opposition began to develop under the leadership of the charismatic figure Kim Dae Jung. His power base was in the relatively impoverished rural districts in southwestern Korea, where the government's land reforms had had only minimal success in raising living standards.

In 1979, Chung Hee Park was assassinated. Once again, a brief interregnum of democratic rule ensued, but in 1980, a new military government under General Chun Doo Hwan seized power. The new regime was as authoritarian as its predecessors, but opposition to autocratic rule had now spread from the ranks of college and high school students, who had led the early resistance, to much of the urban population. Protest against government policies became increasingly frequent. In 1987, massive demonstrations drove government troops out of the southern city of Kwangju, but the troops returned in force and killed an estimated 2,000 demonstrators.

Under increasing pressure from the United States to moderate the oppressive character of his rule, Chun promised national elections in 1987 but then reversed his decision. Amid growing protests, the regime steadily lost credibility, and in 1989, elections were finally held. There were three candidates for president: the government nominee, Roh Tae Woo, and two opposition figures, Democratic Party leader Kim Dae Jung and his rival Kim Young Sam. With the opposition candidates splitting the antigovernment vote, Roh Tae Woo won the election with less than 40 percent of the vote.

The election results discouraged many Koreans, while the violent character of the student protests alienated many moderates. Nevertheless, new elections in 1992 brought Kim Young Sam to the presidency. Kim selected several women for his cabinet and promised to make Korea "a freer and more mature democracy." In the meantime, representatives of South Korea had made tentative contacts with the Communist regime in North Korea on possible steps toward eventual reunification of the peninsula.

During the mid-1990s, Kim Young Sam attempted to crack down on the rising influence of the giant *chaebols*, accused of giving massive bribes in return for favors from government officials. Ex-presidents Chun Doo Hwan and Roh Tae Woo were tried and convicted of using the office to enrich themselves and their families. But the problems of South Korea were more serious than the en-

◆ **Melding Past and Present in South Korea.** South Korea has made a greater effort to preserve aspects of traditional culture than most of its neighbors in East Asia. Here an architect has tried to soften the impact of modernization by camouflaging a gas station in Seoul with a traditional Korean tile roof.

demic problem of corruption. A growing trade deficit, combined with a declining growth rate, led to a rising incidence of unemployment and bankruptcy. Ironically, a second problem resulted from the economic collapse of Seoul's bitter rival, the PRK. Under the rule of Kim Il Sung's son Kim Jong Il, the North Korean economy was in a state of free fall, raising the specter of an outflow of refugees that could swamp neighboring countries. To relieve the immediate effects of a food shortage, the Communist government in Pyongyang relaxed its restrictions on private farming, while Seoul agreed to provide food aid to alleviate the famine.

In the fall of 1997, a sudden drop in the value of the Korean currency, the *won*, led to bank failures and a decision to seek assistance from the International Monetary Fund (IMF). In December, an angry electorate voted Kim Young Sam (whose administration was tarnished by reports of corruption) out of office and elected his rival Kim Dae Jung to the presidency. The new chief executive moved vigorously to attack the deep-seated problems that had led to the financial crisis.

Taiwan: The Other China

South Korea was not the only rising industrial power trying to imitate the success of the Japanese in East Asia. To the south on the island of Taiwan, the Republic of China began to do the same.

After retreating to Taiwan following their defeat by the Communists, Chiang Kai-shek and his followers established a new capital at Taipei and set out to build a strong and prosperous nation based on Chinese traditions and the principles of Sun Yat-sen. The government, which continued to refer to itself as the Republic of China (ROC), contended that it remained the legitimate representative of the Chinese people and that it would eventually return in triumph to the mainland.

In some ways, the Nationalists had much more success on Taiwan than they had achieved on the mainland. In the relatively secure environment provided by a security treaty with the United States, signed in 1954, and the comforting presence of the U.S. Seventh Fleet in the Taiwan Strait, the ROC was able to concentrate on economic growth without worrying about a Communist invasion. The regime possessed a number of other advantages that it had not enjoyed in Nanjing. Fifty years of efficient Japanese rule had left behind a relatively modern economic infrastructure and an educated populace, although the island had absorbed considerable damage during World War II and much of its agricul-

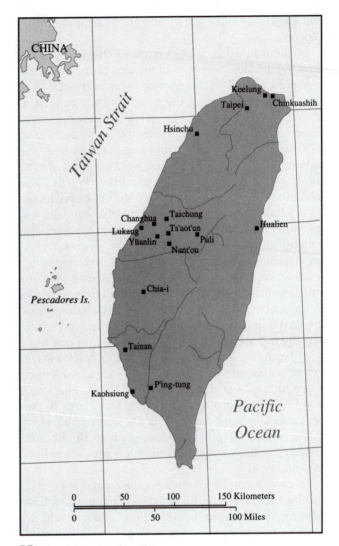

Map 15.3 Modern Taiwan

tural produce had been exported to Japan at low prices. With only a small population to deal with (about 7 million in 1945), the ROC could make good use of foreign assistance and the efforts of its own energetic people to build a modern industrialized society.

The government moved rapidly to create a solid agricultural base. A land reform program, more effectively designed and implemented than the one introduced in the early 1930s on the mainland, led to the reduction of rents, while landholdings over 3 acres were purchased by the government and resold to the tenants at reasonable prices. As in Meiji Japan, the previous owners were compensated by government bonds. The results were gratifying: food production doubled over the next generation and began to make up a substantial proportion of exports.

In the meantime, the government strongly encouraged the development of local manufacturing and commerce. By the 1970s, along with Japan and South Korea, Taiwan was one of the most dynamic industrial economies in East Asia. The agricultural proportion of the gross national product declined from 36 percent in 1952 to only 9 percent thirty years later. At first, the industrial and commercial sector was composed of relatively small firms engaged in exporting textiles and food products, but the 1960s saw a shift to heavy industry, including shipbuilding, steel, petrochemicals, and machinery, and a growing emphasis on exports. The government played a major role in the process, targeting strategic industries for support and investing in infrastructure. Several of the so-called ten major construction projects in the 1970s involved improvements in transportation and communications, including a new international airport, harbor development, and a freeway linking the north and the south. At the same time, as in Japan, the government stressed the importance of private enterprise and encouraged foreign investment and a high rate of internal savings. During the 1960s and 1970s, industrial growth averaged well over 10 percent annually, while the value of exports reached nearly 50 percent of the gross national product. By the mid-1980s more than three-quarters of the population lived in urban areas.

In contrast to the People's Republic of China (PRC) on the mainland, the ROC actively maintained Chinese tradition, promoting respect for Confucius and the ethical principles of the past, such as hard work, frugality, and filial piety. Although there was some corruption in both the government and the private sector, income differentials between the wealthy and the poor were generally less than elsewhere in the region, and the overall standard of living increased substantially. Health and sanitation improved, literacy rates were quite high, and an active family planning program reduced the rate of population growth. Nevertheless, the total population on the island increased to about 20 million in the mid-1980s.

In one respect, however, Chiang Kai-shek had not changed: increasing prosperity did not lead to the democratization of the political process. The Nationalists continued to rule by emergency decree and refused to permit the formation of opposition political parties on the ground that the danger of invasion from the mainland had not subsided. Propaganda material from the PRC was rigorously prohibited, and dissident activities (promoting either rapprochement with the mainland or the establishment of an independent Republic of Taiwan) were ruthlessly suppressed. Although representatives to the provincial government of the province of Taiwan were chosen in local elections, the central government (technically representing the entire population of China) was dominated by mainlanders who had fled to the island with Chiang Kai-shek in 1949.

Some friction developed between the mainlanders, who numbered about 2 million, and the native Taiwanese; except for a few aboriginal peoples in the mountains, most of the natives were ethnic Chinese whose ancestors had emigrated to the island during the Qing Dynasty. While the mainlanders were dominant in government and the professions, the native Taiwanese were prominent in commerce. Mainlanders tended to view the local population with a measure of condescension, and at least in the early years, intermarriage between members of the two groups was rare. Many Taiwanese remembered with anger the events of March 1947, when Nationalist troops had killed hundreds of Taiwanese demonstrators in Taipei. More than 1,000 leading members of the local Taiwanese community were arrested and killed in the subsequent repression. By the 1980s, however, these fissures in Taiwanese society had begun to diminish; by that time, an ever-higher proportion of the population had been born on the island and identified themselves as Taiwanese.

During the 1980s, the ROC slowly began to evolve toward a more representative form of government—a process that was facilitated by the death of Chiang Kai-shek in 1975. Chiang Ching-kuo, his son and successor, was less concerned about the danger from the mainland and more tolerant of free expression. On his death, he was succeeded as president by Lee Teng-hui, a native Taiwanese. By the end of the 1980s, democratization was under way, including elections and the formation of legal opposition parties. A national election in 1992 resulted in a bare majority for the Nationalists over strong opposition from the Democratic Progressive Party

But political liberalization had its dangers; some leading Democratic Progressives began to agitate for an independent Republic of Taiwan, a possibility that aroused concern within the Nationalist government in Taipei and frenzied hostility in the PRC. When a presidential election in early 1996 aroused a political debate over the issue, Beijing responded by holding naval maneuvers in the Taiwan Strait. After his reelection, President Lee calmed the waters by making conciliatory remarks directed toward the mainland, but the fundamental issue about the future of the island remains unresolved.

◆ **The Chiang Kai-shek Memorial in Taipei.** While the Chinese government on the mainland attempted to destroy all vestiges of traditional culture, the Republic of China on Taiwan sought to preserve the cultural heritage as a link between past and present. This policy is graphically displayed in the mausoleum for Chiang Kai-shek in downtown Taipei. The mausoleum, with its massive entrance gate, not only glorifies the nation's leader, but recalls the grandeur of old China.

Whether Taiwan will remain an independent state or be united with mainland is impossible to predict. Certainly, the outcome depends in good measure on developments in the PRC. During his visit to China in 1972, President Richard Nixon said that this was a question for the Chinese people to decide (see Chapter 7). In 1979, President Jimmy Carter abrogated the mutual security treaty between the United States and the ROC that had been in force since 1954 and switched U.S. diplomatic recognition from the Republic of China to the PRC. But the United States continues to provide defensive military assistance to the Taiwanese armed forces and has made it clear that it supports self-determination for the people of Taiwan and that it expects the final resolution of the Chinese civil war to be by peaceful means. In the meantime, economic and cultural contacts between Taiwan and the mainland are steadily increasing. However, the Taiwanese have shown no inclination to accept the PRC's offer of "one country, two systems," under which the ROC would accept the PRC as the legitimate government of China in return for autonomous control over the affairs of Taiwan.

Singapore and Hong Kong: The Littlest Tigers

The smallest, but by no means the least successful, of the "little tigers" are Singapore and Hong Kong. Both are essentially city-states with large populations densely packed into small territories. Singapore, once a British Crown colony and briefly a part of the state of Malaysia, is now an independent state. Hong Kong was a British colony until it was returned to PRC control in 1997. In recent years, both have emerged as industrial powerhouses with standards of living well above the level of their neighbors.

The success of Singapore must be ascribed in good measure to the will and energy of its political leaders.

When it became independent in August 1965, Singapore was in a state of transition. Its longtime position as an entrepôt for trade between the Indian Ocean and the South China Sea was declining in importance. With only 618 square miles of territory, much of it marshland and tropical jungle, Singapore had little to offer but the frugality and industriousness of its predominantly overseas Chinese population. But a recent history of political radicalism, fostered by the rise of influential labor unions, had frightened away foreign investors.

Within a decade, Singapore's role and reputation had dramatically changed. Under the leadership of Prime Minister Lee Kuan-yew (b. 1923), once the firebrand leader of the radical People's Action Party, the government encouraged the growth of an attractive business climate while engaging in massive public works projects to feed, house, and educate its 2 million citizens. The major components of success have been shipbuilding, oil refineries, tourism, electronics, and finance—the city-state has become the banking hub of the entire region.

Like the other little tigers, Singapore has relied on a combination of government planning, entrepreneurial spirit, export promotion, high productivity, and an exceptionally high rate of saving to achieve industrial growth rates of nearly 10 percent annually over the past two decades. Unlike some other industrializing countries in the region, it has encouraged the presence of multinational corporations to provide much needed capital and technological input. Population growth has been controlled by a stringent family planning program, and literacy rates are among the highest in Asia.

As in the other little tigers, an authoritarian political system has guaranteed a stable environment for economic growth. Until his recent retirement, Lee Kuan-yew and his People's Action Party dominated Singaporean politics, and opposition elements were intimidated into silence or arrested. The prime minister openly declared that the Western model of pluralist democracy was not appropriate for Singapore and lauded the Meiji model of centralized development. Confucian values of thrift, hard work, and obedience to authority have been promoted as the ideology of the state. The government has had a passion for cleanliness and at one time even undertook a campaign to persuade its citizens to flush the public urinals. In 1989, the local *Straits Times*, a mouthpiece of the government, published a photograph of a man walking sheepishly from a row of urinals. The caption read "Caught without a flush: Mr. Amar Mohamed leaving the Lucky Plaza [a local shopping center] toilet without flushing the urinal."[12]

But economic success is beginning to undermine the authoritarian foundations of the system, as a more sophisticated citizenry begins to demand more political freedoms and an end to government paternalism. Lee Kuan-yew's successor, Goh Chok Tong, has promised a "kinder, gentler" Singapore, and political restrictions on individual behavior are gradually being relaxed. There is reason for optimism that a more pluralistic political system will gradually emerge.

The future of Hong Kong is not so clear-cut. As in Singapore, sensible government policies and the hard work of its people have enabled Hong Kong to thrive. At first, the prosperity of the colony depended on a plentiful supply of cheap labor. Inundated with refugees from the mainland during the 1950s and 1960s, the population of Hong Kong burgeoned to more than 6 million. Many of them were willing to work for starvation wages in sweatshops producing textiles, simple appliances, and toys for the export market. More recently, Hong Kong has benefited from increased tourism, manufacturing, and the growing economic prosperity of neighboring Guangdong Province, the most prosperous region of the PRC. In one respect, Hong Kong has differed from the other societies discussed in this chapter, in that it has relied on an unbridled free market system rather than active state intervention in the economy. At the same time, by allocating substantial funds for transportation, sanitation, education, and public housing, the government has created favorable conditions for economic development.

Unlike the other little tigers, Hong Kong remained under colonial rule until very recently. British authorities did little to foster democratic institutions or practices, and most residents of the colony cared more about economic survival than political freedoms. In 1983, in talks between representatives of Great Britain and the PRC, the Chinese leaders made it clear they were determined to have Hong Kong return to mainland authority in 1997, when the British ninety-nine-year lease over the New Territories, the food-basket of the colony of Hong Kong, ran out. The British agreed, on condition that satisfactory arrangements could be made for the welfare of the population. The Chinese promised that for fifty years, the people of Hong Kong would live under a capitalist system and be essentially self-governing. Recent statements by Chinese leaders, however, have raised questions about the degree of autonomy Hong Kong will receive under Chinese rule, which began on July 1, 1997 (see box on p. 323).

Hong Kong Returns to the Motherland

After lengthy negotiations, in December 1984, China and Great Britain agreed that on July 1, 1997, the British Crown colony of Hong Kong would return to Chinese sovereignty. In succeeding years, government authorities of the two countries held further talks to work out the details. The final agreement was contained in a Joint Declaration on Hong Kong, which declared that after return to Chinese control, Hong Kong would become a Special Administrative Region (SAR) directly under the authority of the central government in Beijing. According to the text, it would enjoy "a high degree of autonomy, except in foreign and defense affairs which are the responsibility of the Central People's Government."

The nature of authority vested in the government of Hong Kong was spelled out in the text. The SAR would "be vested with executive, legislative and independent judicial power, including that of final adjudication." The laws currently in force in Hong Kong were to remain "basically unchanged." The government was to consist of local residents, with the chief executive appointed by the central government in Beijing "on the basis of elections or consultations to be held locally." The chief executive, in turn, would nominate senior officials for appointment by the central government.

According to the Joint Declaration, Hong Kong residents were promised that the current social and economic system would remain unchanged, as would their lifestyle. Freedom of speech, press, assembly, association, travel, and religious belief was guaranteed, and the rights of private property, inheritance, and foreign investment were protected by law. Still, as the date of transfer approached, many foreign observers and Hong Kong residents worried that Chinese authorities would inevitably chip away at the political and economic freedoms that had gradually been achieved in the colony and place it under direct Chinese control.

Transfer took place as scheduled and without incident in the summer of 1997. The new chief executive, the local shipping magnate Tung Chee-hwa, assured residents of the new SAR that he would scrupulously adhere to the terms of the agreement and protect their rights and their own way of life. Yet there were worrisome signs that times were changing. Chinese sources announced that henceforth organized protests in the SAR must receive prior permission from government authorities, and that textbooks used in local schools were to be revised to delete favorable references to the colonial past and reflect the patriotic interests of the Chinese nation.

In coming years, the situation in Hong Kong will be watched closely, not only by local residents whose own way of life is at issue, but also by foreign economic interests doing business in Hong Kong and by neighboring countries concerned over the future intentions of China as it becomes an increasingly influential power in the region. Particular attention will be paid on the island of Taiwan, which has been offered a similar inducement of "one country, two systems" by Beijing to reunite with the motherland. Chinese authorities will face a major challenge to integrate the onetime Crown colony into Chinese society without destroying the very factors that have made Hong Kong a unique beacon of success and achievement throughout the region.

Source: Kevin Rafferty, *City on the Rocks* (New York: Penguin, 1991).

On the Margins of Asia: Postwar Australia and New Zealand

From a geographic point of view, Australia and New Zealand are not part of Asia, and throughout their short history, both countries have identified themselves culturally and politically with the West rather than with their Asian neighbors. Their political institutions and values are derived from Europe, while in form and content their economies resemble those of the advanced countries of the world rather than the preindustrial societies of much of Southeast Asia. Both are currently members of the British Commonwealth and of the U.S.–led ANZUS alliance (Australia, New Zealand, and the United States), which serves to shield them from political turmoil elsewhere in the region.

Yet trends in recent years have been drawing both states, especially Australia, closer to Asia. In the first place, immigration from East and Southeast Asia has increased rapidly. More than one-half of current immigrants into Australia come from East Asia, and by early in the next century, about 7 percent of the population of about 18 million people will be of Asian descent. In New Zealand, residents of Asian descent represent only about 3 percent of the population of 3.5 million, but about 12 percent of the population are Maoris, Polynesian peoples who settled on the islands about 1,000 years ago. Second, trade relations with Asia are increasing rapidly. About 60 percent of Australia's export markets today are in East Asia, and the region is the source of about one-half of its imports. Asian trade with New Zealand is also on the increase.

At the same time, the links that bind both countries to Great Britain and the United States have been loosening. Ties with London became increasingly distant after Great Britain decided to join the European Community in the early 1970s. There are moves under way in Australia and New Zealand to withdraw from the British Commonwealth at the end of the century, although the outcome is far from certain. Security ties with the United States remain important, but many Australians opposed their government's decision to cooperate with Washington during the Vietnam War, and the government today is seeking to establish closer political and military ties with the ASEAN alliance. Further removed from Asia both physically and psychologically, New Zealand assigns less importance to its security treaty with the United States and has been vocally critical of U.S. nuclear policies in the region.

Whether Australia and New Zealand will ever become an integral part of the Asia-Pacific region is uncertain. Cultural differences stemming from the European origins of the majority of the population in both countries hinder mutual understanding on both sides of the divide, and many ASEAN leaders express reluctance to accept the two countries as full members of the alliance. But economic and geographic realities act as a powerful force, and should the Pacific region continue on its current course toward economic prosperity and political stability, the role of Australia and New Zealand will assume greater significance.

Conclusion

What explains the striking ability of Japan and the four little tigers to follow the Western example and transform themselves into export-oriented societies capable of competing with the advanced nations of Europe and the Western Hemisphere? Some point to the traditional character traits of Confucian societies, such as thrift, a work ethic, respect for education, and obedience to authority. In a recent poll of Asian executives, more than 80 percent expressed the belief that Asian values differ from those of the West, and most add that these values

have contributed significantly to the region's recent success. Others place more emphasis on deliberate steps taken by government and economic leaders to meet the political, economic, and social challenges faced by their societies.

There seems no reason to doubt that cultural factors connected to East Asian social traditions have contributed to the economic success of these societies. Certainly, habits such as frugality, industriousness, and subordination of individual desires have all played a role in their governments' ability to concentrate on the collective interest. As one U.S. scholar of Asian descent has noted:

> In their outward appearance these East Asian *nouveaux riches* are Westernized. Yet behind this facade the people of these countries pursue a way of life that remains essentially Oriental. They prefer to eat Oriental food, observe lunar-calendar-based national festivities, place the family in the center of their social and economic relationships, practice ancestor worship, emphasize frugality in life, maintain a strong devotion to education, and accept Confucianism as the essence of their common culture.[13]

Political elites in these countries have been highly conscious of these factors and willing to use them for national purposes. Prime Minister Lee Kuan-yew of Singapore deliberately fostered the inculcation of such ideals among the citizens of his small nation and lamented the decline of Confucian values among the young. In South Korea, Chung Hee Park noted the connection between economic development and the collective values of traditional East Asian societies:

> Just as a home is a small collective body, so the state is a large community. . . . One who does not maintain a wholesome family order cannot be expected to show strong devotion to his state. A society that puts the national interest above the interests of the individual develops faster than one which does not.[14]

The importance of specifically Confucian values, however, should not be overemphasized as a factor in what authors Roy Hofheinz and Kent E. Calder call the "Eastasia Edge." In the first place, until recently, mainland China did not share in the economic success of its neighbors despite a long tradition of espousing Confucian values. In fact, some historians in recent years have maintained that it was precisely those Confucian values that hindered China's early response to the challenge of the West.

Moreover, while such traits as frugality and hard work have undoubtedly played a significant role in the economic development of East Asian societies, they are not necessarily a direct product of the Confucian tradition. In Japan, for example, indigenous traditions have probably had a greater effect on behavior and attitudes than Confucian teachings, and in societies with a majority Chinese population, it is often precisely those groups least influenced by Confucian doctrine—such as merchant groups in South China—that have participated most actively in the economic revolution of the late twentieth century. Thus, the determining factor is not so much Confucianism as the common emphasis on family values, self-sacrifice, and hard work that characterizes societies throughout the region.

As this and preceding chapters have shown, without active encouragement by political elites, such traditions cannot be effectively harnessed for the good of society as a whole. The creative talents of the Chinese people were not efficiently utilized under Mao Zedong or in the little tigers while they were under European or Japanese colonial rule (although Japanese colonialism did lead to the creation of an infrastructure more conducive to later development than was the case in European colonies). Only when a "modernizing elite" took charge and began to place a high priority on economic development were the stunning advances of recent decades achieved. Rural poverty was reduced if not eliminated by stringent land reform and population control programs. Profit incentives and foreign investment were encouraged, while the development of export markets received high priority.

There was, of course, another common factor in the successes achieved by Japan and its emulators. All the little tigers received substantial inputs of capital and technology from the advanced nations of the West—Taiwan and South Korea from the United States, and Hong Kong and Singapore from Britain. Japan relied to a greater degree on its own efforts, but received a significant advantage by being placed under the U.S. security umbrella and guaranteed access to markets and sources of raw materials in a region dominated by U.S. naval power.

As in parts of Southeast Asia, economic advancement in the region has sometimes been achieved at the cost of political freedom and individual human rights. Until recently, government repression of opposition has been common throughout East Asia except in Japan. As many Western observers have pointed out, the rights of national minorities and women are often still limited in comparison with the advanced countries of the West. Until recently, for example, women in South Korea had no right to inheritance or the legal custody of their children in case of divorce. Some commentators within the region take vigorous exception to such criticism. In a recent article, Singapore's Minister of Foreign Affairs S. Jayakumar has argued that pluralistic political systems could be "very dangerous and destabilizing" in the heterogeneous societies that currently exist in the region. Moreover, he maintains that the central role of the government has been a key factor in the economic success achieved by many Asian countries in recent years.[15]

Recent developments have somewhat tarnished the image of the "Asian miracle," and there is now widespread concern that some of the very factors that contributed to economic success in previous years are now making it difficult for governments in the region to develop increased openness and accountability in their financial systems. Still, it should be kept in mind that progress in political pluralism and human rights has not always been easy to achieve in Europe and North America, and even now frequently fails to match expectations. A rising standard of living, increased social mobility, and a changing regional environment brought about by the end of the Cold War should go far to enhance political freedoms and promote social justice in the countries bordering the western Pacific.

NOTES

1. *Far Eastern Economic Review*, May 19, 1994, p. 32.
2. Ezra F. Vogel, *Japan as Number One: Lessons for America* (Cambridge, MA, 1979), p. 94.
3. Bernard K. Gordon, "Japan's Universities," in *Far Eastern Economic Review*, January 14, 1993.
4. These figures are from Tom Heymann, *On an Average Day in Japan* (New York, 1992), pp. 152–56.
5. *New York Times*, January 30, 1993.
6. *New York Times*, November 19, 1996.
7. Robert Whiting, *You Gotta Have Wa* (New York, 1990).
8. Janet Hunter, *The Emergence of Modern Japan: An Introductory History since 1853* (London, 1989), p. 152.
9. Yukio Mishima and Geoffrey Bownas, eds., *New Writing in Japan* (Harmondsworth, 1972), p. 16.

10. *New York Times*, January 29, 1996.
11. Ezra F. Vogel, *The Four Little Dragons: The Spread of Industrialization in East Asia* (Cambridge, MA, 1991), p. 57.
12. Stan Seser, "A Reporter at Large," *The New Yorker*, January 13, 1992, p. 44.
13. Quoted in Hung-chao Tai, ed., *Confucianism and Economic Development: An Oriental Alternative?* (Washington, DC, 1989), p. 2.

14. Ibid., p. 17, quoting from Roderick MacFarquhar, "The Post-Confucian Challenge," *The Economist*, February 9, 1980.
15. *Far Eastern Economic Review*, May 30, 1996.

PART IV

Reflections

The colonial peoples of Africa and Asia had modest reasons for hope as World War II came to a close. In the Atlantic Charter, issued after their meeting near the coast of Newfoundland in August 1941, Franklin Roosevelt and Winston Churchill had set forth a joint declaration of their peace aims calling for the self-determination of all peoples and self-government and sovereign rights for all nations that had been deprived of them. Although Churchill later disavowed the assumption that he had meant these conditions to apply to colonial areas, Roosevelt on frequent occasions during the war voiced his own intention to bring about the end of colonial domination throughout the world at the close of the conflict.

Although it took many years to complete the process, the promise contained in the Atlantic Charter was eventually fulfilled. Although some colonial powers were reluctant to divest themselves of their colonies, World War II had severely undermined the stability of the colonial order, and by the end of the 1940s, most colonies in Asia had received their independence. Africa followed a decade or two later. In a few instances—notably in Algeria, Indonesia, and Vietnam—the transition to independence was a violent one, but for the most part it was realized by peaceful means.

In their own writings, public declarations, and statements, the leaders of these newly liberated countries set forth three broad goals at the outset of independence: to throw off the shackles of Western economic domination and ensure material prosperity for all their citizens; to introduce new political institutions that would enhance the right of self-determination of their peoples; and to develop a sense of nationhood and establish secure territorial boundaries. It was a measure of their own optimism and the intellectual and cultural influence of their colonial protectors that the governments of most of the newly liberated countries opted to follow a capitalist or moderately socialist path toward economic development. Only in a few cases—China, North Korea, and Vietnam were the most notable examples—did revolutionary leaders opt for the communist model of development

Within a few years of the restoration of independence, reality had set in, for most of the new governments in Asia and Africa did not achieve their ambitious goals. Virtually all of them remained economically dependent on the advanced industrial nations or, in the case of those who chose to follow the socialist model of development, were forced to rely on the USSR. Several faced severe problems of urban and rural poverty. At the same time, fledgling democratic governments were gradually replaced by military dictatorships or one-party regimes that dismantled representative institutions and oppressed dissident elements and ethnic minorities within their borders.

What had happened to tarnish the bright dreams of affluence and political pluralism? During the 1950s and 1960s, one school of thought was dominant among scholars and government officials in the United States. Known as modernization theory, this school adopted the view that the problems faced by the newly independent countries were a consequence of the difficult transition from a traditional agrarian to a modern industrial society. Modernization theorists were convinced that the countries of Asia, Africa, and Latin America were destined to follow the path of the West toward the creation of modern industrial societies, but would need time as well as substantial amounts of economic and technological assistance to complete the journey. In their view, it was the duty of the United States and other advanced capitalist nations to provide such assistance, while encouraging the leaders of these states to follow the path already adopted by the West. Some countries going through this difficult period were especially vulnerable to Communist-led insurgent movements. In such cases, it was in the interests of the United States and its allies to intervene, with military power if necessary, to hasten the transition and put the country on the path to self-sustaining growth.

Beginning in the 1960s, modernization theory began to come under attack from a new generation of younger scholars, many of whom had reached maturity during the Vietnam War, and who had growing doubts about the roots of the problem and the efficacy of the modernization approach. In their view, the responsibility for continued economic underdevelopment in the developing world lay not with the countries themselves, but with their continued domination by the ex-colonial powers. In this view, known as dependency theory, the countries of Asia, Africa, and Latin America were the victims of the international marketplace, which charged high prices for the manufactured goods of the West while dooming preindustrial countries to low prices for their raw material exports. Efforts by such countries to build up their own industrial sectors and move into the stage of self-sustaining growth were hampered by foreign control—through European- and American-owned corporations—over many of their resources. To end this "neocolonial" relationship, the dependency theory advocates argued, developing societies should reduce their economic ties with the West and practice a policy of economic self-reliance, thereby taking control of their own destinies. They should also ignore urgings that they adopt the Western model of capitalist democracy, which had little relevance to conditions in other parts of the world.

Both of these approaches, of course, were directly linked to the ideological divisions of the Cold War and suffered from the political bias of their advocates. Although modernization theorists were certainly correct in pointing out some of the key factors involved in economic development and in suggesting that some traditional attitudes and practices were incompatible with economic change, they were too quick to see the Western model of development as the only relevant one and ignored the fact that traditional customs and practices were not necessarily incompatible with nation building. They also too readily identified economic development in the developing world with the interests of the United States and its allies.

By the same token, the advocates of dependency theory alluded correctly to the unfair and often disadvantageous relationship that continued to exist between the ex-colonies and the industrialized nations of the world, and to the impact that this relationship had on the efforts of developing countries to overcome their economic difficulties. But they often rationalized many of the mistakes made by the leaders of developing countries while assigning all of the blame for their plight on the evil and self-serving practices of the industrialized world. At the same time, the recommendation by some dependency theorists of a policy of self-reliance was not only naive but sometimes disastrous, depriving the new nations of badly needed technology and capital resources.

In recent years, the differences between these two schools of thought have narrowed somewhat as their advocates have attempted to respond to criticism of the perceived weaknesses in their theories. Although the two approaches still have some methodological and ideological differences, there is a growing consensus that there are different roads to development and that the international marketplace can have both beneficial and harmful effects. At the same time, a new school of development theory, known as the world systems approach, has attempted to place recent developments within the broad context of world history. According to world systems theory, during the era of capitalism, the "core" countries of the industrializing West created a strong economic relationship with "peripheral" areas in the Third World to exploit their markets and sources of raw materials. That system is now beginning to develop serious internal contradictions and may be in the process of transformation.

A second area of concern for the leaders of African and Asian countries after World War II was to create a new political culture responsive to the needs of their citizens. For the most part, they accepted the concept of democracy as the defining theme of that culture. Within a decade, however, democratic systems throughout the developing world were replaced by military dictatorships or one-party governments that redefined the concept of democracy to fit their own preferences. Some Western observers criticized the new leaders for their autocratic tendencies while others attempted to explain the phenomenon by pointing out that after traditional forms of authority were replaced, it would take time to lay the basis for pluralistic political systems. In the interval, a strong government party under the leadership of a single charismatic individual could mobilize the population to seek common goals. Whatever the case, it was clear that many had underestimated the difficulties in building democratic political institutions in developing societies.

The problem of establishing a common national identity has in some ways been the most daunting of all the challenges facing the new nations of Asia and Africa. Many of these new states were a composite of a wide variety of ethnic, religious, and linguistic groups that found it difficult to agree on common symbols of nationalism. Problems of establishing an official language and delineating territorial boundaries left over from the colonial era created difficulties in many countries. In some cases, these problems were exacerbated by political and economic changes. The introduction of the concept of democracy sharpened the desire of individual groups to have a separate identity within a larger nation, while economic development often favored some at the expense of others.

The introduction of Western ideas and customs has also had a destabilizing effect in many areas. Often such ideas are welcomed by some groups and resisted by others. Where Western influence has the effect of undermining traditional customs and religious beliefs, it provokes violent hostility and sparks tension and even conflict within individual societies. To some, Western customs and values represent the wave of the future and are welcomed as a sign of progress. To others, they are destructive of indigenous traditions and a barrier to the growth of a genuine national identity based on history and culture.

From the 1950s to the 1970s, the political and economic difficulties experienced by many developing nations in Asia, Africa, and Latin America led to chronic instability in a number of countries and transformed the developing world into a major theater of Cold War confrontation. During the 1980s, however, a number of new factors entered the equation and shifted the focus away from ideological competition. China's shift to a more accommodating policy toward the West removed fears of more wars of national liberation supported by Beijing. At the same time, the Communist victory in Vietnam led not to falling dominoes throughout Southeast Asia but to a bitter war between the two erstwhile Communist allies, Vietnam and China. It was clear that national interests and historic rivalries took precedence over ideological agreement.

In the meantime, the growing success of the "little tigers" and the poor economic performance of socialist regimes led a number of developing countries to adopt a free market approach to economic development. As we have seen, some countries benefited from indigenous cultural and historical factors, and others from a high level of foreign aid and investment. But the role of government leadership in hindering or promoting economic growth should not be ignored. The situation in China is an obvious case in point. While Communist policies in the 1950s may have been beneficial in rectifying economic inequities and focusing attention on building up the infrastructure, the policies adopted during the Great Leap Forward and the Cultural Revolution had disastrous economic effects. Since the late 1970s, China has realized massive progress with a combination of centralized party leadership and economic policies emphasizing innovation and the interplay of free market forces. By some measures, China today has the third largest economy in the world.

Similarly, there have been tantalizing signs in recent years of a revival of interest in the democratic model in various parts of Asia, Africa, and Latin America. The best examples have been the free elections in South Korea, Taiwan, and the Philippines, but similar developments have taken place in a number of African countries. Nevertheless, it is clear that in many areas, democratic institutions are quite fragile, and experiments in democratic pluralism have failed in a number of areas. Many political leaders in Asia and Africa are convinced that such democratic practices as free elections and freedom of the press can be destabilizing and destructive of other national objectives. Many still do not believe that democracy and economic development go hand in hand.

Under the surface, social attitudes are changing as well, as changing economic circumstances have led to more secular attitudes, a decline in traditional hierarchical relationships, and a more open attitude toward sexual practices. In part, this change has been a consequence of the influence of Western music, movies, and television. But it is also a product of the growth of an affluent middle class in many societies of Asia and Africa. This middle class is often strongly influenced by Western ways, and its sons and daughters ape the behavior, dress, and lifestyles of their counterparts in Europe and North America. When Reebok sneakers are worn and coveted in Lagos and Nairobi, Bombay and Islamabad, Beijing and Hanoi, it is clear that the impact of modern Western civilization has been universalized.

PART

V

On the Eve of a
New Millennium

CHAPTER
16

The End of Bipolarity: The Collapse of the Soviet Empire and the Demise of the Cold War

*T*he lights were on late at the Kremlin on the night of March 10, 1985, as eight members of the Politburo met to select a successor for the recently deceased party general secretary, Konstantin Chernenko. To the average Soviet citizen, the logical choice was undoubtedly Mikhail Gorbachev. Young, talented, and vigorous, Gorbachev had risen rapidly in the ranks of the Communist Party leadership in recent years, and had often replaced the aging Chernenko when he was too ill to perform his official du-

ties. But according to inside accounts, conservative party veterans resisted the appointment of Gorbachev, fearing he might launch reforms that would undermine a system that had been in place for more than seventy years. Their fears were well founded. The election, by a bare majority vote, of Gorbachev as the new leader of the Soviet Union set in motion events that would soon destroy the Leninist edifice and bring an end to the Cold War.

. . . .

*T*he Disintegration of the Soviet Empire

The new Soviet leader had shown early signs of promise. Born into a peasant family in 1931, Mikhail Gorbachev combined farmwork with school and received the Order of the Red Banner for his agricultural efforts. This award and his good school record enabled him to study law at the University of Moscow. After receiving his law degree in 1955, he returned to his native southern Russia, where he eventually became first secretary of the Communist Party in the city of Stavropol (he had joined the party in 1952) and then first secretary of the regional party committee. In 1978, Gorbachev was made a member of the party's Central Committee in Moscow. Two years later, he became a full member of the ruling Politburo and secretary of the Central Committee.

During the early 1980s, Gorbachev began to realize the enormity of Soviet problems and the crucial impor-

tance of massive reform in order to transform the system. During a visit to Canada in 1983, he discovered to his astonishment that Canadian farmers worked hard on their own initiative. "We'll never have this for fifty years," he reportedly remarked.[1] On his return to Moscow, he set in motion series of committees to evaluate the situation and recommend measures to improve the system.

The Gorbachev Era

With his election as party general secretary in 1985, Gorbachev seemed intent on taking earlier reforms to their logical conclusions. By the 1980s, Soviet economic problems were obvious. Rigid, centralized planning had led to mismanagement and stifled innovation. Although the Soviets still excelled in space exploration, they had fallen behind the West in high technology, especially in the development and production of computers for private and public use. Most noticeable to the Soviet people was the actual decline in the standard of living.

The cornerstone of Gorbachev's reform program was *perestroika*, or "restructuring." At first it meant only a re-ordering of economic policy, as Gorbachev called for the beginning of a market economy with limited free enterprise and some private property. Initial economic reforms were difficult to implement, however. Radicals demanded decisive measures; conservatives feared that rapid changes would be too painful. In his attempt to achieve compromise, Gorbachev often pursued partial liberalization, which satisfied neither faction and also failed to work, producing only more discontent.

Gorbachev soon perceived that in the Soviet system, the economic sphere was intimately tied to the social and political spheres. Any efforts to reform the economy without political or social reform would be doomed to failure. One of the most important instruments of *perestroika* was *glasnost*, or "openness." Soviet citizens and officials were encouraged to discuss openly the strengths and weaknesses of the Soviet Union. This policy could be seen in *Pravda*, the official newspaper of the Communist Party, where disasters such as the nuclear accident at Chernobyl in 1986 and collisions of ships in the Black Sea received increasing coverage. Soon this type of reporting was extended to include reports of official corruption, sloppy factory work, and protests against government policy. The arts also benefited

◆ **Behind the Mask.** After the Bolshevik Revolution, Soviet writers and artists were expected to follow the dictates of socialist realism. All creative work was expected to glorify the state and the superiority of the socialist system. As official restrictions began to loosen under Gorbachev's policy of *glasnost*, however,

books and paintings began to demonstrate a more critical view of the Soviet system. In the paintings shown here, displayed at an exhibit in Moscow in 1989, an artist seeks to expose the inner natures of hallowed Soviet leaders Lenin and Stalin.

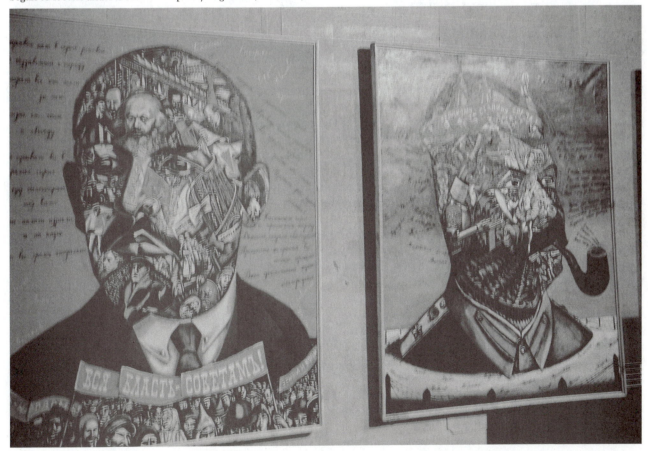

from the new policy, as previously banned works were now published and motion pictures began to depict negative aspects of Soviet life. Music based on Western styles, such as jazz and rock, began to be performed openly.

Political reforms were equally revolutionary. In June 1987, the principle of two-candidate elections was introduced; previously, voters had been presented with only one candidate. Most dissidents, including Andrei Sakharov, who had spent years in internal exile, were released. At the Communist Party conference in 1988, Gorbachev called for the creation of a new Soviet parliament, the Congress of People's Deputies, whose members were to be chosen in competitive elections. It convened in 1989, the first such meeting in Russia since 1918. Because of its size, the Congress chose a Supreme Soviet of 450 members to deal with day-to-day activities. The revolutionary nature of Gorbachev's political reforms was evident in Sakharov's rise from dissident to elected member of the Congress of People's Deputies. As a leader of the dissident deputies, Sakharov called for an end to the Communist monopoly of power and, on December 11, 1989, the day he died, urged the creation of a new, non-Communist party. Early in 1990, Gorbachev legalized the formation of other political parties and struck out Article 6 of the Soviet Constitution, which guaranteed the "leading role" of the Communist Party. Hitherto, the position of first secretary of the party was the most important post in the Soviet Union, but as the Communist Party became less closely associated with the state, the powers of this office diminished. Gorbachev attempted to consolidate his power by creating a new state presidency, and in March 1990, became the Soviet Union's first president.

One of Gorbachev's most serious problems stemmed from the character of the Soviet Union. The Union of Soviet Socialist Republics was a truly multiethnic country, containing 92 nationalities and 112 recognized languages. Previously, the iron hand of the Communist Party, centered in Moscow, had kept a lid on the centuries-old ethnic tensions that had periodically erupted throughout the history of this region. As Gorbachev released this iron grip, tensions resurfaced, a by-product of glasnost that Gorbachev had not anticipated. Ethnic groups took advantage of the new openness to protest what they perceived to be ethnically motivated slights. As violence erupted, the Soviet army, in disarray since the Soviet intervention in Afghanistan in 1979, had difficulty controlling the situation. In some cases, independence movements and ethnic causes became linked, as in Azerbaijan, where the National Front became the

spokesgroup for the Muslim Azerbaijanis in the conflict with Christian Armenians.

The period from 1988 to 1990 witnessed the emergence of nationalist movements throughout the republics of the Soviet Union. Often motivated by ethnic concerns, many of them called for sovereignty of the republics and independence from Russian-based rule centered in Moscow. Such movements sprang up first in Georgia in late 1988 and then in Latvia, Estonia, Moldavia, Uzbekistan, Azerbaijan, and most dramatically in Lithuania.

In December of 1989, the Communist Party of Lithuania declared itself independent of the Communist Party of the Soviet Union. A leading force in this independence movement was the nationalist Lithuanian Restructuring Movement, or "Popular Front for Perestroika," commonly known as *Sajudis*, led by Vytautas Landsbergis. Sajudis favored the radical policy of independence for Lithuania. Gorbachev made it clear that he supported self-determination, but not secession, which he believed would be detrimental to the Soviet Union. Nevertheless, on March 11, 1990, the Lithuanian Supreme Council unilaterally declared Lithuania independent. Its formal name was now the Lithuanian Republic; the adjectives Soviet and Socialist had been dropped. On March 15, the Soviet Congress of People's Deputies, though recognizing a general right to secede from the Union of Soviet Socialist Republics, declared the Lithuanian declaration null and void; the Congress stated that proper procedures must be established and followed before secession would be acceptable.

During 1990 and 1991, Gorbachev struggled to deal with Lithuania and the other problems unleashed by his reforms. On the one hand, he tried to appease the conservative forces who complained about the growing disorder within the Soviet Union. On the other hand, he tried to accommodate the liberal forces, especially those in the Soviet republics, who increasingly favored a new kind of decentralized Soviet federation. Gorbachev especially labored to cooperate more closely with Boris Yeltsin, elected president of the Russian Republic in June 1991.

By 1991, the conservative leaders of the traditional Soviet institutions—the army, government, KGB, and military industries—had grown increasingly worried about the impending dissolution of the Soviet Union and its impact on their own fortunes. On August 19, 1991, a group of these discontented rightists arrested Gorbachev and attempted to seize power. Gorbachev's unwillingness to work with the conspirators and the brave resistance in Moscow of Yeltsin and thousands of Russians who had grown accustomed to their new liber-

✳ Map 16.1   The States of Eastern Europe and the Former Soviet Union

ties caused the coup to disintegrate rapidly. The actions of these right-wing plotters, however, served to accelerate the very process they had hoped to stop—namely, the disintegration of the Soviet Union.

Despite desperate pleas from Gorbachev, the Soviet republics soon opted for complete independence. Ukraine voted for independence on December 1, 1991. A week later, the leaders of Russia, Ukraine, and Belarus announced that the Soviet Union had "ceased to exist" and would be replaced by a Commonwealth of Independent States. Gorbachev resigned on December 25, 1991, and turned over his responsibilities as commander in chief to Boris Yeltsin, the president of Russia. By the end of 1991, one of the largest empires in world history had come to an end, and a new era had begun in its lands.

The New Russia: From Empire to Nation

Within Russia, a new power struggle soon ensued. Yeltsin was committed to introducing a free market economy as quickly as possible. In December 1991, the Congress of People's Deputies granted Yeltsin temporary power to rule by decree. But the former Communist Party members and their allies in the Congress were opposed to many of Yeltsin's economic reforms and tried to place new limits on his powers. Yeltsin fought back. After winning a vote of confidence, both in himself and in his economic reforms, on April 25, 1993, Yeltsin pushed ahead with plans for a new Russian constitution that would abolish the Congress of People's Deputies, create a two-chamber parliament, and establish a strong presidency.

♦ **Tovarishchi (Comrades), Get Out and Vote!** In 1989, the Soviet Union held its first free national elections since the election for the Constituent Assembly in January 1918. Under Gorbachev's policy of *glasnost*, Soviet citizens elected a Congress of People's Deputies to help create a more open system of government in the USSR. In this poster, voters are encouraged to elect deputies who will support the policy of *perestroika*.

Nevertheless, the conflict between Yeltsin and the Congress continued and turned violent. On September 21, Yeltsin issued a decree dissolving the Congress of People's Deputies and scheduling new parliamentary elections for December. A hard-line parliamentary minority resisted and even took the offensive, urging supporters to take over government offices and the central television station. On October 4, Yeltsin responded by ordering military forces to storm the parliament building and arrest hard-line opponents. Yeltsin used his victory to consolidate his power; at the same time, he remained committed to holding new parliamentary elections on December 12.

During the mid-1990s, Yeltsin was able to maintain a precarious grip on power while seeking to implement reforms that would place Russia on a firm course toward a pluralistic political system and a market economy. But the new post-Communist Russia remains as fragile as ever. Burgeoning economic inequality and rampant corruption have aroused widespread criticism and shaken the confidence of the Russian people in the superiority of the capitalist system over that which existed under Communist rule. A nagging war in the Caucasus—where the people of Chechnya have resolutely sought national independence from Russia—has drained the government budget and exposed the decrepit state of the once vaunted Red Army. In presidential elections held in 1996, Yeltsin was reelected, but the rising popularity of a revived Communist Party and the growing strength of nationalist elements led by General Alexander Lebed, combined with Yeltsin's precarious health, raised serious questions about the future of the country.

Eastern Europe: From Soviet Satellites to Sovereign Nations

Stalin's postwar order had imposed Communist regimes throughout Eastern Europe. The process of sovietization seemed so complete that few people believed that the new order could be undone. But discontent with their Soviet-style regimes always simmered beneath the surface of these satellite states, and after Mikhail Gorbachev made it clear that his government would not intervene militarily, their Communist regimes fell quickly in the revolutions of 1989.

POLAND

As had been the case previously, the initial steps took place in Poland. Under Wladyslaw Gomulka, Poland had achieved a certain stability in the 1960s, but economic problems brought his ouster in 1971. His replacement, Edward Gierek, attempted to solve Poland's economic problems by borrowing heavily from the West. But in 1980, when he announced huge increases in food prices in an effort to pay off part of the Western debt, workers' protests erupted once again. This time, however, the revolutionary demands of the workers led directly to the rise of the independent labor movement called Solidarity. Led by Lech Walesa (b. 1943), Solidarity represented 10 million of Poland's 35 million people. Almost instantly, Solidarity became a tremendous force for change and a threat to the government's monopoly of power. With the support of the workers, many intellectuals, and the Catholic Church, Solidarity was able to win a series of concessions. The Polish government seemed powerless to stop the flow of concessions until December 1981, when it arrested Walesa and other Solidarity leaders, outlawed the union, and imposed military rule under General Wojciech Jaruzelski (b. 1923).

But martial rule did not solve Poland's serious economic problems. In 1988, new demonstrations broke out. After much maneuvering and negotiating with Solidarity, the Polish regime finally consented to free parliamentary elections—the first free elections in Eastern Europe for forty years—that led to even greater strength for Solidarity. Bowing to the inevitable, Jaruzelski's regime allowed the Solidarity-led coalition in the lower house of the new legislature to elect Tadeusz Mazowiecki, a leading member of Solidarity, as prime minister. The Communist monopoly of power in Poland had come to an end after forty-five years. In April 1990, it was decided that a new president would be freely elected by the populace by

the end of the year, and in December, Lech Walesa was chosen as the new Polish president.

Poland's new path has not been an easy one. The existence of political parties has fragmented the political process and created the danger of parliamentary stalemate, while rapid free market reforms have created severe unemployment and popular discontent. At the same time, the effort of the powerful Catholic Church to secure abortion law reform and religious education in the schools has raised new issues to divide the Polish people.

HUNGARY

In Hungary, too, the process of liberation from Communist rule had begun before 1989. Remaining in power for more than thirty years, the government of János Kádár tried to keep up with the changing mood by enacting the most far-reaching economic reforms in Eastern Europe. In the early 1980s, he legalized small private enterprises, such as shops, restaurants, and artisan shops. His economic reforms were called "Communism with a capitalist facelift." Hungary moved slowly away from its strict adherence to Soviet dominance and even established fairly friendly relations with the West. Multi-candidate elections with at least two candidates per seat were held for the first time on June 8, 1985.

As the 1980s progressed, however, the economy sagged, and Kádár fell from power in 1988. By 1989, the Hungarian Communist government was aware of the growing dissatisfaction and began to undertake reforms. The more important new political parties united to form an opposition round table, whose negotiations with the Communists led to an agreement that Hungary would become a democratic republic. The Hungarian Communist Party changed its name to the Hungarian Socialist Party in order to have a greater chance of success in the new elections scheduled for March 15, 1990. The party came in fourth, however, winning only 8.5 percent of the vote, a clear repudiation of communism. The Democratic Forum, a right-of-center, highly patriotic party, won the election and formed a new coalition government that committed Hungary to democratic government and a free market economy.

CZECHOSLOVAKIA

Communist regimes in Poland and Hungary had attempted to make some political and economic reforms in the 1970s and 1980s, but this was not the case in

Czechoslovakia. After Soviet troops crushed the reform movement in 1968, hard-line Czech Communists under Gustav Husák purged the party and followed a policy of massive repression to maintain their power. Only writers and other intellectuals provided any real opposition to the government. In January 1977, these dissident intellectuals formed Charter 77 as a vehicle for protest against violations of human rights. By the 1980s, Charter 77 members were also presenting their views on the country's economic and political problems, despite the government's harsh response to their movement.

Regardless of the atmosphere of repression, dissident movements continued to grow in the late 1980s. Government attempts to suppress mass demonstrations in Prague and other Czechoslovakian cities in 1988 and 1989 only led to more and larger demonstrations. By November 1989, crowds as large as 500,000, which included many students, were forming in Prague. A new opposition group, the Civic Forum, emerged and was officially recognized on November 17. The Czechoslovakian Federal Assembly now voted to delete the constitutional articles giving the Communists the leading role in politics. In December 1989, as demonstrations continued, the Communist government, lacking any real support, collapsed. President Husák resigned and at the end of December was replaced by Vaclav Havel, the dissident playwright who had been a leading figure in Charter 77 and had played an important role in bringing down the Communist government. In January 1990, Havel declared amnesty for some 30,000 political prisoners. He also set out on a goodwill tour to various Western countries in which he proved to be an eloquent spokesperson for Czech democracy and a new order in Europe.

The shift to non-Communist rule, however, was complicated by old problems, especially ethnic issues. Czechs and Slovaks disagreed over the makeup of the new state but were able to agree on a peaceful division of the country. On January 1, 1993, Czechoslovakia split into the Czech Republic and Slovakia.

THE REUNIFICATION OF GERMANY

The ruling Communist government in East Germany, led by Walter Ulbricht, consolidated its position in the early 1950s and became a faithful Soviet satellite. Industry was nationalized and agriculture collectivized. After a workers' revolt in 1953 was crushed by Soviet tanks, a steady flight of East Germans to West Germany ensued, primarily through the city of Berlin. This exodus of mostly skilled laborers created economic problems and, in 1961, led the East German government to build the infamous Berlin Wall separating West from East Berlin, as well as equally fearsome barriers along the entire border with West Germany.

After building the Wall, East Germany succeeded in developing the strongest economy among the Soviet union's Eastern European satellites. In 1971, Walter Ulbricht was succeeded by Erich Honecker (b. 1912), a party hard-liner deeply committed to the ideological battle against détente. Propaganda increased, and the use of the *Stasi*, the secret police, became a hallmark of Honecker's virtual dictatorship. Honecker ruled unchallenged for the next eighteen years.

In 1988, however, popular unrest, fueled by the persistent economic slump of the 1980s (which affected most of Eastern Europe) as well as the ongoing oppressiveness of Honecker's regime, caused another mass exodus of East German refugees. Violent repression as well as Honecker's refusal to institute reforms only led to a larger exodus and mass demonstrations against the regime in the summer and fall of 1989. By the beginning of November 1989, the Communist government had fallen into complete disarray. Capitulating to popular pressure on November 9, it opened the entire border with the West. Hundreds of thousands of Germans swarmed across the borders, mostly to visit and return. The Berlin Wall, long the symbol of the Cold War, became the site of a massive celebration, and most of it was soon dismantled by joyful Germans from both sides of the border. By December, new political parties had emerged, and on March 18, 1990, in East Germany's first free elections ever, the Christian Democrats won almost 50 percent of the vote. The Christian Democrats supported rapid monetary unification followed shortly by political unification with West Germany. On July 1, 1990, the economies of West and East Germany were united, with the West German deutsche mark becoming the official currency of the two countries. Political reunification was achieved on October 3, 1990. What had seemed almost impossible at the beginning of 1989 had become a reality by the end of 1990. The country of East Germany had ceased to exist.

The End of the Cold War

The dissolution of the Soviet satellite system in Eastern Europe, combined with the disintegration of the USSR itself, brought a dramatic end to the Cold War at the end of the 1980s. In fact, however, the thaw in relations between the two power blocs had begun with Gorbachev's accession to power in 1985. Gorbachev was willing to rethink many of the fundamental as-

⧫ Gorbachev on the New World Order ⧫

After assuming the leadership of the Communist Party of the Soviet Union in 1985, Mikhail Gorbachev worked to reform and revitalize the Soviet system. With his program called perestroika *(restructuring), he opened the door to rapid changes in Soviet society, as well as in other Eastern European countries. Through the force of his dominant personality (one colleague remarked that he had a nice smile but "iron teeth"), Gorbachev was a dominant force on the Soviet scene for nearly a decade.*

But Gorbachev was determined to introduce "new thinking" in foreign affairs as well. In his book *Perestroika*, he explained that in the new Cold War era, nuclear war could no longer be employed as "a means of achieving political, economic, ideological or any other goals." This viewpoint, he said, was "truly revolutionary," because it discarded the traditional concepts of war and peace. With the advent of nuclear weapons, war was no longer a rational option to achieve national goals, because in a global nuclear conflict, "world civilization would inevitably perish."

It was thus crucial, he continued, to develop a new way of thinking and acting to replace the traditional reliance on force in world politics. In today's world, he said, it was necessary for the first time in history "to base international politics on moral and ethical norms that are common to all mankind." To achieve this form of *perestroika* in the international environment, it would be necessary to humanize interstate relations and increase mutual understanding and mutual communication in a world still marked by serious political, economic, social, and environmental problems.

Gorbachev's words echoed those of U.S. President George Bush, who voiced his own conviction that the world was now entering a period during which it would be necessary to create a new world order based on cooperation rather than on conflict. Yet the course of events since the disintegration of the USSR in 1991 are a vivid indication that the end of the Cold War, by itself, has not given birth to the new era envisioned by these two statesmen. Although the superpower conflict based on a fragile balance of nuclear terror has come to an end, sources of conflict and dispute abound in the world as it prepares to enter a new millennium. Humankind still finds it difficult to place the common concerns of humanity above personal, community, and national interest. The new world order, as it appears at the close of the century, is still characterized primarily by the use or threat of force to achieve national goals.

Source: Mikhail Gorbachev, *Perestroika* (New York: Harper Collins Publishers, 1987).

sumptions underlying Soviet foreign policy, and his "new thinking," as it was called, opened the door to a series of stunning changes (see box above). For one, Gorbachev initiated a plan for arms limitation that led in 1987 to an agreement with the United States to eliminate intermediate-range nuclear weapons (the INF Treaty). Both sides had incentives to dampen the expensive arms race. Gorbachev hoped to make extensive economic and internal reforms, while the United States had serious deficit problems. During the Reagan years, the United States had moved from being a creditor nation to being the world's biggest debtor nation. By 1990, both countries were becoming aware that their large military budgets were making it difficult for them to solve their serious social problems.

During 1989 and 1990, much of the Cold War's reason for being disappeared as the mostly peaceful revolutionary upheaval swept through Eastern Europe. Gorbachev's policy of allowing greater autonomy for the Communist regimes of Eastern Europe meant that the Soviet Union would no longer militarily support Communist governments faced with internal revolt. The unwillingness of the Soviet regime to use force to maintain the status quo, as it had in Hungary in 1956 and in Czechoslovakia in 1968, opened the door to the overthrow of the Communist regimes. The reunification of Germany on October 3, 1990, also destroyed one of the most prominent symbols of the Cold War era. The disintegration of the Soviet Union in 1991 brought an end to the global rivalry between two competing superpowers.

With the end of the Cold War, world leaders began to turn their attention to the construction of what U.S. President George Bush called the New World Order. Certainly both Moscow and Washington hoped to initiate a new era of peace and mutual cooperation. During the first administration of President Bill Clinton, the United States sought to engage Russia as well as its own NATO allies in an effort to resolve the numerous brushfire conflicts that began to arise in various parts of the world in the early 1990s.

Mikhail Gorbachev had already indicated his agreement with this sentiment in a 1992 speech at Westminster College in Fulton, Missouri—the same location where Winston Churchill had announced the opening of the Cold War nearly half a century before. Noting that the United States and the Soviet Union had missed a chance to build a peaceful relationship at the end of World War II, he warned that it would take a major effort to guarantee that the current favorable trends would not be reversed. One danger, he noted, was the rise of an "exaggerated nationalism," the product of centrifugal forces that had for half a century been frozen by the Cold War. Another was the growing inequality in the distribution of wealth between the rich nations and the poor nations.[2]

Yugoslavia: A Tragedy in the Making

Gorbachev's warning about the danger of "exaggerated nationalism" was probably a reference to the rise of nationalist sentiment among ethnic minorities in the Soviet Union that had led to the disintegration of the USSR in the early 1990s. But his comment could as easily have applied to the situation in Yugoslavia, where the fragile union forged by the Communist leader Joseph Tito after World War II came apart after his death.

From its beginning in 1919, Yugoslavia had been an artificial creation. After World War II, Tito had served as a cohesive force for the six republics and two autonomous provinces that constituted Yugoslavia. In the 1970s, Tito had become concerned that decentralization had gone too far in creating too much power at the local level and encouraging regionalism. As a result, he purged thousands of local Communist leaders who seemed more involved with local affairs than national concerns.

After Tito's death in 1980, no strong leader emerged, and his responsibilities passed to a collective state presidency and the presidium of the League of Communists of Yugoslavia (LCY). At the end of the 1980s, Yugoslavia was caught up in the reform movements sweeping through Eastern Europe. On January 10, 1990, the League of Communists called for an end to authoritarian socialism and proposed the creation of a pluralistic political system with freedom of speech and other civil liberties, free elections, an independent judiciary, and a mixed economy with equal status for private property. But division between Slovenes, who wanted a loose federation, and Serbians, who wanted to retain the central-

ized system, caused the collapse of the party congress, and hence the Communist Party. New parties quickly emerged. In multiparty elections held in the republics of Slovenia and Croatia in April and May of 1990 (the first multiparty elections in Yugoslavia in fifty-one years), the Communists fared poorly.

The Yugoslav political scene was complicated by the development of separatist movements that brought the disintegration of Yugoslavia in the 1990s. When new, non-Communist parties won elections in the republics of Slovenia, Croatia, Bosnia-Herzegovina, and Macedonia in 1990, they began to lobby for a new federal structure of Yugoslavia that would fulfill their separatist desires. Slobodan Milosevic, who had become the leader of the Serbian Communist Party in 1987 and had managed to stay in power by emphasizing his Serbian nationalism, rejected these efforts. He maintained that these republics could only be independent if new border arrangements were made to accommodate the Serb minorities in those republics who did not want to live outside the boundaries of a greater Serbian state. Serbs constituted 11.6 percent of Croatia's population and 32 percent of Bosnia-Herzegovina's population in 1981.

After negotiations among the six republics failed, Slovenia and Croatia declared their independence in June 1991. Milosevic's government sent the Yugoslavian army, which it controlled, into Slovenia, but without much success. In September 1991, it began a full assault against Croatia. Increasingly, the Yugoslavian army was the Serbian army, and Serbian irregular forces played an important role in military operations. Before a cease-fire was arranged, the Serbian forces had captured one-third of Croatia's territory in brutal and destructive fighting.

The recognition of Slovenia, Croatia, and Bosnia-Herzegovina by many European states and the United States early in 1992 did not stop the Serbs from turning their guns on Bosnia-Herzegovina. By mid-1993, Serbian forces had acquired 70 percent of Bosnian territory. The Serbian policy of "ethnic cleansing"—killing or forcibly removing Bosnian Muslims from their lands—revived memories of Nazi atrocities in World War II. Nevertheless, despite worldwide outrage, European governments failed to take a decisive and forceful stand against these Serbian activities, and by the spring of 1993, the Muslim population of Bosnia-Herzegovina was in desperate straits. As the fighting spread, European nations and the United States began to intervene to stop the bloodshed, and in the fall of 1995, a fragile cease-fire agreement was reached at a conference held in Dayton, Ohio. An international peacekeeping force was stationed in the area to maintain tranquillity and monitor the accords. Implementation has been difficult, however, as ethnic antagonisms continue to flare, and a final solution seems as far away as ever.

The Shifting Power Balance in Asia

The end of the Cold War had less impact in Asia, where relations among the major countries in the area had been essentially delinked from ideological concerns as a result of the improvement in U.S.–China relations after Nixon's visit to Beijing in 1972. Still, the situation in the Pacific region was in flux. During the 1980s, China began to emerge as an independent power less closely tied to the United States. Chinese relations with the Soviet Union gradually improved, while relations with the United States were impeded by a variety of issues, including continuing U.S. military aid to Taiwan, Chinese arms sales to Middle Eastern countries, and the Chinese government's suppression of student demonstrations in Beijing in the spring of 1989. Discontent among students had been on the rise since the mid-1980s, when thousands demonstrated in the streets of Shanghai to protest against overcrowded dormitories, a lack of meaningful job opportunities, and restrictions on permits to study abroad.

Incident at Tiananmen Square

As long as economic conditions for the majority of Chinese were improving, other classes did not share the students' discontent, and the government was able to isolate them from other elements in society. But in the late 1980s, an overheated economy led to rising inflation and growing discontent among salaried workers, especially in the cities. At the same time, corruption, nepotism, and favored treatment for senior officials and party members were provoking increasing criticism. In May 1989, student protesters carried placards demanding Science and Democracy (reminiscent of the slogan of the May Fourth Movement, whose seventieth anniversary was celebrated in the spring of 1989), an end to official corruption, and the resignation of China's aging party leadership. These demands received widespread support from the urban population (although notably less in rural areas) and led to massive demonstrations in Tiananmen Square (see box on p. 342).

The demonstrations divided the Chinese leaders. Reformist elements around party general secretary Zhao Ziyang were sympathetic to the protesters, but veteran leaders such as Deng Xiaoping saw the student demands for more democracy as a disguised call for an end to Communist Party rule. After some hesitation, the

♦ **Give Me Liberty—or Give Me Death!** The demonstrations that erupted in Tiananmen Square in the spring of 1989 spread rapidly to other parts of China, where students and other local citizens gave their vocal support to the popular movement in Beijing. Here, students from a high school march to the city of Guilin to display their own determination to take part in the reform of Chinese society. Their call to "give me liberty or give me death" (in Patrick Henry's famous phrase) echoes the determination expressed by many of their counterparts in Beijing.

⋟ Students Appeal for Democracy ⋞

In the spring of 1989, thousands of students gathered in Tiananmen Square in downtown Beijing to provide moral support to their many compatriots who had gone on a hunger strike in an effort to compel the Chinese government to reduce the level of official corruption and enact democratic reforms, opening the political process to the Chinese people. The statement that follows was printed on flyers and distributed to participants and passersby on May 17, 1989, to explain the goals of the movement.

"Why Do We Have to Undergo a Hunger Strike?"

By 2:00 P.M. today, the hunger strike carried out by the petition group in Tiananmen Square has been underway for 96 hours. By this morning, more than 600 participants have fainted. When these democracy fighters were lifted into the ambulances, no one who was present was not moved to tears.

Our petition group now undergoing the hunger strike demands that at a minimum the government agree to the following two points:

1) to engage on a sincere and equal basis in a dialogue with the "higher education dialogue group." In addition, to broadcast the actual dialogue in its entirety. We absolutely refuse to agree to a partial broadcast, to empty gestures, or to fabrications that dupe the people.

2) to evaluate in a fair and realistic way the patriotic democratic movement. Discard the label of "trouble-making" and redress the reputation of the patriotic democratic movement.

It is our view that the request for a dialogue between the people's government and the people is not an unreasonable one. Our party always follows the principle of seeking truths from actual facts. It is therefore only natural that the evaluation of this patriotic democratic movement should be done in accordance with the principle of seeking truths from actual facts.

Our classmates who are going through the hunger strike are the good sons and daughters of the people! One by one, they have fallen. In the meantime, our "public servants" are completely unmoved. Please, let us ask where your conscience is.

Source: Flyer, property of the author.

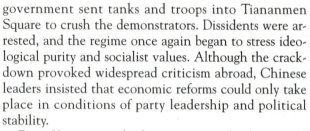

government sent tanks and troops into Tiananmen Square to crush the demonstrators. Dissidents were arrested, and the regime once again began to stress ideological purity and socialist values. Although the crackdown provoked widespread criticism abroad, Chinese leaders insisted that economic reforms could only take place in conditions of party leadership and political stability.

Deng Xiaoping and other aging party leaders turned to the army to protect their base of power and suppress what they described as "counterrevolutionary elements." Deng was undoubtedly counting on the fact that many Chinese, particularly in rural areas, feared a recurrence of the disorder of the Cultural Revolution and craved economic prosperity more than political reform. In the months following the confrontation, the government issued new regulations requiring courses on Marxist-Leninist ideology in the schools, sought out dissidents within the intellectual community, and made it clear that while economic reforms would continue, the CCP's monopoly of power would not be allowed to decay. Harsh punishments were imposed on those accused of undermining the Communist system and supporting its enemies abroad.

Confucius Revived?

In the 1990s, the government began to nurture urban support by reducing the rate of inflation and guaranteeing the availability of consumer goods in great demand among the rising middle class. That policy has paid dividends in bringing about a perceptible decline in alienation among the population in the cities. Industrial production has been increasing rapidly, leading to predictions that China may become one of the economic superpowers in the twenty-first century. But problems in rural areas are on the increase. Farm income has lagged behind in recent years, and high taxes and official corruption have sparked rising resentment among the rural populace. In the meantime, food production has leveled off for a variety of reasons, promoting concerns from some observers that China will no longer be able to feed its growing population in the early years of the new century.

Partly out of fear that such changes could undermine the socialist system and the rule of the CCP, conservative leaders have attempted to curb Western influence and restore faith in Marxism-Leninism. Recently, in what may be a tacit recognition that Marxist exhortations are no longer an effective means of enforcing social discipline, the party has turned to Confucianism as an antidote. Ceremonies celebrating the birth of Confucius now receive official sanction, and the virtues promoted by the master, such as righteousness, propriety, and filial piety, are now widely cited as an antidote to the tide of antisocial behavior. A recent article in *People's Daily* asserted that the current spiritual crisis in contemporary Western culture stems from the incompatibility between science and the Christian religion. The solution, the author maintained, is Confucianism, "a non-religious humanism that can provide the basis for morals and the value of life." Because a culture combining science and Confucianism is taking shape in East Asia today, "it will thrive particularly well in the next century and will replace modern and contemporary Western culture."[3]

In the short term, such efforts may have some success in slowing down the rush toward Westernization because many Chinese are understandably fearful of punishment and concerned for their careers. But one is inevitably reminded of Chiang Kai-shek's failed attempt in the 1930s to revive Confucian ethics as a standard of behavior for modern China—dead ideologies cannot be revived by decree.

Beijing's decision to emphasize traditional Confucian themes as a means of promoting broad popular support for its domestic policies is paralleled in the world arena, where it relies on the spirit of nationalism to achieve its goals. Today, China conducts an independent foreign policy and is playing an increasingly active role in the region. To some of its neighbors, including Japan, India, and post-Soviet Russia, China's new posture is cause for disquiet and gives rise to suspicions that it is once again preparing to assert its muscle as in the imperial era. A striking example of this new attitude took place as early as 1979, when Chinese forces briefly invaded Vietnam as punishment for the Vietnamese occupation of neighboring Cambodia. In the 1990s, China has aroused concern in the region by claiming sole ownership over the Spratly Islands in the South China Sea and over Diaoyu Island (also claimed by Japan) near Taiwan.

To Chinese leaders, however, such actions simply represent legitimate efforts to resume China's rightful role in the affairs of the region. After a century of humiliation at the hands of the Western powers and neighboring Japan, the nation, in Mao's famous words of 1949, "has stood up" and no one will be permitted to humiliate it again. For the moment, at least, a fervent sense of patriotism appears to be on the rise in China, a phenomenon that is actively promoted by the party as a means of holding the country together in uncertain times. Pride

in the achievement of national sports teams is intense, and two young authors recently achieved wide acclaim with the publication of their book, *The China That Can Say No*, an obvious response to recent criticism of the country in the United States and Europe.

Whether the current leaders will be able by such artificial means to prevent further erosion of the party's power and prestige is unclear. Dissatisfaction with the CCP and alienation from the socialist system are running high in China, notably among the educated youth, the professionals, and the middle ranks of the bureaucracy. Although a disintegration of the authority of the Communist regime in China as in the Soviet Union cannot be predicted, the trend toward a greater popular role in the governing process will be difficult to reverse.

Europe Reunited

The fall of Communist governments in Eastern Europe during the revolutions of 1989 brought a wave of euphoria to Europe. The new structures meant an end to a postwar European order that had been imposed on unwilling peoples by the victorious forces of the Soviet Union. In 1989 and 1990, new governments throughout Eastern Europe worked diligently to scrap the remnants of the old system and introduce the democratic procedures and market systems that they believed would revitalize their scarred lands. But the process proved to be neither simple nor easy, and the mood of euphoria largely faded by 1992.

Most Eastern European countries had little or virtually no experience with democratic systems. Moreover, under Communist rule most people had had no chance to participate in public life in general and in democratic debate in particular. Then, too, ethnic divisions that had troubled these areas before World War II and had been forcibly submerged under Communist rule reemerged with a vengeance, making political unity almost impossible. While Czechoslovakia resolved its differences peacefully, Yugoslavia descended into the kind of brutal warfare that had not been seen in Europe since World War II. In the lands of the former Soviet Union, ethnic and nationalist problems threatened to tear some of the new states apart.

The rapid conversion to market economies also proved painful. The adoption of "shock-therapy" austerity measures produced much suffering and uncertainty. Unemployment climbed to more than 15 percent in the former East Germany and to 13 percent in Poland in 1992. Wages remained low while prices skyrocketed.

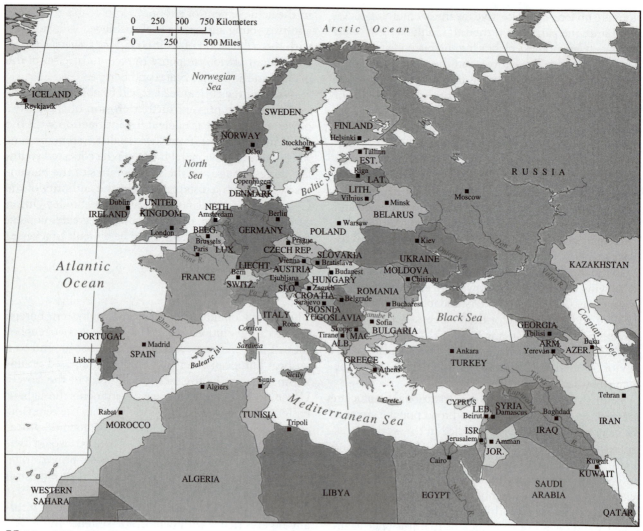

Map 16.2   The New Europe

Russia experienced a 2,000 percent inflation rate in 1992. In many countries, former Communists were able to retain important positions of power or become the new owners of private property. Resentment against former Communists provided yet another source of social instability. For both political and economic reasons, the new non-Communist states of Eastern Europe faced dangerous and uncertain futures.

Germany: The Party's Over

Perhaps the most challenging situation was faced in Germany, where the decision to unify the two zones created serious strains on the economy. Helmut Kohl

was a clever politician who had benefited greatly from an economic boom in the mid-1980s. Gradually, however, discontent with the Christian Democrats increased, and by 1988, their political prospects seemed diminished. But unexpectedly, the 1989 revolution in East Germany led to the reunification of the two Germanies, leaving the new Germany, with its 79 million people, the leading power in Europe. Reunification, accomplished during Kohl's administration, brought rich political dividends to the Christian Democrats. In the first all-German federal election, Kohl's Christian Democrats won 44 percent of the vote, while their coalition partners—the Free Democrats—received 11 percent.

But the euphoria over reunification soon dissipated as new problems arose. All too soon, the realization set in that the revitalization of eastern Germany would take far more money than was originally thought, and Kohl's government was soon forced to face the politically undesirable task of raising taxes substantially. Moreover, the virtual collapse of the economy in eastern Germany led to extremely high levels of unemployment and severe discontent. One reason for the problem was the government's decision to establish a 1:1 ratio between the East and West German marks. This policy raised salaries for East German workers, but it increased labor costs and provoked many companies into hiring workers abroad.

Increasing unemployment, in turn, led to growing resentment against foreigners. For years, foreigners seeking asylum or employment found haven in Germany because of its extremely liberal immigration laws. In 1992, more than 440,000 immigrants came to Germany seeking asylum, 123,000 of them from former Yugoslavia alone. Attacks against foreigners by right-wing extremists—many of them espousing neo-Nazi beliefs—killed seventeen people in 1992 and became an all-too frequent scene in German life.

East Germans were also haunted by another memory from their recent past. The opening of the files of the secret police (the *Stasi*) showed that millions of East Germans had spied on their neighbors and colleagues, and even their spouses and parents, during the Communist era. A few senior *Stasi* officials were placed on trial for their past actions, but many Germans preferred simply to close the door on an unhappy period in their lives.

As the century neared its close, then, Germans struggled to cope with the challenge of building a new, united nation. To reduce the debt incurred because of economic reconstruction in the east, the government threatened to cut back on many of the social benefits West Germans had long been accustomed to receiving. This in turn sharpened resentments that were already beginning to emerge between the two zones. Although the Berlin Wall had been removed, the gap between East and West remained.

France: A Season of Discontent

Although France was not faced with the challenge of integrating two highly different systems into a single society, it encountered many of the same economic and social problems as its neighbor Germany. The policies adopted during the early 1980s by the Socialist majority under President Mitterrand failed to work, and within three years, faced with declining support, the Mitterrand government returned some of the economy to private enterprise. Some economic improvements in the late 1980s enabled Mitterrand to win a second seven-year term in the 1988 presidential election. But France's economic decline continued. In 1993, French unemployment stood at 10.6 percent, and in the elections in March of that year, the Socialists won only 28 percent of the vote while a coalition of conservative parties won 80 percent of the seats in the National Assembly. The move to the right was strengthened when the conservative mayor of Paris, Jacques Chirac, was elected president in May 1995. But conservative policies failed to improve the economic situation, and the Socialists made a comeback with a victory in the elections for the National Assembly in 1997.

As in Germany, resentment against foreign-born residents compounded the problem. Spurred by rising rates of unemployment and large numbers of immigrants from North Africa (often identified in the public mind with terrorist actions committed by militant groups based in the Middle East), many French voters gave their support to Jean-Marie Le Pen's National Front, which openly advocated a restriction on all new immigration and limited assimilation of immigrants already living in France.

Great Britain: Move to the Left

In Great Britain, the conservative prime minister Margaret Thatcher dominated politics in the 1980s. The Labour Party, beset by divisions between moderate and radical wings, offered little effective opposition. Only in 1990 did Labour's fortunes seem to revive when Thatcher's government attempted to replace local property taxes with a flat-rate tax payable by every adult to his or her local authority. Although Thatcher argued that this would make local government more responsive to popular needs, many argued that this was nothing more than a poll tax that would enable the rich to pay the same rate as the poor. After antitax riots broke out, Thatcher's once legendary popularity plummeted to an all-time low. At the end of November, a revolt within her own party caused Thatcher to resign as prime minister. Her replacement was John Major, whose Conservative Party won a narrow victory in the general elections held in April 1992. But Major's lackluster leadership failed to capture the imagination of many Britons, and in new elections in May 1997, the Labour Party won a landslide victory. The new prime minister, Tony Blair, was a moderate whose youth and vigor immediately instilled a new vigor on the political scene.

The Move toward European Unity: Staying the Course?

With the formation of NATO in 1949 and other regional organizations such as EURATOM and the Common Market, Western European governments took the initial moves toward creating a more unified continent. Still, the Common Market, formally known as the European Community (EC), was still primarily an economic union rather than a political one. By 1992, it included within its border nearly 350 million people and constituted the world's largest single trading bloc, transacting almost one-quarter of the world's commerce. In the early 1990s, EC members drafted a new Treaty on European Union (known as the Maastricht Treaty after the city in the Netherlands where the agreement was reached), seeking to create a true economic and monetary union of all members of the organization. The treaty did not go into effect, however, until all member agreed. Finally, on January 1, 1994, the European Community became the European Union.

One of its first goals was to introduce a new common currency, called the euro, by 2002. But problems soon arose. Voters in many countries opposed the austerity measures that their governments would be compelled to take to reduce growing budget deficits. Germans in particular feared that replacing the rock-solid mark with a common European currency could lead to economic disaster. Yet the logic of the new union appeared inescapable if European nations were to improve their capacity to compete with the United States and the powerful industrializing nations of the Pacific Rim.

Although measures to introduce the new all-European currency have gotten under way, in their determination to achieve a greater degree of political and economic integration within the continent, European leaders are running against the strong current of emerging nationalism that has swept through much of the world in recent years and has been making inroads among voters within Europe itself. Although there are persuasive economic reasons for greater European unity, its proponents run the risk of inciting rising popular resentment and a resurgence of the nationalist passions that have swept the region in the past. Today the outcome remains very much in doubt.

The NATO alliance continues to serve as a powerful force for European unity. Yet it too faces new challenges, as Moscow's former satellites in Eastern Europe clamor for membership in the hope that it will spur economic growth and reduce the threat from a revival of Russian expansionism. In 1998, plans were under way to add the Czech Republic, Hungary, and Poland to the alliance. Some observers express concern, however, that an expanded NATO will only reduce the cohesiveness of the organization, while provoking Russia into a new posture of hostility to the outside world.

The United States: Return to Hegemony

During the 1980s, the conservative trend that had begun with the election of Richard M. Nixon as president in 1968 continued. The election of Ronald Reagan in 1980 changed the direction of American policy on several fronts. Reversing decades of the expanding welfare state, Reagan cut spending on food stamps, school lunch programs, and job programs. At the same time, his administration fostered the largest peacetime military buildup in American history. Total federal spending rose from $631 billion in 1981 to more than $1 trillion by 1986. But instead of raising taxes to pay for the new expenditures, which far outweighed the budget cuts in social areas, Reagan convinced Congress to support supply-side economics. Massive tax cuts were designed to stimulate rapid economic growth and produce new revenues. Much of the tax cut went to the wealthy. Between 1980 and 1986, the income of the lowest 40 percent of the workforce fell 9 percent, while the income of the highest 20 percent rose by 5 percent.

Reagan's policies seemed to work in the short run, as the United States experienced an economic upturn that lasted until the end of the 1980s. But the spending policies of the Reagan administration also produced record government deficits, which loomed as an obstacle to long-term growth. In the 1970s, the total deficit was $420 billion; between 1981 and 1987, Reagan budget deficits were three times that amount. The inability of George Bush (b. 1924), Reagan's successor, to deal with the deficit problem or with the continuing economic downslide led to the election of a Democrat, Bill Clinton, in November 1992.

The new president was a southerner who claimed to be a new Democrat—one who favored fiscal responsibility and a more conservative social agenda—a clear indication that the rightward drift in American politics had not been ended by his victory. During his first term in office, Clinton reduced the budget deficit and signed a bill turning the welfare program back to the states, while pushing measures to strengthen the educational system and provide job opportunities for those Americans removed from the welfare rolls. By seizing the center of the American political agenda, Clinton was able to win reelection in 1996, although the Republican Party now held a majority in both houses of Congress.

President Clinton's political fortunes were aided considerably by a lengthy economic revival. Aided by an era of corporate downsizing, major U.S. corporations began to recover the competitive edge they had lost to Japanese and European firms in previous years. At the same time, a steady reduction in the annual government budget deficit strengthened confidence in the performance of the national economy. Although wage increases were modest, inflation was securely in check, and public confidence in the future was on the rise.

Many of the country's social problems, however, remained unresolved. Although crime rates were down, drug use, smoking, and alcoholism among young people were on the rise, while the specter of rising medical costs loomed as a generation of baby boomers neared retirement age. Americans remained bitterly divided over such issues as abortion and affirmative action programs to rectify past discrimination on the basis of gender, race, or sexual preference.

The Other Americas

For other states in the Western Hemisphere, the revival of the United States as an economic juggernaut was a mixed blessing, for the American behemoth was all too often inclined to make use of its power to have its way with its neighbors. Economic recession had brought Brian Mulroney (b. 1939), leader of the Progressive Conservative Party, to power in Canada in 1984. Mulroney's government sought greater privatization of Canada's state-run corporations and negotiated a free trade agreement with the United States. Bitterly resented by many Canadians as a sellout, the agreement cost Mulroney's government much of its popularity. In 1993, the ruling Conservatives were drastically defeated in national elections, winning only two seats in the House of Commons. The Liberal leader, Jean Chrétien, took over as prime minister with the charge of stimulating the nation's sluggish economy.

The new Liberal government was also faced with an ongoing crisis over the French-speaking province of Quebec. In the late 1960s, the Parti Québécois, headed by René Lévesque, campaigned on a platform of Quebec's secession from the Canadian confederation. In 1970, the party won 24 percent of the popular vote in Quebec's provincial elections. To pursue their dream of separation, some underground separatist groups even used terrorist bombings and kidnapped two prominent government officials. In 1976, the Parti Québécois won Quebec's provincial elections and in 1980 called for a referendum that would enable the provincial government to negotiate Quebec's independence from the rest of Canada. Voters in Quebec rejected the plan in 1995, however, and debate over Quebec's status continues to divide Canada as the decade comes to a close.

Washington's southern neighbor, Mexico, was even more vulnerable to changing conditions in the United States. In the late 1970s, vast new reserves of oil were discovered in Mexico. As the sale of oil abroad increased dramatically, the government became increasingly dependent on oil revenues. When world oil prices dropped in the mid-1980s, Mexico was no longer able to make payments on its foreign debt, which had reached $80 billion in 1982. The government was forced to adopt new economic policies, including the increased sale of public-owned companies to private hands.

The debt crisis and rising unemployment increased dissatisfaction with the government. In the 1988 election, the PRI's choice for president, Carlos Salina, who had been expected to win in a landslide, won by only a 50.3 percent majority. The new president continued the economic liberalization of his predecessors and went even further by negotiating a North American Free Trade Agreement (NAFTA) with the United States and Canada. Although NAFTA was highly controversial in the United States because of the fear that U.S. firms would move their factories to Mexico, where labor costs are cheaper and environmental standards less stringent, some observers assert that the immediate impact of NAFTA has been more beneficial to the U.S. economy than to its southern neighbor. Compounding Mexico's continuing economic problems are charges of corruption among leading officials in the ruling party, and rising popular unrest in southern parts of the country.

Elsewhere in Latin America, many countries continue to be plagued with their own economic problems while confronting the challenges of the recent trend away from authoritarian governments toward more democratic systems. In the mid-1970s, only Colombia, Venezuela, and Costa Rica maintained democratic governments. A decade later, pluralistic systems had been installed virtually everywhere except in Cuba, Paraguay, and some of the Central American states. The establishment of democratic institutions, however, has not managed to bring the problem of official corruption under control, nor has it served to reduce the growing gap between rich and poor in many countries in the region.

The two largest states in South America, Argentina and Brazil, have both continued to adhere to democratic principles, sometimes under difficult conditions. In Argentina, in 1989, the civilian president Raúl Alfonsín was defeated in a national election by the Peronist candidate, Carlos Saúl Menem (b. 1930). Reelected in 1995, President Menem has sought to control inflation by curbing government spending.

In Brazil, presidential elections in 1990 brought a newcomer into office—Fernando Collor de Mello (b. 1949). The new president promised to reduce inflation with a drastic reform program, based on squeezing money out of the economy by stringent controls on wages and prices, drastic reductions in public spending, and cuts in the number of government employees. Collor de Mello's efforts were undermined by the corruption in his own administration, however, and he resigned from office at the end of 1992 after having been impeached. In new elections in 1994, Fernando Cardozo was elected president by an overwhelming majority of the popular vote.

Throughout Latin America, the ticking time bomb of rapid population growth threatens the fragile political and economic gains achieved in recent years. In the three decades after 1950, the population of Latin America increased from about 165 million to 400 million. By 1990, there were 29 cities of more than 1 million people, including Mexico City, with 16 million inhabitants. As in other parts of the Third World, the flight to the cities reflected a desire for a better life. Instead, most new arrivals ended up in squalid slums, while all residents suffered from the familiar evils of urban smog and gridlock on crowded streets.

Nowhere is the problem more intimidating than in Brazil, the region's economic giant. With population increase outstripping economic growth, unemployment is on the rise, and more than 30 million Brazilians go hungry each day. Some critics point to the policies of the Roman Catholic Church, which prohibits abortion and the use of contraceptives. In a recent survey, more than three-quarters of those polled in Rio de Janeiro favored the right to abortion in cases of rape or danger to the mother, while 84 percent approved of the use of birth control.[4]

After the Cold War: The "End of History"?

The wave of optimism that accompanied the end of the Cold War was all too brief. After a short period of euphoria—some observers speculated that the world had reached the "end of history," when the major problems still to be encountered would be economic in nature—it soon became clear that, as Mikhail Gorbachev had warned, centrifugal forces were now being released that had long been held in check by the ideological rigidities of the Cold War. The era of conflict that had long characterized the twentieth century was not at an end; it was simply in the process of taking a different form.

Nowhere was this trend more immediately apparent than in Southeast Asia, where even before the end of the Cold War, erstwhile allies in China, Vietnam, and Cambodia turned on each other in a fratricidal conflict that combined territorial ambitions with geopolitical concerns and deep-seated historical suspicions based on the memory of past conflicts. Ideology, it was clear, was no barrier to historical and cultural rivalries. The pattern was repeated elsewhere: in Africa, where several nations erupted into civil war during the late 1980s and 1990s; in the Balkans, where the Yugoslavian Federation broke apart in a bitter conflict that has yet to be resolved; and of course in the Middle East, where the historical disputes in Palestine and the Persian Gulf persistently threaten to break out in open war.

Such outbreaks of virulent nationalism are less common in the advanced industrial countries in Europe, the Western Hemisphere, and eastern Asia. Periodically, however, incidents of terrorism—by militant Palestinian groups, angry Sikhs demanding world recognition of an independent Sikh state in South Asia, or members of the Irish Republican Army (IRA)—are a constant reminder that the passing of the Cold War has not brought an end to our century of conflict. Another reminder is even closer to home—in the ethnic, racial, and religious conflicts and suspicions that continue to divide Western societies from within. The rise of antiforeign sentiment in several European countries, combined with the chronic racial divide that continues to plague the United States, vividly demonstrates that the main sources of conflict and misunderstanding in today's world are not just among nations, but within them as well. It will take all the efforts and talents of a new generation of leaders in the twenty-first century to deal with these issues.

The irony of this explosion of national, ethnic, and religious sentiment is that it has taken place at a time when it is becoming increasingly evident to many observers that the main problems in today's society—such as environmental pollution, overpopulation, and unequal distribution of resources—are shared to one degree or another by all humanity. In a world that is increasingly characterized by global interdependence, how can it be that the world is increasingly being pulled apart?

Conclusion

For four decades after the end of World War II, the world's two superpowers competed for global hegemony. What began as a dispute on the future shape of Eastern Europe spread rapidly to Asia and ultimately penetrated virtually every part of the earth. The Cold War became the dominant feature on the international scene, and dominated the internal politics of many countries around the world as well.

By the early 1980s, some of the tension had gone out of the conflict, as it appeared that both Moscow and Washington had learned to tolerate the other's existence. Skeptical minds even suspected that both countries drew benefits from their mutual rivalry and saw it as an advantage in carrying on their relations with friends and allies. Few suspected that the Cold War, which had for long appeared to be a permanent feature of the political scene, was about to come to an end.

What brought about the collapse of the Soviet Empire? Some argue that the ambitious defense policies adopted by the Reagan administration forced Moscow into an arms race it could not afford, and thus ultimately led to a collapse of the Soviet economy. Others suggest that Soviet problems were more deep-rooted and would have led to the disintegration of the USSR even without outside stimulation. Both arguments have some validity, but the latter is surely closer to the mark. For years, if not decades, leaders in the Kremlin had disguised or ignored the massive inefficiencies of the Soviet system. In the years immediately preceding his ascent to power in the Politburo, the perceptive Mikhail Gorbachev had recognized the crucial importance of instituting radical reforms. At the time, he hoped that by doing so he could save the system. By then, however, it was too late. In the classic formulation of dictatorial regimes the world over, the most dangerous period is when leaders adopt reform measures to prevent collapse.

Why has Communism survived in China, albeit in a substantially altered form, when it collapsed in Eastern Europe and the Soviet Union? Although there may be many reasons, one of the primary factors is probably cultural. Although the doctrine of Marxism-Leninism originated in Europe, many of its main precepts, such as the primacy of the community over the individual and the denial of the concept of private property, run counter to the central trends in Western civilization. This inherent conflict is especially evident in the societies of Central Europe, which were strongly influenced by Enlightenment philosophy and the Industrial Revolution. These forces were weaker in the countries further

◆ **The Monster.** Symbolic of the stunning failure of the Soviet system is this building in the Baltic port of Kaliningrad, once the German city of Königsberg. Twenty years in construction, "the monster," as it was dubbed by locals, was never occupied because of its serious structural flaws. The building was erected on the site of a sixteenth-century castle destroyed during a bombing raid in World War II. The site was then razed by Soviet bulldozers to wipe out all remnants of the past.

to the east, but both had begun to penetrate tsarist Russia by the end of the nineteenth century.

By contrast, Marxism-Leninism found a more receptive climate in China and other countries in the region influenced by Confucian tradition. In its political culture, the Communist system exhibits many of the same characteristics as traditional Confucianism—a single truth, an elite governing class, and an emphasis on obedience to the community and its governing representatives—while feudal attitudes regarding female inferiority, loyalty to the family, and bureaucratic arrogance are hard to break. On the surface, China today bears a number of uncanny similarities to the China of the past.

Yet these similarities should not blind us to the real changes that are taking place in Chinese society today. Although the youthful protesters in Tiananmen Square are comparable in some respects to the reformist elements of the 1890s or the New Culture intellectuals of the early republic—two generations of reformers whose passionate strivings to create a modern China on the Western model helped to destroy the old system but failed to lay firm foundations for a new one—the China of today is fundamentally different from that of the late Qing or even the early republic. Literacy rates and the standard of living, on balance, are far higher; the pressures of outside powers are less threatening; and China has entered the opening stages of its own industrial and technological revolution. Where Sun Yat-sen, Chiang Kai-shek, and even Mao Zadong broke their lances on the rocks of centuries of tradition, poverty, and ignorance, China's present leaders rule a country much more aware of the world and its place in it.

Whether or not communism survives in China—or revives in some form in the lands of the old Soviet Union—the Cold War is not likely to return in its old form, and for that we can be thankful, because it not only kept the earth on the knife edge of a great power conflict but also distracted world leaders from turning their attention to the deeper problems that afflict all of humankind. Still, it is now clear that the end of the Cold War is not necessarily a harbinger of a new era of peace and prosperity. To the contrary, it is more likely to open a new stage of history that will be marked by increased global instability and severe challenges in the areas of environmental pollution, technological change, and population growth. These issues will be addressed in more detail in the final chapter.

NOTES

1. Hedrick Smith, *The New Russians* (New York, 1990), p. 74.
2. *New York Times*, May 7, 1992.
3. Quoted in Frank Ching, "Confucius, the New Saviour," in *Far Eastern Economic Review*, November 10, 1994, p. 37.
4. *New York Times*, October 2, 1997.

CHAPTER
17

Toward a New World Order?

*F*rom a broad historical perspective, World War II can be seen to represent the logical culmination of the imperialist era. Competition among the European powers for markets and sources of raw materials began to accelerate during the early years of the nineteenth century and intensified as the effects of the Industrial Revolution made their way through western and central Europe. By the end of the century, virtually all of Asia and Africa had come under some degree of formal or informal colonial control. World War I weakened the European powers but did not bring the era to an end, and the seeds of a second world confrontation were planted at the Versailles peace conference, which failed to resolve the problems that had led to the war in the first place. Those seeds began to sprout in the 1930s when Hitler's Germany sought to recoup its losses and Japan became an active participant in the race for spoils in the Pacific region.

As World War II came to a close, the leaders of the victorious Allied nations were presented with a second opportunity to fashion a lasting peace based on the principles of social justice and self-determination. There were several issues on their postwar agenda. Europe needed to be revived from the ashes of the war and restored to the level of political stability and economic achievement that it had seemingly attained at the beginning of the century. Beyond the continent of Europe, the colonial system had to be dismantled and

the promise of self-determination enshrined in the Atlantic Charter applied on a global scale. The defeated nations of Germany, Italy, and Japan had to be reintegrated into the world community in order that the *revanchiste* policies of the interwar era not be repeated. Finally, it was vital that the wartime alliance of the United States, Great Britain, and the Soviet Union be maintained into the postwar era in order that bitter national rivalries among the powers did not once again threaten world peace.

In the decades following the end of the war, the first three goals were essentially realized. During the 1950s and 1960s, the capitalist nations managed to recover from the extended economic depression that had contributed to the start of World War II and advanced to a level of economic prosperity never before seen throughout world history. The bloody conflicts that had erupted among European nations during the first half of the twentieth century came to an end, and Germany and Japan were fully integrated into the world community. At the same time, the Western colonial empires in Asia and Africa were gradually dismantled, and the peoples of both continents once again recovered their independence.

But if the victorious nations of World War II had managed to resolve several of the key problems that had contributed to a half century of bloody conflict, the ultimate prerequisite for success—an end to the competitive balance-of-power system that had been a contributing factor in both world wars—was hampered by the emergence of a grueling and sometimes tense ideological struggle between the socialist and capitalist blocs, a competition headed by the only two remaining great powers, the USSR and the United States. While the two superpowers managed to avoid an open confrontation, the postwar world was divided for fifty years into two heavily armed camps in a balance of terror that on one occasion—the Cuban Missile Crisis—brought the world briefly to the brink of a nuclear holocaust.

In retrospect, the failure of the victorious world leaders to perpetuate the Grand Alliance seems virtually inevitable. Although the debate over who started the Cold War has been raging among historians for decades, it seems clear that the underlying causes of the ideological conflict lie not within the complex personalities of world leaders such as Joseph Stalin and Harry Truman (although they may have contributed to the problem), but much deeper in the political, economic, and social conditions that existed in the world at the midpoint of the century. The rapid recovery of Western Europe had reduced the bitterness of class conflict and helped to build strong foundations for the cooperative system of capitalist welfare states that emerged in the postwar era throughout the region, but much of the remainder of the world was just entering the early stages of the Industrial Revolution, and was thus vulnerable to the bitter internecine divisions that had marked the European continent in the previous century.

Under such circumstances, it is hardly surprising that the United States and the Soviet Union would become entangled in a bitter competition over influence in the Third World. Representing dynamic and mutually contradictory ideologies, both Washington and Moscow were convinced that they represented the wave of the future and were determined to shape the postwar world in terms of their own worldview. The particular form that the Cold War eventually took—with two heavily armed power blocs facing each other across a deep cultural and ideological divide—was not necessarily preordained, but given the volatility of postwar conditions and the vast gap in mutual understanding and cultural experience, it is difficult to see how the intense rivalry that characterized the East-West relationship could have been avoided.

End of a Dream

The decline of communism in the final decades of the century brought an end to an era, not only in the Soviet Union, but in much of the rest of the world as well. For more than a generation, thousands of intellectuals and political elites in Asia, Africa, and Latin America had looked to Marxism-Leninism as an appealing developmental ideology that could rush preindustrial societies through the modernization process without the painful economic and social inequities associated with capitalism. Communism, many thought, could make more effective use of scarce capital and resources, while carrying through the reforms needed to bring an end to centuries of inequality in the political and social arena.

The results, however, were much less than advertised. Although such diverse societies as China, Vietnam, and Cuba got off to an impressive start under Communist regimes, after a generation of party rule all were increasingly characterized by economic stagnation, low productivity, and underemployment. Even before the collapse of the USSR, prominent Communist states such as China and Vietnam had begun to adopt reforms that broke with ideological orthodoxy and borrowed liberally from the capitalist model.

To many, the disintegration of the Soviet Union signaled the end of communism as a competitive force in the global environment. In some parts of the world, however, it has survived in the form of Communist parties presiding over a mixed economy combining components of both socialism and capitalism. Why have Communist political systems survived in some areas while the Marxist-Leninist economic model in its classic form has not? In the first place, it is obvious that one of the consequences of long-term Communist rule was the suffocation of alternative political forces and ideas. As the situation in Eastern Europe has demonstrated, even after the passing of communism itself, Communist parties often appeared to be the only political force with the experience, discipline, and self-confidence to govern complex and changing societies.

That monopoly of political experience, of course, is no accident. In its Leninist incarnation, modern communism is preeminently a strategy for seizing and retaining power. The first duty of a Communist Party on seizing control is to determine "who defeats whom" and to establish a dictatorship of the proletariat. As a result, even when perceptive party leaders recognize the failure of the Marxist model to promote the creation of a technologically advanced industrial society, they view the Leninist paradigm as a useful means of maintaining political stability while undergoing the difficult transition through the early stages of the Industrial Revolution. In such countries as China and Vietnam today, Marxism-Leninism has thus become primarily a political technique—a Marxist variant of the single party or military regimes that arose in the Third World during the immediate postwar era. It is still too early to predict how successful such regimes will ultimately be or what kind of political culture will succeed them, but there is modest reason to hope that as their economic reform programs begin to succeed, they will eventually evolve into pluralistic societies such as are now taking shape elsewhere in the region.

Problems of Capitalism

In the meantime, as the century came to a close, the capitalist world began to encounter new challenges of its own. After a generation of rapid growth, beginning in the late 1980s, most of the capitalist states in Europe and North America began to suffer through a general slowdown in their economic performance. This slowdown, in turn, has given rise to a number of related problems, several with serious social and political implications. These problems include an increase in the level of unemployment; government belt-tightening policies to reduce social services and welfare and retirement benefits; and in many countries, an accompanying growth in popular resentment against minority groups or recent immigrants, who are seen as responsible for deteriorating economic prospects.

Europe: Unity or Disunity?

The problem of economic stagnation has been especially prevalent in Western Europe, where unemployment is at its highest level since the 1930s and economic growth in the past five years has averaged less than 1 percent annually. Conditions have been exacerbated in recent years by the need for individual governments to set their financial houses in order in order to comply with the requirements for unification as called for by the Maastricht Treaty of 1991 (see Chapter 16). In order for an individual nation to take part in the process, government deficits must not greatly exceed 3 percent of gross domestic product, nor must the national debt greatly exceed 60 percent of total output. Inflation rates must also be cut to minimal levels.

According to the current schedule, eleven countries that meet these criteria will begin to adopt the new unified monetary unit, to be known as the euro, which will gradually replace the national currencies of the individual states early in the new century. The problem is, many countries are encountering difficulties in adopting the severe economic measures that are needed to qualify for the transition to economic unity. France, concerned at the potential impact on its own fragile economy, has threatened not to carry out the necessary reforms. In Italy, the refusal of the Communist Party to agree to belt-tightening measures almost led to the fall of the coalition government. Even in Germany, long the healthiest of all major Western European states, reductions in social benefits have sharpened tensions between the eastern and western zones and undermined the long-term political dominance of Chancellor Helmut Kohl and his ruling Christian Democratic Union.

But perhaps the most ominous consequence of the new economic austerity has been a rise in antiforeign sentiment. In Germany, attacks against foreign residents—mainly Turks, many of whom have lived in the country for years—have increased substantially. In France, hostility to immigrants from North Africa has led to rising support for Jean-Marie Le Pen's National Front, which advocates strict limits on immigration and the ejection of many foreigners currently living in the country. It seems clear that the ethnic animosities that so often fueled conflict in Europe before World War II have not entirely abated.

By no means do all Europeans fear the costs of economic unity. Official sources argue that it will increase the region's ability to compete with economic powerhouses such as the United States and Japan. But fear of change and a strong legacy of national sentiment have promoted public fears that economic unification could have disastrous consequences. This is especially true in Great Britain, and also in Germany, where many see little benefit and much risk from joining a larger Europe. "The mark is part of us," one German remarked. "What do we need a worthless new money for?"[1]

The United States: Capitalism Ascendant

In some respects, the United States has fared better than other capitalist states in recent years, as the economic revival that has taken place in the 1990s has enabled the government to reduce budget deficits without having to engage in substantial tax increases or a massive reduction in welfare spending. Even there, however, continued increases in social spending have provoked the passage of new legislation to reduce welfare and health-care benefits. Nor has the steady growth in the gross domestic product led to increased prosperity for all Americans. Although the rich have been getting richer, the poorest 20 percent of the population has so far seen little benefit. In fact, one of the reasons for the long period of economic expansion in the 1990s has been the absence of upward pressure on wages. Should the trend continue, it will not simply fail to eradicate a human tragedy but will pose an economic risk as well, because rising consumer demand is a necessary foundation of a growing economy.

The United States has not yet witnessed the emergence of significant antiforeign sentiment on the scale of some countries in Europe, perhaps partly because of the salutary effect of a steadily growing economy. Recent history suggests that tolerance toward immigrants tends to decrease during periods of economic malaise, and vice versa. But there are indications that anger against the growing presence of foreign-born residents—especially those who have arrived illegally—is growing. Legislation to limit social benefits to noncitizens and to expel illegal aliens has been proposed at the state level and has recently been debated in Congress. Many American workers, with the support of labor unions, have vocally opposed the enactment of trade agreements such as the North American Free Trade Association (NAFTA) that would allegedly lead to a flight of jobs overseas as U.S. corporations seek to reduce production costs by hiring cheaper labor. The recent financial crisis in Asia has unsettled the stock market in the United States, spawning criticism that the country is excessively integrated into an unstable global trade network.

Yet, as in the case of European unity, there is solid economic logic in pursuing the goal of increasing globalization of trade. The U.S. industrial machine is increasingly dependent on the importation of raw materials from abroad, while corporate profits are to a rising degree a consequence of sales of U.S. goods in overseas markets. While foreign competition can sometimes lead to a loss of jobs—or entire industries—in the United States, the overall effect is likely to be a growing market for U.S. goods in the international marketplace. Moreover, as the case of the automobile industry has demonstrated, increased competition is crucial for maintaining and enhancing the quality of American products.

It is hardly surprising that the main proponent of the global economic marketplace is the United States, a country well placed to take full advantage of the technological revolution and turn it to its own advantage. Its large market relatively unfettered by onerous government regulations, generous amounts of capital, a tradition of political stability, and an outstanding system of higher education all combine to give the United States an edge over most of its rivals in the relentless drive to achieve a dominant position in the world economy. As Washington applies pressure on other governments to open up their economies to the competition of the international marketplace, and to adopt concepts of human rights that accord with those in the United States, resentment of the U.S. behemoth and fears of U.S. global domination are once again on the rise, as they were during the immediate postwar era.

Asian Miracle, or Asian Myth?

Until quite recently, it was common to observe that the one area in the capitalist world that was in a strong position to advance rapidly in the economic sphere without suffering the social and political strains experienced in the West was East Asia, where Japan and the so-called "little tigers" appeared able to combine rapid economic growth with a minimum of social problems and a considerable degree of political stability. Pundits within the region and abroad opined that the "East Asian miracle" was a product of the amalgamation of capitalist economic techniques and a value system inherited from Confucius that stressed hard work, frugality, and the subordination of the individual to the community—all reminiscent of the alleged "Puritan ethic" of the early capitalist era in the West.

There is indeed some similarity between the recent performance of many East Asian societies and the period of early capitalism in the West. Some commentators in East Asia have pointed with pride to their traditional values and remarked that in the West such values as hard work and a habit of saving have been replaced by a new hedonism that values individual over community interests, present gratification over future needs. Some in the West have agreed with this assessment and lamented the complacency and rampant materialism of Western culture.

As the century nears its end, however, the argument has suddenly become academic, as evidence accumulates that the East Asian miracle itself may be a myth, or at least an overstatement of a more complex reality. The financial crisis of 1997, which began in Thailand and spread rapidly throughout the region, demonstrated that the Pacific nations were not immune to the vicissitudes of capitalism, and that overconfidence and lack of attention to fundamentals could be as destructive on one side of the ocean as the other. Mesmerized by the rhetorical vision of the Confucian work ethic and less experienced in riding the choppy waves of the capitalist business cycle, Asian governments and entrepreneurs alike became too complacent in their view that the bull market in the region would never end. Banks extended loans on shaky projects, and governments invested heavily in expensive infrastructure improvements that exploded budget deficits while promising few financial returns until the distant future. When foreign investors grew wary and began withdrawing their funds, the bubble burst. It has been a sobering experience. As one commentator put it, "It was all too Disneyland; so much glass that was too shiny. Now they are going through a cultural crisis triggered by the economic crisis. These countries have to become more pragmatic."[2]

It would certainly be premature to conclude that the recent vision of a "Pacific century" will fade as surely as Nikita Khrushchev's famous boast to Eisenhower four decades ago that "we will bury you." The economic fundamentals in many East Asian countries are essentially sound, and the region will undoubtedly recover from the current crisis and resume the pace of steady growth that has characterized its performance during the past quarter of the twentieth century. But the fiscal crisis of the late 1990s serves as a warning signal that success—in East Asia as in the West—is the product of hard work, and can never be assumed.

From the Industrial to the Technological Revolution

As many observers have noted, a key aspect of the problem is that the world economy as a whole is in the process of transition to what has been called a "post-industrial age," characterized by the emergence of a system that is not only increasingly global in scope but also increasingly technology-intensive in character. This process, which the futurologist Alvin Toffler has dubbed

◆ **On the Assembly Line.** Automation is sometimes cited as one of the key reasons for the vaunted efficiency of the Japanese industrial machine. Mechanical robots, as shown here, perform tasks in Japan that elsewhere are performed by human beings. In recent years, however, some Japanese companies have discovered that robots are less adaptive to the need for rapid change and innovation on the assembly line than are their human counterparts.

the Third Wave (the first two being the agricultural and industrial revolutions), has produced difficulties for people in many walks of life—for blue-collar workers whose high wages price them out of the market as firms begin to move their factories abroad; for the poor and uneducated who lack the technical skills to handle complex tasks in the contemporary economy; and even for members of the middle class who have been fired or forced into retirement as their employers seek to slim down to compete in the global marketplace.[3]

It is now increasingly clear that the Technological Revolution, like the Industrial Revolution that preceded it, will entail enormous consequences and may ultimately give birth to a level of social and political instability that has not been seen in the developed world since the Great Depression of the 1930s. The success of advanced capitalist states in the second half of the twentieth century has been built on the foundations of a broad consensus on the importance of several propositions: (1) the importance of limiting income inequities in order to reduce the threat of political instability while maximizing domestic consumer demand; (2) the need for high levels of government investment in infrastructure projects such as education, communications, and transportation as a means of meeting the challenges of continued economic growth and technological innovation; and (3) the desirability of cooperative efforts in the international arena as a means of maintaining open markets for the free exchange of goods.

As the century nears an end, all of these assumptions are increasingly under attack, as citizens react with increasing hostility to the high tax rates needed to maintain the welfare state, refuse to support education and infrastructure development, and oppose the formation of trading alliances to promote the free movement of goods and labor across national borders. Significantly, such attitudes are expressed by individuals and groups on all sides of the political spectrum, making the traditional designations of left-wing and right-wing politics increasingly meaningless. Although most governments and political elites have continued to support most of the programs that underpin the welfare state and the global marketplace, they are increasingly under attack from groups within society that feel they have been victimized by the system. The breakdown of the public consensus that brought modern capitalism to a pinnacle of achievement raises serious questions about the likelihood that the coming challenge of the Third Wave can be successfully met without a growing measure of political and social tension.

A Transvaluation of Values

Of course, not all the problems facing the advanced human societies around the world can be ascribed directly to economic factors. It is one of the paradoxes of the second half of the twentieth century that at a time of almost unsurpassed political stability and economic prosperity for the majority of the population in the advanced capitalist states, public cynicism about the system is increasingly widespread. Alienation and drug use among young people in many Western societies are at dangerously high levels, and although crime rates have dropped slightly in some areas, the rate of criminal activities remains much higher than in the immediate postwar era.

The Family

The reasons advanced to explain this paradox vary widely. Some observers place the responsibility for many contemporary social problems on the decline of the traditional family system. The statistics are indeed disquieting. In recent years, there has been a steady rise in the percentage of illegitimate births and single-parent families in countries throughout the Western world. In the United States, approximately one of every two marriages will end in divorce. Even in two-parent families, more and more parents work full-time, thus leaving the children to fend for themselves on their return from school.

Observers point to several factors as an explanation for these conditions: the growing emphasis in advanced capitalist states on an individualistic lifestyle devoted to instant gratification—a phenomenon that is promoted vigorously by the advertising media; the rise of the feminist movement, which has freed women from the servitude imposed on their predecessors, but at the expense of removing them from full-time responsibility for the care and nurturing of the next generation; and the increasing mobility of contemporary life, which disrupts traditional family ties and creates a growing sense of rootlessness and impersonality in the individual's relationship to the surrounding environment.

What is worth noting here is that, to one degree or another, the traditional nuclear family is under attack in societies around the world, not just in the West. Even in East Asia, where the Confucian tradition of filial piety and family solidarity has been endlessly touted as a major factor in the region's economic success, the incidence of divorce and illegitimate births is on the rise, as is the percentage of women in the workforce. Older citizens frequently complain that the Asian youth of today are too materialistic, faddish, and steeped in the individualistic values of the West. Such criticisms are now voiced in mainland China as well as in the capitalist societies around its perimeter. Public opinion surveys suggest that some of the generational differences in Asian societies are only skin deep. When queried about their views, most young Asians express support for the same conservative values of family, hard work, and care for the elderly as their parents.[4] Still, the evidence suggests that the trend away from the traditional family is a worldwide phenomenon.

Religion

While some cite the reduced role of the traditional family as a major factor in the widespread sense of malaise in the contemporary world, others point to the decline in religion and the increasing secularization of Western society. It seems indisputable that one of the causes of the widespread sense of alienation in many societies is the absence of any sense of underlying meaning and purpose in life, which religious faith often provides. Historical experience suggests, however, that while intensity of religious fervor may serve to enhance the sense of community among believers, it can sometimes have a highly divisive impact on society as a whole, as the examples of Northern Ireland, Yugoslavia, and the Middle East vividly attest. Religion, by itself, cannot serve as a panacea for the problems of the contemporary world.

In any event, the issue of religion and its implications for social policy is complicated. While the percentage of people attending church on a regular basis or professing firm religious convictions has been dropping steadily in many Western countries, the intensity of religious belief

◆ **Something Old, Something New.** Under Soviet rule, church weddings were declared illegal and marriage became a simple civil ceremony, lacking the ritual solemnity that religious sanctions had previously provided. With the disintegration of the USSR in 1991, many people began to return to prerevolutionary practices. Here two newlyweds in the Ukrainian port city of Odessa celebrate their marriage ties in the traditional manner.

appears to be growing in many communities. This phenomenon is especially apparent in the United States, where the evangelical movement has become a significant force in politics and an influential factor in defining many social issues. But it has also occurred in Latin America, where a fall in membership in the Roman Catholic Church has been offset by significant increases in the popularity of evangelical Protestant sects. There are significant differences between the two cases, however. Whereas the evangelical movement in the United States tends to adopt conservative positions on social issues such as abortion rights, divorce, and sexual freedom, in Brazil one of the reasons advanced for the popularity of evangelical sects is the stand taken by the Vatican on issues such as divorce and abortion. In Brazil, even the vast majority of Catholics surveyed support the right to abortion in cases of rape or danger to the mother, and believe in the importance of birth control to limit population growth and achieve smaller families.

For many evangelical Christians in the United States, the revival of religious convictions and the adoption of a Christian lifestyle are viewed as necessary prerequisites for resolving the problems of crime, drugs, and social alienation. Some evidence does suggest that children who attend church in the United States are less likely to be involved in crime, and that they perform better in their schoolwork. Some in the evangelical movement, however, not only support a conservative social agenda, but also express a growing suspicion of the role of technology and science in the contemporary world. Some Christian groups have opposed the teaching of evolutionary theory in the classroom or have demanded that public schools present the biblical interpretation of the creation of the earth. Although fear over the impact of science on contemporary life is widespread and understandable, efforts to turn the clock back to a mythical golden age are not likely to succeed in the face of powerful forces for change set in motion by advances in scientific knowledge.

Technology

Concern about the impact of technology on contemporary life is by no means limited to evangelicals. Voices across the political and social spectrum have begun to suggest that scientific advances are at least partly responsible for the psychological malaise now so prevalent in much of the modern world. The criticism dates back at least to the advent of television. Television, in the eyes of its critics, has contributed to a decline in human communication and turned viewers from active participants in the experience of life into passive observers. With the advent of the computer, the process has accelerated, as recent generations of young people raised on video games and surfing the World Wide Web find less and less time for personal relationships or creative activities. At the same time, however, the internet provides an avenue for lonely individuals to communicate with the outside world and seek out others with common interests. The most that can be said at the present time is that such innovations provide both an opportunity and a danger—an opportunity to explore new avenues of communication, and a danger that in the process, the nature of the human experience will be irrevocably changed.

Capitalism

Some argue that the guilty party most responsible for the hedonism and materialism so characteristic of contemporary life is the capitalist system, which has raised narcissism and conspicuous consumerism to the height of the modern consciousness. It is no doubt true that by promoting material consumption as perhaps the supreme good, modern capitalism has encouraged the acquisitive side of human nature and undermined the traditional virtues of frugality and self-denial and the life of the spirit. As Karl Marx perceptively noted more than 100 years ago, under capitalism money is "the universal self-constituted value of all things. It has therefore robbed the whole world, human as well as natural, of its own values."[5]

Perhaps, however, it is more accurate to state that capitalism simply recognizes the acquisitive side of human nature and sets out to make a profit from it. Recent events in China and the USSR suggest that efforts to suppress the acquisitive instinct are ultimately doomed to fail, no matter how stringently they are applied. It is thus left to individual human beings, families, and communities to decide how to supplement material aspirations with the higher values traditionally associated with the human experience. Perhaps it is worth observing that more than once, capitalism has demonstrated the ability to rectify its shortcomings when they threaten the survival of the system. It remains to be seen whether it can successfully deal with the corrosive effects of contemporary materialism on the traditional spiritual longings of humankind (see box on p. 359).

The Family of Man

In their attempt to deal with complex current problems, a number of world leaders have pointed to the need for human beings to adopt a new perspective, especially a moral one, if people are to live in a sane world. Few have spoken on this subject with as much sensitivity as Vaclav Havel, a onetime playwright who is now president of the Czech Republic. In a speech to the U.S. Congress in February 1990, Havel addressed the issues facing humankind in future years.

Pointing out that the salvation of the world lies only in the human heart, in the human power to reflect, and in human responsibility, he warned that in the absence of a dramatic change in the sphere of human consciousness, "the catastrophe toward which this world is headed—be it ecological, social, demographic or a general breakdown of civilization—will be unavoidable." Unfortunately, he warned, the world is still a long way from that "family of man." In fact, "we seem to be receding from the ideal rather than growing closer to it. Interests of all kinds—personal, selfish, state, nation, group, and if you like, company interests—still considerably outweigh genuinely common and global interests."

In effect, Havel observed, human beings are still unable to place moral issues ahead of politics, science, or economics, and still incapable of understanding that the only true backbone of our moral actions is an acceptance of responsibility to something higher than family, corporation, community, country, or individual. What is needed is a sense of responsibility to "the order of being where all our actions are indelibly recorded and where and only where they will be properly judged." The location of that sense of responsibility, he pointed out, was the human conscience.

Source: Speech by Vaclav Havel to the U.S. Congress, quoted in *The Washington Post*, February 22, 1990.

One World, One Environment

Another crucial factor that is affecting the evolution of society and the global economy at the end of the twentieth century is growing concern over the impact of industrialization on the earth's environment. There is nothing new about human beings causing damage to their natural surroundings. It may first have occurred when Neolithic peoples began to practice slash-and-burn agriculture or when excessive hunting thinned out the herds of bison and caribou in the Western Hemisphere. It almost certainly played a major role in the decline of the ancient civilizations in the Persian Gulf and later of the Roman Empire.

Never before, however, has the danger of significant ecological damage been as extensive as during the past century. The effects of chemicals introduced into the atmosphere or into rivers, lakes, and oceans have increasingly threatened the health and well-being of all living species. For many years, the main focus of environmental concern was in the developed countries of the West, where industrial effluents, automobile exhaust, and the use of artificial fertilizers and insecticides led to urban smog, extensive damage to crops and wildlife, and a major reduction of the ozone layer in the upper atmosphere. In recent decades, however, it has become clear that the problem is now global in scope and demands vigorous action in the international arena.

The opening of Eastern Europe after the revolutions of 1989 brought to the world's attention the incredible environmental destruction in that region caused by unfettered industrial pollution. Communist governments had obviously operated under the assumption that production quotas were much more important than environmental protection. The Soviet nuclear power disaster at Chernobyl in 1986 made Europeans acutely aware of potential environmental hazards, and 1987 was touted as the "year of the environment." Many European states now felt compelled to advocate new regulations to protect the environment, and many of them established government ministries to oversee environmental issues.

For some, such official actions were insufficient, and beginning in the 1980s, a number of new political parties were established to focus exclusively on environmental issues. Although these "Green" movements and parties have played an important role in making people aware of ecological problems, they have by no means been able to control the debate. Too often, environmental issues come out second in clashes with economic issues. Still, during the 1990s, more and more European governments were beginning to sponsor projects to safeguard the environment and clean up the worst sources of pollution.

In recent years, the problem has spread elsewhere. China's headlong rush to industrialization has resulted in major ecological damage in that country. Industrial smog has created almost unlivable conditions in many cities, while hillsides denuded of their forests have caused severe problems of erosion and destruction of farmlands. Some environmentalists believe that levels of pollution in China are already higher than in the fully developed industrial societies of the West, a reality that raises serious questions about Beijing's ability to recreate the automotive culture of the modern West in China.

Destruction of the rain forest is a growing problem in many parts of the world, notably in Brazil and in the Indonesian archipelago. With the forest cover throughout the earth rapidly declining, there is less plant life to perform the crucial process of reducing carbon dioxide levels in the atmosphere. In 1997, forest fires in the Indonesian islands of Sumatra and Borneo created a blanket of smoke over the entire region, forcing schools and offices to close and causing thousands of respiratory ailments. Some of the damage could be attributed to the traditional slash-and-burn techniques used by subsistence farmers to clear forest cover for their farmlands, but the primary cause was the clearing of forestland to create or expand palm oil plantations, one of the region's major sources of export revenue.

One of the few salutary consequences of such incidents has been a growing international consensus that environmental concerns have taken on a truly global character. Although the danger of global warming—allegedly caused by the release, as a result of industrialization, of hothouse gases into the atmosphere—has not yet been definitively proven, it has become a source of sufficient concern to bring about an international conference on the subject in Kyoto in December 1997. If, as many scientists predict, worldwide temperatures should increase, the rise in sea levels could pose a significant threat to low-lying islands and coastal areas throughout the world, while climatic change could lead to severe droughts or excessive rainfall in cultivated areas.

It is one thing to recognize a problem, however, and yet another to resolve it. So far, cooperative efforts among nations to alleviate environmental problems have all too often been hindered by economic forces or by political, ethnic, and religious disputes. The 1997 conference on global warming, for example, was marked by bitter disagreement over the degree to which developing countries should share the burden of cleaning up the environment. As a result, it achieved few concrete results. The fact is, few nations have been willing to take unilateral action that might pose an obstacle to economic development plans or lead to a rise in unemployment. India, Pakistan, and Bangladesh have squabbled over the use of the waters of the Ganges and Indus Rivers, as have Israel and its neighbors over the scarce water resources of the Middle East. Pollution of the Rhine River by factories along its banks provokes angry disputes among European nations, while the United States and Canada have argued about the effects of acid rain on Canadian forests.

Today, such disputes represent a major obstacle to the challenge of meeting the threat of global warming. Measures to reduce the release of harmful gases into the atmosphere will be costly and could have significant negative effects on economic growth. Politicians who embrace such measures, then, are risking political suicide. As President Bill Clinton remarked about a proposal to reduce the danger of global warming by raising energy prices, such a measure "either won't pass the Senate or it won't pass muster with the American people." In any event, what is most needed is a degree of international cooperation that would bring about major efforts to reduce pollution levels throughout the world. So far, there is little indication that advanced and developing nations are close to agreement on how the sacrifice is to be divided. At the Kyoto conference, developing nations demanded an exemption to enable them to reach the level of advanced nations, while the latter expressed the fear that unilateral action on their part would simply lead industries to relocate in areas with lower environmental standards.[6]

The Population Debate

At the root of much of the concern about the environment is the worry that global population growth could eventually outstrip the capacity of the world to feed itself. Concern over excessive population growth, of course, dates back to the fears expressed in the early nineteenth century by the British economist Thomas Malthus, who worried that population growth would increase more rapidly than food supply. It peaked in the decades immediately following World War II, when a rise in world birthrates and a decline in infant mortality combined to fuel a dramatic increase in population in much of the Third World. The concern was set aside for a period after the 1970s, when the Green Revolution improved crop yields and statistical evidence appeared to suggest that the rate of population growth was declining in many countries of Asia and Latin America.

Yet some question whether increases in food production through technological innovation (in recent years, the Green Revolution has been supplemented by a

"Blue Revolution" to increase food yields from the world's oceans, seas, and rivers) can keep up indefinitely with world population growth, which continues today although at a slightly reduced rate from earlier levels. From a total of 2.5 billion people in 1950, world population rose to 5.7 billion in 1995 and is predicted to reach 10 billion in the middle of the next century. Today, many eyes are focused on China, where family planning programs have lost effectiveness in recent years and where precious rice lands have been turned to industrial or commercial use in the developmental effort. Some environmentalists fear that as an increasingly affluent population in China switches from staple crops such as rice to meat and other less land-efficient food products, the country will be forced to import food in ever-increasing quantities. China vigorously disputes these estimates.[7]

A Global Village, or a Clash of Civilizations?

For four decades, such global challenges were all too frequently submerged in the public consciousness as the two major power blocs competed for advantage. The collapse of the USSR brought an end to the Cold War, but left world leaders almost totally unprepared to face the consequences. Statesmen, scholars, and political pundits began to forecast the emergence of a "new world order." Few, however, had any real idea of what it would entail. With the division of the world into two squabbling ideological power blocs suddenly at an end, there was little certainty, and much speculation, about what was going to take its place.

One hypothesis that won support in some quarters was that the decline of communism signaled that the industrial capitalist democracies of the West had triumphed in the war of ideas and would now proceed to remake the rest of the world in their own image. That view was frequently expressed during the period of brief euphoria after the fall of the Berlin Wall in 1989, when commentators speculated that with the end of communism, capitalism and democracy had triumphed and would now be applied throughout the entire world. Some cited as evidence a widely discussed book, *The End of History and the Last Man*, by the U.S. scholar Francis Fukuyama. In his book, Fukuyama argues that capitalism and the Western concept of liberal democracy, while hardly ideal in their capacity to satisfy all human aspirations, are at least more effective than rival doctrines in achieving those longings and therefore deserve consider-

ation as the best available ideology to be applied universally throughout the globe.[8]

Fukuyama's thesis provoked a firestorm of debate. Many critics pointed out the absence of any religious component in the liberal democratic model and argued the need for a return to religious faith, with its emphasis on the life of the spirit and traditional moral values. Others, noting that greater human freedom and increasing material prosperity have not led to a heightened sense of human achievement and emotional satisfaction, but rather to increasing alienation and a crass pursuit of hedonistic pleasures, argued that a new and perhaps "postmodernist" paradigm for the human experience must be found.

Whether or not Fukuyama's proposition is true, it is much too early to assume (as he would no doubt admit) that the liberal democratic model has in fact triumphed in the clash of ideas that has dominated the twentieth century. Although it is no doubt true that much of the world is now linked together in the economic marketplace put in place by the Western industrial nations, it seems clear from the discussion of contemporary issues in this chapter that the future hegemony of Western political ideas and institutions is by no means assured, despite their current dominating position as a result of the decline of communism.

For one thing, in much of the world today, Western values are threatened or are now under direct attack. In Africa, even the facade of democratic institutions has been discarded as autocratic leaders rely on the power of the gun as sole justification for their actions. In India, the decline of the once dominant Congress Party has led to the emergence of fragile governments, religious strife, and spreading official corruption, leaving the future of the world's largest democracy in doubt. Even in East Asia, where pluralistic societies have begun to appear in a number of industrializing countries, leading political figures in the region have expressed serious reservations about Western concepts of democracy and individualism and openly questioned their relevance to their societies. The issue was raised at a meeting of the ASEAN states in July 1997, when the feisty Malaysian prime minister Mahathir Mohamad declared that the Universal Declaration of Human Rights, passed after World War II at the behest of the victorious Western nations, was not appropriate to the needs of poorer non-Western countries and should be reviewed. The reaction was immediate. One U.S. official attending the conference retorted that the sentiments contained in the Universal Declaration were "shared by all peoples and all cultures" and had not been imposed by the West. Nevertheless, a number of political leaders in the region echoed Mahathir's views and insisted on the need for a review. Their comments were quickly seconded by Chinese President Jiang Zemin, who declared during a visit to the United States later in the year that human rights were not a matter that could be dictated by the powerful nations of the world, but an issue to be determined by individual societies on the basis of their own traditions and course of development.

Although one factor involved in the debate is undoubtedly the rising frustration of Asian leaders at continuing Western domination of the global economy, in fact political elites in much of the world today do not accept the Western assumption that individual rights must take precedence over community interests, asserting instead the more traditional view that community concerns must ultimately be given priority of place. Some argue that in defining human rights almost exclusively in terms of individual freedom, Western commentators ignore the importance of providing adequate food and shelter for all members of society.[9]

It is possible, of course, that the liberal democratic model will become more acceptable in parts of Africa and Asia to the degree that societies in those regions proceed successfully through the advanced stages of the industrial and technological revolutions, thus giving birth to the middle-class values that underlie modern civilization in the West. There is no guarantee, however, that current conditions, which have been relatively favorable to that process, will continue indefinitely. The fact is, just as the Industrial Revolution in the nineteenth and early twentieth centuries exacerbated existing tensions within and among the nations of Europe, so globalization and the technological revolution are imposing their own strains on human societies today. Should such strains become increasingly intense, they could engender a level of political and social conflict reminiscent of that experienced earlier in the century.

In a recent book, *The Clash of Civilizations and the Remaking of the World Order*, the political scientist Samuel P. Huntington has responded to these concerns by suggesting that the post–Cold War era, far from marking the triumph of the Western idea, will be characterized by increased global fragmentation and a "clash of civilizations" based on ethnic, cultural, or religious differences. According to Huntington, cultural identity has replaced shared ideology as the dominant force in world affairs. As a result, he argues, the coming decades may see an emerging world dominated by disputing cultural blocs in East Asia, Western Europe and the United States, Eurasia, and the Middle East, with the societies in each

region coalescing around common cultural features against perceived threats from rival forces elsewhere around the globe. The dream of a universal order dominated by Western values, he concludes, is a fantasy.[10]

Events in the early 1990s certainly appeared to bear out Huntington's hypothesis. The collapse of the USSR led to the emergence of several squabbling new nations and a general atmosphere of conflict and tension in the Balkans and at other points along the perimeter of the old Soviet Empire. The rise of ethnic and religious conflict in Eastern Europe is, of course, a direct consequence of the collapse of a system that in its own way resembled the transnational empires of the Romanovs, the Austro-Hungarians, and the Ottomans a century ago. But the phenomenon is worldwide in scope and growing in importance. Even as the world becomes more global in culture and interdependent in its mutual relations, centrifugal forces have been at work attempting to redefine the political, cultural, and ethnic ways in which it is divided. This process is taking place not only in developing countries, but also in the West, where fear of the technological revolution and public anger at the impact of globalization and foreign competition have reached measurable levels. Such views are often dismissed by sophisticated commentators as atavistic attempts by uninformed people seeking to return to a mythical past. But perhaps they should more accurately be interpreted as an inevitable consequence of the rising thirst for self-protection and group identity in an impersonal and rapidly changing world. Shared culture is one defense against the impersonal world around us.

In the confusing conditions at the end of the twentieth century, Huntington's thesis serves as a useful corrective to the complacent tendency of many observers in Europe and the United States to see Western civilization as the zenith and the final destination of human achievement. In the promotion by Western leaders of the concepts of universal human rights and a global marketplace there is a recognizable element of the cultural arrogance that was reflected in the doctrine of social Darwinism at the end of the previous century. Both views take as their starting point the assumption that the Western conceptualization of the human experience is universal in scope and will ultimately, inexorably spread to the rest of the world. Neither gives much credence to the view that other civilizations might have seized upon a corner of the truth, and thus have something to offer to the equation.

That is not to say, however, that Huntington's vision of clashing civilizations is necessarily the most persuasive characterization of the probable state of the world in the twenty-first century. In dividing the world into competing cultural blocs, Huntington has probably underestimated the centrifugal forces that exist within the various regions of the world. As many critics have noted, deep-rooted cultural and historical rivalries exist among the various nations in southern and eastern Asia and in the Middle East, as well as in Africa, preventing any meaningful degree of mutual cooperation against allegedly hostile forces in the outside world.[11]

Professor Huntington also tends to ignore the transformative effect of the Industrial Revolution and the emerging global informational network. As the industrial and technological revolutions spread across the face of the earth, their impact is measurably stronger in some societies than in others, thus intensifying political, economic, and cultural distinctions within a given region while establishing links between individual societies in that region and their counterparts undergoing similar experiences in other parts of the world. While the parallel drive to global industrial hegemony in Japan and the United States, for example, has served to divide the two countries on a variety of issues, it has intensified tensions between the former and its competitor South Korea and weakened the political and cultural ties that have historically existed between Japan and China.

The most likely scenario for the next few decades, then, is more complex than either the global village hypothesis or its conceptual rival, the clash of civilizations. The world of the twenty-first century will be characterized by simultaneous trends toward globalization and fragmentation, as the inexorable thrust of the technological and informational revolution both transforms societies and gives rise to counterreactions among individuals and communities seeking to preserve a group identity and a sense of meaning and purpose in a confusing world.

The Arts: Mirror of the Age

In a recent speech at the National Press Club in Washington, D.C., the great Spanish tenor Placido Domingo remarked that "the arts are the signature of its age." If that is so, then what has been happening in literature, art, music, and architecture in recent decades is a reflection of the evolving global response to the rapid changes taking place in human society today. This reaction has sometimes been described as postmodernism, although today's developments are much too diverse to be placed under a single label. As we approach the twenty-first century, some of the arts are still experimenting with the modernist quest for the new and the radical. Others

have begun to return to more traditional styles as a reaction against globalization and a response to the search for national and cultural identity in a bewildering world. (See box on p. 364.)

The most appropriate label for the contemporary cultural scene, in fact, is probably pluralism. The arts today are an eclectic hybrid, combining different movements, genres, and media, as well as incorporating different ethnic or national characteristics. There is no doubt that Western culture has strongly influenced the development of the arts throughout the world in recent decades. In fact, the process has gone in both directions, as art forms from Africa and Asia have profoundly enriched the cultural scene in the West. One ironic illustration is that some of the best literature in the English and French languages today is being written in the nations that were once under British or French colonial rule. Today, global interchange in the arts is playing the same creative role that the exchange of technology between different regions played in stimulating the Industrial Revolution. As one Japanese composer declared recently, "I would like to develop in two directions at once: as a Japanese with respect to tradition, and as a Westerner with respect to innovation. . . . In that way I can avoid isolation from the tradition and yet also push toward the future in each new work."[12]

Such a globalization of culture, however, has its price. Because of the popularity of Western culture throughout the Third World, local cultural forms are being eroded and destroyed as the result of contamination by rock music, mass television, and commercial hype. Although what has been called the "McWorld culture" of Coca-Cola, jeans, and rock is considered merely cosmetic by some, others see it as cultural neoimperialism and a real cause for alarm. How does a society preserve its traditional culture when the young prefer to spend their evenings at a Hard Rock Café rather than attend a traditional folk opera or *wayang* puppet theater? World conferences have been convened to safeguard traditional cultures from extinction, but is there sufficient time, money, or inclination to reverse the tide?

What do contemporary trends in the art world have to say about the changes that have occurred between the beginning and the end of the twentieth century? One reply is that the euphoric optimism of artists during the age of Picasso and Stravinsky has been seriously tempered 100 years later. Naiveté has been replaced by cynicism or irony, which as one critic has remarked, has become the necessary condom for the underlying pessimism of the current age. An exhibit on "the art of distemper" held at the Hirshhorn Museum of Modern Art

❧ An Age of Postmodernism ❧

Postmodernism is the amorphous rubric that has often been attributed to the development of the arts in the latter part of the twentieth century. Appearing first in philosophy, linguistics, and literary criticism in the 1960s, it soon spread to architecture, music, the visual arts, and literature. At its most elemental, postmodernism is a critique and departure from modernism, the avant-garde culture of the first half of the twentieth century, and a return to selected aspects of traditional Western culture. At the same time, it has continued the twentieth-century countertradition of artistic experimentation, distorting and reordering traditional culture through the prism of modernity.

The term *postmodernism* was first coined in 1977 in reference to architecture, at a time when it was apparent that traditional architectural styles were beginning to alter or erode the modernist international style. Of all the arts, it seems logical that architecture would be the most inclined to return to traditional elements, because it interacts most directly with people's daily lives. Architecture thus began to free itself from the repetitiveness and impersonality of the international style. In reaction to the forests of identical glass and steel boxes, and perhaps accelerated by a new enthusiasm for historic preservation and urban renewal, American architects began to reincorporate traditional materials, shapes, and decorative elements into their buildings. Anyone sighting an American city today cannot fail to observe its postmodern skyline of pyramidal and cupolaed skyscrapers of blue-green glass and brick. Even modernist rectangular malls have tacked on Greek columns and Egyptian pyramid-shaped entryways.

Architects elsewhere in the world are following suit by attempting to revive traditional styles in order to reestablish a sense of national or cultural identity in their own physical environment. Modern engineering techniques are being adapted to local climatic and cultural needs. A good illustration of such adaptation is found in a recent high-rise building in Harare, Zimbabwe, which imitates the ingenious heating and cooling system found in local termite mounds as a natural substitute for expensive artificial temperature control.

As we have previously observed, twentieth-century composers experimented radically with the basic components of Western music, from tonality and melody to rhythm and form. But like architecture, music relies on the financial support of a broad segment of the public. Audiences must support orchestras to perform a composer's work. Yet much of twentieth-century music has antagonized concertgoers to the extent that, in order to survive, orchestras have performed mainly premodern music. During the 1970s, composers began to respond, abandoning radical experimentation in favor of a return to more conventional forms. Some use the "quotation" technique, refracting traditional music through a modernist prism, while others strive for more accessibility through a simpler and more romantic style in an effort to bring about a postmodern reconciliation with the past.

When applied to the visual arts, postmodernism consists of several tendencies. At its most basic, however, it implies a return to a nonabstract art grounded in earthly concerns. The 1980s, for example, witnessed a return to the human figure and more traditional art forms, while artists also sought to reach new audiences by addressing racial, feminist, and gay issues in their paintings. Still, modern art retains its popularity, and abstract artists and sculptors continue to reap lucrative financial rewards from an eager public.

Of all the arts, literature is the most difficult to place in a postmodernist framework. Whereas for the other arts, postmodernism implies a hybrid product combining traditional and modern elements, postmodern literature has sometimes been characterized by an attempt to push the modern experiment to its limits, sometimes to the extent that to many, contemporary fiction borders on verbal incomprehension. Still, there has been such an intense search for form and style in recent writing that the era has been labeled by one critic as "an age of no style," with "a peculiar vacancy of meaning." During the 1990s, some writers have returned to a more conservative and less experimental literature. Although science has enlarged human horizons, it has still not solved the paradoxes and indeterminacies of the universe. As a consequence, authors are still writing stories to try to find the meaning of life.

Source: Robert P. Morgan, *Twentieth-Century Music* (New York: W. W. Norton, 1991).

◆ **Workers, Peasants, Soldiers, and Coca-Cola.** In this 1992 painting, the Chinese artist Wang Guangyi combines the social realism of the Cultural Revolution, with its heroic depiction of the revolutionary masses, with a contemporary social commentary on China's current craze of blatant mass consumerism.

in Washington, D.C., in 1996 summarized the uneasy mood since the end of the Cold War and the anxiety and disaffection of our age.

One dominant characteristic of the new art is its reticence—its reserve in expressing the dissonance and disillusioning events of our century. It would appear that we entered the twentieth century with too many expectations, hopes that had been fueled by the promise of revolution and scientific discoveries. Yet however extraordinary the recent advances in medicine, genetics, telecommunications, computer technology, and space exploration have been, humankind seems to remain as befuddled as ever. It is no wonder that despite the mind-boggling recent advances in science, human beings enter the new millennium a little worn and subdued.

What, then, are the prospects for the next century? One critic has complained that postmodernism, "with its sad air of the parades gone by," is spent and exhausted.[13] Others suggest that there is nothing new left to say that has not been expressed previously, and more

effectively. The public itself appears satiated and desensitized after a century of "shocking" art and, as in the case of world events, almost incapable of being shocked any further. Human sensibilities have been irrevocably altered by the media, by technology, and especially by the cataclysmic events that have taken place in our times. Perhaps the twentieth century was the age of revolt, representing "freedom from," while the next 100 years will be an era seeking "freedom for."

What is comforting is that no matter how pessimistic and disillusioned humankind claims to be, individual hope springs eternal, as young writers, artists, and composers continue to grapple with their craft, searching for new ways to express the human condition. How can one not be astonished by architect Frank Gehry's new Guggenheim Museum in Bilbao, Spain, with its thrusting turrets and billowing sails of titanium? Such exuberance can only testify to humanity's indomitable spirit and ceaseless imagination—characteristics that will be badly needed as the world enters its third millennium.

NOTES

1. *New York Times,* September 17, 1997.
2. Henny Sender, "Now for the Hard Part," in *Far Eastern Economic Review,* September 25, 1997.
3. Alvin Toffler and Heidi Toffler, *Creating a New Civilization: The Politics of the Third Wave* (Atlanta, 1995).
4. "Rock Solid," an editorial in the *Far Eastern Economic Review,* December 5, 1996. These traditional family values are apparently less deeply ingrained in the youth of Japan, where many older citizens complain that young people are no longer willing to care for elderly family members.
5. Quoted in John Cassidy, "The Return of Karl Marx," in *The New Yorker,* October 20–27, 1997, p. 250.
6. See "Can We Turn Down the Heat?" in The Economist, reprinted in *World Press Review,* December 1997, pp. 6–7.
7. For references to the controversy, see Barbara Crossette's "Population Debate: The Premises Are Changed," in *The New York Times,* September 14, 1994, and Dennis T. Avery, "Feast or Famine?" in the *Far Eastern Economic Review,* December 1, 1994, p. 40.
8. Fukuyama's original thesis was expressed in his "The End of History," in *The National Interest* (Summer 1989). He has defended his views in Timothy Burns, ed., *After History? Francis Fukuyama and His Critics* (Lanham, MD, 1994); see Chapter 13. Fukuyama contends—rightly in my view—that his concept of the "end of history" has been widely misinterpreted. I hope I have not done so in these comments.
9. For a discussion, see Frank Ching, "Is the UN Declaration Universal?" *Far Eastern Economic Review,* August 28,1997.
10. Samuel P. Huntington, *The Clash of Civilizations and the Remaking of World Order* (New York, 1996). An earlier version was published under the title "The Clash of Civilizations?" in the journal *Foreign Affairs* (Summer 1993).
11. For one commentary, see Richard Bernstein's review of Huntington's book in *The New York Times,* November 6, 1996.
12. The composer was Toru Takemitsu. See Robert P. Moran, *Twentieth-Century Music* (New York, 1991), p. 422.
13. Herbert Muschamp, "The Miracle in Bilbao," *New York Times Magazine,* September 7, 1997, p. 72.

Suggested Readings

Chapter 1. The Rise of Industrial Society in the West

For a useful introduction to the Industrial Revolution, see D. Landes, *The Unbound Prometheus: Technological Change and Industrial Development in Western Europe from 1750 to the Present* (Cambridge, England, 1969). More technical in nature, but also of value, is S. Pollard, *Peaceful Conquest: The Industrialization of Europe, 1760–1970* (Oxford, 1981) and P. Mathias and J. A. David (eds.), *The First Industrial Revolution* (Oxford, 1989). A provocative recent analysis of the roots of industrialization is D. Landes, *The Wealth and Poverty of Nations: Why Some Are So Rich and Some So Poor* (New York, 1997).

On the phenomenon of population growth in the West, see T. McKeown, *The Rise of Population* (London, 1976). Housing reform is discussed in N. Bullock and J. Read, *The Movement for Housing Reform in Germany and France, 1840–1914* (Cambridge, England, 1985), and E. Gauldie, *Cruel Habitations, A History of Working-Class Housing, 1790–1918* (London, 1974). On Karl Marx, the standard work is D. McLellan, *Karl Marx: His Life and Thought* (New York, 1974). On Freud, see P. Gay, *Freud: A Life for Our Time* (New York, 1988).

On trends in modern art, see Robert Hughes, *The Shock of the New* (New York, 1991), and Nikos Stangos (ed.), *Concepts of Modern Art: From Fauvism to Postmodernism* (London, 1994). On music, see Robert P. Morgan, *Twentieth-Century Music: A History of Musical Style in Modern Europe and America* (New York, 1991).

Chapter 2. High Tide of Imperialism: Africa and Asia in an Era of Western Dominance

There are a number of good works on the subject of imperialism and colonialism. For example, see W.

Baumgart, *Imperialism: The Idea and Reality of British and French Colonial Expansion, 1880–1914* (Oxford, 1982) and H. M. Wright (ed.), *The "New Imperialism": Analysis of Late Nineteenth Century Expansion* (New York, 1976). On the new technology, see D. R. Headrick, *The Tentacles of Progress: Technology Transfer in the Age of Imperialism, 1850–1940* (Oxford, 1988).

On the imperialist age in Africa, above all see R. Robinson and J. Gallagher, *Africa and the Victorians: The Official Mind of Imperialism* (London, 1961). Also see T. Pakenham, *The Scramble for Africa* (New York, 1991). For India, see C. A. Bayly, *Indian Society and the Making of the British Empire* (Cambridge, England, 1988). For a comparative approach, see R. Murphey, *The Outsiders: The Western Experience in China and India* (Ann Arbor, MI, 1977).

Chapter 3. Shadows over the Pacific: East Asia under Challenge

The classic general overview of the era is J. K. Fairbank, A. M. Craig, and E. O. Reischauer, *East Asia: Tradition and Transformation* (Boston, 1973). Also see J. Spence's highly stimulating *The Search for Modern China* (New York, 1990). On the Western intrusion, see F. Wakeman, *Strangers at the Gate: Social Disorder in South China, 1839–1861* and P. W. Fay, *The Opium War, 1840–1842* (Chapel Hill, NC, 1975). On the Taiping rebellion, a good recent account is J. Spence, *God's Chinese Son: The Taiping Heavenly Kingdom of Hong Xiuquan* (New York, 1996).

For an overview of the final decades of the Chinese Empire, see F. Wakeman, Jr., *The Fall of Imperial China* (New York, 1975). On Japan, see W.G. Beazley, *The Meiji Restoration* (Stanford, CA, 1972) and C. Gluck, *Japan's Modern Myths: Ideology in the Late Meiji Period* (Princeton, NJ, 1985). Its rise as an imperialist power is discussed in M. R. Peattie and R. Myers, *The Japanese Colonial Empire, 1895–1945* (Princeton, NJ, 1984).

Chapter 4. War and Revolution: World War I and Its Aftermath

A good starting point for the causes of World War I is J. Joll, *The Origins of the First World War* (London, 1984). Two good recent accounts on the war are M. Gilbert, *The First World War* (New York, 1994) and J. M. Winter's lavishly illustrated *The Experience of World War I* (New York, 1989). For a dramatic account, see B. Tuchman, *The Guns of August* (New York, 1962). On the interwar period, see R. I. Sontag, *A Broken World, 1919–1939* (New York, 1971) and S. Marks, *The Illusion of Peace: Europe's International Relations, 1918–1933* (New York, 1976). On the Great Depression, see C. P. Kindleberger, *The World in Depression, 1929–1939*, revised ed. (Berkeley, CA, 1986).

A good introduction to the Russian Revolution can be found in S. Fitzpatrick, *The Russian Revolution, 1917–1932* (New York, 1982) and R. V. Daniels, *Red October* (New York, 1967). On Lenin, see R. W. Clark, *Lenin* (New York, 1988) and A. B. Ulam's *The Bolsheviks* (New York, 1965).

Chapter 5. Nationalism, Revolution, and Dictatorship: Africa, Asia, and Latin America between the Wars

The classic study of nationalism in the non-Western world is R. Emerson, *From Empire to Nation* (Boston, 1960). Also see F. von der Mehden, *Religion and Nationalism in Southeast Asia* (Madison, WI, 1963). For a provocative approach, see B. Anderson, *Imagined Communities* (London, 1983). Also see P. Chatterjee's interesting *The Nation and Its Fragments: Colonial and Postcolonial Histories* (Princeton, NJ, 1993).

There have been a number of interesting studies of Mahatma Gandhi and his ideas. For example, see J. M. Brown, *Gandhi: Prisoner of Hope* (New Haven, CT, 1989), and the psychohistorical study by E. Erikson, *Gandhi's Truth: On the Origins of Militant Nonviolence* (New York, 1969).

For a general survey of events in the Middle East, see H. M. Sachar, *The Emergence of the Middle East, 1914–1924* (New York, 1969). On the early Chinese republic, a good study is L. Yu-sheng, *The Crisis of Chinese Consciousness: Radical Antitraditionalism in the May Fourth Era* (Madison, WI, 1979). The rise of the Chinese Communist Party is discussed in B. Schwartz, *Chinese Communism and the Rise of Mao* (Cambridge, MA, 1958), and A. Dirlik, *The Origins of Chinese Communism* (Oxford, 1989). For a readable and informative biography of Mao Zedong, see S. Schram, *Mao Tse-tung: A Political Biography* (Baltimore, 1966). For an overview of Latin American history in the interwar period, see E. Williamson, *The Penguin History of Latin America* (Harmondsworth, England, 1992). Also see J. Franco, *The Modern Culture of Latin America: Society and the Artist* (Harmondsworth, England, 1970).

Chapter 6. The Crisis Deepens: The Coming of World War II

For a general study of fascism, see S. G. Payne, *A History of Fascism* (Madison, WI, 1996). The best biography of Mussolini is D. Mack Smith's *Mussolini* (New York, 1982). Two brief but sound surveys of Nazi Germany are J. Spielvogel, *Hitler and Nazi Germany: A History*, 3d ed. (Englewood Cliffs, NJ, 1996) and J. Bendersky, *A History of Nazi Germany* (Chicago, 1985). On Hitler, see A. Bullock, *Hitler: A Study in Tyranny* (New York, 1964).

General works on World War II include M. K. Dziewanowski, *War at Any Price: World War II in Europe, 1939–1945*, 2d ed. (Englewood Cliffs, NJ, 1991), and G. Weinberg's celebrated *A World at Arms: A Global History of World War II* (Cambridge, England, 1994). On the Holocaust, see R. Hilberg, *The Destruction of the European Jews*, rev. ed., 3 vols. (New York, 1985) and L. Yahil, *The Holocaust* (New York, 1990). On the war in the Pacific, see R. Spector and T. R. H. Havens, *The Valley of Darkness: The Japanese People and World War Two* (New York, 1978).

Chapter 7. In the Grip of the Cold War

There is a substantial literature on the Cold War. Two general accounts are R. B. Levering, *The Cold War, 1945–1972* (Arlington Heights, IL, 1982) and B. A. Weisberger, *Cold War, Cold Peace: The United States and Russia since 1945* (New York, 1984). Assigning blame for the Cold War to the USSR are H. Feis, *From Trust to Terror: The Onset of the Cold War, 1945–1950* (New York, 1970) and A. Ulam, *The Rivals: America and Russia since World War II* (New York, 1971). Revisionist studies include J. and G. Kolko, *The Limits of Power: The World and United States Foreign Policy, 1945–1954* (New

York, 1972), and W. LaFeber, *America, Russia and the Cold War, 1945–1966*, 2d ed. (New York, 1972). For a critique of the revisionist approach, see R. L. Maddox, *The New Left and the Origins of the Cold War* (Princeton, NJ, 1973).

Recent studies on the Cold War in Asia include O. A. Westad, *Cold War and Revolution: Soviet-American Rivalry and the Origins of the Chinese Civil War* (New York, 1993), D. A. Mayers, *Cracking the Monolith: U.S. Policy against the Sino-Soviet Alliance, 1949–1955* (Baton Rouge, LA, 1986), and S. Goncharov, J. W. Lewis, and Xue Litai, *Uncertain Partners: Stalin, Mao, and the Korean War* (Stanford, CA, 1993). Also see A. Iriye, *The Cold War in Asia: A Historical Introduction* (Englewood Cliffs, NJ, 1974). For a highly readable overall history of the Vietnam War, see S. Karnow, *Vietnam: A History* (New York, 1983).

Chapter 8. Brave New World: The Creation of the Soviet Bloc

For a general overview of Soviet society, see D. K. Shipler, *Russia: Broken Idols, Solemn Dreams* (New York, 1983). On the Khrushchev years, see E. Crankshaw, *Khrushchev: A Career* (New York, 1966). Also see S. F. Cohen, *Rethinking the Soviet Experience* (Oxford and New York, 1985).

For a general study of the Soviet satellites in Eastern Europe, see A. Brown and J. Gary, *Culture and Political Changes in Communist States* (London, 1977) and S. Fischer-Galati, *Eastern Europe in the 1980s* (London, 1981). On Yugoslavia, see L. J. Cohen and P. Warwick, *Political Cohesion in a Fragile Mosaic* (Boulder, CO, 1983). On East Germany, see C. B. Scharf, *Politics and Change in East Germany* (Boulder, CO, 1984).

Chapter 9. The East Is Red: China under Communism

There are a large number of useful studies on postwar China. The most comprehensive treatment of the Communist period is M. Meisner, *Mao's China, and After: A History of the People's Republic* (New York, 1986). For shorter accounts of the period, see J. Grasso et al., *Modernization and Revolution in China* (Armonk, NY, 1991) and C. Dietrich, *People's China: A Brief History* (New York, 1986). For documents, see M. Selden, *The People's Republic of China: A Documentary History of Revolutionary Change* (New York, 1978).

There are many studies on various aspects of the Communist period in China. For a detailed analysis of economic and social issues, see F. Schurmann, *Ideology and Organization in Communist China* (Berkeley, CA, 1968). The Cultural Revolution is treated dramatically in S. Karnow, *Mao and China: Inside China's Cultural Revolution* (New York, 1972). For an individual account, see the celebrated book by Nien Cheng, *Life and Death in Shanghai* (New York, 1986) and Liang Heng and J. Shapiro, *After the Revolution* (New York, 1986). For the early post-Mao period, see O. Schell, *To Get Rich Is Glorious* (New York, 1986). For an interesting biography of Mao's last wife, see R. Witke, *Comrade Chiang Ching* (Boston, 1972). For the most comprehensive introduction to twentieth-century Chinese art, consult M. Sullivan, *Arts and Artists of Twentieth-Century China* (Berkeley, CA, 1996). On literature, see the chapters on Ding Ling and her contemporaries in J. Spence, *The Gate of Heavenly Peace* (New York, 1981).

Chapter 10. Europe and the Western Hemisphere

For a general perspective of the events covered in this chapter, see T. E. Vadney, *The World since 1945* (London, 1987). For a survey of postwar European history, see W. Laqueur, *Europe in Our Time* (New York, 1992). The rebuilding of postwar Europe is examined in A. S. Milward, *The Reconstruction of Western Europe, 1945–1951* (Berkeley, CA, 1984). For a survey of West Germany, see M. Balfour, *West Germany: A Contemporary History* (London, 1983). France under de Gaulle is examined in P. Williams and M. Harrison, *Politics and Society in de Gaulle's Republic* (New York, 1971). On Great Britain, see A. Sampson, *The Changing Anatomy of Britain* (New York, 1982).

For a general survey of U.S. history, see Stephan Thernstrom, *A History of the American People*, 2d ed., (San Diego, 1989). The Truman era is covered in R. J. Donovan, *Tumultuous Years: The Presidency of Harry S Truman* (New York, 1977). On the Eisenhower years, see S. Ambrose, *Eisenhower: The President* (New York, 1984). On social issues, see W. Nugent, *Structure of American Social History* (Bloomington, IN, 1981). On the turbulent 1960s, see W. O'Neill, *Coming Apart: An Informal History of America in the 1960s* (Chicago, 1971). On Nixon and Watergate, see J. Anthony Lukas, *Nightmare: The Underside of the Nixon Years* (New York, 1976).

For general surveys of Latin American history, see E. B. Burns, *Latin America: A Concise Interpretive Survey*,

4th ed. (Englewood Cliffs, NJ, 1976) and E. Williamson, *The Penguin History of Latin America* (London, 1992). Also see T. E. Skidmore and P. H. Smith, *Modern Latin America*, 3d ed. (New York, 1992).

For a survey of contemporary Western society, see A. Sampson, *The New Europeans* (New York, 1968). The changing role of women is examined in A. Cherlin, *Marriage, Divorce, Remarriage* (Cambridge, MA, 1981). On the women's liberation movement, see D. Boudheir, *The Feminist Challenge: The Movement for Women's Liberation in Britain and the United States* (New York, 1983). For a general survey of postwar thought, see R. N. Stromberg, *European Intellectual History since 1789*, 5th ed. (Englewood Cliffs, NJ, 1990). For the most accessible introduction to American literature, consult *The Norton Anthology of American Literature*, shorter 4th ed. (New York, 1995). On Latin America, see Naomi Lindstrom, *Twentieth-Century Spanish American Fiction* (Austin, 1994). Popular culture is treated in R. Maltby (ed.), *Passing Parade: A History of Popular Culture in the Twentieth Century* (New York, 1989).

Chapter 11. A House Divided: South Asia in an Era of Change

For a recent survey of contemporary Indian history, see S. Wolpert, *A New History of India*, rev. ed. (New York, 1989). V. S. Naipaul, *India: A Wounded Civilization* (New York, 1977) is a provocative study of independent India from a friendly but sometimes critical perspective. Also see P. Brass, *The New Cambridge History of India: The Politics of India since Independence* (Cambridge, England, 1990) and C. Baxter, *Bangladesh: From a Nation to a State* (Boulder, CO, 1997). A recent overview, packed with interesting ideas, is Sunil Khilnani, *The Idea of India* (New York, 1998).

On the period surrounding independence, see the dramatic account by L. Collins and D. Lapierre, *Freedom at Midnight* (New York, 1975), or A. Read and D. Fisher's recent *The Proudest Day: India's Long Road to Independence* (London, 1998). On Indira Gandhi, see K. Bhatia, *Indira: A Biography of Prime Minister Gandhi* (New York, 1974).

Social issues are examined in a number of studies. For an overview, see K. Bhatia, *The Ordeal of Nationhood: A Social Study of India since Independence, 1947–1970* (New York, 1971). See also J. M. Freeman, *Untouchable: An Indian Life History* (Stanford, CA, 1979) and W. and C. Wiser, *Behind Mud Walls, 1930–1960*, rev. ed. (New York, 1984). On Indian literature, see D.

Ray and A. Singh (eds.), *India: An Anthology of Contemporary Writing* (Athens, OH, 1983). See also S. Tharu and K. Lalita (eds.), *Women Writing in India*, vol. 2 (New York, 1993). Novels mentioned in the text include A. Desai, *Cry the Peacock* (New Delhi, 1980) and S. Rushdie, *Midnight's Children* (Harmondsworth, England, 1980).

Chapter 12. Nationalism Triumphant: The Emergence of Independent States in Southeast Asia

There are several standard surveys of the history of modern Southeast Asia. Unfortunately, many of them are now out of date because of the changes that have taken place in the region since the end of the Vietnam War. For an introductory survey with a strong emphasis on recent events, see D. R. SarDesai, *Southeast Asia: Past and Present*, 2d ed. (Boulder, CO, 1989). For a more scholarly approach, see D. J. Steinberg (ed.), *In Search of Southeast Asia*, 2d ed. (New York, 1985).

The best way to approach modern Southeast Asia is through individual country studies. On Burma, see J. Silverstein, *Burmese Politics: The Dilemma of National Unity* (New Brunswick, NJ, 1980). On Thailand, see D. Wyatt, *Thailand* (New Haven, CT, 1982). On the Philippines, the best overall survey is D. J. Steinberg, *The Philippines: A Singular and a Plural Place* (Boulder, CO, 1994). For insight into the problem of racial divisions in Malaysia, see M. bin Mohamad, *The Malay Dilemma*. (Kuala Lumpur, 1970).

There is a rich selection of materials on modern Indonesia. On the Sukarno era, see J. Legge, *Sukarno* (New York, 1972). On the Suharto era and its origins, see M. Vatikiotis, *Indonesian Politics under Suharto* (London, 1993). Most of the literature on Indochina in recent decades has dealt with the Vietnam War and related conflicts in Laos and Cambodia. On conditions in Vietnam since the end of the war, see R. Shaplen, *Bitter Victory* (New York, 1986), a study by a veteran journalist, and W. Duiker, *Vietnam: Revolution in Transition*, 2d ed., (Boulder, CO, 1995). For an excellent anthology of contemporary Vietnamese fiction, see *Vietnam: A Traveler's Literary Companion* (San Francisco, 1996).

Chapter 13. Emerging Africa

For a general survey of contemporary African history, see R. Oliver and J. D. Fage, *A Short History of Africa* (Harmondsworth, England, 1986); R. Oliver, *The Afri-*

can *Experience* (New York, 1992), which contains interesting essays on a variety of themes, and K. Shillington, *History of Africa* (New York, 1989), which takes a chronological and geographical approach and includes excellent maps and illustrations. Two recent treatments are B. Davidson, *Africa in History: Themes and Outlines*, rev. ed. (New York, 1991) and P. Curtin et al., *African History* (London, 1995).

On nationalist movements, see P. Gifford and W. R. Louis (eds.), *The Transfer of Power in Africa* (New Haven, CT, 1982). For a poignant analysis of the hidden costs of nation-building, see N. F. Mostert, *The Epic of South Africa's Creation and the Tragedy of the Xhosa People* (London, 1992). For a survey of economic conditions, see *Sub-Saharan Africa: From Crisis to Sustainable Growth* (Washington, DC, 1989), issued by the World Bank. Also see J. Illiffe, *The African Poor* (Cambridge, England, 1983). On recent political events, see S. Decalo, *Coups and Army Rule in Africa* (New Haven, CT, 1990).

On African literature, see L. S. Klein (ed.), *African Literatures in the Twentieth Century: A Guide* (New York, 1986), and C. H. Bruner (ed.), *African Women's Writing* (Oxford, 1993). Also see Chinua Achebe, *Things Fall Apart* (New York, 1994), Ngugi Wa Thiong-o, *A Grain of Wheat*, rev. ed. (Oxford, 1986), and Ama Ata Aidoo, *No Sweetness Here* (New York, 1995). On art, see F. Willett, *African Art: An Introduction* (New York, 1985).

Chapter 14. Ferment in the Middle East

Good general surveys of the modern Middle East include A. Goldschmidt, Jr., *A Concise History of the Middle East* (Boulder, CO, 1991) and G. E. Perry, *The Middle East: Fourteen Islamic Centuries* (Elizabeth City, NJ, 1992).

On Israel and the Palestinian question, see B. Reich, *Israel: Land of Tradition and Conflict* (Boulder, CO, 1985) and C. C. O'Brien, *The Siege: The Saga of Israel and Zionism* (New York, 1986). For a dramatic account by a journalist, see Thomas L. Friedman, *From Beirut to Jerusalem* (New York, 1989). On U.S.–Israel relations, see S. Green, *Living by the Sword: America and Israel in the Middle East, 1968–1997* (London, 1998). The issue of oil is examined in G. Luciani, *The Oil Companies and the Arab World* (New York, 1984). Also see M. H. Kerr and El Sayed Yassin (eds.), *Rich and Poor States in the Middle East: Egypt and the New Arab Order* (Boulder, CO, 1985).

On the Iranian Revolution, see S. Bakash, *The Reign of the Ayatollahs* (New York, 1984) and B. Rubin, *Iran since the Revolution* (Boulder, CO, 1985). On politics, see J. A. Bill and R. Springborg, *Politics in the Middle East*

(London, 1990) and R. R. Anderson, R. F. Seibert, and J. G. Wagner, *Politics and Change in the Middle East: Sources of Conflict and Accommodation* (Englewood Cliffs, NJ, 1993). For a general anthology of literature in the Middle East, see J. Kritzeck, *Modern Islamic Literature from 1800 to the Present* (New York, 1970). For a scholarly but accessible overview, also see M. M. Abdawi, *A Short History of Modern Arab Literature* (Oxford, 1993). For an introduction to women's issues, see Geraldine Brooks, *Nine Parts of Desire* (New York, 1995).

Chapter 15. Toward the Pacific Century: The Emergence of Modern Societies in East Asia

The number of books in English on modern Japan has increased in virtually direct proportion to Japan's rise as a major industrial power. Though many deal with economic and financial issues and cater to the business world, increased attention is also being paid to political, social, and cultural issues. For a contemporary view, see R. Buckley, *Japan Today* (Cambridge, England, 1985). For a topical approach with strong emphasis on social matters, J. E. Hunter, *The Emergence of Modern Japan: An Introductory History since 1853* (London, 1989), is excellent.

Relatively little has been written on Japanese politics and government. A good treatment, if somewhat outdated, is J. A. A. Stockwin, *Japan: Divided Politics in a Growth Economy* (London, 1982). Political dissent and its consequences are dealt with in N. Fields, *In the Realm of the Dying Emperor* (New York, 1991). Japanese social issues are treated in R. J. Hendry, *Understanding Japanese Society* (London, 1987). Also see, for a local approach, R. P. Dore, *Shinohata: A Portrait of a Japanese Village* (New York, 1978) and T. C. Bestor, *Neighborhood Tokyo* (Stanford, CA, 1989). On the role of women in modern Japan, see D. Robins-Mowry, *The Hidden Sun: Women of Modern Japan* (Boulder, CO, 1983), N. Bornoff, *Pink Samurai: Love, Marriage and Sex in Contemporary Japan* (New York, 1991), and K. Fujimura-Fanselow and A. Kameda (eds.), *Japanese Women* (New York, 1995).

Books attempting to explain Japanese economic issues have become a growth industry. The classic account of the Japanese miracle is E. F. Vogel, *Japan as Number One: Lessons for America* (Cambridge, MA, 1979). For a provocative response providing insight into Japan's current economic weakness, see J. Woronoff, *Japan as—Anything but—Number One* (Armonk, NY 1991). On the role of government in promoting business in Japan, see C. Johnson, *MITI and the Japanese Miracle* (Stanford, CA, 1982). For the impact of economics on society, see R. J. Smith, *Kurusu: The Price of Progress in a Japanese Village* (Stanford, CA, 1978).

On Japanese literature after World War II, see D. Keene, *Dawn to the West: Japanese Literature in the Modern Era* (New York, 1984) and A. Birnbaum, *Monkey Brain Sushi: New Tastes in Japanese Fiction* (Tokyo, 1991). On Japanese women authors, see N. M. Lippit and K. I. Selden (eds.), *Stories by Contemporary Japanese Women Writers* (New York, 1982).

On the four little tigers and their economic development, see E. F. Vogel, *The Four Little Dragons: The Spread of Industrialization in East Asia* (Cambridge, MA, 1991); J. W. Morley (ed.), *Driven by Growth: Political Change in the Asia-Pacific Region* (Armonk, NY, 1992); and J. Woronoff, *Asia's Miracle Economies* (New York, 1986). For individual treatments of the little tigers, see Hakkyu Sohn, *Authoritarianism and Opposition in South Korea* (London, 1989); D. F. Simon, *Taiwan: Beyond the Economic Miracle* (Armonk, NY, 1992); C. M. Turnbull, *A History of Singapore, 1819–1975* (Oxford, 1977); and K. Rafferty, *City on the Rocks: Hong Kong's Uncertain Future* (London, 1991).

Chapter 16. The End of Bipolarity: The Collapse of the Soviet Empire and the Demise of the Cold War

On the end of the Cold War, see B. Denitch, *The End of the Cold War* (Minneapolis, MN, 1990); W. G. Hyland, *The Cold War Is Over* (New York, 1990); and W. Laqueur, *Soviet Union 2000: Reform or Revolution?* (New York, 1990). On the Gorbachev era, see M. Lewin, *The Gorbachev Phenomenon* (Berkeley, CA, 1988); G. Hosking, *The Awakening of the Soviet Union* (London, 1990); and S. White, *Gorbachev and After* (Cambridge, England, 1991). The collapse of the Soviet Union is analyzed acutely in J. F. Matlock, Jr., *Autopsy on an Empire: The American Ambassador's Account of the Collapse of the Soviet Union* (New York, 1995). On the crisis in the Balkans, see L. Silber and A. Little, *Yugoslavia: Death of a Nation* (New York, 1997).

Recent studies on China include journalist O. Schell's *Discoes and Democracy: China in the Throes of Reform* (New York, 1988) and L. Feigon's eyewitness account of the 1989 demonstrations, *China Rising: The Meaning of Tiananmen* (Chicago, 1990). For commentary by Chinese dissidents, see Liu Binyan, *China's Crisis, China's Hope* (Cambridge, MA, 1990) and Fang Lizhi, *Bringing*

Down the Great Wall: Writings on Science, Culture, and Democracy in China (New York, 1991). Recent writing on Chinese literature includes E. Widmer and D. DrWei Wang (eds.), *From May Fourth to June Fourth: Fiction and Film in Twentieth-Century China* (Cambridge, MA, 1993). An excellent appraisal of Chinese women writers is found in M. S. Duke (ed.), *Modern Chinese Women Writers: Critical Appraisals* (Armonk, NY, 1989).

Chapter 17. Toward a New World Order?

For divergent visions of the future world order (or disorder), see Samuel P. Huntington, *The Clash of Civilizations and the Remaking of World Order* (New York, 1996), and Francis Fukuyama, *The End of History and the Last Man* (New York, 1992). Also of interest is J. Scott's *Seeing Like a State: How Certain Schemes to Improve the Human Condition Have Failed* (New Haven, CT, 1998). An account of the impact of the fall of Communism is contained in R. Skidelsky, *The Road from Serfdom: The Economic and Political Consequences of the End of Communism* (New York, 1996).

On the technological revolution and its impact, see A. and H. Toffler's latest vision, entitled *Creating a New Civilization: The Politics of the Third Wave* (Atlanta, 1997). On global warming and its potential dangers, see the series of articles entitled "Feuding over Global Warming," in the *World Press Review* (July 1995). For a fascinating analysis of the contrasting pulls of globalization and diversification in the world today, see B. R. Barber's *Jihad vs. McWorld* (New York, 1995).

Recent studies dealing with changes taking place in eastern Asia are listed in Chapter 15. For an impressive recent study, see I. P. Hall, *Cartels of the Mind: Japan's Intellectual Closed Shop* (New York, 1997). On the emergence of an unbridled capitalist system in Russia, see J. R. Blasi, M. Kroumova, and D. Kruse, *Kremlin Capitalism: The Privatization of the Russian Economy* (Ithaca, NY, 1997).

On current trends in the cultural field, see D. Sharp and L. Humphries, *Twentieth Century Architecture: A Visual History* (London, 1991) and R. P. Morgan, *Twentieth Century Music: A History of Musical Style in Modern Europe and America* (New York, 1991). Also see B. Nettl et al., *Excursions in World Music*, 2d ed., (Englewood Cliffs, NJ, 1997). For a concise introduction to postmodernism in literature, see R. Ruland and M. Bradburg, *From Puritanism to Postmodernism: A History of American Literature* (New York, 1991). On art, see Nikos Stangos (ed.), *Concepts of Modern Art: From Fauvism to Postmodernism* (London, 1994).

Photo Credits

1 Hulton Getty/Corbis-Bettmann.

5 FPG International.

21 Erich Lessing/Art Resource, NY. Munch, Edvard (1863–1944). *The Scream*. 1893. National Gallery, Oslo, Norway.

23 Pablo Picasso, *Les Demoiselles d'Avignon*, Paris (begun May, reworked July 1907). Collection, The Museum of Modern Art, New York. Acquired through the Lillie P. Bliss Bequest.

32 Bildarchiv Preussischer Kulturbesitz, Berlin.

33 Aberdeen University Library.

41 Courtesy of William J. Duiker.

45 Courtesy of William J. Duiker.

57 Courtesy of William J. Duiker.

59 *Leslie's Weekly*, 10/14/1900.

63 U.S. Naval Academy.

69 Scala/Art Resource, NY.

73 Paul Dorsey, *Life Magazine*, © 1938 Time, Inc.

77 Roger-Viollet/ Liaison Agency, Inc.

93 Gerasimov, Alexander. *Lenin at the Tribune*, 1930. Tretyakov Gallery, Moscow, Russia. Scala/Art Resource, NY.

94 Kandinksy, Vasily, *Black Lines*, December 1913. Gift, Solomon R. Guggenheim, 1927, The Solomon R. Guggenheim Museum, New York. Photograph by David Heald/© The Solomon R. Guggenheim Foundation, New York.

95 © Peter Mauss/ Esto.

103 AP/Wide World Photos.

106 Culver Pictures.

113 Earl Lea/Rapho/Liaison Agency, Inc.

120 Brown Brothers.

128 Hugo Jaeger, *Life Magazine*, © Time Warner, Inc.

130 Picasso, Pablo (1881–1973). *Guernica*, 1937. © 1999 Estate of Pablo Picasso. Copyright ARS, NY. Museo del Prado, Madrid, Spain.

147 E.T. Archives.

153 AP/Wide World Photos.

157 Corbis-Bettmann.

162 Jack Wiles, *Life Magazine* © 1945 Time Warner, Inc.

169 AP/Wide World Photos.

174 Courtesy of William J. Duiker.

179 Courtesy of William J. Duiker.

182 Corbis-Bettmann.

188 Courtesy of William J. Duiker.

191 AP/ Wide World Photos.

197 Courtesy of William J. Duiker.

199 Courtesy of William J. Duiker.

207 © Raimond-Dityvon/Viva/Woodfin Camp & Associates.

214 Bob Adelman/Magnum Photos.

220 Corbis-Bettmann.

226 Hans Namuth/ Photo Researchers.

233 Courtesy of William J. Duiker.

239 Courtesy of William J. Duiker.

246 Courtesy of William J. Duiker.

247 Courtesy of William J. Duiker.

248 Courtesy of William J. Duiker.

258 Courtesy of William J. Duiker.

260 Courtesy of William J. Duiker.

263 John Elk/Stock Boston.

276 Abbas/Magnum Photos.

279 Corbis-Bettmann.

282 Courtesy of William J. Duiker.

290 UPI/Corbis-Bettmann.

294 Courtesy of William J. Duiker.

301 Corbis-Bettmann.

312 Courtesy of William J. Duiker.

318 Courtesy of William J. Duiker.

321 Courtesy of William J. Duiker.

331 David Heald © The Solomon R. Guggenheim Foundation, New York.

333 Courtesy of William J. Duiker.

336 Courtesy of William J. Duiker.

341 Courtesy of William J. Duiker.

349 Courtesy of William J. Duiker.

355 Reuters/Susumu Takahashi/Archive Photos.

357 Courtesy of William J. Duiker.

365 Guangyi Wang, "Great Criticism: 1.25 Liters Coca Cola," © 1994, Hanart T Z Gallery.

Index

Japan, World War II *(continued)*
    militarism in 1930s, 116–118, 132, 135–136
    takeover of Manchuria and advance into China, 123, 132, 160
    post–World War II
        Allied occupation, 305–306, 311–312
        economy, 306, 309–312
        politics and government, 305–309
        religion and culture, 315–317
        social changes and role of women, 307–308, 312–315
Japan's Emergence as a Modern State (Norman), 68
Japan That Can Say No, The (Shintaro), 310
Jaruzelski, Wojciech, 337
Jews (in the 20th century), 108. *See also* Israel
    Balfour Declaration and, 107, 289
    Holocaust, 208, 303
    Nazi Germany, 126–129, 142–144
    in the USSR, 171, 177
    Zionism, 289, 291
Jiang Qing, 191–192
Jiang Zemin, 362
Jinnah, Mohammed Ali, 235, 239–240
Johnson, Lyndon B., 168–169, 213–214
Jordan, 107, 288–289, 290–291, 300
Joyce, James, 94–95, 228
July Days, 88
Junichiro Tanizaki, 116

Kabila, Lauren, 280
Kádár, János, 181–182, 337
Kanagawa Treaty, 64
Kangxi (K'ang Hsi, Chinese emperor), 50
Kang Youwei (K'ang Yu-wei), 57–59
Kapital, Das (Marx), 18
Kapoor, Karisma, 248
Kashmir, 235, 237
Kazakhstan, 175
Keiretsu, The (Ikko Shimizu), 310
Kellogg, Frank B., 89
Kellogg-Briand pact, 89
Kennan, George, 157
Kennedy, John F., 166, 213–214, 216, 219
Kentucky Fried Chicken, 244–245, 312
Kenya, 46, 271–272, 275
    independence and aftermath, 271, 275, 277–278, 285–286
Kenya African National Union (KANU), 271–272
Kenyatta, Jomo, 272, 274–275, 278
Kenzaburo Oe. *See* Oe, Kenzaburo
Kerensky, Alexander, 86
Keynes, John Maynard, 84, 91, 213
KGB, 174, 176, 334

Khalidi, Wahid, 293
Khan, Ayub, 240
Khan, Yahya, 240
Khmer Rouge, 267–268
Khomeini, Ayatollah, 171, 217, 250, 288, 295–297, 303
Khrushchev, Nikita, 165–168, 170, 175–176, 181, 184, 231, 355
    and Cuban Missile Crisis, 166
Kibbutz, 303
Kim Dae Jung, 318–319
Kim Jong-il, 319
Kim Young Sam, 318–319
King, Martin Luther, Jr., 214–215
Kingoro, Hashimoto, 137
Kipling, Rudyard, 36–38, 102
Kishwar, Madhu, 249
Kissinger, Henry, 169, 292
Klee, Paul, 94
Kohl, Helmut, 208, 344–345, 353
Kokutai (national polity), 61, 69, 116–118, 314
Kolkhoz. *See* Collective farms
Korea
    annexed in 1908, 54, 67, 117, 164
    Japanese and, 54, 56, 66–67, 117, 164, 309, 318
    Korean War, 163–164, 208, 213
    People's Republic of, 317
    South Korea, contemporary, 304, 317–319
Kornilov, Lavr, 86
Kosygin, Alexei, 170, 176
Kowtow, 50
Kristallnacht, 129
Kurds, 295–296
Kurile Islands, 146, 307
Kursk, battle of (1943), 141
Kuwait, 296–299

Labour party (Britain), 91, 205, 209, 236, 254, 345
Lanier, Wilfried, 16
Laos, 30, 68, 268
    under French rule, 30, 44, 165
Latin America. *See also specific countries*
    colonial period, 16–17
    in the 19th century, 118, 121
    20th-century authoritarian regimes, 16–17, 118–121
    post-World War II, 204, 217–223, 347
Latvia, 83, 334
Law, 8
    in China, 59
    in India, 42
    in Japan, 64
Lawrence, T. E. (Lawrence of Arabia), 80, 105

Lay, Camara, 285
League of Combat, 124
League of Nations, 83–85, 89–90, 123, 133
Leary, Timothy, 212
Lebanon, 83, 107, 288–289, 292
    Arab-Israeli conflict and, 289, 292
    independence, 289
Lebed, Alexander, 336
Le Corbusier, 94
Lee Kuan-yew, 260–261, 322, 324
Lee Teng-hui, 320
Leghari, Farooq, 240
Lenin, Vladimir, 97, 131–133, 186
    on imperialism, 61–62, 85, 88, 92, 109, 168
    New Economic Policy, 92–93, 333
    program for revolution in non-Western societies, 108–111
Leopold II, Belgian king, 34
Le Pen, Jean-Marie, 353
Lesotho, 47
Lesseps, Ferdinand de, 33
Lévesque, René, 347
Lewis, Sinclair, 95
Liang Heng, 192–193
Liberal Democratic Party (Japan), 308–309
Liberalism, 10–13, 15–17
Liberia, 32, 280
Libya
    conquest by Italy, 15, 33–34, 288
    under Qadhafi, 278, 298
Life and Death in Shanghai (Nien Cheng), 193
Life and Ritual in Old Siam (Rajadhon), 262
Lin Zexu (Lin Tse-hsu), 54
Literature, 228
    in Africa, 285
    in China
        under Communism, 201–202
        Western influence in the early 20th century, 115, 201
    in Europe, 22–23, 94–96
        naturalism, 22
        realism, 23
        symbolists, 22–23
    in Japan
        Western influence in early 20th century, 116
Lithuania, 88, 334
Liu Shaoqi (Liu Shao-ch'i), 191
Livingstone, David, 32, 24, 48
Lloyd George, David, 83
Locarno, treaty of, 89–90
Lo Liyong, Taban, 278
Long March, 113
Louis-Philippe (French king), 12
Lubis, Mochtar, 263
Ludendorff, Erich von, 82